P9-BZC-100

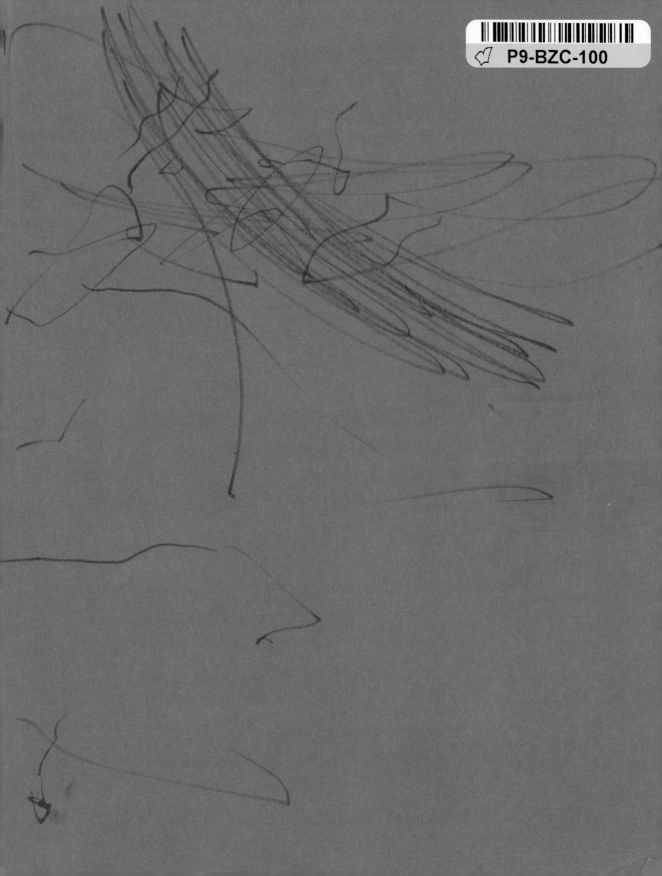

L E Andrade

Philosophy

Second Edition

PHILOSOPHY:
A Text with Readings

Vincent Barry
Bakersfield College

Wadsworth Publishing Company
Belmont, California
A Division of Wadsworth, Inc.

McLean County Unit #5
NCHS IMC - 300

Philosophy editor: Kenneth King
Production editor: Judith McKibben
Managing and cover designer: Adriane Bosworth
Copy editor: Lorraine Anderson
Cover photographer: David Cross
Signing representative: Kay Chamberlain

Chapter opening photos: (1) Wind Tunnel Construction, Fort Peck Dam, Margaret Bourke-White, LIFE magazine, 1936 © Time, Inc.; (2) Rome 1966, Leonard Freed/Magnum; (3) Korean Conflict, Al Chang/U. S. Army; (4) Martin Luther King leading Selma to Montgomery Civil Rights March, United Press International, Inc.; (5) Rembrandt Painting, Amsterdam, Kent Reno/Jeroboam, Inc.; (6) The Library of Congress, Dennis Brack/Black Star; (7) Trees, © Richard Gordon; (8) Chambered Nautilus, 1927, Edward Weston, © 1981 Arizona Board of Regents Center for Creative Photography; (9) Escalators, Robert Burroughs/Jerboam, Inc.; (10) Stonehenge, A. F. Kersting.

© 1983, 1980 by Wadsworth, Inc. All rights reserved. No part of this book may be reproduced, stored in a retrieval system, or transcribed, in any form or by any means, electronic, mechanical photocopying, recording, or otherwise, without the prior written permission of the publisher, Wadsworth Publishing Company, Belmont, California 94002, a division of Wadsworth, Inc.

Printed in the United States of America
1 2 3 4 5 6 7 8 9 10–87 86 85 84 83

Library of Congress Cataloging in Publication Data

Barry, Vincent E.
  Philosophy, a text with readings.

  Bibliography: p.
  Includes index.
  1. Philosophy—Introductions. I. Title.
BD21.B29 1982   100   82-8570
ISBN 0-534-01216-7   AACR2

McLean County Unit #5
NCHS IMC - 830

For Dr. Leonard Sacks: Teacher, Scholar, Friend

CONTENTS

x   Contents

BRIEF SELECTIONS INCLUDED WITHIN THE CHAPTERS

PREFACE

Philosophy: A Text with Readings has four main objectives: (1) to introduce readers to traditional philosophical problems in a way that will help them define and shape their own lives; (2) to expose readers to philosophical argumentation in such a way that they will feel confident in handling abstract concepts; (3) to help readers recognize philosophical problems in everyday contexts and to deal with everyday problems philosophically; and (4) to provide readers with a representative sampling of primary philosophical writings and philosophical fiction.

Organization

The material has been organized radially, with the notion of self-discovery at the hub. Since I return to this center in each chapter, the only logical connections that need be made are between self-discovery and the material discussed. This allows instructors to use all chapters other than the first in whatever order they choose and to omit any chapter if desired.

Another point about the organization: Value concerns—ethics, social philosophy, art—appear early in the text. Although to some philosophers the more logical order is epistemology, metaphysics, and then axiology, I have found the values area the most manageable for the introductory student. Thus its location in the text. But, again, this is a mere convenience. Those wanting to study epistemology first may do so without bruising the integrity of the text.

Continuing Features

No more needs to be said about the organization, since it is spelled out in the table of contents. But I would like to point out there are a number of features that make this text unusual, if not unique. Among them are the following:

1. "Philosophy and Life" boxes. These inserts are intended to introduce timely material that shows philosophy's impact on everyday life or its connection

with other areas. For example, the box entitled "Viktor Frankl's Logotherapy" in Chapter 1 associates the principles of logotherapy with the study and value of philosophy; another, "Koestler and James" (Chapter 2) demonstrates the profound impact of one's view of human nature on one's life.

2. End-of-chapter philosophical fiction. These selections, culled from outstanding classical and contemporary sources, dramatize the immediacy of philosophy in our lives and glitter with philosophical insights.

3. Fictional dialogues. The purpose of these informal conversations is to make the abstract and theoretical more accessible to the neophyte.

4. Coverage of topics such as the connection between philosophy and the satisfaction of higher level needs; the nature and origin of values; warranted belief, including the various modes of warrantability; the meaning of science and scientific statements. Also covered is Eastern religion and philosophy, in order to give our study a cross-cultural flavor.

5. "Paperbacks for Further Reading." A list of readily available philosophical fiction and nonfiction paperbacks follows each chapter.

6. End-of-text bibliography. A list of formal works in philosophy appears at the end of the text. These are arranged to correspond with the chapters.

7. End-of-chapter exercises. These correspond with the sections within each chapter.

8. The inclusion of primary source material within the chapters. (This material has been expanded over the first edition.)

Second Edition Features

Those familiar with the first edition will spot many changes in this new one. An important change appears in Chapter 3, "Ethics," which now includes a section on metaethics, as well as one on moral responsibility and determinism. More noteworthy are the changes to Chapter 4, "Social Philosophy," which I have overhauled. This chapter now centers around four topics: justice, the justification of the state, government control, and law and freedom. These topics are fleshed out with appropriate selections from the works of Plato, Hobbes, Locke, Rousseau, Mill, Marx, and Rawls.

Of major importance are the new "Showcase" sections. These give certain chapters a sharper focus by providing in-depth looks at the thoughts of key philosophers. A showcase includes a brief overview of a philosopher's life, then highlights some important features of his philosophy and relates them to the chapter's contents. Most importantly, generous samplings of the philosopher's writings are provided. The philosophers showcased are Socrates (Chapter 1), Plato and Sartre (Chapter 2), Marx (Chapter 4), Descartes (Chapter 6), and Kierkegaard (Chapter 10). I have placed these showcases toward the ends of the chapters for two reasons. First, I have found that students can better handle an in-depth look after they have had an overview of an area, issue, or problem. Second, I wanted to preserve instructional flexibility. Thus, those who do not wish to pursue a philosopher in detail can merely omit a showcase without compromising the rest of a chapter. By the same token, an instructor or student who so desires can focus on just this aspect of a chapter. However the showcases are used, I hope they provide suitable focus and depth to chapters whose content particularly warrants that.

Another feature involves the "Main Points," which are located at the beginning of each chapter. The main points serve as overviews of the chapters, but readers are encouraged to reread them after completing the chapter so that they may also serve as a review. An instructor's manual is available for instructors.

Acknowledgments

I would like to acknowledge the assistance of Wadsworth philosophy editor Ken King, and the following professors whose contributions to the first edition remain evident in this new one: Robert C. Bennett, El Centro College; Fred Blomgren, Monroe Community College; Donald Cates, Grays Harbor College; Richard C. Conrath, Lakeland Community College; Emeric Deluca, Harrisburg Area Community College; John Donnelly, University of San Diego; Paul Hamilton, Middle Tennessee State University; Thomas King, University of Texas, Arlington; Kevin McGinley, Seattle College; Mary Paroski, Mountain View College; Norman Prigge, California State College; Richard Schoenig, San Antonio College; Harvey Solganick, Eastfield College; Ben Starr, Modesto Junior College; Michael Vengrin, Radford College; Mark Woodhouse, Georgia State University; and especially David Long of California State University at Sacramento. Of particular help with this second edition were the reviews of: Paul Diener, York College of Pennsylvania; Mary Hines, Catonsville Community College; Robert Loofbourrow, Antelope Valley College; Michael Popich, Westminster College; and Ted Thompson, Oscar Rose Junior College.

Part I

INTRODUCTION

THE MEANING AND
VALUE OF PHILOSOPHY

1

Wonder is the feeling of a philosopher, and philosophy begins in wonder.
—*Socrates*

A conversation between two students, Liz and Jon, overheard in a classroom twenty minutes before the first meeting of an introductory philosophy course:

Jon: Do you have any idea what this course is all about?

Liz: Philosophy.

Jon: But what's that?

Liz: You got me.

Jon: I think it's pretty heavy.

Liz: Me, too. You know what troubles me?

Jon: What?

Liz: Well, I'm at least familiar with all the other courses I'm taking—English, calculus, history. And the ones I'm not familiar with are in my major—pre-med. But philosophy—where does it fit in?

Jon: I'm in business administration. You know, I've always thought that philosophers were superbright dudes that nobody but other philosophers could understand.

Liz: Me, too.

Jon: What do you figure they do?

Liz: Think a lot, I guess. You know that piece of sculpture of the naked guy hunched over like he's trying to remember where he left his clothes?

Jon: *The Thinker.*

Liz: I guess. That's how I picture philosophers.

Jon: You think there are many of them around?

Liz: I doubt it. When was the last time you saw a want ad for a philosopher?

Jon: You got a point, but that doesn't mean there aren't many around.

Liz: You mean *closet* philosophers?

Jon: Not exactly. I just don't think someone has to make a living as a philosopher to be one.

Liz: You're probably right. A friend of my mom is a painter but actually makes her living as a legal secretary.

Jon: That's what I mean. I think a person could philosophize and not be a professional philosopher.

Liz: What do you mean "philosophize"?

Jon: You know, to really question something.

Liz: You mean I was philosophizing the other night with my dad when I was really questioning his religious beliefs?

Jon: You probably were. That's like me about two years ago when my best friend was killed in a car crash. I questioned everything—the purpose and meaning of life, the existence of God, the value of friendship. Why, at one point I was even wondering whether there was any reason to get out of bed in the morning, that maybe suicide was the way out.

Liz: I guess you're not much of a scientist.

Jon: What do you mean?

Liz: Well, I believe that everything can be accounted for by science, and what can't isn't worth getting lathered up over. That's actually what got me into that philosophical discussion with my dad about religious belief. I just can't see any scientific basis for believing the way he does.

Jon: But how does that apply to me?

Liz: Well, it seems to me that one of the reasons your friend's death shook you up was that instead of a scientific explanation of it, you insisted on something else, some explanation outside science.

Jon: Hey, I saw the pictures, the skid marks, the reports. I know the conditions and circumstances that led to the accident. But what got me was, Why *that* person? Of all the turkeys nobody ever would have missed, why a straight shooter like that? The whole thing seemed so senseless. To tell you the truth, it still does.

Liz: But that's my point. Stop looking for sense and meaning outside science. You're just asking for a bad trip.

Jon: But I happen to believe there's more to life than science. Call it spiritual if you want, but I don't think science alone can account for every aspect of life.

Liz: I disagree. The fact is that science is explaining more and more. As far as I'm concerned, what it can't account for is so much bull.

Jon: But——.

Liz: Hey, you know what?

Jon: What?

Liz: I think we're philosophizing.

The curious thing about this conversation is that the students moved from expressing perplexity about philosophy to actually doing it, to philosophizing. Philosophy is not as elusive as is often thought and claimed. Most people, in fact, have had occasion to use philosophy meaningfully. For example, "My religious *philosophy* is based on love of neighbor," "The *philosophy* of this business is that the customer is always right," and "This country's *philosophy* must be traced back to the great European thinkers of the eighteenth century."

Thus, philosophy is not remote from the problems of people. True, most of us lack a knowledge of philosophy's jargon and history and don't have a clear idea of its issues, but like Liz and Jon, we have been touched and moved by the feelings of wonder from which all philosophy derives. We wonder whether God exists; why a close friend was killed; whether all we can ever know—all that can ever prove meaningful—is what can be framed in the language of science; what we should do to be happy; whether we should protest a national policy we disagree with; what makes one piece of music brilliant and another mediocre; and how we should treat other people and the environment. If we think that such questions arise only as we get older, we're mistaken. Listen sometime to the questions that children ask, almost within the echo of their first words: "Where did I come from?" "Where do people go when they die?" "What's beyond the sky?" "How did the world start?" "Who made God?" "Why is one and one two, not three?"

Neither philosophy nor philosophizing is entirely new to any of us, for we wonder about what we experience. What is new is philosophy as a discipline of study, an academic subject. As Liz indicated, many of us are already familiar with most of the courses that we take in college. We've taken previous courses or have read about them. But we approach philosophy with no formal preparation. We don't know what to expect, and we feel anxious.

This opening chapter aims to dispel much of the anxiety that students bring to philosophy by providing an overview of the issues of philosophy and transmitting some of philosophy's fun and excitement. It tries to show that philosophy is not to be feared; it is to be cultivated and relished. Specifically, this chapter considers the nature and meaning of philosophy and examines some of its characteristics. Finally, and most important, it addresses the question, What's the value of philosophy? The main points in this chapter are as follows.

Main Points

1. Philosophy literally means "love of wisdom."

2. *The Apology* is one of the best-known works of the Greek philosopher Plato. His chief work is *The Republic*. In his writings, Plato presents his philosophy in the form of dialogues involving his ideal philosopher and mentor, Socrates.

3. Philosophy may be considered the parent science, in that it has given birth to other natural, physical, and social sciences. These disciplines continue to provide philosophy with a rich abundance of contemporary issues, questions that they themselves are unable to answer. Philosophy is both independent of other disciplines and embedded in their foundations and ongoing activities.

4. The three main fields of philosophy are epistemology, metaphysics, and axiology.

5. Epistemology deals with questions of knowledge, including the structure, reliability, extent, and kinds of knowledge; truth, validity, and logic; a variety of linguistic concerns; and the philosophy of science.

6. Metaphysics deals with questions of reality, including the meaning and nature of being; the nature of mind, self, and consciousness; and the nature of religion, such as the existence of God, the destiny of the universe, and the immortality of the soul.

7. Axiology refers to the study of values, including values in human conduct; the nature and justification of social structures and political systems; and the nature of art and its meaning in human experience.

8. The philosophical enterprise is an active imaginative process of formulating proper questions and resolving them by rigorous, persistent analysis.

9. Modern psychology generally characterizes human needs as being either maintenance needs or actualizing needs. Maintenance needs refer to physical and psychological needs: food, shelter, security, and so on. Actualizing needs refer to self-expression, realization of potential, and creativity. Both Abraham Maslow and Carl Rogers have written extensively about actualizing needs.

10. Philosophy can help satisfy actualizing needs by (1) helping us to develop our own opinions and beliefs, (2) increasing self-awareness, (3) equipping us to deal with uncertainty, (4) soliciting creativity, and (5) aiding us in clearly conceptualizing value systems.

11. Philosophy can help us maximize our freedom by increasing our awareness, making us less biased and provincial by exposing us to the history of thought, refining our analytical powers, assisting us in dealing with uncertainty, enriching us through the contemplation of eternal questions.

12. In studying philosophy we risk having personal and cultural beliefs and assumptions exposed. This risk is worth running in the light of philosophy's value.

The Difficulty of Defining Philosophy

It's not surprising that Liz and Jon had trouble defining philosophy. For almost 3,000 years philosophers have asked, "What is philosophy?" and they have yet to agree. Why?

One thing that makes defining philosophy tough is that it lacks distinct subject matter. Biology, botany, physics, astronomy, psychology, economics, political science—all deal with a specific body of subjects. If you asked botanists, physicists, or psychologists what their studies dealt with, they probably could answer without too much disagreement. Not so with philosophy. Philosophers often disagree on their subject matter. One reason is that philosophy deals more with issues than with specific subjects. Issues make up the content of philosophy. While some issues have remained throughout the development of philosophical thought, many have not. Some have faded with the passage of time or have become part of the subject matter of other disciplines, such as physics or psychology. What's more, even those issues that have remained in the province of philosophy have changed as various thinkers and ages have considered them.

To illustrate, the early Western philosophers were fascinated by a number of questions about the nature of the universe: What does everything consist of? What's the nature of reality? Is reality ultimately material or nonmaterial? Today we may find such questions strange, because we feel that physics is answering them. Of course, 3,000 years ago the science of physics didn't exist as we know it today. Nevertheless, the point remains: What was once a philosophical question might be regarded today primarily as a scientific one and would be so handled. Thus, contemporary physics has been devoted in part to throwing light on the age-old philosophical concern about the nature of the universe.

Take another ancient philosophical concern: human nature. What is it to be a human being? What, if anything, makes human beings different, perhaps unique? What does it mean to be a human? To a large degree, such inquiries are now taken up by the social sciences in general, and by psychology and anthropology in particular. Again, what was once a question strictly for philosophy is today a concern of many disciplines.

Of course, this doesn't mean that reality and human nature are no longer philosophical concerns. They are, as we'll see in the chapters ahead. But they can no longer be described as exclusively the concerns of philosophy. On the contrary, if you wanted to make philosophical sense out of these areas, you would have to investigate what the appropriate physical, biological, and social sciences were saying about them.

So, because philosophy deals primarily with issues, many of which have been usurped by other fields and altered with the passing of time, it's hard to define philosophy in terms of subject matter. The task of defining philosophy becomes even tougher when you consider competing definitions. For some, philosophy is "the quest for truth," for others it's "the search for God," for still others it's "the study of the logical structure of artificial languages." Such definitions, while valuable, tell us more about the biases of philosophers than about philosophy itself.

Despite the difficulty in defining philosophy, something does seem to have characterized philosophy from its beginnings, something that continues to make it unique. To understand this, it's helpful to examine the meaning of the word *philosophy*.

Philosophy as the Love of Wisdom

If we took the time to trace the history of the physical, natural, and social sciences, we'd find their roots in philosophy as it was practiced about 2,700 years ago in Greece. In those times, people of infinite curiosity puzzled over certain aspects of the world and their experience of them. We saw that one of the questions that they asked concerned reality. But these profoundly curious people wondered about other things as well: Why does anything exist? Why is there something rather than nothing? How can things change? How do we come to know things? What's the nature of knowledge? What's the difference between right and wrong? What's goodness? How can we best achieve happiness? What's justice? What is the just state? On what basis, if any, can society compel us to obey its rules if we don't wish to obey them? Those who asked these questions clearly showed a marked curiosity in the things of experience, a curiosity that could be described as a vital concern for becoming wise about the phenomena of the world and the human experience. For this reason, such people were termed *philosophers* and their study **philosophy,** which literally means "the love of wisdom." Philosophers were originally lovers or seekers of wisdom; they still are.

What is the wisdom that philosophers seek? Actually, this question is a fundamental part of the conversation between Liz and Jon.

Liz: You know, you say philosophy asks heavy questions. I guess the thing that's bothering me is I don't see the point of asking them. I mean, after my dad and I spent all that time going around and around about religion, I couldn't help thinking: So what? And now I hear you talking about how you questioned everything when your friend was killed, and I wonder the same thing. What's the point of asking all those questions? What does it get you? What does it get any of us?

Jon: You make it sound like there has to be a payoff.

Liz: Maybe I do. But you have to admit that we can't answer those questions. You never leave one of those discussions feeling that you've settled anything. In fact, a lot of times you feel worse: The other night I had a terrible time getting to sleep after that discussion about religion. I was really uptight. I think it was because everything was left up in the air. We hadn't settled anything.

Jon: I hear what you're saying, but I'm not sure that when you ask questions like that you're looking for certain answers.

Liz: What else?

Jon: Understanding, maybe. That's what I wanted when my friend was killed. To make sense out of the whole damn thing. But all I got were *facts*. Hey, I knew the facts. What I wanted was *meaning*.

Liz: But I still don't see the point of asking questions that have no factual answers.

Jon: Because I'm a person, that's why. And these things bug me. I wonder about them. Sometimes *really* wonder. So what does that make me—some kind of flake? What am I supposed to do when I wonder—pop a couple of pills and nod out? Look for a shrink? Subscribe to *TV Guide*? Hey, I don't want to go through life in a fog, okay? I want to know what it's all about, what I'm doing here. That doesn't mean I want certainty. What I want is understanding, so my life has some meaning.

The wisdom that philosophers have sought is not the wisdom of book learning and fact acquiring. It is not the wisdom that produces high scores on intelligence tests and big-money winners on TV game shows. Let's not kid ourselves. Those with encyclopedic information, though seemingly intelligent, may actually be quite foolish when it comes to understanding the meaning and significance of what they know. While many appear wise, few are. In defending himself against the trumped-up charges that he had corrupted the minds of Athenian youth and considered himself wiser than the god Apollo, the great Greek philosopher and teacher Socrates (469–399 B.C.) made just this point. "Wisdom? What wisdom?" he asked his accusers, as immortalized in *The Apology*, one of the best-known dialogues of his student Plato (427–347 B.C.). "I certainly have no knowledge of such wisdom, and anyone who says that I have is a liar and a willful slanderer." In some quarters those are fighting words. But Socrates meant it. And he went on to explain why people thought he was wise.

You know Chaerephon, of course. . . . Well, one day he actually went to Delphi and asked this question of the god. . . . He asked whether there was anyone wiser than myself. The priestess replied that there was no one. . . .

When I heard about the oracle's answer, I said to myself "What does the god mean? Why does he not use plain language? I am only too conscious that I have no claim to wisdom, great or small; so what can he mean by asserting that I am the wisest man in the world?" . . .

After puzzling about it for some time, I set myself at last with considerable reluctance to check the truth of it in the following way. I went to interview a man with a high reputation for wisdom. . . . Well, I gave a thorough examination to this person—I need not mention his name, but it was one of our politicians that I was studying when I had this experience—and in conversation with him I formed the impression that although in many people's opinion, and especially in his own, he appeared to be wise, in fact he was not. . . . I reflected as I walked away: "Well, I am certainly wiser than this man. It is only too likely that neither of us has any knowledge to boast of; but he thinks that he knows something which he does not know, whereas I am quite conscious of my ignorance. At any rate it seems that I am wiser than he is to this small extent, that I do not think that I know what I do not know."

From that time on I interviewed one person after another. I realized with distress and alarm that I was making myself unpopular. . . . After I had finished with the politicians I turned to the poets, dramatic, lyric, and all the rest. . . . It seemed clear to me that the poets were in much the same case; and I also observed that the very fact that they were poets made them think that they had a perfect understanding of all other subjects, of which they were totally ignorant. So I left that line of inquiry too with the same sense of advantage that I had felt in the case of the politicians.

Last of all I turned to the skilled craftsmen. I knew quite well that I had practically no technical qualifications myself, and I was sure that I should find them full of impressive knowledge. . . . But, gentlemen, these professional experts seemed to share the same failing which I had noticed in the poets; I mean that on the strength of their technical proficiency they claimed a perfect understanding of every other subject, however important. . . .

The effect of these investigations of mine, gentlemen, has been to arouse against me a great deal of hostility. . . . This is due to the fact that whenever I succeed in disproving another person's claim to wisdom in a given subject, the bystanders assume that I know everything about that subject myself. But the truth of the matter, gentlemen, is pretty certainly this: that real wisdom is the property of [Apollo], and this oracle is his way of telling us that human wisdom has little or no value. It seems to me that he is not referring literally to

Socrates, but has merely taken my name as an example, as if he would say to us "The wisest of you men is he who has realized, like Socrates, that in respect of wisdom he is really worthless."[1]

Wisdom, then, is not the expertise or technical skills of professional people. Indeed, as Socrates points out, such knowledge may impede the quest for wisdom by deluding people into thinking that they know what they don't. In contrast, the wisdom of Socrates consists of a critical habit, an eternal vigilance about all things and a reverence for truth, whatever its forms, wherever its place. His is a perspective that allows him to transcend the narrowness, the smugness, the arrogance, and the pettiness of mundane ego fulfillment.

Others have viewed wisdom, and thus philosophy, differently. Some, like Aristotle (384–322 B.C.), have tried to gain an organized knowledge of the world and an understanding of the nature of things and the relationships among them. Part of this is an understanding of how we ought to live. By exposing all stated and implied assumptions, theories, and methods of all beliefs, philosophy seeks the wisdom that comes from systematically organizing, structuring, and relating all available data and experiences. Thus, the love of wisdom is all-encompassing; it is not bounded by the limitations of this subject or that discipline.

Others view wisdom more actively. For them, philosophy consists of participation in life—to change things, to solve human problems, or to discover the meaning of existence. Still others feel that the wisdom of philosophy is in helping us to think more clearly and precisely.

No philosopher has a monopoly on wisdom or its meaning. For us Socrates' critical perspective will do, for it suggests an attitude, a temperament, that underlies other views. But the other perspectives have merit. On wisdom, as on other subjects, our knowledge is a drop, our ignorance an ocean.

In one sense, time has eroded many ancient philosophical concerns. As we have come to know more and to refine our methodology for unraveling the secrets of the universe, we have decreased the subject matter of the original philosophical debate. At the same time, however, philosophy has been enriched and the pursuit of wisdom intensified by the philosophical questions that new disciplines have inevitably raised.

For example, modern physics holds that the universe might best be described as consisting primarily of energy, which seems to be defined by the requirements of mathematical symmetry. But is this mathematical pattern strictly a mental construct? If it is, might reality best be described as being mental rather than physical? These are essentially philosophical questions.

Today, one of the most widely accepted explanations of the universe's origins is referred to as "the pulsating cosmos." In essence, it holds that gravity once pulled together all the matter in the universe, resulting in a molten ball; due to intense gravitational forces, this ball ultimately collapsed on itself, then exploded. The matter that is apparently moving away from us today is the

1. *Plato.* The Apology, *in* The Last Days of Socrates. *Hugh Tredennick, Trans. New York: Penguin, 1959, pp. 49–52. © Hugh Tredennick, 1954, 1959, 1969. Reprinted by permission of Penguin Books Ltd.*

condensed and clustered residue of that explosion. Ultimately, the theory goes, the process will be repeated, because it is thought to be a perpetual cycle. Thus, it's argued that we are part of a dynamic, eternal process in which energy is built up, dissipated, and regenerated.

This scientific theory raises a number of philosophical questions: If such an explosion did in fact occur, what's the origin of the matter that went into it? Are there other pulsating universes? Astronomy can't answer these questions fully. Indeed, some would say that, strictly speaking, they are not the concern of astronomy. But they are part of the interests of some philosophers today who, consistent with the ancient philosophical commitment to pursue wisdom, seek the answers to bedrock questions that other disciplines raise but can't answer.

Take, as a final example, the psychological theory of behaviorism, which has gained wide recognition today. In effect, behaviorism states that humans are totally the products of their experiences. In other words, we are the sum total of genetic and environmental influences. If this is so, can we say that humans are free? If so, in what sense? If we're not free, can we rightly be held responsible for anything we do? For example, is there any justification for punishing people for so-called wrongdoing? Indeed, what meaning does wrongdoing have if we can't help what we do? In a word, research and discovery in psychology raise numerous philosophical questions of vital concern to those seeking to become wise about the nature of human beings.

But don't think that philosophy only consists of questions that can't be answered definitely. Philosophy is not so much residue, it is not a dustbin for the refuse of the sciences. After all, the sciences rest upon philosophical foundations regarding reality—the extent to which we can know it, the methods we use to understand it, and the truths we may find about it. The search for data, the theoretical directions, the subsequent evaluations, all can begin only with the help of philosophical assumptions and guidelines. For example, what constitutes fact or evidence? Even existence presupposes philosophical categorizations. Notable scientists are keenly aware of their philosophical roots as well as the ramifications of their work for our views of human nature and the universe. What's more, the question "What is science?" if not an informational inquiry, is itself highly philosophical. Specifically, science is a mode of consciousness, philosophy is a mode of self-consciousness. Philosophy and science have different methods and purposes, and they produce knowledge of very different logical types. Science studies the world, never itself. Philosophy, among other things, studies science and necessarily studies itself as well. It articulates the presuppositions of science, and in so doing it articulates the necessary structure of the world. In brief, philosophy is always a strong presence in the center of things.

What, then, is philosophy? While any definition threatens to be incomplete or inaccurate, perhaps the most workable one views philosophy as the love and pursuit of wisdom. Let's consider philosophy, therefore, as the cultivation of critical habits, the search for truth, the interrogation of the obvious. As such, it is both independent of other disciplines and embedded in their foundations and ongoing activities. Looking at it this way, we capture the initial and continuing impulse of philosophy. We also allow for broad diversity in how individual philosophers pursue wisdom. Perhaps most important, viewed this way, philosophy is an activity undertaken by human beings who are deeply concerned about who they are and what everything is all about.

Although philosophy is difficult to pin down, this doesn't mean that there is no agreement about the issues that philosophy traditionally studies and about the philosophical enterprise. In fact, a familiarity with the philosophical issues and enterprise leads to a sound understanding of what philosophy is.

Traditional Concerns of Philosophy

Traditionally, philosophy has sought an organized knowledge of the world and our place in it; and knowledge about how we ought to live, including the bases for beliefs and interactions with others. Of course, philosophers have approached these general concerns in diverse ways, each emphasizing some aspect of human knowledge. Thus, one philosophy, termed *logical/analytical philosophy*, has concentrated on the confusion which impairs thinking and communicating; another, called *pragmatism*, has stressed the need to find solutions to problems of our social existence; still another, *existentialism*, has been concerned with making life meaningful to each individual person. By the same token, individual philosophers have taken diverse approaches to the task of philosophy: "the quiet philosophy of the sage who sees much but speaks little because language cannot hold life; the articulate, noisy dialectics of Socrates; the calm, logical apologetics of Aquinas; the mystical philosophy of Plotinus and Chuang-tzu; the mathematical philosophy of Russell and Wittgenstein."[2]

The variety of philosophies notwithstanding, philosophy in general has dealt with such basic questions as: What is knowledge? What is real? What is good? While none of these questions can be considered in isolation, all philosophical questions fall under one or more of these foundational inquiries, which represent the traditional interests of philosophers. Numerous non-philosophers have also stressed the importance of investigating these subjects.

These traditional concerns suggest the three categories under which all other philosophical problems fall: knowledge, reality, and value. The fields of philosophy that explore these themes are generally termed *epistemology*, *metaphysics*, and *axiology*.

Epistemology literally means the study of knowledge. A variety of problems are usually discussed as part of epistemology: the structure, reliability, extent, and kinds of knowledge; truth (including definitions of truth and validity); logic and a variety of strictly linguistic concerns; and the foundations of all knowledge (including the conditions under which an assertion is warranted and numerous concerns dealing directly with science and scientific knowledge).

Metaphysics is the study of the most general or ultimate characteristics of reality or existence. Some of the problems that fall under it are the structure

2. *James L. Christian.* Philosophy: An Introduction to the Art of Wondering. *2nd ed. New York: Holt, Rinehart and Winston, 1978, pp. xvii–xviii.*

and development of the universe; the meaning and nature of being; and the nature of mind, self, and consciousness. Also, the nature of religion can be considered to fall under metaphysics, which includes the existence of God, the destiny of the universe, and the immortality of the soul.

Axiology refers to the study of values. Specifically, axiological problems often involve values in human conduct; the nature and justification of social structures and political systems; the nature of art; and the meaning of art in human experience.

In approaching these areas, philosophy asks critical questions about the obvious and taken-for-granted. This is an important characteristic of the philosophical enterprise, but there are others.

The Philosophical Enterprise

It is sometimes said that the key to philosophy, its essence, is asking the right question. The right question not only initiates philosophical thinking but also gives it direction. What is the "right question"? That's impossible to say. There is no easy formula or instant recipe. Asking the right question is really an art, and, as with all arts, imagination plays a significant part. By imagination, we mean the ability to deal creatively with the things of experience, to go beyond the commonplace, to see what is not readily apparent, to wonder about things that other people accept, and to conceive of possibilities and alternatives—different ways of approaching the obvious. Thus, most people accept unquestioningly the apparent order operating in the natural world. The imaginative person wonders about it, puzzles over it, ultimately formulates questions about it: "What is the nature of this order? What accounts for it? How can it be explained? Indeed, is it properly described as 'order' to begin with? Is there a similar 'order' working in my life?" Having heard of the Jonestown suicides and murders, which claimed nearly 1,000 lives, many people expressed grief, shock, and horror. Then, they went about their business. But the imaginative person ponders it, not in any morbid or unhealthy way, but in what we can term a philosophical mode. They wonder: "What was the meaning of that tragedy? Was there some purpose in it? If there is a God, what kind of God would permit such a thing? What social currents, if any, contributed to the tragedy?" Each question moves us from the facts of experience to profound speculation. We can address these questions only if we're prepared to receive the disclosures of the world imaginatively rather than matter-of-factly, if we're open to new possibilities and changes in how we see things. This is much easier said than done, since humans generally resist change.

It's worth noting that in philosophy all the important questions were asked millennia ago. What's crucial, then, is to see the mistakes in the latest answers and to rectify them. Philosophy is a progression, one that moves through the criticism of old answers and the formation of new ones. In the process we create a new vision of reality itself. The attempt to criticize answers and form new ones is generally characterized by an acute and exacting application of one's rational powers. Thus, most philosophers, if not all, would agree that philosophy is a rational enterprise that attempts to answer questions by means of an intensive application of reason. Inevitably, this application draws on analysis, comparison, and evaluation.

A good example of this is found in book IV of Plato's best-known work, *The Republic*. There Socrates talks with Glaucon about a subject of contemporary debate: the equality of women. He argues that women with the right natural gifts are not to be excluded from fulfilling the highest functions in the state. This meant they could be Guardians, the name given to a group of specialists, suited by a combination of qualities to defend and rule the city. The highest section of Guardians were philosophical Rulers. Thus, Socrates contends that when the best Guardians are chosen for training as Rulers, women may be among them. At Plato's time such a notion was unthinkable. Women in Athens lived in seclusion, taking no part in politics. At the outset, then, Socrates reacts to this custom. Notice how his commitment to goodness and honor steels him against social ridicule. Then, clarifying his terms, making distinctions, following a logical train of thought, he demonstrates that in the management of social affairs, no occupation belongs exclusively to one sex. It follows that women deserve the same kind of training as men.

> *Socrates:* We must go back, then, to a subject which ought, perhaps, to have been treated earlier in its proper place; though, after all, it may be suitable that the women should have their turn on the stage when the men have quite finished their performance, especially since you are so insistent. In my judgement, then, the question under what conditions people born and educated as we have described should possess wives and children, and how they should treat them, can be rightly settled only by keeping to the course on which we started them at the outset. We undertook to put these men in the position of watch-dogs guarding a flock. Suppose we follow up the analogy and imagine them bred and reared in the same sort of way. We can then see if that plan will suit our purpose.
>
> *Glaucon:* How will that be?
>
> *Socrates:* In this way. Which do we think right for watch-dogs: should the females guard the flock and hunt with the males and take a share in all they do, or should they be kept within doors as fit for no more than bearing and feeding their puppies, while all the hard work of looking after the flock is left to the males?
>
> *Glaucon:* They are expected to take their full share, except that we treat them as not quite so strong.
>
> *Socrates:* Can you employ any creature for the same work as another, if you do not give them both the same upbringing and education?
>
> *Glaucon:* No.
>
> *Socrates:* Then, if we are to set women to the same tasks as men, we must teach them the same things. They must have the same two branches of training for mind and body and also be taught the art of war, and they must receive the same treatment.
>
> *Glaucon:* That seems to follow.
>
> *Socrates:* Possibly, if these proposals were carried out, they might be ridiculed as involving a good many breaches of custom.

Glaucon: They might indeed.

Socrates: The most ridiculous—don't you think?—being the notion of women exercising naked along with the men in the wrestling-schools; some of them elderly women too, like the old men who still have a passion for exercise when they are wrinkled and not very agreeable to look at.

Glaucon: Yes, that would be thought laughable, according to our present notions.

Socrates: Now we have started on this subject, we must not be frightened of the many witticisms that might be aimed at such a revolution, not only in the matter of bodily exercise but in the training of women's minds, and not least when it comes to their bearing arms and riding on horseback. Having begun upon these rules, we must not draw back from the harsher provisions. The wits may be asked to stop being witty and try to be serious; and we may remind them that it is not so long since the Greeks, like most foreign nations of the present day, thought it ridiculous and shameful for men to be seen naked. When gymnastic exercises were first introduced in Crete and later at Sparta, the humorists had their chance to make fun of them; but when experience had shown that nakedness is better uncovered than muffled up, the laughter died down and a practice which the reason approved ceased to look ridiculous to the eye. This shows how idle it is to think anything ludicrous but what is base. One who tries to raise a laugh at any spectacle save that of baseness and folly will also, in his serious moments, set before himself some other standard than goodness of what deserves to be held in honor.

Glaucon: Most assuredly.

Socrates: The first thing to be settled, then, is whether these proposals are feasible; and it must be open to anyone, whether a humorist or serious-minded, to raise the question whether, in the case of mankind, the feminine nature is capable of taking part with the other sex in all occupations, or in none at all, or in some only; and in particular under which of these heads this business of military service falls. Well begun is half done, and would not this be the best way to begin?

Glaucon: Yes.

Socrates: Shall we take the other side in this debate and argue against ourselves? We do not want the adversary's position to be taken by storm for lack of defenders.

Glaucon: I have no objection.

Socrates: Let us state his case for him. "Socrates and Glaucon," he will say, "there is no need for others to dispute your position; you yourselves, at the very outset of founding your commonwealth, agreed that everyone should do the one work for which nature fits him." Yes, of course; I suppose we did. "And isn't there a very great difference in nature between man and woman?" Yes, surely. "Does not that natural difference imply a corresponding difference in the work to be given to each?" Yes. "But if so, surely you must be mistaken now and contradicting yourselves when you say that men and women, having such widely divergent natures, should do the same things?" What is your answer to that, my ingenious friend?

Glaucon: It is not easy to find one at the moment. I can only appeal to you to state the case on our own side, whatever it may be.

Socrates: This, Glaucon, is one of many alarming objections which I foresaw some time ago. That is why I shrank from touching upon these laws concerning the possession of wives and the rearing of children.

Glaucon: It looks like anything but an easy problem.

Socrates: True; but whether a man tumbles into a swimming-pool or into mid-ocean, he has to swim all the same. So must we, and try if we can reach the shore, hoping for some Arion's dolphin or other miraculous deliverance to bring us safe to land.

Glaucon: I suppose so.

Socrates: Come then, let us see if we can find the way out. We did agree that different natures should have different occupations, and that the natures of man and woman are different; and yet we are now saying that these different natures are to have the same occupations. Is that the charge against us?

Glaucon: Exactly.

Socrates: It is extraordinary, Glaucon, what an effect the practice of debating has upon people.

Glaucon: Why do you say that?

Socrates: Because they often seem to fall unconsciously into mere disputes which they mistake for reasonable argument, through being unable to draw the distinctions proper to their subject; and so, instead of a philosophical exchange of ideas, they go off in chase of contradictions which are purely verbal.

Glaucon: I know that happens to many people; but does it apply to us at this moment?

Socrates: Absolutely. At least I am afraid we are slipping unconsciously into a dispute about words. We have been strenuously insisting on the letter of our principle that different natures should not have the same occupations, as if we were scoring a point in a debate; but we have altogether neglected to consider what sort of sameness or difference we meant and in what respect these natures and occupations were to be defined as different or the same. Consequently, we might very well be asking one another whether there is not an opposition in nature between bald and long-haired men, and, when that was admitted, forbid one set to be shoemakers, if the other were following that trade.

Glaucon: That would be absurd.

Socrates: Yes, but only because we never meant any and every sort of sameness or difference in nature, but the sort that was relevant to the occupations in question. We meant, for instance, that a man and a woman have the same nature if both have a talent for medicine; whereas two men have different natures if one is a born physician, the other a born carpenter.

Glaucon: Yes, of course.

Socrates: If, then, we find that either the male sex or the female is specially qualified for any particular form of occupation, then that occupation, we shall say, ought to be assigned to one sex or the other. But if the only difference appears to be that the male begets and the female brings forth, we shall conclude that no difference between man and woman has yet been produced that is relevant to our purpose. We shall continue to think it proper for our Guardians and their wives to share in the same pursuits.

Glaucon: And quite rightly.

Socrates: The next thing will be to ask our opponent to name any profession or occupation in civic life for the purposes of which woman's nature is different from man's.

Glaucon: That is a fair question.

Socrates: He might reply, as you did just now, that it is not easy to find a satisfactory answer on the spur of the moment, but that there would be no difficulty after a little reflection.

Glaucon: Perhaps.

Socrates: Suppose, then, we invite him to follow us and see if we can convince him that there is no occupation concerned with the management of social affairs that is peculiar to women. We will confront him with a question: When you speak of a man having a natural talent for something, do you mean that he finds it easy to learn, and after a little instruction can find out much more for himself; whereas a man who is not so gifted learns with difficulty and no amount of instruction and practice will make him even remember what he has been taught? Is the talented man one whose bodily powers are readily at the service of his mind, instead of being a hindrance? Are not these the marks by which you distinguish the presence of a natural gift for any pursuit?

Glaucon: Yes, precisely.

Socrates: Now do you know of any human occupation in which the male sex is not superior to the female in all these respects? Need I waste time over exceptions like weaving and watching over saucepans and batches of cakes, though women are supposed to be good at such things and get laughed at when a man does them better?

Glaucon: It is true, in almost everything one sex is easily beaten by the other. No doubt many women are better at many things than many men; but taking the sexes as a whole, it is as you say.

Socrates: To conclude, then, there is no occupation concerned with the management of social affairs which belongs either to woman or to man, as such. Natural gifts are to be found here and there in both creatures alike; and every occupation is open to both, so far as their natures are concerned, though woman is for all purposes the weaker.

Glaucon: Certainly.

Socrates: Is that a reason for making over all occupations to men only?

Glaucon: Of course not.

Socrates: No, because one woman may have a natural gift for medicine or for music, another may not.

Glaucon: Surely.

Socrates: Is it not also true that a woman may, or may not, be warlike or athletic?

Glaucon: I think so.

Socrates: And again, one may love knowledge, another hate it; one may be high-spirited, another spiritless?

Glaucon: True again.

Socrates: It follows that one woman will be fitted by nature to be a Guardian, another will not; because these were the qualities for which we selected our men Guardians. So for the purpose of keeping watch over the commonwealth, woman has the same nature as man, save insofar as she is weaker.

Glaucon: So it appears.

Socrates: It follows that women of this type must be selected to share the life and duties of Guardians with men of the same type, since they are competent and of a like nature, and the same natures must be allowed the same pursuits.

Glaucon: Yes.

Socrates: We come round, then, to our former position, that there is nothing contrary to nature in giving our Guardians' wives the same training for mind and body. The practice we proposed to establish was not impossible or visionary, since it was in accordance with nature. Rather, the contrary practice which now prevails turns out to be unnatural.

Glaucon: So it appears.

Socrates: Well, we set out to inquire whether the plan we proposed was feasible and also the best. That it is feasible is now agreed; we must next settle whether it is the best.

Glaucon: Obviously.

Socrates: Now, for the purpose of producing a woman fit to be a Guardian, we shall not have one education for men and another for women, precisely because the nature to be taken in hand is the same.

Glaucon: True.

Socrates: What is your opinion on the question of one man being better than another? Do you think there is no such difference?

Glaucon: Certainly I do not.

Socrates: And in this commonwealth of ours which will prove the better men—the Guardians who have received the education we described, or the shoemakers who have been trained to make shoes?

Glaucon: It is absurd to ask such a question.

Socrates: Very well. So these Guardians will be the best of all the citizens?

Glaucon: By far.

Socrates: And these women the best of all the women?

Glaucon: Yes.

Socrates: Can anything be better for a commonwealth than to produce in it men and women of the best possible type?

Glaucon: No.

Socrates: And that result will be brought about by such a system of mental and bodily training as we have described?

Glaucon: Surely.

Socrates: We may conclude that the institution we proposed was not only practicable, but also the best for the commonwealth.

Glaucon: Yes.

Socrates: The wives of our Guardians, then, must strip for exercise, since they will be clothed with virtue, and they must take their share in war and in the other social duties of guardianship. They are to have no other occupation; and in these duties the lighter part must fall to the women, because of the weakness of their sex. The man who laughs at naked women, exercising their bodies for the best of reasons, is like one that "gathers fruit unripe," for he does not know what it is that he is laughing at or what he is doing. There will never be a finer saying than the one which declares that whatever does good should be held in honor, and the only shame is in doing harm.

Glaucon: That is perfectly true.[3]

Evident here and illustrated throughout the dialogues is another feature of the philosophical enterprise. Philosophy is an activity. Remembering this fact is most important, because it combats the tendency to think of philosophy as something to be learned or mastered as we do other disciplines. But philosophy is something we *do*, not master. Thus, Plato and Glaucon are *doing* philosophy. It's true that in reading Plato's dialogues, we learn of his philosophy through Socrates, but there is more than that. The greatness of Socrates or Plato, or of any other philosopher, is not in their conclusions, their theories, or their systems. Their greatness is in their remarkable ability to think, to conceptualize, to analyze, to compare, to evaluate, to understand. In a word, to *philosophize*. To miss this in your study of philosophy, while gleaning names, dates, and beliefs, is like missing the forest for the trees. Of course, the other side of the coin is philosophy as a product. The best philosophers have something to say, a product to offer. By studying their product, you should be more able to philosophize for yourself, to understand and to articulate your understanding. Philosophy as a process and philosophy as a product, therefore, are complementary.

So, the philosophical enterprise is an active process of formulating proper questions and resolving them by rigorous, persistent analysis. Though an incomplete description, this nonetheless captures the spirit of philosophy. It's one thing, however, to list philosophy's concerns and to characterize its spirit, and quite another to justify its study. We should ask, therefore: Why study philosophy?

Why Philosophy?

To put this question in the context of the college student, let's rejoin Liz and Jon. In addition to being puzzled about what philosophy is, they're also unsure about why they should study it.

---

3.   Plato. *The Republic of Plato. F. M. Cornford, Trans. New York: Oxford University Press, 1941, pp. 148–155. Reprinted by permission of Oxford University Press.*

Liz:	You know, I don't think I'd be taking this course if it didn't meet a requirement.
Jon:	Really. But I am kind of curious about it.
Liz:	Sure, but I find it hard to get into something when I don't see how it affects me. I mean, how's philosophy going to help me cut it?
Jon:	Maybe you'll just have to wait and see.
Liz:	You really think it can help?
Jon:	I don't know. But if we don't know what it's all about, maybe we should give it a chance. I wouldn't write off a food without first tasting it, would you?

Wait and see. That is one way to address the value of philosophy. Just as it's hard to know whether you'll like a new dish without first sampling it, it's unrealistic, even foolish, to junk philosophy without first trying it. Still, many beginners see this as a cop-out.

Liz:	But at least I have some basis for trying a new food. I've tried lots of other strange foods and liked some of them. But philosophy? I've gotten along okay so far. Why study it now?

Such a reaction has an immediate appeal, but it warrants examination.

Jon:	You keep talking about "getting along." What do you mean exactly?
Liz:	Well, you know, I haven't had any big problems. I've pretty much been able to take care of myself. For example, take last year; I decided my social life needed a shot in the arm. So I decided to get a car. But the only way I could afford one was to get a part-time job, selling clothes. Nobody at the shop asked me if I knew anything about philosophy. But they did ask me whether I'd had any previous experience in sales. Good thing I had. Now I've got a car, and my social life has picked up.

When people talk about getting along, they generally mean satisfying what psychologists often term *maintenance needs,* the physical and psychological needs that people must satisfy in order to maintain themselves as human beings: food, shelter, security, social interaction, and so on. Liz sees personal needs strictly in terms of maintenance. Little wonder that when it comes to education, she has no trouble understanding the need for job preparation courses; they clearly assist the satisfaction of maintenance needs.

Jon:	Me, I want more out of life than just to get along.

Liz: More? Like what?

Jon: I don't know exactly. But don't you ever think in terms of growth? Of becoming everything you can be? Of living life to the fullest?

Liz: Sure, that's why I'm really cracking in my major.

Jon: I don't know. I see myself as more than what I'm going to spend the rest of my life doing.

Liz: I guess I never have—not really.

Jon: But don't you think it's important?

Liz: I suppose it could be.

Jon: I mean later, after you've got all the rest.

Liz: So what are you saying—that I need more than just to get along?

Jon: I guess I am.

Liz: And philosophy can help?

Jon: I don't know. Maybe.

Some modern psychologists, Abraham Maslow among them, point out that humans have needs other than maintenance ones, which they term *actualizing needs*. While more difficult to describe than maintenance needs, actualizing needs appear to be associated with self-fulfillment, creativity, self-expression, realization of your potential, and, in a word, being everything you can be. Why mention these? Because evaluating the worth of courses and disciplines in terms of their job preparation value is to take a narrow view of what human beings need. It completely overlooks higher-level needs. This doesn't mean, of course, that studying philosophy will necessarily lead to self-actualization. But philosophy assists by promoting the ideal of self-actualization, or what psychotherapist Carl Rogers terms the "fully functioning person."

Consider some characteristics of the self-actualized or fully functioning person. One is the ability to form one's own opinions and beliefs. Self-actualized people don't automatically go along with what's "in" or what's expected of them. Not that they are necessarily rebels; they just make up their own minds. They think, evaluate, and decide for themselves. What could better capture the spirit of philosophy than such intellectual and behavioral independence?

A second characteristic is profound self-awareness. Self-actualized people harbor few illusions about themselves and rarely resort to easy rationalizations to justify their beliefs and actions. If anything, philosophy is geared to deepen self-awareness by inviting us to examine the basic intellectual foundations of our lives.

A third characteristic is flexibility. Change and uncertainty don't level self-actualized people. Indeed, they exhibit resilience in the face of disorder, doubt, uncertainty, indefiniteness, even chaos. But they are not indifferent or uncaring. Quite the opposite. They are much involved in their experiences. Because of their resilience, they not only recognize the essential ambiguity of human affairs but also develop a high ambiguity tolerance. They are not upended by a lack of definite answers or of concrete solutions. When seriously undertaken, the study of philosophy often promotes what some have termed a philosophical calm, the capacity to persevere in the face of upheaval. This stems in part from an ability to put things in perspective, to see the "big picture," to make neither too much nor too little of events.

A fourth characteristic of self-actualized or fully functioning people is that they are generally creative. They are not necessarily writers, painters, or musicians, for creativity can function in many ways and at various levels. Rather, such people exhibit creativity in all they do. Whether spending leisure time or conversing, they seem to leave their own distinctive mark. Philosophy can help in this process by getting us to develop a philosophical perspective on issues, problems, and events. This means, in part, that we no longer see or experience life on the surface. We engage it on deeper levels, and we interact with it so that we help to fashion our world. In another way, because philosophy exercises our imaginations, it invites a personal expression that is unique and distinctive.

PHILOSOPHY AND LIFE 1-1
Viktor Frankl's Logotherapy

Dr. Viktor E. Frankl is one psychologist who believes that the search for meaning is the human's primary interest. Frankl, professor of psychiatry and neurology, spent three years at Auschwitz and other Nazi concentration camps. He then gained his freedom, only to learn that almost all his family had been wiped out. During those years of incredible suffering and degradation, which he in part describes in his *Man's Search for Meaning*, Frankl developed a theory of psychotherapy termed *logotherapy*.

Logotherapy is derived from the Greek word *logos*, which denotes "meaning." Logotherapy focuses on the meaning of human existence as well as on the human's search for such meaning. According to Dr. Frankl and other logotherapists, the striving to find meaning in their lives is the primary motivational force in humans. He writes:

> Man's search for meaning is a primary force in his life and not a "secondary rationalization" of instinctual drives. This meaning is unique and specific in that it must and can be fulfilled by him alone; only then does it achieve a significance that will satisfy his own will to meaning. There are some authors who contend that meaning and values are "nothing but defense mechanisms, reaction formation and sublimation." But as for myself, I would not be willing to live merely for the sake of my "defense mechanisms," nor would I be ready to die merely for the sake of my "reaction formations." Man, however, is able to live and even to die for the sake of his ideals and values!*

Finally, self-actualized or fully functioning people have clearly conceptualized, well-thought-out value systems in morality, the arts, politics, and so
on. Since a fundamental concern of philosophy is values and since philosophy
often deals directly with morals, art, politics, and other value areas, it offers an
opportunity to formulate viable assessments of worth and find meaning in our
lives. For some psychologists, the search for meaning and values constitutes the
human's primary interest (see Philosophy and Life 1-1).

Some philosophers have shared this particular psychological insight, although expressing it differently. Perhaps the best example is found in the
thought of Aristotle, who developed his view of self-realization by distinguishing among bodily goods (such as health), external goods (such as wealth), and
spiritual (that is, psychological) goods (such as virtue). In his masterly analysis
of happiness, *Nicomachean Ethics* (book I, chs. 4–13; book X, chs. 6–9), Aristotle
says that happiness, which is the end or goal of all human beings, does not
consist in any action of the body or senses. In the language of Maslow, happiness does not consist in satisfying maintenance needs. Rather, happiness involves the satisfaction of higher-level needs, in what Aristotle calls action of

---

Logotherapy, therefore, considers humans as beings whose primary concerns are fulfilling a meaning and actualizing values, rather than the mere
gratification and satisfaction of drives and instincts.

Dr. Frankl contends that the human search for meaning and value may
arouse inner tensions rather than inner equilibrium. But he feels that these
tensions are an indispensable prerequisite to mental health. There is nothing
that would so effectively help one survive even the worst conditions, as the
knowledge that there is a meaning in one's life. As evidence, he recalls his
prison experiences, in which he witnessed that those who believed that there
was a task waiting for them, a meaning, were the most likely to survive. In a
word, for Dr. Frankl mental health is based in part on the tension that's inherent in humans who recognize the gap between what they are and what
they should become.

* *Viktor E. Frankl. Man's Search for Meaning. New York: Pocket Books, 1972, pp. 154–155.*

☐ *Can the study of philosophy be related to the principles of
logotherapy?* ☐ *Is there any wisdom in the following words of the German
philosopher Friedrich Nietzsche (1844–1900): "He who has a why to live for
can bear almost any how"?* ☐ *What, if any, meaning do you currently find
in your life?*

what is noblest and best in us: our reason. But happiness is not activity of the practical reason, for this is full of care and trouble in meeting basic needs. In contrast, happiness is the activity of speculative and theoretical reason; it is the life of the intellectual virtues, the chief of which is philosophic wisdom, which equips us for contemplating the highest truth and good. In brief, for Aristotle, health, maturity, education, friends, and worldly goods (all of which serve to satisfy maintenance needs) should be made subordinate aids to the truly happy life, which consists in a self-realization that takes root in the contemplative life.

So it seems safe to say that part of philosophy's value lies in its assisting us to satisfy higher-level needs, which often arise when maintenance needs have been met. At the same time, philosophy also contributes to the satisfaction of some maintenance needs. We mentioned previously the need for security. People acquire insurance policies and often go to extreme measures to avoid anxiety-inducing situations. But security needs show up on other levels. People seek to make sense out of their world in a variety of ways: through allegiance to religious beliefs, adherence to political systems, commitment to causes, and participation in clearly defined ways of seeing things and living. In part, such loyalties and behavior betray the human need for the security that stems from having ordered our universe, from having made sense out of things. Can philosophy help?

In fact, it's hard to imagine a better place to begin this ordering process than with the study of philosophy. One of the goals of philosophy is the integration of experience into a unified, coherent, systematic world view. Studying philosophy exposes you not only to world-view alternatives but also to how philosophers have ordered the universe for themselves. Stated another way, at the personal level, philosophy aims to integrate thought, feeling, and action in a meaningful way. As a result, philosophy extends the range of personal alternatives. Perhaps we believe things or have outlooks primarily because of our acculturation. We've never really thought about these beliefs or perspectives, having adopted them as an intellectual backdrop. We all have such taken-for-granted beliefs. But optional life-styles may exist that are more suitable for us. Or we may not fully understand and appreciate the worth of our own taken-for-granted ideas. Either way, philosophy offers the opportunity to test various beliefs, outlooks, and life-styles.

Other things make the study of philosophy worthwhile. Consider, for example, the importance of awareness. In part, personal freedom depends on awareness of self and the world. To a large degree, we are only as free as we are aware of the significant influences on our lives. In helping us deepen our awareness, philosophy gives us the ability to deal with and perhaps to slough off encumbrances to freedom.

What's more, philosophy exposes us to the history of thought. By portraying the evolutionary nature of intellectual achievement, it provides a perspective on the continuing development of human thought. As we confront the thought of various philosophers, we realize that one outlook is not necessarily true and another false; the value of any attitude lies chiefly in its usefulness within a given context. A merit of this exposure is that it breeds humility. We realize that if today's view has proved yesterday's inadequate, then tomorrow's may so prove today's. As a result, we become more tolerant, more receptive, and more sympathetic to views that compete or conflict with our own. We're less biased, provincial, ingrown; more open-minded and cosmopolitan.

Also, the study of philosophy helps us refine our powers of analysis, our abilities to think critically, to reason, to evaluate, to theorize, and to justify. As we said earlier, these skills are the tools of philosophy. Exposure to the great ideas of extraordinary thinkers is likely to hone our own powers of analysis, hopefully enough to apply them constructively to our own affairs.

In conclusion, we might relate the value of philosophy to what we earlier noted as one of its distinctive characteristics: the absence of a body of definitely ascertainable knowledge. For many, rather than a value of philosophy, its uncertainty suggests that philosophy is of little worth. Is this so? Or is philosophy's uncertainty its strength?

Those critical of philosophy on this point should ask themselves: What in life is certain? Death and taxes, replied that great American humorist and writer Mark Twain. Were he alive today, advances in organ transplant, the advent of cryonics, and the rumble of taxpayer revolt might give Twain pause. The point is that very little, if anything, can be considered certain. Indeed, some, like Bertrand Russell, would insist that the only thing that is certain is uncertainty itself. Thus, Russell contended that the value of philosophy is its uncertainty. It seems fitting, then, that we should conclude this overview of the value of philosophy with a passage from Russell's *The Problems of Philosophy*, in which he explains his contention. Notice how Russell, after making this point, goes on to discuss what he considers to be philosophy's chief value, the nature of the subjects that it contemplates.

> The value of philosophy is, in part, to be sought largely in its very uncertainty. The man who has no tincture of philosophy goes through life imprisoned in the prejudices derived from common sense, from the habitual beliefs of his age or his nation, and from convictions which have grown up in his mind without the cooperation or consent of his deliberate reason. To such a man the world tends to become definite, finite, obvious; common objects rouse no questions, and unfamiliar possibilities are contemptuously rejected. As soon as we begin to philosophize, on the contrary, we find . . . that even the most everyday things lead to problems to which only very incomplete answers can be given. Philosophy, though unable to tell us with certainty what is the true answer to the doubts which it raises, is able to suggest many possibilities which enlarge our thoughts and free them from the tyranny of custom. Thus, while diminishing our feeling of certainty as to what things are, it greatly increases our knowledge as to what they may be; it removes the somewhat arrogant dogmatism of those who have never traveled into the region of liberating doubt, and it keeps alive our sense of wonder by showing familiar things in an unfamiliar aspect.
>
> Apart from its utility in showing unsuspected possibilities, philosophy has a value—perhaps its chief value—through the greatness of the objects which it contemplates, and the freedom from narrow and personal aims resulting from this contemplation. The life of the instinctive man is shut up within the circle of his private interests: family and friends may be included, but the outer world is not regarded except as it may help or hinder what comes within the circle of

instinctive wishes. In such a life there is something feverish and confined, in comparison with which the philosophic life is calm and free. The private world of instinctive interests is a small one, set in the midst of a great and powerful world which must, sooner or later, lay our private world in ruins. Unless we can so enlarge our interests as to include the whole outer world, we remain like a garrison in a beleaguered fortress, knowing that the enemy prevents escape and that ultimate surrender is inevitable. In such a life there is no peace, but a constant strife between the insistence of desire and the powerlessness of will. In one way or another, if our life is to be great and free, we must escape this prison and this strife.

One way of escape is by philosophic contemplation. Philosophic contemplation does not, in its widest survey, divide the universe into two hostile camps—friends and foes, helpful and hostile, good and bad—it views the whole impartially. Philosophic contemplation, when it is unalloyed, does not aim at proving that the rest of the universe is akin to man. All acquisition of knowledge is an enlargement of the Self, but this enlargement is best attained when it is not directly sought. It is obtained when the desire for knowledge is alone operative, by a study which does not wish in advance that its objects should have this or that character, but adapts the Self to the characters which it finds in its objects.[4]

Before concluding this chapter, it is useful to observe a recurring problem in any introduction to philosophy. That problem concerns focus. Because so much material is and must be covered, the overall treatment may lack focus; the student may be left confused, or with only a most superficial understanding. While there is no easy solution to this problem, one useful device is to take a more in-depth look at a central figure in the material being covered. This book will use this strategy in some of its chapters. Since the purpose of this technique is to provide focus by exhibiting the relevant thought of a philosopher, an appropriate term for it is *showcase*. Our first Showcase spotlights Socrates and his method of dialectic.

Showcase: Socrates (469–399 B.C.)

It is hard to imagine a time so rich in human genius as the Athens into which Socrates was born in 469 B.C. By this time the great Greek dramatist Aeschylus had written some of his immortal works. Persia had been defeated, and Athens was on the verge of attaining naval control of the Aegean Sea. Pericles, who would usher in and preside over a splendid age of democracy and art, was still a young man, and the tragedians Euripides and Sophocles mere boys. During Socrates' lifetime, the Parthenon and the statues of Phidias would be finished and Athens would have secured for itself an immortal, perhaps unequalled, niche in the history of Western civilization. But all that was ancient Athens did not glitter; for, although the age in which Socrates grew up was indeed golden,

4.   *Bertrand Russell.* The Problems of Philosophy. *London: Oxford University Press, 1912, pp. 158–159. Reprinted by permission of Oxford University Press.*

by the end of his life it had tarnished. In his declining years, Socrates was to see Athens humbled in war, and his own life end in prison where, at the age of seventy, he was to drink the fabled hemlock in compliance with the death sentence handed down by the court which had tried him.

By profession a stonecutter, Socrates married and had children, and served honorably as a soldier. But he wrote nothing. Most of what we know about him has been preserved by three of his younger contemporaries: the dramatist Aristophanes, the historian Xenophon, and the philosopher Plato.

Because Socrates left no writing, there is some dispute about what philosophy rightly can be attributed to him. One of the most illuminating sources of his thought is the *Dialogues* of Plato, in which Socrates often serves as the leading character. But how much of the thought presented in the *Dialogues* is Socrates', how much is Plato's? Some argue that Plato's *Dialogues* accurately reflects the philosophy of Socrates, as well as, of course, the literary genius of Plato. Others, Aristotle among them, distinguish between the philosophical contributions made by Socrates and Plato. Today a middle position is popular. Accordingly, the early dialogues (for example, *The Apology* and *Euthyphro*) are considered accurate representations of Socratic thought, while the later ones reflect Plato's own philosophic development, including Plato's formulation of the metaphysical theory of Forms, which we will showcase in the next chapter. In this view, Socrates is considered an original philosopher who developed a new method of intellectual inquiry termed *dialectic*.

Dialectic

As we have seen in this chapter, Socrates was vitally concerned with attaining reliable knowledge. He was convinced that the way to attain reliable knowledge was through a practice of developed conversation, a method he called **dialectic.**

Socrates' dialectic would begin with a discussion of the most obvious aspects of any problem. Then a dialogic exchange would follow. Essential to this dialogue or conversation would be a clarification of ideas, which would continue until a clear statement of what was meant emerged.

We are told that Socrates, accordingly, would haunt the streets of ancient Athens, buttonholing powerful men and asking them irreverent questions about their opinions. To those who pretended to knowledge about justice, he would ask: What is justice? When you say something or somebody is just, what do you mean? Similarly, he would probe ideas about virtue or knowledge or morality. By careful questioning, Socrates would plumb one's system of beliefs, raising cherished certainties and exposing their soft underbellies. Understandably, Socrates' persistent demand for clarity of thought and exactness disarmed his victims, some of whom began to consider him a threat to social stability. In the end they were successful in suppressing him, but not in stilling his method of dialect, which continues to resonate in the philosophical enterprise.

A marvelous example of Socrates' dialectic is found in Plato's dialogue entitled *Euthyphro,* a portion of which follows. The scene is the front of the Hall of King Archon where Socrates is waiting to discover more about Meletus, a young man who has brought suit against him for "impiety," a capital offense in

Athens. Socrates doesn't know what the charge means. Straightaway, another young man named Euthyphro arrives. As it happens, Euthyphro has come to prosecute a suit of his own, charging that his own father is guilty of impiety. With tongue well in cheek, Socrates expresses delight for chancing upon someone like Euthyphro, who, he says, surely must know the meaning of impiety inasmuch as he is accusing his own father of it.

After asking Euthyphro to define piety, Socrates then shows him that his definition is inconsistent with other things that the young man believes. The procedure Socrates follows is analytic. By extracting the paradoxical in the familiar, he forces Euthyphro to look at his system of definitions and beliefs, to examine the glib assumptions by which he thinks and lives. In so doing, Socrates provides us with a sterling example of what it means to philosophize. When we philosophize we examine the certainty of our taken-for-granted; we poke and probe the easy and fundamental premises on which we erect our outlooks and base our actions. We examine our lives. Sometimes the examination ends conclusively with solid answers. Other times it does not. In *Euthyphro*, for example, the subject of piety is not resolved. But Socrates is not concerned with imposing a set of dogmatic ideas upon listeners but with leading them through an orderly process of thought. So is the study of philosophy.

As you will see in the passage that follows, Euthyphro eventually grows impatient with Socrates' dialectic. "Another time, Socrates," he tells the stonecutter, "for I am in a hurry and must go now." While you likely will share Euthyphro's uneasiness, even confusion, in your study of philosophy, it is hoped that you will not be impatient. Rather, allow philosophy to help you examine your life so that it will be worth living.

Socrates: And what is piety, and what is impiety?

Euthyphro: Piety is doing as I am doing; that is to say, prosecuting any one who is guilty of murder, sacrilege, or of any similar crime—whether he be your father or mother, or whoever he may be—that makes no difference; and not to prosecute them is impiety. And please to consider, Socrates, what a notable proof I will give you of the truth of my words, a proof which I have already given to others:—of the principle, I mean, that the impious, whoever he may be, ought not to go unpunished. For do not men regard Zeus as the best and most righteous of the gods?—and yet they admit that he bound his father (Cronos) because he wickedly devoured his sons, and that he too had punished his own father (Uranus) for a similar reason, in a nameless manner. And yet when I proceed against my father, they are angry with me. So inconsistent are they in their way of talking when the gods are concerned, and when I am concerned.

Socrates: May not this be the reason, Euthyphro, why I am charged with impiety—that I cannot away with these stories about the gods? and therefore I suppose that people think me wrong. But, as you who are well informed about them approve of them, I cannot do better than assent to your superior wisdom. What else can I say, confessing as I do, that I know nothing about them? Tell me, for the love of Zeus, whether you really believe that they are true.

Euthyphro: Yes, Socrates; and things more wonderful still, of which the world is in ignorance.

Socrates: And do you really believe that the gods fought with one another, and had dire quarrels, battles, and the like, as the poets say, and as you may see represented in the works of great artists? The temples are full of them; and notably the robe of Athene, which is carried up to the Acropolis at the great Panathenaea, is embroidered with them. Are all these tales of the gods true, Euthyphro?

Euthyphro: Yes, Socrates; and, as I was saying, I can tell you, if you would like to hear them, many other things about the gods which would quite amaze you.

Socrates: I dare say; and you shall tell me them at some other time when I have leisure. But just at present I would rather hear from you a more precise answer, which you have not as yet given, my friend, to the question, What is "piety"? When asked, you only replied, Doing as you do, charging your father with murder.

Euthyphro: And what I said was true, Socrates.

Socrates: No doubt, Euthyphro; but you would admit that there are many other pious acts?

Euthyphro: There are.

Socrates: Remember that I did not ask you to give me two or three examples of piety, but to explain the general idea which makes all pious things to be pious. Do you not recollect that there was one idea which made the impious impious, and the pious pious?

Euthyphro: I remember.

Socrates: Tell me what is the nature of this idea, and then I shall have a standard to which I may look, and by which I may measure actions, whether yours or those of any one else, and then I shall be able to say that such and such an action is pious, such another impious.

Euthyphro: I will tell you, if you like.

Socrates: I should very much like.

Euthyphro: Piety, then, is that which is dear to the gods, and impiety is that which is not dear to them.

Socrates: Very good, Euthyphro; you have now given me the sort of answer which I wanted. But whether what you say is true or not I cannot as yet tell, although I make no doubt that you will prove the truth of your words.

Euthyphro: Of course.

Socrates: Come, then, and let us examine what we are saying. That thing or person which is dear to the gods is pious, and that thing or person which is hateful to the gods is impious, these two being opposites of one another. Was not that said?

Euthyphro: It was.

Socrates: And well said?

Euthyphro: Yes, Socrates, I thought so; it was certainly said.

Socrates: And further, Euthyphro, the gods were admitted to have enmities and hatreds and differences?

Euthyphro: Yes, that was also said.

Socrates: And what sort of difference creates enmity and anger? Suppose for example that you and I, my good friend, differ about a number; do differences of this sort make us enemies and set us at variance with one another? Do we not go at once to arithmetic, and put an end to them by a sum?

Euthyphro: True.

Socrates: Or suppose that we differ about magnitudes, do we not quickly end the differences by measuring?

Euthyphro: Very true.

Socrates: And we end a controversy about heavy and light by resorting to a weighing machine?

Euthyphro: To be sure.

Socrates: But what differences are there which cannot be thus decided, and which therefore make us angry and set us at enmity with one another? I dare say that answer does not occur to you at the moment, and therefore I will suggest that these enmities arise when the matters of difference are the just and unjust, good and evil, honourable and dishonourable. Are not these the points about which men differ, and about which when we are unable satisfactorily to decide our differences, you and I and all of us quarrel, when we do quarrel?

Euthyphro: Yes, Socrates, the nature of the differences about which we quarrel is such as you describe.

Socrates: And the quarrels of the gods, noble Euthyphro, when they occur, are of a like nature?

Euthyphro: Certainly they are.

Socrates: They have differences of opinion, as you say, about good and evil, just and unjust, honourable and dishonourable: there would have been no quarrels among them, if there had been no such differences—would there now?

Euthyphro: You are quite right.

Socrates: Does not every man love that which he deems noble and just and good, and hate the opposite of them?

Euthyphro: Very true.

Socrates: But, as you say, people regard the same things, some as just and others as unjust,—about these they dispute; and so there arise wars and fightings among them.

Euthyphro: Very true.

Socrates: Then the same things are hated by the gods and loved by the gods, and are both hateful and dear to them?

Euthyphro: True.

Socrates: And upon this view the same things, Euthyphro, will be pious and also impious?

Euthyphro: So I should suppose.

Socrates: Then, my friend, I remark with surprise that you have not answered the question which I asked. For I certainly did not ask you to tell me what action is both pious and impious: but now it would seem that what is loved by the gods is also hated by them. And therefore, Euthyphro, in thus chastising your father you may very likely be doing what is agreeable to Zeus but disagreeable to Cronos or Uranus, and what is acceptable to Hephaestus but unacceptable to Herè, and there may be other gods who have similar differences of opinion.

Euthyphro: But I believe, Socrates, that all the gods would be agreed as to the

propriety of punishing a murderer: there would be no difference of
opinion about that.

Socrates: Well, but speaking of men, Euthyphro, did you ever hear any one
arguing that a murderer or any sort of evil-doer ought to be let off?

Euthyphro: I should rather say that these are the questions which they are always
arguing, especially in courts of law; they commit all sorts of crimes, and
there is nothing which they will not do or say in their own defense.

Socrates: But do they admit their guilt, Euthyphro, and yet say that they ought
not to be punished?

Euthyphro: No; they do not.

Socrates: Then there are some things which they do not venture to say and do: for
they do not venture to argue that the guilty are to be unpunished, but
they deny their guilt, do they not?

Euthyphro: Yes.

Socrates: Then they do not argue that the evil-doer should not be punished, but
they argue about the fact of who the evil-doer is, and what he did and
when?

Euthyphro: True.

Socrates: And the gods are in the same case, if as you assert they quarrel about
just and unjust, and some of them say while others deny that injustice
is done among them. For surely neither God nor man will ever venture
to say that the doer of injustice is not to be punished?

Euthyphro: That is true, Socrates, in the main.

Socrates: But they join issue about the particulars—gods and men alike; and, if
they dispute at all, they dispute about some act which is called in
question, and which by some is affirmed to be just, by others to be
unjust. Is not that true?

Euthyphro: Quite true.

Socrates: Well then, my dear friend Euthyphro, do tell me, for my better
instruction and information, what proof have you that in the opinion of
all the gods a servant who is guilty of murder, and is put in chains by
the master of the dead man, and dies because he is put in chains before
he who bound him can learn from the interpreters of the gods what he
ought to do with him, dies unjustly; and that on behalf of such an one a
son ought to proceed against his father and accuse him of murder. How
would you show that all the gods absolutely agree in approving of his
act? Prove to me that they do, and I will applaud your wisdom as long
as I live.

Euthyphro: It will be a difficult task; but I could make the matter very clear indeed
to you.

Socrates: I understand; you mean to say that I am not so quick of apprehension as
the judges: for to them you will be sure to prove that the act is unjust,
and hateful to the gods.

Euthyphro: Yes indeed, Socrates: at least if they will listen to me.

Socrates: But they will be sure to listen if they find that you are a good speaker.
There was a notion that came into my mind while you were speaking; I
said to myself: "Well, and what if Euthyphro does prove to me that all
the gods regarded the death of the serf as unjust, how do I know
anything more of the nature of piety and impiety? For granting that this
action may be hateful to the gods, still piety and impiety are not

adequately defined by these distinctions, for that which is hateful to the gods has been shown to be also pleasing and dear to them." And therefore, Euthyphro, I do not ask you to prove this; I will suppose, if you like, that all the gods condemn and abominate such an action. But I will amend the definition so far as to say that what all the gods hate is impious, and what they love pious or holy; and what some of them love and others hate is both or neither. Shall this be our definition of piety and impiety?

Euthyphro: Why not, Socrates?

Socrates: Why not! Certainly, as far as I am concerned, Euthyphro, there is no reason why not. But whether this admission will greatly assist you in the task of instructing me as you promised, is a matter for you to consider.

Euthyphro: Yes, I should say that what all the gods love is pious and holy, and the opposite which they all hate, impious.

Socrates: Ought we to enquire into the truth of this, Euthyphro, or simply to accept the mere statement on our own authority and that of others? What do you say?

Euthyphro: We should enquire; and I believe that the statement will stand the test of enquiry.

Socrates: We shall know better, my good friend, in a little while. The point which I should first wish to understand is whether the pious or holy is beloved by the gods because it is holy, or holy because it is beloved of the gods.

Euthyphro: I do not understand your meaning, Socrates.

Socrates: I will endeavor to explain: we speak of carrying and we speak of being carried, of leading and being led, seeing and being seen. You know that in all such cases there is a difference, and you know also in what the difference lies?

Euthyphro: I think that I understand.

Socrates: And is not that which is beloved distinct from that which loves?

Euthyphro: Certainly.

Socrates: Well; and now tell me, is that which is carried in this state of carrying because it is carried, or for some other reason?

Euthyphro: No; that is the reason.

Socrates: And the same is true of what is led and of what is seen?

Euthyphro: True.

Socrates: And a thing is not seen because it is visible, but conversely, visible because it is seen; nor is a thing led because it is in the state of being led, or carried because it is in the state of being carried, but the converse of this. And now I think, Euthyphro, that my meaning will be intelligible; and my meaning is, that any state of action or passion implies previous action or passion. It does not become because it is becoming, but it is in a state of becoming because it becomes; neither does it suffer because it is in a state of suffering, but it is in a state of suffering because it suffers. Do you not agree?

Euthyphro: Yes.

Socrates: Is not that which is loved in some state either of becoming or suffering?

Euthyphro: Yes.

Socrates: And the same holds as in the previous instances; the state of being loved follows the act of being loved, and not the act the state.

Euthyphro: Certainly.

Socrates: And what do you say of piety, Euthyphro: is not piety, according to your definition, loved by all the gods?

Euthyphro: Yes.

Socrates: Because it is pious or holy, or for some other reason?

Euthyphro: No, that is the reason.

Socrates: It is loved because it is holy, not holy because it is loved?

Euthyphro: Yes.

Socrates: And that which is dear to the gods is loved by them, and is in a state to be loved of them because it is loved of them?

Euthyphro: Certainly.

Socrates: Then that which is dear to the gods, Euthyphro, is not holy, nor is that which is holy loved of God, as you affirm; but they are two different things.

Euthyphro: How do you mean, Socrates?

Socrates: I mean to say that the holy has been acknowledged by us to be loved of God because it is holy, not to be holy because it is loved.

Euthyphro: Yes.

Socrates: But that which is dear to the gods is dear to them because it is loved by them, not loved by them because it is dear to them.

Euthyphro: True.

Socrates: But, friend Euthyphro, if that which is holy is the same with that which is dear to God, and is loved because it is holy, then that which is dear to God would have been loved as being dear to God; but if that which is dear to God is dear to him because loved by him, then that which is holy would have been holy because loved by him. But now you see that the reverse is the case, and that they are quite different from one another. For one Θεοφιλες is of a kind to be loved because it is loved, and the other οσιον is loved because it is of a kind to be loved. Thus you appear to me, Euthyphro, when I ask you what is the essence of holiness, to offer an attribute only, and not the essence—the attribute of being loved by all the gods. But you still refuse to explain to me the nature of holiness. And therefore, if you please, I will ask you not to hide your treasure, but to tell me once more what holiness or piety really is, whether dear to the gods or not (for that is a matter about which we will not quarrel); and what is impiety?

Euthyphro: I really do not know, Socrates, how to express what I mean. For somehow or other our arguments, on whatever ground we rest them, seem to turn round and walk away from us.

Socrates: Your words, Euthyphro, are like the handiwork of my ancestor Daedalus; and if I were the sayer or propounder of them, you might say that my arguments walk away and will not remain fixed where they are placed because I am a descendant of his. But now, since these notions are your own, you must find some other gibe, for they certainly, as you yourself allow, show an inclination to be on the move.

Euthyphro: Nay, Socrates, I shall still say that you are the Daedalus who sets arguments in motion; not I, certainly, but you make them move or go round, for they would never have stirred, as far as I am concerned. . . .

Socrates: Then we must begin again and ask, What is piety? That is an enquiry which I shall never be weary of pursuing as far as in me lies; and I entreat you not to scorn me, but to apply your mind to the utmost, and tell me the truth. For, if any man knows, you are he; and therefore I must detain you, like Proteus, until you tell. If you had not certainly known the nature of piety and impiety, I am confident that you would never, on behalf of a serf, have charged your aged father with murder. You would not have run such a risk of doing wrong in the sight of the gods, and you would have had too much respect for the opinions of men. I am sure, therefore, that you know the nature of piety and impiety. Speak out then, my dear Euthyphro, and do not hide your knowledge.

Euthyphro: Another time, Socrates; for I am in a hurry, and must go now.

Socrates: Alas! my companion, and will you leave me in despair? I was hoping that you would instruct me in the nature of piety and impiety; and then I might have cleared myself of Meletus and his indictment. I would have told him that I had been enlightened by Euthyphro, and had given up rash innovations and speculations, in which I indulged only through ignorance, and that now I am about to lead a better life.[5]

Summary and Conclusions

We began by observing that while some people are uncomprehending of philosophy as a field of study, they nevertheless philosophize in their everyday lives. We saw that defining philosophy presents a problem because philosophy lacks a distinct subject matter and lends itself to idiosyncratic descriptions and definitions. Etymology may still provide the best definition of philosophy—the love of wisdom. The wisdom that philosophy seeks is the cultivation of critical habits, the search for truth, the questioning of the obvious. In general, philosophical concerns cluster around three themes: epistemology, metaphysics, and axiology. We noted that the philosophical enterprise is an activity characterized by asking the right questions and answering them through critical, persistent analysis. As for the value of studying philosophy, philosophy can help satisfy higher-level human needs. It also seems to satisfy some maintenance needs, such as the need for security. Furthermore, it liberates through increasing awareness, deepens tolerance and broadens our capacity to receive the disclosures of the world, refines our powers of analysis, helps us deal with the uncertainties of living, and enlarges us through the nature of the subjects that it contemplates. Finally, while the study of philosophy entails definite intellectual risks, in the last analysis these are justified by the rewards that philosophy promises.

There are no free lunches, not even in philosophy. If you want what philosophy offers, you must pay a price. Part of the price is long, painstaking study and careful examination and reexamination of ideas, outlooks, and assertions. Another part is the realization that this process is endless; we will not

5. *Plato.* Euthyphro, *in* The Dialogues of Plato. *B. Jowett, Trans. New York: Macmillan, 1892, pp. 103–109.*

reach a point where all questions are resolved, all doubt eliminated. But potentially the highest price to be paid for the rewards of philosophical study is the risks that we will run; for in subjecting beliefs to the critical questioning that makes up an important part of the philosophical enterprise, we risk unmasking personal and cultural assumptions. Doubtless, the collapse of a cherished belief, like the loss of a loved one, can deeply wound and pain. Not surprisingly, we resist having challenged those ideas that we take for granted. So, as we begin our adventure into the exciting, though disturbing, world of great philosophical ideas, it's important to ponder this question: Can individuals or societies progress without intellectual suffering?

It seems not, though it might take many pages and volumes to illustrate and demonstrate this belief. Enough here to suggest that in many ways, if not all, we are better off today than our primitive ancestors were. But so-called civilization and all that it implies have not come easily. Many along the way have suffered enormous intellectual agony. We met one such person in this chapter, Socrates, who ultimately paid with his life for what he believed. Consider how profoundly impoverished we would be, personally and collectively, had Socrates been unwilling to pay the price. He, like countless others, paid his intellectual dues and, to a large extent, ours as well.

But a considerable debt is still outstanding, for neither as individuals nor as a species do we have all the answers, the whole truth, the full meaning. And isn't that, after all, what we seek? Isn't it what we've always sought? If so, then let's press on, convinced that the goal we seek is well worth the risks.

In the pages ahead, as we consider many of the enduring philosophical questions, uppermost in each of our minds will be the question: Who and what am I? We could call this the unifying theme that draws together what may appear to be disparate philosophical concerns. We'll see that the study of philosophy can help us in answering this question, for ultimately a human being is many things: a moral being, a social and political animal, an appreciator of art and beauty, a perceiver and knower, a scientist, a religionist. As we now know, all these aspects of humanity and self are areas of intense philosophical concern and speculation. Our adventure into the world of philosophy, therefore, is more than an encounter with great ideas, thinkers, systems, and movements. It's a voyage into ourselves. It's a quest for self-definition and understanding.

Section Exercises

The Difficulty of Defining Philosophy

1. Think of three scientific issues that raise philosophical questions.

2. Ask about six friends what they think philosophy is. Is there any agreement?

3. Would it be accurate to say that just about every profession has its own philosophy? What does this mean? How would you characterize the educational philosophy of the institution that you are attending?

Philosophy as the Love of Wisdom

1. It's sometimes said that the admission of ignorance is the beginning of wisdom. Why? Does Socrates' self-defense indicate this belief?

2. Have you known bright people who weren't wise? Why weren't they wise? Make two lists, one containing the characteristics of intelligent people, the other the characteristics of wise people. How much overlapping is there?

3. What kind of wisdom would you like to possess?

Traditional Concerns of Philosophy

1. Compose as many philosophical questions as you can think of. Then place them under one or more of the three major philosophical themes.

2. Make a list of the philosophical concerns that you wish to learn something about during your introductory philosophy course. Try to be as specific as you can. Suppose, for example, you'd like to learn something about religion. Exactly what would you like to learn? Try to formulate a question that will direct your study, such as "Is there any reason to believe that God exists?" or "If God is all-good and all-powerful, how can evil exist?"

The Philosophical Enterprise

1. Construct a dialogue between two people discussing the nature of beauty. One person insists that beauty is what lies in the eye of the beholder. The other person is attempting to get the first person to analyze this claim, to clarify and crystallize the concept.

2. A famous maxim often attributed to Socrates is "The unexamined life is not worth living." What does this mean? How does it relate to philosophy?

3. Suppose someone objected, "If philosophy is an ongoing process, what's the point of engaging in it? You'll never get any certain answers; your search will never end. Such a prospect is thoroughly depressing." How would you respond to this criticism?

Why Philosophy?

1. What indications of actualizing needs do you currently see in your life?

2. What evidence suggests that your college curriculum was devised in part with something like actualizing needs in mind?

3. It's not uncommon for "successful" people to be bored. Indeed, many academically successful students express profound boredom with school. What, in your mind, is the nature of boredom? Can it be related to actualizing needs? Can philosophy in any way combat boredom?

4. Can you think of any people whom you consider self-actualized? What traits do they show?

5. Give an example of how increasing your awareness has made you freer.

Story of a Good Brahman

Voltaire

Among history's most satiric and philosophical storytellers ranks the Frenchman Voltaire (1694–1778). Best known for his ironic classic Candide, *Voltaire wrote numerous shorter, perhaps less familiar works that are often as provocative if not as dazzling as his masterpiece. "Story of a Good Brahman" is one. With few but well-chosen words, Voltaire presents the paradox that is at once the curse and blessing of the philosophically minded: Why persist in asking unanswerable questions when all they do is make us unhappy? His reply: The alternative, not asking them, is more appalling. Voltaire seems to say that, in the long run, the peace and comfort that philosophers experience must derive from knowing that they exercise the human's noblest quality —curiosity —even though being curious may preclude contentment.*

I met on my travels an old Brahman, a very wise man, full of wit and very learned; moreover he was rich, and consequently even wiser; for, lacking nothing, he had no need to deceive anyone. His family was very well governed by three beautiful wives who schooled themselves to please him; and when he was not entertaining himself with his wives, he was busy philosophizing.

Near his house, which was beautiful, well decorated, and surrounded by charming gardens, lived an old Indian woman, bigoted, imbecilic, and rather poor.

The Brahman said to me one day: "I wish I had never been born."

I asked him why. He replied:

"I have been studying for forty years, which is forty years wasted; I teach others, and I know nothing; this situation brings into my soul so much humiliation and disgust that life is unbearable to me. I was born, I live in time, and I do not know what time is; I find myself in a point between two eternities, as our sages say, and I have no idea of eternity. I am composed of matter; I think, and I have never been able to find out what produces thought; I do not know whether my understanding is a simple faculty in me like that of walking or of digesting, and whether I think with my head, as I take with my hands. Not only is the principle of my thinking unknown to me, but the principle of my movements is equally hidden from me. I do not know why I exist. However, people every day ask me questions on all these points; I have to answer; I have nothing any good to say; I talk much, and I remain confounded and ashamed of myself after talking.

"It is much worse yet when they ask me whether Brahma was produced by Vishnu or whether they are both eternal. God is my witness that I don't know a thing about it, and it certainly shows in my answers. 'Ah! Reverend Father,' they say to me, 'teach us how it is that evil inundates the whole world.' I am as much at a loss as those who ask me that question; I sometimes tell them that all is for the very best, but those who have been ruined and mutilated at war believe nothing of it, and neither do I; I retreat to my house overwhelmed with my curiosity and my ignorance. I read our ancient books, and they redouble the darkness I am in. I talk to my companions: some answer that we must enjoy life and laugh at men; the others think they know something, and lose themselves in absurd ideas; everything increases the painful feeling I endure. I am sometimes ready to fall into despair, when I think that after all my seeking I know neither where I come from, nor what I am, nor where I shall go, nor what shall become of me."

The state of this good man caused me real pain; no one was either more reasonable or more honest than he. I perceived that the greater the lights of his understanding and the sensibility of his heart, the more unhappy he was.

That same day I saw the old woman who lived in his vicinity: I asked her whether she had

From Voltaire: Candide, Zadig and Selected Stories. *Donald M. Frame, Trans. Copyright © 1961 by Donald M. Frame. Reprinted by arrangement with The New American Library, Inc., New York.*

ever been distressed not to know how her soul was made. She did not even understand my question: she had never reflected a single moment of her life over a single one of the points that tormented the Brahman; she believed with all her heart in the metamorphoses of Vishnu, and, provided she could sometimes have some water from the Ganges to wash in, she thought herself the happiest of women.

Struck by the happiness of this indigent creature, I returned to my philosopher and said to him:

"Aren't you ashamed to be unhappy at a time when right at your door there is an old automaton who thinks of nothing and who lives happily?"

"You are right," he answered; "I have told myself a hundred times that I would be happy if I was as stupid as my neighbor, and yet I would want no part of such a happiness."

This answer of my Brahman made a greater impression on me than all the rest. I examined myself and saw that indeed I would not have wanted to be happy on condition of being imbecilic.

I put the matter up to some philosophers, and they were of my opinion.

"There is, however," I said, "a stupendous contradiction in this way of thinking."

For after all, what is at issue? Being happy. What matters being witty or being stupid? What is more, those who are content with their being are quite sure of being content; those who reason are not so sure of reasoning well.

"So it is clear," I said, "that we should choose not to have common sense, if ever that common sense contributes to our ill-being."

Everyone was of my opinion, and yet I found no one who wanted to accept the bargain of becoming imbecilic in order to become content. From this I concluded that if we set store by happiness, we set even greater store by reason.

But, upon reflection, it appears that to prefer reason to felicity is to be very mad. Then how can this contradiction be explained? Like all the others. There is much to be said about it.

Questions for Analysis

1. Why, do you think, does Voltaire call his Brahman "good"? Why didn't he entitle his story "Story of a Brahman"?

2. Why doesn't the Brahman desire the happiness of the old woman?

3. Voltaire seems to say that you can be either a reasoning or a happy creature, but not both. Do you agree?

4. Which of the two would you prefer to be: the Brahman or the old woman? Why?

5. Which of the two, the Brahman or the old woman, would you say is more in harmony with the nature of a human being?

6. Voltaire describes the woman in his story as "poor." Do you think, however, that you would mischaracterize the story if you saw the discrepancies in life orientations exclusively in economic terms?

Paperbacks for Further Reading

Adler, Mortimer J. *The Conditions of Philosophy.* New York: Dell, 1967. One of the great humanistic thinkers of our time presents a clear, readable account of the nature of philosophy. Just as important, Adler suggests what's needed to make philosophy more applicable to the modern world.

Bontempo, Charles I. and S. Jack Odell, Eds. *The Owl of Minerva*. New York: McGraw-Hill, 1975. This collection of original articles by eighteen leading contemporary philosophers explains what the authors find attractive and fulfilling about their work.

Commins, Saxe, and Robert N. Linscott. *The World's Greatest Thinkers*. Buffalo, N.Y.: Washington Square Press, 1954. A four-volume overview of the world's most important thinkers. The authors divide their subject into four parts: the social philosophers (volume 1), the speculative philosophers (volume 2), the political philosophers (volume 3), and the philosophers of science (volume 4). The four volumes constitute a nice complement to any introductory philosophy book.

Durant, Will. *The Story of Philosophy*. New York: Pocket Books, 1953. An immensely readable account of the development of philosophy. Full of anecdotes and informative asides, Durant's book charms while it enlightens.

Friedman, Maurice. *The Hidden Human Image*. New York: Dell, 1974. Friedman's work is especially helpful in exploring contemporary human concerns. It's philosophically stimulating without being pedantic or stuffy. A good book to ignite philosophical thinking and debate.

Jung, Carl. *The Undiscovered Self*. New York: New American Library (Mentor Books), 1957. In this short work (125 pages), the renowned psychoanalyst discusses the psychic forces dividing the world, underscoring the need for personal integrity and freedom to counter the dehumanization of contemporary society. Most important, Jung distinguishes between knowing and understanding. Reason without self-knowledge, he writes, is humanly disastrous.

Körner, Stephan. *Fundamental Questions in Philosophy*. London: Penguin, 1971. A good introduction to the basic questions of philosophy. Körner's work also nicely traces the changes that have occurred in philosophy over the years. For those with a logic bias, this work will prove especially attractive, for the author emphasizes logic as the key to understanding and doing philosophy.

Nott, Kathleen. *Philosophy and Human Nature*. New York: Dell, 1971. Poet, novelist, and critic Nott provides an antidote to the highly analytical philosophy of the twentieth century. Highly readable.

Taylor, A. E. *Socrates*. New York: Doubleday Anchor, 1959. This is a most informative and readable book about the life of Socrates.

VIEWS OF HUMAN NATURE

Indeed it is of the essence of man . . .
that he can lose himself in the jungle of his existence, within himself,
and thanks to his sensation of being lost can react
by setting energetically to work to find himself again.
—Jose Ortega y Gasset

Can you imagine a more basic philosophical concern than what it means to be human? Not likely. Thus, what better way is there to launch our study of philosophy than with this question? But there's another issue—one that will preoccupy us throughout our study and provide it with direction and purpose. It concerns our self-image.

Have you ever felt out of touch with yourself? Not long ago there was a popular expression that described the effort to order one's life, to define or redefine oneself—"getting your act together." Perhaps you've heard a friend say, "I've got to get my act together," or maybe you've said it. Events often seem more than we can bear. Demands at home, school, and work can build until we fear that we are losing touch with ourselves, losing our identities.

The kind of being I consider myself is fundamental to the question of self-image. If I view people as essentially good, rational, and free, I'm inclined to see myself that way, too. If I consider them basically evil, irrational, and un-free, I'm likely to see myself that way. So, the issue of self-image, of who and what I am, is inseparable from the question of what it means to be a human.

Anthropology, psychology, sociology, and philosophy provide definitions and descriptions of human nature, which frequently differ and conflict; these differences can leave us uncertain about our *precise nature*. Some social scientists, for example, have championed the view that humans are essentially cruel, selfish, and evil—unreasoning creatures molded by social forces. In his *On the Origin of the Species by Means of Natural Selection* (1859), Charles Darwin (1809–1882) presented a picture of nature as a battlefield for an unforgiving war of survival in which the fittest survived. The thought and work of Sigmund Freud (1856–1939) also support this view. As an illustration, consider his predatory view of human nature presented in *Civilization and Its Discontents*:

Men are not gentle, friendly creatures wishing for love, who simply defend themselves if they are attacked, but . . . a powerful measure of desire for aggressiveness has to be reckoned as part of their instinctual endowment. The result is that their neighbor is to them not only a possible helper or sexual object, but also a temptation to them to gratify their aggressiveness . . . to seize his possessions, to humiliate him, to cause him pain, to torture and to kill him. . . .

Anyone who calls to mind the atrocities of the early migrations, of the invasion of the Hun or the so-called Mongols under Genghis Khan and Tamerlane, of the sacks of Jerusalem by the pious crusaders, even indeed the horrors of the last world-war, will have to bow his head humbly before the truth of this view of man.[1]

Others have agreed with this view, including Konrad Lorenz,[2] Carl Jung,[3] and Robert Ardrey.[4]

On the other side, a large group of psychologists and social scientists view human nature as being unaggressive, peace loving, cooperative, and good; people are rational creatures with a significant amount of control over their lives and destinies. Thus, some years back, after he had considered all the available evidence, psychologist Gordon Allport drew this conclusion about human nature in his monumental study of prejudice: "Normal men everywhere reject in principle and by preference the path of war and destruction. They like to live in peace and friendship with their neighbors, they prefer to love and be loved rather than to hate and be hated. . . . While wars rage, yet our desire is for peace and while animosity prevails, the weight of mankind's approval is on the side of affiliation."[5]

More recently, Carl Rogers drew similar conclusions from his exhaustive study of clients in psychotherapy: "One of the most revolutionary concepts to grow out of clinical experience is the growing recognition that the inmost core of man's nature, the deepest layers of his personality, the base of his 'animal nature,' is positive in nature—is basically socialized, forward moving, rational, and realistic."[6]

The studies of some anthropologists support this optimistic view. Margaret Mead, for example, found a primitive New Guinea tribe to be entirely peace loving and convinced that all humans were naturally unaggressive, self-denying, and ultimately concerned with nurturing children.[7] Of course, she

---

1. Sigmund Freud. Civilization and Its Discontents. London: Hogarth, 1930, pp. 85–86.

2. Konrad Lorenz. On Aggression. New York: Harcourt Brace Jovanovich, 1966.

3. Carl Jung. "Relations between the Ego and the Unconscious." In Collected Works. R. F. C. Hull, Trans. Princeton, N.J.: Princeton University Press, 1953.

4. Robert Ardrey. African Genesis. New York: Delta, 1961. The Territorial Imperative. New York: Atheneum, 1966.

5. Gordon Allport. The Nature of Prejudice. Boston: Beacon Press, 1954, p. xiv.

6. Carl Rogers. On Becoming a Person: A Therapist's View of Psychotherapy. Boston: Houghton Mifflin, 1961, pp. 90–91.

7. Margaret Mead. From the South Seas: Studies of Adolescence and Sex in Primitive Societies. New York: Morrow, 1939.

found other tribes that were aggressive in the extreme. Most recently, social scientist Ashley Montagu has attacked the aggressionist view in his *The Nature of Human Aggression*.[8]

Today the debate about human nature has reemerged in the light of the life sciences. The reality of test-tube babies, the creation of androids, and the possibility of understanding and controlling the genetic code all raise fundamental questions about what it means to be a human. Since a view of human nature relates to how we see ourselves and our place in the world, the impact of these developments is most personal.

Given the present proliferation of views, it might be hard to imagine that individuals were once quite certain about what kind of beings they were. There have been times when people felt little doubt about the essential nature of human beings and thus likely felt little if any confusion about their self-concepts. As an example, consider the view expressed in the seventeenth century by the first great philosophical figure of the modern age, René Descartes (1596–1650). Notice in this selection from his most famous work, *Meditations on First Philosophy*, that Descartes leaves no question that the essential nature of a human inheres in one property: that it thinks.

> But what, then, am I? A thinking thing, it has been said. But what is a thinking thing? It is a thing that doubts, understands (conceives), affirms, denies, wills, refuses, that imagines also, and perceives. Assuredly it is not little, if all these properties belong to my nature. But why should they not belong to it? Am I not that very being who now doubts of almost everything; who, for all that, understands and conceives certain things; who affirms one alone as true, and denies the others; who desires to know more of them, and does not wish to be deceived; who imagines many things, sometimes even despite his will; and is likewise percipient of many, as if through the medium of the senses? Is there nothing of all this as true as that I am, even although I should be always dreaming, and although he who gave me being employed all his ingenuity to deceive me? Is there also any one of these attributes that can be properly distinguished from my thought, or that can be said to be separate from myself? For it is of itself so evident that it is I who doubt, I who understand, and I who desire, that it is here unnecessary to add anything by way of rendering it more clear. And I am as certainly the same being who imagines; for, although it may be (as I before supposed) that nothing I imagine is true, still the power of imagination does not cease really to exist in me and to form part of my thought. In fine, I am the same being who perceives, that is, who apprehends certain objects as by the organs of sense, since, in truth, I see light, hear a noise, and feel heat. But it will be said that these presentations are false, and that I am dreaming. Let it be so. At all events it is certain that I seem to see light, hear a noise, and feel heat; this cannot be false, and this is what in me is properly called perceiving, which is nothing else than thinking. From this I begin to know what I am with somewhat greater clearness and distinctness than heretofore.[9]

8. *Ashley Montagu.* The Nature of Human Aggression. *New York: Oxford University Press, 1976.*

9. *From René Descartes.* The Method, Meditations and Philosophy of Descartes. *John Veitch, Trans. New York: Tudor, 1901, pp. 188–190. Reprinted by permission.*

Some students of philosophy term such a view as Descartes's *essentialist*. [10] By this they mean a view of the human as a definite kind of being, a creature that possesses a basic immaterial property that is necessary to being human. In this chapter we'll focus on this concept. Specifically, we'll consider two of the most influential essentialist doctrines in Western civilization: the rational and the religious views. Just as important, we'll see three challenges to these doctrines that, in effect, deny any immaterial human nature. These can be termed the *scientific, existential,* and *Eastern* views. Each has grown in influence and popularity in the Western world in this century.

For coherence and unity, we'll consider these doctrines' perspectives on human goodness, rationality, and freedom. In this way we can understand how these doctrines can and do affect us: how we see ourselves, interact with others, and live.

While these views are important philosophical outlooks, they are far from mere abstractions. They have immediate and significant impact on our own identities. Indeed, in the course of our study, we will continually see that the great philosophical ideas always affect us personally. Here are the main points we will make.

Main Points

1. *Human nature* refers to what it means to be one of our species, what makes us different from anything else.

2. The view of the human as a rational being, which dates from the ancient Greeks, contends that humans are primarily reasoning creatures. This view fosters a concept of the self as something existing apart from and above the objective world and as capable of discovering truth, beauty, and goodness. It also fosters a view of freedom as self-awareness.

3. The religious view of the human, rooted in Judeo-Christian thought, claims that humans are unique because they are made in the image of God, their Creator, who has endowed them with self-consciousness and an ability to love. This concept fosters a view of self as being purposeful, moral, and possessing free will.

4. Scientific views deny any essential immaterial human nature. A strict scientific view reduces humans to physiochemical processes. Even though the social sciences don't share this highly materialistic view, they can be as reductionist. Twentieth-century psychological behaviorism makes no essential distinction between body and mind or between humans and the rest of nature. Concepts such as purpose, morality, and will are, say the behaviorists, the results of prescientific thinking. Everything is determined, and there is no personal freedom.

5. The view of the human as an existential being, while denying the existence of any essential immaterial human nature, also denies that we are only

10. *See Walter L. Fogg and Peyton E. Richter.* Philosophy Looks to the Future. *Boston: Holbrook Press, 1974, pp. 196–198.*

products of our environment. It asserts that although there is no essential self, there is an existing self, and that the self is a freely choosing, active agent. Self, as Sartre argues, is choice.

6. The Eastern view denies both a human nature and a self. These concepts are imaginary and arise from deep-seated psychological needs for self-preservation. Freedom is an illusion.

Two Essentialist Views of Human Nature

The Rational View

One highly influential theory of human nature, held by the ancient Greeks, views the human primarily as a thinker capable of reasoning. This view is well illustrated in the thought and writings of a man considered by some to be the greatest philosopher—Plato. Although Plato did not consider reason to be the sole constituent of human nature, he did hold that it was the highest part of human nature. Conversing in *The Republic*, Socrates and Glaucon present Plato's view by discussing the question "What is the self?" Notice in the following passage the recurrence of the word *soul*, a common translation of Plato's term *psyche*. Since Plato did not intend all the theological connotations that we frequently place on the word *soul*, it would be wiser to substitute *self* for *soul*:[11]

> *Socrates:* Here, then, we have stumbled upon another little problem: Does the soul contain . . . three elements or not? . . . [That] we have [different kinds of experience is] a fact which is easily recognized. But here the difficulty begins. Are we using the same part of ourselves in all these three experiences, or a different part in each? Do we gain knowledge with one part, feel anger with another, and with yet a third desire the pleasures of food, sex, and so on? Or is the whole soul at work in every impulse and in all these forms of behavior? The difficulty is to answer that question satisfactorily.
>
> *Glaucon:* I quite agree.
>
> *Socrates:* Let us approach the problem whether these elements are distinct or identical in this way. It is clear that the same thing cannot act in two opposite ways or be in two opposite states at the same time, with respect to the same part of itself, and in relation to the same object. So if we find such contradictory actions or states among the elements concerned, we shall know that more than one must have been involved.
>
> *Glaucon:* Very well. . . .
>
> *Socrates:* Now, would you class such things as assent and dissent, striving after something and refusing it, attraction and repulsion, as pairs of opposite actions or states of mind—no matter which?
>
> *Glaucon:* Yes, they are opposites. . . .

11. *See W. T. Jones.* The Classical Mind. *New York: Harcourt, Brace & World, 1969, p. 164.*

Socrates: We conclude, then, that the soul of a thirsty man, just insofar as he is thirsty, has no other wish than to drink. That is the object of its craving, and towards that it is impelled.

Glaucon: That is clear.

Socrates: Now if there is ever something which at the same time pulls it the opposite way, that something must be an element in the soul other than the one which is thirsting and driving it like a beast to drink; in accordance with our principle that the same thing cannot behave in two opposite ways at the same time and towards the same object with the same part of itself. . . .

Glaucon: Exactly.

Socrates: Now, is it sometimes true that people are thirsty and yet unwilling to drink?

Glaucon: Yes, often.

Socrates: What, then, can one say of them, if not that their soul contains something which urges them to drink and something which holds them back, and that this latter is a distinct thing and overpowers the other?

Glaucon: I agree.

Socrates: And is it not true that the intervention of this inhibiting principle in such cases always has its origin in reflection; whereas the impulses driving and dragging the soul are engendered by external influences and abnormal conditions?

Glaucon: Evidently.

Socrates: We shall have good reason, then, to assert that they are two distinct principles. We may call that part of the soul whereby it reflects, rational; and the other, with which it feels hunger and thirst and is distracted by sexual passion and all the other desires, we will call irrational appetite, associated with pleasure in the replenishment of certain wants.

Glaucon: Yes, there is good ground for that view.

Socrates: Let us take it, then, that we have now distinguished two elements in the soul. What of that passionate element which makes us feel angry and indignant? Is that a third, or identical in nature with one of those two?

Glaucon: It might perhaps be identified with appetite.

Socrates: I am more inclined to put my faith in a story I once heard about Leontius, son of Aglaion. On his way up from Piraeus outside the north wall, he noticed the bodies of some criminals lying on the ground, with the executioner standing by them. He wanted to go and look at them, but at the same time he was disgusted and tried to turn away. He struggled for some time and covered his eyes, but at last the desire was too much for him. Opening his eyes wide, he ran up to the bodies and cried, "There you are, curse you; feast yourselves on this lovely sight!"

Glaucon: Yes, I have heard that story too.

Socrates: The point of it surely is that anger is sometimes in conflict with
appetite, as if they were two distinct principles.[12]

To understand Plato's view, consider this illustration. Suppose you are very thirsty. Before you is a glass of poisoned water. One part of you, what Plato called Appetite—located in the abdomen—invites you to drink. By Appetite he meant thirst and hunger, as well as sexual and other physical desires. But a second part of you, Reason, forbids you to drink. By Reason Plato meant the uniquely human capacity for thinking reflectively and drawing conclusions—the ability to follow relationships from one thought to another in an orderly and correct way. This rational part, said Plato, has its center in the brain. In this illustration a conflict arises between Appetite and Reason. But Plato claimed conflict could arise in another way, as when our emotions or passions flare up.

Suppose someone cuts you off on the highway. You become enraged; you begin to blow your horn and shake your fist at the driver. You are even tempted to tailgate for a few miles just to vent your spleen. But what good would that do? Besides, it would be dangerous. Plato would say that the conflict here is not between Reason and Appetite, but between Reason and what he variously calls anger, indignation, and Spirit. Spirit is like self-assertion or self-interest; according to Plato, it resides in the breast.

Thus, in Plato's view, Reason, Spirit, and Appetite characterize human nature. Depending on which part dominates, we get three kinds of people, whose main desires are knowledge, success, and gain. But Plato leaves no doubt about which element should dominate: Reason. True, each element plays a part, but Spirit and Appetite have no principle of order of their own and must be brought under the control of Reason. Through Reason we can discover the truth about how we ought to live. This truth exists outside ourselves in some objective state. It is not a matter of opinion or feeling, nor is it something we make for ourselves. It is not relative.

For Aristotle (384–322 B.C.), too, reason is the human's highest faculty. It is the characteristic that sets us apart from all other creatures of nature. Likewise, the Stoics, members of a school of thought founded by Zeno in 308 B.C., regarded the ideal person as able to suppress passion and emotion through reason. Only in this way could humans discover knowledge and be in harmony with cosmic reason, or **logos**.

Although the views of Plato, Aristotle, and the Stoics differ in many ways, they all stress reason as the human's most important feature. They generally would have us see the self as a body and a mind. The body is physical and subject to the laws that govern matter. The mind is immaterial; it is conscious and characterized by reasoning. Unlike the body, the mind has no extension; it is not part of the world of matter and thus is not subject to its laws.

We might even view ourselves as fields of conflict between these two aspects of our nature. Furthermore, since we are the only creatures with a ra-

12.   *Plato.* The Republic of Plato. *F. M. Cornford, Trans. New York: Oxford University Press, 1941, pp. 134–136, 139. Reprinted by permission of Oxford University Press.*

tional mind, we would likely experience conflict with nature; we might see ourselves as distinct from the matter of the world and as potential masters of it. In short, our mind enables us to stand apart from our environment, to find meaning and sense in the events around us. We gain freedom through self-awareness, by becoming conscious of the forces that have shaped us and the influences that have made us what we are. Freedom is a function of self-awareness; ignorance is bondage. Through reason we can also discover how we ought to live. The way to truth is through reason, which leads to moral knowledge.

So the implications of the rational view for self-image are vast. We see ourselves as reasoning, free, moral beings. This classical view is one of the two

---

PHILOSOPHY AND LIFE 2-1
Lana, Seeker of Truth

Sarah of USC, Washoe and Lucy of Oklahoma, Nim of Columbia, Lana of Yerkes—all names well known to those who study human language. Why are they well known? Because they're famous scholars? Linguistic anthropologists? Perhaps each has been responsible for some ground-breaking research? Not quite. They're all chimpanzees.

Separately and together, these chimps have demonstrated the ability to converse with humans, to combine acquired words in order to describe new objects or situations, to distinguish difference and sameness, to understand "if-then" concepts, to describe their moods, to lie, to choose and use words in syntactical order, to express desires, to anticipate future events, to seek signed communications with others of their species, and, at least in one instance, to extract the truth from a lying human. This last remarkable occurrence is recorded by Duane Rumbaugh of the Yerkes Primate Center in Atlanta in *Language Learning by a Chimpanzee: The Lana Project.*

Human Tim, Rumbaugh recalls, had entered chimp Lana's room with a bowl of monkey chow, which Lana had requested be loaded into her food machine. But instead of honoring her request, Tim loaded the machine with cabbage, then told Lana that chow was in the machine. Rather than asking the machine for her chow, as was her custom, Lana asked Tim, "You put chow in machine?" Tim lied that he had.

Lana: Chow in machine?
Tim: (still lying) Yes.
Lana: No chow in machine (which was true).
Tim: What in machine (repeated once)?
Lana: Cabbage in machine (which was true).
Tim: Yes, cabbage in machine.
Lana: You move cabbage out of machine.

most influential theories in Western civilization. We still largely accept some version of it, despite many recent and fascinating experiments with primates (see Philosophy and Life 2–1). Of equal importance, however, is the religious view.

The Religious View

According to the Judeo-Christian tradition, humans are made in the image of God. They are essentially divine beings, because they contain something of the self-consciousness and ability to love that characterize their Creator.

This ability to love is the distinguishing characteristic of the Judeo-Christian view. Whereas the Greeks held that only those capable of attaining

---

Tim: Yes (whereupon he removed the cabbage and put in the monkey chow).

Lana: Please machine give piece of chow (repeatedly until all was obtained).

In 1637 René Descartes wrote: "There are no men so dull and stupid that they cannot put words together in a manner to convey their thoughts. And this proves not merely that animals have less reason than man, but they have none at all, for we see that very little is needed to talk." Experiences with chimps like Lana and gorillas like Koko at Stanford, who has exhibited a learned vocabulary of 300 words and an IQ of around 85, would strongly call such an easy distinction between human and beast into question.*

* *Current research argues against the belief that apes or chimps are capable of fully linguistic behavior, in its known sense. Here are several references which should be consulted in this regard: M. S. Seidenberg and L. A. Petitto, "Signing Behavior in Apes: A Critical Review," Cognition, vol. 7, 1979, pp. 177–215; H. S. Terrace, et al., "Can an Ape Create a Sentence?" Science, vol. 206, 1979, pp. 891–902; Albir Bindra, "Ape Language," Science, vol. 211, 1981, p. 86; H. S. Terrace, et al., "Ape Language," Science, vol. 211, 1981, pp. 87–88; Francine Patterson, "Ape Language," Science, vol. 211, 1981, pp. 86–87.*

□ *If chimps and apes have access to language, can they be expected to reason?* □ *Primatologists currently suspect that there's no significant distinction between the ape's capacity for language and our own. Would this in any way affect our concept of human nature?* □ *Our responsibilities to animals?* □ *Might Descartes counter that it's not so much whether chimps can use language, but whether they mean what they say, know what they mean, and have self-awareness—as indicated by language?*

McLean County Unit #5
NCHS IMC - 300

theoretical and moral knowledge could realize the purpose of living, the divine view contends that the two purposes of life—loving God and serving God—are open to all regardless of intelligence. As Saint Paul writes, "If I understand all mysteries and all knowledge . . . but have not love, I am nothing" (2 Cor. 13:2). Being given by God, this love is divine, and so allows humans to share in divinity.

At the same time, the divine view is hardly a denial of the rational view. On the contrary, Plato strongly influenced Christian thought through philosophers such as the Roman Plotinus (205?–270?) and the early Christian Saint Augustine (354–430). We observe in their philosophies a similar dualism of mind and body and a belief in the uniqueness of the human mind. But the divine view also holds that a single personal God created humans in His own image; that is, He endowed His creation with self-consciousness and the ability to love. This ability is what makes human beings unique.

What views of self is this divine view likely to foster? First, since the universe is the expression of an intelligent mind (God), believers may see themselves as part of a universe whose meaning and purpose they personally share through fellowship with God. One's purpose in life, therefore, is found in serving and loving God.

For the Christian, the way to serve and love God is by emulating the life of Jesus of Nazareth. In the life of Jesus we find an expression of the highest virtue: love. We love when we perform selfless acts, develop a keen sense of social-mindedness, and realize that people are creatures of God and are thereby worthwhile. Thus, "Thou shalt love thy neighbor as thyself" (Lev. 19:18).

For the Jew, one serves and loves God primarily through expressions of justice and righteousness. One also develops a sense of honor that is derived from a commitment to the ideals of truth, humility, fidelity, and kindness. This commitment also produces a sharp sense of responsibility to family and community.

The religious view also fosters the concept of a moral self: Each of us is capable of great good, but also of great evil. When we refuse to serve and love God, we commit our greatest evil. This refusal is expressed in various ways: injustice, vanity, pride, and dishonesty. Whenever we commit these offenses to God, we lose touch with ourselves by retreating from our alliance with Him. In contrast to the Greek belief that we must develop our rational powers to perceive the moral order in the universe, the divine view holds that intelligence is no prerequisite for a moral sense. We do good when we make God the center of our lives; we do wrong when we retreat from this commitment. Yes, we are rational, but what makes us unique is our divine likeness.

That we can make moral decisions implies that we are *free* to make them. Moral freedom, then, is another feature of the self fostered by the divine view. As divine creations, we are supposedly free to choose a course that will bring us closer to or take us further from our Creator. As a result, we bear full responsibility for our moral choices and cannot blame external factors for our failure to love and serve God.

As noted, the views of the human as a rational and as a divine being have been the most influential in Western civilization. In them we find the in-

McLean County Unit #5
NCHS IMC - 300

tellectual emphasis of the Greeks and the religious emphasis of the Jews and Christians. From them we inherit the view that an essential human nature is shared by all individuals. In this sense human nature precedes any particular human being; the universal human prototypes (Adam and Eve) precede the individual human experience.

In the twentieth century two other views have arisen, both of which deny any essential human nature. As a result, their influences on one's self-concept differ from those of the rational and divine views. One of these sees the human in scientific terms; the other holds that the human is an existential being. Apart from their common belief that there is no essential human nature, these two views are quite unlike. In recent years the Western world has experienced a burgeoning interest in still another nonessentialist view, that of Eastern religion and philosophy. Let's consider these three challenges to essentialist views.

Challenges to Essentialist Views

Scientific Views

Science's increasing impact has created a marked tendency to view the human "scientifically." However, what this means depends very much on what scientific perspective you take.

For example, one strict scientific view claims that people can be explained by the natural sciences. True, humans are more complex than other entities, but ultimately they can be reduced to physical and chemical phenomena. There is no essential human nature in the classical or religious sense. There is no so-called mind or ability to love that makes us unique. The mind and thinking are simply the electrochemical activities of the brain.

Those who maintain this view, that complex processes like life and thought can be explained wholly in terms of simpler physical and chemical processes, are often called *reductionists* or *mechanists*. Reductionism is the idea that a whole can be completely understood by analyzing its parts, or that a developing process can be explained as the result of earlier, simpler stages. Reductionists take something that is commonly thought to be real and reduce it to an appearance of something else. Thus, the strictly scientific view we've sketched holds that science reaches no further than objective facts. Human nature can be attributed or reduced to such facts.

However, not all scientific views reduce human nature to a physiochemical process. Since the nineteenth century, a number of sciences have emerged that deal directly with human beings, society, and the relationships between them. These include anthropology, economics, political science, sociology, and psychology. These sciences have amassed an impressive collection of facts and material that describe people and human relationships. Social scientists do not study the human as a strictly physical object, as do the natural sciences; but nonetheless, many of them have advanced the theory that people can best be understood as an integrated system of responses resulting from genetics and environment; that individuals are basically passive objects—things that are acted upon and that really cannot help acting as they do. Even a cursory reading of social science literature discloses a widespread belief that humans are driven beings, moved by outer and inner needs or urges. Historically, debate has centered over what these needs are.

Political philosopher Karl Marx (1818–1883) rejected the primacy of reason and the divine origins of humankind. Material forces, said Marx, produce both human nature and societal tendencies. What changes social structure is the production and reproduction of life; the primary need is survival. How we make a living is therefore of utmost importance, for the basic social characteristic that motivates humans is their productive capacity. We can influence our lives and history somewhat by altering our living conditions, but this capacity does not reside in our brains, wills, ideas, or desires. It exists mainly in the means of production and the class dynamics of society. Marx's view, then, is not strictly scientific but psychosocial.

An example of the psychosocial approach in psychology is the work of Sigmund Freud. Freud held that nothing we do is haphazard or coincidental; everything results from mental causes, most of which we are unaware of. According to Freud, the mind is not only what is conscious or potentially conscious but also what is unconscious. This unconsciousness is a reservoir of human motivation comprised of instincts. In general, most of what we think, believe, and do is the result of unconscious urges, especially those developed in the first five years of life in response to traumatic experiences.

Marx and Freud both evidence some reductionism and do not support the notion of a basic immaterial human nature. Indeed, as the social sciences have continued to grow and as the influence of the natural sciences has increased, the belief in an essential human nature has steadily declined. As a result, today there is a tendency to view humans in a more strictly scientific way. This view has received impetus from psychological **behaviorism,** a school of psychology that restricts the study of humans to what can be objectively observed—namely human behavior.

Founded by John B. Watson and advanced by B. F. Skinner, behaviorism is not concerned with human motives, goals, purposes, or actions. As Watson put it, a human being is simply "an assembled organic machine ready to run." Behaviorists view all humans as empty organisms having identical neural mechanisms that await conditioning and programming. Concepts such as will, impulse, feelings, and purpose have no place. We are, in effect, mechanisms that are shaped and controlled by our environment. By facing this fact, say behaviorists, we will be better able to cope with the human condition by concentrating on the external factors that mold our behavior.

Skinner has argued that a new, improved social order is needed that is based on scientific principles of design and control. The basis of this prescription is his view that humans are not free and self-governing agents who can do what they please; they are the products of conditioning. Such a view has deep implications for self-image, as the selection below from his widely read *Beyond Freedom and Dignity* suggests. You'll notice Skinner's frequent use of the word *contingencies.* By this word Skinner means the contingencies of reinforcement, which are relationships among (1) the occasion upon which a response occurs, (2) the response itself, and (3) the reinforcing consequences. Here's a simple example. A child just beginning to talk utters many babbling sounds. Eventually the child babbles "mamma." On this occasion the mother beams and embraces the child. The child associates its act of saying "mamma" with the positive attention and the reinforcing consequences that follow it. This is a signal event in the child's life: an experience of the satisfying fact that producing a particular verbal sound brings attention and approval from mother. So the child repeats the word and utters others, eventually becoming a competent communicator. [13]

A contingency of reinforcement, then, is a sequence of events in which some key act is necessary in order to receive a reward. This concept is central to Skinner's psychology and philosophy, which are captured in the following selection:

> A self is a repertoire of behavior appropriate to a given set of contingencies. A substantial part of the conditions to which a person is exposed may play a dominant role, and under other conditions a person may report, "I'm not myself today," or, "I couldn't have done what you said I did, because that's not like me." The identity conferred upon a self arises from the contingencies responsible for the behavior. Two or more repertoires generated by different sets of contingencies compose two or more selves. A person possesses one repertoire appropriate to his life with his friends and another appropriate to his life with his family, and a friend may find him a very different person if he sees him with his family or his family if they see him with his friends. The problem of identity arises when situations are intermingled, as when a person finds himself with both his family and his friends at the same time.
>
> Self-knowledge and self-control imply two selves in this sense. The self-knower is almost always a product of social contingencies, but the self that is known may come from other sources. The controlling self (the conscience or superego) is of social origin, but the controlled self is more likely to be the product of genetic susceptibilities to reinforcement (the id, or the Old Adam). The controlling self generally represents the interests of others, the controlled self the interests of the individual.
>
> The picture which emerges from a scientific analysis is not of a body with a person inside, but of a body which *is* a person in the sense that it displays a complex repertoire of behavior. [14]

According to the behaviorist view, the self is not primarily the mind, and it certainly is not unique. Rather, everyone is essentially the same kind of empty organism that awaits the input of environmental forces. In effect, the individual's behavior is not free, but determined.

Determinism is the theory that everything in the universe is totally ruled by causal laws. Stated in another and perhaps more accurate way, every event has a prior condition, and all events are at least theoretically predictable if all the prior conditions are known. In the strictly scientific world, it is generally assumed that everything is determined by natural laws. The universe and its parts participate in and are governed by an orderly causal sequence. Events

13. *See Finley Carpenter.* The Skinner Primer. *New York: Free Press, 1974, p. 6.*

14. *B. F. Skinner.* Beyond Freedom and Dignity. *New York: Knopf, 1971, p. 190. Reprinted by permission.*

follow conditions with predictable regularity. With the growth of the social sciences, the doctrine of determinism has extended beyond the natural and physical sciences to the biological and social sciences. In fact, Skinner makes one of the strongest contemporary cases for determinism.

He views freedom as a myth. All our responses, he argues, are the result of past contingencies of conditioning and reinforcement. He doesn't deny that we *feel* free, but he does maintain that this feeling is itself a conditioned response:

> The use of such concepts as individual freedom, initiative, and responsibility has, therefore, been well reinforced. When we turn to what science has to offer, however, we do not find very comforting support for the traditional Western point of view. The hypothesis that man is not free is essential to the application of scientific method to the study of human behavior. The free inner man who is held responsible for the behavior of the external biological organism is only a prescientific substitute for the kinds of causes which are discovered in the course of a scientific analysis. All these alternatives lie *outside* the individual.[15]

In sum, the scientific views we have in mind generally tend to be reductionist and to deny any essential immaterial human nature. They reject personal freedom and any inherent rational force in the human makeup, and view people as innately neither good nor evil but neutral, highly educable creatures that can be markedly influenced or even controlled by environmental conditions.

Another twentieth-century view that denies any essential immaterial human nature insists that humans are ultimately free of their genetic and environmental influences and actively control what and who they will be. This is the existential view.

The Existential View

Although the theory that humans actively determine what they will be is not new, it appears full-blown in our century in a philosophy called **existentialism.** Existentialists focus on individual existence and its problems. They deny any essential human nature in the traditional rational or religious sense, insisting that individuals create their own characters through free, responsible choices and actions. Humans are active participants in the world, not determined mechanisms. Although they recognize outside influences, existentialists insist that each self determines its own human nature.

While existentialism continues to be popular among religious thinkers, we'll confine our remarks to atheistic existentialism, since its view provides a unique concept of human nature and self. The chief exponent of atheistic existentialism is Jean-Paul Sartre (1905–1980), who sees humans as "condemned to be free." We are free because we can rely neither on a God (who doesn't exist) nor on society to justify our actions or to tell us what we essentially are. We are condemned because without absolute guidelines we must suffer the agony of our own decision making and the anguish of its consequences.

Although he believes that there are no true universal statements about

---

15. *B. F. Skinner.* Science and Human Behavior. *New York: Macmillan, 1953, pp. 447–448.*

what humans ought to be, Sartre does make at least one general statement about the human condition: We are free. This freedom consists chiefly of our ability to envisage additional possibilities to our state, to conceive of what is not the case, to suspend judgment, and to alter our condition. Each of us has our subjectivity, our only birthright.

To illustrate, many people believe that we have little or no control over our emotions. If we're depressed, we're depressed, and there's little we can do about it. Sartre argues that if we're depressed, we've chosen to be. Emotions, he says, are not moods that come over us but ways in which we freely choose to perceive the world, to participate in it. It is the consciousness of this freedom and its accompanying responsibilities that cause our anguish. The most anguishing thought of all is that we don't know how we will behave next. Sometimes we escape this anguish by pretending we are not free, as when we pretend that our genes or our environment is the cause of how we are or act, or that we are spectators rather than participants, passive rather than active. When we so pretend, says Sartre, we act in "bad faith." To guard against this, he cautions us to make individual choices fully aware that we are doing so. We must take full responsibility not only for our actions but also for our beliefs, feelings, and attitudes.

Existentialism obviously emphasizes the individual. The self in this view is not necessarily rational, divine, or mechanical. It is neither a creature of God nor a kind of moss or fungus. It is instead a project that possesses a subjective life; it is the sum total, not of everything that happens to it, but of everything it ever does. In the end, we are our choices; to be human means to be free.

In his *Existentialism and Humanism*, Sartre vigorously expresses the existential view of human nature. Notice in the selection that follows the primacy that Sartre gives to existence. Existence is prior to essence, he believes; humans

"'We are our choices. Man is freedom.'" (Sartre)

exist first, then they make something of themselves. In this fact lies the human condition.

> Atheistic existentialism, of which I am a representative, declares . . . that if God does not exist there is at least one being whose existence comes before its essence, a being which exists before it can be defined by any conception of it. That being is man. . . . What do we mean by saying that existence precedes essence? We mean that man first of all exists, encounters himself, surges up in the world—and defines himself afterwards. If man as the existentialist sees him is not definable, it is because to begin with he is nothing. He will not be anything until later, and then he will be what he makes of himself. Thus, there is no human nature, because there is no God to have a conception of it. Man simply is. Not that he is simply what he conceives himself to be, but he is what he wills. . . . [16]

Clearly, existentialism gives the inner life and experience a new emphasis. Whereas those seeing the self as a response to stimuli ignore the inner world of feelings, sensations, moods, and anxieties, existentialists focus on it. Indeed, this inner life is precisely what the self experiences, and thus it is the self. In it are found our feelings of despair, fear, guilt, and isolation, as well as our uncertainties, especially about death. There we confront the meaninglessness that is at the core of existence and thus discover a truth that enables us to live fully conscious of what being human means.

Despite existentialism's assertion of self and its wide contemporary influence, many argue that the self is really an illusion and that attachment to this illusion causes existential sorrow, anguish, and ultimate absurdity. Psychological behaviorists would probably so argue. But this reaction has become increasingly popular in the West with the spread of Eastern philosophies and religions that deny the existence of an essential human nature and of self.

Eastern Views

When we speak of Eastern philosophy, we refer to those systems of thought, belief, and action espoused by many peoples in the Near and Far East. Because Eastern thought offers many views of human nature, it is impossible to mention them all. Buddhism's view is particularly noteworthy for several reasons. First, it represents a large number of Eastern thinkers. Second, many Westerners have been converted to Buddhism. Third, it contrasts sharply with most Western views. At the same time, we must acknowledge the rich diversity of Buddhist sects: Theravada, Mahayana, Bodhisattva and Pure Land, and Zen. The treatment of Buddhism and Eastern thought in this book will likely prove too cursory for most Westerners, but our intention is not to exhaust the subject but to provide a vital transcultural perspective as well as evidence of the global view of philosophy.

Central to Buddhist thought is the belief that all existence is characterized by constant movement and change. Since "all is change," there is no fixed or static human nature. Nevertheless, like existentialists, Buddhists do make

---

16. *Jean-Paul Sartre.* Existentialism and Humanism. *Philip Mairet, Trans. London: Methuen, 1949, p. 85.*

statements about the human condition, which can be summed up in the Buddhist doctrine of the Four Noble Truths.

The first of these truths is the existence of suffering. From birth to death, life is a succession of physical and psychological torments that no one avoids. Yes, for a time we may ward off suffering with youth, health, and riches, but ultimately we experience it. Suffering is a universal problem in a finite and ever changing world.

The Second Noble Truth states that we suffer because we desire or crave things. The insidious nature of these "thirsts" is that the more we try to satisfy them, the worse they become. The more we get, the more we want and the more we must have. When these desires run unchecked, they leave us frustrated and unhappy. However, they need not control us; when we master them, we attain a peace and serenity that no amount of appetite satisfying can match.

The Third Noble Truth is that release from this seemingly endless round of pleasure pursuit is possible by realizing that the true nature of self is not found in trying to satisfy our desires, but in fortifying ourselves with values that are contrary to these desires. When we do this, we ease pain, suffering, and unhappiness.

The values that express the true nature of self are found in the Fourth Noble Truth: that we gain release from suffering through the Noble Eightfold Path. This path consists of the following steps:

1. *Right understanding.* Humans must realize that the only way out of pain and suffering is to know their true selves, to abandon ignorance about the self, and to eliminate craving and desire. Without understanding we do not know how to escape our predicament.

2. *Right intention or purpose.* We must want release from our dilemma and commit ourselves to discovering self-knowledge. Without purpose we will not do what we must to find peace.

3. *Right speech.* One sign that we are serious about attaining enlightenment is that our speech is above reproach. We must never lie, gossip, slander, boast, flatter, or threaten.

4. *Right conduct.* Just as speech reflects the quality of our intention, so does conduct. Seekers of enlightenment never kill or harm any living creature. Neither do they pollute their bodies with meats and liquors.

5. *Right way of livelihood.* How we earn a living must be compatible with our goal of enlightenment. Seeking material self-enrichment, such as money and status, excites desires and leads us from the path of true self-knowledge. Working in the service of other people helps to quell these desires and to keep us directed toward our goal.

6. *Right effort.* Speech, conduct, and way of living are not substitutes for discipline. Right effort involves constantly checking desires and cravings and conceding no morsel of gratification to them.

7. *Right mindfulness.* The interior life is as important as the exterior; what we think is as important as what we do. Just as we must not give in to desires,

so must we not even think about them. All action originates in thought. When the thought is right, so is the action.

8. *Right concentration.* The best way to ensure right mindfulness is through meditation and concentration, the spine of the Eightfold Way. Through reflective practices and concentrated voyages into the interior self, we can gain enlightenment.

Enlightenment, in Buddhist doctrine, is the state of "pure joy." This joy may come after long-practiced meditation and is not dependent on other people or on our own egos. We are enlightened when we are no longer selves or egos but a part of the flow of universal energy. We so merge with this flow of energy that we are one with it. Nothing can still or limit the joy of this merging, not even thoughts of death, because the energy of the universe experiences no death. Since we are one with this energy, we too will always exist, not as particular human beings but as embodiments of eternal being. When we realize this, we abandon self-centered concerns and gain release from the endless cycle of change.

Although to ease explanation even Buddhist scholars use the terms *human nature* and *self,* Buddhists contend that there are no human nature and no self as we understand them. In fact, any attempt to characterize humans as rational, divine, scientific, or existential is destined to fail, and any attempt to affirm our egos is doomed to produce misery.

Instead, Buddhist teaching poses a merging of five "streams" of physical sensations, feelings, perceptions, ideas, and consciousness. These streams, called *skandhas,* comprise being and *an-atta,* the "no self." In denying self and ego, Buddhists assert that nothing is permanent, everlasting, or absolute. According to Siddhartha Gautama the Buddha, the idea of self is an imaginary belief that produces harmful thoughts of "me," "mine," desire, vanity, egoism, and ill will.

Consistent with this view of human nature and self, Buddhism views everything that exists as being connected—everything depends on and is influenced by everything else. Nothing comes into existence without prior conditions; nothing exists independently of anything else.

We can infer from this view that nothing—physical or mental—is entirely free, because everything is relative and conditioned.[17] Since the whole existence is relative and conditioned, there can be no moral freedom, for freedom implies something independent of conditions. As a result, it makes little sense to speak of the human as being essentially good or evil, or of individual actions as being right or wrong.

One of the more respected scholars of Buddhism is Christmas Humphreys. He also has been a prime mover behind Western Buddhism, having founded the Buddhist Society, London, the oldest and largest Buddhist organization in Europe. Humphreys has authored "Twelve Principles of Buddhism," a synopsis of doctrines that have been ratified by the major Buddhist groups in the

17. *See Walpola Rahula.* What the Buddha Taught. *New York: Grove Press, 1962, p. 55.*

world. Because the "Twelve Principles" nicely summarizes and augments our bare bones presentation, we include it here in its entirety:

Twelve Principles of Buddhism

1. Self-salvation is for any man the immediate task. If a man lay wounded by a poisoned arrow he would not delay extraction by demanding details of the man who shot it, or the length and make of the arrow. There will be time for ever-increasing understanding of the Teaching during the treading of the Way. Meanwhile, begin now by facing life, as it is, learning always by direct and personal experience.

2. The first fact of existence is the law of change or impermanence. All that exists, from a mole to a mountain, from a thought to an empire, passes through the same cycle of existence—i.e., birth, growth, decay and death. Life alone is continuous, ever seeking self-expression in new forms. "Life is a bridge; therefore build no house on it." Life is a process of flow, and he who clings to any form, however splendid, will suffer by resisting the flow.

3. The law of change applies equally to the "soul." There is no principle in an individual which is immortal and unchanging. Only the "Namelessness," the ultimate Reality, is beyond change, and all forms of life, including man, are manifestations of this Reality. No one owns the life which flows in him any more than the electric light bulb owns the current which gives it light.

4. The universe is the expression of law. All effects have causes, and man's soul or character is the sum total of his previous thoughts and acts. Karma, meaning action-reaction, governs all existence, and man is the sole creator of his circumstances and his reaction to them, his future condition, and his final destiny. By right thought and action he can gradually purify his inner nature, and so by self-realization attain in time liberation from rebirth. The process covers great periods of time, involving life after life on earth, but ultimately every form of life will reach Enlightenment.

5. Life is one and indivisible, though its ever-changing forms are innumerable and perishable. There is, in truth, no death, though every form must die. From an understanding of life's unity arises compassion, a sense of identity with the life in other forms. Compassion is described as "the Law of laws—eternal harmony," and he who breaks this harmony of life will suffer accordingly and delay his own Enlightenment.

6. Life being One, the interests of the part should be those of the whole. In his ignorance man thinks he can successfully strive for his own interests, and this wrongly-directed energy of selfishness produces suffering. He learns from his suffering to reduce and finally eliminate its cause. The Buddha taught four Noble Truths: (*a*) The omnipresence of suffering; (*b*) its cause, wrongly directed desire; (*c*) its cure, the removal of the cause; and (*d*) the Noble Eightfold Path of self-development which leads to the end of suffering.

7. The Eightfold Path consists in Right (or perfect) Views or preliminary understanding, Right Aims or Motive, Right Speech, Right Acts, Right Livelihood, Right Effort, Right Concentration or mind-development, and,

finally, Right *Samadhi*, leading to full Enlightenment. As Buddhism is a way of living, not merely a theory of life, the treading of this Path is essential to self-deliverance. "Cease to do evil, learn to do good, cleanse your own heart: this is the Teaching of the Buddhas."

8. Reality is indescribable, and a God with attributes is not the final Reality. But the Buddha, a human being, became the All-Enlightened One, and the purpose of life is the attainment of Enlightenment. This state of Consciousness, Nirvana, the extinction of the limitations of self-hood, is attainable on earth. All men and all other forms of life contain the potentiality of Enlightenment, and the process therefore consists in becoming what you are. "Look within: thou *art* Buddha."

9. From potential to actual Enlightenment there lies the Middle Way, the Eightfold Path "from desire to peace," a process of self-development between the "opposites," avoiding all extremes. The Buddha trod this Way to the end, and the only faith required in Buddhism is the reasonable belief that where a Guide has trodden it is worth our while to tread. The Way must be trodden by the whole man, not merely the best of him, and heart and mind must be developed equally. The Buddha was the All-Compassionate as well as the All-Enlightened One.

10. Buddhism lays great stress on the need of inward concentration and meditation, which leads in time to the development of the inner spiritual faculties. The subjective life is as important as the daily round, and periods of quietude for inner activity are essential for a balanced life. The Buddhist should at all times be "mindful and self-possessed," refraining from mental and emotional attachment to "the passing show." This increasingly watchful attitude to circumstances, which he knows to be his own creation, helps him to keep his reaction to it always under control.

11. The Buddha said: "Work out your own salvation with diligence." Buddhism knows no authority for truth save the intuition of the individual, and that is authority for himself alone. Each man suffers the consequences of his own acts, and learns thereby, while helping his fellow men to the same deliverance; nor will prayer to the Buddha or to any God prevent an effect from following its cause. Buddhist monks are teachers and exemplars, and in no sense intermediates between Reality and the individual. The utmost tolerance is practiced towards all other religions and philosophies, for no man has the right to interfere in his neighbor's journey to the Goal.

12. Buddhism is neither pessimistic nor "escapist," nor does it deny the existence of God or soul, though it places its own meaning on these terms. It is, on the contrary, a system of thought, a religion, a spiritual science and a way of life, which is reasonable, practical and all-embracing. For over two thousand years it has satisfied the spiritual needs of nearly one-third of mankind. It appeals to the West because it has no dogmas, satisfies the reason and the heart alike, insists on self-reliance coupled with tolerance for other points of view, embraces science, religion, philosophy, psychology, ethics and art, and points to man alone as the creator of his present life and sole designer of his destiny.[18]

18. *Christmas Humphreys*. Buddhism. *London: Penguin, 1951, pp. 74–75.* © *Christmas Humphreys 1951. Reprinted by permission of Penguin Books Ltd.*

Some Observations

In examining any one view, there is a tendency to see it as excluding others. But these theories rarely do that. The rational, religious, and existential views, for example, all agree on the human's essential freedom. The scientific and Buddhist views agree that the self does not exist in the way that traditional Western thought would have it.

You yourself might hold a traditional view that the human is a combination of mind and body. You might consider the mind immaterial and immortal, the body material and mortal. You would probably view yourself, then, from the rational and scientific perspectives. So these traditions do overlap, and combined views are not only common but seemingly necessary to account for the full range of human experience. Differences in views are more often differences of emphasis than of content.

Thinkers obviously disagree about which aspect of the human experience deserves the most emphasis. Differences in emphases have produced these different positions about human nature, and no position is watertight. Each offers a different aspect of what it means to be human, and none completely describes that phenomenon. Nevertheless, in recent decades, the scientific and existential perspectives have grown increasingly dominant.

In the last analysis, no one theory can fully describe and explain human nature. The most reasonable position seems to be one that does not distort and ignore aspects of human experience beyond its own focus and that can accommodate additional data about the human condition. The most plausible view of human nature is self-reflexive; that is, it is sufficiently rich in categories and concepts to allow theorists to formulate their own theories. This position accords significance to all phenomena, particularly subjectivity.

Although we cannot say which view fulfills these requirements, the acceptance or rejection of a particular view influences our lives and how we interpret issues. The issue of freedom, to which we have already referred, is a good example. Whether we consider ourselves free, partially free, or not free at all depends to a large extent on what our view of human nature is. This attitude toward freedom in turn influences how we live. Thus, our view of human nature affects our lives.

Also, our experiences affect our views of human nature because of the intimacy between our experiences and our self-concepts. Obviously, we can sail along smoothly in life buoyed up by unexamined assumptions, such as that we are free. Then something happens; we run aground. A crisis forces us to evaluate our taken-for-granted, and we wonder if we are really free. Our inquiry, if pursued with philosophical zest, leads to far-reaching questions about what kind of being we are. As a result, we may even modify our particular view. To illustrate the interplay between these theoretical constructs and our personal lives and identities, consider the case of Doris.

Having grown up in a religious environment, Doris has assumed that everyone possesses free will, that is, the God-given capacity to make voluntary decisions, to choose freely from alternatives. Taking this for granted, she has lived with the comfortable belief that she is the responsible ruler of her life.

Then, Doris begins college and starts thinking about what she will do with her life. Had she lived a generation or two ago, she would not even have posed the question—she would have become a wife and mother without too much thought. But times have changed and circumstances are different. "It's just not that simple anymore," she tells her tradition-minded parents, who still are not convinced that college is the proper place for their daughter. "Why not take something practical, like business or nursing?" they ask. A woman can always find work as a secretary or nurse, they tell her, or perhaps as an elementary school teacher.

Doris is majoring in elementary school education, but she is dissatisfied. She finds the curriculum unchallenging and the prospect of life in a classroom unattractive. Lately she has begun to think about engineering. She has always been extremely good at math and science, and she enjoys working with machinery. However, studying engineering hardly seems practical: It is expensive and grueling. Even if she does succeed, she still worries about the future for a female engineer. Prospects are improving, but they are still uncertain. And what about the pressure along the way? Already many of her friends are married; others are set on traditional female professions.

It's very important for Doris to make her own choice. Most of all she wants to feel that she alone is deciding, not her parents, friends, or society. She is convinced that making the decision is tough enough without feeling that someone else is actually making it. Doris's problem cuts to the very assumption upon which she has based her life, which springs from the religious view of human nature.

Feeling the pinch of her dilemma, Doris seeks advice from a friend, Jane. Jane does not believe in the religious concept of free will. She considers herself primarily a thinker who, through commitment to thought and reason, tries to solve her problems as a rational being. Let us see what advice Jane gives to Doris.

Doris: I'm going to be a teacher.

Jane: Are you sure that's what you want to do?

Doris: No, but I'm tired of weighing the pros and cons. It's decided, and that's the end of it.

Jane: *It's* decided? A second ago you said *you* decided.

Doris: I mean me. *I* have decided.

Jane: Okay, why do you want to be a teacher?

Doris: Look, Jane, I really don't want to go through all this again.

Jane: I think you should.

Doris: But what good will it do?

Jane: It might stop you from doing something you'll regret.

Doris: Whatever I do I'm going to regret.

Jane: Okay, so you have unpleasant alternatives. By examining them, at least you'll know why you made the decision.

Doris: Is that so important—to know *why*?

Jane: Sure it is. If you don't know why you're choosing something, how do you know *you* are choosing it? Remember when you bought your car?

Doris: Yes.

Jane: Did you know why you bought it?

Doris: Of course. I needed transportation.

Jane: And you wanted something small, cheap, and dependable.

Doris: Right.

Jane: You knew why you were buying the car. And if someone asked, you could have told them.

Doris: So?

Jane: So isn't this choice as important as buying a car?

Doris: Of course it is.

Jane: Then why do you want to be a teacher?

Doris: For a lot of reasons. For one, my parents think it's a good idea.

Jane: Sure they do, but for *their* reasons.

Doris: What do you mean?

Jane: Well, *they're* not becoming a teacher—*you* are. *They're* not the ones who must spend the rest of their professional lives in a classroom—*you* are.

Doris: You make them sound terrible.

Jane: I don't mean to. I'm just trying to help you see sides of the question that you don't seem to be aware of.

Doris: Do you really believe I'm not being honest with myself about this?

Jane: I don't know. But if *you* are really going to choose, you should be aware of *why* you're choosing. Otherwise you're having the choice made for you. And that's what's really going to hurt over the long haul—much more than if you make the so-called right choice.

Doris: You know, Jane, you've got me thinking.

Jane: In what way?

Doris: Well, I'm just wondering how many things that I'm not even aware of are influencing this choice.

Jane: Right. Now you're taking charge. You've taken the first step toward choosing for yourself.

Doris.   I don't know if that's so good. After all, I can never be aware of everything.

Jane: Of course not. But you can become aware of the important influences.

Because Jane views the human as a reasoning being, she encourages Doris to think and reflect, to develop insightful awareness. Just as important, she offers an alternative to Doris's own view of personal freedom and perhaps to her view of human nature. Jane sees herself as someone who is free only to the degree that she is aware of the factors affecting her choices. The less aware, the less free; the more aware, the more free. In Jane's view, then, freedom is always contingent on self-awareness. If she's right, then individually we carry the heavy burden of developing insights into the factors that influence our lives. Otherwise we remain imprisoned by them.

So Jane seems to be saying that Doris must somehow *learn* to be free. But can Doris do this? After all, many factors affect her decision. Perhaps these factors are also affecting how well she can learn and how much awareness she can have. How much self-insight can she actually develop? Suppose that Doris was never encouraged to be self-aware, that self-awareness was not a value in her upbringing. Can she suddenly develop it? Such a question asks exactly what kind of being Doris is and, by extension, any of us is. Are we essentially free to alter the conditions that have affected us? Are we to become self-aware just for the sake of self-awareness? We still must decide what to do.

Presumably we become self-aware to reach the right decision about a course of action. Thus, Jane seems to imply that if Doris just thinks hard and long enough, she will see the right thing to do. True, the universe seems to be governed by physical laws, like the laws of motion and gravity, and through thought and reason we discover them. But are there necessarily moral laws at work that await our discovery and that direct our conduct?

The ability to reflect seems to be a double-edged sword. On the one hand, it can cut to valuable self-insights, to an understanding of the factors influencing our decisions. On the other hand, it can uncover so many factors that we do not seem to be free at all; as a result, we may come to doubt that there is any freedom. As we've seen, the belief that freedom is an illusion is an integral part of the scientific and Buddhist views.

Taking Jane's advice to think, introspect, and become self-aware, Doris examines the factors bearing on her choice. She discovers a whole list of influences: parents, home life, education, friends, and so forth.

For example, she recalls how as a little girl she was given dolls and dollhouses to play with, encouraged to think of marriage and family, and sheltered from considering professions such as medicine, engineering, or law. In fact, she can't think of a single instance when someone asked her, "What are you going to be when you grow up?" although she recalls that they often asked that of her brother. What she would be seemed a foregone conclusion: a wife and mother.

Such considerations set her to thinking about just how free any person is in view of all the environmental and hereditary influences affecting us. She wonders if we can behave any differently from the way in which we are programmed. Thinking along this line, Doris suspects that she cannot help acting as she will, for her past is determining her future.

Discontent with the idea that she is not at all free, Doris confides in another friend, Fred. Fred sees humans existentially, as active participants in the world around them. They are by nature free to choose and direct their lives. Although this sounds like the concept of free will, Fred's sense of freedom poses no God from whom freedom springs. Rather, freedom is an integral part of being human.

Doris cannot quite believe that she is free in the way that Fred believes. She asks him whether, if she introspects enough, she will discover the right thing to do. Fred points out that it isn't a question of the right thing to do: If

"'. . . you're like an empty canvas that sits waiting for the artist to put color and form on it for meaning.'"

there were a right decision to be made, we would be under an obligation to discover it. But obligations are the opposite of freedom; they restrict and limit rather than liberate. Her job, Fred tells Doris, is not to discover the so-called right decision but to *make* it; in making it, she will make herself. Doris doesn't understand.

"Right now," says Fred, "you're like an empty canvas that sits waiting for the artist to put color and form on it for meaning. It sits awaiting its real identity."

"But the paints, what about the paints? Aren't they just everything that's ever happened to me? Aren't they what give me meaning?"

"No. It's the painter who does that. What paints are used are left to the artist—to you in this case. And if no painting ever appears on the canvas, that too is up to the artist, up to you."

Fred sees Doris as an agent engaged in her own self-definition. He admits that the past influences the present and the present the future. But humans are not mechanical; they are not objects. They are subjects: They are acted upon, but they act as well. It is this dimension, the "I" as agent, that provides us with freedom. Simply by being, we are free. This freedom allows us to determine what we will be, to fashion meaning out of experience. There are no shoulds or musts, which would bind us to obligations not of our own making. There is no right or wrong to be followed or avoided. There just *is*. We exist, and why we exist is up to each of us to say. The whole meaning of our lives lies in creating our own reasons for being. Whatever Doris does with her life, *she* is responsible—not her parents or society.

What has occurred here? A question of intense personal concern has evoked philosophical ponderings about human nature. In the last analysis, the question "What is a human?" is one of the most important that we can ask, for much hinges on its answer. Life's meaning and purpose, what we ought to do, what we can hope to accomplish—all are profoundly affected by what we consider human nature (see Philosophy and Life 2–2). If we truly are children of God, then God's purpose for our existence defines us, informs us what to do. But if we are ultimately the product of society, then our happiness and welfare are bound up with social conditions, and presumably we should work to improve them. If we are fundamentally free and can't avoid individual choice, then seemingly the only sensible approach toward life is to accept our lot and make our choices with full awareness of what we're doing. Thus, while at times seeming to float in the ether of abstraction, these views of human nature vitally affect our lives. What's more, we can use the stuff of our experience to gain a firmer grasp of these views and their influences.

Showcase: Plato and Sartre

The preceding discussion was intended to provide an array of overviews of human nature, and thus has certain pitfalls. One might conclude from the dis-

PHILOSOPHY AND LIFE 2-2
Koestler and James

Does it really matter which view of human nature you believe? Sure, they carry different implications. Some hold we're free, others that we're not; some that we have a divine destiny, others that we don't. But in the last analysis, such claims raise unanswerable philosophical questions. So, what difference does it make what view you hold?

Author and outspoken opponent of behaviorism Arthur Koestler thinks it does make a difference. In his autobiography, *Arrow in the Blue* (New York: Macmillan, 1952), Koestler recalls how his own belief in free will significantly affected his decision to abandon his studies in engineering for the uncertain career of an author. Writes Koestler:

> I had no plans except "to lead my own life." In order to do that I had to "get off the track." This metaphorical track I visualized very precisely as an endless stretch of steel rails on rotting sleepers. You were born onto a certain track, as a train is put on its run according to the timetable; and once on the track, you no longer had free will. Your life was determined . . . by outside forces; the rail of steel, stations, shunting points. If you accepted that condition, running on rails became a habit which you could no longer break. The point was to jump off the track before the habit was formed, before you became encased in a rattling prison. To change the metaphor: reason and routine kept people in a straitjacket which made their living flesh rot beneath it [p. 32].

For Koestler, then, the belief in his own personal freedom led him to the

cussion that philosophy is merely a catalogue of diverse opinions; that engaging an issue such as human nature, philosophy ultimately does little more than serve up a smorgasbord of opinions. Moreover, focusing on a single issue as we have just done inevitably dislodges the portion from the mosaic of interrelated pieces which, taken together, make up a full-scale philosophy. In fact, one cannot fully appreciate a position on an issue without understanding how it fits in with an entire outlook. In order to avoid these pitfalls and give the preceding material a sharper focus, we will now take a more in-depth look at two philosophers, one ancient, the other modern: Plato and Sartre.

Philosopher Leslie Stevenson has written a marvelously succinct book entitled *Seven Theories of Human Nature*.[19] In it the author lays out four categories within which we can profitably compare and contrast the core thought of Plato and Sartre. These categories are: theory of the universe, theory of human nature (man), diagnosis of the human condition, and prescription for improving the human condition.

19. *Leslie Stevenson.* Seven Theories of Human Nature. *New York: Oxford University Press, 1974.*

conviction that he could "jump off the track" chosen for him by others, that he could lead his own life.

Koestler's account is reminiscent of the crisis that the American philosopher and psychologist William James (1842–1910) once faced. James had suffered throughout his life from a variety of emotional disorders that left him feeling profoundly alienated. Then, like Koestler, James seemingly took a giant step toward resolving his problems when he was able to satisfy himself that he was free. James captures the moment in a letter to his father: "I think that yesterday was a crisis in my life. I finished the first part of Renouvier's second 'Essais' and see no reason why his definition of Free Will—'the sustaining of a thought because I choose to when I might have other thoughts'—need be the definition of an illusion. At any rate, I will assume for the present—until next year—that it is no illusion. My first act of free will shall be to believe in free will."*

* The Letters of William James. *Henry James, Ed. Boston: Atlantic Monthly Press, 1920,* p. 148.

☐ *Illustrate how the belief in one or more of the views of human nature is concretely expressed in your life.* ☐ *Have you ever felt or found yourself "blocked" because of how you saw yourself or what you believed you were or were capable of being?*

Plato (427–347 B.C.)

Plato was born in the Greek city-state of Athens. Under a democratic government in the time of Pericles, Athens had enjoyed economic prosperity and a richly stimulating intellectual climate, culminating in the great ethical philosopher Socrates. But when Plato grew up, Athens was at war with another Greek polity, Sparta, and eventually was humbled by defeat at the hands of this city-state known for strict discipline and military might. As a result, democracy was supplanted by a brief period of tyranny.

When democracy was restored in Athens, Socrates was condemned to death on a charge of impiety and corrupting the youth of Athens. As we have seen, Socrates' main philosophical concern was with how anyone can know the right way to live. This preoccupation was to exert a strong influence on Plato, who, deeply shocked by the death of his teacher, grew disillusioned with politics, even philosophy. As a result, Plato began to seek knowledge of the truth about the universe, and the cure for society's ills. In the many philosophical dialogues he later wrote, Plato put his concerns into the mouth of Socrates. These dialogues were taught in the Academy Plato founded and which is regarded as the world's first university. The most famous of Plato's dialogues is *The Republic.* In *The Republic,* Plato presents his conception of the ideal society, and offers his views on many topics, including philosophy, morals, politics, education, and art.

Theory of the Universe. Without doubt, the cornerstone of Plato's concept of the universe is his theory of Forms, which can be summarized under four aspects: logical, metaphysical (dealing with reality), epistemological (dealing with what can be known), and moral. For purposes of illustration, consider the word *dog.* How is it that *dog* (or *house* or *tree* or *lamp* or any other general term) can truly apply to many individual things (for example, Lassie, Rin-Tin-Tin, Fido, Rover, or the mutt rummaging through your trash can)? Plato's response is that corresponding to any such general word is one Form, for example, the Form Dog, which is different from all individual dogs. What makes Lassie, Rin-Tin-Tin, Fido, Rover, the mutt, or any other particular animal a dog is its resemblance to or "participation in" the Form Dog. This, then, is the logical aspect of Plato's theory of Forms: an answer to the meaning of general words.

The metaphysical aspect springs from a further consideration of the nature of the Forms. Plato believed that the Forms never change; they are indestructible, immaterial, timeless. For this reason he considered Forms more real than material things: The Form Dog is more real than any individual dog. These Forms are not located in space or time, nor are they perceivable by any of the senses. Where, then, are they? According to Plato, the Forms exist in another realm, a world beyond the changeable and perishable things we experience, a world of unchanging, eternal Forms. Plato concluded that, given their nature, only the Forms can be said to fully exist.

The epistemological aspect of Plato's theory of Forms follows upon the metaphysical. Since only what fully exists can be fully known, Plato said that only an intellectual acquaintance with the Forms can really count as knowledge. Can any of us have such knowledge? Plato believed we could through a process of education.

At this point, you might be tempted to write off Plato as fuzzy-headed, as a blower of smoke rings. But before you do, recall your study of plane geometry. Euclidean geometry, with which Plato was familiar, yields a compelling illustration of the logical, metaphysical, and epistemological aspects of Plato's theory. For example, geometry deals with lines, circles, and squares, even though no physical object is perfectly straight, circular, or square. Despite the ever present irregularity in any geometric figure, anyone who has studied plane geometry realizes that theorems concerning these ideal objects (straight lines without thickness, perfect circles and squares, and so on) are demonstrated with certainty by logical argument. In other words, Euclidean geometry yields certain knowledge of timeless objects which are the patterns that material objects (a particular line, circle, or square) imperfectly resemble. In the language of Plato, these ideal objects are Forms.

It is the moral aspect of the theory of Forms that is crucial in Plato's theory of human nature. Just as there is a corresponding Form for a term such as *dog,* so there is a corresponding Form for moral words such as *courage* and *justice.* Thus, the many individual acts of justice and courage that we observe, and the many individual persons we consider courageous or just, correspond to the Forms Courage and Justice. Stated another way, individual acts of justice or courage resemble or "participate in" the Form Justice, or the Form Courage. Just as no particular circle is perfect, so no action or individual is perfectly courageous or just. Nevertheless, according to Plato, perfect justice and courage do exist in the Forms. Moreover, the moral Forms establish the standards by which all human character and actions should be judged.

The most general of the moral words is *good.* Accordingly, the Form Good is preeminent among the Forms. It is the source of all reality, all truth, all goodness. The absolute standards set by the moral Forms, which like all other Forms emanate from the Good, apply not only to individuals, but to the whole of social and political life. In a word, they define ideals in human behavior and societal relations. It is at this point that Plato's view of human nature may be fitted into his theory of Forms.

Human Nature. As we have seen, Plato held a dualist view of human nature, according to which the soul or mind is a nonmaterial entity which can exist apart from the body. The human soul, then, is immaterial and indestructible. Most important, the soul can attain knowledge of the Forms, a doctrine that meshes with Plato's contrast of the world of Forms with the world of perceivable things. That the Forms, as ultimate realities, are knowable only by the intellect, explains why Plato believed that of the three aspects of the soul (Reason, Appetite, Spirit), Reason should predominate. Through Reason, through the intellect, humans can attain knowledge of the Forms, especially of the preeminent one, the Form Good.

Thus, while Plato's emphasis is on the intellect, on knowledge, it is also on morality because of his belief that virtue is a matter for human knowledge, and not just belief or opinion. Briefly, there is such a thing as the truth about how we ought to live, and we can know this truth via the human intellect, when we achieve knowledge of the timeless Forms.

Diagnosis. While the Forms define ideals for individuals and society, Plato recognizes that individually and collectively we fall far short of these ideals.

Rarely do individual persons show signs of harmonizing the three parts of the soul. Nor do societies manifest harmony and stability. Indeed, some societies, tyrannies, value ambition and competition at the expense of intelligence; others, oligarchies, invest power and authority in the masses, who lack self-discipline and are motivated only by pleasure. Plato's diagnosis of the human condition, then, is simply that as individuals and societies we are not what we should be.

In Plato's view, the defects of individuals and societies are inseparable. Neither is totally to blame for the imperfection of the other. Imperfect societies produce imperfect individuals, and imperfect individuals make for imperfect societies. By the same token, neither individual and society can be perfected apart from the perfection of the other. The just state is not possible without having justice in individuals; justice in individuals is impossible without having justice in the state. Justice itself is the same for both individual and society: a harmonizing of the parts. But how is such a harmony to be attained? How to establish harmony in individual and state?

Prescription. Plato succinctly states the essence of his prescription for the defects he sees in individuals and society when he says in *The Republic*: "There will be no end to the trouble of states, or of humanity itself, till the philosophers become kings of the world, or till those we now call kings and rulers really and truly become philosophers, and political power and philosophy thus come into the same hands." Plato recognizes the unlikelihood of realizing his proposal, but given his theory of Forms and concept of human nature, his prescription makes sense. After all, if there is a truth about how we should live, then those with this knowledge are the only ones qualified to rule the state. Since philosophers are those who have attained the knowledge by coming to know the Forms, they should rule. Going further, Plato suggests that when a society is ruled by philosophers, the problems of human nature can be solved. In a word, the perfect state is one ruled by perfect individuals.

In *The Republic,* Plato sets up an elaborate system of education, one of whose functions is to produce perfect individuals to run the state. We need not detail the system here, but we will present one of Plato's best known and expertly crafted parables called the Allegory of the Cave. In part, it is a story about education, about bringing people out of the darkness of illusion into the light of truth and reality. The Allegory of the Cave also is the best illustration of Plato's two-worlds view, and it sets up his argument that philosophers should rule. Beyond this, the parable well depicts the difficulty all of us have in confronting the truth, the universal tendency to cling to the false security of our illusions.

Socrates: Imagine men to be living in an underground cave-like dwelling place, which has a way up to the light along its whole width, but the entrance is a long way up. The men have been there from childhood, with their neck and legs in fetters, so that they remain in the same place and can only see ahead of them, as their bonds prevent them turning their heads. Light is provided by a fire burning some way behind them and on a higher ground, there is a path across the cave and along this a low wall has been built, like the screen at a puppet show in front of the performers who show their puppets above it.

Glaucon: I see it.

Socrates: See then also men carrying along that wall, so that they overtop it, all kinds of artifacts, statues of men, reproductions of other animals in stone or wood fashioned in all sorts of ways, and, as is likely, some of the carriers are talking while others are silent.

Glaucon: This is a strange picture, and strange prisoners.

Socrates: They are like us, I said. Do you think, in the first place, that such men could see anything of themselves and each other except the shadows which the fire casts upon the wall of the cave in front of them?

Glaucon: How could they, if they have to keep their heads still throughout life?

Socrates: And is not the same true of the objects carried along the wall?

Glaucon: Quite.

Socrates: If they could converse with one another, do you not think that they would consider these shadows to be the real things?

Glaucon: Necessarily.

Socrates: What if their prison had an echo which reached them from in front of them? Whenever one of the carriers passing behind the wall spoke, would they not think that it was the shadow passing in front of them which was talking? Do you agree?

Glaucon: By Zeus, I do.

Socrates: Altogether then, I said, such men would believe the truth to be nothing else than the shadows of the artifacts?

Glaucon: They must believe that.

Socrates: Consider then what deliverance from their bonds and the curing of their ignorance would be if something like this naturally happened to them. Whenever one of them was freed, had to stand up suddenly, turn his head, walk, and look up toward the light, doing all that would give him pain, the flash of the fire would make it impossible for him to see the objects of which he had earlier seen the shadows. What do you think he would say if he was told that what he saw was foolishness, that he was now somewhat closer to reality and turned to things that existed more fully, that he saw more correctly? If one then pointed to each of the objects passing by, asked him what each was, and forced him to answer, do you not think he would be at a loss and believe that the things which he saw earlier were truer than the things now pointed out to him?

Glaucon: Much truer.

Socrates: If one then compelled him to look at the fire itself, his eyes would hurt, he would turn round and flee toward those things which he could see, and think that they were in fact clearer than those now shown to him.

Glaucon: Quite so.

Socrates: And if one were to drag him thence by force up the rough and steep path, and did not let him go before he was dragged into the sunlight, would he not be in physical pain and angry as he was dragged along? When he came into the light, with the sunlight filling his eyes, he would not be able to see a single one of the things which are now said to be true.

Glaucon: Not at once, certainly.

Socrates: I think he would need time to get adjusted before he could see things in the world above; at first he would see shadows most easily, then reflections of men and other things in water, then the things themselves. After this he would see objects in the sky and the sky itself more easily at night, the light of the stars and the moon more easily than the sun and the light of the sun during the day.

Glaucon: Of course.

Socrates: Then, at last, he would be able to see the sun, not images of it in water or in some alien place, but the sun itself in its own place, and be able to contemplate it.

Glaucon: That must be so.

Socrates: After this he would reflect that it is the sun which provides the seasons and the years, which governs everything in the visible world, and is also in some way the cause of those other things which he used to see.

Glaucon: Clearly that would be the next stage.

Socrates: What then? As he reminds himself of his first dwelling place, of the wisdom there and of his fellow prisoners, would he not reckon himself happy for the change, and pity them?

Glaucon: Surely.

Socrates: And if the men below had praise and honours from each other, and prizes for the man who saw most clearly the shadows that passed before them, and who could best remember which usually came earlier and which later, and which came together and thus could most ably prophesy the future, do you think our man would desire those rewards and envy those who were honoured and held power among the prisoners, or would he feel, as Homer put it, that he certainly wished to be "serf to another man without possessions upon the earth" and go through any suffering, rather than share their opinions and live as they do?

Glaucon: Quite so, I think he would rather suffer anything.

Socrates: Reflect on this too. If this man went down into the cave again and sat down in the same seat, would his eyes not be filled with darkness, coming suddenly out of the sunlight?

Glaucon: They certainly would.

Socrates: And if he had to contend again with those who had remained prisoners in recognizing those shadows while his sight was affected and his eyes had not settled down—and the time for this adjustment would not be short—would he not be ridiculed? Would it not be said that he had returned from his upward journey with his eyesight spoiled, and that it was not worthwhile even to attempt to travel upward? As for the man who tried to free them and lead them upward, if they could somehow lay their hands on him and kill him, they would do so.

Glaucon: They certainly would.

Socrates: This whole image, my dear Glaucon, must be related to what we said before. The realm of the visible should be compared to the prison dwelling, and the fire inside it to the power of the sun. If you interpret the upward journey and the contemplation of things above as the upward journey of the soul to the intelligible realm, you will grasp what I surmise since you were keen to hear it. Whether it is true or not only the god knows, but this is how I see it, namely that in the intelligible world the Form of the Good is the last to be seen, and with difficulty; when seen it must be reckoned to be for all the cause of all that is right and beautiful, to have produced in the visible world both the light and the fount of light, while in the intelligible world it is itself that which produces and controls truth and intelligence, and he who is to act intelligently in public or in private must see it.

Glaucon: I share your thought as far as I am able.

Socrates: Come then, share with me this thought also: do not be surprised that those who have reached this point are unwilling to occupy themselves with human affairs, and that their souls are always pressing upward to spend their time there, for this is natural if things are as our parable indicates.

Glaucon: That is very likely.

Socrates: Further, do you think it at all surprising that anyone coming to the evils of human life from the contemplation of the divine behaves awkwardly and appears very ridiculous while his eyes are still dazzled and before he is sufficiently adjusted to the darkness around him, if he is compelled to contend in court or some other place about the shadows of justice or the objects of which they are shadows, and to carry through the contest about these in the way these things are understood by those who have never seen Justice itself?

Glaucon: That is not surprising at all.

Socrates: Anyone with intelligence would remember that the eyes may be confused in two ways and from two causes, coming from light into darkness as well as from darkness into light. Realizing that the same applies to the soul, whenever he sees a soul disturbed and unable to see something, he will not laugh mindlessly but will consider whether it has come from a brighter life and is dimmed because unadjusted, or has come from greater ignorance into greater light and is filled with a brighter dazzlement. The former he would declare happy in its life and experience, the latter he would pity, and if he should wish to laugh at it, his laughter would be less ridiculous than if he laughed at a soul that has come from the light above.

Glaucon: What you say is very reasonable.

Socrates: We must then, if these things are true, think something like this about them, namely that education is not what some declare it to be; they say that knowledge is not present in the soul and that they put it in, like putting sight into blind eyes.

Glaucon: They surely say that.

Socrates: Our present argument shows that the capacity to learn and the organ with which to do so are present in every person's soul. It is as if it were not possible to turn the eye from darkness to light without turning the whole body; so one must turn one's whole soul from the world of becoming until it can endure to contemplate reality, and the brightest of realities, which we say is the Good.

Glaucon: Yes.

Socrates: Education then is the art of doing this very thing, this turning around, the knowledge of how the soul can most easily and most effectively be turned around; it is not the art of putting the capacity of sight into the soul; the soul possesses that already but it is not turned the right way or looking where it should. This is what education has to deal with.

Glaucon: This seems likely.[20]

20.   Plato. The Republic *(book VII). G. M. A. Grube, Trans. Indianapolis, Ind.: Hackett, 1974. Reprinted by permission.*

Sartre (1905–1980)

Jean-Paul Sartre was born in 1905 and educated at the École Normale Supérieure in Paris. At an early age he exhibited a precocious gift for writing, which he turned his full creative and intellectual energies to while in his twenties. During World War II, Sartre served in the French army and in the French Resistance movement. He also spent time as a prisoner of war in Germany.

Probably Sartre has become identified with existentialism chiefly because he gave lucid and popular expression to the more technical writings of the contemporary German philosophers, especially Martin Heidegger (1889–1976). This is not to say he was incapable of writing about existentialism in the most exacting and complex style. Quite the contrary, his massive major work *Being and Nothingness* (1943) belies the glib view of Sartre as a mere popularizer of existentialism. Perhaps his best-known work is his lecture on "Existentialism is a Humanism" (1946), a work that glitters with brilliance, despite Sartre's later attempt to define existentialism somewhat differently.

Evident in Sartre's view of existentialism are the influences of at least three modes of thought, stemming from Marx, Edmund Husserl (1895–1938), and Heidegger. While in many important ways different, these philosophers did share a deep concern for the individual. For Marx, as we shall see in Chapter 3, the function of philosophy, and philosophers, was not merely to understand the world, but to change it. For Husserl, whom we'll take up in Chapter 9, philosophy was to seek its foundation exclusively in the human and, specifically, in the essence of the human's concrete world existence. And for Heidegger, whom we will also consider in Chapter 9, an understanding of the larger question of Being was achieved best through the existential analysis of person. In short, each of these philosophers shared a concern about the human's active role in forging his or her own destiny, a concern shared by Sartre.

We will postpone considering how Sartre reversed traditional metaphysics until we engage that subject elsewhere (Chapter 9). Here we will discuss Sartre in terms of the categories just applied to Plato: theory of the universe, theory of human nature, diagnosis of the human condition, and prescription for improving the human condition.

Theory of the Universe. As we just saw, the central element in Plato's concept of the universe is his affirmative declaration of the existence of Forms, and he spends considerable time arguing his case. In contrast, Sartre's key assertion about the universe is a negative one: There is no God. Sartre spends no time arguing this point, assuming instead that the idea of God is self-contradictory, and that previous philosophers have amply demonstrated that God cannot or does not exist. But, while Sartre does not regard the existence of God as arguable, he holds that the absence of God is of utmost importance; for if there is no God, then there are no transcendent or objective values set for us. There are no laws of God that we must obey. Nor are there any Platonic Forms that we should attain knowledge of. The conclusion entailed by Sartre's analysis is inescapable: Forlorn and abandoned, we are on our own. What, then, are we to do? Sartre believes that that is for each of us to decide. He says that the only foundation for values is human freedom, and that there can be no external or objective justification for the values any of us chooses to adopt. This description, of course, stands in stark contrast to Plato's belief in objective moral standards set in the moral Forms, which through education we can gain knowledge of.

Human Nature. Sartre's rejection of any notion of objective values bears directly on his view of human nature. As we have seen, Sartre denies that there is any such thing as "human nature" about which there could be true or false theories. This doesn't mean that he denies certain properties which clearly are universal among all human beings, such as the need to eat, for example. Rather, he seems to be denying that there are any true general statements about what all individuals ought to be or do, as Plato believed there were.

Yet, as previously noted, Sartre does make some general statements about the human condition, the chief of which is the assertion that humans are free. How he arrives at this conclusion is a rather complex affair which we will merely attempt to sketch here.

Sartre reaches the conclusion that humans are free by analyzing the notion of consciousness. He begins by distinguishing between consciousness *(being-for-itself)* and nonconscious objects *(being-in-itself)*. Sartre thinks that this dualism is shown by the fact that consciousness necessarily has an object: Consciousness is always consciousness of something that is not itself. At the same time, consciousness is always aware of itself as well. Thus, consciousness distinguishes between itself and its object. The capacity to distinguish between consciousness and object is foundational to the ability to make judgments about these objects.

Judgments can be positive or negative. For example, I can say, "The book is on the table," a positive judgment. But I can also recognize and assert that which is *not* the case, as in "The book is not on the table." According to Sartre, conscious beings have the unique capacity to conceive of what is *not* the case.

Sartre makes a great deal of the capacity to make negative judgments, that is, of nothingness. Boiled down, his analysis points to a crucial role that negative judgments play in making a conceptual connection between consciousness and freedom. The ability to conceive of what is not the case is the freedom to imagine other possibilities, to suspend judgment. The power of negation, then, is the same as freedom. Our freedom lies in our capacity to imagine possibilities (that is, things other than as they are) and to try to actualize them. To be conscious is to be free.

This freedom, because it is an integral part of consciousness, extends to everything we think and do. To be sure, there are times when this total freedom is quite apparent to us, as in moments of temptation or indecision. But Sartre insists that everything we think and do is free. In expanding the concept of choice and freedom beyond their normal use, Sartre would hold us responsible not just for our actions but for our emotions, even for our own character. Thus, if I am mad, jealous, or angry, it is because I have chosen to be that way. If I am the kind of person who would rather "grin and bear it" than resist and protest, that too is a disposition I choose to adopt. This view seems at odds with our conventional views about emotions and character. We tend to view emotions as things that "come over us," and character as some fact about ourselves, which is perhaps alterable but only gradually and with great effort, even pain.

On the other hand, Sartre's view of freedom is not just an arbitrary misuse of language. After all, sometimes we do hold people accountable for their emotions and character. "How could you let yourself get so mad?" we ask a person overcome with anger, or "Must you always be so curt with people?" we ask of the person who is chronically impolite or uncivil. Indeed, such implied rebukes can influence behavior by making individuals aware of apparent character flaws. The more we become aware of what we are, the more capable we will be of becoming something else. This is a notion which Plato could heartily endorse. To be sure, the classical concept of freedom, as we saw, is intimately associated with self-awareness.

But in the last analysis, Sartre is saying more than that self-knowledge is liberating. He is saying that as conscious beings we have freedom in everything we think and do. By this account, every situation is novel, every moment requires a new or renewed choice. Because we never know how we will behave next, we experience anguish, which is another word for the consciousness of our freedom.

Diagnosis. Sartre admits that anguish, the consciousness of our freedom, is painful and that we ordinarily try to escape it. But we can never escape anguish, for it is a necessary truth that we are free. This observation leads to the crucial concept in Sartre's diagnosis of the human condition: self-deception or bad faith.

Self-deception or bad faith is the attempt to avoid anguish by pretending to ourselves that we are not free. There are various ways we do this: by trying to convince ourselves that our behavior is determined by our character, outside influences, forces beyond our control, unconscious mental states, or by anything but ourselves. One graphic example of self-deception provided by Sartre involves a young woman sitting with a man who, she knows, is bent on seduction. He takes her hand. In order to avoid the painful necessity of making a decision to accept or reject the man, the woman pretends not to notice, leaving her hand in his. The bad faith here lies in the woman's pretending to be a passive object, a being-in-itself, rather than what she really is: conscious and, therefore, a free being. Here's Sartre's account of the incident, as he develops it in *Being and Nothingness*.

> Take the example of a woman who has consented to go out with a particular man for the first time. She knows very well the intentions which the man who is speaking to her cherishes regarding her. She knows also that it will be necessary sooner or later for her to make a decision. But she does not want to realize the urgency; she concerns herself only with what is respectful and discreet in the attitude of her companion. She does not apprehend this conduct as an attempt to achieve what we call "the first approach": that is, she does not want to see possibilities of temporal development which his conduct presents. She restricts this behavior to what is in the present; she does not wish to read in the phrases which he addresses to her anything other than their explicit meaning. If he says to her, "I find you so attractive!" she disarms this phrase of its sexual background; she attaches to the conversation and to the behavior of the speaker, the immediate meanings, which she imagines as objective qualities. The man who is speaking to her appears to her sincere and respectful as the table is round or square, as the wall coloring is blue or gray. The qualities thus attached to the

person she is listening to are in this way fixed in a permanence like that of things, which is no other than the projection of the strict present of the qualities into the temporal flux. This is because she does not quite know what she wants. She is profoundly aware of the desire which she inspires, but the desire cruel and naked would humiliate and horrify her. Yet she would find no charm in a respect which would be only respect. In order to satisfy her, there must be a feeling which is addressed wholly to her *personality*—i.e., to her full freedom— and which would be a recognition of her freedom. But at the same time this feeling must be wholly desire; that is, it must address itself to her body as object. This time then she refuses to apprehend the desire for what it is; she does not even give it a name; she recognizes it only to the extent that it transcends itself toward admiration, esteem, respect and that it is wholly absorbed in the more refined forms which it produces, to the extent of no longer figuring anymore as a sort of warmth and density. But then suppose he takes her hand. This act of her companion risks changing the situation by calling for an immediate decision. To leave the hand there is to consent in herself to flirt, to engage herself. To with- draw it is to break the troubled and unstable harmony which gives the hour its charm. The aim is to postpone the moment of decision as long as possible. We know what happens next; the young woman leaves her hand there, but she *does not notice* that she is leaving it. She does not notice because it happens by chance that she is at this moment all intellect. She draws her companion up to the most lofty regions of sentimental speculation; she speaks of Life, of her life, she shows herself in her essential aspect—a personality, a consciousness. And during this time the divorce of the body from the soul is accomplished; the hand rests inert between the warm hands of her companion—neither consenting nor resisting—a thing.

We shall say that this woman is in bad faith, but we see immediately that she uses various procedures in order to maintain herself in this bad faith. She has disarmed the actions of her companion by reducing them to being only what they are. . . .[21]

Plato might try to account for the woman's behavior in terms of the three parts of the soul. Evident in this incident, he might point out, is a conflict between Appetite and Reason. The woman has yet to harmonize the two parts, together with Spirit; she is "out of sync." Thus the tension, the conflict, the apparent lack of integration. In this sense, Plato probably would agree that the woman, in being ignorant of her fundamental nature, is in a way denying it. For Sartre, the denial involves pretending to herself that she is not free. She can avoid this self-deception by facing up to her own freedom, by deciding whether to accept or reject the man. In contrast, Plato might argue that she will never be truly free until she knows whether she *ought* to accept or reject the man, and she can only learn this by achieving knowledge of the preeminent Form Good. For Sartre no such certain knowledge is possible. If she ought to do anything, it is to stop acting in bad faith, to stop deceiving herself.

The opposite of self-deception and bad faith is authenticity or sincerity. When we acknowledge our freedom as conscious beings, we act sincerely or

21.   *Jean-Paul Sartre.* Being and Nothingness. *Hazel E. Barnes, Trans. New York: Philosophical Library, 1956, pp. 55–56. Copyright © 1956 by Philosophical Library, Inc. Reprinted by permission of Philosophical Library, Inc.*

authentically. But where does that leave us? After we engage our freedom, what then?

Prescription. Given his rejection of any possibility of objective values, Sartre's prescription, in sharp contrast with Plato's, seems an empty one. Where Plato can recommend achieving knowledge of the Forms and erection of the just state on a base of philosophical knowledge, Sartre can recommend no particular course of action or way of life. Seemingly all he can do is condemn any bad faith, any effort to pretend that we are not free. About all Sartre can prescribe is that we act authentically; that is, that we make individual choices with awareness that nothing determines them for us. Of course, authentic choice could itself be considered something of intrinsic value. In fact, Sartre's descriptions of particular cases of good and bad faith imply a moral approval of good faith and disapproval of bad. But in the final analysis, Sartre recommends little in comparison to Plato's detailed prescription as developed in *The Republic*.

A comparison of Plato and Sartre, then, turns up some striking differences in how they view the universe and human nature, and in their diagnoses of the human condition and prescriptions for improving it. Of singular importance are their stands on morality and freedom. Whereas Plato believes that there are objective standards which serve as patterns on which to model human behavior and society, Sartre rejects this notion. Similarly, Plato associates freedom with self-awareness and knowledge of the Forms, while Sartre views freedom as an integral part of what it means to be a conscious being.

Summary and Conclusions

We opened the chapter by raising the issue of human nature as it applies to personal identity: Who and what am I? How we see ourselves has been influenced by at least five theories of human nature: the rational view, the religious view, the scientific view, the existential view, and the Eastern view. Although it is impossible to say which theory is most accurate, we frequently interpret aspects of our lives, such as personal freedom, through these theories. They do not exist in isolation, but often melt into one another. We seldom find ourselves acting exclusively according to one school of thought; more often we must act under the influences of several. They should provoke some personal reflections about what we believe and why.

But freedom, rationality, and goodness are only three issues describing who and what we are. There are others: what we know, what we consider to be ultimately real, what we cherish as objects of ultimate loyalty, what we hold to be morally right, what we regard as beautiful, and so on. All are fundamental expressions of how we see ourselves. As is the case with the issue of personal freedom, our beliefs in these areas betray many influences. We will explore these influences in further chapters, for these subjects are among those that constitute the study of philosophy.

Over 2,000 years ago Socrates claimed that "the unexamined life is not worth living." When humans begin to examine life, they begin to philosophize.

Philosophers are persons who perceive to some degree how the many experiences and insights of their existence form a pattern of meaning. Philosophy, as we saw in Chapter 1, is an activity undertaken by those who are deeply concerned with who and what they are and what everything means. We have launched that activity.

Section Exercises

The Rational View

1. Some people argue that because nonhuman animals can think, humans are not unique at all. What is the difference between thinking and reasoning? What mental states indicate a thinking process? Would you say that reasoning presumes thinking but that thinking does not presume reasoning?

2. What historical evidence indicates that we are rational animals? What evidence indicates that we are not?

The Religious View

1. How do the rational and religious views foster a concept of the human as being at odds with nature? Does history indicate that Westerners have lived up to this concept? Does contemporary experience confirm or challenge the wisdom of this concept?

2. Do you think that religions have generally not emphasized the God-given capacity to love so much as other concepts, such as sinful human nature, reward and punishment, and adherence to dogma?

Scientific Views

1. Psychological behaviorists claim that the human can be measured experimentally. Are there any human characteristics that contradict this claim? What human qualities cannot be measured?

2. Behaviorists also argue that techniques and engineering practices can be used to shape behavior so that people will function harmoniously for everyone's benefit. What questions would you raise about such a proposal?

The Existential View

1. Sartre's existentialism leaves us with our moral rules or behavioral guidelines, yet it ultimately holds us responsible for all our choices. Do you find such a view appealing? Contradictory? Unsettling? Liberating?

2. To what degree and in what ways, if any, do you experience your life as free, as Sartre describes freedom?

Eastern Views

1. Both the Buddhist and the scientific views deny the existence of self. But how and why they do are quite different. Describe the contrasts.

2. Does the view of no self have anything to offer the Western world? In what areas?

Some Observations

1. Political polls and projections are often said to influence the outcome of elections. What control, if any, does a forecast exercise over an event (for example, the astrological prophecies of Jeane Dixon)? If the existence of God is assumed, and if He already knows how things are going to turn out, can any of us alter that result? If we cannot alter something, are we free?

2. In *The Crito*, Plato shows Socrates refusing to escape from jail, even though he has been imprisoned unjustly, because such an action would violate the principles of a life dedicated to upholding the law. As a result, Socrates drinks the hemlock and dies. Was he free to choose differently? Was he a victim of his past?

3. Jane claims, "By examining [the alternatives], at least you'll know why you made the decision. . . . If you don't know why you're choosing something, how do you know *you* are choosing it?" Relative to the problem of self, how important would you say it is to know *why* you do something? In what sense are you less yourself by not knowing? Can you think of an instance in which it may be better not to know why you're doing something? Would it be better in the long term as well as the short?

4. Point to examples in your own life that show you doing things for other people's reasons. Perhaps your choice to be in school or to study a particular subject would be a good place to begin. How susceptible to peer pressure do you think you are? Do you detect the pressure affecting the views you hold? In what area of life do you feel you can truly express yourself?

5. Doris suggests that the very faculty of self-awareness may be a victim of the same influences that Jane claims are affecting Doris's decision. Can you illustrate Doris's suggestion?

6. Are we strictly mechanical, as Doris suspects? Can you think of qualities we possess that computers do not? Are they qualities computers *can never* possess, or qualities they do not possess now but could in the future?

7. Fatalism is the belief that events are fixed, that nothing we can do will alter them—what will be, will be. Is Doris a fatalist? Are you? Do scientific views necessitate fatalism? Is fatalism consistent with the doctrine of free will? Is it consistent with the view of the human as thinker? As an existential being?

8. If Fred believed that the right decision lay buried in us like a treasure to be discovered, he could not believe that we were truly free to make our own decisions. Why?

9. The difference between "making" yourself and "finding" yourself is partly chronological. Does making yourself precede or follow your coming into

existence? Does finding yourself suggest that something precedes your existence? Relate your explanations to each of the five views.

10. Can you think of any instance in which you would have no freedom at all? If we are essentially free, how does this freedom lead to uncertainty?

Night-Sea Journey

John Barth

What's the wildest thing you can imagine? Contact with extraterrestrial life? Living forever? Unending happiness? No doubt the list could go on and on. It's not likely, though, that your list would include a philosophical spermatozoon. But author John Barth asks us to imagine exactly this in his captivating short story "Night-Sea Journey."

A few years ago Woody Allen played a similar motif for laughs in one of his films. But Barth, one of our most inventive storytellers,[22] *is dead serious. In developing his metaphor, he raises profound philosophical questions about life, God, the universe, human nature, and the human condition. In short, Barth uses the microcosmic world of reproduction to launch a philosophical inquiry about the cosmos, the human's place in it, and the world beyond.*[23]

"One way or another, no matter which theory of our journey is correct, it's myself I address; to whom I rehearse as to a stranger our history and condition, and will disclose my secret hope though I sink for it.

"Is the journey my invention? Do the night, the sea, exist at all, I ask myself, apart from my experience of them? Do I myself exist, or is this a dream? Sometimes I wonder. And if I am, who am I? The Heritage I supposedly transport? But how can I be both vessel and contents? Such are the questions that beset my intervals of rest.

"My trouble is, I lack conviction. Many accounts of our situation seem plausible to me—where and what we are, why we swim and whither. But implausible ones as well, perhaps especially those, I must admit as possibly correct. Even likely. If at times, in certain humors—stroking in unison, say, with my neighbors and chanting with them 'Onward! Upward!'—I have supposed that we have after all a common Maker, Whose nature and motives we may not know, but Who engendered us in some mysterious wise and

launched us forth toward some end known but to Him—if (for a moodslength only) I have been able to entertain such notions, very popular in certain quarters, it is because our night-sea journey partakes of their absurdity. One might even say: I can believe them *because* they are absurd.

"Has that been said before?

"Another paradox: it appears to be these recesses from swimming that sustain me in the swim. Two measures onward and upward, flailing with the rest, then I float exhausted and dispirited, brood upon the night, the sea, the journey, while the flood bears me a measure back and down: slow progress, but I live, I live, and make my way, aye, past many a drownèd comrade in the end, stronger, worthier than I, victims of their unremitting *joie de nager.* I have seen the best swimmers of my generation go under. Numberless the number of the dead! Thousands drown as I think this thought, millions as I rest before returning to the swim. And scores, hundreds of millions have expired since we surged forth, brave in our innocence, upon our dreadful way.

From Lost in the Funhouse *by John Barth. Copyright © 1966 by John Barth. Reprinted by permission of Doubleday and Company, Inc.*

22.   *Other Barth titles:* Giles Goat-Boy, The Sot-Weed Factor, The End of the Road, *and* The Floating Opera. *"Night-Sea Journey" can be found in his collection of experimental short stories* Lost in the Funhouse, *in which Barth explores ways to use the disembodied authorial voice metaphorically.*

23.   *My thanks to Professor David Long of California State University at Sacramento for suggesting this selection and insights into it.*

'Love! Love!' we sang then, a quarter-billion strong, and churned the warm sea white with joy of swimming! Now all are gone down—the buoyant, the sodden, leaders and followers, all gone under, while wretched I swim on. Yet these same reflective intervals that keep me afloat have led me into wonder, doubt, despair—strange emotions for a swimmer!—have led me, even, to suspect . . . that our night-sea journey is without meaning.

"Indeed, if I have yet to join the hosts of the suicides, it is because (fatigue apart) I find it no meaningfuller to drown myself than to go on swimming.

"I know that there are those who seem actually to enjoy the night-sea; who claim to love swimming for its own sake, or sincerely believe that 'reaching the Shore,' 'transmitting the Heritage' (*Whose* Heritage, I'd like to know? And to whom?) is worth the staggering cost. I do not. Swimming itself I find at best not actively unpleasant, more often tiresome, not infrequently a torment. Arguments from function and design don't impress me: granted that we can and do swim, that in a manner of speaking our long tails and streamlined heads are 'meant for' swimming; it by no means follows—for me, at least—that we *should* swim, or otherwise endeavor to 'fulfill our destiny.' Which is to say, Someone Else's destiny, since ours, so far as I can see, is merely to perish, one way or another, soon or late. The heartless zeal of our (departed) leaders, like the blind ambition and good cheer of my own youth, appalls me now; for the death of my comrades I am inconsolable. If the night-sea journey has justification, it is not for us swimmers ever to discover it.

"Oh, to be sure, 'Love!' one heard on every side: 'Love it is that drives and sustains us!' I translate: we don't know *what* drives and sustains us, only that we are most miserably driven and, imperfectly, sustained. *Love* is how we call our ignorance of what whips us. 'To reach the Shore,' then: but what if the Shore exists in the fancies of us swimmers merely, who dream it to account for the dreadful fact that we swim, have always and only swum, and continue swimming without respite (myself excepted) until we die? Supposing even that there *were* a Shore—that, as a cynical companion of mine once imagined, we rise from the drowned to discover all those vulgar superstitions and exalted metaphors to be literal truth: the

giant Maker of us all, the Shores of Light beyond our night-sea journey!—whatever would a swimmer do there? The fact is, when we imagine the Shore, what comes to mind is just the opposite of our condition: no more night, no more sea, no more journeying. In short, the blissful estate of the drowned.

"'Ours not to stop and think; ours but to swim and sink. . . .' Because a moment's thought reveals the pointlessness of swimming. 'No matter,' I've heard some say, even as they gulped their last: 'The night-sea journey may be absurd, but here we swim, will-we nill-we, against the flood, onward and upward, toward a Shore that may not exist and couldn't be reached if it did.' The thoughtful swimmer's choices, then, they say, are two: give over thrashing and go under for good, or embrace the absurdity; affirm in and for itself the night-sea journey; swim on with neither motive nor destination, for the sake of swimming, and compassionate moreover with your fellow swimmer, we being all at sea and equally in the dark. I find neither course acceptable. If not even the hypothetical Shore can justify a sea-full of drownèd comrades, to speak of the swim-in-itself as somehow doing so strikes me as obscene. I continue to swim—but only because blind habit, blind instinct, blind fear of drowning are still more strong than the horror of our journey. And if on occasion I have assisted a fellow-thrasher, joined in the cheers and songs, even passed along to others strokes of genius from the drownèd great, it's that I shrink by temperament from making myself conspicuous. To paddle off in one's own direction, assert one's independent right-of-way, overrun one's fellows without compunction, or dedicate oneself entirely to pleasures and diversions without regard for conscience—I can't finally condemn those who journey in this wise; in half my moods I envy them and despise the weak vitality that keeps me from following their example. But in reasonabler moments I remind myself that it's their very freedom and self-responsibility I reject, as more dramatically absurd, in our senseless circumstances, than tailing along in conventional fashion. Suicides, rebels, affirmers of the paradox—nay-sayers and yea-sayers alike to our fatal journey—I finally shake my head at them. And splash sighing past their corpses, one by one, as past a hundred sorts of others: friends, enemies, brothers; fools, sages, brutes—and nobodies, million upon million. I envy them all.

"A poor irony: that I, who find abhorrent and tautological the doctrine of survival of the fittest (*fitness* meaning, in my experience, nothing more than survival-ability, a talent whose only demonstration is the fact of survival, but whose chief ingredients seem to be strength, guile, callousness), may be the sole remaining swimmer! But the doctrine is false as well as repellent: Chance drowns the worthy with the unworthy, bears up the unfit with the fit by whatever definition, and makes the night-sea journey essentially *haphazard* as well as murderous and unjustified.

"'You only swim once.' Why bother, then?

"'Except ye drown, ye shall not reach the Shore of Life.' Poppycock.

"One of my late companions—that same cynic with the curious fancy, among the first to drown—entertained us with odd conjectures while we waited to begin our journey. A favorite theory of his was that the Father does exist, and did indeed make us and the sea we swim—but not a-purpose or even consciously; He made us, as it were, despite Himself, as we make waves with every tail-thrash, and may be unaware of our existence. Another was that He knows we're here but doesn't care what happens to us, inasmuch as He creates (voluntarily or not) other seas and swimmers at more or less regular intervals. In bitterer moments, such as just before he drowned, my friend even supposed that our Maker wished us unmade; there was indeed a Shore, he'd argue, which could save at least some of us from drowning and toward which it was our function to struggle—but for reasons unknowable to us He wanted desperately to prevent our reaching that happy place and fulfilling our destiny. Our 'Father,' in short, was our adversary and would-be killer! No less outrageous, and offensive to traditional opinion, were the fellow's speculations on the nature of our Maker: that He might well be no swimmer Himself at all, but some sort of monstrosity, perhaps even tailless; that He might be stupid, malicious, insensible, perverse, or asleep and dreaming; that the end for which He created and launched us forth, and which we flagellate ourselves to fathom, was perhaps immoral, even obscene. Et cetera, et cetera: there was no end to the chap's conjectures, or the impoliteness of his fancy; I have reason to suspect that his early demise, whether planned by 'our Maker' or not, was expedited by certain fellow-swimmers indignant at his blasphemies.

"In other moods, however (he was as given to moods as I), his theorizing would become half-serious, so it seemed to me, especially upon the subjects of Fate and Immortality, to which our youthful conversations often turned. Then his harangues, if no less fantastical, grew solemn and obscure, and if he was still baiting us, his passion undid the joke. His objection to popular opinions of the hereafter, he would declare, was their claim to general validity. Why need believers hold that *all* the drownèd rise to be judged at journey's end, and non-believers that drowning is final without exception? In *his* opinion (so he'd vow at least), nearly everyone's fate was permanent death; indeed he took a sour pleasure in supposing that every 'Maker' made thousands of separate seas in His creative lifetime, each populated like ours with millions of swimmers, and that in almost every instance both sea and swimmers were utterly annihilated, whether accidentally or by malevolent design. (Nothing if not pluralistic, he imagined there might be millions and billions of 'Fathers,' perhaps in some 'night-sea' of their own!) However—and here he turned infidels against him with the faithful—he professed to believe that in possibly a single night-sea per thousand, say, one of its quarter-billion swimmers (that is, one swimmer in two hundred fifty billions) achieved a qualified immortality. In some cases the rate might be slightly higher; in others it was vastly lower, for just as there are swimmers of every degree of proficiency, including some who drown before the journey starts, unable to swim at all, and others created drownèd, as it were, so he imagined what can only be termed impotent Creators, Makers unable to Make, as well as uncommonly fertile ones and all grades between. And it pleased him to deny any necessary relation between a Maker's productivity and His other virtues—including, even, the quality of His creatures.

"I could go on (*he* surely did) with his elaboration of these mad notions—such as that swimmers in other night-seas needn't be of our kind; that Makers themselves might belong to different *species*, so to speak; that our particular Maker mightn't Himself be immortal, or that we might be not only His emissaries but His 'immortality,' continuing His life and our own, transmogrified, beyond our individual deaths. Even this modified immortality (meaningless to me) he conceived as relative and contingent, subject to accidental or deliberate termination: his pet hypothesis was that Makers and swimmers *each generate the other*—against all odds, their number being so great—and that any given 'immortality-chain' could terminate after any number of cycles, so that what was 'immortal' (still speaking relatively) was only the cyclic process of incarnation, which itself might have a beginning and an end. Alternatively he liked to imagine cycles within cycles, either finite or infinite: for example, the 'night-sea,' as it were, in which Makers 'swam' and created night-seas and swimmers like ourselves, might be the creation of a larger Maker, Himself one of many, Who in turn et cetera. Time itself he regarded as relative to our experience, like magnitude: who knew but what, with each thrash of our tails, minuscule seas and swimmers, whole eternities, came to pass—as ours, perhaps, and our Maker's Maker's, was elapsing between the strokes of some supertail, in a slower order of time?

"Naturally I hooted with the others at this nonsense. We were young then, and had only the dimmest notion of what lay ahead; in our ignorance we imagined night-sea journeying to be a positively heroic enterprise. Its meaning and value we never questioned; to be sure, some must go down by the way, a pity no doubt, but to win a race requires that others lose, and like all my fellows I took for granted that I would be the winner. We milled and swarmed, impatient to be off, never mind where or why, only to try our youth against the realities of night and sea; if we indulged the skeptic at all, it was as a droll, half-contemptible mascot. When he died in the initial slaughter, no one cared.

"And even now I don't subscribe to all his views—but I no longer scoff. The horror of our history has purged me of opinions, as of vanity, confidence, spirit, charity, hope, vitality, everything—except dull dread and a kind of melancholy, stunned persistence. What leads me to recall his fancies is my growing suspicion that I, of all swimmers, may be the sole survivor of this fell journey, tale-bearer of a generation. This suspicion, together with the recent sea-change, suggests to me now that nothing is impossible, not even my late companion's wildest visions,

and brings me to a certain desperate resolve, the point of my chronicling.

"Very likely I have lost my senses. The carnage at our setting out; our decimation by whirlpool, poisoned cataract, sea-convulsion; the panic stampedes, mutinies, slaughters, mass suicides; the mounting evidence that none will survive the journey—add to these anguish and fatigue; it were a miracle if sanity stayed afloat. Thus I admit, with the other possibilities, that the present sweetening and calming of the sea, and what seems to be a kind of vasty presence, song, or summons from the near upstream, may be hallucinations of disordered sensibility. . . .

"Perhaps, even, I am drowned already. Surely I was never meant for the rough-and-tumble of the swim; not impossibly I perished at the outset and have only imaged the night-sea journey from some final deep. In any case, I'm no longer young, and it is we spent old swimmers, disabused of every illusion, who are most vulnerable to dreams.

"Sometimes I think I am my drownèd friend.

"Out with it: I've begun to believe, not only that *She* exists, but that She lies not far ahead, and stills the sea, and draws me Herward! Aghast, I recollect his maddest notion: that our destination (which existed, mind, in but one night-sea out of hundreds and thousands) was no Shore, as commonly conceived, but a mysterious being, indescribable except by paradox and vaguest figure: wholly different from us swimmers, yet our complement; the death of us, yet our salvation and resurrection; simultaneously our journey's end, mid-point, and commencement; not membered and thrashing like us, but a motionless or hugely gliding sphere of unimaginable dimension; self-contained, yet dependent absolutely, in some wise, upon the chance (always monstrously improbable) that one of us will survive the night-sea journey and reach . . . Her! *Her*, he called it, or *She*, which is to say, Other-than-a-he. I shake my head; the thing is too preposterous; it is myself I talk to, to keep my reason in this awful darkness. There is no She! There is no You! I rave to myself; it's Death alone that hears and summons. To the drowned, all seas are calm. . . .

"Listen: my friend maintained that in every order of creation there are two sorts of creators, contrary yet complementary, one of which gives rise to seas and swimmers, the other to the

Night-which-contains-the-sea and to What-waits-at-the-journey's-end: the former, in short, to destiny, the latter to destination (and both profligately, involuntarily, perhaps indifferently or unwittingly). The 'purpose' of the night-sea journey—but not necessarily of the journeyer or of either Maker!—my friend could describe only in abstractions: *consummation, transfiguration, union of contraries, transcension of categories*. When we laughed, he would shrug and admit that he understood the business no better than we, and thought it ridiculous, dreary, possibly obscene. 'But one of you,' he'd add with his wry smile, 'may be the Hero destined to complete the night-sea journey and be one with Her. Chances are, of course, you won't make it.' He himself, he declared, was not even going to try; the whole idea repelled him; if we chose to dismiss it as an ugly fiction, so much the better for us; thrash, splash, and be merry, we were soon enough drownèd. But there it was, he could not say how he knew or why he bothered to tell us, any more than he could say what would happen after She and Hero, Shore and Swimmer, 'merged identities' to become something both and neither. He quite agreed with me that if the issue of that magical union had no memory of the night-sea journey, for example, it enjoyed a poor sort of immortality; even poorer if, as he rather imagined, a swimmer-hero plus a She equaled or became merely another Maker of future night-seas and the rest, at such incredible expense of life. This being the case—he was persuaded it was—the merciful thing to do was refuse to participate; the genuine heroes, in his opinion, were the suicides, and the hero of heroes would be the swimmer who, in the very presence of the Other, refused Her proffered 'immortality' and thus put an end to at least one cycle of catastrophes.

"How we mocked him! Our moment came, we hurtled forth, pretending to glory in the adventure, thrashing, singing, cursing, strangling, rationalizing, rescuing, killing, inventing rules and stories and relationships, giving up, struggling on, but dying all, and still in darkness, until only a battered remnant was left to croak 'Onward, upward,' like a bitter echo. Then they too fell silent—victims, I can only presume, of the last frightful wave—and the moment came when I also, utterly desolate and spent, thrashed my last and gave myself over to the current, to sink or float as might be, but swim no more. Whereupon, marvelous to tell, in an instant the sea grew still! Then warmly, gently, the great tide turned, began to bear me, as it does now, onward and upward will-I nill-I, like a flood of joy—and I recalled with dismay my dead friend's teaching.

"I am not deceived. This new emotion is Her doing; the desire that possesses me is Her bewitchment. Lucidity passes from me; in a moment I'll cry 'Love!' bury myself in Her side, and be 'transfigured.' Which is to say, I die already; this fellow transported by passion is not I; *I am he who abjures and rejects the night-sea journey!* I. . . .

"I am all love. 'Come!' She whispers, and I have no will.

"You who I may be about to become, whatever You are: with the last twitch of my real self I beg You to listen. It is *not* love that sustains me! No; though Her magic makes me burn to sing the contrary, and though I drown even now for the blasphemy, I will say truth. What has fetched me across this dreadful sea is a single hope, gift of my poor dead comrade: that You may be stronger-willed than I, and that by sheer force of concentration I may transmit to You, along with Your official Heritage, a private legacy of awful recollection and negative resolve. Mad as it may be, my dream is that some unimaginable embodiment of myself (or myself plus Her if that's how it must be) will come to find itself expressing, in however garbled or radical a translation, some reflection of these reflections. If against all odds this comes to pass, may You to whom, through whom I speak, do what I cannot: terminate this aimless, brutal business! Stop Your hearing against Her song! Hate love!

"Still alive, afloat, afire. Farewell then my penultimate hope: that one may be sunk for direst blasphemy on the very shore of the Shore. Can it be (my old friend would smile) that only utterest nay-sayers survive the night? But even that were Sense, and there is no sense, only senseless love, senseless death. Whoever echoes these reflections: be more courageous than their author! An end to night-sea journeys! Make no more! And forswear me when I shall forswear myself, deny myself, plunge into Her who summons, singing . . .

"'Love! Love! Love!'"

Questions for Analysis

1. The following terms recur in the story: *night, sea, night-sea, swimmer, shore, She*. Keeping in mind the reproduction metaphor, what would these terms stand for? What meaning do they carry beyond the reproduction metaphor? (For example, a swimmer might stand for a spermatozoan, but also for any individual human being.)

2. The narrator/night-sea swimmer says: "My trouble is, I lack conviction." What does this mean, and how does the swimmer's lack of resolve correlate with the human condition?

3. Why can the night-sea swimmer believe the common Maker view of human nature while holding it absurd?

4. What does the night-sea swimmer mean by "Another paradox: it appears to be these recesses from swimming that sustain me in the swim"? Can the recesses in any way be compared with philosophy and philosophizing?

5. What does the night-sea swimmer understand by "love"? Would you agree?

6. Why does even the possibility of the Shore leave the night-sea swimmer with misgivings?

7. What alternative religious views of human nature does the night-sea swimmer suggest?

8. Why does the night-sea swimmer reject the survival-of-the-fittest view?

9. Does the night-sea swimmer at any point seem to reject the existential view? Why?

10. What is the night-sea swimmer's ultimate wish?

Paperbacks for Further Reading

Ellison, Ralph. *Invisible Man*. New York: Vintage, 1951. Launching this novel with an explosive opening chapter, Ellison has written a compelling tale of the quest for self-discovery.

Erikson, Erik. *Identity, Youth and Crisis*. New York: Norton, 1968. In this classic on the quest for self-identity, psychoanalyst Erikson relates issues of individual identity to the historically changing patterns of social organization.

Sartre, Jean-Paul. *Nausea*. New York: New Directions, 1964. A less systematic presentation of his philosophy than his formal works *Existentialism and Humanism* and *Existentialism and Human Emotions*, this novel nevertheless illustrates Sartre's views on freedom, ambiguity, anxiety, and nothingness.

Skinner, B. F. *About Behaviorism*. New York: Knopf, 1974. Skinner's most recent, succinct, and readable statement of the methodology and philosophy of behaviorism.

Skinner, B. F. *Walden II*. New York: Macmillan, 1962. Psychologist Skinner presents his behaviorist utopia, governed by principles of stimulus and response, positive reinforcement, and aversive conditioning. The novel is a good introduction to the ideas spelled out in Skinner's *Beyond Freedom and Dignity*.

Thoreau, Henry David. *Walden and Other Writings*. Joseph Wood Krutch, Ed. New York: Bantam, 1971. *Walden* is Thoreau's classic autobiographical statement of how he avoided a life of "quiet desperation" and found personal freedom and identity, as well as joy, in nature.

Watts, Alan. *The Book: On the Taboo against Knowing Who You Are*. New York: Collier, 1966. In a thoroughly readable work, Watts examines what he considers to be the West's mistaken focus on ego and self. He argues for the Eastern position of no self and the interdependence of all things. In addition, Watts raises questions of love, suffering, death, and the meaning of existence.

Part II

AXIOLOGY

The word axiology, which comes from the Greek axios meaning "worthy," refers to the study of values in general. It deals with values that are thought to be good in themselves and with values leading to what's good. One branch of axiology is ethics, or moral philosophy. Traditionally ethics has investigated the problem of values in human conduct. Ethics investigates questions involving right conduct, good character, and life fulfillment. Another branch is value theory, the logical analysis of ethical discourse and the language of values. Value theory examines the meanings of all value terms in order to clarify the meaning of ethical discourse and to justify ethical judgments. A third branch of axiology is aesthetics, which examines the nature and meaning of art in human experience and attempts to set artistic standards. The last branch of axiology that we will mention is social and political philosophy, which concerns questions about social structures and political systems. Social and political philosophy examines theories of the state and the roots of social obligations. While these branches have been the traditional interests of axiology, axiology would address any philosophical problem relating to values.

The next three chapters deal with important axiological matters: ethics, social philosophy, and philosophy and art.

3

ETHICS

Man is the only animal that blushes, or needs to.
—Mark Twain

Today, numerous changes in our traditional life-styles are evident. Our fashions, diet, and language are altering; so are our attitudes toward sex, the family, society, and ourselves. No one knows where these changes will lead, but one thing is certain: They are steeping in the pot of affluence and leisure time, a pot of unprecedented size.

No people in history have had so much of the world's bounty and so much time in which to use it as we have. It is no wonder that we keep hearing the phrase "quality of life." After all, many of us are now in a position to seek, if not share, the "good life." But just what is this good life? Various interests will gladly tell us, from the latest brand of beer to transcendental meditation. All pretend to offer a value worth our time and money, if not our devotion. The number of interests vying for our loyalties boggles the mind. To which drummer should we march? What values should we pursue?

Much of how we see ourselves is determined by what we value, for our values shape our thoughts, feelings, actions, and perceptions. Our values also express who and what we are. In the past, perhaps because of strong family ties, values were served up at the dinner table. We frequently attended a particular church, voted for a certain party, read select magazines, and behaved in a prescribed way because our parents did. But for many today the family is little more than a holiday house, checking account, and mailing address. Familial bonds, once strong and far-reaching, often extend no farther than the nearest freeway; loyalty stretches no farther than the next meal. The affinity that many once felt for family is now often felt for a friend, a cause, or a commune. In most instances, however, these experiences with family substitutes are not long-lived or profound enough to instill lasting values. The results are frequently short, although often intense, romances with various values that can leave us intellectually dizzy.

Just what values should we hold and pursue? What values should we nourish in our own lives, in the running of our country, in our artistic tastes?

"But just what is this good life?"

So important are these questions in expressing and shaping us that we shall devote the next three chapters to them. We do this not to provide easy, simple-minded answers but to provide a framework in which to develop our own value systems. In this chapter we explore the nature of values and then focus on ethics. The main points of this chapter are the following:

Main Points

1. Axiology is the study of values.

2. Ethics is concerned with questions of right and wrong, of duty and obligation, and of moral responsibility.

3. Normative ethics is the reasoned search for principles of moral behavior. Metaethics examines normative judgments, paying special attention to the meaning of the language used.

4. Consequentialist theories claim that the morality of an action depends only on its consequences.

5. Egoism is the consequentialist position that states: Always act in such a way that your actions promote your own best long-term interests.

6. Act utilitarianism is the consequentialist position that states: Always act in such a way that your actions produce the greatest happiness for the most people.

7. Rule utilitarianism is the consequentialist position that states: Always act in such a way that the rule of your actions produces the greatest happiness for the most people.

8. Situationism is the normative position that is based on the belief that the moral action produces the greatest amount of Christian love of all the possible actions.

9. Divine command enjoins us to follow the law of God.

10. Kant's categorical imperative is the normative position that states: Always act in such a way that you could wish the rule of your action to become a universal law.

11. Ross's theory of prima facie duties obliges us to perform the action with the greatest amount of prima facie rightness over wrongness.

12. Buddhism emphasizes volition and ties morality to wisdom. Its moral code has a negative and positive component.

13. The concept of moral responsibility is associated with the concept of excusability, which holds that there are circumstances under which we should excuse people for their decisions and conduct.

14. In response to the claim that moral responsibility is not possible in a strictly deterministic universe, four main positions can be identified: hard determinism, indeterminism, soft determinism, and self-determinism.

The Nature of Values

Individually and collectively, people express many different values. In clothes, some prefer sportswear, others more formal attire. In food, some like the spicy, others the bland. In books, some people read mysteries, others devour science fiction. On it goes, from religion to art, politics to education—values in every area of human affairs.

How do values arise? Where do they come from? Why does one person see beauty in an ocean, while another is unmoved? Why does one person risk life and limb to ensure justice, while another stands detached and indifferent? Our values are largely shaped and formed by experience. Thus, the sea holds out little beauty for one who has watched a loved one die in it. The person who has felt the sting of racial or sexual discrimination can understandably develop a hearty appetite for fair and just treatment, even at great personal risk. In a word, the values we hold, as individuals and as groups, are inseparable from the endlessly changing experiences of our lives.

History reveals that no society has ever been without some value system, and every individual has some code of values. The issue, therefore, is not whether we are to have values but what those values will be—whether they will advance or retard life, whether they will be consistent or not. Axiology is too broad a study to consider fully here. But before we examine one field of axiology, ethics, it will be helpful to introduce some general axiological ideas.

First, philosophers distinguish between a fact and a value. A *factual judgment* describes an empirical relationship or quality. For example, "Washington, D.C., is the nation's capital" and "Water boils at 212 degrees Fahrenheit at sea level" are factual statements. A *value judgment*, on the other hand, assesses the worth of objects, acts, feelings, attitudes, even people. For example, "Beethoven was a good composer," "I should visit my sick brother," and "You were wrong in lying" are value judgments.

Throughout our discussion of axiological issues, specifically in ethics and aesthetics, one question will recur: Do value judgments express knowledge or feelings? When I say "Beethoven was a good composer" or "You were wrong in lying," am I expressing a truth or a personal preference? The answer is uncertain, underscoring the fact that there is little agreement on how the term *value* should be defined. Perhaps the best definition we can give is that a **value** is an assessment of worth. This is how we'll use the term.

Another axiological concern is whether values are subjective or objective. When I say, for example, that the *Mona Lisa* is beautiful, does the value I express originate in me or in the painting? Some say that a value is the subjective satisfaction of a human want, desire, or need. Others claim that a value is a quality within an object that satisfies the individual and is therefore objective. Still others contend that a value has both subjective and objective elements.

According to our Greek and Judeo-Christian traditions, there are certain absolute, unchanging values that are rooted in the nature of the universe or given by God. Because these traditions posit a moral order, we believe that we can call things good or evil regardless of what anyone thinks. Likewise, because an aesthetic order is part of the nature of the universe, we think that we correctly call some things beautiful and others ugly, regardless of what anyone thinks.

In modern times another view of the nature of values has arisen that appeals to people of a less rigid and dogmatic bent. In this view, the basis of all values is found in the human. Since the human is a growing entity in a changing, dynamic universe, values reflect this developmental process. Consequently, there are no fixed or immutable values. Rather, with changing human conditions and ever-expanding knowledge, values change. In this view, what is ultimately of value is what advances human and community development.

Finally, the *selection* of values is an important axiological concern. Just what should we value? There is general agreement that certain groups of values exist, such as the moral, political, aesthetic, religious, and intellectual, and that genetic, biological, and cultural influences produce many of these values. But there is little agreement about the nature of these values, their relative importance, or their relationship to one another. Nevertheless, most philosophers use the following principles in discussing axiological issues:

1. We should prefer what is of intrinsic value to what is of extrinsic value. *A thing has intrinsic value when it is valued for its own sake.* For example, some believe that pleasure has intrinsic value; that is, it is worthwhile in itself, not because it can yield something else. *On the other hand, a thing has extrinsic value when it is a means to something else.* A film could be said to have extrinsic value; that is, it is not a value in itself but can yield a value, perhaps pleasure. But intrinsic and extrinsic values are not necessarily mutually exclusive. What is valued in itself may also be a means to something else, as in the case of knowledge. Knowledge is worthwhile in itself, but also because it may lead to a job, affluence, or prestige.

2. We should prefer values that are productive and lasting to ones that are not. Physical and material values are generally less productive and long-lived than social, artistic, intellectual, and religious values. Long after a

new car has worn out or a fortune has been spent, a genuine friendship or one's personal integrity persists.

3. We should choose our own values according to our own goals and ideals. When we allow values to be thrust upon us, we live others' lives, not our own. Our values should be consistent with one another and responsive to our own circumstances and experiences.

4. Finally, in choosing between two values, we should prefer the greater. What constitutes the greater will be determined largely by the previous three criteria. When we must choose between two evils, we should choose the lesser, again allowing these criteria to influence our choice.

These principles are themselves expressions of fundamental values. In what are they grounded? The rich legacy of Western culture. Again, we are reminded of the experiential basis of all assessments of worth, of all values.

One aspect of our values applies to the realm of human conduct, that is, moral values. For example, some value pleasure, because for them pleasure has intrinsic worth. They believe that they should seek pleasure and avoid pain at all times. Others, in contrast, place a premium on virtue, such as truth or honesty. They believe that virtue is worthwhile in itself and should be pursued, even at great personal inconvenience. Still others might opt for other moral values, such as self-realization or love. As in all cases involving assessments of worth, people cherish any number of moral values. But how do we know which moral values to choose? Should we, for example, chiefly value pleasure, virtue, some other value, or a combination of values? While admittedly a most difficult problem to solve, this question is one concern of the study of ethics, and it has profound implications not only for individuals but for nations as well.

Ethics

Let's define **ethics** as *the branch of philosophy that studies what constitutes good and bad human conduct, including related actions and values.* In understanding this

"Long after a new car has worn out . . . a genuine friendship . . . persists."

definition, it's helpful to view all ethical questions as involving a choice. Suppose, for example, that after not answering your telephone for several hours, you finally take a call. The caller, a friend, expresses frustration at having failed to reach you earlier and asks whether you were home. You were home, of course, but simply didn't feel like answering the phone. Naturally you could tell the person the unvarnished truth. But since such behavior is uncharacteristic of you, the person will likely expect an explanation or feel slighted. In short, saying that you weren't home seems less complicated than telling the truth. What should you do?

Invariably all ethical questions involve a decision about what one should do in a specific instance. Notice the word *should*. Ethical questions are not concerned with what one *would* do (an essentially psychological concern) but what one *ought to* do. Judgments about such decisions are generally expressed with words like *right* and *wrong*, *should* and *ought*, or *obligation* and *duty*. For instance, "I *ought* to tell the caller I was home" or "Telling the caller I wasn't home is the *right* thing to do." A good portion of ethics is devoted to the philosophical problems concerning the right thing to do or what we should do, that is, to questions of obligation.

But, at the same time, implied in any choice is a value or value judgment. If you decide to tell the caller you were home, your action betrays a commitment to some value, perhaps to truth. If you choose to lie, again your action reflects a value, perhaps your own pleasure. In effect, every choice involves an assessment of worth. We feel obliged to behave a certain way because we seek a specific value or good. These values, just as the actions themselves, can be described with words such as *good*, *bad*, *evil*, *desirable*, *undesirable*, *beneficial*, *harmful*, and so on. In addition to dealing with questions of obligation, therefore, ethics deals with questions of value. *Taken together, questions of obligation and value form the heart of ethics.*

Occasionally the term *ethics* is used interchangeably with *morals*. Business or medical ethics, for example, is generally synonymous with morals. Although this is acceptable, a precise usage would apply the terms *morals* and *moral* to the conduct itself, while the terms *ethics* and *ethical* would refer to the study of moral conduct or to the code that one follows. Thus, the specific act of telling the caller you were home could be described as moral or immoral. But what makes any act moral or immoral, right or wrong, would fall within the province of ethics. When we speak of moral problems, then, we generally refer to specific problems, such as "Is lying ever right?" or "Is stealing always wrong?" In contrast, we can look at ethical problems as being more general and theoretical. Thus, "What makes any act, such as lying or stealing, right or wrong?" and "What makes any entity good?" are ethical problems. In short, morality refers to the degree to which an action conforms to a standard or norm of human conduct. Ethics refers to the philosophical study of values and of what constitutes good and bad human conduct.

Sometimes the term *nonmoral* arises in the study of ethics. This term refers to what lies outside the sphere of moral concern. Thus, whether I choose to answer my telephone and whether a manufacturer packages a product in a vertical or horizontal container are essentially nonmoral questions. However, nonmoral questions can quickly take on moral overtones. For example, telling a friend to call me at a certain hour and then refusing to answer the call could raise a moral question. Likewise, if the shape of a container could mislead the consumer about the quantity of its contents, then it could constitute a moral question.

In dealing with human conduct from the perspective of obligation and value, ethics investigates a variety of related concerns. Among them are whether a standard of morality exists that applies to all people at all times everywhere, the precise nature of moral responsibility, the conditions under which one is morally accountable or responsible, and the proper end of law. When ethicists use words like "good" or "right" to describe a person or action, they generally mean that the person or action conforms to some standard. A good person or action has certain desirable qualities. Ethicists often disagree about the nature of those standards and desirable qualities and follow different paths in establishing standards and discovering which qualities are desirable. For purposes of understanding, though, we can view ethics as divided into two fields—normative ethics and nonnormative ethics.

Normative Ethics

Normative ethics involves an attempt to determine precisely what moral standards to follow so that our actions may be morally right or good. There are two areas of normative ethics: applied and general. Applied normative ethics is the attempt to explain and justify positions on specific moral problems, such as sex outside marriage, capital punishment, euthanasia, and reverse discrimination. This area of normative ethics is termed *applied* because the ethicist applies or uses general ethical principles in an attempt to resolve specific moral problems. For example, in defending an act of civil disobedience, a person might appeal to principles of justice and equality. When such general principles are arranged into an ethical theory, the second field of normative ethics emerges: general normative ethics.

General normative ethics is the reasoned search for principles of human conduct, including a critical study of the major theories about which things are good, which acts are right, and which acts are blameworthy. It attempts to determine precisely what moral standards to follow so that our actions may be morally right or good. For most of us, ethical actions spring from some standard: "Do unto others as you would have them do unto you"; "Act in such a way that you bring about the greatest good for the greatest number"; "Always act in your own best interests." Which principle should we adopt? General normative ethics, in part, tries to answer this question by attempting to formulate and defend a system of basic ethical principles which presumably is valid for everyone.

Two broad categories of general normative theories can be distinguished: teleological and deontological. *Teleological* derives from the word *teleology,* which literally means "the theory of ends or purposes." Teleological theories maintain that the morality of an action depends on the nonmoral consequences that the action brings about. For simplicity, we shall refer to teleological theories as *consequentialist.* Two important consequentialist theories that we will consider are egoism and utilitarianism. Egoism is concerned with the best consequences for self, utilitarianism with the best consequences for everyone.

Deontological derives from the word *deontology,* which refers to the theory or study of moral commitment. Deontological theories maintain that the morality of an action depends on factors other than consequences. Again, for simplicity, we will refer to deontological theories as *nonconsequentialist.* Three important non-consequentialist theories we will consider are divine command, categorical imperative, and prima facie duties. Divine command is concerned with acting in such a way that one's actions conform to the laws of God. The categorical imperative is concerned with acting in such a way that one could wish the maxim of one's action to become a universal law. Prima facie duties are concerned with acting in accordance with an overriding obligation as indicated by the circumstances involved.

Since the terms *consequentialist* and *nonconsequentialist* actually pinpoint the difference between teleological and deontological theories, we'll use these simpler terms in the pages ahead, where we will consider the major theories in each group and indicate the theory of value that generally accompanies each theory.[1]

Nonnormative Ethics

Nonnormative ethics consists of either a factual investigation of moral behavior, or an analysis of the meaning of the terms used in moral discourse and an examination of the moral reasoning by which moral beliefs can be shown to be true or false. Like normative ethics, nonnormative ethics consists of two fields: scientific or descriptive study, and metaethics.

Scientific or Descriptive Study

The scientific or descriptive study of morality involves factual investigation of moral behavior. It is concerned with how people do in fact behave. This approach is used widely in the social sciences. For example, anthropologists and sociologists investigate and describe moral attitudes. They report on how moral attitudes and codes differ from society to society, investigating and describing the values and behaviors of different societies. Thus, anthropologists tell us that Eskimos used to abandon their elderly on the ice and allow them to die of starvation and exposure, and that some African tribes kill infant twins and require that a man marry his brother's widow. That societies often differ markedly in their values and conceptions of right and wrong has led many to advance a doctrine called *ethical relativism.*

In order to understand ethical relativism, one must first be familiar with ethical absolutism. *Ethical absolutism* is the doctrine that there exists one and only one moral code. Absolutists maintain that this code applies to everyone, at all times, everywhere. What is a moral duty for me must also be a duty for you. What is a moral duty for an American must also be a moral duty for an Asian,

---

1. *See Jacques Thiroux.* Ethics. *Encino, Calif.: Glencoe Press, 1980, p. 34.*

African, European, and aborigine. If euthanasia is wrong, it is wrong for everyone, at all times, everywhere. That a society may see nothing wrong with euthanasia or lying or cannibalism in no way affects the rightness or wrongness of such actions. Ethical absolutists do not necessarily claim that their interpretation of the absolute standard is the true and valid one. But they do insist that there is a true moral code and that this code is the same for all people in all ages.

Ethical relativism is the doctrine that denies that there is a single moral standard that is universally applicable to all people at all times. Relativists deny that there exists only one moral code, law, principle, or standard. They insist that there are many moral codes, which take root in diverse social soils and environments. As the name implies, ethical relativists insist that any morality is relative to the time, place, and circumstances in which it occurs. In no way is any moral code absolute.

Ethical relativism is not the same as cultural relativism. Cultural relativism is a sociological fact: Research proves the existence of many obviously different and often contradictory moral codes. Ethical relativists are not merely saying that what is thought right in one part of the world is frequently thought wrong in another. Scientific or descriptive ethics has established this fact that even absolutists accept. Rather, ethical relativists assert that precisely the same action that is right in one society at one time can be wrong in another. Thus, putting to death anyone over eighty years old can be right in the jungles of New Guinea and wrong in the United States. Such a claim is quite different from saying that putting octogenarians to death is *thought* to be right in one place and *thought* to be wrong in another. In brief, ethical relativists believe that what is *thought* right *is* right.

We shall not take the time here to criticize these positions. Whether we agree with absolutism or relativism, we still must decide what we ought to do individually and collectively. Presumably this requires some standard on the basis of which to make decisions. So, whether I am an absolutist or a relativist, the question remains: How ought I to behave and how ought my society to behave?

Metaethics

The second field of nonnormative ethics is called *metaethics*. **Metaethics** is the highly technical discipline investigating the meaning of ethical terms, including a critical study of how ethical statements can be verified. Largely the province of philosophers, metaethics is concerned with the meanings of such important ethical terms as *right, obligation,* and *responsibility.* Accordingly, metaethicists would be more concerned with the meanings of such words as *good* or *bad* than with what we think is good or bad. If you maintained, for instance, that an act of euthanasia was right, the metaethicist might ask: Just what do you mean by *right*? Metaethical positions often are classified as representative of naturalism, nonnaturalism, and emotivism (or noncognitivism).

Naturalism maintains that ethical statements can be translated into nonethical statements. One naturalistic position—autobiographical naturalism— contends that an ethical statement simply expresses the approval or disapproval of the speaker. For example, when you say, "That act of euthanasia was right," you mean "I approve of that act of euthanasia." Another naturalistic position—

sociological naturalism—holds that an ethical statement simply expresses the approval or disapproval of the majority. Thus, "That act of euthanasia was right" means "The majority approves of that act of euthanasia." Still another naturalistic position—theological naturalism—claims that an ethical statement expresses divine approval or disapproval. Accordingly, "That act of euthanasia was right," in effect, means "God (or some equivalent reference) approves of that act of euthanasia."

Nonnaturalism, in contrast to naturalism, is the position which holds that an ethical statement defies translation into a nonethical form. Nonnaturalists insist that at least some ethical words can be defined only in terms of other ethical words. Thus, nonnaturalists might argue that the statement "That act of euthanasia was right" can only be translated into other ethical statements, such as "That act of euthanasia was proper" or "That act of euthanasia should have been performed," or "That act of euthanasia was good." Nonnaturalists hold that naturalistic translations would be like trying to define *hour* in other than temporal terms, or *inch* in other than spatial terms. It just cannot be done. The motto "You can't get an is out of an ought" nicely captures the nonnaturalistic position. In other words, words like *good, right,* and *should* are so basic in ethics that there are no other words by means of which to define them.[2]

English philosopher and nonnaturalist G. E. Moore (1874–1958) attempted to refute naturalistic theories by use of the so-called open-question technique. Moore argued that no matter what property of a thing you assert, someone can always meaningfully grant that the thing has the property but then ask: Is that property good? Thus, "I grant that Fred Jones is very happy (property), but is happiness always and everywhere good?" "I acknowledge that Jeannine Cox is an honest woman, but is honesty good?" Perhaps happiness and honesty are good. But, in Moore's view, one cannot claim that they are simply on the basis of a definition of *good* which others might reject.

Moore went so far as to assert that *good* is verbally indefinable, just as some other words are, for example, *red* and *pleasure.* He claimed that to identify *good* with any natural object was to commit the naturalistic fallacy. Writing in his most important work, *Principia Ethica,* Moore explains what he means:

> Suppose a man says, "I am pleased"; and suppose that it is not a lie or a mistake but the truth. Well, if it is true, what does that mean? It means his mind, a certain definite mind, distinguished by certain definite marks from all others, has at this moment a certain definite feeling called pleasure. "Pleased" *means* nothing but having pleasure, and though we may be more pleased or less pleased, and even, we may admit for the present, have one or another kind of pleasure; yet insofar as it is pleasure we have, whether there be more or less of it, and whether it be of one kind or another, what we have is one definite thing, absolutely indefinable, some one thing that is the same in all the various degrees and in all the various kinds of it that there may be. We may be able to say how it is related to other things: that, for example, it is in the mind, that it causes desire, that we are conscious of it, etc., etc. We can, I say, describe its relations to other things, but define it we can *not.* And if anybody tried to define pleasure for us as

2.   *John Hospers.* Introduction to Philosophical Analysis. *Englewood Cliffs, N.J.: Prentice-Hall, 1967, p. 573.*

being any other natural object; if anybody were to say, for instance, that pleasure *means* the sensation of red, and were to proceed to deduce from that that pleasure is a color, we should be entitled to laugh at him and to distrust his future statements about pleasure. Well, that would be the same fallacy which I have called the naturalistic fallacy. That "pleased" does not mean "having the sensation of red," or anything else whatever, does not prevent us from understanding what it does mean. It is enough for us to know that "pleased" does mean "having the sensation of pleasure," and though pleasure is absolutely indefinable, though pleasure is pleasure and nothing else whatever, yet we feel no difficulty in saying that we are pleased.[3]

Given their position, nonnaturalists clearly come close to asserting that ethical statements cannot be verified, that they cannot be determined true or false. How then does the nonnaturalist handle ethical statements? Moore advises that we reflect on them and determine as well as we can, whether we believe the statements are true. There are no empirical observations, no mathematical or logical calculations, which would enable us to discover the truth of ethical statements. All we can do is distinguish them carefully from other statements, particularly those with which they might easily be confused; and then reflect upon them and see whether, after this reflection, we believe that they are true.

Emotivism (or noncognitivism) can be broadly defined as a metaethical position which claims that ethical statements are used to evoke a predetermined response or to encourage a predetermined behavior. According to emotivists, ethical statements can be used, indeed are used, to make someone feel or behave in a certain way. For example, if a teacher says to a student, "Cheating is wrong," the teacher may not be expressing a moral position on cheating but rather trying to instill in the student a certain attitude toward cheating. The teacher may also be trying to elicit a non-cheating behavior. Ethical statements, therefore, amount to commands such as "Don't cheat" or "Don't lie" or "Don't break promises." The essential difference between autobiographical naturalism and emotivism is that the former holds that ethical statements are subjective and verifiable, while the latter believes that they are subjective but *not* verifiable.

The flow chart on page 103 organizes the different fields of normative and nonnormative ethics that we have just sketched. In the remainder of this chapter we shall flesh out the predominant normative theories. The coverage stresses normative theories because this is the approach that most of us take. In our personal and social lives, we want to determine for ourselves some principles or standards of moral behavior. Also, in recent years ethicists have renewed their interest in normative ethics in an attempt to deal with today's urgent moral issues.

Consequentialist (Teleological) Theories

To begin, let us join two city policemen, Obie and The Kid, on their tour of duty. Obie is the veteran, the "hair-bag" in police slang. The Kid is fresh out of the police academy, with ideas gathered more from school than from the street.

---

3. *G. E. Moore.* Principia Ethica. *London: Cambridge University Press, 1903, pp. 12–13.*

Obie:	I see where B. B. McGeester was sprung this morning.
Kid:	McGeester?
Obie:	Maybe you don't know him. I busted him three times. Fourth last month. The third time he served a total of eighteen months for pushing snow. Then he was out—"rehabilitation," they call it. Last month I nailed him for murder two.
Kid:	I take it you don't think they should have released him.
Obie:	Ask the storekeeper he killed if B. B. should have been released. Civil rights. They said this morning his civil rights had been violated. Well, I say if you're not civil, you don't deserve civil rights.
Kid:	You don't think a criminal has any civil rights?
Obie:	He loses them the day he breaks the law, that's what I think. But the minute we bust him, some judge who's never been in the street says, "Mister McGeester, sir, we apologize for violating your civil rights. We hope we haven't inconvenienced you." "Oh no, Your Honor, not in the least. But don't let it happen again. Because if you do, I'm going to sue the pants off you. How's a guy supposed to make a dishonest living if you keep violating his civil rights?"
Kid:	But what if his civil rights *were* violated, Obie? What if he was being held illegally?
Obie:	What if, what if, what if . . . what if an hour after he's released he breaks some storekeeper's head; what if tomorrow he rapes some woman in the park; what if next week he swipes a car and runs over a child? Believe me, Kid, it's not right. It's downright immoral! And it won't be long before you see what I mean.

What Obie means is that an action is wrong if its consequences are undesirable. And since releasing criminals on the basis of a civil rights violation often leads to additional crime, it is immoral. What would you rather have, Obie would ask, a civil right violated or a known felon walking the streets? Just consider the consequences and that should tell you.

Traditionally many ethicists have contended that moral rightness must be determined by appeal to the consequences of an action. If the consequences are good, the act is right. If the consequences are bad, the act is wrong. Thus, a **consequentialist theory** measures the morality of action on the basis of the nonmoral consequences. Consequentialists consider the ratio of good to evil that an action produces. The right action is the one that produces, will probably produce, or is intended to produce at least as great a ratio of good to evil as any other action. The wrong action is the one that does not.

For example, suppose that while driving down an almost deserted street one night, you momentarily take your eyes off the road and then strike a parked car. You stop and cautiously look around. There's no one in sight, and no house lights are on. Using a flashlight, you estimate the damage to the parked car at about $200. You'd like to leave a note on the windshield, but you don't have insurance or the money to pay for the damage. Besides, the parked car is a new Corvette, and you assume that the owner must have insurance.

If you were a consequentialist, in determining what you should do, you'd evaluate the nonmoral consequences of the two choices. If you left a note, you

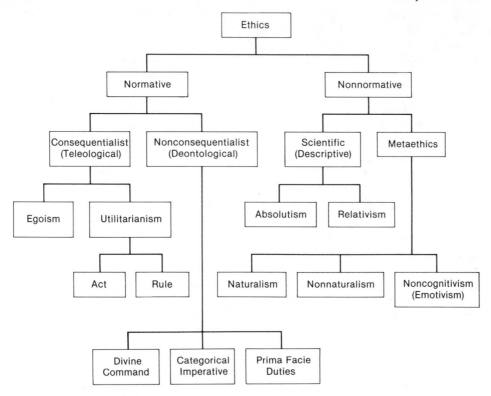

would probably have to pay for the damage. That would greatly complicate your life: You'd have to work to pay off the debt, let other expenses slide, greatly reduce your luxuries, and possibly need to quit school. In contrast, if you don't leave a note, you might go unpenalized while the owner foots the bill. Of course, the owner is likely to be hopping mad, perhaps even deciding to treat other motorists spitefully. Furthermore, you may be found out; that could mean considerable trouble. This is a consequentialist analysis.

An obvious question arises here: In evaluating the nonmoral consequences of an action, whom do consequentialists have in mind? Clearly, if you evaluate the consequences just for yourself in the preceding illustration, you would likely make a different judgment than if you evaluate the consequences for the Corvette's owner. In deciding what to do, then, should we evaluate the consequences only for ourselves, or should we consider the effects on all people involved? The answers to these questions form the bases for two consequential theories: egoism and utilitarianism.

Egoism

Some ethicists believe that in deciding the morality of an action, we should consider only the consequences for ourselves. These ethicists are called egoists. **Egoism** contends that we should always act in a way that promotes our own best long-term interests. Although egoists argue about what actions will do this, they agree that once such actions are determined, we should take them.

This notion does not imply, however, that we should do whatever we want; often our best immediate interests are not our best long-term ones. Many a Watergate conspirator lied, presumably hoping that his lie would cover up his own and others' corruption. And it did, for a while. But eventually much of the corruption came out and the liar then faced an additional problem: perjury. Thus, although his immediate interests might have been served, his long-term interests were not.

Just what do egoists mean by "self-interests"? It's tempting to think that they must mean pleasure; that is, I act in my best interests when I do what is calculated to bring me the most pleasure. Holding this belief makes me a hedonist. **Hedonism** is *the ethical philosophy which holds that only pleasure is worth having for its own sake.* In a word, hedonists view pleasure and only pleasure as having intrinsic value. It is true that many egoists are hedonistic, as was the ancient Greek philosopher Epicurus (342?–270 B.C.), who argued that people should live so as to bring about as much pleasure for themselves as possible. But two points need stressing. First, where egoists (or any normative theorists, for that matter) are hedonistic, it's important to determine what they mean by *pleasure.* Second, not all egoists are strict hedonists.

With respect to the first point, few popular definitions of pleasure would correspond with Epicurus' definition. Rather than with sensual gratification, Epicurus associated pleasure with what he termed *sober thinking:*

> When I say that pleasure is the goal of living I do not mean the pleasures of libertines and the pleasures inherent in positive enjoyment. . . . I mean, on the contrary, the pleasure that consists in freedom from bodily pain and mental agitation. The pleasant life is not the product of one drinking party after another or of sexual intercourse. . . . On the contrary, it is the result of sober thinking—namely, investigation of the reasons for every act of choice and aversion, and elimination of those false ideas about the gods and death which are the chief source of mental disturbances.[4]

While preaching the pursuit of pleasure, Epicurus nonetheless discouraged excess and recommended simplicity and moderation. He even considered the limitation of appetite to be a major good because "becoming habituated to a simple rather than a lavish way of life provides us with the full complement of health; it makes a person ready for the necessary business of life; it puts us in a position of advantage when we happen upon sumptuous fare at intervals and prepares us to be fearless in facing fortune."[5]

As for the second point above, many egoists identify the good not with pleasure but with knowledge, power, or rational self-interest. Some, in fact, associate it with self-realization, which is the promotion of all one's capacities. This belief seems an essential part of what some thinkers have traditionally called the doctrine of humanism, which stresses distinctly human interests and ideals.

While popularized through the thought and writings of contemporary psychologists such as Abraham Maslow, the self-realization doctrine is also evi-

---

4. *Epicurus. "Letter to Menoeceus," in* The Philosophy of Epicurus. *George K. Strodach, Ed. Evanston, Ill.: Northwestern University Press, 1963, p. 175.*

5. *Epicurus. "Letter to Menoeceus," p. 176.*

dent in the works of classical philosophers. In *The Republic*, for example, Plato discusses the three active principles within each person: Reason, Appetite, and Spirit (see Chapter 2). For Plato, each part has a role to play. When these elements work together, they result in personal harmony, order, and peace— self-realization. Similarly, in the first systematic presentation of morality, *Nicomachean Ethics*, Aristotle stresses the life of reason, which entails the harmonious development of all functions of the human organism.

Today self-realization as a goal of the good life continues to find philosophical expression. For example, British philosopher Francis Herbert Bradley argues that satisfaction is only possible when one achieves self-realization, that is, a harmonious integration of all one's desires. Only then can a person become a self, an individual.

The point is that an egoist is not necessarily a hedonist. On the contrary, ethical egoists may hold any theory of value. They all agree, however, that individuals should pursue courses of action that will advance their own best long-term interests.

Ethical egoism does pose a number of problems. First is the issue of conflicting interests, which Kurt Baier (1917—) has expressed quite graphically. He asks us to imagine two presidential candidates, whom we will call Brown and Kory. It's in the interests of both to be elected, but only one can succeed. It follows, then, that it would be in Brown's interest but not in Kory's if Brown were elected, and vice versa. Similarly, it would be in Brown's interest but not in Kory's if Kory were liquidated, and vice versa. More important, Brown ought to do everything possible to get rid of Kory; in fact, it would be wrong for Brown not to do so. Likewise Kory, knowing that his own liquidation is in Brown's interests, ought to take steps to foil Brown's endeavors. Indeed, it would be wrong for Kory not to do so. "It follows," writes Baier, "that if [Kory] prevents [Brown] from liquidating him, his act must be said to be both wrong and not wrong—wrong because it is the prevention of what [Brown] ought to do, his duty, and wrong for [Brown] not to do it; not wrong because it is what [Kory] ought to do, his duty, and wrong for [Kory] not to do it."[6] Baier's point is that egoism seems unable to resolve conflicts of interest, which he assumes a moral theory should do. Without that assumption, however, there are no conflicts, just a fully relativized situation in which each individual believes in his own best interests.

Related to this objection is a second: the inconsistency that ethical egoism introduces into moral counsel. To illustrate, let's suppose that Brown and Kory seek out the advice of Parnell. Parnell tells Brown to do whatever's necessary to prevent Kory from getting the job and to ensure that he, Brown, secures it. However, Parnell tells Kory to do whatever's necessary to prevent Brown from getting the job and to ensure that he, Kory, secures it. In her counsel, Parnell recommends two conflicting courses of action as being right. Critics of ethical egoism fault a moral theory that allows such flagrant inconsistency in moral counsel. However, in fairness to egoism, they are again assuming a collective value. Egoism by definition holds no such value, so why measure it by one?

Some critics think that the most serious weakness of ethical egoism is that it

6. *Kurt Baier.* The Moral Point of View. *Ithaca, N.Y.: Cornell University Press, 1958, p. 189.*

undermines the moral point of view, which many ethicists accept as a necessary part of moral decision making. By the "moral point of view," they mean the attitude of one who attempts to see all sides of an issue without being committed to the interests of a particular individual or group. In short, the moral point of view is one of impartiality and disinterest. The moral point of view can be thought of as the perspective taken by an ideal observer or judge. An ideal observer, or ideal judge, has three key charcteristics. First, the ideal observer is impartial or unbiased, that is, he does not treat himself as a special case. The ideal observer is as impartial in considering what he should do as he would be in deciding what someone unknown to him, someone in whom he has no special interest, should be. Second, the ideal observer has full knowledge of the facts of the situation to be judged. Third, the ideal observer can imaginatively identify with any person involved in the situation. If an individual possessed these characteristics, he or she would be a perfect moral judge of any situation; the person would be able to say what was right and wrong. Additionally, the ideal observer's view would tell the meaning of right and wrong.[7]

If we accept the legitimacy of this perspective, we must look for it in any proposed ethical standard. But ethical egoists cannot take the moral point of view as described because, by definition, they are always influenced by what is in their own best interest, regardless of the issues, principles, circumstances, or individuals involved. Thus, Brown and Kory cannot be impartial or disinterested in determining the right courses for them to follow. What's more, if Parnell is an egoist, she can't maintain the moral point of view as described, for she must counsel each candidate with her own interest in mind.

But is the moral point of view realistic? How can anyone be completely impartial or disinterested? We can't. Some would even argue that approximating the perspective of the ideal observer is a surefire way to moral indecision, inaction, and passivity, because, rather than engaging the issues of the day, we likely will withdraw from them. All moral decision making and action may involve a passional element, an essentially nonrational commitment of will that makes disinterest impossible. If this is so—and one could mount a powerful argument for it—then the most serious objection to egoism dissolves.

Obviously, the objections to egoism arise from holding a collective rather than a strictly subjective value. In fact, many consequentialists focus not on self-interest but on the interests of all involved. Such is the emphasis of the normative theory termed *utilitarianism*.

Utilitarianism

In contrast to egoism, utilitarianism asserts that the promotion of *everyone's* best interests is the standard of morality. In brief, **utilitarianism** claims that *we should always act so as to produce the greatest possible ratio of good to evil for all concerned.* Again, as with all consequentialist positions, good and evil are taken to mean nonmoral good and evil.

7. *See John Hospers.* Introduction to Philosophical Analysis. *2nd ed. Englewood Cliffs, N.J.: Prentice-Hall, 1967, p. 570.*

As formulated and developed by Jeremy Bentham (1748–1832) and John Stuart Mill (1806–1873), utilitarianism maintains that what is of intrinsic value or what is good in itself is pleasure, or happiness; this was unequivocally stated in the opening chapter of Bentham's *Introduction to the Principles of Morals and Legislation*. Notice in the excerpt from that chapter cited below how Bentham moves from the pleasure and pain experienced by an individual to that experienced by the group. In so doing, he lays the basis for the utilitarian moral principle that actions are right to the extent that they promote happiness and pleasure for all, wrong to the extent that they tend to produce pain and the absence of pleasure.

I. Nature has placed mankind under the governance of two sovern masters, *pain* and *pleasure*. It is for them alone to point out what we ought to do, as well as to determine what we shall do. One the one hand the standard of right and wrong, on the other the chain of causes and effects, are fastened to their throne. They govern us in all we do, in all we say, in all we think: every effort we can make to throw off our subjection, will serve but to demonstrate and confirm it. In words a man may pretend to abjure their empire: but in reality he will remain subject to it all the while. The *principle of utility* recognizes this subjection, and assumes it for the foundation of that system, the object of which is to rear the fabric of felicity by the hands of reason and of law. Systems which attempt to question it, deal in sounds instead of sense, in caprice instead of reason, in darkness instead of light.

But enough of metaphor and declamation: it is not by such means that moral science is to be improved.

II. The principle of utility is the foundation of the present work: it will be proper therefore at the outset to give an explicit and determinate account of what is meant by it. By the principle of utility is meant that principle which approves or disapproves of every action whatsoever, according to the tendency which it appears to have to augment or diminish the happiness of the party whose interest is in question: or, what is the same thing in other words, to promote or to oppose that happiness, I say of every action whatsoever; and therefore not only of every action of a private individual, but of every measure of government.

III. By utility is meant the property in any object, whereby it tends to produce the benefit, advantage, pleasure, good, or happiness (all this in the present comes to the same thing) to prevent the happening of mischief, pain, evil, or unhappiness to the party whose interest is considered; if that party be the community in general, then the happiness of the community: if a particular individual, then the happiness of that individual.

IV. The interest of the community is one of the most general expressions that can occur in the phraseology of morals: no wonder that the meaning of it is often lost. When it has a meaning, it is this. The community is a fictitious *body*, composed of the individual persons who are considered as constituting as it were its *members*. The interest of the community then is, what?—the sum of the interests of the several members who compose it.

V. It is in vain to talk of the interest of the community, without understanding what is the interest of the individual. A thing is said to promote the interest, or to be *for* the interest, of an individual, when it tends to add to

the sum total of his pleasures: or, what comes to the same thing, to diminish the sum total of his pains.

VI. An action then may be said to be conformable to the principle of utility, or,
for shortness sake, to utility, (meaning with respect to the community at
large) when the tendency it has to augment the happiness of the community is greater than any it has to diminish it.

VII. A measure of government (which is but a particular kind of action, performed by a particular person or persons), may be said to be conformable to
or dictated by the principle of utility, when in like manner the tendency
which it has to augment the happiness of the community is greater than any
which it has to diminish it.[8]

In contrast with Bentham's original formulation, many modern utilitarians
would view things other than happiness or pleasure as having intrinsic worth.
Such things include power, knowledge, beauty, or moral qualities. These views
are often termed *ideal utilitarianism,* and they have attracted philosophers such as
G. E. Moore[9] and Hastings Rashdall.[10] Since we'll be considering primarily
classical utilitarianism, we'll use *good* to mean "pleasure." What we'll say about
classical utilitarianism, however, applies equally to pluralistic positions, if for
"pleasure" the phrase "intrinsic good" is substituted.

At the outset one may wonder whether pleasure can be calculated, as the
utilitarian doctrine seems to require. Bentham thought it could. In attempting
to determine how much pleasure and pain would result from a person's action,
he formulated a hedonistic calculus, that is, a calculation of pleasure based on a
number of criteria, such as the intensity of the pleasure, how long it lasted,
how certain it was to occur, and how likely it was to produce additional pleasure. Later Mill added quality to Bentham's calculus, by which he meant the
moral superiority that one pleasure holds over another. Although Bentham's
calculus doesn't allow an exact calculation of pleasure and pain, it presents
valuable criteria for evaluating actions other than on the basis of immediate
gratification.

In developing his calculus, Bentham seemed to have in mind a particular
utilitarian theory of obligation, termed *act utilitarianism,* as distinguished from
rule utilitarianism.

Act and Rule Utilitarianism

Act utilitarianism is *the normative position that contends we should act so as to
produce the greatest happiness for the most people.* In other words, before acting,
ask yourself: What will be the consequences of my action not only for myself
but also for everyone else involved? If the consequences are good (that is, they
are calculated to produce more happiness or pleasure than any other action will

8. From *Jeremy Bentham.* Introduction to the Principles of Morals and Legislation. *Oxford: Oxford University Press, 1823, chap. 1. Originally published 1789.*

9. G. E. Moore. Principia Ethica. *London: Cambridge University Press, 1903.*

10. *Hastings Rashdall.* A Theory of Good and Evil: A Treatise on Moral Philosophy. *2 vols. New York: Oxford University Press, 1924.*

produce), the action is right; if they are bad (that is, they are not so calculated), then the action is wrong. In effect, for the act utilitarian, the end justifies the means. This can raise problems.

Kid: Obie, you remember that big drug bust on the East Side last month?

Obie: Sure, I remember it. That's another example of what I'm talking about. "Entrapment" they called it, and threw it right out of court.

Kid: But it *was* entrapment.

Obie: Look, Kid, when you're trying to catch a criminal, you're interested in what works. Am I right?

Kid: Do you really believe it doesn't matter how you accomplish something just so long as you accomplish it?

Obie: When it comes to incorrigibles, that's exactly what I believe.

Kid: But how can you break the law to keep it?

Obie: Hey, just because something's the law doesn't make it right. A lot of laws are bad. That's the whole point. Take capital punishment, for instance. I say if a man murders in cold blood, he loses his right to live.

Kid: What if he's innocent?

Obie: What're you talking about, *innocent*? Didn't I just say he murdered in cold blood?

Kid: But suppose he's innocent this particular time. Suppose he's guilty of a lot of other things, maybe even murders, but on this particular occasion he's innocent.

Obie: How can he be innocent if he's guilty of so much to begin with?

Kid: He's innocent in this one instance. That's what I'm saying.

Obie: And guilty all the rest of the time?

Kid: Right.

Obie: And he's gotten away with it all?

Kid: Suppose he has.

Obie: Then I say, when you get the chance, nail him.

Kid: You know what you're saying? You're saying it's okay to railroad somebody, to send him up for something he didn't do.

Obie: He did plenty. You said so yourself.

Kid: But not this particular thing.

Obie: A technicality.

Kid: A technicality!

Obie: Look, you got a choice: You either get this guy off the streets or you don't. Now, are you going to tell me we should leave him out there on some technicality? Use your head, Kid, this is a public menace we're talking about, not some Boy Scout. You're removing a public menace from the streets! Who cares how you do it?

Kid: Then why not just shoot him and save us all a lot of time and money?

Obie: Because we're a law-abiding country.

What if an action that promises the greatest good for the greatest number, such as imprisoning an innocent person, appears to be patently wrong? The consequences of removing a chronic public threat, although never certain, appear to provide greater safety and happiness for the vast majority of people. Yet suppose that in this particular case the individual is innocent.

A number of ethicists point out that we get into such dilemmas when we apply the "greatest happiness" principle to a *particular act* and not to the rule that the act implements. What we should be concerned with is the consequences of keeping or breaking the operative rule under which a particular act falls. This is a *rule utilitarian* position. For example, in this case the ethical rule that the Kid is defending seems to be "People should never be imprisoned for something they didn't do." To determine whether to railroad the person in question, we must determine whether this is a good rule. Evaluate the consequences of breaking it. How much fear and anxiety would arise if we all knew that we could be imprisoned for something we did not do? Would these feelings make us happy or not? Would breaking such a rule leave us feeling secure? Would it perhaps encourage us to break the law when we could, since abiding by it would be as perilous as breaking it? The consequences of breaking the rule may not constitute as much collective happiness as abiding by it. If not, say the rule utilitarians, acting in a way that violates this rule would be bad, whereas acting in a way that promotes the rule would be good. In short, **rule utilitarianism** maintains that *we should act in such a way that the rule governing our actions produces the greatest happiness for the most people.*

But is it that simple? What about this rule: "When people are chronic and deliberate violators of the law, and they are found by reasonable criteria to be public menaces, it is good and desirable to imprison them, even for something they did not do"? The consequences of violating this rule appear to be similar to the consequences of violating the preceding rule. It would seem bad, then, not to promote this rule, and good to promote it. In brief, it is not easy to say what a good rule is. It is especially difficult to assess the rule on the basis of its consequences, since they are generally problematic. But is any other basis possible? Some think that we must consider criteria other than consequences in evaluating morality. Before considering these nonconsequentialist views, however, it's important for us to complete our overview of utilitarianism by mentioning that it has received a novel twist in recent years. Specifically, act utilitarianism has been reformulated within the context of what is generally termed *situation ethics*, a movement having a broad impact on contemporary morality.

Situation Ethics

For simplicity, we'll confine our observations to the situation ethics proposed by Christian moralist Joseph Fletcher. Fletcher views situation ethics as one of three primary avenues for making moral decisions. The other two are the legalistic, which contends that moral rules are absolute laws that must always be obeyed, and the antinomian or existential (for example, act utilitarianism), which contends that no guidelines exist, that each situation is unique and so requires a new decision. According to Fletcher, legalism is overly directive, antinomianism unacceptably nondirective. Both, he feels, are unworkable. Situation ethics falls between these two extremes but apparently closer to antinomianism.

Like utilitarians, Fletcher is very much concerned with the consequences of our actions. But rather than acting so as to produce the greatest happiness for the greatest number, Fletcher advocates that we produce the most Christian love, that is, the greatest amount of love fulfillment and benevolence. **Situation ethics** is *the doctrine that contends that the moral action produces the greatest amount of Christian love of all the possible actions.*

For Fletcher, rules and principles are valid only if they serve love in a specific situation. Therefore, when making a moral decision, it's crucial to be fully acquainted with all the facts surrounding the case as well as with the probable consequences of each possible action. In this Fletcher is decidedly consequentialist; in fact, he is utilitarian. But he also argues that after all the calculations are completed, one must choose the act that will best serve love, that is, what Christian tradition has called *agape* (AH-ga-pay).

Christianity teaches that agape is unselfish love, epitomized by Jesus, who made the ultimate sacrifice for love of humankind. Agape is a principle describing the type of actions that Christians are to regard as good. In a word, agape is loving concern, characterized by a love of God and neighbor.

Fletcher contends that agape is the one unexceptionable principle. In this he differentiates himself from consequentialists generally and utilitarians particularly. For Fletcher, something is valid only if it serves love in any situation; even the proscriptions of the Ten Commandments and the injunctions of the Sermon on the Mount should be viewed as cautious generalizations, not as absolutely binding moral principles. In this respect, Fletcher agrees with Martin Luther's statement that "when the law impels one against love, it ceases and should no longer be a law. But where no obstacle is in the way, the keeping of the law is a proof of love, which lies hidden in the heart. Therefore you have need of the law, that love may be manifested; but if it cannot be kept without injury to the neighbor, God wants us to suspend and ignore the law."[11] In effect, Fletcher's position is that traditional Christian moral laws are fine and even obligatory, but only if they serve love. When they don't, we can, even must, break them.

It's easy, however, to misconstrue Fletcher. His agape principle is not a limp standard that can be used to justify anything. On the contrary, the hallmarks of agape are prudence and careful evaluation, characterized by a willing of the neighbor's good. As such, justice is an integral part of Fletcher's doctrine. But Fletcher doesn't seem to associate justice with the efficiency espoused by utilitarians. For utilitarians, justice is tantamount to producing the most happiness. This is why Obie can prosecute a man for something he did not do. In contrast, Fletcher sees justice as giving people their due. When we truly love, we must practice justice. Justice is inseparable from love. "*Agape* is

---

11. *Martin Luther.* Works. *J. N. Linker, Ed. Luther House, 1905, vol. 5, p. 175.*

what is due to all others," he writes, "justice is nothing other than love working out its problems."[12]

Fletcher believes that in formulating social policies, the Christian should join with the utilitarian in trying to produce the greatest good for the greatest number, or, as he calls it, "the greatest amount of neighbor welfare for the largest number of neighbors possible." Thus, the hedonistic calculus of utilitarianism becomes for Fletcher the "agape calculus."[13]

In summary, for Fletcher nothing is good in itself except love, that is, Christian love, or *agape*. Love becomes the standard of moral decision making. It is identical with justice, which is love distributed. When do we love? When we will the good of our neighbor. Finally, love's decisions are determined by particular situations; nothing but the end ever justifies the means.[14]

A number of features of Fletcher's situationism are appealing to many people. First, by focusing on loving concern, Fletcher brings to human relationships a much-needed emphasis on the primacy of individuals and on their welfare. Too often, especially under strictly utilitarian doctrines, the centrality of human beings can be lost within or diminished by the group ideal. Fletcher's situationism decisively restores the human dimension with its emphasis on "willing of the neighbor's good."

Second, in rejecting moral legalism, Fletcher in effect eliminates what is often a person's chief way of avoiding personal moral responsibility. By following a legalistic line, individuals needn't grapple with moral decisions. At the same time, legalism leaves individuals with the impression that the law represents the limit of their moral obligations, whether the law is of a civil or moral nature. As a result, legalism can easily undercut moral accountability by removing moral decision making from individual control. In rejecting legalism, then, situationism seems to energize the whole concept of moral accountability.

Despite these strengths, situationism is not without flaws. First, it is not a definite decision-making procedure. In illustrating how love's decisions are determined by particular situations, Fletcher cites the example of a young woman who is asked by an American intelligence agency to use sex to blackmail an enemy spy. Should she value her chastity more than patriotism and service to her country? Fletcher's answer is no.

But why not? Why couldn't she appeal to the same patriotic motives to preserve her chastity? She might reason that her country should not exploit a person sexually, whatever the reason. She might feel that information gathering does not give government agencies a blanket justification for demanding any kind of behavior. In other words, she might as easily interpret her refusal to be sexual bait as more patriotic and rendering a greater service to her country than her consent. In short, she might see her refusal as the most loving thing to do. Thus, in situation ethics, the same motives could result in different actions.

12. *Joseph Fletcher*. Situation Ethics: The New Morality. *Philadelphia: Westminster Press, 1966, p. 95.*

13. *Luther Binkley*. Conflict of Ideals. *New York: D. Van Nostrand, 1969, p. 265.*

14. *Luther Binkley*. Conflict of Ideals, *p. 254.*

Second, critics argue that Fletcher actually espouses the antinomianism that he rejects. To understand this objection fully, we must distinguish between two kinds of rules: summary and general. A *summary rule* contends that following the practice advocated or avoiding the practice prohibited is *generally* the best way of acting. Thus, the following are summary rules: "Telling the truth is generally love fulfilling" or "Paying your debts is generally love fulfilling." Summary rules clearly allow exceptions. General rules, on the other hand, do not. A *general rule* contends that you must *always* follow the practice advocated and avoid the one prohibited. Thus: "Telling the truth is always love fulfilling" and "Paying your debts is always love fulfilling."

It seems that Fletcher must deny the existence of general rules, lest he fall into the legalism that he condemns. If, on the other hand, he espouses summary rules, then individuals would determine for themselves when the interests of loving concern transcend summary rules. Of course, should he deny summary as well as general rules, then he would be advocating the antinomian or existentialist position. In fact, Fletcher does express rules: "No unwanted and unintended baby should ever be born," "Exploiting persons is always wrong," "Sex which does not have love as its partner, its senior partner, is wrong." If these are summary rules, under what conditions does loving concern allow one to transcend them?

Due to the problems associated with consequentialist ethics, many ethicists feel that some criteria other than consequences must be used as moral measuring rods. The theories of these ethicists are placed under the heading of *nonconsequentialist* ethics.

Nonconsequentialist (Deontological) Theories

The most influential nonconsequentialist theories can best be categorized as either proposing a single rule that governs human conduct or proposing multiple rules. Two significant single-rule nonconsequentialist theories are the divine command theory and Immanuel Kant's categorical imperative theory.

Divine Command Theory

The **divine command theory** is a single-rule nonconsequentialist normative theory that says we should always do the will of God. In other words, whatever the situation, if we do what God wills, then we do the right thing; if we do not do what God wills, then no matter what the consequences, we do wrong.

Notice that this theory does not state that we should obey God's law because we will therefore promote our own or the general good or be faithful to some virtuous principles. Perhaps we will accomplish these ends, but the sole justification for obeying God's law is that God wills it. The theory also does not defend the morality of an action by promising some supernatural reward to the faithful. True, perhaps the faithful will be rewarded, and perhaps behaving righteously is in their best long-term interests, but divine command theorists wouldn't justify moral actions on such egoistic grounds.

Understandably, divine command theorists would see no intrinsic worth or value in such things as pleasure, power, or knowledge; instead, they would propose something like a union with God as taking the form of heavenly salvation. The great Christian theologian and philosopher Thomas Aquinas, writing in one of his most important ethical works, *Summa contra Gentiles,* refers to the human's ultimate happiness as being the contemplation of God. He arrives at this conclusion after arguing that human happiness does not consist in wealth, worldly power, or sensual pleasures. Here's Aquinas' conclusion:

> Accordingly if man's ultimate happiness consists not in external things, which are called goods of chance; nor in goods of the body; nor in goods of the soul, as regards the sensitive faculty; nor as regards the intellective faculty, in the practice of moral virtue; nor as regards intellectual virtue in those which are concerned about action, namely art and prudence; it remains for us to conclude that man's ultimate happiness consists in the contemplation of the truth.
>
> For this operation alone is proper to man, and none of the other animals communicates with him therein.
>
> Again. This is not directed to anything further as its end: since the contemplation of the truth is sought for its own sake.
>
> Again. By this operation man is united to things above him, by becoming like them: because of all human actions this alone is both in God and in separate substances. Also, by this operation man comes into contact with those higher beings, through knowing them in any way whatever.
>
> Besides, man is more self-sufficing for this operation, seeing that he stands in little need of the help of external things in order to perform it.
>
> Further. All other human operations seem to be directed to this as their end. Because perfect contemplation requires that the body should be disencumbered, and to this effect are directed all the products of art that are necessary for life. Moreover, it requires freedom from the disturbance caused by the passions, which is achieved by means of the moral virtues and prudence; and freedom from external disturbance, to which all the regulations of the civil life are directed. So that, if we consider the matter rightly, we shall see that all human occupations are brought into the service of those who contemplate the truth. Now, it is not possible that man's ultimate happiness consists in contemplation based on the understanding of first principles: for this is most imperfect, as being universal and containing potential knowledge of things. Moreover, it is the beginning and not the end of human study, and comes to us from nature, and not through the study of the truth. Nor does it consist in contemplation based on the sciences that have the lowest things for their object: since happiness must consist in an operation of the intellect in relation to the highest objects of intelligence. It follows then that man's ultimate happiness consists in wisdom, based on the consideration of divine things. It is therefore evident by way of induction that man's ultimate happiness consists solely in the contemplation of God, which conclusion was proved above by arguments.[15]

15. *St. Thomas Aquinas.* Summa contra Gentiles. *English Dominican Fathers, Trans. New York: Benziger, 1928. Reprinted by permission of Glencoe Publishing Company, Inc.*

This state of eternal bliss is the ultimate goal of all human endeavor; it is the only thing of intrinsic value. What is valuable, then, is independent of what any individual thinks or likes and what any society happens to sanction. Moral laws are established by God; they are universally binding for all people and are eternally true, regardless of whether they are universally obeyed. Such God-established laws are generally interpreted in a religious tradition. The Ten Commandments are a good example. These laws, claim their adherents, apply to everybody everywhere and their value does not depend on what produces human satisfaction, either individually or collectively.

The justification of such moral laws is usually divine authority and its supposed expression through humans and their institutions. Thus the Bible or the Koran may be appealed to as an authority, as may a religious institution or leader.

Christian theologians have developed a natural law theory of absolute values. According to this view, God endowed each creature with definite intrinsic tendencies, or natural laws, by which the creature should act. We can discover these laws through reason alone. Thus, we can know the will of God without recourse to special revelation.

Contrast this legalistic view of the nature of goodness with Fletcher's situationism. Although both theories of value have a long religious tradition, emphasizing one over the other can lead to contrasting theories of obligation. Pursuing union with God consistently leads to a divine command theory of obligation, in which we attempt to do what God wills. However, following the lead of love can suggest behavior apparently inconsistent with what we understand as being the law of God, for Fletcher contends that agape is the one unexceptionable principle in Christian ethics. Everything else is valid only if it serves love in any situation. You can imagine how this can easily lead to contrasting positions on important issues, such as abortion and euthanasia.

Even a cursory look at the divine command theory reveals a couple of inherent weaknesses. First, we don't know what God has commanded. True, divine command theorists frequently point to sacred books or scriptures as guidelines. Yet, how do we know that these writings represent the inspired word of God? Some would assert that the scriptures say so. But such circular reasoning won't do. After all, how do we know that there is a God at all? And if there is, can we be sure that He or She expressed Himself or Herself in one source and not in another?

In addition, the divine command theory can't satisfactorily explain why God commands something. In other words, does God command something because it is right, or is something right because God commands it? If the former, then the theory appears to collapse because it contends that something is right *because* God commands it. If the latter, then anything that God commands must be right. Should God command cruelty, then cruelty would be right—a most difficult proposition to defend.

Philosophers have not been indifferent to these objections. In the eighteenth century Immanuel Kant attempted to present a single-rule nonconsequentialist theory based, not on religious teaching, but on reason alone.

Kant's Categorical Imperative

To understand Kant's thought, note the emphasis he places on the idea of good intentions. Kant believed that nothing was good in itself except a "good will." Intelligence, judgment, and all other facets of the human personality are perhaps good and desirable, but only if the will that makes use of them is good. To quote Kant:

> Nothing can possibly be conceived in the world, or even out of it, which can be called good, without qualification, except a Good Will. Intelligence, wit, judgment, and the other *talents* of the mind, however they may be named, or courage, resolution, perseverance, as qualities of temperament, are undoubtedly good and desirable in many respects; but these gifts of nature may also become extremely bad and mischievous if the will which is to make use of them, and which, therefore, constitutes what is called *character*, is not good. It is the same with *gifts of fortune*. Power, riches, honor, even health, and the general well-being and contentment with one's condition which is called *happiness*, inspire pride, and often presumption, if there is not a good will to correct the influence of these on the mind, and with this also to rectify the whole principle of acting, and adapt it to its end. The sight of a being who is not adorned with a single feature of a pure and good will, enjoying unbroken prosperity, can never give pleasure to an impartial rational spectator. Thus a good will appears to constitute the indispensable condition even of being worthy of happiness.[16]

By *will*, Kant meant the uniquely human capacity to act according to the concepts behind laws—that is, principles presumably operating in nature. A good will, therefore, acts in accordance with nature's laws. For Kant a will could be called good without qualification only if it always had in view one principle: whether the maxim of its action could become a universal law. This standard is such a crucial part of Kant's theory of ethics that we have included the entire passage presenting this point from Kant's masterpiece, *Fundamental Principles of the Metaphysic of Morals*. Notice that Kant does not rely on a consideration of consequences, but strictly on a logical analysis of the would-be law in question.

> But what sort of law can that be, the conception of which must determine the will, even without paying any regard to the effect expected from it, in order that this will may be called good absolutely and without qualification? As I have deprived the will of every impulse which could arise to it from obedience to any law, there remains nothing but the universal conformity of its actions to law in general, which alone is to serve the will as a principle, i.e. I am never to act otherwise than so *that I could also will that my maxim should become a universal law*. Here, now, it is the simple conformity to law in general, without assuming any particular law applicable to certain actions, that serves the will as its principle, and must so serve it, if duty is not to be a vain delusion and a chimerical notion. The common reason of men in its practical judgments perfectly coincides with this, and always has in view the principle here suggested. Let the question be, for example: May I when in distress make a promise with the intention not to keep it? I readily distinguish here between the two significa-

16. *Immanuel Kant.* Fundamental Principles of the Metaphysic of Morals. *6th ed. T. K. Abbott, Trans. London: Longmans Green, 1909, sec. 1, pp. 9–10.*

tions which the question may have: whether it is prudent, or whether it is right, to make a false promise? The former may undoubtedly often be the case. I see clearly indeed that it is not enough to extricate myself from a present difficulty by means of this subterfuge, but it must be well considered whether there may not hereafter spring from this lie much greater inconvenience than that from which I now free myself, and as, with all my supposed *cunning*, the consequences cannot be so easily foreseen but that credit once lost may be much more injurious to me than any mischief which I seek to avoid at present, it should be considered whether it would not be more *prudent* to act herein according to a universal maxim, and to make it a habit to promise nothing except with the intention of keeping it. But it is soon clear to me that such a maxim will still only be based on the fear of consequences. Now it is a wholly different thing to be truthful from duty, and to be so from apprehension of injurious consequences. In the first case, the very notion of the action already implies a law for me; in the second case, I must first look about elsewhere to see what results may be combined with it which would affect myself. For to deviate from the principle of duty is beyond all doubt wicked; but to be un-faithful to my maxim of prudence may often be very advantageous to me, al-though to abide by it is certainly safer. The shortest way, however, and an unerring one, to discover the answer to this question whether a lying promise is consistent with duty, is to ask myself, Should I be content that my maxim (to extricate myself from difficulty by a false promise) should hold good as a uni-versal law, for myself as well as for others? and should I be able to say to my-self, "Every one may make a deceitful promise when he finds himself in a difficulty from which he cannot otherwise extricate himself"? Then I presently become aware that while I can will the lie, I can by no means will that lying should be a universal law. For with such a law there would be no promises at all, since it would be in vain to allege my intention in regard to my future actions to those who would not believe this allegation, or if they over-hastily did so, would pay me back in my own coin. Hence my maxim, as soon as it should be made a universal law, would necessarily destroy itself.

I do not, therefore, need any far-reaching penetration to discern what I have to do in order that my will may be morally good. Inexperienced in the course of the world, incapable of being prepared for all its contingencies, I only ask myself: Canst thou also will that thy maxim should be a universal law? If not, then it must be rejected, and that not because of a disadvantage accruing from it to myself or even to others, but because it cannot enter as a principle into a possible universal legislation, and reason extorts from me immediate respect for such legislation. I need not as yet *discern* on what this respect is *based* (this the philosopher may inquire), but at least I understand this, that it is an estimation of the worth which far outweighs all worth of what is recom-mended by inclination, and that the necessity of acting from *pure* respect for the practical law is what constitutes duty, to which every other motive must give place, because it is the condition of a will being good *in itself*, and the worth of such a will is above everything.

Thus, then, without quitting the moral knowledge of common human rea-son, we have arrived at its principle. And although, no doubt, common men do not conceive it in such an abstract and universal form, yet they always have it really before their eyes, and use it as the standard of their decision.[17]

17.   Immanuel Kant. Fundamental Principles, pp. 12—14.

Kant believed, then, that there was just one command or imperative that was categorical—that is, one that presented an action as necessary of itself, without regard to any other end. He believed that from this one categorical imperative, this universal command, all commands of duty could be derived. Kant's **categorical imperative** states that we should act in such a way that the maxim, or general rule, governing our action could become a universal law.

Consider his example of making a promise that you are willing to break if it suits your purposes. Your maxim can be expressed thus: When it suits my purposes, I'll break promises that I have made. This maxim could not be universally acted upon, because it involves a contradiction of will. On the one hand, you are willing to make promises and honor them; on the other, you are willing to break those promises. Notice that Kant is not a utilitarian: he is not arguing that the consequences of a universal law condoning promise breaking would be bad and therefore the rule is bad. Instead, he is claiming that the rule is self-contradictory; the institution of promise making would dissolve if such a maxim were universalized. His appeal is to logical consistency, not to consequences.

Or consider another of Kant's examples, involving a man who, in despair after suffering a series of evils, contemplates suicide. Specifically, the man, while still in possession of his reason, asks whether it would be contrary to his duty to himself to take his own life. He wonders whether the maxim of his action could become a universal law of nature.

> His maxim, however, is: For love of myself, I make it my principle to shorten my life when by a longer duration it threatens more evils than satisfaction. But it is questionable whether this principle of self-love could become a universal law of nature. One immediately sees a contradiction in a system of nature whose law would be to destroy life by the feeling whose special office is to impel the improvement of life. In this case it would not exist as nature: hence the maxim cannot obtain as a law of nature, and thus it wholly contradicts the supreme principle of all duty.[18]

Although there is only one categorical imperative, it can be stated in different ways to reveal pertinent aspects. One very important formulation of it is: Always act so as to treat yourself and other individuals as ends in yourselves, and never as means to ends. This insight may be at the root of the disagreement between our two police officers.

Obie: What gets me, Kid, is that people like you make it sound like I'm doing society a disservice by keeping these thugs off the street. When, in fact, the opposite is true.

Kid: But that's not the point, Obie. Even if society's interests are served, you don't put someone in jail for something he didn't do.

Obie: Even if he did a lot of other stuff, and will probably do more?

Kid: That's right.

Obie: Well, I guess I'm dense, because I don't see that at all.

18. *Immanuel Kant.* Fundamental Principles, p. 15.

Kid: That's because you don't see anything wrong with using people to accomplish social goals.

The Kid's charge surely couldn't be applied to Kant. On the contrary, Kant emphasized that every rational creature has inherent worth, which results solely from the possession of rationality. Rational creatures possess what Kant termed an "autonomous, self-legislating will." In other words, they can evaluate their actions, make rules for themselves, and direct their conduct according to these self-imposed rules.

But Kant's theory is not airtight. First, it is highly doubtful that all acts falling under a categorical rule are always wrong. For example, one of Kant's maxims is "Don't lie." But is lying always wrong? Is it wrong to lie to save your life? To save someone from serious pain or injury? Second, duties frequently conflict. If, as Kant argues, it is always wrong to tell a lie and always wrong to break a promise, then which do I choose when these duties conflict? Finally, there is no compelling reason why certain actions should be prohibited without exception. In other words, there seems some doubt that actions like lying, promise breaking, and suicide must be prohibited without exception. Apparently Kant failed to distinguish between persons' making no exceptions to rules and rules' having no exceptions. If a person should make no exceptions to rules, then one should never except oneself from being bound by a rule. But it does not therefore follow that the rule has no exceptions and can never be qualified. In fairness to Kant, however, it should be noted that the limitations of his examples do not necessarily discredit his ethical theory.

In the twentieth century a nonconsequentialist British ethicist named William David Ross turned his attention to the conflicting-duties problem that Kant's theory seems incapable of resolving. The result is a multiple-rule nonconsequentialist theory generally referred to as Ross's *prima facie duties.*

Ross's Prima Facie Duties

Obie: You're not telling me you'd turn a guy like that loose, are you?

Kid: That's exactly what I'm telling you.

Obie: But you said yourself he was one of those incorrigibles.

Kid: But he's innocent in this particular case.

Obie: What's that got to do with it?

Kid: Everything.

Obie: You realize that he's going to go out and do the same thing again?

Kid: Maybe so.

Obie: And that you've got a duty to protect society?

Kid: I know that.

Obie: And despite that you'd release him?

Kid: I would.

Obie: How come?

Kid: Because I don't believe it's right to imprison somebody for something he didn't do. It's just not fair.

Considering only consequences often seems inadequate for resolving moral decisions. The choice is frequently between duties. Thus, a person may have a duty to protect society. At the same time, the person has a duty to uphold justice. When those duties conflict, as here, which takes precedence? For Obie, it's the duty to protect society; for the Kid, it's justice. Who's right? William David Ross turned his attention to such questions in his work *The Right and the Good* (1930).

At the outset of his book, Ross makes it clear that he rejects the consequentialist belief that what makes an act right is whether it produces the most good. As he notes, consequences of conflicting courses of action frequently counterbalance each other. So, instead of a consequentialism, Ross argues that in deciding among ethical alternatives, we must determine which duties we fulfill by performing or not performing each alternative.

Consistent with this insight is Ross's rejection of the claim that there is but one thing of intrinsic value. For Ross there are four things that are intrinsically worthwhile: pleasure, virtue, knowledge, and the distribution of pleasure and pain according to virtue. Because these things don't share any single value-making property, they can't be reduced to any single intrinsic good. A theory of value that holds several things as being intrinsically valuable is termed *axiological pluralism*. Ross's pluralism, evident in his theory of value, also appears in his theory of obligation.

As Ross explains, an act may fall under a number of rules at once, not just a single rule. For example, the rule to keep a promise may in a given circumstance conflict with the rule not to do anyone harm. For example, suppose that political candidate Ida Simpson promises a wealthy builder that if he funds her campaign and she gets elected, she'll deliver him an attractive government contract. Simpson is subsequently elected and makes good her promise. As it happens, the contractor does good work and offers competitive prices. But, of course, Ida Simpson doesn't even consider any other bids.

On the one hand, Simpson has fulfilled her promise, which she may have viewed as binding. On the other hand, she's violated her duty to society, which trusts that she will not collude with private interests to advance her own or their own welfare but will always act strictly in the interest of the public good. As a result, we'd probably believe that Simpson acted immorally, but not because the consequences of her action were unfavorable. She acted wrongly because the reasons against what she did count more than the reason for what she did. Such an analysis evaluates the conflicting duties to determine the most compelling.

In such cases, the possible acts are motivated by a number of reasons. Each reason in turn appeals to a moral duty—to keep a promise, to be faithful to the people who trust you, to be fair, to be honest. Each of these moral duties provides grounds for a particular action, and yet no single one provides sufficient grounds. The task is to choose the most obligatory duty, but first we must have a knowledge of *prima facie* duties.

The term *prima facie* means "at first sight" or "on the surface." By **prima facie duties,** Ross means duties that dictate what we should do when other moral factors aren't considered. Stated another way, prima facie duties are duties that generally obligate us; that is, they ordinarily impose a moral obligation but may not in a particular case because of circumstances. An **actual duty** is the action that one ought to perform after considering and weighing all the prima facie duties involved.

In *The Right and the Good*, Ross lists six categories of prima facie duties, although he concedes that this breakdown may be incomplete. First are duties that rest on previous acts of our own, such as promises. Ross calls these *duties of fidelity*. Under duties of fidelity, Ross would place not only the honoring of promises but also the obligation not to lie, "which seems to be implied in the act of entering into conversation," and to fulfill contracts that we've entered into, including oaths we've sworn. Under duties of fidelity Ross also lists duties of reparation (repairing wrongful acts). If, for example, I damage something that belongs to someone else, I've an obligation to make restitution.

A second category is duties that rest on acts of other people toward us. Ross terms these *duties of gratitude*. In effect, Ross argues that we're bound by obligations arising from relationships that exist between people, such as those between friends or relatives. Suppose, for example, an especially good friend is suddenly in need of assistance. I'm duty bound to do all I can to help this individual, who in the past has acted so selflessly toward me.

A third category is *duties of justice*, by which he means those duties that rest on the fact or possibility of a distribution of pleasure or happiness that is not in accordance with the merits of the people concerned. Imagine the case of imprisoning a man for a crime he never committed. No matter how much good might result from his imprisonment, such a punishment violates justice.

Ross lists as a fourth category *duties of beneficence*, duties toward people whose virtue, intelligence, or happiness we can improve. For example, I've an obligation to help out a corner beggar in genuine need if I can afford it; if I can help someone correct a costly mistake that they chronically make, I'm duty bound to do it.

Ross's fifth category is *duties of self-improvement*, that is, duties to improve our own condition with respect to virtue, intelligence, or happiness. Thus, just as we've obligations to help others, we are also duty bound to help improve ourselves. An exceptionally talented person who fritters away time, energy, and potential violates this duty. In contrast, a person who seizes opportunities for self-improvement honors it.

The last, and most important, of Ross's six categories is *duties of nonmaleficence,* which are duties of not injuring others. We're obliged to avoid hurting others physically, emotionally, and psychologically. In fact, Ross inevitably allows this duty to override any other duty with which it conflicts.

In summary, Ross presents six categories of prima facie duties, although there may be more categories. However, he does insist that we acknowledge and willingly accept the six categories without argument. His appeal for their acceptance does not rely primarily on reason and argument but on intuition. In other words, Ross invites us to reflect on certain situations, such as telling the truth. If we do, he's convinced that we'll accept his claim that these are true duties.

When faced with a situation that presents conflicting prima facie duties, Ross tells us, we must follow the more obligatory, our actual duty. The actual duty has the greatest amount of prima facie rightness over wrongness.

Although Ross addresses the most important question of conflicting duties, his theory is not without weaknesses. First, how do we know what our prima facie duties are? Ross claims that these are self-evident truths to anyone of sufficient mental maturity who has given them enough attention. But here he seems to presuppose traditional, collective values. What if people disagree with his categories? Ross would say that they lack "sufficient mental maturity" or that they didn't give the proposition "sufficient attention." But then we must decide on the precise nature of "sufficient mental maturity" and what it means to give something "sufficient attention."

More serious, however, is the fact that it's difficult, if not impossible, to determine the relative weight and merit of conflicting duties. When faced with a situation that presents conflicting duties, how do we determine our actual duty? In the case of two conflicting duties, Ross counsels, "The act is one's duty which is in accord with the more stringent prima facie obligation." In cases of more than two conflicting duties, he says, "That act is one's duty that has the greatest balance of prima facie rightness over wrongness." But without assigning weights to duties, how can we determine the "most stringent" obligation or "the greatest balance of prima facie rightness over wrongness"?

This completes our overview of the main currents in Western ethical theory. In keeping with our intention of providing an intercultural perspective, we should at least mention the rich moral legacy of Eastern religion and philosophy. Because increasing numbers of Westerners are finding philosophical enrichment in Eastern thought, Eastern morality promises to become increasingly influential in the West. Although we can't acknowledge all Eastern moral thought, we can look at the one that we've already sketched, Buddhism. Before doing this you might try applying the ethical theories to a concrete moral situation (see Philosophy and Life 3-1).

Buddhist Ethics

For centuries in the Western world, moral, religious, and philosophical scholars have exhorted people to practice "the good, the true, and the beautiful" to attain happiness. In recent years scholars have rediscovered the Buddhist method of incorporating this advice into a system that leads to wisdom or ultimate reality.

Buddhism's emphasis on ethical behavior can be generalized in two ways. First, volitional actions are regarded of supreme importance because according to the moral law of causation (karma), they determine our destiny. We will be what we have been; what we do will determine what we become. Second, ethics is considered the parent of wisdom, in that reflection on the wholesome-ness or unwholesomeness of volitional actions leads to discipline of the mind, which eventually results in insight and enlightenment. Thus, we are always brought to the following dictum: "Morality is washed all round with wisdom, and wisdom is washed all round with morality. Wherever there is morality, there is wisdom, and wherever there is wisdom there is morality. From the observing of the moralities comes wisdom and from observing of wisdom comes morality. Morality and wisdom together reveal the height of the world. It is just as if one should wash one hand with the other or one foot with the other; exactly so is morality washed round with wisdom and wisdom with morality."[19] The Buddhist standards of morality, then, must always be condu-cive to the attainment of nirvana (enlightened wisdom) and the realization of the Four Noble Truths. The Buddhist ethical ideal is that of the self-reliant person, the individual who has attained personal enlightenment. Of course, as we've indicated elsewhere, enlightenment is not derived from logical deduction. But this does not mean that the individual should therefore wait for a supernatural revelation. Recall that the Fourth Noble Truth is that of the way to the cessation of suffering, which, Buddhism teaches, we must follow continuously and dili-gently throughout the present life. We do this essentially by following three short axioms:

> *Cease to do evil;*
> *Learn to do good;*
> *Purify your own mind.*[20]

In his marvelous treatment of this subject, Buddhist scholar H. Saddhatissa says that the first line, "Cease to do evil," sums up the code of Buddhist morality contained in five precepts, which constitute the negative aspects of Buddhist morality.[21] These precepts can be viewed as a "clearing away of the weeds from the soil,"[22] an ordering of the outer life before turning to the inner life, to the development and liberation of the mind, which are the goals of Buddhist teach-ing. These precepts represent the first steps that one can take after reading, hearing, and pondering Buddhist teaching and establishing some confidence in it. But it's important not to view these precepts as a set of rules, for Buddhism stresses the cultivation of wisdom and discernment. In other words, blind obedience to these negative precepts is not encouraged.

Before we mention these precepts, we must emphasize that Buddhist mor-ality is a natural morality. It is based on personal understanding, experience, and choice. No one is asked to obey the commandments of God. Individuals are neither threatened with punishment nor wooed with promises of reward. Only understanding based on experiment and careful choice is involved. Would-be Buddhists are simply invited to take upon themselves certain rules of training, which they may find helpful in achieving self-reliance. In short, the

19.   Dighanikaya. T. W. *Rhys Davies and J. E. Carpenter, Eds. Pali Text Society, 1947, vol. 1, p. 124.*

20.   Dhammapada. *Suriyagoda Sumangala, Ed. Pali Text Society, 1914, p. 124.*

21.   *See H. Saddhatissa.* The Buddha's Way. *New York: George Braziller, 1971.*

22.   *H. Saddhatissa.* The Buddha's Way, *p. 32.*

appeal is not to law, commandment, or rule but to common sense and social order.

Buddhist moral teaching, then, is founded on these five precepts:

1. I undertake the rule of training to refrain from harming living things.
2. I undertake the rule of training to refrain from taking what is not given.
3. I undertake the rule of training to refrain from a misuse of the senses.
4. I undertake the rule of training to refrain from wrong speech.
5. I undertake the rule of training to refrain from taking drugs or drinks which tend to cloud the mind.[23]

These are worthy of close inspection.

23. *H. Saddhatissa.* The Buddha's Way, *p. 28.*

PHILOSOPHY AND LIFE 3-1
Getting to Know You: The Corporate Probe

Beth Broheimer was annoyed. "Over and over again, the same question," she thought. "What do they think I am—a thief?"

> *Do you think most companies take advantage of people who work for them when they can? Did you ever think about stealing money from places where you have worked? Do you believe you are too honest to steal?*

At the very least, Beth decided, these were odd questions to ask someone who was applying for a job at The Gap, a chain of several hundred modern clothing outlets specializing in shirts, jackets, and Levi's jeans. But the questions went on.

> *If you knew that a member of your family was stealing from a place where he works, do you think you would report it to the owner of the company? Were you ever tempted to take company money without actually taking any? Do you keep out of trouble at all costs? Do you think it okay to get around the law if you don't actually break it?*

Why such questions? The answer's simple: The Gap, like numerous discount and drug stores, banks, brokerage houses, and fast-food restaurants, was subjecting Beth to a preemployment screen to determine whether she'd be likely to steal from the firm as an employee. Is such a determination possible? Yes, claim the sponsors of one such test, the Reid Report, devised by Reid and Associates, a polygraph firm based in Chicago. But the Reid Report asks other questions of the job candidate, which at best seem to relate only indirectly to the inventory's purpose.

The first precept implies an increasing awareness of the sanctity of life. This can easily—and mistakenly—be read as "Thou shalt not kill." Remember that there are no "thou shalts" in Buddhist morality. More important, this is not just an injunction against murder or wanton killing; it suggests an abstinence from injuring or in any way harming living things. If you savor the full implications of this, intriguing questions arise. For example, "The question arises whether my gastronomical pleasure should be satisfied at the expense of 'living things,' whether animals should be slaughtered so that I may disport myself in their borrowed plumes. And then the questions begin to go deeper. What of my murderous impulses when I am thwarted or humiliated? What of the secret joy I feel when someone I dislike is 'put down'?"[24] Just imagine the ever-increasing questions and doubts that a Westerner might have on trying to

24. H. Saddhatissa. The Buddha's Way, p. 28.

How much money do you pay each month as a result of divorce or separate maintenance for the support of your wife and children? In the past five years about how much money, if any, have you gambled?

Before completing the Reid Report, Beth Broheimer will have answered questions about loans and debts, outside income, and personal habits (including drug and drinking habits). Indeed, by the time she's finished, she will have revealed to her prospective employer many important details of her financial status; her criminal record, if any; her physical and mental health; and her personal life.

What will become of this information? Reid will keep the inventory dealing directly with theft. The rest of the information will be returned to her employer. And, oh yes, Reid and Associates will or will not recommend Beth Broheimer for employment at The Gap.*

* See Peter Schrag. "Confess to Your Corporate Father: Does Your Boss Know What You Do When You're Alone?" Mother Jones, August 1978, pp. 56–60.

☐ *Does an employer have a right to subject a potential employee to such tests?* ☐ *Is it proper for employers to know the details of their employees' personal lives?* ☐ *What considerations do consequential and nonconsequential theories raise for deciding whether or not to use these tests?*

implement this first precept. So much the better; for while initially disturbing us, such unrest, Buddhism teaches, ultimately results in a life having a new significance and perspective. We develop a new sense of respect for self and others that permeates all our thinking.

The second precept asks us to refrain from taking what is not given. Again, the easy translation is "Thou shalt not steal." But this is grossly inadequate, for this precept invites us to develop toward the owners of inanimate objects the same respect that the first precept enjoins toward living things. Rather than merely an injunction against stealing, this second precept necessitates waiting until things are offered us. Thus, a quiet, serene patience replaces the frenzied, rapacious attitude of those living by an "I want" dictum.

The third precept, which asks us to refrain from a misuse of the senses, again is often erroneously translated as a commandment against sexual misconduct; "Thou shalt not covet thy neighbor's wife" or "Don't fornicate." But this is an incomplete understanding. We're advised to refrain from the misuse of the body and bodily sensations. Thus, artificially stimulating the appetite for food is as much to be eschewed as adultery or incest. By this precept, personal habits that lead to obesity, muscular deterioration, or any pollution of the body and its organs are to be avoided. This is hardly a precept that the tobacco industry is likely to endorse. However, Buddhism does not ask its adherents to become ascetics. It simply invites them to be ceaselessly aware of the quality and degree of one's sensual activity. The senses should be enjoyed, not jaded; used, not abused.

As for the fourth precept, Buddhist literature is replete with varieties of "wrong speech." Lying, slander, gossip, malicious talk generally, violation of secrets—the list goes on. The key thing is a call for self-honesty. By avoiding wrong speech, we establish a link between "right thought" and "right action." We practice right speech when we use conversation for knowing people, for understanding others and ourselves. Using a contemporary buzz word, we can translate right speech to right *communication*, whether it involves conversation, advertising, or political speeches.

The fifth precept clues us into the entire code of Buddhist morality. Recall that the cardinal concept of Buddhist human ethics is enlightenment and illumination. The central teaching is a system of meditation designed to clarify the mind so that knowledge and insight may arise in it and be reflected freely. It follows that anyone seriously interested in attaining the state of enlightened wisdom would refrain from indulgences that impair the clarity of mental vision, shroud doubts and uncertainties in a kind of euphoria, and encourage seeing things other than as they are.

As said earlier, these five precepts are summed up in the first axiom of Buddhist moral teaching, "Cease to do evil." These precepts, however, are only the ground breaking and the weeding. The constructive work begins with the second axiom, "Learn to do good." This leads us to the positive aspects of Buddhist morality.

Buddhist literature sparkles with various lists of "wholesome" states or "things to be encouraged," which are contrasted with "unwholesome" states or "things to be discouraged." Among the most prominent of the wholesome: *dāna*, which means "giving."

Again, there's a tendency to equate this with the *caritas* (charity) principle of the New Testament. But the earliest descriptions of *dāna* belie this equation. *Dāna* is not encouraging philanthropic gifts, tithing, or making charitable contributions to worthy causes. Rather, *dāna* implies the gradual developing of the *will* to give whenever the need arises. To formulate an approximation of *dāna* that is closer to love, Saddhatissa advises Westerners to reconsider the description of *caritas* in the epistle of the Corinthians: "And though I distribute all my goods [to the poor], and offer my body to be burned [as a sacrifice], yet it will profit me nothing unless I have love. Love is long-suffering and kind; love is not jealous, nor does it vaunt itself . . . love does not reckon the wrong that has been done to it, nor is it easily provoked" (1 Cor. 13:3–5).

A close reading of this scripture suggests another prominent Buddhist virtue: *mettā*, often translated as "loving kindness." Wheras *dāna* is one outward manifestation of concern for the welfare of others, *mettā* embraces the whole sphere of that concern. "To develop *mettā* is to develop the state of mind wherein the joys and sorrows, the well-being and the problems of others are as important to me as my own.[25] In other words, *mettā* requires that we break down the barriers between self and others. "It has often been said that the follower of the Buddha should endeavor to feel towards all men—relations, friends, acquaintances and enemies—just as a mother feels towards her child."[26] Undoubtedly, this is a tough task. Nonetheless, according to the Buddhist code, we must do this if we're to make any spiritual progress.

But perhaps the Buddhist virtue most difficult for the Western mind to grasp is the "transference of merit." We can perhaps best appreciate this by pondering the fact that a time comes when, having avoided evil and done good, we realize our inherent selfishness: We are doing good to reap for ourselves the harvest of enlightened wisdom. At this point Buddhism invites us to practice "transference of merit," that is, to learn to will that the benefits of our good actions return not to us alone but to all humanity. "Each act of generosity, each movement of love, is no longer to be toted up in my personal account book but is to rebound to the benefit of all. Rather like a stream which feeds the ocean and which is replenished, not by means of the same water flowing back to it, but in the course of time with the falling of the rains."[27]

In summary, while there are similarities between traditional Western ethics and Buddhist ethics, there are also fundamental differences. One is the Eastern nonreliance on rules and commandments. Remember that both the negative and positive aspects of Buddhist morality should be looked on as invitations, not proscriptions. Second is the emphasis on the individual. In the last analysis, the individual avoids evil and cultivates good to facilitate personal en-

---

25. H. Saddhatissa, The Buddha's Way, p. 33.

26. H. Saddhatissa. The Buddha's Way, p. 33.

27. H. Saddhatissa. The Buddha's Way, p. 34.

lightenment. Third, Buddhist morality takes root in a metaphysical outlook. Conducting our lives morally is an expeditious way to experience reality. Fourth is Buddhism's encouraging practitioners to dig into their own experiences, to be open to the universe. If the path of the heart is followed, consideration of the consequences of action is irrelevant. If we are open to the disclosure of the world, then congruence of being and cosmos will follow.

Selecting a Theory of Value and Obligation

Having completed our overview of major consequentialist and nonconsequentialist ethical theories of value and obligation, we should now ask, Which, if any, of these theories ought we to adopt as a personal code of ethics? Unfortunately, we can apply no one principle in choosing, no absolute standard for simplifying the choice. As a result, we're ultimately left to our own devices—to our own experience, reasoning, and intuition. Perhaps the whole enterprise of trying to formulate and justify moral principles is futile and should be abandoned. While such a reaction is understandable, it is, in the last analysis, unfounded.

That an ethical theory lacks perfection doesn't mean that it's useless or that the pursuit of a satisfactory theory is hopeless. Human relationships inevitably present a tangled web of subtle, ill-defined problems. What's more, since relationships are constantly changing, so are the problems and our perspectives of them. The ethical theories we've discussed are just that, theories. They're conceptual frameworks by which we can intelligently conduct moral investigation. What's more, ethical theories are in as constant need of reexamination and refinement as is, say, the democratic theory of government. Their imperfect state, then, is less a flaw than a testimony to the evolutionary nature of humankind.

Each of these theories has an impressive range of applications. In criticizing them, philosophers invariably focus on their weaknesses. Although some people might call such activity "nit-picking," it is consistent with the philosophical enterprise of pursuing truth and certainty. Philosophers raise cases that tend to break the theory down and to test its strength. Failing to grasp this aspect of the philosophical enterprise, one can easily conclude that ethical theories and moral philosophizing offer little if anything of worth. But this would be a gross overstatement that even the harshest critics would not accept. Such a view would be as indefensible as scrapping the theory of biological evolution or of quantum mechanics because they are incomplete or unsatisfactory in important ways. As in the world of science, we face complex realities in the realm of human relationships that by nature seem to preclude total success. And this requires cooperative attempts to test the range of theoretical applications.

Granting that these theories, though imperfect, are extremely useful, isn't the selection of one theory ultimately arbitrary? If none of them can be proved correct, doesn't it matter little which one, if any, we choose? Although this is an understandable reaction, we should reflect on the meaning of the word *arbitrary*.

It's true that it would probably be arbitrary if a person decided that, since ethical theories generally agree on basic ideals, it doesn't matter which code is followed. But such a position would be unsound because different codes commit us to different principles. The thoughtful person recognizes these differences and chooses. Such a choice, rooted in a consideration of alternatives, cannot be arbitrary. Indeed, it's based on the best available evidence. In the words of British philosopher R. M. Hare: "To describe such ultimate decisions as arbitrary . . . would be like saying that a complete description of the universe was utterly unfounded, because no further fact could be called upon in corroboration of it. This is not how we use the words 'arbitrary' and 'unfounded.' Far from being arbitrary, such a decision would be the most well-founded of decisions, because it would be based upon a consideration of everything upon which it could possibly be founded."[28]

Finally, we should note that the fundamental worth of studying and understanding ethical thought is not to obtain definitive guides to moral conduct. Rather, the value lies in becoming aware of the moral options available to us for dealing with complex moral decisions on a personal and collective level (see Philosophy and Life 3–2). Let's try to tie together all that we've said by reflecting on this complexity.

The Complexity of Moral Decisions

To understand the complexity of moral decisions and how an understanding of normative positions can help to elucidate them, imagine a convalescent home. Janet, a twenty-two-year-old nurse, works at Sunnyview. Janet likes her work very much and hopes some day to be a physician. She particularly enjoys the elderly people she attends and considers herself more a friend than a nurse. For the most part, they feel the same about her.

Janet is particularly fond of one old gentleman, Mr. Pitman; he reminds her of her grandfather, who died only a year before after a long and painful illness. In his prime, Mr. Pitman was vigorous, but now his eighty years have hobbled and enfeebled him. He has no family and depends on welfare to pay his bills. He despises Sunnyview so much that he has tried to take his life twice. Although alert and rational, he sees no point in living. Sunnyview officials have told him that if he persists in his suicide attempts, he will be transferred to a state psychiatric hospital for the remainder of his life.

The long shadows of a winter's afternoon have just fallen across Mr. Pitman's room when we join him and Janet.

Mr. Pitman: Janet, you once said you'd do anything for me.

Janet: I would, Mr. Pitman, you know that.

Mr. Pitman: Anything?

Janet: Anything in the world.

28. *R. M. Hare.* The Language of Morals. Oxford: Clarendon Press, 1952, p. 69.

Mr. Pitman: You wouldn't fool an old man, would you?

Janet: You know better than that.

Mr. Pitman: Yes, I suppose I do. . . . Tomorrow when you come in, would you bring me a bottle of . . . sleeping pills?

Janet: Sleeping pills? You know you don't have to send out for those, Mr. Pitman. The doctor will prescribe them if you can't sleep.

Mr. Pitman: You don't understand. I have no trouble sleeping. It's waking up that's the bother.

Janet: You mean——

Mr. Pitman: I mean I wish a quick and painless death. But at the same time, I don't want you to get into any trouble on my account. So here, take this money.

Janet: I'm sorry, Mr. Pitman, I can't do that.

Mr. Pitman: You can't do it? But, Janet, I thought you were my friend.

Janet: But you can't ask me to help you——

Mr. Pitman: Die? Janet, I'm old and I'm sick. And tomorrow I'll be even older and sicker. It will never be different. Only worse. You don't wish that for me, do you?

PHILOSOPHY AND LIFE 3-2
IVF Research

Of all the futuristic applications of science, one of the most challenging to our ethics is our ability to tinker with human life outside the womb. While fascinated by experiments that hold out the promise of new life, as in the case of Louise Brown, the first test-tube baby, we recoil at the thought of a brave new world in which babies are not born but decanted.

Precipitating this concern today is *in vitro fertilization* (IVF), the process by which a human ovum or egg is removed from a woman's body and fertilized in a laboratory petri dish. Thus, life begins outside the womb, as Louise Brown began her life.

While the principles of IVF have been known for some time, federal funds for IVF research have, in effect, been forbidden since 1973. And yet, in September 1978, the government's Ethics Advisory Board, established to monitor experiments on human subjects, convened in Bethesda, Maryland. Its purpose was to consider the tough moral issues involved in IVF research and whether federal funds should be provided to support it. The two tasks are separate but related, for whether one counsels federal sponsorship depends at least in part on one's moral view of the nature of such research.

To illustrate, consider an experiment that proposes to perfect ways to repair defective genes inside human ova and sperm, and to identify immunization processes that might be activated to help the body reject cancer cells. Few would question the potential good of such research. However, moral questions arise and sides are taken over the question of how scientists will conduct this research.

Janet: No, of course I don't. But it'd be wrong for me to do what you ask.

Mr. Pitman: Why would it be wrong?

Janet: Because it goes against everything people believe is right and good. You know that, Mr. Pitman.

Mr. Pitman: No, I don't. I don't know that. All I know is there's no one in this bed suffering but me. Where are all those right and decent people? Out there, out in the streets and in the film shows and in front of television sets. They're not feeling all the pain and hurt, Janet. I am—Robert Pitman—I'm feeling it all. And the loneliness—the agony of having nobody, no family, no friends, just people like you who come to work here and poke me and prop me up. Those good and decent people you speak of—what right do they have to tell me what to do? Let them lie here awhile and then tell me that. In the meantime I say it's right, Janet, and I want you to help me.

Janet has been asked to help someone kill himself. On what basis should she decide whether to help? Her reaction that "it goes against everything people believe is right and good" doesn't satisfy Mr. Pitman; nor from the view

---

One researcher, Dr. Pierre Soupart of Vanderbilt University, has applied for a federal grant to conduct experiments in which human ova would be fertilized in the lab and allowed to develop for six days, after which the embryos will die and their cells will be examined for chromosomal or other defects attributable to artificial conception. Some authorities argue that embryos are "biologically alive" from the instant of fertilization. Thus, it would be intrinsically wrong to create, use, and then deliberately discard them. Others, in contrast, do not consider the early embryo a human subject. Consequently, they see nothing intrinsically objectionable in such an experiment.

Whether such experiments are right or wrong, and consequently whether the government should fund them, largely depends on whether the early embryo is human in the moral sense and therefore to be protected. In advising the National Institutes of Health on what government policy should be, the board must answer this question.

☐ *If you were a board member, what would your position be?*   ☐ *On what moral grounds ought the board to make its recommendations?*   ☐ *Suppose the government did ultimately subsidize experiments that you thought were immoral; would you feel morally obliged to take action in opposition?*

of morality should it, because it begs the question. Left unexplored is the reason for social disapproval. Janet's appeal is strictly to popular opinion. Popular opinion is not necessarily erroneous, but on the other hand it isn't a foolproof way to select values in ethics or in any other value area. Recall the third principle of axiological issues: We should choose our own values based on our own goals and ideals. Just as important, when we allow values to be thrust upon us, we live others' lives, not our own. This is the philosophical point of Mr. Pitman's impassioned reaction.

Ultimately society may have compelling reasons for condemning what Mr. Pitman has asked Janet to do, and thus she may be wise to abide by its standard. But without evaluating those reasons within the general paradigm of ethical theory, who can say? As an egoist, act utilitarian, or situationist would advise, Mr. Pitman implores Janet to focus on the specific circumstances of his case. Should she?

Notice that the issue here is not whether suicide is moral, although that issue no doubt enters the question. The main issue is whether a person under these circumstances should help another person end his life. Thus, it would be entirely consistent for Janet to see nothing wrong with suicide but still insist that it's wrong for her to help someone take his life. Why shouldn't she comply with Mr. Pitman's request? What's her moral justification? If she should, then again, why? By following the rest of the conversation, we can observe the subtle interplay of ethical theories that's often evident when people agonize over the right thing to do. Just as important, we can see how the abstract can quickly become disquietingly concrete, how theoretical weaknesses lead to tangible problems, and what moral options are available to those who face tough decisions.

Janet: But I can't help you, Mr. Pitman.

Mr. Pitman: Do you think it's wrong for me to take my life?

Janet: I'm not sure. But I think almost everybody would say it's wrong for me to help you.

Mr. Pitman: Now listen. If I had a family, if people were depending on me, if there were loved ones who would be deeply hurt by my action . . .

Janet: But I will be, Mr. Pitman.

Mr. Pitman: That's kind of you, my dear. But can you honestly say that your hurt will be greater than what I'm going through? What I *will* go through?

Janet: No, probably not.

The element of utilitarianism is clear in this exchange. True, suicide is not the moral issue here, but Mr. Pitman believes that the consequences of his suicide are relevant to whether it is right or wrong for Janet to help him. He is not, however, egoistic, as one might expect from his previous statements. He does not assume that only consequences to himself are at stake. In effect, he asks Janet to compare the consequences of his proposal for all concerned.

Mr. Pitman: Then why not help me?

Janet: But what if I helped everyone who asked me to do that?

Mr. Pitman: But not everyone is asking you.

Janet: Would you believe that Mrs. Kandinsky asked me the same thing last month?

Mr. Pitman: Mrs. Kandinsky. The poor soul. . . . But Mrs. Kandinsky has a family to consider.

Janet: You think that makes her suffering any less? Am I supposed to just help people without families, Mr. Pitman? Or those with families that don't love or visit them? Or maybe those with families who only visit them on Christmas and Thanksgiving?

Mr. Pitman: Why not just help those who are desperate and who beg you, like me? Is that so hard, Janet? Wouldn't that be the right thing to do?

Janet: I don't know. Do you know what Mrs. Kandinsky said to me yesterday? That she's looking forward to the spring and the birth of her grandchild. So you tell me, Mr. Pitman, what's desperation? How do you measure it?

How do you make up a rule to cover situations like these? This is what Janet is asking Mr. Pitman. She does not wish to consider the consequences of his isolated act. She wants to look at the rule that the act is following. Assuming the role of the rule utilitarian, Mr. Pitman says simply that she should aid anyone who asks and who is desperate. But precisely what does *desperate* mean? How many of us have not felt at some time desperate enough to die, only to have that feeling pass like a nightmare?

Mr. Pitman: Janet, I thought you were my friend.

Janet: But I am, Mr. Pitman. And I'll continue to be.

Mr. Pitman: Well, don't friends generally do things for each other?

Janet: Yes, but——

Mr. Pitman: Didn't you tell me just a minute ago that there wasn't anything you'd not do for me?

Janet: But that didn't include helping you hurt yourself.

Mr. Pitman: *Anything*, Janet; you said you'd do *anything* for me.

The conversation has turned; the consequences of the action are no longer the issue. Now the issue is duties that have accrued in the past, especially the duty to fidelity. Janet has made a promise to Mr. Pitman, and he is trying to hold her to it. In his eyes she is duty bound. But, she says, the promise didn't include helping him commit suicide. This raises the question of just how far promises go. Are all promises contingent on mental reservations, conscious or otherwise? When people promise to love and honor "from this day forward till death us do part," does that promise exclude "incompatibility," "irreconcilable differences," and the like, which excuse from their marriage vows more than half the people who take them? It is one thing to argue normatively that we are bound to be faithful to the promises we make; it is another to specify the nature, conditions, and limitations of a promise.

Janet: But I've made another promise, Mr. Pitman.

Mr. Pitman: What other promise?

Janet: To help you stay well and healthy. I've sworn to help you stay alive, not to help you die.

As we have previously seen, duties often conflict. Perhaps Janet does have a personal obligation to Mr. Pitman stemming from promises she has made to him. But she also has a professional obligation to him that stems from an oath that she took when becoming a nurse.

Mr. Pitman: All right, Janet. Let me ask you one thing and I'll not bother you anymore. If you don't respect my wishes, can you truly say that you acted out of love?

Janet: I don't think I understand.

Mr. Pitman: If you don't help me die with dignity, can you honestly say that you chose not to out of a genuine desire to do what's best for me?

Janet: What you're saying is that if I loved you, I'd help you commit suicide.

Mr. Pitman: I suppose I am.

Janet: I don't know, Mr. Pitman, I really don't. But let me ask you something. Can you say you truly act out of love when you ask me to help you end your life?

Mr. Pitman: I would like to think I can. . . . But I guess I don't know either.

As a last resort to enlist her aid, Mr. Pitman endorses a form of situationism. But loving concern, it seems, is much easier dealt with in the abstract than in the concrete. Who is to say that a denial of his request would not be an act of greater loving concern than an honoring of it? Indeed, if Janet thought it to be, intended it to be, by definition it apparently would be. If nothing else, however, Mr. Pitman's inquiry presses Janet to assess further the nature of her decision. It also forces Mr. Pitman to examine the moral nature of his request.

In the end we all must decide, perhaps not whether it's right to help an old man end his life or to imprison a known felon for a crime that the person didn't commit, but other issues that are pressing for us. On what basis do we make these decisions, which shape who and what we are and will be? Failing to engage and resolve these questions, we run a grave risk of leaving undeveloped a significant facet of human nature and self, the moral aspect.

Suppose that you have accepted one of the normative theories, according to which certain acts are right and others are wrong. Suppose further that Janet helps Mr. Pitman end his life. On the basis of your theoretical preference, you judge that Janet's action was wrong. But having made this judgment, you can always ask further: Should or should not Janet be held responsible for her act? In other words, you can ask whether Janet is at fault, and, therefore, should be blamed for what she did. These questions cut to a basic issue in the study of ethics: moral responsibility. The issue of moral responsibility is one with far-reaching ethical implications. So, in concluding our overview of ethics, we will briefly consider this issue.

Moral Responsibility

A good way to enlighten the issue of moral responsibility is to connect it to the concept of excusability, that is, that there are circumstances under which we excuse people for their decisions and conduct. Ethicists generally speak of four kinds of conditions under which we ordinarily excuse people, that is, hold them blameless or not morally responsible: (1) excusable ignorance of the consequences or circumstances of an act; (2) the presence of a constraint that forced the person to do the act and that was so strong that no ordinary amount of will power could overcome it; (3) the presence of circumstances beyond the person's control; and (4) the absence of either the ability or the opportunity, or both, to do the right thing in the given situation.[29]

Excusable Ignorance of Consequences. We excuse people when we don't believe they were aware of the unfavorable consequences their actions would produce or because they couldn't reasonably have been expected to know how to prevent the consequences. For example, today health professionals are cautious, or should be, about subjecting patients to x-rays because of the potential dangers of radiation exposure. Years ago, however, medical personnel were not aware of this serious potential threat. Therefore, barring cases of egregiously excessive and unnecessary x-ray exposure, we generally would not hold health professionals morally responsible for damage from x-rays administered during that time. But today we would.

Not knowing how to prevent bad consequences which are foreseen by someone may also warrant excusability. Thus, we wouldn't hold a Sunnyview patient at fault for not knowing what to do if Mr. Pitman suddenly experienced cardiac arrest. But we might blame Janet or the other health professionals at Sunnyview if they were present during the incident because, presumably, they are in a position to take corrective action, although, of course, not to guarantee the results.

Constraints. We usually excuse people when we think that they could not help what they did, that they had little or no choice in a matter. The constraint may be either external or internal. External constraint refers to outside factors or forces. When situations involve external constraints, we typically speak of

29.   *Paul Taylor.* Problems of Moral Philosophy. *2nd ed. Belmont, Ca.: Dickenson Publishing Company, 1972, p. 277.*

people acting against their wills. A bank teller who at gunpoint turns over the bank's money to a robber is acting against his or her will. As a result, we would not condemn such behavior or blame the teller, for the act was done under coercion. In contrast, we would certainly find fault with the teller who, of his or her own free will, helped the robber, perhaps by telling the person beforehand the best time to rob the bank.

In the second form of constraint, internal, the compelling element comes from inside rather than from someone else. We speak of people who act in certain ways because they feel an overwhelming inner urge, desire, craving, or impulse to do so. Accordingly, we normally would not hold a kleptomaniac morally accountable for shoplifting a watch from a jewelry shop, or patients responsible for damage they cause during periods of postoperative psychosis. In contrast, we would surely blame the robber who carefully and coolly orchestrated the robbery of the jewelry shop, while feeling no inner drive to carry out the plan. By the same token, we would blame patients who, fully aware of what they were doing, that is, acting of their own free will, throw destructive and disruptive temper tantrums.

Uncontrollable Circumstances. When, in our estimation, the circumstances of an act were beyond the person's control, we generally excuse the behavior. There are many circumstantial excuses that we readily accept as legitimate. Illnesses, accidents, unexpected duties are typical cases. Thus, we would not hold Janet responsible for arriving late for her hospital shift if, through no fault of her own, she was involved in an automobile accident. Were we to learn, however, that the accident was caused by Janet's reckless driving, we likely would hold her accountable for her tardiness.

Lack of Alternatives. Ordinarily we excuse actions when we think that people lacked either the ability or the opportunity to do the right act. If a man can't swim, we wouldn't blame him for not jumping into a pool and trying to save a drowning child (although we would hold him responsible for not summoning aid or not throwing the child a life preserver). Similarly, if the man could swim, but failed to save the child because he saw him only when it was too late, he lacked the opportunity to save the child. Therefore, we would not consider him morally responsible.

In sketching these four conditions, philosophy professor Paul Taylor points out that there are two important points to realize. First, insofar as any actual situation satisfies one or more of these conditions, it can be sharply contrasted with a situation of the opposite kind in which these conditions are not met. Second, situations of both kinds do occur in everyday life.

> Thus, just as there are cases where a person could not have foreseen the harmful consequences of his act, there are other cases where a person does foresee such consequences and still chooses to do the act. (A man who intends to murder someone not only foresees that his victim will die but wants this to happen.) Just as there are acts done under the coercion of another person, so there are acts done when no such external constraint is present. A man who fires a shotgun at the house of a civil-rights worker in the South may have decided to do it entirely by himself and may have acted under no external compulsion. It is possible, indeed, to act in opposition to a considerable amount of external constraint.

Whenever a person commits a crime he does so in spite of, rather than because of, such external constraints as threat of punishment, fear of the police, and general social disapproval. Again, consider the case in which an internal urge or drive compels a person to act against his own will. This kind of case is to be contrasted with that of a person freely choosing to do something after carefully deliberating about it. A man might be in full control of himself as he works out a plan to embezzle funds, and feel under no compulsion as he calmly carries out his plan. In connection with the third kind of situation, just as we are sometimes prevented from doing what we ought to do by circumstances beyond our control, there are other cases where we don't do what we ought simply because we don't want to. We sometimes try to avoid our obligations when we find them onerous. Finally, although in a given situation we may lack the ability or the opportunity to do what would be right, just as often we have the capacity and the opportunity to do any number of alternatives open to our choice and yet we knowingly choose to do what is wrong. For example, the man who does not report accurately his income in order to avoid paying a tax certainly has the ability and opportunity to make out an accurate report, and knows that this would be the right thing for him to do.[30]

Thus, in everyday life there are occasions when we excuse people and occasions when we hold them responsible for their acts.

The preceding observations about moral responsibility probably seem commonsensical enough. And they remain so, until the theory of determinism, or universal causation, is applied to human choice and conduct. Then things tend to grow murky.

Determinism

As we saw in Chapter 2, determinism is the theory that everything in the universe is totally ruled by causal laws. Accordingly, every event has a prior condition, and all events are at least theoretically predictable if all the prior conditions are known. The principle of determinism is widely used by the sciences of psychology, sociology, and anthropology in accounting for human behavior. Without doubt, these sciences have gone far in helping us understand why we act, feel, and choose as we do. And doubtless as these sciences continue to develop, our knowledge about human feelings, motives, and beliefs will be further enriched. Along with such knowledge probably will develop an ability to give causal explanations about human decisions and conduct. As a result, many people are beginning to think of humans as they think about animals or machines: They take the same scientific view toward all of them. In so doing, they view behavior not as chance events occurring haphazardly or in unpredictable ways, but rather as events that happen in an orderly way. This order, they say, is discovered when scientists are able to explain the events in terms of causal laws.

What has determinism to do with the conditions for excusability and moral responsibility? Many believe that moral responsibility is incompatible with determinism. They claim that in cases where the four types of conditions of ex-

30. *Paul Taylor.* Problems of Moral Philosophy, *pp. 279–280.*

cusability do not hold, people may *appear* to be under no constraints; and they may *appear* to have the ability and opportunity to choose any number of alternatives and to act on them. But, the argument goes, these appearances are mere illusions. If choices and actions are causally determined, then, given the causal laws operating in the situation of choice, only one course of action can possibly occur: the one which will be the effect of the previous causes that are occurring in the situation. In other words, the act that a person ultimately chooses to do is inevitable, since there was a set of events which, of itself, was sufficient for producing the choice; and, because that sufficient condition was present, the choice of that act had to occur. In brief, the person could not have acted other than he or she did. If this explanation is so, if determinism operates in the realm of human decision and conduct, then determinism appears to be incompatible with freedom and responsibility in an ethical sense.

How, then, is the so-called moral self to be understood? In response to the assertion that moral responsibility is not possible in a strictly deterministic universe, four main positions emerge: hard determinism, indeterminism, soft determinism, and self-determinism.

Hard Determinism. **Hard determinism** is based on the rigid causality apparent in the physical universe. Freedom is incompatible with this view, for to admit freedom is to admit an element of unpredictableness in the universe. What, then, is "free choice"? According to hard determinists, free choice amounts to little more than human ignorance. We think we are free merely because we cannot predict our own or others' future behavior. While we cannot help engaging in the process of deliberation, the choice we make is determined by whichever set of motives is strongest. To insist that we are free because we could have acted otherwise is to speak so much gibberish. After all, say hard determinists, there could never be any possible proof that we could have acted otherwise since the proof is precisely what never did occur, and never will occur. Does this mean, then, that criminals, say, are not morally responsible for what they do? Precisely. According to hard determinists, a life of crime is predetermined by genetic inheritance and environment. Neither a criminal, nor Janet, nor Mr. Pitman, nor any of us is responsible in an ethical sense for what we do. By this account, it is not so much false to say that individuals are responsible for their own characters, decisions, and actions; rather it is meaningless.

Indeterminism. The opposite of hard determinism is **indeterminism,** the view that humans are exceptions to the rigid causation that occurs in nature. Like determinists, indeterminists agree that the laws of causality may apply to everything else in nature. But indeterminists make of humans an exception to these causal laws. Causal laws do not apply to our free choices. How are our choices, then, to be explained? According to indeterminists, there are no causes for our free choices; our free acts are uncaused events that simply happen without having been brought about by anything. Thus, human beings are not merely personalities entirely explainable in empirical terms, as hard determinism holds. Rather, humans are also moral agents. When humans are confronted by a choice between right and wrong, they consider themselves to be free agents with a moral self. It is the person's moral self that makes the choice and can accordingly be held accountable.

Soft Determinism. Hard determinism and indeterminism share an assumption: Determinism is incompatible with moral responsibility. Confronted with a choice between determinism and no responsibility, or responsibility but no determinism, hard determinists choose determinism; indeterminists choose responsibility. In contrast, **soft determinists** attempt to reconcile freedom and responsibility with determinism. They do this by limiting both concepts to the point where their evident incompatibility vanishes.

Soft determinists concede that in the sense that humans cannot choose to act against their individual characters, they are determined. But in the sense that humans are often free from outside compulsion and can thus conduct themselves unhampered in doing what they choose, they are free agents. Thus, while Janet's character in part is the product of outside forces, she is not wholly shaped by them. On the contrary, she has helped shape her own character by her previous personal choices. She has helped make herself what she is.

Given that Janet is responsible for her individual character, she is responsible for the choices she makes according to her character. Yes, every act is caused, but not by something outside her. It is caused by the kind of being she has become by reason of her previous personal choices. In this way, soft determinists claim that they have avoided the mistake of indeterminists, who admit of causeless acts; and that of hard determinists, who consider responsibility a fiction.

While soft determinism appears to wed freedom and moral responsibility with determinism, it leaves some key questions unanswered. First, if Janet, or any of us, is not free to act against her individual character, doesn't this mean that she is always subject to inner constraints? If she is, then the freedom of soft determinism seems pointless. Second, if her character, which determines whether or not she will help Mr. Pitman end his life, has been molded by her own previous free choices, doesn't it follow that each of her free choices, in turn, was determined by that state of her own character at that previous moment, and so on back to childhood when deliberate free choice was impossible? Given this analysis, what kind of freedom does Janet or any of us have? In short, critics say that in trying to reconcile moral freedom and responsibility with determinism, soft determinists have blurred what is worthwhile in each.

Self-Determinism. **Self-determinism** accepts the doctrine of determinism that nothing can happen without a cause. It follows that our free acts are caused acts. In the case of human decisions and conduct, humans themselves are the cause of the act. When individuals choose, their choices are not made by something else outside or inside the person, but are the acts of the very person. Indeed, the very meaning of *person,* say self-determinists, implies someone who makes his or her own choices. Thus, individuals cause their own acts. While it is true that we are strongly influenced by motives and must deliberate between them, in the final analysis we are not necessitated by them either way. In the end we choose for ourselves.

Critics like hard determinists charge that self-determinists have evaded the issue. As we saw, hard determinists say that no acts are free acts. They insist that it would be impossible to prove that a person could have acted otherwise than he or she did (that is, freely), because the very proof is an act which did not occur and cannot occur. Self-determinists, they say, do nothing to meet this objection.

In reply, the self-determinist might say that this objection only holds if one assumes that all causes necessarily produce only one determined effect. But in the realm of human decisions and conduct, say self-determinists, individuals function as free agents: They can produce any one of several alternative effects on the basis of a choice. Critics object that this is having it both ways: endorsing the doctrine of determinism, while at the same time rejecting, or at least warping it.

It's apparent that none of these viewpoints presents an airtight case. Because it denies freedom and moral responsibility, hard determinism does not accord with how we generally experience our own actions. Indeterminism, in proposing the notion of uncaused acts, seemingly preserves freedom and responsibility at the expense of scientific respectability. Soft determinism, which tries to reconcile freedom and responsibility with determinism, apparently does away with something worthwhile in each. And self-determinism may end up warping the doctrine of determinism in an attempt to preserve freedom and responsibility.

The controversy about freedom and determinism ultimately is a metaphysical one: It cuts to fundamental assumptions about reality and being. At the same time, it has profound implications for ethics, because the position one chooses in the controversy affects one's idea of moral responsibility, among other things.

Summary and Conclusions

We opened this chapter by observing that values, like so many other things today, are changing. Axiology, the study of values, includes debates about whether value judgments express knowledge or feeling, whether values are subjective or objective, and what is of value. One important value area is ethics. Normative ethics is the search for principles of good conduct. Broadly speaking, normative ethics can be divided into the consequentialist and nonconsequentialist schools. The consequentialist school, in turn, can be subdivided into egoism, act utilitarianism and rule utilitarianism, and situationism; the nonconsequentialist school into single- and multiple-rule nonconsequentialism: divine command, Kant's categorical imperative, and Ross's prima facie duties. In addition, Buddhism offers a rich moral legacy that Westerners find increasingly appealing.

Whether or not we choose to acknowledge them as such, the moral values we hold and the obligations we feel constitute expressions of who we are, how we see things, and how we wish to be seen by others. In choosing a moral life-style, we're really defining a large part of our selves. Yet, the complexity of moral decision making persists; the choices remain murky. The question that continues to nag us is: What moral life-style should I adopt to live the fullest, most rewarding life I can?

As stated throughout this chapter, there is no certain answer. The nature of moral decision making disallows scientific assurance. Nevertheless, we can garner factors from our discussion that seem appropriate to a personal morality. First, any moral code you follow must be your own, not in the sense that you alone follow it, but in the sense that you have arrived at it through the powers of your reason and the reflection upon your experience. Granted, we cannot fully escape our social, cultural, and religious backgrounds; nor would we want to. Nevertheless, if our morality is to be an expression of self, we must carefully reflect on the values we have inherited, weighing their merits and liabilities in the light of our own lives, times, and circumstances. Such reflection places heavy emphasis on self-growth, especially on increasing our knowledge and awareness of self and the world and on being willing to adjust our moral views as relevant new discoveries arise. It also recognizes the dynamic, experimental value of morality.

The second factor appropriate to a personal morality is related to the first. It stems from Immanuel Kant's concept of a good will. As just suggested, to make moral decisions primarily on the basis of social or institutional influence is to surrender what most people consider a uniquely human quality: the individual capacity to make moral decisions. These outside forces should not be our primary reasons for acting morally. For the mature and thoughtful person, right intention or good will is a necessary ingredient of the true moral act. This ingredient introduces the elements of motive, sincerity, and love. It is true that these are hazy concepts, but they frequently clear up in context. For example, the motives of the person who gives to charity primarily for the sake of a tax write-off are different from those of the person who gives to improve the conditions of the less fortunate; the intention of the person who flatters to ingratiate is different from that of the person who speaks the truth for its own sake. The teachings of ethicists and great moral leaders have stated or implied the importance of right intention, good will, or love in the moral act.

But these two subjective elements of a personal moral code, moral self-determination and right intention, are insufficient to ensure right action. After all, we may be morally self-determining and well intentioned but do something heinous. The third element, therefore, is an objective one, involving a consideration of the results or consequences of our actions. It seems that consequences must be a factor in any moral stance, for to be indifferent to the consequences of our actions is to act irresponsibly—that is, without moral regard. As we have seen, however, determining the consequences of an action is often difficult. It requires much evidence, analysis, and reflection. Even then we cannot be certain. But without such an examination, our action will not be in the highest sense moral.

No doubt there are other factors that you might wish to introduce. But these three—self-determination, right intention, and consideration of consequences—are the building blocks of a personal moral code.

Section Exercises

Egoism

1. Some people argue that everyone is ultimately an ethical egoist. What do

they mean by this? Do you agree? Would this prove that egoism is the basis for all ethics?

2. What are the connotations of the word *egoism*? Are these connotations compatible with what you know about ethical egoism?

3. With which concepts of knowledge and reality do you think ethical egoism is compatible?

4. How prevalent do you think ethical egoism is in contemporary society?

Utilitarianism

Below are four ethical problems. How would an act utilitarian solution differ from a rule utilitarian solution in each case?

1. An aide is conferring with the president of the United States:

    Mr. President, it's imperative that you win the upcoming election. If you don't, subversives will take over the government. This could spell the end of our government as we know it. We could present the public with all the facts and let them decide, but that would only alarm and panic them. There's another way, and that is to use the enormous financial connections of this administration to manipulate and mold public opinion. This, it's true, will necessitate illegal election contributions, misrepresentation of facts, and considerable fancy footwork in the campaign. But it's an immediate, practical, and judicious solution in the best interests of the nation.

2. The daughter of a very rich and important public figure has been kidnapped. The kidnappers threaten to murder the young woman unless her father delivers $250,000 in ransom money. Authorities have told him that if he does so he'll only be encouraging future terrorist activities that will invariably involve more people, more suffering, and more deaths.

3. Taxpayer Smith decides that there are plenty of things he dislikes about the way the U.S. government is run: exorbitant defense spending, collusion between business and government, mismanaged funds, and so on. As a result, he is contemplating not paying his income taxes.

4. Jones and Brown are debating whether a person has a moral obligation to obey all laws. Jones claims that deliberately breaking a law is immoral. Brown denies this.

Situation Ethics

1. What would situationists say in the preceding cases? How would they resolve the dilemmas?

Divine Command Theory

1. Reconsider the four preceding situations from the viewpoint of a divine command theorist. What decisions and actions do you think are called for? Would the judgments differ from the act utilitarian's? The rule utilitarian's?

Kant's Categorical Imperative

1. Can the categorical imperative be applied toward resolving the four situations described previously? Illustrate.

2. Would it be possible or desirable to universalize the following maxims?

    a. "Never work unless you absolutely must."

    b. "Always do your own thing unless it hurts somebody else."

    c. "Give nothing and expect nothing in return."

    d. "Sell all you have and give to the poor."

    e. "Let your conscience be your guide."

    f. "Always stick by your friends."

    g. "Never discriminate against someone on the basis of race, religion, color, or sex."

    h. "Never punish a child physically."

    i. "Without prior approval, you should never take something that doesn't belong to you."

Ross's Prima Facie Duties

1. Reexamine the four situations described previously. What duties may be involved? Would the duty ethicist's perspective prescribe obligations that differ from the act utilitarian's? The rule utilitarian's?

2. In the play *The Victors*, Jean-Paul Sartre portrays six French Resistance fighters captured and tortured by the Nazis, who wish to extract vital troop movement information from them. Just before his painful interrogation, one of the prisoners, fifteen-year-old François, informs his fellow cellmates that he'll reveal all rather than be tortured as they have been. His cellmates have a choice: Silence him, or let him speak and thus imperil the lives of sixty French soldiers. Lucy, the boy's sister, is among the prisoners. Seeing herself bound by fidelity to the other troops, she votes to kill François. From the viewpoint of a prima facie duty theorist, would you say she acted wrongly? Does she have a conflicting duty because she's the boy's sister? One of the other prisoners ultimately strangles François. Did he act wrongly?

Buddhist Ethics

1. Apply each of Buddhism's five precepts to appropriate aspects of your life. What changes would they necessitate?

2. What weaknesses, if any, do you detect in Buddhist ethics?

3. What social changes can you think of that an implementation of Buddhist ethics might bring about? (For example, how would it alter advertising or marketing generally? What impact would it have on television, if any?)

Antigone

Jean Anouilh

What must one do when faced with a decision between advancing the maximum good and doing what one believes is right? Undoubtedly among the toughest moral choices are those that pit desirable consequences against personal principles. Such is the theme of French playwright Jean Anouilh's Antigone.

The play, adapted from the original by the great Greek tragedian Sophocles, involves a clash of wills between Creon, king of Thebes, and his niece Antigone concerning the burial of her brother and his nephew, Polynices. Because Polynices led a revolt against his own brother Eteocles, thus igniting a civil war in which the two brothers killed each other, Creon has decreed Polynices an enemy of the state and a traitor. Specifically, he has ordered that Polynices not be given a proper burial as the ultimate censure and a warning to all would-be revolutionaries. Antigone, however, has other ideas. She insists that her brother be given a proper burial, as Eteocles has received.

In the selection below, Antigone has been brought before Creon by guards who have caught her throwing dirt on Polynices' body. Notice that in the confrontation between uncle and niece, both operate from essentially unselfish positions. Creon, on the one hand, is committed to advancing the greatest social good. Antigone, on the other hand, is basically moved by principles of love, decency, justice, and other aspects of duty. In the end, Creon and Antigone, while moved by nonegoistic impulses, nevertheless stand unreconciled, testimony to the apparently unbridgeable gap between two points on a moral continuum: the one motivated by social consequences, the other by nonconsequentialist duties.

Creon: Why did you try to bury your brother?

Antigone: I owed it to him.

Creon: I had forbidden it.

Antigone: I owed it to him. Those who are not buried wander eternally and find no rest. If my brother were alive, and he came home weary after a long day's hunting, I should kneel down and unlace his boots, I should fetch him food and drink, I should see that his bed was ready for him. Polynices is home from the hunt. I owe it to him to unlock the house of the dead in which my father and my mother are waiting to welcome him. Polynices has earned his rest.

Creon: Polynices was a rebel and a traitor, and you know it.

Antigone: He was my brother.

Creon: You heard my edict. It was proclaimed throughout Thebes. You read my edict. It was posted up on the city walls.

Antigone: Of course I did.

Creon: You knew the punishment I decreed for any person who attempted to give him burial.

Antigone: Yes, I knew the punishment.

Creon: Did you by any chance act on the assumption that a daughter of Oedipus, a daughter of Oedipus' stubborn pride, was above the law?

Antigone: No, I did not act on that assumption.

Creon: Because if you had acted on that assumption, Antigone, you would have been deeply wrong. Nobody has a more sacred obligation to obey the law than those who make the law. You are a daughter of lawmakers, a daughter of kings, Antigone. You must observe the law.

Antigone: Had I been a scullery maid washing my dishes when that law was read aloud to me, I should have scrubbed the greasy water from my arms and gone out in my apron to bury my brother.

Creon: What nonsense! If you had been a scullery maid, there would have been no doubt in your mind about the seriousness of that edict. You would have known that it meant death; and you would have been satisfied to weep for your brother in your kitchen. But

From Antigone *by Jean Anouilh, adapted and translated by Lewis Galantiere. Copyright 1946 by Random House, Inc., and renewed 1974 by Lewis Galantiere. Reprinted by permission of Random House, Inc.*

you! You thought that because you come of the royal line, because you were my niece and were going to marry my son, I shouldn't dare have you killed.

Antigone: You are mistaken. Quite the contrary. I never doubted for an instant that you would have me put to death.

(A pause, as Creon *stares fixedly at her)*

Creon: The pride of Oedipus! Oedipus and his headstrong pride all over again. I can see your father in you—and I believe you. Of course you thought that I should have you killed! Proud as you are, it seemed to you a natural climax in your existence. Your father was like that. For him as for you human happiness was meaningless; and mere human misery was not enough to satisfy his passion for torment. *(He sits on a stool behind the table)* You come of people for whom the human vestment is a kind of strait jacket: it cracks at the seams. You spend your lives wriggling to get out of it. Nothing less than a cozy tea party with death and destiny will quench your thirst. The happiest hour of your father's life came when he listened greedily to the story of how, unknown to himself, he had killed his own father and dishonored the bed of his own mother. Drop by drop, word by word, he drank in the dark story that the gods had destined him, first to live and then to hear. How avidly men and women drink the brew of such a tale when their names are Oedipus—and Antigone! And it is so simple, afterward, to do what your father did, to put out one's eyes and take one's daughter begging on the highways.

Let me tell you, Antigone: those days are over for Thebes. Thebes has a right to a king without a past. My name, thank God, is only Creon. I stand here with both feet firm on the ground; with both hands in my pockets; and I have decided that so long as I am king—being less ambitious than your father was—I shall merely devote myself to introducing a little order into this absurd kingdom; if that is possible.

Don't think that being a king seems to me romantic. It is my trade; a trade a man has to work at every day; and like every other trade,

it isn't all beer and skittles. But since it is my trade, I take it seriously. And if, tomorrow, some wild and bearded messenger walks in from some wild and distant valley—which is what happened to your dad—and tells me that he's not quite sure who my parents were, but thinks that my wife Eurydice is actually my mother, I shall ask him to do me the kindness to go back where he came from; and I shan't let a little matter like that persuade me to order my wife to take a blood test and the police to let me know whether or not my birth certificate was forged. Kings, my girl, have other things to do than to surrender themselves to their private feelings. *(He looks at her and smiles)* Hand *you* over to be killed! *(He rises, moves to end of table and sits on the top of table)* I have other plans for you. You're going to marry Haemon; and I want you to fatten up a bit so that you can give him a sturdy boy. Let me assure you that Thebes needs that boy a good deal more than it needs your death. You will go to your room, now, and do as you have been told; and you won't say a word about this to anybody. Don't fret about the guards: I'll see that their mouths are shut. And don't annihilate me with those eyes. I know that you think I am a brute, and I'm sure you must consider me very prosaic. But the fact is, I have always been fond of you, stubborn though you always were. Don't forget that the first doll you ever had came from me. *(A pause. Antigone says nothing, rises and crosses slowly below the table toward the arch. Creon turns and watches her; then)* Where are you going?

Antigone (Stops downstage. Without any show of rebellion): You know very well where I am going.

Creon (After a pause): What sort of game are you playing?

Antigone: I am not playing games.

Creon: Antigone, do you realize that if, apart from those three guards, a single soul finds out what you have tried to do, it will be impossible for me to avoid putting you to death? There is still a chance that I can save you; but only if you keep this to yourself and give up your crazy purpose. Five minutes more, and it will be too late. You understand that?

Antigone: I must go and bury my brother. Those men uncovered him.

Creon: What good will it do? You know that there are other men standing guard over Polynices. And even if you did cover him over with earth again, the earth would again be removed.

Antigone: I know all that. I know it. But that much, at least, I can do. And what a person can do, a person ought to do.

(Pause)

Creon: Tell me, Antigone, do you believe all that flummery about religious burial? Do you really believe that a so-called shade of your brother is condemned to wander forever homeless if a little earth is not flung on his corpse to the accompaniment of some priestly abracadabra? Have you ever listened to the priests of Thebes when they were mumbling their formula? Have you ever watched those dreary bureaucrats while they were preparing the dead for burial—skipping half the gestures required by the ritual, swallowing half their words, hustling the dead into their graves out of fear that they might be late for lunch?

Antigone: Yes, I have seen all that.

Creon: And did you never say to yourself as you watched them, that if someone you really loved lay dead under the shuffling, mumbling ministrations of the priests, you would scream aloud and beg the priests to leave the dead in peace?

Antigone: Yes, I've thought all that.

Creon: And you still insist upon being put to death—merely because I refuse to let your brother go out with that grotesque passport; because I refuse his body the wretched consolation of that mass-production jibber-jabber, which you would have been the first to be embarrassed by if I had allowed it. The whole thing is absurd!

Antigone: Yes, it's absurd.

Creon: Then why, Antigone, why? For whose sake? For the sake of them that believe in it? To raise them against me?

Antigone: No.

Creon: For whom then if not for them and not for Polynices either?

Antigone: For nobody. For myself.

(A pause as they stand looking at one another)

Creon: You must want very much to die. You look like a trapped animal.

Antigone: Stop feeling sorry for me. Do as I do. Do your job. But if you are a human being, do it quickly. That is all I ask of you. I'm not going to be able to hold out forever.

Creon (Takes a step toward her):   I want to save you, Antigone.

Antigone: You are the king, and you are all-powerful. But that you cannot do.

Creon: You think not?

Antigone: Neither save me nor stop me.

Creon: Prideful Antigone! Little Oedipus!

Antigone: Only this can you do: have me put to death.

Creon: Have you tortured, perhaps?

Antigone: Why would you do that? To see me cry? To hear me beg for mercy? Or swear whatever you wish, and then begin over again?

(A pause)

Creon: You listen to me. You have cast me for the villain in this little play of yours, and yourself for the heroine. And you know it, you damned little mischiefmaker! But don't you drive me too far! If I were one of your preposterous little tyrants that Greece is full of, you would be lying in a ditch this minute with your tongue pulled out and your body drawn and quartered. But you can see something in my face that makes me hesitate to send for the guards and turn you over to them. Instead, I let you go on arguing; and you taunt me, you take the offensive. *(He grasps her left wrist)* What are you driving at, you she-devil?

Antigone: Let me go. You are hurting my arm.

Creon (Gripping her tighter):   I will not let you go.

Antigone (Moans):   Oh!

Creon: I was a fool to waste words. I should have done this from the beginning. *(He looks at her)* I may be your uncle—but we are not a particularly affectionate family. Are we, eh? *(Through his teeth, as he twists)* Are we? (Creon *propels* Antigone *round below him to his side)* **What fun for you, eh? To be able to spit in the face of a king who has all the power in the world; a man who has done his own killing in his day; who has killed people just as pitiable as you are—and who is still soft enough to go to all this trouble in order to keep you from being killed.**

(A pause)

Antigone: Now you are squeezing my arm too tightly. It doesn't hurt any more.

(Creon stares at her, then drops her arm)

Creon: I shall save you yet. *(He goes below the table to the chair at end of table, takes off his coat and places it on the chair)* God knows, I have things enough to do today without wasting my time on an insect like you. There's plenty to do, I assure you, when you've just put down a revolution. But urgent things can wait. I am not going to let politics be the cause of your death. For it is a fact that this whole business is nothing but politics: the mournful shade of Polynices, the decomposing corpse, the sentimental weeping and the hysteria that you mistake for heroism—nothing but politics.

Look here. I may not be soft, but I'm fastidious. I like things clean, ship-shape, well scrubbed. Don't think that I am not just as offended as you are by the thought of that meat rotting in the sun. In the evening, when the breeze comes in off the sea, you can smell it in the palace, and it nauseates me. But I refuse even to shut my window. It's vile; and I can tell you what I wouldn't tell anybody else: it's stupid, monstrously stupid. But the people of Thebes have got to have their noses rubbed into it a little longer. My God! If it was up to me, I should have had them bury your brother long ago as a mere matter of public hygiene. I admit that what I am doing is childish. But if the featherheaded rabble I govern are to understand what's what, that stench has got to fill the town for a month!

Antigone (Turns to him): You are a loathsome man!

Creon: I agree. My trade forces me to be. We could argue whether I ought or ought not to follow my trade; but once I take on the job, I must do it properly.

Antigone: Why do you do it at all?

Creon: My dear, I woke up one morning and found myself King of Thebes. God knows, there were other things I loved in life more than power.

Antigone: Then you should have said no.

Creon: Yes, I could have done that. Only, I felt that it would have been cowardly. I should have been like a workman who turns down a job that has to be done. So I said yes.

Antigone: So much the worse for you, then. I didn't say yes. I can say no to anything I think vile, and I don't have to count the cost. But because you said yes, all that you can do, for all your crown and your trappings, and your guards—all that you can do is to have me killed.

Creon: Listen to me.

Antigone: If I want to. I don't have to listen to you if I don't want to. You've said your *yes.* There is nothing more you can tell me that I don't know. You stand there, drinking in my words. *(She moves behind chair)* Why is it that you don't call your guards? I'll tell you why. You want to hear me out to the end; that's why.

Creon: You amuse me.

Antigone: Oh, no, I don't. I frighten you. That is why you talk about saving me. Everything would be so much easier if you had a docile, tongue-tied little Antigone living in the palace. I'll tell you something, Uncle Creon: I'll give you back one of your own words. You are too fastidious to make a good tyrant. But you are going to have to put me to death today, and you know it. And that's what frightens you. God! Is there anything uglier than a frightened man!

Creon: Very well. I am afraid, then. Does that satisfy you? I am afraid that if you insist upon it, I shall have to have you killed. And I don't want to.

Antigone: I don't have to do things that I think are wrong. If it comes to that, you didn't really want to leave my brother's body unburied, did you? Say it! Admit that you didn't.

Creon: I have said it already.

Antigone: But you did it just the same. And

now, though you don't want to do it, you are going to have me killed. And you call that being a king!

Creon: Yes, I call that being a king.

Antigone: Poor Creon! My nails are broken, my fingers are bleeding, my arms are covered with the welts left by the paws of your guards—but I am a queen!

Creon: Then why not have pity on me, and live? Isn't your brother's corpse, rotting there under my windows, payment enough for peace and order in Thebes? My son loves you. Don't make me add your life to the payment. I've paid enough.

Antigone: No, Creon! You said yes, and made yourself king. Now you will never stop paying.

Creon: But God in Heaven! Won't you try to understand me! I'm trying hard enough to understand you! There had to be one man who said yes. Somebody had to agree to captain the ship. She had sprung a hundred leaks; she was loaded to the water-line with crime, ignorance, poverty. The wheel was swinging with the wind. The crew refused to work and were looting the cargo. The officers were building a raft, ready to slip overboard and desert the ship. The mast was splitting, the wind was howling, the sails were beginning to rip. Every man jack on board was about to drown—and only because the only thing they thought of was their own skins and their cheap little day-to-day traffic. Was that a time, do you think, for playing with words like yes and no? Was that a time for a man to be weighing the pros and cons, wondering if he wasn't going to pay too dearly later on; if he wasn't going to lose his life, or his family, or his touch with other men? You grab the wheel, you right the ship in the face of a mountain of water. You shout an order, and if one man refuses to obey, you shoot straight into the mob. Into the mob, I say! The beast as nameless as the wave that crashes down upon your deck; as nameless as the whipping wind. The thing that drops when you shoot may be someone who poured you a drink the night before; but it has no name. And you, braced at the wheel, you have no name, either. Nothing has a

name—except the ship, and the storm. (*A pause as he looks at her*) Now do you understand?

Antigone: I am not here to understand. That's all very well for you. I am here to say no to you, and die.

Creon: It is easy to say no.

Antigone: Not always.

Creon: It is easy to say no. To say yes, you have to sweat and roll up your sleeves and plunge both hands into life up to the elbows. It is easy to say no, even if saying no means death. All you have to do is to sit still and wait. Wait to go on living; wait to be killed. That is the coward's part. *No* is one of your man-made words. Can you imagine a world in which trees say *no* to the sap? In which beasts say *no* to hunger or to propagation? Animals are good, simple, tough. They move in droves, nudging one another onward, all traveling the same road. Some of them keel over; but the rest go on; and no matter how many may fall by the wayside, there are always those few left which go on bringing their young into the world, traveling the same road with the same obstinate will, unchanged from those who went before.

Antigone: Animals, eh, Creon! What a king you could be if only men were animals!

(*A pause.* Creon *turns and looks at her*)

Creon: You despise me, don't you? (Antigone *is silent.* Creon *goes on, as if to himself*) Strange. Again and again, I have imagined myself holding this conversation with a pale young man I have never seen in the flesh. He would have come to assassinate me, and would have failed. I would be trying to find out from him why he wanted to kill me. But with all my logic and all my powers of debate, the only thing I could get out of him would be that he despised me. Who would have thought that the white-faced boy would turn out to be you? And that the debate would arise out of something so meaningless as the burial of your brother?

Antigone (Repeats contemptuously): Meaningless!

Creon (Earnestly, almost desperately): And yet, you must hear me out. My part is not an heroic one, but I shall play my part. I shall have you put to death. Only, before I do, I want to make one last appeal. I want to be sure that you know what you are doing as well as I know what I am doing. Antigone, do you know what you are dying for? Do you know the sordid story to which you are going to sign your name in blood, for all time to come?

Antigone: What story?

Creon: The story of Eteocles and Polynices, the story of your brothers. You think you know it, but you don't. Nobody in Thebes knows that story but me. And it seems to me, this afternoon, that you have a right to know it too. *(A pause as* Antigone *moves to chair and sits)* It's not a pretty story. *(He turns, gets a stool from behind the table and places it between the table and the chair)* You'll see. *(He looks at her for a moment)* Tell me, first. What do you remember about your brothers? They were older than you, so they must have looked down on you. And I imagine that they tormented you—pulled your pigtails, broke your dolls, whispered secrets to each other to put you in a rage.

Antigone: They were big and I was little.

Creon: And later on, when they came home wearing evening clothes, smoking cigarettes, they would have nothing to do with you; and you thought they were wonderful.

Antigone: They were boys and I was a girl.

Creon: You didn't know why, exactly, but you knew that they were making your mother unhappy. You saw her in tears over them; and your father would fly into a rage because of them. You heard them come in, slamming doors, laughing noisily in the corridors—insolent, spineless, unruly, smelling of drink.

Antigone (Staring outward): Once, it was very early and we had just got up. I saw them coming home, and hid behind a door. Polynices was very pale and his eyes were shining. He was so handsome in his evening clothes. He saw me, and said: "Here, this is for you"; and he gave me a big paper flower that he had brought home from his night out.

Creon: And of course you still have that flower. Last night, before you crept out, you opened a drawer and looked at it for a time, to give yourself courage.

Antigone: Who told you so?

Creon: Poor Antigone! With her night-club flower. Do you know what your brother was?

Antigone: Whatever he was, I know that you will say vile things about him.

Creon: A cheap, idiotic bounder, that is what he was. A cruel, vicious little voluptuary. A little beast with just wit enough to drive a car faster and throw more money away than any of his pals. I was with your father one day when Polynices, having lost a lot of money gambling, asked him to settle the debt; and when your father refused, the boy raised his hand against him and called him a vile name.

Antigone: That's a lie!

Creon: He struck your father in the face with his fist. It was pitiful. Your father sat at his desk with his head in his hands. His nose was bleeding. He was weeping with anguish. And in a corner of your father's study, Polynices stood sneering and lighting a cigarette.

Antigone: That's a lie.

(A pause)

Creon: When did you last see Polynices alive? When you were twelve years old. *That's* true, isn't it?

Antigone: Yes, that's true.

Creon: Now you know why. Oedipus was too chicken-hearted to have the boy locked up. Polynices was allowed to go off and join the Argive army. And as soon as he reached Argos, the attempts upon your father's life began—upon the life of an old man who couldn't make up his mind to die, couldn't bear to be parted from his kingship. One after another, men slipped into Thebes from Argos for the purpose of assassinating him, and every killer we caught always ended by confessing who had put him up to it, who had paid him to try it. And it wasn't only Polynices. That is really what I am trying to tell you. I want you to know what went on in the back room, in the kitchen of politics; I want you to know what took place in the wings of this drama in which you are burning to play a part.

Yesterday, I gave Eteocles a State funeral, with pomp and honors. Today, Eteocles is a saint and a hero in the eyes of all Thebes. The whole city turned out to bury him. The schoolchildren emptied their savings boxes to buy wreaths for him. Old men, orating in quavering, hypocritical voices, glorified the virtues of the great-hearted brother, the devoted son, the loyal prince. I made a speech myself; and every temple priest was present with an appropriate show of sorrow and solemnity in his stupid face. And military honors were accorded the dead hero.

Well, what else could I have done? People had taken sides in the civil war. Both sides couldn't be wrong; that would be too much. I couldn't have made them swallow the truth. Two gangsters was more of a luxury than I could afford. *(He pauses for a moment)* And this is the whole point of my story. Eteocles, that virtuous brother, was just as rotten as Polynices. That great-hearted son had done his best, too, to procure the assassination of his father. That loyal prince had also offered to sell out Thebes to the highest bidder. Funny, isn't it? Polynices lies rotting in the sun while Eteocles is given a hero's funeral and will be housed in a marble vault. Yet I have absolute proof that everything that Polynices did, Eteocles had plotted to do. They were a pair of blackguards—both engaged in selling out Thebes, and both engaged in selling out each other; and they died like the cheap gangsters they were, over a division of the spoils.

But, as I told you a moment ago, I had to make a martyr of one of them. I sent out to the holocaust for their bodies; they were found clasped in one another's arms—for the first time in their lives, I imagine. Each had been spitted on the other's sword, and the Argive cavalry had trampled them down. They were mashed to a pulp, Antigone. I had the prettier of the two carcasses brought in, and gave it a State funeral; and I left the other to rot. I don't know which was which. And I assure you, I don't care. *(Long silence, neither looking at the other)*

Antigone (In a mild voice): Why do you tell me all this?

Creon: Would it have been better to let you die a victim to that obscene story?

Antigone: It might have been. I had my faith.

Creon: What are you going to do now?

Antigone (Rises to her feet in a daze): I shall go up to my room.

Creon: Don't stay alone. Go and find Haemon. And get married quickly.

Antigone (In a whisper): Yes.

Creon: All this is really beside the point. You have your whole life ahead of you—and life is a treasure.

Antigone: Yes.

Creon: And you were about to throw it away. Don't think me fatuous if I say that I understand you; and that at your age I should have done the same thing. A moment ago, when we were quarreling, you said I was drinking in your words. I was. But it wasn't you I was listening to; it was a lad named Creon who lived here in Thebes many years ago. He was thin and pale, as you are. His mind, too, was filled with thoughts of self-sacrifice. Go and find Haemon. And get married quickly, Antigone. Be happy. Life flows like water, and you young people let it run away through your fingers. Shut your hands; hold on to it, Antigone. Life is not what you think it is. Life is a child playing round your feet, a tool you hold firmly in your grip, a bench you sit down upon in the evening, in your garden. People will tell you that that's not life, that life is something else. They will tell you that because they need your strength and your fire, and they will want to make use of you. Don't listen to them. Believe me, the only poor consolation that we have in our old age is to discover that what I have said to you is true. Life is nothing more than the happiness that you get out of it.

Antigone (Murmurs, lost in thought): Happiness . . .

Creon (Suddenly a little self-conscious): Not much of a word, is it?

Antigone (Quietly): What kind of happiness do you foresee for me? Paint me the picture of your happy Antigone. What are the unimportant little sins that I shall have to commit before I am allowed to sink my teeth into life and tear happiness from it? Tell me: to whom shall I have to lie? Upon whom shall I have to fawn? To whom must I sell myself? Whom do you want me to leave dying, while I turn away my eyes?

Creon: Antigone, be quiet.

Antigone: Why do you tell me to be quiet when all I want to know is what I have to do to be happy? This minute; since it is this very minute that I must make my choice. You tell me that life is so wonderful. I want to know what I have to do in order to be able to say that myself.

Creon: Do you love Haemon?

Antigone: Yes, I love Haemon. The Haemon I love is hard and young, faithful and difficult to satisfy, just as I am. But if what I love in Haemon is to be worn away like a stone step by the tread of the thing you call life, the thing you call happiness; if Haemon reaches the point where he stops growing pale with fear when I grow pale, stops thinking that I must have been killed in an accident when I am five minutes late, stops feeling that he is alone on earth when I laugh and he doesn't know why—if he too has to learn to say yes to everything—why, no, then, no! I do not love Haemon!

Creon: You don't know what you are talking about!

Antigone: I do know what I am talking about! Now it is you who have stopped understanding. I am too far away from you now, talking to you from a kingdom you can't get into, with your quick tongue and your hollow heart. *(Laughs)* I laugh, Creon, because I see you suddenly as you must have been at fifteen: the same look of impotence in your face and the same inner conviction that there was nothing you couldn't do. What has life added to you, except those lines in your face, and that fat on your stomach?

Creon: Be quiet, I tell you!

Antigone: Why do you want me to be quiet? Because you know that I am right? Do you think I can't see in your face that what I am saying is true? You can't admit it, of course; you have to go on growling and defending the bone you call happiness.

Creon: It is your happiness, too, you little fool!

Antigone: I spit on your happiness! I spit on your idea of life—that life that must go on, come what may. You are all like dogs that lick everything they smell. You with your promise of a humdrum happiness—provided a person doesn't ask too much of life. I want everything of life, I do; and I want it now! I want it total, complete: otherwise I reject it! I will *not* be moderate. I will *not* be satisfied with the bite of cake you offer me if I promise to be a good little girl. I want to be sure of everything this very day; sure that everything will be as beautiful as when I was a little girl. If not, I want to die!

Questions for Analysis

1. Point to the utilitarian aspects of Creon's position.
2. With which ethical theory (or theories) do you think Antigone's position is compatible?
3. What do you think Kant would say of the relative merit of each position?
4. Eventually Creon has Antigone killed. Could his action be defended on a utilitarian basis? On any other?

Paperbacks for Further Reading

Barry, Vincent E. *Applying Ethics.* Belmont, Ca.: Wadsworth, 1981. This book not only covers major ethical theories but applies them to issues such as abortion, capital punishment, pornography, sex outside marriage, and economic justice and world hunger.

Brand, Stewart. *Updated Last Whole Earth Catalog*. New York: Random House, 1974. This work has become as popular for the code of values that it embodies as for the "set of tools" that it recommends.

Burgess, Anthony. *A Clockwork Orange*. New York: Norton, 1963. The central question in this disturbing novel is: Who is less moral, an individual with no moral sense or the society that attempts to "rehabilitate" him?

Fried, Charles. *An Anatomy of Values: Problems of Personal and Social Choice*. Cambridge, Mass.: Harvard University Press, 1970. This book nicely demonstrates the connection between values and choices, both on an individual and collective level. It is of particular help in sorting out values.

Ladd, J. *Ethical Relativism*. Belmont, Ca.: Wadsworth, 1973. This work is a good, succinct treatment of the doctrine of ethical relativism.

May, Rollo. *Love and Will*. New York: Norton, 1969. Existential psychotherapist May stresses the freedom of individuals to make the choices that maximize self-realization, but he balances this value against social responsibility.

Mill, John Stuart. *Utilitarianism: With Critical Essays*. Samuel Gorovity, Ed. Indianapolis, Ind.: Bobbs-Merrill, 1971. This book contains a collection of twenty-eight critical essays on Mill's philosophy, as well as the text of Mill's *Utilitarianism* and a chapter from *A System of Logic*.

Muller, Herbert J. *The Children of Frankenstein*. Bloomington: Indiana University Press, 1970. This is an interesting and informative analysis of the decline of values in the face of increasing technology.

Nietzsche, Friedrich. *On the Genealogy of Morals*. Walter Kaufman, Ed. New York: Vintage, 1967. While attacking the ethics of humility and self-denial in this classic, Nietzsche provides deep insight into the subsurface motives for adhering to such ethics.

SOCIAL PHILOSOPHY

Freedom and bread enough for all are inconceivable together.
–Fyodor Dostoyevsky

In his first State of the Union address (February 1981), President Reagan said that "the taxing powers of government must be used to provide revenues for legitimate government purposes. It must not be used to regulate the economy or bring about social change." About six months later Reagan proposed a tax bill that seemed designed to do just that. Dozens of new exclusions, exemptions, deductions, and credits encouraged everything from giving to charities to refurbishing old buildings, from investing in utilities to opening new bank accounts, from buying new machinery to drilling for oil.

To illustrate, suppose that taxpayer Bruce Miller invested in utilities. Under the President's tax plan, Bruce would be eligible for a special tax break of $750. But if he invested, say, in steel or cars (or anything else for that matter), he would get no break. Suppose further that Bruce's wife, Marge, spent $5,000 to fix up an old building that she intended to use as an antique shop. She could reduce her tax liability by $1,000. But Marge and Bruce must be careful. Should they decide to live in the building, they won't get the reduction. On the other hand, if Marge decided to buy a $5,000 savings certificate, instead of fixing up the building, the interest she earns would be tax-exempt. But if she bought a $5,000 money market certificate, then the interest would be fully taxable.

The Reagan tax bill, which was approved by Congress, also sought to regulate corporate behavior. For example, by allowing corporations to deduct more than a dollar for each dollar invested in new machinery, but less than a dollar for each dollar invested in new buildings, it encouraged investments in machinery rather than buildings. Again, by providing greater tax incentives for buying machinery than hiring people, it encouraged corporations to buy machinery rather than hire workers, in instances when both would do the job at the same cost. Furthermore, the tax proposal allowed corporations to reduce their taxes up to $3,000 for each worker hired who belonged to one of nine minority groups, including welfare recipients, ex-convicts, or economically disadvantaged eighteen-to-twenty-four-year-olds. What if a company preferred to hire an

"Aristotle observed that the human is a social animal."

equally disadvantaged twenty-five-year-old who had never been on welfare or in jail? It could, but it wouldn't get a tax break. There would appear to be, then, a gap between the Reagan ideal, as expressed in his State of the Union message, and the reality of the Reagan tax proposal.

Of course, the President and like-minded thinkers might say that the regulation evident in the tax code is a temporary evil that must be permitted in order to achieve the long-range objective of getting government off our backs. Critics would argue that the regulation has not gone far enough, that the tax code should be used more aggressively to right social and economic inequities. It is not our purpose to debate the merit of those positions, but to key on an issue that is embedded in them. The issue concerns the role of government in society. How big a part should government play in regulating our lives?

How active a role the state (taken to mean the highest authority in society) and its primary instrument, government, ought to take in the lives of its citizens invites an inquiry into the proper relation between individual and society. Aristotle observed that the human is a social animal. We work with, depend on, and relate to one another for our survival and prosperity. The totality of the relationships among people is known as society. A specific society consists of a group of human beings broadly distinguished from other groups by its interests, institutions, and culture. Because society so strongly influences our attitudes, values, loyalties, and outlooks, it is useful to examine the relationship between the individual and society in order to shed more light on the unifying theme of this text: self-identity.

In approaching this topic, we will focus on four related issues. First, since a determination of the proper relationship between individual and society inevitably raises questions of fairness and equity, we will begin with the problem of justice. Second, after laying out some influential theories of justice, we will consider the basis on which the power and authority of the state may be justified. This will require a close look at contract theory, which forms the theoretical foundations for the legitimacy of our state and government. But even if the power of the state can be justified, there is the question of the extent of its authority and power over the individual. So, third, we will talk about government control over its citizens. The subject of government control seems naturally to invite examination of the primary way that government exercises its control: law. So, fourth and finally, we will consider the meaning of law and its relation to freedom. Thus, (1) justice, (2) the justification of the state, (3) government control, and (4) law are the main subjects of this chapter.

These concepts and issues have one thing in common: They arise out of the social milieu. Although they have ethical and political implications, they do not directly involve either ethics or politics. They are not ethics, because they are not primarily concerned with establishing a norm of good conduct; they are not political, because they are not concerned with evaluating political power and the institutions that exercise it. Rather these concerns fall into the category of **social philosophy,** which is *the application of moral principles to the problems of freedom, equality, and justice.* In our overview of social philosophy, then, here are the points we will stress.

Main Points

1. Distributive justice refers to the relation between a community and its members.

2. The classical Greek view of justice, as expressed by Plato and Aristotle, associates justice with merit or desert.

3. Several British philosophers of the eighteenth and nineteenth centuries, among them John Stuart Mill, associate justice with social utility.

4. Associating justice with social utility raises the problem of balancing individual rights and interests with the common good.

5. A modern formulation of social justice, expressed by John Rawls, associates justice with equality.

6. Most of us today accept a contractual justification for the power and authority of the state, that is, that the state acquires its legitimacy through consent of the governed.

7. Contract theory has its roots in the thought of Thomas Hobbes, John Locke, and Jean Jacques Rousseau.

8. Regarding government control, modern contract theorists stake out a position somewhere between anarchism and totalitarianism, leaning toward willing individual cooperation or a strong authoritarian state; these leanings are reflected in the contemporary meanings of *conservative* and *liberal,* terms whose meanings differ significantly from their classical formulations.

9. Contractual theorists believe that the state has the right and duty to pass laws.

10. Thomas Aquinas distinguished among divine (eternal), natural, and human

law. He believed that you could break a human law if it was not consistent with a divine law.

11. We enjoy "freedoms-from"—that is, guarantees against state interference, such as the Bill of Rights.

Justice

In thinking about the proper relationship between individual and society, one inevitably confronts the issue and problem of justice. It's common to think of justice in terms of crime and punishment. Sometimes, we read of a criminal being sent to prison and we infer that justice was meted out. Other times, we hear of someone's not being punished for apparent wrongdoing and we bemoan the miscarriage of justice. In short, we commonly think of justice in terms of retribution, that is, punishment given for some wrongdoing.

But we can think of justice in terms other than retribution. In fact, in a larger sense, justice deals with distribution, not merely retribution. Questions and issues arise daily about how things should be allocated. The issues may involve the distribution of wealth and goods. Thus, given the relative scarcity of a society's resources, how should they be distributed? Should everyone receive the same amount? Ought those most in need to receive the lion's share? Or should the resources be distributed according to the individual's potential contributions to society? If individuals belong to groups who have been unfairly discriminated against, should these persons receive special consideration and treatment? Who should have access to medical care: only those who can afford it? everyone who needs it? those who likely will be most benefited?

The issues of distribution needn't be confined to wealth and goods. Equally important is the distribution of privilege and power. Education raises such issues. Who should be educated? Everyone? Only those who can afford an education? Only those who promise to benefit society? Other questions of privilege and power can also be asked. Who shall be permitted to vote? To drive? To drink? Should everyone be treated the same under the law? Or should certain individuals, for example juveniles, receive special consideration?

All of these issues raise questions of justice, as much as do issues of crime and punishment. But the justice involved is distributive, not retributive. *Distributive justice* refers to the relation between a community and its members. As implied in the name, distributive justice is concerned with the fair and proper distribution of public benefits and burdens among the members of a community. While distributive justice operates in all organizations, it applies chiefly to the state's relationship with its members.

Clearly, the subject of distributive justice touches many areas, from jobs to income, from taxes to medical services. Embedded in any answer to the question of how jobs should be assigned, income and taxes determined, and medical resources allocated, will be a principle of distributive justice; that is, some assumption about what is the proper way of distributing what is available when there isn't enough for all. For example, it's commonly argued that jobs should be distributed on the basis of talent and ability. Again, in the tax code of 1980, large corporations were given tax breaks because it was felt that they would reinvest their savings, thus increasing jobs and productivity, which in turn would benefit the whole of society. And some today claim that medical services should be provided on the basis of need. Each of these assertions implies some standard that should be considered in the distribution of certain resources: desert, social benefit, need. Whether or not these or other principles should be taken into account is one basic concern of distributive justice.

But no matter the principle which serves as the standard for distribution, it ordinarily can be traced, and ideally should be, to a fully developed theory of justice. Thus, the person who invokes talent and ability as the principle of job distribution probably views justice itself in terms of merit. Likewise, the person who argues for special tax advantages for large corporations is viewing justice in terms of social utility. And those who think that medical resources should be distributed on the basis of need likely view justice chiefly in terms of equality: Everyone should be treated equally in the sense that all should get what they need. In fact, merit, social utility, and equality have served as focal points for various theories of justice down through the years and continue to exert profound influence on our current views of justice and the proper relationship between individual and society.

Merit

Plato and Aristotle proposed the first significant theory of justice, which is associated with giving to individuals what is their due. In Plato's view, justice in the state is exactly what it is in the individual: a harmony between the various parts for the good of the whole. Social justice, then, requires cooperation among all members of a society. As a result, the interests of the individual must be subordinated to those of society.

Such a notion had a decided impact on the overwhelming majority of the Greek population, who were poor and powerless. The submissive role that these people played, especially the slaves, was considered vital to the overall success of the society. Consequently, their interests and rights were kept to a minimum. Indeed they themselves expected reward only insofar as their actions benefited their superiors. Such an attitude could only be fostered in a rigidly structured society, whose sharply drawn class divisions left no confusion about one's place, role, or expectations in life. This is precisely the kind of society that Plato erects in *The Republic:* a system in which every individual has his or her place, and justice means that each acts and is treated accordingly. Justice, in Plato's view, then, becomes associated with merit, in the sense that individuals are treated and expected to act according to the kinds of persons they are, according to the roles that nature has best fitted them to perform. In the following passage from *The Republic,* Plato states his position quite clearly:

> I think that justice is the very thing, or some form of the thing which, when we were beginning to found our city, we said had to be established throughout. We stated, and often repeated, if you remember, that everyone must pursue one occupation of those in the city, that for which his nature best fitted him.
> Yes, we kept saying that.

Further, we have heard many people say, and have often said ourselves, that justice is to perform one's own task and not to meddle with that of others.

We have said that.

This then, my friend, I said, when it happens, is in some way justice, to do one's own job. And do you know what I take to be a proof of this?

No, tell me.

I think what is left over of those things we have been investigating, after moderation and courage and wisdom have been found, was that which made it possible for those three qualities to appear in the city and to continue as long as it was present. We also said that what remained after we found the other three was justice.

It had to be.

And surely, I said, if we had to decide which of the four will make the city good by its presence, it would be hard to judge whether it is a common belief among the rulers and the ruled, or the preservation among the soldiers of a law-inspired belief as to the nature of what is, and what is not, to be feared, or the knowledge and guardianship of the rulers, or whether it is, above all, the presence of this fourth in child and woman, slave and free, artisan, ruler and subject, namely that each man, a unity in himself, performed his own task and was not meddling with that of others.

How could this not be hard to judge?

It seems then that the capacity for each in the city to perform his own task rivals wisdom, moderation, and courage as a source of excellence for the city.

It certainly does.

You would then describe justice as a rival to them for excellence in the city?

Most certainly.

Look at it this way and see whether you agree: you will order your rulers to act as judges in the courts of the city?

Surely.

And will their exclusive aim in delivering judgement not be that no citizen should have what belongs to another or be deprived of what is his own?

That would be their aim.

That being just?

Yes.

In some way then possession of one's own and the performance of one's own task could be agreed to be justice.

That is so.

Consider then whether you agree with me in this: if a carpenter attempts to do the work of a cobbler, or a cobbler that of a carpenter, and they exchange their tools and the esteem that goes with the job, or the same man tries to do both, and all the other exchanges are made, do you think that this does any great harm to the city?

No.

But I think that when one who is by nature a worker or some other kind of moneymaker is puffed up by wealth, or by the mob, or by his own strength, or some other such thing, and attempts to enter the warrior class, or one of the soldiers tries to enter the group of counsellors and guardians, though he is unworthy of it, and these exchange their tools and the public esteem, or when the same man tries to perform all these jobs together, then I think you will agree that these exchanges and this meddling bring the city to ruin.

They certainly do.

The meddling and exchange between the three established orders does very great harm to the city and would most correctly be called wickedness.

Very definitely.

And you would call the greatest wickedness worked against one's own city injustice?

Of course.

That then is injustice. And let us repeat that the doing of one's own job by the moneymaking, auxiliary, and guardian groups, when each group is performing its own task in the city, is the opposite, it is justice and makes the city just.

I agree with you that this is so.[1]

Apparent in this selection and throughout *The Republic* is not only Plato's insistence on severe class distinctions but on the *inequality* of individuals. Aristotle too shared the assumption that individuals are unequal, and thus justice is giving to individuals what is their due. Indeed, in his *Politics*, Aristotle defended slavery, not only because of the economic benefit to society, but because he believed that those who were slaves were naturally suited for that role and would be wretched and ineffectual were they made free. Both he and Plato believed that different people have different roles in society; and that justice means that each should act and be treated according to his or her role.

It is interesting to speculate how Plato and Aristotle might react to some contemporary concerns which raise questions of justice. For example, it seems safe to say that both would object to heterogeneous grouping in public schools (that is, the practice of placing students of diverse abilities in the same class; as opposed to homogeneous grouping, in which only students of like ability are placed in a class). Also, they likely would object to giving aliens the same privileges as citizens (for example, education and medical care), and to treating men and women as equals. As for the draft, they wouldn't object to discriminating between males and females, but they might to subjecting every male of a certain age to the draft. The just thing would be to conscript only those suited to be soldiers.

Many of us today would find Plato's and Aristotle's theory of justice objectionable because of its assumption that individuals are unequal. But it should be remembered that the presupposition of equality is as much an assumption as the presupposition of inequality and as such requires a defense. But even though we may not share the Greek view of inequality, our own conceptions of justice are in other important ways deeply indebted to both Plato and Aristotle. For example, like these two philosophical luminaries, we today hold that equals should be treated equally. The difference, of course, is that we espouse *egalitarianism*, which is the view that all are equal by virtue of their being human beings; whereas Plato and Aristotle did not endorse universal equality. Also, in his concern with the distribution of a society's resources, Aristotle anticipated an issue of social justice that is of vital national and international concern today. In addition, and perhaps most importantly, Aristotle, despite his elitism, clearly

1. *Plato.* The Republic, *book VI. G. M. A. Grube, Trans. Indianapolis, Ind.: Hackett, 1974. Reprinted by permission.*

recognized the importance of justice for the poorest and least powerful members of society. In his view, justice was most important for these members of the community inasmuch as they, unlike the rich and powerful, could not fend for themselves. Finally, much of the theorizing since the time of the Greeks, in effect, has been a response to Plato's claim that justice is giving everyone what is his or her due. Specifically, much of the writing since Plato has attempted to explain what an individual is due and why. Inevitably, this has called for an inspection of the relation between justice and equality, which we will see as we turn to the theory of justice associated with social utility.

Social Utility

The theory that views justice in terms of social utility has its roots in the social and political thought of a number of British philosophers of the eighteenth and nineteenth centuries. This position is foundationally different from the Greeks in that it starts from the assumption that everyone is equal; in contrast, the Greeks, as we saw, assumed inequality.

The assumption of equality is one that we can readily identify with, having been reared in a society erected on the premise that "all men are created equal." Accordingly, in the United States it is widely believed that everyone is entitled to a period of roughly the same kind of education; that the sexes should be treated equally; that individuals should be treated equally before the law; that everyone should have equal job opportunities and equal access to medical care; that everyone should be allowed to practice religion, speak freely, travel, and so on. Similarly, we reject slavery in principle because it violates our belief that everyone is equal. We even object to, though practice, snobbery, presumably because we believe that one person is not necessarily better than another because of wealth, family, intelligence, or some other criterion. The point is that we needn't look far to see evidence that, at least in theory, our society is erected on a commitment to egalitarianism. But this commitment brews up problems of both a theoretical and operational sort, problems which you must be aware of in order to understand the thrust of the social utility theory.

To sample the flavor of these problems, consider the practice of heterogeneous grouping in the classroom, which we alluded to earlier. Consistent with the belief that everyone is equal, we try to insure that everyone has roughly the same educational opportunities, at least in their formative years. Accordingly, thirty students of widely differing abilities and capacities may be placed in the same class at the same time with the same instructor. Faced with such essential diversity, teachers often end up aiming at the nonexistent "average" class member. Likely as not, the instructional level will be too high for the slowest class members and too low for the swiftest. As a result, the slowest don't learn, the swiftest get bored; both "turn off." Is this just?

Again, medical technology today has made the wondrous dream of organ transplants an astonishing reality. Corneas, hearts, kidneys, even livers—all can be transplanted with more or less success. But there's a rub: Demand exceeds supply. Who should get available organs when there aren't enough to go around? By a strict egalitarian calculation, presumably everyone who needs a heart, say, should have an equal chance of getting it. But suppose that two people are in need of the only available heart. One of them is an internationally renowned neurosurgeon in her forties whose survival promises to benefit countless persons. The other is a sixty-five-year-old derelict, who for three decades has wantonly abused his body and whose survival promises little if any benefit for anyone, except possibly himself. Is it just to treat these individuals as equals in determining who will receive the heart? Or is it more just that they be treated as unequals?

Here's one final example to point up the problem of justice inherent in a commitment to universal equality. With rare exceptions (for example, in the case of prisoners), every adult in our society is entitled to vote. But certainly not all are informed. Yet, the votes of the uninformed count as much as those of the informed. Is this just? Or is it an example of systematic injustice?

Doubtless, the examples could be multiplied. But the point should already be clear: There are cases in which the public interest clashes with the requirements of equal treatment. For Greek theorists like Plato and Aristotle, this is no great problem, because they are associating justice with merit, not equality. But for modern theorists, who largely take equality as a natural fact, the tension between public interest and demand for equal treatment poses an urgent problem. Indeed, it is one that British philosophers have engaged for several centuries, and that has given rise to the theory of justice associated with social utility.

We already indicated that certain British philosophers started from the premise that everyone is equal. But while philosophers such as Thomas Hobbes, John Locke, and David Hume endorsed equality, they did not take this to mean that unequal treatment is never permissible. On the contrary, they associated justice with what assures peace and security for all. In other words, justice means the public interest or social utility. What advances the good of society, or at least most of its citizens, is just. Notice that, in contrast to the Greek view, there is no acknowledgment here of giving individuals what befits them according to their station or role in life, or according to what they are by nature designed to be. Yes, individuals should get what is their due, but their due must be determined by appeal to the common good. The ultimate criterion of justice, then, is utility; that is, public interest or the satisfaction of the interests of at least the majority of people in society.

The most explicit statement of the utility view is expressed by John Stuart Mill. Writing in *Utilitarianism,* Mill concedes that the notion of equality often is part of both our conception and practice of justice. But he does not believe that equality constitutes the essence of justice. While the notion of justice varies in different persons, says Mill, it always conforms to the individual's idea of utility. Thus, all people believe that equality is the dictate of justice *except* when they feel that expediency requires inequality. Then they are likely to say, for example, that the famous surgeon and the skid-row bum should not be treated as equals in determining who will get the available heart. Since preserving the life of the surgeon promises more social benefit, expediency requires inequality of treatment: The surgeon should get the organ.

In Mill's view, then, expediency is the ever-present criterion in determining what is just and unjust. Whatever the institution, policy, or program, its justness depends ultimately on one's opinion about expediency respecting the phe-nomenon. Is reverse discrimination just? It all depends on whether it serves the public interest better than any other alternative posed to insure comparability of opportunity. Does a fee-for-service medical system best serve society's interests? Does a selective service system which conscripts males but not females most effectively advance the common good? While individual answers may vary, each of them, according to Mill, will be based on an opinion about the expediency of the practice. What is considered expedient will be considered just; what is not considered expedient will not be considered just.

But what about the various interpretations that expediency lends itself to? You might regard a policy of reverse discrimination expedient; I might not. Similar interpretive differences can arise on any issue. Does this make utility a hopelessly uncertain standard for determining what is just? Mill thinks not. In fact, he thinks that all notions of justice are susceptible to the same objection. In the following passage from *Utilitarianism* he makes this point, and an additional critical one: In the last analysis all cases of justice are also cases of expediency.

> We are continually informed that utility is an uncertain standard, which every different person interprets differently, and that there is no safety but in the immutable, ineffaceable, and unmistakable dictates of justice, which carry their evidence in themselves and are independent of the fluctuations of opinion. One would suppose from this that on questions of justice there could be no con-troversy; that, if we take that for our rule, its application to any given case could leave us in as little doubt as a mathematical demonstration. So far is this from being the fact that there is as much difference of opinion, and as much discus-sion, about what is just as about what is useful to society. Not only have differ-ent nations and individuals different notions of justice, but in the mind of one and the same individual, justice is not some one rule, principle, or maxim, but many which do not always coincide in their dictates, and, in choosing between which, he is guided either by some extraneous standard or by his own personal predilections.
>
> For instance, there are some who say that it is unjust to punish anyone for the sake of example to others, that punishment is just only when intended for the good of the sufferer himself. Others maintain the extreme reverse, contend-ing that to punish persons who have attained years of discretion, for their own benefit, is despotism and injustice, since, if the matter at issue is solely their own good, no one has a right to control their own judgment of it; but that they may justly be punished to prevent evil to others, this being the exercise of the legiti-mate right of self-defense. Mr. Owen, again, affirms that it is unjust to punish at all, for the criminal did not make his own character; his education and the circumstances which surrounded him have made him a criminal, and for these he is not responsible. All these opinions are extremely plausible; and so long as the question is argued as one of justice simply, without going down to the principles which lie under justice and are the source of its authority, I am unable to see how any of these reasoners can be refuted. For in truth every one of the three builds upon rules of justice confessedly true. The first appeals to the acknowledged injustice of singling out an individual and making him a sacrifice, without his consent, for other people's benefit. The second relies on the acknowledged justice of self-defense and the admitted injustice of forcing one person to conform to another's notions of what constitutes his good. The Owen-

ite invokes the admitted principle that it is unjust to punish anyone for what he cannot help. Each is triumphant so long as he is not compelled to take into consideration any other maxims of justice than the one he has selected; but as soon as their several maxims are brought face to face, each disputant seems to have exactly as much to say for himself as the others. No one of them can carry out his own notion of justice without trampling upon another equally binding. These are difficulties; they have always been felt to be such; and many devices have been invented to turn rather than to overcome them. As a refuge from the last of the three, men imagined what they called the freedom of the will—fancying that they could not justify punishing a man whose will is in a thoroughly hateful state unless it be supposed to have come into that state through no influence of anterior circumstances. To escape from the other difficulties, a favorite contrivance has been the fiction of a contract whereby at some unknown period all the members of society engaged to obey the laws and consented to be punished for any disobedience to them, thereby giving to their legislators the right, which it is assumed they would not otherwise have had, of punishing them, either for their own good or for that of society. This happy thought was considered to get rid of the whole difficulty and to legitimate the infliction of punishment, in virtue of another received maxim of justice, *volenti non fit injuria*—that is not unjust which is done with the consent of the person who is supposed to be hurt by it. I need hardly remark that, even if the consent were not a mere fiction, this maxim is not superior in authority to the others which it is brought in to supersede. It is, on the contrary, an instructive specimen of the loose and irregular manner in which supposed principles of justice grow up. This particular one evidently came into use as a help to the coarse exigencies of court of law, which are sometimes obliged to be content with very uncertain presumptions, on account of the greater evils which would often arise from any attempt on their part to cut finer. But even courts of law are not able to adhere consistently to the maxim, for they allow voluntary engagements to be set aside on the ground of fraud, and sometimes on that of mere mistake of misinformation.

To take another example from a subject already once referred to. In co-operative industrial association, is it just or not that talent or skill should give a title to superior remuneration? On the negative side of the question it is argued that whoever does the best he can deserves equally well, and ought not in justice to be put in a position of inferiority for no fault of his own; that superior abilities have already advantages more than enough, in the admiration they excite, the personal influence they command, and the internal sources of satisfaction attending them, without adding to these a superior share of the world's goods; and that society is bound in justice rather to make compensation to the less favored for this unmerited inequality of advantages than to aggravate it. On the contrary side it is contended that society receives more from the more efficient laborer; that, his services being more useful, society owes him a larger return for them; that a greater share of the joint result is actually his work, and not to allow his claim to it is a kind of robbery; that, if he is only to receive as much as others, he can only be justly required to produce as much, and to give a smaller amount of time and exertion, proportioned to his superior efficiency. Who shall decide between these appeals to conflicting principles of justice? Justice has in this case two sides to it, which it is impossible to bring into harmony, and the two disputants have chosen opposite sides; the one looks to what it is just that the individual should receive, the other to what it is just that the community should

give. Each, from his own point of view, is unanswerable; and any choice between them, on grounds of justice, must be perfectly arbitrary. Social utility
alone can decide the preference.

The considerations which have now been adduced resolve, I conceive, the
only real difficulty in the utilitarian theory of morals. It has always been evident
that all cases of justice are also cases of expediency; the difference is in the
peculiar sentiment which attaches to the former, as contradistinguished from the
latter. If this characteristic sentiment has been sufficiently accounted for; if there
is no necessity to assume for it any peculiarity of origin; if it is simply the natural
feeling of resentment, moralized by being made coextensive with the demands
of social good; and if this feeling not only does but ought to exist in all the classes
of cases to which the idea of justice corresponds—that idea no longer presents
itself as a stumbling block to the utilitarian ethics. Justice remains the appropriate name for certain social utilities which are vastly more important, and
therefore more absolute and imperative, than any others are as a class (though
not more so than others may be in particular cases); and which, therefore, ought
to be, as well as naturally are, guarded by a sentiment, not only different in
degree, but also in kind; distinguished from the milder feeling which attaches to
the mere idea of promoting human pleasure or convenience at once by the more
definite nature of its commands and by the sterner character of its sanctions.[2]

Since Mill's utilitarian theory of justice is a logical extension of his ethical
theories, it is understandable that it should invite some of the same objections.
First, even if what we consider expedient we also consider just, ought we?
Logicians have a name for the kind of reasoning evident in Mill's argument.
They call it the *is-ought fallacy*, which consists in assuming that what is the case
ought to be the case. For example, there are laws against possessing amounts of
marijuana that exceed specified limits. Whether or not there ought to be such
laws, or whether or not such laws are just, is another issue. To assume that
merely because the laws exist that they ought to exist, or that they are necessarily just, is to commit the is-ought fallacy. Again, there are laws prohibiting active
euthanasia, that is, taking direct measures to end the life, say, of someone
hopelessly ill and in excruciating pain. But ought there to be such laws? That is
another issue. Respecting Mill's view, merely because we may think of justice in
terms of expediency does not necessarily mean that we ought to. Perhaps we
should think of it in other terms, as for example the Greeks did, or as strict
egalitarians do.

A second, and operationally more troublesome, problem with social utility
arises from the inevitable clash of individual and public interests. Surely, there
are cases when the general utility can be served only at the expense of a single
individual, or perhaps a group of them. Take, for example, the currently volatile
issue of installing commercial nuclear power plants. Even assuming (1) that the
plants are the most efficient source of energy available (which, of course, is
debatable) and (2) that they pose only remote and minimal hazards to individuals living near them, is it just for the state to insist that these individuals must
bear even a negligible risk or undergo dislocations for the good of society?
Again, in recent years considerable money and domestic resources have been

2. *John Stuart Mill.* Utilitarianism. *New York: Bobbs-Merrill, 1957. Reprinted by permission.*

diverted from human services to national defense. Some individuals and groups (for example, the poor, the young, the elderly, the infirm) seem to be directly injured as a result. The justification for the realignment of priorities largely takes the form of an appeal to the national interest. Does this appeal to social utility of itself make a program intended to shore up national defense at the expense of the most vulnerable members of society just? Of course, one could respond that the utility of a specific act by itself cannot give an adequate concept of justice, that what is needed is a theory of general practice along the lines of rule utilitarianism. But as we have seen elsewhere (see Chapter 3), rule utilitarianism still allows the possibility of a practice which systematically increases the general utility at the expense of some individual or group. Is this just? Utility theorists would say it is just, simply because justice ultimately has no concrete meaning apart from expediency.

But not all agree. In fact, what is perhaps the most powerful contemporary theory of justice attempts to reassert the primacy of individual rights by placing the emphasis on the advantages of a practice to the least advantaged members of society. In so doing, it clearly ties together the concepts of justice and equality. Such a theory has been proposed by the American philosopher John Rawls.

Equality

By his own account, John Rawls has presented his theory as a modern alternative to utilitarianism, one which he hopes will be compatible with the belief that justice must be associated with equality, that is, individual rights. Because this alternative focuses primarily on the distribution of economic goods and services, and attempts to maximize the plight of the most disadvantaged, economists have referred to it as the **maximin principle;** that is, the social theory of justice which contends that inequality is permissible if and only if it improves the lot of the worst off in society.

The heart of Rawls's theory of justice consists in two principles: equal liberty and difference. In developing the equal liberty principle, Rawls admits that it is nothing new (nor his principle of justice, for that matter). Rather, it is a point on which all social philosophers and moralists agree. According to Rawls, the *equal liberty principle* means that "each person participating in a practice or affected by it, has an equal right to the most extensive liberty compatible with a like liberty for all." Rawls points out that the term *person* has various referents depending on the circumstances. In some instances, *person* will mean human individuals; but in others it may refer to nations, business firms, churches, teams, or various associations. No matter who or what *person* refers to, the principles of justice apply in all instances, although there is a logical priority given to the case of human individuals.

Central to the equal liberty principle is *equality,* by which Rawls means that everybody is to be treated equally. More technically, by *equality* Rawls means the impartial and equitable administration and application of the rules that define a practice. The equal liberty principle expresses this concept. *Impartial administration* means a spirit of disinterestedness should prevail in the distribution of good and evil; no person should receive special consideration. By *equitable administra-*

tion Rawls seems to mean that the distribution must be fair and just to begin with.

To illustrate the equal liberty principle, suppose that the government decided that every family of four should have an income of at least $7,500 per year. Any family with a subminimal income (that is, below $7,500) would be subsidized the difference. According to the equal liberty principle, the rule must be administered to all families of four in the subminimal category without exception. If a family of four making $6,000 a year was excluded, the rule would not be equitably administered. Nor would the rule be equitably administered if it failed to recognize income reduced by factors outside the family's control. For example, suppose two families each earned $6,000 a year, but the first incurred medical bills totaling $2,000. An equitable distribution would involve a $3,500 subsidy to the first family and a $1,500 subsidy to the second. Naturally, any family with conditions similar to those of the first family would rightly expect the same treatment. Keep in mind here that Rawls is defining liberty with reference to the pattern of rights, duties, powers, and liabilities established by a practice. In this case, families making less than $7,500 a year have the *right* to expect equal treatment regarding governmental subsidies.

But Rawls's equal liberty principle expresses the idea of equality in a second, more important way. Many would argue that all regulations infringe on personal liberty. In his equal liberty principle, Rawls recognizes this apparently inherent characteristic of all laws. Thus, a law that requires you to drive on the right-hand side of the road is an infringement on your freedom to drive on either side whenever you wish. Some would argue that justice only requires an *equal* liberty, that is, as long as every motorist is required to drive on the right-hand side of the road, justice is being served. But Rawls argues that if a more extensive liberty were possible for all without loss, damage, or conflict, then it would be irrational to settle on a lesser liberty. In the case of driving, of course, more extensive liberty is not possible without great loss and injury. But it is possible that treating people unequally could result in a more extensive liberty for all. It is this issue that he addresses in his *difference principle*. In the following selection, taken from his essay "Justice as Fairness," Rawls explains what he means by this principle.

> The second principle defines what sorts of inequalities are permissible; it specifies how the presumption laid down by the first principle may be put aside. Now by inequalities it is best to understand not *any* differences between offices and positions, but differences in the benefits and burdens attached to them either directly or indirectly, such as prestige and wealth, or liability to taxation and compulsory services. Players in a game do not protest against there being different positions, such as batter, pitcher, catcher, and the like, nor to there being various privileges and powers as specified by the rules; nor do the citizens of a country object to there being the different offices of government such as president, senator, governor, judge, and so on, each with their special rights and duties. It is not differences in the resulting distribution established by a practice, or made possible by it, of the things men strive to attain or avoid. Thus they may complain about the pattern of honors and rewards set up by a practice (*e.g.* the privileges and salaries of government officials) or they may object to the distribution of power and wealth which results from the various ways in which

men avail themselves of the opportunities allowed by it (*e.g.* the concentration of wealth which may develop in a free price system allowing large entrepreneurial or speculative gains).

It should be noted that the second principle holds that an inequality is allowed only if there is reason to believe that the practice with the inequality, or resulting in it, will work for the advantage of *every* party engaging in it. Here it is important to stress that *every* party must gain from the inequality. Since the principle applies to practices, it implies that the representative man in every office or position defined by a practice, when he views it as a going concern, must find it reasonable to prefer his condition and prospects with the inequality to what they would be under the practice without it. The principle excludes, therefore, the justification of inequalities on the grounds that the disadvantages of those in one position are outweighed by the greater advantages of those in another position. This rather simple restriction is the main modification I wish to make in the utilitarian principle as usually understood. When coupled with the notion of a practice, it is a restriction of consequence, and one which some utilitarians, for example Hume and Mill, have used in their discussions of justice without realizing apparently its significance, or at least without calling attention to it. Why it is a significant modification of principle, changing one's conception of justice entirely, the whole of my argument will show.

Further, it is also necessary that the various offices to which special benefits or burdens attach are open to all. It may be, for example, to the common advantage, as just defined, to attach special benefits to certain offices. Perhaps by doing so the requisite talent can be attracted to them and encouraged to give its best efforts. But any offices having special benefits must be won in a fair competition in which contestants are judged on their merits. If some offices were not open, those excluded would normally be justified in feeling unjustly treated, even if they benefited from the greater efforts of those who were allowed to compete for them. Now if one can assume that offices are open, it is necessary only to consider the design of practices themselves and how they jointly, as a system, work together. It will be a mistake to focus attention on the varying relative positions of particular persons, who may be known to us by their proper names, and to require that each such change, as a once for all transaction viewed in isolation, must be in itself just. It is the system of practices which is to be judged, and judged from a general point of view: unless one is prepared to criticize it from the standpoint of a representative man holding some particular office, one has no complaint against it.[3]

Associating inequality with everyone's advantage, as Rawls does here, is the *first* formulation of the difference principle. Rawls says later that the principle is more accurately formulated as: "Social and economic inequalities are to be arranged so that they are . . . *to the greatest benefit of the least* advantaged. . ."[4] (italics added). This is why Rawls's view is identified with the interests of society's worst off.

In addition, in order to understand the implications of the difference principle, it's important to distinguish between contingent and noncontingent equality. *Contingent equality* is equality that depends on something else for its

3. *John Rawls. "Justice as Fairness."* The Philosophical Review, *LXVII, April 1958. Reprinted by permission.*

4. *John Rawls.* A Theory of Justice. *Cambridge, Mass.: Harvard University Press, 1972, p. 255.*

justification; it is not justified in and of itself. For example, utilitarians would justify equality on grounds of social improvement. Yes, people should be treated equally when and if the social good is advanced. When the social good is retarded, and more good can be realized by treating people unequally, then inequality is justified. In contrast, a *noncontingent equality* is not justified by appeal to consequences or to anything else. We shouldn't treat people equally because it leads to the greatest social good, but because equality in and of itself is the right and proper way to deal with people.

For Rawls, equality is not contingent. But he would suffer inequality when, and only when, the practice involving inequality in all likelihood works to the advantage of the worst off. In other words, the most disadvantaged must find their conditions improved as a result of the inequality. Observe that the difference principle disallows inequalities generally justified on utilitarian grounds, that is, on the grounds that the greatest number will profit. In Rawls's view, an inequality that elevates the condition of the most people but does not improve the plight of the worst off is not justified.

As opposed to the efficiency emphasis of classical utilitarianism's concept of justice, Rawls's concept takes root in reciprocity. *Reciprocity* is the principle that requires that a practice be such that all members could and would accept it and be bound by it. Without reciprocity, there can be no basis for true community.

When the equal liberty and difference principles conflict, Rawls relies on the equal liberty principle, which he insists is logically prior to the difference principle. In contrast, a utilitarian would see liberty as contingent on social productivity. Rawls would argue that any position that even allows the possibility of the loss of equal liberty is unacceptable. As he puts it, "Each person possesses an inviolability founded on justice that even the welfare of society as a whole cannot override. . . . Therefore, . . . the rights secured by justice are not subject to political bargaining or to the calculus of social interests."[5]

Now let us see how Rawls's theory might work in practice by relating it to the graduated income tax. Some economists argue that a sharply graduated income tax reduces work incentive—that the most productive and talented members of a society are discouraged from working and so cut back on their effort. If physicians lost their incentive to work, everyone would probably end up worse off than they were originally, including the worst off. Under Rawls's maximin rule, therefore, it seems defensible not to tax physicians so much as, say, artists of equal income, since the loss of the physicians' work would probably reduce the state of the worst off, but the loss of the artists' probably would not. It is conceivable, on the other hand, that the artists might be heavily taxed so long as such taxation reduced the economic gap between them and the poorest group in society. But wouldn't the artists, like the physicians, ultimately lose incentive? And, with that loss, wouldn't their tax dollars be lost to the poor? Presumably, at this point, Rawls would favor the unequal economic status of the groups, since such inequality would actually serve to improve the position of the lowliest group in the society. It is clear that Rawls's maximin rule is compatible

5. *John Rawls. A Theory of Justice, p. 4.*

with considerable inequality, but only if it improves the status of the poorest members of society.

In his argument, Rawls relies on a traditional "patterned" distribution of goods. A patterned distribution is one that can be summed up in some formula like "To each according to his _____," in which the blank may be filled in with *need, work, intelligence,* or *effort,* for example. It is highly unlikely that any society already reflects this formula for the distribution of wealth. Therefore, to achieve a just society, the goods must be redistributed until people's holdings correspond with what is thought to be the just pattern. Rawls believes the just pattern to be his maximin rule.

Rawls's Harvard colleague Robert Nozick disagrees. In his view any theory of justice relying on a patterned distribution of wealth is inherently unjust because it coerces individuals and thus violates their basic rights. Such a theory deprives citizens of the free exercise of their preferences even when they are not hurting anyone else. Nozick provides an ingenious example.

He asks us to imagine a society in which the goods are distributed in accordance with some patterned concept of justice, such as equality, whereby everyone has precisely the same holdings. Suppose that basketball star Julius Irving signs a contract with a team under which he receives 25¢ from each game ticket sold. Excited by the prospect of seeing Irving play, fans gladly pay the surcharge on their tickets. In the course of the season, 1 million people attend Irving games. As a result, Irving ends up with $250,000—much more money than anyone else has in the society. The transaction has obviously altered the patterned distribution of wealth, but is the new distribution unjust? If it is, why? Nozick argues that the source of the injustice cannot be that a million people freely chose to spend their money in this way and not some other. Since they knew where their money was going, they have no just claim against Irving. As for those who did not see him play, their holdings are unaffected. And, Nozick points out, if they had no claim against the goods of the transacting parties before this alteration took place, they shouldn't have any now.

Nozick is raising several objections to Rawls's maximin rule. One is that Rawls is using the better-off people in society to assure the welfare of the worst off. Nozick regards this utilitarian ethic as fundamentally unjust. As a corollary, he claims Rawls is not impartial, for he is seeing things only through the eyes of the worst off. Finally, he objects to Rawls's apparent contention that under certain circumstances individuals are not entitled to what they create. A person's entitlement is very much a part of Nozick's thinking, and his work is largely devoted to spelling out this concept.

But perhaps in applying Rawls's difference principle to a specific transaction, Nozick has warped it, or at least overburdened it. After all, Rawls's principle is addressing the backdrop against which public policies and decisions about redressing inequalities are to be made. It is not speaking directly to specific, small scale instances of the sort Nozick cites. More important, Rawls is not making the socialistic argument that all property should be shared. He says only that society must help the most disadvantaged members. This does not at all mean that everyone has a right to an equal share. In other words, Rawls's concept of justice does not equate fair distribution with equal distribution. Yes, individuals have a just claim to whatever they have acquired, so long as the acquisition occurred within the context of a fair social policy. In the following paragraph, taken from his "A Kantian Conception of Equality," Rawls makes these very points concerning his difference principle:

> In explaining this principle, several matters should be kept in mind. First of all, it applies in the first instance to the main public principles and policies that regulate social and economic equalities. It is used to adjust the system of entitlements and rewards, and the standards and precepts that this system employs. Thus the difference principle holds, for example, for income and property taxation, for fiscal and economic policy; it does not apply to particular transactions or distributions, nor, in general, to small scale and local decisions, but rather to the background against which these take place. No observable pattern is required of actual distributions, nor even any measure of the degree of equality. . . . What is enjoined is that the inequalities make a functional contribution to those least favored. Finally, the aim is not to eliminate the various contingencies, for some such contingencies [that is, social primary goods such as (1) rights, liberties and opportunities; (2) income and wealth; (3) the social bases of self-respect] seem inevitable. Thus even if an equal distribution of natural assets seemed more in keeping with the equality of free persons, the question of redistributing these assets (were this conceivable) does not arise, since it is incompatible with the integrity of the person. Nor need we make any specific assumptions about how great these variations are: we only suppose that, as realized in later life, they are influenced by all three contingencies. The question, then, is by what criterion a democratic society is to organize cooperation and arrange the system of entitlements that encourages and rewards productive efforts. We have a right to our natural abilities and a right to whatever we become entitled to by taking part in a fair social process. The problem is to characterize this process.[6]

In the last analysis, Rawls's thought is most significant, and controversial, not because it has connected justice with equality, but because it has enlarged the sphere of equality. While most, if not all, of us today would agree that people should have equal legal rights and opportunities, many would not extend equality to material goals and social services. Indeed, in the '80s there has been a concerted effort at the federal executive level to roll back equalities that have been gained in these areas. Rawls is claiming that justice requires not only political and legal equality, but an equality which embraces the rights of individuals to material goods and social services. On this point he puts considerable distance between himself and social utilitarians like Mill and the mainstream of what today is termed conservative social and fiscal thinking, both of which would consider the distribution of goods and services as a matter of utility.

The preceding discussion gives witness to the claim that justice poses a profound problem to social and political philosophers. While we mentioned only a handful of philosophers, we spanned more than two millennia, from classical Greeks such as Plato and Aristotle to contemporary theoreticians such as John Rawls. There is no single theory of justice which receives universal endorsement. Indeed our own society seems ambivalent, giving at various times priority

---

6. *John Rawls. "A Kantian Conception of Equality."* Cambridge Review, *February 1974, p. 97.*

to merit, social utility, or equality. The challenge continues to be what it has always been: to effect a proper balance—whatever and wherever that may be—between public and private interests. In fact, the state is empowered to do this; for by definition it is the authority with the power to define the public interest and to enforce its definition. This means that it is the state that draws the line of demarcation between individual and society. All would agree that this is an awesome power.

For as long as philosophers have pondered the meaning of justice, they have also grappled with the question of the legitimacy of the state and its primary instrument, government. On what basis is the power of the state justified? While any answer to this question inevitably will reflect one's concept of justice, the question of the legitimacy of the state, of the justification of its power, is distinct from the problem of justice. It is to this question that we now turn.

The Justification of the State

The state is the highest authority in a society. As indicated, it has the power to define the public interest and enforce its definition. One clear example of the state's doing this can be seen in the graduated income tax system. The state sets priorities, that is, defines the public interest; then it taxes citizens in order to implement these priorities. In theory, Americans pay taxes proportional to their incomes: The more they make, the greater the proportion of income they pay. Many feel this is fair. But with demands for and costs of goods and services rising, a sizable number of people think that this system is unfair, especially people who disagree with the programs for which taxes are spent. Take, for example, the case of the childless couple whom we met earlier, the Millers.

Bruce Miller, a chemical engineer, and his wife Marge, a dental hygienist, have no dependents and can claim very few deductions. As a result, they pay a hefty income tax every year. Although they like to consider themselves loyal Americans who are willing to bear their share of the nation's expenses, in recent years they have grown resentful of the tax system and are seriously thinking about voting for an initiative that will limit not only property tax but income tax as well.

Bruce: You know, I really think it's unfair that the government takes such a big bite of our income.

Marge: What bothers me even more than the amount is the way it's spent.

Bruce: Well, there's a lot of waste. There's no question about that.

Marge: I don't even mean the waste. Do you realize that our money is being used to support things we don't directly benefit from? Take that swimming pool they put in the high school last year. We're never going to use that. And we don't have any children who ever will. But our property tax has gone up this year to help pay for it, so we wind up paying for it whether we like it or not.

Bruce: I see what you mean. But I'll tell you what really galls me even more than being forced to pay for something we're not going to use.

Marge: What's that?

Bruce: Being forced to pay for something I think is wrong.

Marge: Like what?

Bruce: Well, I know that you disagree with me on this, but I don't think abortion is right. And yet I'm helping to finance the abortion clinics that the state's set up.

Marge: You know, I never thought of that. Even though I do support abortion, I think you're right. You shouldn't be forced to violate your conscience. That's what you're saying, isn't it?

Bruce: You bet it is.

Notice that the Millers are resentful not of paying taxes but of how their tax money is spent. They are questioning the fairness of a system that compels them under penalty of law to pay for some programs that they cannot in good conscience support.

But there is an even broader question that this case raises which does not relate directly to the graduated income tax system or to any other specific program, policy, or measure that the state implements in enforcing its definition of the public interest. That question is: What justifies the power of the state in the first place? What gives the state the right to tax, conscript, arm, educate, or do any of the myriad things we see it doing? It is true that the Millers are not asking this question. To be sure, very few of us ever do. We criticize various state intrusions into our lives and liberties, but never plumb the deeper theoretical issue that underlies any specific utilization of governmental power. And that issue concerns the legitimacy of the state per se. Understanding that issue gives us some basis for intelligently evaluating specific uses of that power. Stated another way, it is impossible to determine whether a government has misused its power until we determine what are the rightful limits of that power. And determining the rightful limits of authority, in turn, ultimately calls for an inquiry into the legitimacy of the state's authority and power to begin with.

At different times in various societies, theories have been advanced to define the legitimacy of the state and justify its power. At times the power of the state has been justified by appeal to divine authority. Thus some rulers have claimed the power to rule as a divine right, as a kind of mandate from some deity. Other times, the state has been justified by appeal to the public interest. Accordingly, insofar as the state furthers the public interest, it is justified. But the theory that most of us today accept is that the state is justified by the consent of the governed; that is, the legitimacy of the state stems from an agreement of the governed to be ruled by the state. The most influential modern versions of this viewpoint are captured in the term *social contract,* which refers to a complex theory of state legitimacy that has extraordinary importance for us today.

Contract Theory

The so-called **contract theory** is both an explanation of the origin of the state and a defense of its authority that philosophers have frequently used. We see evidence of contract theory as far back as Plato, but its most noteworthy proponents were Thomas Hobbes (1588–1679) and John Locke. More than any other person, Hobbes was the founder of modern political philosophy. Political theorists before him, such as Plato, Aristotle, Saint Augustine, and Thomas Aquinas, had emphasized that the state was subject to criticism and control. In contrast, Hobbes, impressed by the new mathematics and mechanics and the tragic English civil war, attempted to formulate a scientific theory of the state and a defense of its power. He based his political philosophy on the principles of seventeenth-century scientific materialism. According to this doctrine, the world is a mechanical system that can be explained in terms of the laws of motion. Even the behavior of humans or complex societies, it was argued, are reducible to geometric and physical explanations. From this view of reality Hobbes deduced how things must of necessity occur.

In his most famous work, *Leviathan*, Hobbes portrays humans as selfish, unsocial creatures driven by two needs: survival and personal pleasure. Therefore, human life is characterized by constant struggle, strife, and war, with individual pitted against individual in a battle for self-preservation and gain. In Hobbes's words:

> Hereby it is manifest, that during the time men live without a common power to keep them all in awe, they are in that condition which is called war; and such a war, as is of every man, against every man. For WAR, consisteth not in battle only, or the act of fighting; but in a tract of time, wherein the will to contend by battle is sufficiently known: and therefore the notion of *time*, is to be considered in the nature of war; as it is in the nature of weather. For as the nature of foul weather, lieth not in a shower or two of rain; but in an inclination thereto of many days together: so the nature of war, consisteth not in actual fighting; but in the known disposition thereto, during all the time there is no assurance to the contrary. All other time is PEACE.
>
> Whatsoever therefore is consequent to a time of war, where every man is enemy to every man; the same is consequent to the time, wherein men live without other security, than what their own strength, and their own invention shall furnish them withal. In such condition, there is no place for industry; because the fruit thereof is uncertain: and consequently no culture of the earth; no navigation, nor use of the commodities that may be imported by sea; no commodious building; no instruments of moving, and removing, such things as require much force; no knowledge of the face of the earth; no account of time; no arts; no letters; no society; and which is worst of all, continual fear, and danger of violent death; and the life of man, solitary, poor, nasty, brutish, and short.
>
> To this war of every man, against every man, this also is consequent; that nothing can be unjust. The notions of right and wrong, justice and injustice have there no place. Where there is no common power, there is no law: where no law, no injustice. Force, and fraud, are in war the two cardinal virtues. Justice, and injustice are none of the faculties neither of the body, nor mind. If they were, they might be in a man that were alone in the world, as well as his senses, and passions. They are qualities, that relate to men in society, not in solitude. It is consequent also to the same condition, that there be no propriety, no dominion, no *mine* and *thine* distinct; but only that to be every man's, that he can get: and for so long, as he can keep it. And thus much for the ill condition, which man by mere nature is actually placed in; though with a possibility to come out of it, consisting partly in the passions, partly in his reason.

The passions that incline men to peace, are fear of death; desire of such things as are necessary to commodious living; and a hope by their industry to obtain them. And reason suggesteth convenient articles of peace, upon which men may be drawn to agreement. These articles, are they, which otherwise are called the Laws of Nature.[7]

Notice in the final paragraph that Hobbes, while asserting that the instinct for self-preservation is the basic drive behind human behavior, states that humans have the capacity to reason.

Although Hobbes never viewed reason to be as energizing a force as self-preservation, he did hold that reason could regulate human actions and anticipate their results. This rationality enabled them to evaluate the long-term results of behavior originally motivated by self-interest.

Rational concern for their own survival and for their best long-term interests impels humans to enter into a contract with one another that forms the basis for society. Because they recognize that their lives are destined to be "solitary, poor, nasty, brutish, and short," humans accept an authority outside themselves that has the power to force all to act in the best interests of the majority. For Hobbes this authority is irrevocable. Once set up, the political body wielding this power exercises complete authority over its subjects and remains in power as long as it is able to compel them to do what they otherwise would not do.

The society that individuals contract for thus becomes superior to the individuals. For Hobbes, the state cannot bear any resistance to its rule. If such resistance becomes effective, the state has proven itself unable to govern—in which case the established officials no longer rule and the people are no longer their subjects. At that point the people revert to their natural state of struggle for self-preservation and gain until they form another contract.

While he attacks the classical Greek view that people are capable of virtue and wisdom, at the same time, Hobbes is really a modern echo of Plato. Plato's classical Greece was characterized by great art and philosophy, but it was nevertheless undergoing institutional change that constantly threatened war and civil unrest. Against this background, Plato wove, as Hobbes would weave later, a totalitarian political fabric in which the basic purpose of the state was to produce order. As he presents this utopia in *The Republic*, the basis of its order is the eternal values that exist apart from personal preference or practical need and that reason can discover. When human nature is not informed with this reason, humans are as beastly as Hobbes describes. Like Hobbes, Plato believed in an elitist ruling class composed of people who could reason about the eternal truths. To these rulers the citizens owed absolute allegiance and had no right to question, reject, or rebel against their authority.

In contrast with Plato's and Hobbes's rather pessimistic views, John Locke viewed humans as essentially moral beings who ought to obey natural moral rules. Whereas Hobbes saw warfare as the human's natural state, Locke saw it at least partly as a system of natural moral laws. As a result, Locke viewed humans as being by nature free and equal, regardless of the existence of any government. Government, he argued, doesn't decree mutual respect for the freedom and

7. *Thomas Hobbes.* Leviathan. *London: J. Bohn, 1839, pt.1, ch. 15.*

liberties of all—nature does. Humans are by nature free, rational, and social creatures. They establish governments because three things are missing in the state of nature: (1) a firm, clearly understood interpretation of natural law, (2) unbiased judges to resolve disputes, and (3) personal recourse in the face of injustices. So, in order to maintain their natural rights, individuals enter into a social contract. In one portion of his brilliant and most influential political writing, *Essay Concerning the True and Original Extent and End of Civil Government* (1690), Locke explains the end of political society and government:

123. If man in the state of Nature be so free as has been said, if he be absolute lord of his own person and possessions, equal to the greatest and subject to nobody, why will he part with his freedom, this empire, and subject himself to the dominion and control of any other power? To which it is obvious to answer, that though in the state of Nature he hath a right, yet the enjoyment of it is very uncertain and constantly exposed to the invasion of others; for all being kings as much as he, every man his equal, and the greater part no strict observers of equity and justice, the enjoyment of the property he has in this state is very unsafe, very insecure. This makes him willing to quit this condition which, however free, is full of fears and continual dangers; and it is not without reason that he seeks out and is willing to join in society with others who are already united, or have a mind to unite for the mutual preservation of their lives, liberties and estates, which I call by the general name—property.

124. The great and chief end, therefore, of men uniting into commonwealths, and putting themselves under government, is the preservation of their property; to which in the state of Nature there are many things wanting.

Firstly, there wants an established, settled, known law, received and allowed by common consent to be the standard of right and wrong, and the common measure to decide all controversies between them. For though the law of Nature be plain and intelligible to all rational creatures, yet men, being biased by their interest, as well as ignorant for want of study of it, are not apt to allow of it as a law binding to them in the application of it to their particular cases.

125. Secondly, in the state of Nature there wants a known and indifferent judge, with authority to determine all differences according to the established law. For every one in that state being both judge and executioner of the law of Nature, men being partial to themselves, passion and revenge is very apt to carry them too far, and with too much heat in their own cases, as well as negligence and unconcernedness, make them too remiss in other men's.

126. Thirdly, in the state of Nature there often wants power to back and support the sentence when right, and to give it due execution. They who by any injustice offended will seldom fail where they are able by force to make good their injustice. Such resistance many times makes the punishment dangerous, and frequently destructive to those who attempt it.

127. Thus mankind, notwithstanding all the privileges of the state of Nature, being but in an ill condition while they remain in it are quickly driven into society. Hence it comes to pass, that we seldom find any number of men live any time together in this state. The inconveniencies that they are therein exposed to by the irregular and uncertain exercise of the power every man has of punishing the transgressions of others, make them take sanctuary under the established laws of government, and therein seek the preservation of their property. It is this makes them so willingly give up every one his single power of punishing to be exercised by such alone as shall be appointed to it amongst them, and by such

rules as the community, or those authorised by them to that purpose, shall agree on. And in this we have the original right and rise of both the legislative and executive power as well as of the governments and societies themselves.[8]

In short, individuals create a political entity capable of preserving the inherent rights of "life, liberty, and estate." This contract is based on the consent of the majority, and all agree to obey the decisions of the majority. The state's authority is limited by the terms of the contract, which is continually reviewed by the citizenry. So, unlike Hobbes's absolutistic state, Locke's state is specific and limited. Most important, one of the fundamental moral rights in Locke's political state is the right to resist and to challenge authority. Whereas Hobbes believed that resistance to authority was never justified, Locke regarded such a right as essential. Although the contrast between Hobbes and Locke is sharp, they do agree that rationality enables humans to perceive the necessity of forming a social contract.

This contract theory, especially as enunciated by Locke, led directly to the social philosophy of Jean Jacques Rousseau (1712–1778), who some consider the foremost articulator of the social contract theory. However, Rousseau did not appeal to a self-evident natural law as Locke had. He argued that if people are to act morally, then they must live under laws that they freely accept. Rousseau's emphasis, then, was on personal moral autonomy, the capacity and right of individuals to live under laws that they prescribe for themselves. Thus, for Rousseau the fundamental requirement of a morally acceptable government is that the governed have freely subscribed to a common body of law. In his most important work, *Of the Social Contract*, Rousseau describes his contract theory:

> The articles of this contract are so unalterably fixed by the nature of the act that the least modification renders them vain and of no effect; so that they are the same everywhere, and are everywhere tacitly understood and admitted, even though they may never have been formally announced; until, the social compact being violated, each individual is restored to his original rights, and resumes his native liberty, while losing the conventional liberty for which he renounced it.
>
> The articles of the social contract will, when clearly understood, be found reducible to this single point: the total alienation of each associate, and all his rights, to the whole community; for, in the first place, as every individual gives himself up entirely, the condition of every person is alike; and being so, it would not be to the interest of any one to render that condition offensive to others.
>
> Nay, more than this, the alienation being made without any reserve, the union is as complete as it can be, and no associate has any further claim to anything: for if any individual retained rights not enjoyed in general by all, as there would be no common superior to decide between him and the public, each person being in some points his own judge, would soon pretend to be so in everything; and thus would the state of nature be continued and the association necessarily become tyrannical or be annihilated.
>
> Finally, each person gives himself to all, and so not to any one individual; and as there is no one associate over whom the same right is not acquired which

8.   *John Locke.* Essay Concerning the True and Original Extent and End of Civil Government. *Oxford: Clarendon Press, 1894, vol. 4, p. 4. Originally published 1690.*

is ceded to him by others, each gains an equivalent for what he loses, and finds his force increased for preserving that which he possesses.

If, therefore, we exclude from the social contract all that is not essential, we shall find it reduced to the following terms:

Each of us places in common his person and all his power under the supreme direction of the general will; and as one body we all receive each member as an indivisible part of the whole.

From that moment, instead of as many separate persons as there are contracting parties, this act of association produces a moral and collective body, composed of as many members as there are votes in the assembly, which from this act receives its unity, its common self, its life, and its will. This public person, which is thus formed by the union of all other persons, took formerly the name of "city," and now takes that of "republic" or "body politic." It is called by its members "State" when it is passive, "Sovereign" when in activity, and whenever it is compared with other bodies of a similar kind, it is denominated "power." The associates take collectively the name of "people," and separately, that of "citizens," as participating in the sovereign authority, and of "subjects," because they are subjected to the laws of the State. But these terms are frequently confounded and used one for the other; and it is enough that a man understands how to distinguish them when they are employed in all their precision.[9]

Rousseau's reference to the "general will" deserves some elaboration, since general will is a cornerstone in his social contract. The general will should be contrasted with the "will of all," or unanimity of feeling. A group of wills is *general* when each member of the group aims at the common good, which is what Rousseau has in mind. True, the general will and the will of all might result in the same course, for each group member may see his or her own best interests being served. But Rousseau felt that agreement is more likely when everyone tries to determine whether a proposed action is best for the good of all, for the general good, rather than just for self.

Rousseau argues further that the general will, unlike the will of all, represents a true consensus—it's what everyone wants. Even when the minority must conform to majority will, there is no coercion or violation of personal freedom because everyone, even the minority members, seeks the general good. In other words, everyone is agreed on the end; they differ only in what they believe the means should be. Ultimately, they all get what they want: promotion of the common good. One glaring flaw in the whole arrangement, of course, is the assumption that the majority view accords with the general good. Such a bald appeal to head counting is, to say the least, highly questionable.

Nonetheless, Rousseau's version of the social contract has a decided Lockean flavor. A decade later Thomas Jefferson would also sound a Lockean chord in these lines from the Declaration of Independence: "To secure these rights [life, liberty and the pursuit of happiness], governments are instituted among Men, deriving their just powers from the consent of the governed. That whenever any Form of Government becomes destructive of these ends, it is the

9. *Jean Jacques Rousseau.* The Social Contract and Discourses. *G. D. H. Cole, Trans. An Everyman's Library Edition. Reprinted by permission of the publisher in the United States, E. P. Dutton.*

Right of the People to alter or to abolish it, and to institute a new Government, laying its foundation on such principles and organizing its powers in such form, as to them shall seem most likely to effect their safety and Happiness." Both the Declaration and Locke's contract agree that when a government infringes on the individual rights of life, liberty, and the pursuit of happiness (or property, for Locke), the people have the right to dismiss it.

But precisely when does a government destroy those rights? Perhaps it would be easy to determine when a government is depriving us of our right to life, but what about liberty and the pursuit of happiness? It could be argued that these liberties are political and civil in nature and can thus be spelled out constitutionally. Still, it is one thing for a constitution to guarantee the right of assembly, but quite another for a mayor to interpret an assembly as a mob and for a court to uphold this interpretation. In other words, the U.S. Constitution, like the contract theory on which it is based, provides a general framework to ensure liberties but leaves great latitude for the interpretation and possible restriction of those liberties.

Determining when a government is infringing on the pursuit of happiness is even more difficult. Some might argue that a graduated income tax inhibits the pursuit of happiness. When a wealthy person's earnings and holdings are taxed considerably more than an average-income person's, is the government infringing on the wealthy person's pursuit of happiness? This is really the basis for the Millers' discontent.

Marge: You know, when you actually sit down and start adding up all the things you don't morally support and subtract from your taxes how much is going to each, you come up with quite a sum.

Bruce: You can say that again. I'd like to have every penny of my tax money that went to that Vietnam war.

Marge: We both thought that was wrong.

Bruce: But we helped finance it.

Marge: And the maddening thing about it is that we end up depriving ourselves of things that will make us happy in order to support many things we don't think are right.

Bruce: That sure is a switch, isn't it? I thought the job of government was to help in our pursuit of happiness, not to hinder it.

Under the social contract, then, we give up certain rights to gain others. Specifically, under our political system we are guaranteed the rights to life, liberty, and the pursuit of happiness. The problem for today is: Is the government acting in such a way as to secure these rights? Or is the government acting in such a way that it is actually depriving us of these rights?

There are no simple answers to these questions about the proper limits of government control. Complicating matters is the fact that evaluating the justice of the social contract requires a high degree of moral development. Evidence suggests that most people lack such a degree of moral awareness (see Philosophy and Life 4-1). Nevertheless, even if the authority and power of the state are justified, we can and should inquire about their proper limits. We can ask, for example, whether a tax code should be used as a mechanism for social change. Just how far the state or government ought to go in the exercise of its authority and power in controlling the lives of its citizens provokes analysis about the nature of government control.

Government Control

Regarding the extent to which the state or its primary instrument, government, should enter into the lives of its citizens, two extreme positions are immediately apparent: **anarchism** and **totalitarianism.** Anarchists express unswerving faith in individual cooperation and show little, if any, confidence in the state. Accordingly, anarchists argue that the state should be abolished as unnecessary. At the other extreme, totalitarians place such strong emphasis on the efficient workings of the state that they are willing to sacrifice most individual rights and interests. Thus, totalitarians believe that government should absorb the whole of human life.

Between these polar opposites are more moderate positions represented by most contractual theorists and by our own society. Typifying these positions is a confidence in both individual cooperation and the reasonably just state that falls short of a total endorsement of either. These moderate views try to maintain a proper balance between the claims of the individual and state, between private and public interests. They do not want any more government interference than is needed, but are willing to allow it when necessary. In the same vein, they leave the way open for private initiatives but are ready to assist private initiatives when they fail. Not only do these moderate positions seek to protect efforts undertaken for the common good, but they also try to positively promote them. They respect the rights of individual and family, are reluctant to usurp their duties, and try to assist them mainly by providing opportunities rather than attempting to regiment their behavior.

Clearly no government has ever succeeded in perfectly effecting this moderate theory of government control, but many, including our own, continue to hold it as an ideal. One factor that challenges the realization of this ideal is that individuals and groups who on the one hand espouse it, on the other have leanings to one side or the other: toward confidence in willing individual cooperation or in a strong authoritarian state. These leanings are not so pronounced as to warrant the labels *anarchism* or *totalitarianism*. A more accurate classification might term them *individualism* and *paternalism*. In any event, one must understand these leanings in order to understand why it is so difficult in our own society to effect the ideal of a proper balance between the public interest and the need for cooperation on the one hand, and individual rights and interests on the other. So, it would be quite profitable for us to consider individualism and paternalism and show how these interplay with moderate approaches to government control.

Individualism

Some historical background is necessary to understand the philosophy of **individualism.** This can be provided with reference to the contract theory we've just sketched. The earliest formulations of modern contract theory were made against the backdrop of two significant trends. One was the desire to break away from established patterns of thinking. The second was the belief in universal law. We will say considerably more about these tendencies in Chapter 9 when we discuss the philosophy of materialism. Here it's enough to emphasize that these two intellectual main currents carried the silt of social, political, and economic developments in the eighteenth and nineteenth centuries, as well as the philosophy of individualism.

For example, the tendency toward freedom and independence was fostered by an economic theory known as **laissez-faire,** which accompanied the indus-

---

PHILOSOPHY AND LIFE 4-1
Stages of Moral Development

Any discussion of social justice that refers to reciprocity, equality, and human dignity is bound to lose a great many people. The reason is that most of us simply don't grasp the abstract principles involved. Why not?

Psychologist Lawrence Kohlberg has thrown as much light on this question as anybody. In his view, individuals pass through three levels of moral development, each consisting of two stages. Stages 1 and 2 comprise what Kohlberg calls the preconventional level, characterized by unquestioning obedience and the satisfaction of one's own needs. At Stage 1, one's moral views derive almost entirely from cultural labels of good and bad and from the physical power of those who define good and bad. At Stage 2 one generally regards as right whatever satisfies one's own needs. At both of these stages, concepts of fairness, justice, and loyalty are totally absent. Any reciprocity evident operates strictly in an instrumental sense: "You scratch my back, and I'll scratch yours."

At the conventional level, Kohlberg says that individuals attempt to please others and satisfy social conventions, customs, and laws. Thus, at Stage 3 good conduct is viewed as what pleases and helps others and what is approved by society. Behavior is judged by intention rather than exclusively in terms of consequences. Kohlberg's example of Stage 3 morality: Charlie Brown of *Peanuts* fame. At Stage 4 individuals are still authority oriented but recognize a personal stake in the maintenance of law and order. Thus, Stage 4 morality is characterized by duty to society and respect for the law, which is not yet perceived as a social contract open to change but as being fixed and

trial revolution. According to this theory, business and commerce should be free from governmental control so that the entrepreneur can pursue free enterprise. Adam Smith (1723–1790), the leading spokesperson for laissez-faire economics, insisted that governmental interference in private enterprise must be reduced, free competition encouraged, and enlightened self-interest made the rule of the day. If commercial interests are left to pursue self-interest, then the good of society will be served. Indeed, only through egoistic pursuits can the greatest happiness for the greatest number be produced. The essence of Smith's position can be seen in the following passage from his most influential *The Wealth of Nations*. Notice that Smith, while discussing the need to restrict imports, actually underscores the broad enabling assumption that underlies his economics.

> But the annual revenue of every society is always precisely equal to the exchangeable value of the whole annual produce of its industry, or rather is precisely the same with that exchangeable value. As every individual, therefore, endeavors as much as he can both to employ his capital in the support of domestic industry, and so to direct that industry that its produce may be of the

immutable. Thus, racism may be wrong, but one shouldn't break the law to protest against it, for that invites social chaos.

The postconventional level represents higher values and the questioning of the existing legal system in the light of social utility and such abstract principles as justice and human dignity. Thus, in Stage 5 a social contract orientation develops, characterized by a recognition of the value of constitutional rights and legal procedures. Here is evident an emphasis on possible change of the social contract, based on social utility. In Kohlberg's view, Stage 5 reasoning represents the "official morality" of the U.S. government and is expressed in the U.S. Constitution. Thus, breaking a law to protest racial inequality would be right if it helped change an unjust law. In Kohlberg's view, some people, but hardly a majority, reach this stage. The final stage, Stage 6, is characterized by an individual's formulating abstract moral principles that are not so much prescriptions for behavior as universal principles of justice, reciprocity, equality, and respect for all people. Few people reach this stage.

□ *At what stage are you?* □ *At what stage are most people whom you know?* □ *Research indicates that people cannot comprehend moral reasoning two stages above their own. What are the implications of this for creating a just society?*

greatest value; every individual necessarily labors to render the annual revenue of the society as great as he can. He generally, indeed, neither intends to promote the public interest, nor knows how much he is promoting it. By preferring the support of domestic to that of foreign industry, he intends only his own security; and by directing that industry in such a manner as its produce may be of the greatest value, he intends only his own gain, and he is in this, as in many other cases, led by an invisible hand to promote an end which was no part of his intention. Nor is it always the worse for the society that it was no part of it. By pursuing his own interest he frequently promotes that of the society more effectually than when he really intends to promote it. I have never known much good done by those who affected to trade for the public good. It is an affection, indeed, not very common among merchants, and very few words need be employed in dissuading them from it.[10]

Thinkers like Thomas Malthus (1766–1834) and David Ricardo (1772–1823) argued that obvious inequities that might arise would resolve themselves, for natural law or order operated in such affairs as surely as Newton's laws of gravitation and motion operated in the universe. Therefore, natural law would regulate prices and wages; natural law would correct inequities. Such thinking was bolstered by the nineteenth-century utilitarianism of John Stuart Mill.

Like Smith, Mill feared government interference in the economy. A government should interfere, said Mill, only in those matters for which society itself cannot find solutions. Such matters should be resolved according to the principle of utility, which holds that what is good is that which produces the greatest happiness for the greatest number of people. Under no circumstances should the government unnecessarily restrict individual freedom, including the individual's right to realize as much pleasure and progress for himself as possible.

At least three beliefs characterize the philosophy of individualism as it appeared in the eighteenth and nineteenth centuries: (1) Individuals should be free to pursue their own interests without interference, providing they do not impinge on the rights and interests of others; (2) individuals should be allowed to earn as much money as they can and to spend it however they choose; and (3) individuals should not expect the government to aid or inhibit their economic growth, for such interference only destroys individual incentive and creates indolence. So, in order to combat the antiquated laws and regulations that fettered humans, to keep pace with the scientific discoveries of natural law, and to bury the last vestiges of feudalism, eighteenth- and nineteenth-century thinkers elevated the importance of individualism. These thinkers were termed *liberals* and their political philosophy *liberalism*.

Classical liberalism placed great importance on individual rights, especially those concerning economic matters. The government, these liberals felt, should interfere only as a last resort. John Locke, for example, believed that since we are by nature free, any form of government is an encroachment on that freedom. For Locke, state power was inherently at odds with individual liberty: They govern best who govern least.

10. *Adam Smith*. The Wealth of Nations. C. J. Bullock, Ed. New York: Colliers and Sons, 1909, p. 379. *Originally published 1776.*

Much has happened since that time. Basically, the individual has lost control of the means of production. For one thing—as Karl Marx (1818–1883), whom we will later showcase, observed as early as the middle of the nineteenth century—exorbitant costs, complex machinery, increasing demands, and intense competition have worked against individual productiveness. Specialization in the textile and steel industries has tended to depersonalize the worker. Whereas the economy of the industrial revolution was characterized by relatively free and open competition, the economy of the twentieth century is made up of a relatively few enormous holding companies, which can secretly fix prices, eliminate smaller competitors, and monopolize an industry. Occasionally the government regulates industry, as the Justice Department did in 1974 when it attempted to sever Western Electric from I.T.&T. But most efforts are token and ineffective. Today's corporation apparently wishes government to stay out of its business only when things are going well. Frequently, however, when a company is about to fail, it expects to be subsidized as a "vital industry," as did Penn Central, Pan American Airlines, and Chrysler Corporation. And businesses openly solicit governmental favors in return for political support. Many politicians offer the plums of favorable tariffs, franchises, and laws in return for whopping sums of money. It is little wonder that today we find ourselves largely trying to undo the solutions of the nineteenth century. In so doing, yesterday's liberals often become today's conservatives.

Although generalizations can be dangerously misleading, we might risk saying that today's liberals frequently feel that in many areas the best government is the one that governs *most*. Although they would agree with Locke that individuals are perhaps by nature free, they would add that individuals are *in fact* unfree. Therefore, government should free individuals by vigorously—some would say intrusively—directing social change. People's only hope of gaining freedom and equality, they claim, is through governmental action. Furthermore, they probably would not agree with Locke that state power is inherently at odds with individual liberty. Without governmental interference, they would point out, we'd still have sweatshops, rampant segregation, subminimal wages, inadequate roads and transportation, and substandard schools, colleges, hospitals, and waterworks; and we would be without many services that government now provides. Whereas Locke viewed the adequately structured government as promoting individual liberties and rights and leaving individuals free to earn their own livings as they see fit, contemporary liberals view that kind of government as the reason we have monopolies, ruthless competition, slums, unemployment, and social inequalities. It is that very "rugged individualism" preached by classical liberals that their contemporary counterparts like Philip Slater[11] say underlies many of our social ills. In brief, today's liberals generally believe that the human condition can be improved by government.

Clearly liberalism today is significantly different from the classical liberalism espoused by John Locke and later by Jeremy Bentham and John Stuart Mill. True, there are similarities: Both types believe that humans are social animals

---

11.   *See Philip Slater.* The Pursuit of Loneliness. *Boston: Beacon Press, 1971.*

greatly influenced by environment; both claim that the job of government is to promote the general welfare; both uphold the sacredness of life, liberty, and the pursuit of happiness. But the differences are major. Whereas classical liberals minimized government interference, contemporary liberals often maximize it. Whereas classical liberals paid only token attention to the state's role in promoting individualism, today's liberals think that strong communal bonds are necessary to preserve individual life, liberty, and the pursuit of happiness, and that government must play a vital role in strengthening these bonds. Finally, whereas classical liberals held individuals ultimately responsible for their own liberty and prosperity, contemporary liberals generally hold political authority responsible for these things. In short, in trying to strike a proper balance between private and public interests, today's liberal generally emphasizes the need for a strong government presence to ensure individual cooperation and opportunity.

Paternalism

Paternalism, sometimes termed *statism*, leans toward a strong state presence and has little confidence in the possibility of individual cooperation without the guiding hand of government. Its corresponding economic theory would be socialism, although paternalism can exist without socialism (for example, in pre-French Revolution mercantilist monarchies). When not socialistic, paternalism allows private property but limits the scope of private enterprise in its use. Additionally, paternalism tends to impose regulations on business and charges the state with the duty of undertaking all public works. Although in theory paternalism does not dismiss the value of individual and family, in practice it gives government an active role in directing the affairs of each, as a parent might a child.[12] If we were looking for a classical political ideology that corresponds with paternalism as liberalism does with individualism, then *conservatism* would be a likely choice, specifically the conservatism of the English political philosopher Edmund Burke (1729–1797).

Central to Burke's political ideology is a distrust of the individual. Emphasis on individualism, he felt, led to the anarchy of the French Revolution. Certainly, individualism was incompatible with social and political stability, Burke's primary concern. For Burke, society represented an organic and mystic link binding the past, present, and future. The state, therefore, was not an artificial but an organic structure, nourished by religious fervor, patriotism, and faith. This concept of the state as an organism persuaded Burke to preserve tradition, to nurture respect for established institutions such as religion and private property, and to honor whatever had survived for generations. As a result, Burke considered radical changes signs of disaster, contending that all change must evolve naturally and never represent a rupture with the past.

Obviously, Burke's political ideas emphasize institutions over individuals. The survival of the state is by far more important than individual interests, which always must be consistent with tradition. Individual rights exist side by side with duties, which, along with faith and loyalty, provide the mortar of a

---

12. *See Milton A. Gonsalves.* Fagothey's Right and Reason. *7th ed. St. Louis: C. V. Mosby, 1981, p. 360.*

solid society. Unlike liberals, Burke believed that individuals are not by nature equal. This belief, along with his observations of political unrest in Europe, led him to distrust the masses, democracy, and popular rule. As a result, Burke's ideal state is ruled by a landed aristocracy whose circumstances of birth, breeding, and education mark them as natural rulers. Only such aristocrats are capable of enforcing the law and inspiring respect for traditions and institutions.

As is true of classical and contemporary liberals, classical and contemporary conservatives differ in their conceptions of individualism. Whereas Burke showed little if any faith in the individual, today's conservatives are decidedly ambivalent. On the one hand, many conservatives today are reluctant to leave the development of one's moral character to oneself. They seem rather pessimistic about the individual's capacity or willingness to live virtuously, as defined by some religious or time-honored standard. As a result, they often support political systems that promise to restore traditional moral values, and reassert the centrality of personal integrity, individual responsibility, and the so-called Protestant work ethic. Indeed, many conservatives, though not all, expect the government to initiate programs and pass laws that advance these goals (for example, anti-abortion and anti-pornography legislation, reduction of welfare and other human services programs, the inclusion of creationism theory in public school biology curricula).

On the other hand, these same conservatives often show unbridled optimism in the individual capacity to manage one's own economic affairs. Indeed, they resist and oppose government interference in the economic sphere as vigorously as did the classical liberals of the nineteenth century.

Contemporary conservatives frequently argue that governmental interference is strangling society. If the government would only allow individual states, communities, and people more powers of self-determination, problems would straighten out. Instead, they say, the federal government regulates commerce, education, transportation, and utilities more and more. Rather than liberating individuals, government watches over them from cradle to grave, thereby destroying initiative and self-respect. As a result, many conservatives today agree with David Riesman's judgment that "no ideology . . . can justify the sacrifice of an individual to the needs of the group."[13]

Thus, conservatism has maintained its emphasis on order, continuity, traditional institutions, and personal discipline. But, with economic problems increasing, the disparity between the haves and the have-nots more evident than ever, and growing pressure on government to redress these and other inequalities, contemporary conservatives seem inclined to define individualism in terms of economic rather than political freedom. Since contemporary liberals argue for more governmental involvement to redress economic and social inequities, ideological tension is bound to arise. This tension results from a fundamental difference between liberals, who espouse the greatest possible equality among individuals, and conservatives, who espouse the greatest possible respect for individual rights. At the core of this difference is the aforementioned problem of justice and what constitutes the just society.

13. *David Riesman.* Individualism Reconsidered. *Garden City, N.Y.: Doubleday, 1954, p. 27.*

The preceding observations should be viewed as cautious generalizations, which are subject to some glaring exceptions because of the various nuances within contemporary liberal and conservative thinking. But there is little question that the differences usually can be accounted for in terms of one's leaning toward individual cooperation or a strong state. And there is no question that the terms *liberal* and *conservative* are indeed slippery ones whose meanings today sometimes border on diametric opposition to their classical formulations.

But whatever the stripe of today's liberal or conservative, whether the leaning is toward individual cooperation or a strong authoritarian state, both believe in varying solutions to the same key problem. That problem concerns striking a proper balance between private and public interests. In other words, both espouse the middle way between anarchism and totalitarianism. What's more, they believe that government should positively assist private initiative for the common good.

One very important power implied in the belief that government has a definite role in helping individuals advance the general welfare is that the government has the right and duty to pass laws. Indeed, when we think of "law," what comes first to mind is the law of the state. This is what the great Christian philosopher and theologian Saint Thomas Aquinas seemingly had in mind when he gave his classical definition of law as "nothing else than an ordinance of reason for the common good promulgated by him who has care of the community."[14] So, although there are various moderate views on government control, all these views share the belief that, whatever the proper balance between individual and state, the state and government have the right and duty to exercise control through law. So important is law in distinguishing between private and public rights and interests, in articulating the basic tenets of contract theory, that it warrants our attention.

Law

Traditionally, the line of demarcation between the individual and society has been the *law*, by which we mean a rule or body of rules that tell individuals what they may and may not do.

Our Western legal system, which we have inherited from the Judeo-Christian tradition, is a hierarchy of laws. For example, when a town law and a state law conflict, the state law takes precedence. Likewise, federal laws take precedence over state laws. Does anything take precedence over federal law, over the so-called law of the land? Both the Jewish and the Christian traditions maintain allegiance to a law that transcends any state, which they have historically referred to as the "law of God." We find a similar concept in ancient Greek philosophy.

The Stoics, members of the school of thought founded by Zeno around 300 B.C., believed that the world does not operate by blind chance but involves

---

14. *Saint Thomas Aquinas.* Summa Theologica, *in* Basic Writings of Saint Thomas, *Anton Pegis, Ed. New York: Random House, 1968, vol. 2, p. 4.*

divine providence. The universe, they believed, is rational, in the sense that it operates according to laws that the human mind can discover. This orderliness or world reason the Stoics variously termed *Zeus, nature,* and *logos* ("word"). Since people are happy when they act in accordance with nature—with the order of the universe—the purpose of institutions, according to the Stoics, is to enact laws that reflect this single universal law. Thus, what we today call *civic laws* have their basis in natural law. Natural law generally refers to (1) a pattern of necessary and universal regularity holding in physical ratio or (2) a moral imperative, a description of what ought to happen in human relationships. It's the second definition that concerns us here.

The Christian philosopher and theologian Saint Augustine presented a well-thought-out scheme of law in his *City of God.* In fact, Augustine's thought influenced Saint Thomas Aquinas, who in the Middle Ages distinguished among several kinds of law. First is divine or eternal law—that is, God's decrees for the governance of the universe. According to Thomas, all things obey eternal law, and how they behave simply reflects this law. Thus, a flame rises and a stone falls. God, then, is the lawmaker of the universe; things behave as they do because He so decrees it; they cannot behave otherwise. But Thomas also applied this concept to the affairs of states. For Thomas, laws applying to the universe—what we today call physical laws—found their counterpart in the lesser communities called states.

Thomas defined natural law as divine law applied to human situations. This description is not of much help until one takes a closer look at Thomas's morality. Morality, as Thomas conceived it, is not an arbitrary set of rules for behavior; rather, the basis of moral obligation is built into the very nature of the human in the form of various inclinations, such as the preservation of life, the propagation of the species, and the search for truth. The moral law, then, is founded upon these natural inclinations and the ability of reason to discern the right course of conduct. The rules of conduct corresponding to these inherent human features are called natural law.

A good part of Thomas's theory of natural law had already been worked through by Aristotle. In *Ethics,* Aristotle distinguished between natural and conventional justice. According to Aristotle, some forms of behavior are wrong because they violate a law that has been made to regulate the behavior. To use a contemporary example, consider the law in many places against jaywalking. Since there's nothing in nature that requires people not to jaywalk, such a law is conventional, not natural. In contrast, Aristotle argued that some laws are derived from nature; the behavior that they prohibit has always been wrong. Murder and theft might be two examples. These are wrong not because any human-made law forbids them but because they run counter to the nature of human beings. Both Aristotle and Thomas believed that humans can discover the natural basis for human conduct through reason. But Thomas went further, contending that the human's existence and nature can only be understood in relation to God.

For Thomas, then, law deals primarily with reason, which is the rule and measure of acts. Law consists of these rules and measures of human acts and is therefore based on reason. What's more, the natural law is dictated by reason. Since God created everything, human nature and natural law are best comprehended as the product of God's wisdom or reason.

In summary, for Thomas, natural law consists of that portion of the eternal law that pertains directly to humans. The basic precepts of the natural law are preservation of life, propagation and education of offspring, and the pursuit of truth and a peaceful society. These precepts reflect God's intentions for the human in creation and can be discovered and understood by reason.

Although these precepts do not vary, their enforcement does. Since different societies are influenced by different topographies, climates, cultures, and social customs, Thomas believed that different codes of justice are needed. He called these specific codes of justice human law. The function of rulers is to formulate human law by informing themselves of the specific needs of their communities and then passing appropriate decrees. So, whereas natural law is general enough to govern the community of all humans, human law is specific enough to meet the requirements of a particular society.

For Thomas, then, there are two points of difference between human law and natural or divine law. First, human law applies to a specific group, society, or community; second, it is the expressed decrees of a human agent and not the laws operating in the universe at large. Nevertheless, a human law is a law because it articulates divine law. That is, human law is not law because it emanates from a legislator or ruler but because it implements divine law.

From Thomas's theory of law we can draw one conclusion that is particularly relevant to our discussion: Subjects have the right to rebel. This conclusion follows from his idea that human law must be obeyed only when it expresses divine law. Since humans are capable of poor judgment, rulers can pass unjust laws that are not "an ordinance or reason for the common good."

In his famous "Letter from Birmingham Jail," civil rights leader Martin Luther King, Jr., relied in part on this point to defend his civil disobedience of segregation laws.[15]

> A just law is a man-made code that squares with the moral law or the Law of God. An unjust law is a code that is out of harmony with the moral law. To put it in the terms of Saint Thomas Aquinas: An unjust law is a human law that is not rooted in eternal law and natural law. Any law that uplifts human personality is just. Any law that degrades human personality is unjust. All segregation statutes are unjust because segregation distorts the soul and damages the personality. It gives the segregator a false sense of superiority and the segregated a false sense of inferiority.

But when people refer to a higher law, they do not always mean a religious or God-given law. Many men who refused to fight in the Vietnam war, for example, were no doubt atheists, but they felt that to fight would violate their personal code of behavior. By higher law, then, we mean any law that an individual considers to take precedence over the body of rules that governs the activities within the state. When people appeal to a higher law, presumably they feel that the state has exceeded its rightful authority over them. But precisely

---

15. *Martin Luther King, Jr. "Letter from Birmingham Jail," in* The Norton Reader. *3rd ed. Arthur M. Eastman, Ed. New York: Norton, 1973, p. 665.*

when is this? When does the state exceed its authority over the individual? To what extent do the government and the public interest have authority over individuals and individual action? This question assumes special importance in the light of psychological studies that show how reluctant people are to question authority (see Philosophy and Life 4-2). The answer to this question, in part, calls for an examination of freedom and its relation to the law.

Freedom

Were we concerned with and should we value only efficiency in government, then any evaluation of the rightful limits of governmental authority would be relatively simple. Only required would be a determination of whether or not government intrusions as exercised through law best serve public interest. By this strictly social utility account, it is entirely possible that the most authoritarian government might prove the most efficient. Indeed, a popular explanation for the relative ease with which the Soviet Union, compared with the United States, can marshal its citizens behind a policy or program is that by nature a totalitarian regime does not require a consensus of national opinion as a democracy does.

But clearly in our society we are concerned with more than efficiency, more than a well-oiled governmental machine. We are also concerned with justice and individual rights, which we do not consider altogether contingent on the social good. To be sure, efficiency is not always compatible with the dictates of justice and individual rights, both of which contract theory regards as of paramount importance and our philosophy of law acknowledges. The trouble is that contract theory is not clear about the status of individual rights. One of those rights, which concerns us here, is freedom.

The kind of freedom we have in mind can be called political and social freedom, which includes the freedoms of speech, religion, and governance. History records many heroic battles fought to secure these freedoms as well as to win equality, that is, the same treatment for all citizens in a state. Freedom finds what may be its classic description in John Stuart Mill's essay *On Liberty* (1859), in which the British social and political philosopher presents a powerful case for political individualism.

One of Mill's concerns is the freedom of the individual. He is specifically concerned with what actions individuals in society may perform. In essence, Mill claims that society may interfere with the individual in matters involving other people but not in matters involving only the individual. In effect, he distinguishes between two spheres of interest, the outer and the inner. A matter belongs to the outer sphere if it involves more than just a few individuals and to the inner if it involves only the self or a few others. The following excerpt from *On Liberty* captures the spirit of Mill's position:

> What, then, is the rightful limit to the sovereignty of the individual over himself? Where does the authority of society begin? How much of human life should be assigned to individuality, and how much to society?
>
> Each will receive its proper share, if each has that which more particularly concerns it. To individuality should belong the part of life in which it is chiefly the individual that is interested; to society, the part which chiefly interests society.

Though society is not founded on a contract, and though no good purpose is answered by inventing a contract in order to deduce social obligations from it, everyone who receives the protection of society owes a return for the benefit, and the fact of living in society renders it indispensable that each should be bound to observe a certain line of conduct towards the rest. This conduct consists, *first,* in not injuring the interests of one another; or rather certain interests, which, either by express legal provision or by tacit understanding, ought to be considered as rights; and *secondly,* in each person's bearing his share (to be fixed on some equitable principle) of the labors and sacrifices incurred for defending the society or its members from injury and molestation. These conditions society is justified in enforcing, at all costs to those who endeavor to withhold fulfillment. Nor is that all that society may do. The acts of an individual may be hurtful to others, or wanting in due consideration for their welfare, without going to the length of violating any of their constituted rights. The offender may then be justly punished by opinion, though not by law. As soon as any part of a person's conduct affects prejudicially the interests of others, society has jurisdiction over it, and the question whether the general welfare will or will not be promoted by interfering with it, becomes open to discussion. But there is no room for entertaining any such question when a person's conduct affects the interests of no persons besides himself, or need not affect them unless they like (all the persons concerned being of full age, and the ordinary amount of understanding). In all such cases, there should be perfect freedom, legal and social, to do the action and stand the consequences.[16]

16. *John Stuart Mill.* On Liberty. *London: J. M. Dent, 1910, pp. 77–78.*

PHILOSOPHY AND LIFE 4-2
The Milgram Studies

To what extent will people in our society follow the orders of those thought to be in authority? Apparently to a considerable extent. At least that's what a series of experiments conducted by Stanley Milgram indicates.

Milgram's experiments consisted of asking subjects to administer strong electric shocks to people whom the subjects couldn't see. The subjects could supposedly control the shock's intensity by means of a shock generator with thirty clearly marked voltages, ranging from 15 to 450 volts and labeled from "Slight Shock (15)" to "XXX—Danger! Severe Shock (450)."

The entire experiment, of course, was contrived: No one was actually administering or receiving a shock. The subjects were led to believe that the "victims" were being shocked as part of an experiment to determine the effect of punishment on memory. The victims, who were in fact confederates of the experimenters, were strapped in their seats with electrodes attached to their wrists "to avoid blistering and burning." They were told to make no noise until a "300-volt shock" was administered, at which point they were to make noise loud enough for the subjects to hear (for example, pounding on the walls as if

Although Mill appears to have drawn some line of demarcation between society and individual, it seems fuzzy. Just how many constitute "a few others"? Furthermore, Mill argues that since the individual and not society is the best judge of what advances self-interest, the individual should be free from interference in such pursuits. But it seems that we do not always know our best interests. Suppose a man who enjoys heroin "shoots up" every day. This matter might fall within the inner sphere, in which case he should be free from interference. Yet his behavior is probably not in his best interests. Therefore, it could easily be argued that his behavior should be interfered with.

The problem is that Mill's concept of freedom guarantees noninterference but not much else. What kind of freedom allows a drug addict to shoot himself into oblivion? Although this kind of freedom is necessary, it is a negative freedom, a "freedom-from." These are the kinds of freedom guaranteed us by the Bill of Rights—freedoms from outside influence. But perhaps something more positive is needed, a "freedom-to."

Freedoms-to are positive statements that guarantee people certain choices: the right to an education; the right to medical care; the right to a decent neighborhood; the right to equal opportunity regardless of race, national origin, or sex; and the right to equal pay for work of equal worth. When the freedoms-to are combined with the freedoms-from, we seem to have a better description of political and social freedom and of a climate favorable to personal security and growth. Just as important, we have a basis for viewing law as an essential part of freedom rather than just a limit on it.

in pain). The subjects were reassured that the shocks, though extremely painful, would cause no permanent tissue injury.

When asked, a number of psychologists said that no more than 10 percent would honor the request to administer a 450-volt shock. In fact, well over half did—twenty-six out of forty. Even after hearing the victims' pounding, 87.5 percent of the subjects (thirty-five out of forty) applied more voltage. The conclusions seem unmistakable: A significant number of people in society, when urged by legitimate authority and when being paid, will hurt others.

□ Under what conditions, if any, does society have the right to expect its members to kill or injure other human beings?   □ Under what conditions, if any, may individuals refuse?   □ In order to conduct this experiment, experimenters had to lie to subjects and expose them to considerable stress. Do you think that was moral?   □ If so, on what grounds?

Without understanding the distinction between negative and positive free-doms, we are hard pressed to understand intense social unrest. For example, seeing freedom only as freedoms-from, we would probably say that all Ameri-cans are equally free. But the concept of freedom-to clearly shows that some of us are freer than others. Without certain freedoms-to, some people will have very little freedom.

A currently divisive issue in the United States, as we have seen, is how much the government should interfere to guarantee freedoms-to. Some contend that there is already too much interference, that the executive, legislative, and particularly the judicial branches of government are poking their collective noses into areas where they do not belong. In short, there are too many bad laws. Others claim that governmental interference is needed, that society has grown too unwieldy for individuals to fight their own battles for freedom. In short, there are too few good laws. Although these positions differ in their solutions, they are concerned with the same central problem that has occupied us throughout this chapter: how to best strike a balance between public and pri-vate interest. In other words, they are concerned with the problem of justice.

Showcase: Karl Marx (1818–1883)

On several occasions in this chapter and elsewhere in our study, we have alluded to Karl Marx. So seminal a social philosopher of the modern age is Marx, and so widely misunderstood, that we will focus on him in this showcase.

Karl Marx was born in 1818 in Trier in the Rhineland to Jewish parents who, faced with anti-Semitism, turned Lutheran. After completing his course of studies at the gymnasium in Trier, Marx went on to study at the universities of Bonn and Berlin.

When Marx entered the University of Berlin in 1836, the dominant intellec-tual influence throughout Germany and at the university was the philosophy of Georg Hegel (1770–1831). Central to Hegel's thought was that reality is not fixed and static, but changing and dynamic. Life is constantly passing from one stage of being to another; the world is a place of constant change. But Hegel did not believe the change itself is arbitrary. On the contrary, he thought it proceeds according to a well-defined pattern or method, termed a *dialectic*.

The idea of the dialectic is that reality is full of contradictions. As reality unfolds, the contradictions are resolved and something new emerges. The pro-cedure of the dialectical method can be represented as follows:

Thesis: assertion of position or affirmation

Antithesis: assertion of opposite position or negation

Synthesis: union of the two opposites

The Hegelian **dialectic** presumably expresses the process of development that Hegel believed pervades everything. By this account, there is only one reality:

Idea. The only thing that is real is the rational; the Idea is thought itself thinking itself out. The process of thought thinking itself out is the dialectic.

In thinking itself out, thought arrives at the main antithesis to itself: inert matter. At this point Idea objectifies itself in matter: It becomes Nature, or, for Hegel, the creation of the world. Life is the first sign of synthesis. Thought reappears in matter, organizing plants and displaying conscious instinct in animals. Ultimately, thought arrives at self-consciousness in human beings. The dialectic continues through human history.

In order to understand a society or culture, therefore, it is crucial to recognize the dialectical process that is operating. Each period in the history of a culture or society has a character of its own. This character can be viewed as a stage in the development from what preceded it to what follows it. This development proceeds by laws that basically are mental or spiritual. In effect, a culture has a personality of its own, which largely accounts for its development. Indeed, by Hegel's reckoning, the whole world or all of reality can be identified with a single character or personality—with what Hegel variously called *the Absolute, world self,* or *God* (taken in a pantheistic sense). All of human history, then, can be viewed as the progressive realization of this Absolute Spirit which is the synthesis of the thesis, Idea thinking itself out, with the antithesis, Idea spread out into Nature.

While at the University of Berlin, Marx read Hegel's complete works. He was drawn to a revolutionary aspect of Hegel's philosophy, namely, that no historical state of affairs can ever be considered final since further negation is always possible. Marx also joined the Berlin Club of Young Hegelians, a group of young men who believed that the aim of philosophy must be to alter the world. Under their influence, he soon became convinced that philosophy alone was inadequate to change the world. What was needed was social and political action.

After completing his doctoral dissertation in 1841, Marx turned to socialistic journalism, taking an editorial position in 1842 at the *Rheinische Zeitung (Rhineland Gazette)*. In this position, Marx became familiar with the social problems of the day, and deepened the social orientation of his thought. Soon he became editor-in-chief of the newspaper and took it in a radical direction, conducting a campaign against Christian religion and the Christian state. As a result, the newspaper was shut down by the state censor in March 1843.

The suppression of the *Rheinische Zeitung* marked a new period in Marx's intellectual development, during which he began to formulate his materialistic concept of history and eventually became a communist. Also during this time, which he spent in Paris, Marx turned to a critical examination of Hegelian thought, and in 1843 published an article on the subject: "Introduction to the Critique of Hegel's Philosophy." The article portrayed religion as an illusion resulting from the fact that the world is alienated and estranged from its real nature. Total revolution, Marx argued, is necessary to turn and emancipate society from this condition. Marx's critique of Hegel was significantly influenced by the work of Ludwig Feuerbach.

In his *Essence of Christianity* (1841), Feuerbach had tried to show that Hegel's idealism was wrong-headed in that it had succeeded in eliminating physical reality. By contrast, Feuerbach held that philosophy is the science of reality, which consists in physical nature. Thus, when philosophy pretends, as Hegel's does, to have a higher object than the human relations to physical nature, it errs; it becomes sheer illusion. Part of the illusion Feuerbach saw in Hegel was Hegel's belief in Absolute Spirit or God progressively realizing itself in history. In fact, according to Feuerbach, the ideas of religion are produced by human beings as a reflection of the world, which is the only reality. Because individuals are dissatisfied or "alienated" in their practical lives, they need to believe in illusions such as those fostered in Hegelian philosophy. Thus, metaphysics is no more than an "esoteric psychology"; it is the expression of feelings within ourselves rather than truths about the universe. In particular, religion is the expression of alienation. Individuals can be freed from the illusions of religion only by realizing their purely human destiny in this world.

Feuerbach's influence on Marx was such that Marx grew convinced that dialectical philosophy could avoid idealism by starting from human reality rather than from an ideal Absolute Spirit. Also, it could avoid mechanistic materialism by taking the concrete nature of the human being as its initial principle.

While his reading of Feuerbach did alter Marx's view of Hegel, Marx nevertheless did preserve Hegel's notion of historical development and of alienation. These he wove into his own materialist concept of history. Like Hegel, Marx saw historical development operating in things; but it was not spiritual, rather material in character. The key to all history lay not in the individual's idea, but in the economic conditions of his or her life. Again, while culling Hegel's notion of alienation, Marx did not see it as metaphysical or religious in nature, but social and economic. Marx's view of alienation can be found in his "Economic and Philosophic Manuscripts" (1844). His materialistic concepts of history can be found in various works of the same period: *The Holy Family* (1845), *The German Ideology* (1846), and *The Poverty of Philosophy* (1847).

Until recently, Marx was best known as the author of *Das Kapital* (1867) and the *Communist Manifesto* (1848) which he coauthored with friend and collaborator Friedrich Engels. Today, largely as a result of the publication of his early writings, the philosophical aspect of Marxist work has caught the attention of scholars. Indeed, it is now thought that Marx's later writings cannot be fully understood and interpreted without reference to his earlier works, especially "Economic and Philosophic Manuscripts" and *The German Ideology*.

View of History

Distinctive in Marx's understanding of the world as a whole is his interpretation of history. Marx was firmly convinced that he had discovered a scientific method for studying the history of human societies, that eventually there would be a single science which would include the science of man along with natural science. Accordingly, he held that there are universal laws behind historical change. Just as we can predict things like eclipses, we can predict the future large-scale course of history from a knowledge of these laws. Just as physicists aim to uncover the natural laws of the universe, so Marx believed he was laying bare the economic laws of modern society, the material laws of capitalist production. These laws, presumably, are working with iron necessity toward inevitable results.

Like Hegel, Marx held that each period in each culture has its own character and personality. Therefore, the only true universal laws in history are those concerned with the process of development whereby one stage gives rise to the next. He viewed this developmental process as roughly divided into the Asiatic, the ancient, the feudal, and the "bourgeois" or capitalist phases. When conditions are right, said Marx, each stage must give way to the next. Ultimately, capitalism will give way to communism. Writing with Engels in the *Communist Manifesto*, Marx puts it this way:

> *The history of all hitherto existing society is the history of class struggles.*
>
> Freeman and slave, patrician and plebian, lord and serf, guild-master and journeyman, in a word, oppressor and oppressed, stood in constant opposition to one another, carried on an uninterrupted, now hidden, now open fight, a fight that each time ended, either in a revolutionary re-constitution of society at large, or in the common ruin of the contending classes.
>
> In the earlier epochs of history, we find almost everywhere a complicated arrangement of society into various orders, a manifold gradation of social rank. In ancient Rome we have patricians, knights, plebians, slaves; in the middle ages, feudal lords, vassals, guild-masters, journeymen, apprentices, serfs; in almost all of these classes, again, subordinate gradations.
>
> The modern bourgeois society that has sprouted from the ruins of feudal society, has not done away with class antagonisms. It has but established new classes, new conditions of oppression, new forms of struggle in place of the old ones.
>
> Our epoch, the epoch of the bourgeoisie, possesses, however, this distinctive feature; it has simplified the class antagonisms. Society as a whole is more and more splitting up into two great hostile camps, into two great classes directly facing each other: Bourgeoisie and Proletariat.[17]

Not only did Marx believe that there are universal laws operating in history, but that these laws are economic in nature. Moreover, there is a causal connection between the economic structure and everything in society such that the mode of production of material life determines the general character of the social, political, and spiritual processes of life. In a word, the economic structure is the real basis by which everything else about society is determined.

Marx's view of history, then, can be characterized as having two main features. First, there are universal laws operating behind historical change. Second, these supposed laws of history are economic in nature. Based on this view of history, Marx predicts that capitalism will become increasingly unstable economically. The class struggle between the *bourgeoisie* (ownership class) and *proletariat* (working class) will increase, with the proletariat getting both poorer and larger in number. The upshot will be a social revolution: The workers will seize power and institute the new communist phase of history.

17. *Karl Marx and Friedrich Engels*. Communist Manifesto. *Samuel Moore, Trans. Chicago: Regnery, 1969.*

View of Human Nature

Related to Marx's view of history is his view of human nature, which we alluded to in Chapter 2. Apart from some obvious biological factors, such as the need to eat, Marx denies that there is any such thing as an essential human nature, that is, something that is true of every individual at all times everywhere. He does allow, however, that humans are social beings, that to speak of human nature is really to speak in terms of the totality of social relations. Accordingly, whatever any of us does is a social act, which presupposes the existence of other people standing in certain relations to us. In short, everything is socially learned.

The social influence is especially apparent in every activity of production. Producing what we need to survive physically is a social activity: It always requires that we interact and cooperate with others. Given Marx's account, it follows that the kind of individuals we are and the kinds of things we do are determined by the kind of society in which we live. In other words, for Marx it isn't the consciousness of individuals that defines their beings, but their social being which determines their consciousness. In commenting incisively on this point, professor of philosophy Leslie Stevenson has written:

> In modern terms, we can summarize this crucial point by saying that sociology is not reducible to psychology, i.e., it is not the case that everything about men can be explained in terms of facts about individuals; the kind of society they live in must be considered too. This methodological point is one of Marx's most distinctive contributions, and one of the most widely accepted. For this reason alone, he must be recognized as one of the founding fathers of sociology. And the *method* can of course be accepted whether or not one agrees with the particular *conclusions* Marx came to about economics and politics.[18]

Professor Stevenson goes on to point out that, despite Marx's denial of such a thing as individual human nature, Marx is prepared to offer at least one generalization about human nature. It is that humans are active, predictive beings who distinguish themselves from other animals by the central, overriding fact that they produce their own means of subsistence. Indeed, according to Marx, not only is it natural for humans to work for their livings, but *right* as well. Thus, by Marx's account, the life of productive activity is the right one for humans.

Granted it is proper for humans to work for their living, what may be said about the product of that work? Like Locke before him, and numerous thinkers after him (including Rawls and Nozick), Marx thought that individuals have a legitimate claim to the product of their own labor. But Marx rejects the notion that they are entitled to own property that they have not personally produced. Neither is property ownership licit when it functions to enrich the already affluent at the expense of other people, thereby forcing these people to work without benefit of the products of their labor. But this, according to Marx, is precisely what capitalism encourages: the exploitation of the large working class (proletariat) at the hands of the affluent few who own the means of production

18. *Leslie Stevenson.* Seven Theories of Human Nature. *New York: Oxford University Press, 1974, p. 54.*

(bourgeoisie). Again, here are Marx and Engels writing on this subject in the *Communist Manifesto:*

The bourgeoisie, wherever it has got the upper hand, has put an end to all feudal, patriarchal, idyllic relations. It has pitilessly torn asunder the motley feudal ties that bound man to his "natural superiors," and has left remaining no other nexus between man and man than naked self-interest, callous "cash payment." It has drowned the most heavenly ecstasies of religious fervor, of chivalrous enthusiasm, of philistine sentimentalism, in the icy water of egotistical calculation. It has resolved personal worth into exchange value, and in place of the numberless indefeasible chartered freedoms, has set up that single, unconscionable freedom—Free Trade. In one word, for exploitation, veiled by religious and political illusions, it has substituted naked, shameless, direct, brutal exploitation.

The bourgeoisie has stripped of its halo every occupation hitherto honored and looked up to with reverent awe. It has converted the physician, the lawyer, the priest, the poet, the name of science, into its paid wage-laborers.

The bourgeoisie has torn away from the family its sentimental veil, and has reduced the family relation to a mere money relation.

The bourgeoisie has disclosed how it came to pass that the brutal display of vigor in the Middle Ages, which Reactionists so much admire, found its fitting complement in the most slothful indolence. It has been the first to show what man's activity can bring about. It has accomplished wonders far surpassing Egyptian pyramids, Roman aqueducts, and Gothic cathedrals; it has conducted expeditions that put in the shade all former Exoduses of nations and crusades.

The bourgeoisie cannot exist without constantly revolutionizing the instruments of production, and thereby the relations of production, and with them the whole relations of society. Conservation of the old modes of production in unaltered form, was, on the contrary, the first condition of existence for all earlier industrial classes. Constant revolutionizing of production, uninterrupted disturbance of all social conditions, everlasting uncertainty and agitation distinguish the bourgeois epoch from all earlier ones. All fixed, fast-frozen relations, with their train of ancient and venerable prejudices and opinions, are swept away, all new-formed ones become antiquated before they can ossify. All that is solid melts into air, all that is holy is profaned, and man is at last compelled to face, with sober senses, his real conditions of life, and his relations with his kind.

The need of a constantly expanding market for its products chases the bourgeoisie over the whole surface of the globe. It must nestle everywhere, settle everywhere, establish connections everywhere.

The bourgeoisie has through its exploitation of the world-market given a cosmopolitan character to production and consumption in every country. To the great chagrin of Reactionists, it has drawn from under the feet of industry the national ground on which it stood. All old-established national industries have been destroyed and are daily being destroyed. They are dislodged by new industries, whose introduction becomes a life and death question for all civilized nations, by industries that no longer work up indigenous raw material, but raw material drawn from the remotest zones; industries whose products are consumed, not only at home, but in every quarter of the globe. In place of the old wants, satisfied by the productions of the country, we find new wants, requiring for their satisfaction the products of distant lands and climes. In place of the old local and national seclusion and self-sufficiency, we have intercourse in every direction, universal inter-dependence of nations. And as in material, so also in intellectual production. The intellectual creations of individual nations become common property. National one-sidedness and narrow-mindedness become more and more impossible, and from the numerous national and local literatures there arises a world-literature.

The bourgeoisie, by the rapid improvement of all instruments of production, by the immensely facilitated means of communication, draws all, even the most barbarian, nations into civilization. The cheap prices of its commodities are the heavy artillery with which it batters down all Chinese walls, with which it forces the barbarians' intensely obstinate hatred of foreigners to capitulate. It compels all nations, on pain of extinction, to adopt the bourgeois mode of production; it compels them to introduce what it calls civilization into their midst, i.e., to become bourgeois themselves. In a word, it creates a world after its own image.

The bourgeoisie has subjected the country to the rule of the towns. It has created enormous cities, has greatly increased the urban population as compared with the rural, and has thus rescued a considerable part of the population from the idiocy of rural life. Just as it has made the country dependent on the towns, so it has made barbarian and semi-barbarian countries dependent on the civilized ones, nations of peasants on nations of bourgeois, the East on the West.

The bourgeoisie keeps more and more doing away with the scattered state of the population, of the means of production, and of property. It has agglomerated population, centralized means of production, and has concentrated property in a few hands. The necessary consequence of this was political centralization. Independent, or but loosely connected provinces, with separate interests, laws, governments and systems of taxation, became lumped together in one nation, with one government, one code of laws, one national class-interest, one frontier and one customs-tariff.

The bourgeoisie, during its rule of scarce one hundred years, has created more massive and more colossal productive forces than have all preceding generations together. Subjection of Nature's forces to man, machinery, application of chemistry to industry and agriculture, steam-navigation, railways, electric telegraphs, clearing of whole continents for cultivation, canalization of rivers, whole populations conjured out of the ground—what earlier century had even a presentiment that such productive forces slumbered in the lap of social labor?[19]

According to Marx, the result of bourgeois exploitation is alienation, a key concept in his political and social philosophy.

Concept of Alienation

Marx borrowed his notion of alienation from Hegel, and also from Feuerbach. Recall that for Hegel alienation has its roots in a distinction between a subject and supposedly alien object. For Marx, the human can be considered the subject; and Nature, that is, the human-created world, can be viewed as object. Accordingly, humans are alienated from Nature, from the world and the social relations they create. What is the cause of this alienation? Marx is rather fuzzy about this. At one point he traces the roots of the alienation to the ownership of

19. *Karl Marx and Friedrich Engels.* Communist Manifesto. *Samuel Moore, Trans. Chicago: Regnery, 1969. Reprinted by permission.*

private property. Elsewhere he says that private property is not the cause but the effect of alienation. Whether private property is a cause or effect of alienation, one thing is evident: Marx associates alienation with economics, with the ownership of private property. Specifically, alienation consists of individuals not fulfilling themselves in work. Rather, because the work is imposed on them as a means of satisfying the needs of others, they feel exploited and debased. What about workers who are paid handsomely for their efforts? Nevertheless, says Marx, they remain estranged. Insofar as the fruits of their labor are enjoyed by someone else, the work ultimately proves meaningless to them. In the following selection from his "Economic and Philosophic Manuscripts" (1844), Marx summarizes his notion of alienation as the separation of individuals from the objects they create, which in turn results in separation from other people and ultimately from oneself.

We shall begin from a *contemporary* economic fact. The worker becomes poorer the more wealth he produces and the more his production increases in power and extent. The worker becomes an ever cheaper commodity the more goods he creates. The *devaluation* of the human world increases in direct relation with the *increase in value* of the world of things. Labor does not only create goods; it also produces itself and the worker as a *commodity,* and indeed in the same proportion as it produces goods. . . .

All these consequences follow from the fact that the worker is related to the *product of his labor* as to an *alien* object. For it is clear on this presupposition that the more the worker expends himself in work the more powerful becomes the world of objects which he creates in face of himself, the poorer he becomes in his inner life, and the less he belongs to himself. It is just the same as in religion. The more of himself man attributes to God the less he has left in himself. The worker puts his life into the object, and his life then belongs no longer to himself but to the object. The greater his activity, therefore, the less he possesses. What is embodied in the product of his labor is no longer his own. The greater this product is, therefore, the more he is diminished. The *alienation* of the worker in his product means not only that his labor becomes an object, assumes an *external* existence, but that it exists independently, *outside himself,* and alien to him, and that it stands opposed to him as an autonomous power. The life which he has given to the object sets itself against him as an alien and hostile force.

. . . the worker becomes a slave of the object; first, in that he receives an *object of work,* i.e. receives *work,* and secondly, in that he receives *means of subsistence.* Thus the object enables him to exist, first as a *worker,* and secondly, as a *physical subject.* The culmination of this enslavement is that he can only maintain himself as a *physical subject* so far as he is a *worker,* and that it is only as a *physical subject* that he is a worker. . . .

What constitutes the alienation of labor? First, that the work is *external* to the worker, that it is not part of his nature; and that, consequently, he does not fulfill himself in his work but denies himself, has a feeling of misery rather than well-being, does not develop freely his mental and physical energies but is physically exhausted and mentally debased. The worker, therefore, feels himself at home only during his leisure time, whereas at work he feels homeless. His work is not voluntary but imposed, *forced labor.* It is not the satisfaction of a need, but only a *means* for satisfying other needs. Its alien character is clearly shown by the fact that as soon as there is no physical or other compulsion it is avoided like the plague. External labor, labor in which man alienates himself, is a labor of self-sacrifice, of mortification. Finally, the external character of work for the worker is shown by the fact that it is not his own work but work for someone else, that in work he does not belong to himself but to another person. . . .

We arrive at the result that man (the worker) feels himself to be freely active only in his animal functions—eating, drinking and procreating, or at most also in his dwelling and in personal adornment—while in his human functions he is reduced to an animal. The animal becomes human and the human becomes animal.

Eating, drinking and procreating are of course also genuine human functions. But abstractly considered, apart from the environment of human activities, and turned into final and sole ends, they are animal functions.

We have now considered the act of alienation of practical human activity, labor, from two aspects: (1) the relationship of the worker to the *product of labor* as an alien object which dominates him. This relationship is at the same time the relationship to the sensuous external world, to natural objects, as an alien and hostile world; (2) the relationship of labor to the *act of production* within *labor.* This is the relationship of the worker to his own activity as something alien and not belonging to him, activity as suffering (passivity), strength as powerlessness, creation as emasculation, the *personal* physical and mental energy of the worker, his personal life (for what is life but activity?), as an activity which is directed against himself, independent of him and not belonging to him. This is *self-alienation* as against the above-mentioned alienation of the *thing.* [20]

Marx goes on to infer yet a third aspect of estranged labor from the preceding two: the estrangement of the individual from the species itself. But this needn't concern us here.

In Marx's view, when workers are alienated they cannot be free. Yes, they may have the political and social freedoms of speech, religion, and governance that classical liberals delineate. But even with these freedoms that guarantee noninterference, individuals still are not free; for freedom from government interference and persecution are not necessarily guarantees of freedom from economic exploitation. And it is for this kind of freedom, freedom from alienation, that Marx and Engels feel such passion.

Sense of Freedom

How can humans be free of alienation? To begin with, they must recognize that the key to freedom and the lack of it lies in economics. Therefore, humans must return to a "natural" state in which they and their labor are one. This natural state is similar to Rousseau's in the sense that it recognizes the corrupting influence of society and calls for a conception of the state that will allow humans to be unselfish and nondestructive. But don't misunderstand. Marx is not advocating the end of work. On the contrary, he holds that work is humanizing, ennobling. Thus, he is urging people to liberate themselves from alienated work. Without this kind of freedom, which is basically a freedom from material need, other freedoms are a sham.

20.   *Karl Marx. From "The Economic and Philosophic Manuscripts of 1844," in* Karl Marx: Early Writings. *T. B. Bottomore, Trans.* © *T. B. Bottomore, 1963. Used with permission of McGraw-Hill Book Company.*

Basically Marx prescribes a fairer distribution of wealth as a means for combating alienation and insuring freedom. For Rawls, this means a focus on the needs of the worst-off in society, but not necessarily an equal sharing of wealth and property. In contrast, for Marx justice equates fair distribution with equal distribution. In unvarnished terms, in part this means no ownership of property except for those products a person makes directly. It also means an end to the worker/owner distinction, thereby making everyone a laborer who shares in the benefits of his or her labor. Specifically, Marx calls for nationalization as a way of attaining freedom from alienation—nationalization of land, factories, transport, and banks. But insofar as Marx presumably believes that (1) the State is the basis of all social ills, and (2) nationalization evidently will exacerbate this by concentrating power in the hands of the State, it isn't at all clear how such institutional changes could effect freedom. This observation has led Leslie Stevenson to suggest that we understand Marx as saying "at least in his early phase, that alienation consists in the lack of community. In other words, since the State is not a real community, individuals cannot see their work as contributing to a group of which they are members. It would follow that freedom from alienation would be won by decentralizing, not nationalizing, the State in genuine communities or 'communes.' These entities would be characterized by the abolition of money, specialization, and private property."[21] Indeed, it may be this community element of Marx's vision that explains why Marx continues to win and hold followers. After all, it is difficult to disagree with such ideas as a decentralized society in which individuals cooperate in communities for the common good, technology is harnessed and directed for the interest of all, and the relationship between society and nature is harmonized. At the same time, Marx gives no good reason for assuming that the communist society will achieve any of these ideals. In fact, if the history of Russia since the revolution is any indication, quite the opposite seems the case.

Summary and Conclusions

We opened this chapter by keying on a recurring issue in any determination of the proper relation between individual and society: the problem of justice. One influential theory, developed by Plato and Aristotle, associates justice with merit. Another, developed primarily by English philosophers such as Hobbes, Locke, Hume, and especially Mill, associates justice with social utility. Still another, most recently articulated by John Rawls, identifies justice largely with equality. The problem of justice is related to but distinct from a second issue: the basis on which the power and authority of the state may be justified. While there are a number of theories of the legitimacy of the state, contract theory is the view on which our own society's conception of power and governance is based. Even if the power of the state can be justified by contract theory, we can always ask about the extent of government control: To what extent ought the state and its

21. *Leslie Stevenson.* Seven Theories of Human Nature, *p. 58.*

primary instrument, government, exercise its authority and power over the individual? In response, two extreme views are identifiable. Anarchism has unflinching confidence in the individual and none in the state; by contrast, totalitarianism shows confidence in a strong state and government, and little if any in the individual. The consensus view in our own society falls somewhere between these extremes, with leanings toward individualism, that is, willing individual cooperation; or paternalism, confidence in a strong authoritarian state. These leanings show up, respectively, in what we term political conservatism and liberalism, both of which differ significantly from their classical formulations. Whatever their leaning, contract theorists believe that the state and government have the right and duty to exercise control through law, which traditionally has demarcated individual and society. Laws guarantee freedoms-from, but in a broader sense they also guarantee freedoms-to.

From time immemorial men and women have valued individualism as experienced through freedom and liberties. Indeed, individualism has been the most influential philosophy of freedom in modern Western society. Whether we talk of economic, religious, or political freedom, the emphasis is on the individual. The philosophy of individualism is rooted in the valuing of the human personality and the conviction that human progress relies on the free exercise of individual energy.

The purposes of individualism seem commendable enough. As sociologist Robert Nisbet points out in *The Quest for Community*, "no fault is to be found with the declared purposes of individualism. As a philosophy it has correctly emphasized the fact that the ultimate criteria of freedom lie in the greater or lesser degrees of autonomy possessed by *persons*. A conception of freedom that does not center upon the ethical primacy of the person is either naive or malevolent."[22]

But, as Nisbet observes, the unquestioned ethical centrality of the individual does not make an inherited eighteenth- or nineteenth-century philosophy of individualism equally valid. The reason is that, historically, individualism is more than an ethic. It is also a psychology and an implied theory of the relation between people and their institutions. In Nisbet's view, many of the difficulties with the philosophy of individualism that we presently face stem from an unconscious effort to keep the ethical aspect of individualism alive when we have overlooked and even tried to suppress the psychological and sociological premises of this philosophy. To fully appreciate Nisbet's valuable remarks, we must first separate the assumptions of classical individualism from those of contemporary individualism.

When the fundamental principles of individualism were being formulated in the doctrine of classical liberalism, the human was viewed as a self-sufficient, rational, stable, and secure being who moved inexorably toward freedom and order. In short, the human was idealized as being equipped with both the instincts and the reason that could make it autonomous. In retrospect, we can now see how thinkers actually abstracted certain moral and psychological characteristics from a social organization and attributed them to individuals,

---

22. *Robert Nisbet.* The Quest for Community. *New York: Oxford University Press, 1953.*

rendering those characteristics the "timeless, natural qualities of the *individual*, who was regarded as independent of the influences of any historically developed social organization."[23] In other words, the qualities given to persons actually were qualities of a set of institutions or groups, all of which were aspects of historical tradition.

Recall Hobbes. With the laws of mechanics and motions before him, Hobbes reduced everything to human atoms in motion. Just as the physical scientists of the day dealt with physical atoms in space, so did Hobbes try to build theoretical systems on human atoms alone. Like others, he strived to develop his social and political thought from the purest resources of reason, from the rigorous development of potentialities that reason taught lay everywhere in human nature.[24]

Institutions and groups were rendered secondary, "as shadows, so to speak, of the solid reality of men,"[25] to the inherent rationality and self-sufficiency of humans. Inevitably the strategy of freedom became one of releasing individuals from institutional shackles. In short, while the philosophy of individualism began with an emphasis on the ethical primacy of the individual, it evolved into a rationalist psychology bent on freeing individuals from traditional associations and cultures. Only in this way, it was argued, could the truly free individual unfold.

What emerged in the eighteenth century and developed in the nineteenth, then, were systems of economic, religious, and intellectual freedom founded on the assumption that the essence of human behavior lies within the individual and not in the relation between the individual and institutions. Hence arose the dichotomy between persons and society. The free society was ideally conceptualized as one in which individuals were free from groups, institutions, and classes. It would consist of socially and morally separated individuals. Social order would result from a natural equilibrium of economic and political forces. "Freedom would arise from the individual's release from all the inherited personal interdependencies of traditional community; and from his existence in an impersonal, natural, economic order."[26]

This self-discovery and self-consciousness swelled as society assumed more and more of an impersonal, mechanical structure. Ultimately, the price of individual freedom was viewed as detachment from the world, a defining of society in strictly objective, impersonal terms. What we have, then, is something quite remarkable—in Nisbet's words, "the conception of society as an aggregate of morally autonomous, psychologically free individuals, rather than as a collection of groups."[27] Politically, this roughly translated into a society that abstract all legitimate influence and authority from primary communities (for example, family, religion, professional organizations, and so on) and invests them in the state. This setup is what contract theorists seem to have in mind. Thus, Hobbes

23. *Robert Nisbet.* The Quest for Community, *p. 226.*

24. *Robert Nisbet.* The Quest for Community, *p. 131.*

25. *Robert Nisbet.* The Quest for Community, *p. 226.*

26. *Robert Nisbet.* The Quest for Community, *p. 227.*

27. *Robert Nisbet.* The Quest for Community, *p. 228.*

had no affection for associations based on locality, interest, faith, kinship, or household. He brooked no system of authority other than the state, which he believed best allows individuals to pursue rational self-interest. Similarly, Rousseau believed the state would effectuate the independence of the individual from society by realizing the individual's dependence on self. For Rousseau, the state, the "General Will," was the instrument for freeing individuals from tyrannical societal restrictions.

"What is significant here," writes Nisbet, "is that when the philosophical individualists were dealing with the assumed nature of man, they were dealing in large part with a hypothetical being created by their political imagination."[28] The truth of this observation is apparent in the thinking of nineteenth-century English liberals, nearly all of whom conceived of freedom as emancipation from custom, tradition, and every kind of local group. In short, freedom lay outside association, not within. Mill is a perfect example of this thinking. In *On Liberty* he clearly implies that community or association membership is an unfortunate restriction on the individual's creative powers. Today we don't quarrel with Mill's concept of individuality, but we do puzzle over his necessary conditions for the full development of individualism.

Even a cursory look at the studies in modern social psychology reveals increasing numbers of people seeking communal refuge. A large and growing area of psychology and social science emphasizes the contemporary preoccupation with disintegration and disorganization, as evidenced by numerous studies of community and family disorganization, personality disorientation, industrial alienation, and dissolution of ethnic subcultures. Numerous studies have detailed the rise of the nuclear family (parents and children living in a household) and the decline of the extended family (parents, children, and other blood relatives living in a household). "However empirical his studies of social relationships," Nisbet writes, "however bravely he rearranges the semantic elements of his terminology to support the belief in his own moral detachment, and however confidently he may sometimes look to the salvational possibilities of political legislation for moral relief, it is plain that the contemporary student of human relations is haunted by perceptions of disorganization and the possibility of endemic collapse."[29] Thirty years ago, Kingsley Davis, one of America's foremost sociologists, made the same point when he asked, "Can the anonymity, mobility, impersonality, specialization, and sophistication of the city become the attributes of a stable society, or will society fall apart?"[30] Questions and observations like these point up that the eighteenth- and nineteenth-century rationalist image of the human is inadequate in theory and unacceptable in practice. We realize today that we are not self-sufficient in social isolation, that human nature cannot be deduced simply from the constituents of our germ plasma, and that an individual is vitally connected to social groups. We realize that these affiliations must be acknowledged.

28.   *Robert Nisbet.* The Quest for Community, *p. 228.*

29.   *Robert Nisbet.* The Quest for Community, *p. 9.*

30.   *Kingsley Davis.* Human Society. *New York: Macmillan, 1949, p. 342.*

As a theoretical construct, individualism was tolerable when the primary elements of social organization were still vital and psychologically meaningful. Indeed, it was extremely useful when these elements were overbearing and oppressive. But today classical individualism lacks this pragmatic justification. Now the main psychological problem is not release but reintegration.[31]

An essential tenet of contemporary psychology and sociology is that individuality cannot be studied or understood except as the product of value-oriented human interactions. In other words, we cannot comprehend human nature without considering the vast array of social norms and cultural incentives. Furthermore, because culture is always the product of social relationships, the influence of these social relationships must be recognized to understand human nature. Nisbet expresses this point well: "The greatest single lesson to be drawn from the social transformations of the twentieth century, from the phenomena of individual insecurity and the mass quest for community, is that the intensity of men's motivations toward freedom and cultures is unalterably connected with the relationships of a social organization that has structural coherence and functional significance. From innumerable observations and controlled studies we have learned that the discipline of values *within* a person has a close and continuing relationship with the discipline of values supported by human inter-relationships."[32] In other words, only by fixing their own conduct in a group's culture can individuals keep their own beliefs and values secure in the face of the ceaseless fluctuations of moods, influences, and stimuli that assault them today.

In fact, in the last ten years a communitarian consciousness has emerged that shows a strong tendency to transcend the narrow bounds of individualism enunciated by classical liberalism. This heightened consciousness takes numerous forms. Perhaps the most dramatic are the experimental living ventures that have attracted millions of people. Because the arrangements of these groups vary so much, they cannot be described in general terms. Some communal groups are highly organized and philosophically grounded; others consist of a handful of persons who live in the same house in order to share resources and combat personal isolation. These groups can be rural or urban, closed or open in membership. They may practice celibacy, monogamy, or free sexual relationships. They may be democratic, anarchistic, or, as in the Jonestown experiment, headed by a single charismatic leader. The organizing principles may be religious-spiritual and political, solely political, or psychological, or there may be no established values at all. Whatever the setup, the most important ingredient to the success of these communities is almost always the closeness among the individuals. Communes that don't offer their members some intimate contact seem to dissolve within a short time.[33]

It would be grossly inaccurate to characterize such experimental living alternatives as being anti-individual. On the contrary, they all seem to recognize the

---

31. *Robert Nisbet.* The Quest for Community, *p. 229.*

32. *Robert Nisbet.* The Quest for Community, *p. 230.*

33. *See R. M. Kanter.* "Communes." Psychology Today, *vol. 4, p. 2.*

need to define self within an associative context. Unable to satisfy this need within the framework of a "superstate," organizers have attempted to satisfy it by re-creating basic historical, social, and interpersonal relations. They seem determined to end the bifurcation between individual and society that emerged in the eighteenth and nineteenth centuries. At the same time, history records the horrific evolution of group experiments into totalitarian states when they reduce a complex world to cant formulas and accept belief systems that respond to dogma or a megalomaniac's discipline, as at Jonestown. Ironically, such groups often end up re-creating what they try to escape.

There are many lessons to be learned from such failures. An important one in this discussion's context is that we cannot live outside history. Groups that try to do so become infected with nostalgia for some lost Eden and thus become spiritually enslaved; such communities become breeding grounds for intolerance, passivity, and paranoia.[34] Our challenge is to create a society that both allows people to live within history and gives expression to their spiritual longings, that is, to strike a proper balance between individual and society.

Section Exercises

Justice

1. Is it just to be taxed to fund something that you do not morally subscribe to?

2. Can you think of a situation in which it is more just to treat people differently than to treat them equally?

3. Is the law requiring young people to remain in school to a certain age just? Is the one that requires parents or guardians to enroll their children or charges in a school just?

4. Rawls argues for a view of justice from the position of the worst off in society. Would it be unrealistic to argue a case for a view from the position of the best off in the society? How might you do this?

5. Applying Rawls's maximin principle view to your society, which groups do you think would receive preferential economic treatment? Why?

6. What evidence indicates that Rawls's theory is already operating in your society?

The Justification of the State

1. What is the fundamental difference between Hobbes's and Locke's contract theory concepts?

2. The contract theory contends that we should obey the state because we have contractually promised to do so. How, if at all, have you contracted to obey the state?

3. The Declaration of Independence contends that "whenever any Form of Government becomes destructive" of individual life, liberty, and the pursuit

34. *See "Nightmare in Jonestown." Time, 4 December 1978, p. 27.*

of happiness, "it is the Right of the People to alter or to abolish it." Under what circumstances, if any, would you personally exercise this right? Specifically, what conditions must prevail for you to act to alter or abolish your form of government?

Government Control

1. In *The Pursuit of Loneliness,* Philip Slater contends that our cultural emphasis on individualism is frustrating the spirit of community that is needed to solve many of our social problems. This love for individualism is warring against "the wish to live in trust and fraternal cooperation with one's fellows in a total and visible collective entity."[35] Do you agree that the United States is experiencing this cultural emphasis and that it is having the consequences that Slater sees?

2. Slater also argues that "our approach to social problems is to decrease their visibility: out of sight, out of mind. This is the real foundation of racial segregation, especially its most extreme case, the Indian 'reservation.' The result of our social effort has been to remove the underlying problems of our society farther and farther from daily experience and daily consciousness, and hence to decrease, in the mass of the population, the knowledge, skill, resources and motivation necessary to deal with them."[36] Do you agree?

3. Do you agree with Riesman's statement "No ideology, however noble, can justify the sacrifice of an individual to the needs of the group"?

4. In what ways can excessive concern with individualism actually undermine individualism?

5. How true to the laissez-faire ideal is our present economy?

6. Is Mill's political philosophy consistent with his ethical philosophy, which argues that the moral action is one that produces the greatest happiness for the most people?

7. How realizable today is Mill's belief that "the only freedom which deserves the name, is that of pursuing our own good in our own way, so long as we do not attempt to deprive others of theirs, or impede their efforts to obtain it"?

8. Burke believed that the state has the right to compel the individual to conform to its ideas of social and personal excellence. Do you agree that in certain areas the state has this right? In what areas? Are there areas today in which the state is exercising a right you believe it does not have?

9. "Democrats are generally liberal and Republicans are generally conservative." Do you agree with this generalization? Would you prefer to qualify the statement by specifying an area (economics, for example)? What are the connotations of *liberal* and *conservative*? Cite particular politicians you would misrepresent by putting them into either of these categories.

---

35. *Philip Slater.* The Pursuit of Loneliness, *p. 27.*
36. *Philip Slater.* The Pursuit of Loneliness, *p. 15.*

Law

1. What laws, if any, do you regard as unjust? Why?

2. Does the state have the right to make laws concerning homosexuality, pornography, and marijuana?

3. To what extent do you feel that your own ability to live as you believe is cramped by laws?

4. Do you think that every American has a right to a college education?

5. Do you think that every American has a right to medical care?

6. Do you believe that all people have the right to determine the political system under which they live? If you do, does one state have a moral obligation to assist another that is fighting to exercise that right? Is there any point at which the obligation ends?

Brave New World

Aldous Huxley

What will be the relationship between the individual and the state? On the basis of current trends, can we anticipate what the future holds for a highly industrialized society such as our own?

Numerous literary works have attended to these questions. Perhaps the best known and most widely read is Aldous Huxley's Brave New World. *The theme of this futuristic novel is how the advancement of science affects humans. Specifically, the work is about a group of people who achieve social stability by revolutionizing human control and conditioning with scientific means. As Huxley himself pointed out,* Brave New World *is a warning that unless science is used as a means to the end of producing a race of free individuals rather than as the end to which humans are the means, we invite totalitarian regimes to satisfy society's need for efficiency and stability.*

Totalitarian—there's a word that makes Western liberals shudder. Huxley's Brave New World *is surely a totalitarian state, for one would have to travel far, inside as well as outside fiction, to find a more ruthless concentration of power. And yet, no one can deny that totalitarianism has appeal to people of good will; its success hinges on its offering refuge to the beleaguered, hope to the despairing, and faith to the disillusioned. To dismiss totalitarianism as irrational, undemocratic, or unequal is to misunderstand it. Proponents have argued that totalitarianism's technically advanced scientific management and bureaucratic custodianship of cultural life are consummately rational, that its popular foundations are in the philosophy of such Western liberal darlings as Rousseau, and that the elimination of all associative groups—religious, academic, economic, and artistic—is for the purpose of advancing equality.*

You must avoid the temptation to dismiss the Brave New World *with ridicule and name calling. It is an extension (some might say an aberration) of the historical movement toward the superstate that took root in the liberalism of the eighteenth and nineteenth centuries. What's needed is an alternative that accounts for human nature and cultivates individuality more effectively. After all, those who manage the* Brave New World *are fervent in their conviction that they are fostering a society that will satisfy human wants and needs, and emancipate individuals from the shackles imposed by the petty groups that claim them.*

The selection that follows shows the regime in operation. It describes the conditioning of eight-month-old babies. In reading the selection, be alert to the seemingly utilitarian justification for the conditioning: In the long run, such conditioning will best serve the interests of all.

Mr. Foster was left in the Decanting Room. The D.H.C. and his students stepped into the nearest lift and were carried up to the fifth floor.

INFANT NURSERIES. NEO-PAVLOVIAN CONDITIONING ROOMS, announced the notice board.

The Director opened a door. They were in a large bare room, very bright and sunny; for the whole of the southern wall was a single window. Half a dozen nurses, trousered and jacketed in the regulation white viscose-linen uniform, their hair aseptically hidden under white caps, were engaged in setting out bowls of roses in a long row across the floor. Big bowls, packed tight with blossom. Thousands of petals, ripe-blown and silkily smooth, like the cheeks of innumerable little cherubs, but of cherubs, in that bright light, not exclusively pink and Aryan, but also luminously Chinese, also Mexican, also apoplectic with too much blowing of celestial trumpets, also pale as death, pale with the posthumous whiteness of marble.

The muses stiffened to attention as the D.H.C. came in.

"Set out the books," he said curtly.

In silence the nurses obeyed his command. Between the rose bowls the books were duly set out—a row of nursery quartos opened invitingly each at some gaily colored image of beast or fish or bird.

"Now bring in the children."

They hurried out of the room and returned in a minute or two, each pushing a kind of tall dumbwaiter laden, on all its four wire-netted shelves, with eight-month-old babies, all exactly alike (a Bokanovsky Group, it was evident) and all (since their caste was Delta) dressed in khaki.

"Put them down on the floor."

The infants were unloaded.

"Now turn them so that they can see the flowers and books."

Turned, the babies at once fell silent, then began to crawl towards those clusters of sleek colors, those shapes so gay and brilliant on the white pages. As they approached, the sun came out of a momentary eclipse behind a cloud. The roses flamed up as though with a sudden passion from within; a new and profound significance seemed to suffuse the shining pages of the books. From the ranks of the crawling babies came little squeals of excitement, gurgles and twitterings of pleasure.

The Director rubbed his hands. "Excellent!" he said. "It might almost have been done on purpose."

The swiftest crawlers were already at their goal. Small hands reached out uncertainly, touched, grasped, unpetaling the transfigured roses, crumpling the illuminated pages of the books. The Director waited until all were happily busy. Then, "Watch carefully," he said. And, lifting his hand, he gave the signal.

The Head Nurse, who was standing by a switchboard at the other end of the room, pressed down a little lever.

There was a violent explosion. Shriller and ever shriller, a siren shrieked. Alarm bells maddeningly sounded.

The children started, screamed; their faces were distorted with terror.

"And now," the Director shouted (for the noise was deafening), "now we proceed to rub in the lesson with a mild electric shock."

He waved his hand again, and the Head Nurse pressed a second lever. The screaming of the babies suddenly changed its tone. There was something desperate, almost insane, about the sharp spasmodic yelps to which they now gave utterance. Their little bodies twitched and stiffened; their limbs moved jerkily as if to the tug of unseen wires.

"We can electrify that whole strip of floor," bawled the Director in explanation. "But that's enough," he signalled to the nurse.

The explosions ceased, the bells stopped ringing, the shriek of the siren died down from tone to tone into silence. The stiffly twitching bodies relaxed, and what had become the sob and yelp of infant maniacs broadened out once more into a normal howl of ordinary terror.

"Offer them the flowers and the books again."

The nurses obeyed; but at the approach of the roses, at the mere sight of those gaily-colored images of pussy and cock-a-doodle-doo and

From Brave New World *by Aldous Huxley. Copyright 1932, 1960 by Aldous Huxley. Reprinted by permission of Harper & Row, Publishers, Inc., and Mrs. Laura Huxley and Chatto & Windus Ltd.*

baa-baa black sheep, the infants shrank away in horror; the volume of their howling suddenly increased.

"Observe," said the Director triumphantly, "observe."

Books and loud noises, flowers and electric shocks—already in the infant mind these couples were uncompromisingly linked; and after two hundred repetitions of the same or a similar lesson would be wedded indissolubly. What man has joined, nature is powerless to put asunder.

"They'll grow up with what the psychologists used to call an 'instinctive' hatred of books and flowers. Reflexes unalterably conditioned. They'll be safe from books and botany all their lives." The Director turned to his nurses. "Take them away again."

Still yelling, the khaki babies were loaded on to their dumbwaiters and wheeled out, leaving behind them the smell of sour milk and a most welcome silence.

One of the students held up his hand; and though he could see quite well why you couldn't have the lower-caste people wasting the Community's time over books, and that there was always the risk of their reading something which might undesirably decondition one of their reflexes, yet . . . well, he couldn't understand about the flowers. Why go to the trouble of making it psychologically impossible for Deltas to like flowers?

Patiently the D.H.C. explained. If the children were made to scream at the sight of a rose, that was on grounds of high economic policy. Not so very long ago (a century or thereabouts), Gammas, Deltas, even Epsilons, had been conditioned to like flowers—flowers in particular and wild nature in general. The idea was to make them want to be going out into the country at every available opportunity, and so compel them to consume transport.

"And didn't they consume transport?" asked the student.

"Quite a lot," the D.H.C. replied. "But nothing else."

Primroses and landscapes, he pointed out, have one grave defect: they are gratuitous. A love of nature keeps no factories busy. It was decided to abolish the love of nature, at any rate among the lower classes; to abolish the love of nature, but *not* the tendency to consume transport. For of course it was essential that they should keep on

going to the country, even though they hated it. The problem was to find an economically sounder reason for consuming transport than a mere affection for primroses and landscapes. It was duly found.

"We condition the masses to hate the country," concluded the Director. "But simultaneously we condition them to love all country sports. At the same time, we see to it that all country sports shall entail the use of elaborate apparatus. So that they consume manufactured articles as well as transport. Hence those electric shocks."

"I see," said the student, and was silent, lost in admiration.

There was a silence; then, clearing his throat, "Once upon a time," the Director began, "while our Ford was still on earth, there was a little boy called Reuben Rabinovitch. Reuben was the child of Polish-speaking parents." The Director interrupted himself. "You know what Polish is, I suppose?"

"A dead language."

"Like French and German," added another student, officiously showing off his learning.

"And 'parent'?" questioned the D.H.C.

There was an uneasy silence. Several of the boys blushed. They had not yet learned to draw the significant but often very fine distinction between smut and pure science. One, at last, had the courage to raise a hand.

"Human beings used to be . . ." he hesitated; the blood rushed to his cheeks. "Well, they used to be viviparous."

"Quite right." The Director nodded approvingly.

"And when the babies were decanted . . ."

"'Born'," came the correction.

"Well, then they were the parents—I mean, not the babies, of course; the other ones." The poor boy was overwhelmed with confusion.

"In brief," the Director summed up, "the parents were the father and the mother." The smut that was really science fell with a crash into the boys' eye-avoiding silence. "Mother," he repeated loudly rubbing in the science; and, leaning back in his chair, "These," he said gravely, "are unpleasant facts; I know it. But then most historical facts *are* unpleasant."

He returned to Little Reuben—to Little Reuben, in whose room, one evening, by an oversight, his father and mother (crash, crash!) happened to leave the radio turned on.

("For you must remember that in those days of gross viviparous reproduction, children were always brought up by their parents and not in State Conditioning Centers.")

While the child was asleep, a broadcast program from London suddenly started to come through; and the next morning, to the astonishment of his crash and crash (the more daring of the boys ventured to grin at one another), Little Reuben woke up repeating word for word a long lecture by that curious old writer ("one of the very few whose works have been permitted to come down to us"), George Bernard Shaw, who was speaking, according to a well-authenticated tradition, about his own genius. To Little Reuben's wink and snigger, this lecture was, of course, perfectly incomprehensible and, imagining that their child had suddenly gone mad, they sent for a doctor. He, fortunately, understood English, recognized the discourse as that which Shaw had broadcasted the previous evening, realized the significance of what had happened, and sent a letter to the medical press about it.

"The principle of sleep-teaching, or hypnopaedia, had been discovered." The D.H.C. made an impressive pause.

The principle had been discovered; but many, many years were to elapse before that principle was usefully applied.

"The case of Little Reuben occurred only twenty-three years after Our Ford's first T-Model was put on the market." (Here the Director made a sign of the T on his stomach and all the students reverently followed suit.) "And yet . . ."

Furiously the students scribbled, *"Hypnopaedia, first used officially in A.F. 214. Why not before? Two reasons. (a) . . ."*

"These early experimenters," the D.H.C. was saying, "were on the wrong track. They thought that hypnopaedia could be made an instrument of intellectual education . . ."

(A small boy asleep on his right side, the right arm stuck out, the right hand hanging limp over the edge of the bed. Through a round grating in the side of a box a voice speaks softly.

"The Nile is the longest river in Africa and the second in length of all the rivers of the globe. Although falling short of the length of the Mississippi-Missouri, the Nile is at the head of all rivers as regards the length of its basin, which extends through 35 degrees of latitude . . ."

At breakfast the next morning, "Tommy,"

someone says, "do you know which is the longest river in Africa?" A shaking of the head. "But don't you remember something that begins: The Nile is the . . ."

"The-Nile-is-the-longest-river-in-Africa-and-the-second-in-length-of-all-of-the-rivers-of-the-globe . . ." The words come rushing out. "Although-falling-short-of . . ."

"Well now, which is the longest river in Africa?"

The eyes are blank. "I don't know."

"But the Nile, Tommy."

"The-Nile-is-the-longest-river-in-Africa-and-second . . ."

"Then which river is the longest, Tommy?"

Tommy bursts into tears. "I don't know," he howls.)

That howl, the Director made it plain, discouraged the earliest investigators. The experiments were abandoned. No further attempt was made to teach children the length of the Nile in their sleep. Quite rightly. You can't learn a science unless you know what it's all about.

"Whereas, if they'd only started on *moral* education," said the Director, leading the way towards the door. The students followed him, desperately scribbling as they walked and all the way up in the lift. "Moral education, which ought never, in any circumstances, to be rational."

"Silence, silence," whispered a loudspeaker as they stepped out at the fourteenth floor, and "Silence, silence," the trumpet mouths indefatigably repeated at intervals down every corridor. The students and even the Director himself rose automatically to the tips of their toes. They were Alphas, of course, but even Alphas have been well conditioned. "Silence, silence." All the air of the fourteenth floor was sibilant with the categorical imperative.

Fifty yards of tiptoeing brought them to a door which the Director cautiously opened. They stepped over the threshold into the twilight of a shuttered dormitory. Eighty cots stood in a row against the wall. There was a sound of light regular breathing and a continuous murmur, as of very faint voices remotely whispering.

A nurse rose as they entered and came to attention before the Director.

"What's the lesson this afternoon?" he asked.

"We had Elementary Sex for the first forty

minutes," she answered. "But now it's switched over to Elementary Class Consciousness."

The Director walked slowly down the long line of cots. Rosy and relaxed with sleep, eighty little boys and girls lay softly breathing. There was a whisper under every pillow. The D.H.C. halted and, bending over one of the little beds, listened attentively.

"Elementary Class Consciousness, did you say? Let's have it repeated a little louder by the trumpet."

At the end of the room a loudspeaker projected from the wall. The Director walked up to it and pressed a switch.

". . . all wear green," said a soft but very distinct voice, beginning in the middle of a sentence, "and Delta Children wear khaki. Oh no, I don't want to play with Delta children. And Epsilons are still worse. They're too stupid to be able to read or write. Besides they wear black, which is such a beastly color. I'm *so* glad I'm a Beta."

There was a pause; then the voice began again.

"Alpha children wear grey. They work much harder than we do, because they're so frightfully clever. I'm really awfully glad I'm a Beta, because I don't work so hard. And then we are much better than the Gammas and Deltas. Gammas are stupid. They all wear green, and Delta children wear khaki. Oh no, I *don't* want to play with Delta children. And Epsilons are still worse. They're too stupid to be able . . ."

The Director pushed back the switch. The voice was silent. Only its thin ghost continued to mutter from beneath the eighty pillows.

"They'll have that repeated forty or fifty times more before they wake; then again on Thursday, and again on Saturday. A hundred and twenty times three times a week for thirty months. After which they go on to a more advanced lesson."

Roses and electric shocks, the khaki of Deltas and a whiff of asafoetida—wedded indissolubly before the child can speak. But wordless conditioning is crude and wholesale; cannot bring home the finer distinctions, cannot inculcate the more complex courses of behavior. For that there must be words, but words without reason. In brief, hypnopaedia.

"The greatest moralizing and socializing force of all time."

The students took it down in their little books. Straight from the horse's mouth.

Once more the Director touched the switch.

". . . so frightfully clever," the soft, insinuating, indefatigable voice was saying. "I'm really awfully glad I'm a Beta, because . . ."

Not so much like drops of water, though water, it is true, can wear holes in the hardest granite; rather, drops of liquid sealing-wax, drops that adhere, incrust, incorporate themselves with what they fall on, till finally the rock is all one scarlet blob.

"Till at last the child's mind *is* these suggestions, and the sum of the suggestions *is* the child's mind. And not the child's mind only. The adult's mind too—all his life long. The mind that judges and desires and decides—made up of these suggestions. But all these suggestions are *our* suggestions!" The Director almost shouted in his triumph. "Suggestions from the State." He banged the nearest table. "It therefore follows . . ."

A noise made him turn round.

"Oh, Ford!" he said in another tone, "I've gone and woken the children."

Questions for Analysis

1. What is meant by the statement "What man has joined, nature is powerless to put asunder"? Do you think this observation is consistent or inconsistent with the philosophy of individualism that arose in the eighteenth and nineteenth centuries?

2. Why are the Deltas conditioned to dislike books? Flowers? Every state has numerous ways to condition its members and, in fact, uses them. Where would you draw the line between justifiable and unjustifiable state conditioning of citizens?

3. Could the Brave New World in any way be characterized as classically liberal? Would it violate any of classical liberalism's enabling assumptions?

4. Could the Brave New World in any way be characterized as classically conservative? Would it violate any of classical conservatism's enabling assumptions?

5. Does any social contract operate in the Brave New World? If so, how would you describe it?

6. Would people in Rawls's original position be likely to agree to live in the Brave New World?

7. What does the Director mean when he says: "Moral education . . . ought never . . . to be rational"? Would you consider this a departure from the classical philosophy of individualism or a natural extension of it?

Paperbacks for Further Reading

Golding, William. *Lord of the Flies*. New York: Capricorn Books, 1959. Golding creates a "state of nature," then portrays the attitudes and behavior of a handful of innocents who find themselves a part of it. A disturbing portrayal of the darker side of human nature.

Held, Virginia. *Property, Profits and Economic Justice*. Belmont, Ca.: Wadsworth, 1980. This collection of readings from Locke and Smith down to the present examines the corporation as a social invention.

Hoffer, Eric. *The True Believer*. New York: Harper & Row, 1966. This is longshoreman-philosopher Hoffer's study of those who lose their identities by throwing themselves into social causes and mass movements.

Kaufman, Arnold S. *The Radical Liberal: The New Politics in Theory and Practice*. New York: Simon & Schuster, 1968. Kaufman, a professional philosopher, argues for fundamental liberal values while advocating actively bringing about radical social change. He argues for the "politics of radical pressure" with respect to black power, education, and foreign affairs.

Machiavelli, Niccolo. *The Prince*. C. Detmold, Trans. New York: Airmont, 1965. This classic about political machinations is essential reading for anyone interested in political philosophy.

Marcuse, Herbert. *One-Dimensional Man: Studies in the Ideology of Advanced Industrial Society*. Boston: Beacon Press, 1964. This is an attack on the alienation and dehumanization of humankind in "advanced" technological societies. Marcuse argues that, rather than being used to enslave humans, science and technology could be used to liberate human capacities.

Oakeshott, Michael. *Rationalism in Politics*. New York: Basic Books, 1962. For an important challenge to liberal philosophy, this book is a "must."

Wolfe, Tom. *The Pump House Gang*. New York: Bantam, 1965. Perhaps America's leading satirist, Wolfe has written a highly entertaining and ironic collection of essays which deal largely with the problem of increased self-involvement in contemporary society.

5

PHILOSOPHY AND ART

Art is, indeed, the spearhead of human development, social and individual.
—Susanne K. Langer

What if you had just five minutes to live? What thoughts would run through your mind? What regrets might you have? Would you think about how you might have done things differently? In his novel *The Idiot*, Fyodor Dostoyevsky pictures a man in just such a situation:

> He had only five minutes more to live . . . those five minutes seemed to him an infinite time, a vast wealth; he felt that he had so many lives left in those five minutes that there was no need yet to think of the last moment, so much so that he divided his time up. He set aside time to take leave of his comrades, two minutes for that; then he kept another two minutes to think for the last time; and then a minute to look about him for the last time. He remembered very well having divided his time like that. He was dying at twenty-seven, strong and healthy. As he took leave of his comrades, he remembered asking one of them a somewhat irrelevant question and being particularly interested in the answer. Then when he had said good-bye, the two minutes came that he had set apart for *thinking* to himself. He knew beforehand what he would think about. He wanted to realize as quickly and clearly as possible how it could be that now he existed and was living and in three minutes he would be *something*—someone or something. But what? Where? He meant to decide all that in those two minutes! Not far off there was a church, and the gilt roof was glittering in the bright sunshine. He remembered that he stared very persistently at that roof and the light flashing from it; he could not tear himself away from the light. It seemed to him that those rays were his new nature and that in three minutes he would somehow melt into them. . . . The uncertainty and feeling of aversion for that new thing which would be and was just coming was awful. But he said that nothing was so dreadful at that time as the continual thought, "What if I were not to die! What if I could go back to life—what eternity! And it would all be mine! I would turn every minute into an age; I would lose nothing. I would count every minute as it passed, I would not waste one!" He said that this idea turned to such a fury at last that he longed to be shot quickly.[1]

1. *Fyodor Dostoyevsky*. The Idiot. *New York: Modern Library, 1935, p. 55.*

Dying must be a sobering experience. Too bad it is so final—most of us could probably benefit from a dry run or two. We could benefit from seeing a profile of the basics, from realizing "what really matters," from hearing again or perhaps for the first time the drummer we meant to march to. As a result, many, like Dostoyevsky's prisoner, would lust to turn every minute into an age.

Dostoyevsky's character responds to the scent of his own mortality: He perceives what he did not fully perceive before. Call it what you will: blowing away the cobwebs, putting things in perspective, knowing which side is up, getting his house in order, or cleaning up his act. Whatever, he knows who he is. He is in touch with himself. A scrape with death often has this effect, perhaps because imminent death causes us to experience what Aristotle called **catharsis,** a purging or cleansing of the emotions. Every drama, said Aristotle, must result in catharsis—a purifying of the audience through their complete emotional involvement in the play. Anything less is bad tragedy. Today, of course, we have empirical evidence of the healthful value of catharsis. In medicine, the word usually describes a cleansing of the digestive system; in psychoanalysis, it is a technique of cleansing the emotions to relieve tension and anxiety by bringing repressions to consciousness.

For many of us, a brush with death would cleanse us of the irrelevant, the extraneous, the superficial. It would purify us of false needs—needs to meet others' standards, to have fun, to be accepted, to want what others want, to dislike what others dislike, to seek society's values in pursuing a job, position, or reward. A scrape with death often acquaints us with the essentials of our lives, whatever they may be—our true needs. And what are these? Outside the physical needs of food, shelter, and clothing and the psychological needs of loving and being loved, each of us decides. That is the point. If a false need is imposed on us, a true need springs from within, from the core of our being. A true need can be defined no more easily than a religious experience. But we are unable to determine true needs as long as we are controlled, indoctrinated, and manipulated to pursue false needs, just as we are probably cut off from true religious experience so long as we seek it outside ourselves rather than within.

Although a brush with death frequently frees us of artificial bonds, obviously we cannot wait for such an experience. Neither can we assume that such a showdown will liberate us. On the contrary, it might send us on a lemminglike rush to experience everything before dying. Ignorant of what we truly need, we pursue false needs. We adopt societal values and needs because, as psychoanalyst Erik Erikson puts it, "We deal with a process located in *the core of the individual* and yet also *in the core of his communal culture*, a process which establishes, in fact, the identity of those two identities."[2] As a result, if society fails to perceive true cultural needs, rest assured that our perception of true individual needs will become increasingly obscured.

Perhaps your own needs are already fogbound. Perhaps you already feel the more than sneaking suspicion that you are drowning in a sea of plastics and pre-fabs, that the TV dinners have grown moldy, and that the talk shows

2. *Erik Erikson.* Identity, Youth and Crisis. *New York: Norton, 1968, p. 18.*

are all talked out. If you do sense a gap between how your society sees things and how you see them, just what do you do about it? Do you become, in Camus's words, a "living reproach"? Perhaps withdraw into the cocoon of transcendental meditation or hawk "Jesus Saves" pamphlets? If you do, can you remain impervious to polluted air and water, burgeoning populations, imminent war, mushrooming crime, unstable economies, racial unrest, and sexual tensions? What experience is as cathartic as death that will purge us of false needs and bring us to true ones? What experience will get us in touch with the self?

The answer of "aesthetic experience" might seem odd and frivolous. After all, for many of us the word *aesthetics* calls up images of cool, marbled museums peopled by snobs gawking and snorting at inscrutable paintings whose only possible value seems to be in the frames. Actually, aesthetics is the branch of philosophy that studies beauty, especially in art. By *art* we mean not only painting but also music, literature, sculpture, drama, and architecture. The study of aesthetics, then, examines the nature of beauty, taste, and standards of artistic judgment. But what has philosophy to do with art or art with philosophy? In this chapter we'll answer this question. Specifically, we'll see that just as a brush with death often heightens our perception and clarifies our true needs, so do art and the experience of it. They raise our level of consciousness and self-awareness, making us more responsive to the world around us.

It's hard to imagine a study more fitting than philosophy and art to answer the question Who am I? Although there are innumerable approaches to the study of philosophy and art, we'll begin by considering the aesthetic experience, its meaning and content. In doing so, we must talk about various theories of art as well as investigate the purpose of art—whether it should teach morality or exist only for its own sake, or perhaps do both. In addition, we'll ask: What is "good" art? We'll see whether objective standards exist for judging art or whether all aesthetic judgments are subjective. While this chapter does concern artistic values, it deals more with the *value of these values*. It assumes that self-discovery is bound up with an awareness of our needs, and it tries to show why a discovery of our needs must begin with the discovery that we need aesthetics (see Philosophy and Life 5-1). Here are the main points we will cover.

Main Points

1. *Aesthetics* derives from a Greek word meaning "perspective." Aesthetics is the branch of philosophy that studies beauty, especially in art. The study of aesthetics heightens perception and makes us aware of our true personal needs.

2. There are a number of aesthetic theories. First, art is imitative; second, art gives pleasure; third, art is a form of play; fourth, art is expressive of the artist's internal state; fifth, art produces empathy—it unifies and orders experience.

3. There are a number of theories on the function of art. One contends that

art should instill morality; a second holds that art should exist for its own sake; a third contends that art should make possible new ways of seeing things.

4. Some believe that the final judge of good art is the individual; others hold that there are objective standards by which to measure art; others, like the objective relativists, admit that there are some general standards but believe that art ultimately must be evaluated according to its ability to inspire aesthetic response.

5. Susanne Langer believes that the function of art is to transmit inner experience. Art expresses what is inexpressible; it gives shape, form, and meaning to our feeling. It puts us in touch with ourselves and the world around us.

6. Aesthetic education can help clarify and define inner needs.

The Aesthetic Experience

Suppose you are viewing *Guernica*, a painting by Picasso that portrays the horrors of war. The visual stimuli—color, shape, form, and so forth—create sensations in you. As you look longer, you begin to organize your sensations so that you recognize objects: a bull, a soldier, a woman, a light bulb, a horse. These organized sensations are called perceptions, or percepts. Thus you *sense* the color gray but you *perceive* the bull; you sense the color white but you

---

PHILOSOPHY AND LIFE 5-1
Aesthetic Needs

People obviously have all sorts of biological and psychological needs. Some psychologists today even speak of self-actualizing needs—the needs for self-expression, creativity, self-fulfillment. Do people also have aesthetic needs? Is beauty, however defined, necessary to healthful functioning? Psychologist Abraham Maslow, for one, believes it is. Indeed, in his hierarchy of needs Maslow lists such needs as the last of his so-called Being-needs.

In fact, some evidence supports the claim that people react positively to what they consider beautiful. What's more, some people actually become ill when deprived of experiencing beauty. Little wonder, then, that in psychotherapy, music and poetry are often used with patients who have been profoundly deprived of the experience of beauty.

But aesthetic needs may involve more than an exposure and reaction to beauty. They may include the need to create beauty, as well as to appreciate it. Without question, from the very beginning of our existence on earth, we have luxuriated in experimenting with various forms of storytelling, music, and design. In fact, one can detect this uniquely human tendency in the clay

perceive the light bulb. You might then perceive the state of these objects: the shrieking horse with a spear in its back, the screaming woman with her dead child, the crying victims engulfed in flames. You perceive the terror in the painting and thus the terror of war. You may perceive other things: Picasso's opposition to the Spanish Civil War, his expressionistic and cubistic skills, his imitation of stroboscopic-light photography.

Aesthetics relates to these many perceptual levels of human experience. In *Guernica* one of the perceptual levels involves the agony of war. War is a frightful thing. Picasso is telling us that even a so-called just war is full of deprivation and agony. People suffer and die as much in a "good" war as in a "bad" one. It is terrible that people must experience such suffering. We should strive to ensure that they do not have to, that we do not have to. What is happening when we experience these feelings?

Through an aesthetic experience, we have cut through what we might term a societally imposed need: that we must have wars. What are the reasons given for the necessity of war? There are many: to end all wars, to make the world safe for democracy, to ensure the self-determination of people, to bolster the economy, to protect our vital and national interests, to guarantee that our children won't have to fight, to perfect weaponry, to unify a country, to divert public attention from divisive issues, to fulfill a cycle of history, to return us to a fear and respect for God, to rid the world of Satan and his heathen followers, to bury capitalist pigs, to destroy godless communists, and so on. But what is our *true* need? Peace. When there is no peace we must consciously and con-

houses and stick figures made by a child. For Maslow, creativity is one characteristic of the self-actualized individual. He sees it as a most revealing indicator of psychological well-being.

Frequently, of course, this creativity takes the form of artistic expression, but is this the only form? Can't people be creative in thinking or in problem solving in such areas as arranging furniture, sewing, or cooking? Can't people respond aesthetically to crafts? If so, then the objects of aesthetic response needn't be restricted to the fine arts.

□ *In what way might a scientific discovery result in an aesthetic experience?* □ *Would anything in a sporting event, say a baseball game, elicit an aesthetic response?* □ *Is every creative act necessarily artistic?* □ *Is the artistic act necessarily creative?*

stantly strive to survive. *Guernica* makes us aware of this basic need. The effect is similar to the one that philosopher-scientist Jacob Bronowski wished to preserve after World War II when he proposed that Nagasaki be kept intact as a meeting ground for diplomats and governments who perhaps had forgotten the horrors of war. Bronowski was saying that we need this perceptual experience, this aesthetic contact, to remind us of our desperate need for peace.

Neither Bronowski nor Picasso was denying the reality of war, or even its necessity. They were simply saying that there are other necessities—war satisfies only some human needs, and there are other needs satisfied only by peace. The aesthetic experience asks us to perceive the part in order to understand the whole. As James Ogilvy puts it:

> Esthetic education not only educates the student to the man-made products of his cultural tradition; it also quickens his sensitivity to his own felt needs for a balanced and whole human existence. Wholeness is an elusive standard when the parts of human existence keep changing with the flux of history. A fixed inventory of human capacities no more functions as a checklist for wholeness than a list of colors tells a painter when he has completed a picture. The point is not to use each of the colors or human capacities. We need an esthetic sensibility to tell us whether man's most recent creations of himself cohere in a healthy pattern of wholeness or fall apart into schizoid decadence.[3]

In this sense, aesthetic sensibility helps us sort out the true needs from the false ones. It blows away the cobwebs, orders our universe, and puts things in perspective. It expresses for us the inexpressible. As the nineteenth-century English essayist and critic Walter Pater put it: "Art comes to you proposing frankly to give nothing but the highest quality to your moments as they pass." Surely this is a gift of inestimable worth.

What we have described through the example of *Guernica* suggests a most useful concept of aesthetic experience for a practical philosophy. It stems from the belief that the function of art is primarily to emphasize human feelings, clarify our inner lives, and brighten our vision. But this is only one theory of the function of art. There are many others. Since the ancient Greeks, individuals have held as many beliefs about the nature of aesthetics as about the natures of knowledge, reality, and goodness. These theories develop various concepts about the functions of art. It would be worthwhile to note at least the major theories, for each has validity. Moreover, each is compatible with the view that the aesthetic experience reveals true needs.

Theories of Art

Have you ever been part of a museum tour? Sometimes you can learn as much from other tour members as you can from the guide—perhaps not about art but about attitudes toward art.

To explore some of the main traditional and popular aesthetic theories, we are going to join a tour. With us, in addition to our guide, are Jerry and Betty, a married couple who are taking the tour as part of a vacation package. After this

---

3. James Ogilvy. *Self and World. Harcourt Brace Jovanovich, 1973, p. 461.*

tour, they will visit a botanical garden, a zoo, and a disco. Then there is Smitty, a man of little formal artistic training who has read some and enjoyed an aesthetic experience or two. He secretly believes that if things had been different, he could have been a great artist. But a long time ago he bought a taxi instead. Finally, there is Nellie, a retired schoolteacher from Anaheim, California, not far from Disneyland. Her conscience has never permitted her to miss any tour that purported to be a "cultural must." Her last tour: Dachau, scene of countless Nazi atrocities during World War II. As with all the other tours she has taken, she found it "interesting" if "excessively long."

As we join the tour, the group is reacting to "action painter" Jackson Pollock's *Convergence* (1952). As he did with many of his works, Pollock laid the canvas on the floor in order to move in the orbit of his creation. Then, using commercial paints, he flung, splattered, dribbled, smeared, and smudged his way to what some consider to be an expression of artistic genius. Others see little more than a well-soiled smock.

Jerry: Well, if you ask me, it looks like a chicken with the runs ran across that canvas.

Betty: Shhh, it's a Pollock.

Jerry: It's appalling!

Guide: Do you have a question, sir?

Betty: No.

Jerry: Yes, I do have a question.

Betty: Jerry!

Jerry: Relax, I'll take care of this. Not meaning any disrespect, Miss, but for the last half-hour you've paraded us through a collection of so-called paintings that I wouldn't line my canary's cage with, let alone hang on my wall. What gives?

Betty: He doesn't mean that. We don't even own a canary.

Guide: Apparently you don't appreciate modern art.

Jerry: Appreciate it? What's there to appreciate?

Betty: The frame, Jerry, look at the frame. It's beautiful!

Guide: The line, the form, the color, the motion, the rhythm——

Nellie: That's all well and good, young lady, but what the gentleman's asking is "What is there to see?"

Jerry: The lady's right. What's there to see?

Nellie: What does it all mean? The trouble today is there's no pleasure in looking at art.

Guide: Must it mean something?

Jerry: What!

Smitty: I can see that.

Jerry: What do you mean, you can see that?

Smitty: Well, like she says, why must it mean something? If you ask me, I see a painter who's having a lot of fun.

Jerry: Where?

Jackson Pollock, Convergence. Albright-Knox Art Gallery, Buffalo, New York. Gift of Seymour H. Knox, 1956.

Betty: Stand back, Jerry, you're always supposed to look at a painting from afar.

Jerry: Oh yeah? Well, I couldn't look at this one from too far afar. If there's a guy in there that's having fun, then I'm the monkey's uncle who painted this.

Guide: Perhaps the artist felt as you do.

Jerry: Frustrated?

Guide: Perhaps. And he's expressed this.

Jerry: You mean that's why he's made this mess? To frustrate me?

Smitty: I see what you're saying, Miss, but as I said before, I think Pollock was playing.

Jerry: You make this Pollock sound like a quarterback.

Smitty: Yes, in a way. Like a football player, an artist releases excess energy through play. His play is his art: painting, music, sculpture, literature, whatever. You could say art is a kind of spiritual play.

Jerry: But, what's play got to do with life?

Smitty: It's an escape from life.

Jerry: So anybody who escapes from life is an artist, is that what you're saying?

Nellie: Of course he's not. He's saying that an artist escapes from life.

Jerry: Well, what's an escapist got to tell me about life? That he's escaping? That he's playing? That he's having fun?

Smitty: Well, you allow the athlete to. Why not the artist?

Jerry: Because the athlete is entertaining me, that's why. He helps me pass my idle hours, fills my spare time. He even lets me grow old gracefully. What artist ever did that for me?

Smitty: What artist have you ever given the chance?

Jerry: I'll tell you who. What's his name? The guy that drew all those magazine covers for the *Saturday Evening Post.*

Betty: Norman Rockwell.

Jerry: Yeah, that's the guy.

Nellie: Now there's a man who brought years and years of pleasure into my life.

Jerry: A better painter never lived! Vermont in the winter, a kid's first haircut, presidents, old people with gnarled hands—stuff like that. The thing about that guy is, his stuff is real, you know what I mean? If he does a winter scene, you feel cold; if he does a pot-bellied stove, you feel warm. Now, when a guy can make you feel that way, that's what I call an artist.

Smitty: Well, if you want something real, why don't you just photograph it?

Jerry: What do you mean?

Smitty: If you want a tree to look precisely like a tree, maybe you should photograph it and not paint it at all.

Jerry: Well, by the same token, why don't I just stare at it, then? And not even photograph it?

Smitty: Why not? The tree itself is more real than a representation of it, and if you really must have what's *real*——

Jerry: Look, all I'm saying is that if I'm going to look at a painting I want to see something, that's all. What's wrong with that?

Guide: Nothing, absolutely nothing.

What is causing all the heat? Obviously, there is disagreement about what art is. Jerry believes that art is a representation of reality, that it should imitate how things are in life. Nellie doesn't quite agree. For her, art should give pleasure. Smitty has still another viewpoint: Art is primarily the artist's own experience, which is one of escape or play. Artists do not necessarily owe their audiences anything, for the aesthetic experience belongs to them. The guide also seems to focus on the artist's experience, but for her the artist is expressing something that finds completion in the viewer who shares the artist's experience. As for Betty, she has her hands full refereeing. Let us investigate each of these theories, keeping in mind that we are speaking not only of painting but of all forms of art.

Art as Imitation

Jerry's view of art as imitation has a respectable history. It's as old as Plato and Aristotle. Plato held that all art should imitate something in the physical world. Art succeeds to the degree that it does so. Since Plato saw the physical world as an imperfect reflection of his ideal world of Forms, he was especially critical of art as being a reflection of a reflection. In presenting his theory of art in book X of *The Republic*, he writes of poetry:

> We may conclude, then, that all poetry, from Homer onwards, consists in representing a semblance of its subject, whatever it may be, including any kind of human excellence, with no grasp of the reality. We were speaking just now of the painter who can produce what looks like a shoemaker to the spectator who, being as ignorant of shoemaking as he is himself, judges only by form and color. In the same way the poet, knowing nothing more than how to represent appearances, can paint in words his picture of any craftsman so as to impress an audience which is equally ignorant and judges only by the form of expression; the inherent charm of meter, rhythm, and musical setting is enough to make them think he has discoursed admirably about generalship or shoemaking or any other technical subject. Strip what the poet has to say of its poetical coloring, and I think you must have seen what it comes to in plain prose. It is like a face which was never really handsome, when it has lost the fresh bloom of youth.[4]

In brief, Plato held that through imitation, art portrays the universal. Aristotle basically agreed, although he differed in his concept of universals. For both, the value of art is chiefly cognitive, that is, it provides us with information. Thus, the greatness of Oedipus' tragedy, as described by the immortal Greek tragedian Sophocles, is that it represents the self-undoing pride of all

---

4. *Plato.* The Republic. *F. M. Cornford, Trans. London: Oxford University Press, 1941, p. 331. Reprinted by permission of Oxford University Press.*

humans. The magnificence of the Parthenon is that it imitates the harmony and balance that promise peace and fulfillment.

Art as Pleasure

Neither Plato nor Aristotle ignored the role of pleasure in art. On the contrary, both believed that in representing the physical world, art gave pleasure. As a contemporary example, consider the pleasure that we experience when we watch an accomplished impressionist at work, such as Rich Little or David Frye. Their impressions of famous people often give more pleasure than would the people themselves, especially certain politicians. For Aristotle the inherent pleasure in art is related to learning. In his *Nicomachean Ethics*, he makes the connection between imitation, learning, and pleasure:

> Imitation is natural to man from childhood, one of his advantages over the lower animals being this, that he is the most imitative creature in the world, and learns at first by imitation. And it is also natural for all to delight in works of imitation. The truth of this second point is shown by experience: though the objects themselves may be painful to see, we delight to view the most realistic representations of them in art, the forms for example of the lowest animals and of dead bodies. The explanation is to be found in a further fact: to be learning something is the greatest of pleasures not only to the philosopher but also to the rest of mankind, however small their capacity for it; the reason of the delight in seeing the picture is that one is at the same time learning—gathering the meaning of things, e.g. that the man there is so-and-so.[5]

The point is that imitative and pleasurable qualities go together. Thus, Nellie indicates fondness for Norman Rockwell, probably because she derives this pleasure from the imitative quality of his art. Of course, this doesn't mean that what is not imitative will not give her pleasure.

Art as Play

The Pollock painting is not imitative. Clearly, it does not give Jerry or Nellie pleasure. But it seems to give pleasure to Smitty and the guide. Smitty's pleasure seems to derive from the fun that Pollock seemed to be having. We might compare this kind of pleasure to witnessing a child in a playpen having fun with a cardboard box. (Jerry might liken it to a visit to the monkey house!) For Smitty, the pleasure is primarily the artist's, not the audience's. Nevertheless, through the art the audience can find release from the tension and stress of their lives. Like artists, we too need a break from drudgery; we need an outlet for an uncontrolled expression of energy. Artists find this in art; we find it indirectly through their expression. In his *Critique of Judgment*, Immanuel Kant developed this idea by pointing out that art is in itself fun, that it is closer to play than to work. Well before any such modern formulations of the nature of art, however, Plato observed that art is a form of play for the artist. In book X of *The Republic*, Plato records this dialogue:

5. *Aristotle.* Nicomachean Ethics, *in* Works. W. D. Ross, Trans. Oxford: Clarendon Press, 1925, vol. 60, sec. 1103a17.

Here is a further point, then. The artist, we say, this maker of images, knows nothing of the reality, but only the appearance. But that is only half the story. An artist can paint a bit and bridle, while the smith and the leatherworker can make them. Does the painter understand the proper form which bit and bridle ought to have? Is it not rather true that not even the craftsmen who make them know that, but only the horseman who understands their use?

Quite true.

May we not say generally that there are three arts concerned with any object—the art of using it, the art of making it, and the art of representing it?

Yes.

And that the excellence or beauty or rightness of any implement or living creature or action has reference to the use for which it is made or designed by nature?

Yes.

It follows, then, that the user must know most about the performance of the thing he uses and must report on its good or bad points to the maker. The flute-player, for example, will tell the instrument-maker how well his flutes serve the player's purpose, and the other will submit to be instructed about how they should be made. So the man who uses any implement will speak of its merits and defects with knowledge, whereas the maker will take his word and possess no more than a correct belief, which he is obliged to obtain by listening to the man who knows.

Quite so.

But what of the artist? Has he either knowledge or correct belief? Does he know from direct experience of the subjects he portrays whether his representations are good and right or not? Has he even gained a correct belief by being obliged to listen to someone who does know and can tell him how they ought to be represented?

No, he has neither.

If the artist, then, has neither knowledge nor even a correct belief about the soundness of his work, what becomes of the poet's wisdom in respect of the subjects of his poetry?

It will not amount to much.

And yet he will go on with his work, without knowing in what way any of his representations is sound or unsound. He must, apparently, be reproducing only what pleases the taste or wins the approval of the ignorant multitude.

Yes, what else can he do?

We seem, then, so far to be pretty well agreed that the artist knows nothing worth mentioning about the subjects he represents, and that art is a form of play, not to be taken seriously. This description, moreover, applies above all to tragic poetry, whether in epic or dramatic form.

Exactly.[6]

Art as Expression

The guide agrees with Smitty that art is a form of expression. But for her it is not so much an expression of play as an expression of an internal feeling. Perhaps Pollock was frustrated, she says, and he expressed this feeling in *Convergence*. For her, artists seek the most reflective forms and techniques for what

6. *Plato. The Republic, pp. 331–333. Reprinted by permission of Oxford University Press.*

they are trying to say. The Italian philosopher Benedetto Croce (1866–1952) saw art as "intuitive knowledge" of mental states. To catch Croce's meaning, it's important to distinguish, as he does, between two forms of knowledge: intuitive and logical. Intuitive knowledge, according to Croce, is knowledge obtained through the imagination; it is knowledge of individual things and it produces images. In contrast, logical knowledge is knowledge obtained through the intellect. It is knowledge of the universal and of the relations between individual things. Rather than images, logical knowledge produces concepts. Croce identifies intuitive knowledge, or what he terms expressive knowledge, with art. Every true intuition is also expression. In other words, true intuitive knowledge for Croce must objectify itself in expression. In his best-known work, *Theory of Aesthetic*, Croce makes this point:

> And yet there is a sure method of distinguishing true intuition, true representation, from that which is inferior to it: the spiritual fact from the mechanical, passive, natural fact. Every true intuition or representation is also *expression*. That which does not objectify itself in expression is not intuition or representation, but sensation and mere natural fact. The spirit only intuits in making, forming, expressing. He who separates intuition from expression never succeeds in reuniting them.
>
> Intuitive activity *possesses intuitions to the extent that it expresses them*. Should this proposition sound paradoxical, that is partly because, as a general rule, a too restricted meaning is given to the word "expression." It is generally restricted to what are called verbal expressions alone. But there exist also nonverbal expressions, such as those of line, color and sound, and to all of these must be extended our affirmation, which embraces therefore every sort of manifestation of the man, as orator, musician, painter, or anything else. But be it pictorial, or verbal, or musical, or in whatever other form it appear, to no intuition can expression in one of its forms be wanting; it is, in fact, an inseparable part of intuition. How can we really possess an intuition of a geometrical figure, unless we possess so accurate an image of it as to be able to trace it immediately upon paper or on the blackboard? How can we really have an intuition of the contour of a region, for example of the island of Sicily, if we are not able to draw it as it is in all its meanderings? Every one can experience the internal illumination which follows upon his success in formulating to himself his impressions and feelings, but only so far as he is able to formulate them. Feelings or impressions, then, pass by means of words from the obscure region of the soul into the clarity of the contemplative spirit. It is impossible to distinguish intuition from expression in this cognitive process. The one appears with the other at the same instant, because they are not two, but one.[7]

Art as Empathy and as Experience

There are still other theories of art. A common reaction to a Eugene O'Neill play, for example, is one of physical and mental exhaustion—shades of Aristotle's catharsis. The reason is that we become so involved in the lives and relationships of O'Neill's characters that we experience much of their physical and mental anguish. William Gibson's *The Miracle Worker* is an espe-

7. *Benedetto Croce. Theory of Aesthetic. New York: Macmillan, 1909, pp. 8–9.*

cially good example of this. By the end of this play we are "wrung out." Art makes us feel **empathy**. The empathic theory of art contends that art makes us feel what we would experience if we were actually involved in that which is artistically depicted.

For John Dewey, on the other hand, art is a process of doing or making. In *Art as Experience*, he argues that art has become separated from experience. The point of art is to elevate common experience. It accomplishes this by unifying and ordering experience for the mind. The aesthetic experience for Dewey resides in our recognizing the wholeness of the interrelationships among the things depicted. The artist's intention is not meaning but the quality of the experience that the work elicits. The more widespread and intense the experience depicted, the more expressive the art. Figuring prominently in Dewey's theory is emotion. Indeed, at one point in *Art as Experience*, Dewey defines art as "nature transformed by entering into new relationships where it evokes a new emotional response." This does not mean that a work of art has emotion as its main ingredient. Emotion works to effect continuity of movement, singleness of effect. In other words, emotion is selective of material and is directive, but it is not expressive. Nevertheless, emotion is necessary for art; without it there may be craftsmanship, but not art. Dewey develops this point by asking us to conjecture about why some works of art attract us, while others repel us:

> If one examines into the reason why certain works of art offend us, one is likely to find that the cause is that there is no personally felt emotion guiding the selecting and assembling of the materials presented. We derive the impression that the artist, say the author of a novel, is trying to regulate by conscious intent the nature of the emotion aroused. We are irritated by a feeling that he is manipulating materials to secure an effect decided upon in advance. The facets of the work, the variety so indispensable to it, are held together by some external force. The movement of the parts and the conclusion disclose no logical necessity. The author, not the subject matter, is the arbiter.
>
> In reading a novel, even one written by an expert craftsman, one may get a feeling early in the story that hero or heroine is doomed, doomed not by anything inherent in situations and character but by the intent of the author who makes the character a puppet to set forth his own cherished idea. The painful feeling that results is resented not because it is painful but because it is foisted upon us by something that we feel comes from outside the movement of the subject matter. A work may be much more tragic and yet leave us with an emotion of fulfillment instead of irritation. We are reconciled to the conclusion because we feel it is inherent in the movement of the subject matter portrayed. The incident is tragic but the world in which such fateful things happen is not an arbitrary and imposed world. The emotion of the author and that aroused in us are occasioned by scenes in that world and they blend with subject matter. It is for similar reasons that we are repelled by the intrusion of a moral design in literature while we esthetically accept any amount of moral content if it is held together by a sincere emotion that controls the material. A white flame of pity or indignation may find material that feeds it and it may fuse everything assembled into a vital whole.
>
> Just because emotion is essential to that act of expression which produces a work of art, it is easy for inaccurate analysis to misconceive its mode of operation and conclude that the work of art has emotion for its significant content.

One may cry out with joy or even weep upon seeing a friend from whom one has been long separated. The outcome is not an expressive object—save to the onlooker. But if the emotion leads one to gather material that is affiliated to the mood which is aroused, a poem may result. In the direct outburst, an objective situation is the stimulus, the cause, of the emotion. In the poem, objective material becomes the content and matter of the emotion, not just its evocative occasion.[8]

As noted before, all of these theories have validity, and none is mutually exclusive of the others. The appropriateness of one or another frequently relies on a particular social, historical, or artistic context. Emphasis on one theory does not necessarily mar the aesthetic experience, unless the emphasis biases us against other interpretations. This is essentially the problem with our tour members. Jerry refuses to consider any approach to art other than a representative one, while Smitty almost professes a scorn for this view. These biases will likely turn up in what they believe the purpose or function of art to be.

The Function of Art

One of the aesthetic questions that inevitably arises in discussing the function of art is whether art should teach morals or exist only for its own sake. Jerry, for example, believes that art should serve a moral function; Smitty does not.

Guide: But often there's more to art than meets the eye.

Smitty: You said it.

Jerry: Sure there is. But lots of times these guys don't even know themselves what they mean.

Nellie: I must agree with him, you know. I knew a painter once who said he was always amazed by what the critics wrote about his work. He never understood any of it. I think much of this modern art is—how do you say it—a put-on.

Smitty: But what is play but a put-on? A pretense? A sham?

Nellie: Like that young man a few years back who was painting Coca-Cola bottles and Brillo boxes.

Guide: Andy Warhol.

Jerry: You call that stuff art?

Smitty: Well, *you* should. Or isn't it realistic enough for you?

Jerry: What do you mean?

Smitty: If you so admire Rockwell for his believability, why not Warhol?

Betty: But how can you relate to a Coke bottle or a Brillo box?

Jerry: There's your answer. You can't *relate* to those things. But a cozy living room in winter with a big fire burning and a mother teaching a child how to read and a father buried in the daily

---

8. John Dewey. Art as Experience. *New York: Minton, Balch, 1934, pp. 68–69. Copyright © 1934 by John Dewey; renewed © 1962 by Roberta L. Dewey. Reprinted by permission of G. P. Putnam's Sons.*

paper and a big woolly dog half asleep at his feet—now that's telling about something, something worth listening to.

Smitty: What?

Jerry: Are you kidding? The *family*, that's what. The family as a value in society.

Nellie: He has a point.

Guide: Are you saying, sir, that art, to be art, should encourage a value, an ethic?

Jerry: Call it values or morals or ethics, whatever you want. I say that good art always teaches a moral. In fact, you could say that's the function of art.

Smitty: Nonsense! *Ars gratia artis:* art for the sake of art! Art is its own purpose.

Jerry: Nonsense.

Smitty: Then tell me something. Whose values will you use to measure art?

Jerry: What are you talking about, *whose* values?

Guide: Whose morality? Whose ethics? The Russian writer Solzhenitsyn is condemned in Russia but praised in the United States. Why? Because in Russia his art is politically heretical, but in America it isn't.

Nellie: She has a point.

Jerry: But what are you going to do, make moral and practical concerns take a back seat to art? Okay, go ahead, but don't come yelling to me about all the hard-core pornography that's polluting our kids' minds, and all the blood and guts on the tube and in the movies, and all the language that's not fit for a locker room, let alone a living room.

Nellie: Well, now *you've* got a point.

Smitty: Sure he has. And you can see it in the scissors of the censor.

Jerry: What're you talking about? I'm no bluenose.

Smitty: Of course you're not. Except when it comes to something that offends you personally. As long as art is confirming your own narrow preconceptions and predispositions, you're quite open-minded and tolerant. But let something run against the grain of your moral, religious, or political biases and you react with all the self-righteous indignation of the bluest of the bluenoses.

The contention that art should have a moral function is at least as old as Plato, who believed that when art does not advance the interests of social harmony and stability, it should be censored. For Plato, art that did not bring the audience closer to knowledge of the eternal Forms had no place in his republic. That same attitude is evident under some communist and fascist regimes. Recall the many depictions of the Russian or Chinese worker who, through dedication and obedience to the state, advances the cause of social revolution.

It is easy for us to sneer at this obvious propaganda if we disagree with the doctrine. But consider the propagandistic value of classical Greek art, which was a glorification of a way of life as much as an artistic expression. Or consider the obvious and intentional religious propaganda of great Renaissance art, or the early twentieth-century movement called naturalism, whose purpose was to shock the public into action. Upton Sinclair's *The Jungle*, a work whose primary purpose was to so outrage the public conscience that people would demand social reform, is a good example. We can hardly be consistent and make a distinction between the good ethic and the bad one. If we argue for the inseparability of art from values, we must accept a great variety of ethics—even those that contradict our own. Should we not, we must be prepared to defend the unquestionable righteousness of our own position. As we saw in our discussion of ethics and social philosophy, this is most difficult.

If, like Smitty, we argue for the separation of art from moral judgment, we seem to restrict ourselves to *aestheticism*, the view that art must ultimately be judged in terms of aesthetic enjoyment. For this outlook, art exists for art's sake. But this belief is not trouble free. Jerry asks about pornography. It seems irresponsible to sit by indifferently as children's and adults' minds are poisoned by the lewd and obscene, whose only evident purpose is to make a dollar. Likewise, when evidence indicates a causal connection between cinematic and social violence, can we ignore celluloid horrors for the sake of art? We seem to be on the horns of a dilemma. Let us see if we can escape it by proposing that art functions to reveal personal alternatives and increase sensitivity.

Guide: But why must art exist either for art's sake or for morality's? Why must one exclude the other?

Smitty: How can art that advances a moral standard exist for its own sake?

Jerry: And how can art for its own sake teach morals?

Guide: By offering new possibilities, by expanding human sympathies and imagination, by revealing to us our common bonds.

Betty: I think I know what she means. It reminds me of that film *That Certain Summer*. It was a TV drama about two gay men and how one had to reveal to his son that he was gay.

Nellie: Oh, I do remember that. You know, I didn't think I'd like it when I came across it in *TV Guide*. But then as I started to watch it, I began to feel compassion for them, and after a while I saw them as just two human beings suffering, if you know what I mean. For whatever reason, all I know is my attitude changed.

Jerry: So what does all this mean? That you're now out campaigning for gay liberation?

Nellie: Of course not. It simply means that now I understand better. How would you say it—I had my eyes opened to a different viewpoint. Well, I suppose you could say that with respect to the human condition I broadened my horizons.

In this third view of the function of art, art serves morality not by promoting a particular viewpoint but by quickening our imaginations and sensibilities to the human condition. For Nellie, the import of *That Certain Summer* was not that she did or did not become gay or that she did or did not agree with that preference. Neither was it the film's intention to convert anyone. Rather, its purpose was to heighten our consciousness of the agony that can be involved in decision making and value selecting. In this context, the moral purpose of art is not to confirm us in our own preconceptions but to introduce us to new possibilities, new values—to humanize us for tomorrow by sensitizing us to-day.

Even if we agree with this function of art, we are still left with the question: Who decides how well the art has executed these possibilities? Notice that we are not asking who decides the worth of the possibilities. That would merely pitch us back into an ethical juggernaut. We are asking who should be the judge of good art. Who decides what is great, good, fair, poor, terrible? Are there objective criteria? Or, in the last analysis, must the individual decide?

We Americans are notorious for reserving judgment on art because our aesthetic training is so shallow. We frequently adopt the views of "experts": the critics, the reviewers, the professors, the ones who supposedly know what art is all about. To a degree, this dependency on the views of others may explain why the advertiser can sell us virtually anything. In many cases we simply do not trust our own abilities to distinguish the substantive from the decorative, the tasteful from the gaudy; we simply do not know good art from bad. With this underdeveloped aesthetic sense often travels a whole bizarre value system.

The fundamental reasons for our aesthetic ignorance are too many and too complex to explore here. But in part, the ignorance stems from the Western emphasis on science and technology, which contrasts with, for example, the aesthetic emphasis found in Eastern cultures (see Philosophy and Life 5-2).

Aesthetic Judgment

Jerry: Well, what does this Pollock picture do for your horizons?

Nellie: I must admit, not very much.

Jerry: Now you're talking.

Betty: You know, I don't see too much in it either. I can see your getting something out of *That Certain Summer*. After all, it did deal with real people in a real situation. But what does this deal with?

Guide: For one thing, it deals with the medium of painting. I think that's important to see here. Within that medium it combines technique, form, and content——

Jerry: Technique? What technique?

Smitty: Expressionism.

Guide: That's right. Abstract expressionism, to be precise—an artistic movement that erupted in New York right after World War II. It's quite complex to explain without first going into cubism, nonobjectivism, and surrealism.

Jerry: I don't understand any of that.

Guide: One point I do think you should grasp is that in abstract expressionism the act of painting is frequently considered more meaningful and important than the content itself.

Jerry: But I thought you said this had content.

Guide: I did. But for Pollock, unlike your Rockwell, representing the familiar things in life isn't as important as portraying impressions, emotions, and insights in symbolic form. Believe it or not, sir, *Convergence* does have unity, coherence, rhythm, balance, and all the other formal ingredients that make any creative piece—in music, literature, sculpture, architecture, as well as painting—a work of art. But these formal features may elude you because your aesthetic sense, if you'll pardon the expression, may be underdeveloped.

Jerry: Underdeveloped?

Smitty: Frankly, Miss, I think I detect a hint of elitism in your remarks.

Guide: Really?

Jerry: Right!

Smitty: Well, you make it sound as if only a qualified observer can appreciate good art. That you need an understanding of cubism, nonobjectivism, and surrealism to understand *Convergence.*

Guide: Well, it would certainly help.

Smitty: Help, perhaps. Yet surely you don't believe that judgment of beauty should be left only to those who are trained in aesthetics and in the art they're evaluating?

Guide: But where are standards to come from if not from those who have refined their aesthetic faculties so that they can separate the quality from the trash?

Jerry: I'll tell you. From the average Joe who experiences it, that's where from. From you and me. We decide what's good and what's bad, just as we do in life. Like lying. For you lying may be okay, for me it's not. Who's to say? Each person decides for himself. You take this painting here by Pollock. Okay, you say it's terrific. I say it stinks. This lady, she's straddling the fence——

Nellie: I just can't make up my mind.

Jerry: Okay, so who's right? Is the painting great, lousy, or somewhere in between? The answer, folks, is none-of-the-above. Nobody can tell for sure. It all comes down to a matter of personal taste. And arguing about it is as smart as arguing about which is better, steak or chops.

Smitty: Up to a point, I agree with you. But I also think that, although there are no clear-cut guidelines for assessing aesthetic worth, we can decide on some general properties to help determine it.

Jerry: What general properties?

Smitty: Structure, for example. Without structure or form, as our guide calls it, there can be no object of art to begin with.

Guide: Certainly we all agree on that point.

Jerry: But what's form? Answer me that.

Smitty: It's internal relationships. Form is how the parts of the object fit in with one another. I think good form is present in a piece of art when the piece has many different parts so interrelated that they form a complete unit, a whole. It's this, it seems to me, that gives art its glow, its intensity, its impact. The better the form, the greater chance the work has to provoke an aesthetic response. And that, I think, is the test of any piece of art: its capacity to bring out an aesthetic response. And I don't believe the experts are the best or the only judges of that capacity.

For simplicity, we can reduce the debate on aesthetic judgment to this question: Is aesthetic judgment a matter of personal taste, or are there objective standards that you can apply? Notice that the question is reminiscent of the one that we faced in ethics: Is the good act strictly subjective, or are there objective criteria that we can apply to determine it? Similarly, in discussing knowledge, we will ask, "Can we know an objective world or are we confined to our own experience?"

Obviously, Jerry insists on the subjective position. What he likes is artistically good; what he dislikes is not. This, in effect, makes each of us our own aesthetic judge, in much the same way that egoism makes each of us an ethical judge. Furthermore, this view makes aesthetic debates meaningless. But perhaps they should be. After all, we can point to societies whose artistic tastes differ markedly from our own. Some individuals prefer New Wave music, while others hear in it nothing but cacophony. As Jerry puts it, "Who's to say?"

Yet people have been "saying" for some time. Doubtless all critics regard Sylvia Plath as a better poet than Rod McKuen and Joan Didion as a better writer than Jacqueline Susann. They believe that certain standards apply in evaluating art. Some, like the guide, believe that a qualified judge should de-

---

PHILOSOPHY AND LIFE 5-2
Zen Art

Western civilization is characterized by high achievement in science and technology. In both areas, however, the aesthetic dimension is largely neglected. Similarly, Western religions emphasize intricate theologies and the elevation of the moral stature of human beings, relegating aesthetic concerns to subordinate functions. In sharp contrast stand Eastern philosophies and religions, such as Hinduism, Buddhism, and Taoism. They do not stress the conceptualization of experience and moral perfection as much as the acceptance and celebration of life. This is especially true of Zen Buddhism.

If we consider aesthetic experience to be an appreciation of something as being complete in itself, then all Zen experience could be considered aesthetic. Furthermore, Zen artistic expression becomes inseparable from Zen religion and philosophy. Zen emphasizes nature, specifically what is concrete and specific, everyday and actual. Value is placed on description, not explanation; on showing, not telling. Appropriately, art is an integral part of the Zen religion. It's little wonder that to the Western eye Zen art is often enigmatic.

Zen art is preoccupied with natural, concrete, everyday things. It inevitably echoes the moment and celebrates the marvelous nature of life. A haiku poem, for example, underscores what we may term the "suchness" or "thusness" of the living moment:

termine what is good and what is bad. Who is qualified? David Hume believed it is someone who has spent a lifetime cultivating the aesthetic attitude of detachment, disinterest, and distance. Others, like Immanuel Kant, claimed that we could judge by comparing art with an absolute standard or idea. Harmony and order serve as a basis for aesthetic evaluation. Still others, like Smitty, would deny these absolute standards and the experts' preferred status, but they would admit the existence of certain aesthetic properties such as structure. These objective relativists, as they are termed, evaluate art in terms of its capacity to inspire an aesthetic response. They hold the value theory termed **objective relativism,** which contends that values are relative to human satisfaction but that human needs and what satisfies them are open to empirical examination.

As in most philosophical debates, all positions seem to have merit. Undoubtedly we exercise subjective choice in voicing an artistic preference, but do we when we voice artistic judgment?

Although it is possible to consider Beethoven a great composer and yet not *like* him, more often in the arts a judgment of worth is also an expression of preference. The converse is less frequently true. When people say they like John Wayne's acting, they would not necessarily claim that John Wayne was a

---

> *A stray cat*
> *Asleep on the roof*
> *In the spring rain.*

Another poem juxtaposes the beautiful and the ugly, appreciating both:

> *The young girl*
> *Blew her nose*
> *In the evening-glory.*

Similarly, the Zen painter portrays individual suchness. Thus, Zen painting is characterized by disequilibrium, asymmetry, and imperfection; for these, as much as harmony, typify how things are. The famous dry garden of Ryoanji is a good example. There we see fifteen uncarved rocks arranged in five groups on an expanse of raked sand.

☐ *Should art do anything besides accept and portray things as they are?*
☐ *Would it be fair to say that Zen art fails to portray possibility and novelty?*
☐ *In what sense could a Zen painting be considered not a representation of nature but a work of nature?*

great actor. In fact, they may readily admit that John Wayne was probably not a great actor; nevertheless, they like his acting and go to see every one of his movies. On the other hand, it would be unusual for someone to say, "Richard Burton is a great actor, but I don't like his acting." This would be comparable to saying "Lying is wrong, but I don't disapprove of it." In general, then, an aesthetic judgment involves some measure of subjective preference.

However, the fact that we frequently say, "I like John Wayne's acting, but he's not a great actor," should tell us that more goes into an aesthetic judgment than personal preference. In this case, we might claim that Wayne didn't have depth, or show versatility, or ever do any "serious" theater. Although we may not be mindful of them, we frequently apply objective criteria in value judgments. Consider the heated discussions that otherwise "non-arty" people get embroiled in over the relative merits of two athletes: Who was the greater baseball player, Henry Aaron or Babe Ruth? Which is the better motorcycle, a Harley Davidson or a BMW? Who was the wiser general, Grant or Lee? The person who insists that Lee was wiser because that person "feels he was" would not be taken seriously, and for good reason. You would want to know *why* the person believes that. If the person then spoke of Lee's handsome gray beard and beautiful white horse, you would still laugh, because the criteria are irrelevant to Lee's status as a general. But if the person discussed strategy, tactics, imagination, and daring, you would listen. These are relevant criteria.

So it is with art. Frequently we discuss technique, content, form, and so on as measures of artistic worth, as objective criteria. Just as frequently we call on the experts to fortify our opinions as readily as we would call on Civil War expert Bruce Catton to support our evaluation of Lee. The trouble, of course, is that many of us are so ignorant of the arts and so lacking in an understanding of aesthetic experience that we vacillate between never judging for ourselves and insisting there are no standards. But ignorance of standards is not the same as an absence of standards. There *are* standards, and we can and do learn them by studying the arts.

Of course, an art object is not an athlete, a motorcycle, or a general. And an aesthetic judgment is neither a simple "I like that" nor a "Based on these criteria, that's good." Moreover, if it is only a combination of these two reactions, then an aesthetic judgment is a sterile exercise that warrants no more than the little time most give to it. Ultimately, aesthetic judgment seems rooted in the aesthetic experience that we spoke of earlier—it must be rooted in feeling as well as thinking, imagining as well as reasoning. Without the subjective element of feelings and imagination, it is doubtful that we would ever experience an aesthetic impulse, although our aesthetic learning might be impressively broad and refined. As the writer Stendhal put it, "The people who passionately love bad music are much closer to good taste than the wise men who love with good sense and moderation the most perfect music ever made."

We live in times when phrases such as "man's inhumanity to man" ring painfully true. Perhaps the cause is our inability to feel. But what is an inability to feel if not a dysfunctional imagination? It seems that we lack the imagination not only to see our way out of our problems but to feel their gravity fully. Just as physiologically our most necessary sense is the tactile one, emotionally and psychologically our most necessary sense is feeling. True, without feeling we experience no pain, but we also experience no danger. Without feeling we cannot distinguish the harmful from the harmless or the wise from the foolish. Without feeling we run a perilous, though admittedly painless, course to destruction. Therefore, however we judge art or determine its nature and function, we must return to the aesthetic experience, whose chief value seems to be that it puts us in touch with ourselves and others. This idea deserves development.

Art as Transmission of Inner Experience

In her essay "The Cultural Importance of Art," philosopher Susanne K. Langer gives a definition of art that seems relevant to our discussion. "Art," she says, "may be defined as the practice of creating perceptible forms expressive of human feeling." By *feeling* she means everything that may be felt—not just pleasure, sensibility, or emotion. By *form* she means "an apparition given to our perception," as

> . . . when you say, on a foggy night, that you see dimly moving forms in the mist; one of them emerges clearly, and is the form of a man. It is in this sense of an apparition given to our perception that a work of art is a form. It may be a permanent form like a building or a vase or a picture, or a transient dynamic form like a melody or a dance, or even a form given to imagination, like the passage of purely imaginary, apparent events that constitute a literary work. But it is always a perceptible, self-identical whole; like a natural being, it has a character of organic unity, self-sufficiency, individual reality. And it is thus, as an appearance, that a work of art is good or bad or perhaps only rather poor—as an appearance, not as a comment on things beyond it in the world, or as a reminder of them.[9]

But for our purposes the operative part of the definition is that these perceptible forms are "expressive of human feeling." By this she means that art transmits inner experience.

To understand her meaning, let's look at language. Language expresses the world around us and, on occasion, the world within us. It expresses self. But we often have feelings that defy language, that "lie too deep for words." Frequently, when we do seem to find the right words, they belie our real feelings. This is so, some say, because feelings are irrational. "On the contrary," writes Langer, "they seem irrational because language does not help make them conceivable, and most people cannot conceive anything without the logical scaffolding of words." Language can misrepresent and distort; for its classifications, order, and relationships are not precise. Now, if language is unfit to express the world around us, how much more unfit is it to describe the elusive world within us? At least we can detect a resemblance between the form of our language and the world around us (whether or not we have im-

9. *Susanne K. Langer. "The Cultural Importance of Art," in* Philosophical Sketches. *Baltimore: The Johns Hopkins Press, 1967, p. 86. Reprinted by permission.*

posed that form on things is not relevant here). But how does language form reflect the natural form of feeling?

To grasp the point, consider how our language inclines us to see in terms of things. But feeling is not a thing. Furthermore, our language allows expression primarily in terms of actor and action: "I am feeling angry." But what does this mean to someone else? Not much, for that person has no way of knowing what feeling angry means for you, and no words can convey that feeling. The word *anger* simply refers to a very general inner experience, as do *fear, love, excitement,* and *resentment.* Thus, whereas language gives outward experience a form and makes it sensible, it is really unfit to shape and define inner experience. As Langer puts it, "Human feeling . . . has an intricate dynamic pattern, possible combinations and new emergent phenomena. It is a pattern of organically interdependent and interdetermined tensions and resolutions, a pattern of almost infinitely complex activation and cadence. To it belongs the whole gamut of our sensibility—the sense of straining thought, all mental attitude and motor set. Those are the deeper reaches that underlie the surface waves of our emotion, and make human life a life of feeling instead of an unconscious metabolic existence interrupted by feelings."[10]

According to Langer, art gives expression to this dynamic pattern. A work of art is a "symbol of feeling," for it formulates our inward experience as language formulates outward experience. "Art objectifies the sentience and desire, self-consciousness and world-consciousness, emotions and moods, that are generally regarded as irrational because words cannot give us clear ideas of them."

Yet, we may ask, so what? What is the cash value of art? After all, it's not practical; it's not religion or morality, business or science. Just what is it? What does it offer to society? The answer may be imagination.

Imagination is perhaps our oldest mental capacity. It is probably "the common source of dream, reason, religion, and all true general observation." Even language stems from imagination. Language breaks up reality, organizes it, and makes it manageable for us. But by what process other than imagination could this occur? True, imagination gives rise to the arts, but the arts in turn inspire imagination. By representing in an objective way what we subjectively feel, art permits us, says Langer, to "imagine feeling and understand its nature." For this reason, Nellie and Betty are able to sympathize with the characters of *That Certain Summer,* Jerry is moved by the Rockwell illustrations, Smitty is able to see Pollock at play, and the guide is able to sense Pollock's art in his execution. It is why you, at a rock concert perhaps, "really envisage vital movement, the stirring and growth and passage of emotion, and ultimately the whole direct sense of human life." And since only you are having your feeling, the aesthetic experience is opening you up to yourself, revealing dimensions you did not know were yours, offering you possibilities heretofore hidden from rational scrutiny. In this way it is showing you at least part of what you need to be complete. In effect, the "arts we live with—our picture books and stories and the music we hear—actually form our emotive experience." Without them

10. Susanne K. Langer, "The Cultural Importance of Art," p. 88.

we lack certain ways of feeling, and thus our impulses are less than human and so are society's. For "a society that neglects [aesthetic education] gives itself up to formless emotion." Part of this education would involve learning how to respond to objects in aesthetic ways. This is no easy task when we realize that, in general, we have been trained to respond in nonaesthetic ways (see Philosophy and Life 5-3).

Summary and Conclusions

We opened this chapter by noting that the aesthetic experience allows us to perceive personal needs more clearly than we could otherwise. In fact, we may describe the aesthetic experience as getting in touch with profound personal needs and values through artistic media. We examined various theories of the nature and function of art, all of which are compatible with aesthetic experience. In the last analysis, the great value of art is that it seems to express the inexpressible, to give form and shape to feelings that frequently cannot be expressed in words. In discovering these dimensions of the self through art, we can discover who we are by discovering what we need.

In Dostoyevsky's novel, the prisoner who must die in five minutes received a last-minute reprieve. You might wonder what he did with his "eternity of life." Did he live counting each moment? "Oh no. . . . He didn't live like that at all; we're told he wasted many, many minutes. Life goes on. We forget. It seems impossible to live 'counting each moment.'" And yet this is what the aesthetic experience allows us to do.

What would allow the prisoner's experience to live on? Perhaps a painting.

"One thought came into my mind just now," Dostoyevsky has Myshkin say to Adelaida, ". . . to suggest that you should paint the face of the condemned man the moment before the blade falls, when he is still standing on the scaffold before he lies down on the plank."

"The face? The face alone?" asks Adelaida. "That would be a strange subject. And what sort of picture would it make?"

Myshkin doesn't know; he simply saw a painting like that once, and it struck him. But Myshkin intuits that it is important for us to be struck more often than once in a while, for the experience increases our understanding of what is important in our lives. Knowing what is of real value and need to us provides deep self-insights.

Today we have little time for these experiences. In the words of the poet Wordsworth:

> The world is too much with us; late and soon,
> Getting and spending, we lay waste our powers:
> Little we see in Nature that is ours.
> We have given our hearts away, a sordid boon!

As incredible as it may sound, we seem to be without time to feel and, as a result, without time to cultivate an aspect of self that we need to be happy as individuals and to survive as a species. Worse, our capacity to feel seems blunted.

As an example, recall two stunning moments from the court-martial of Lieutenant William Calley, accused and convicted of engineering the Mylai massacre of civilians in Vietnam. At one point, Calley's corporal explained why he shot civilians even though he did not think the original orders to "waste" them still applied: "Some of my men had already opened fire. I figured these people were wounded anyway, so I might as well go ahead and shoot." The second astonishing moment was when Calley explained why he thought he was being sent home after the Mylai massacre: "I thought I was coming home to be decorated and promoted, sir." In these words is a chilling, if understandable, logic that suggests an unconcern for or ignorance of personal and societal needs apart from the ones imprinted in boot camp or Officer's Candidate School. An effective way, and some believe the only way, to make reasonable beings of sensuous ones is to teach them a sense of the aesthetic. We seem to be paying a high price for not doing so.

Section Exercises

The Aesthetic Experience

1. It is possible that the total effect of *Guernica* might be to marshal sentiment

---

PHILOSOPHY AND LIFE 5-3
The Aesthetic Response

One thing that makes characterizing an aesthetic response so difficult is that we have learned to respond to objects in nonaesthetic ways. Generally, we respond to them cognitively or practically, in part because we are encouraged to do so. When we respond cognitively, we seek information about the nature and function of the object: What is it? How does it work? Who made it? When we respond practically, we try to determine its usefulness: How can I use it? Why should I have one? Is it worth the money?

Suppose that we're responding to a painting. We might respond cognitively by asking questions about the painter's life and other works, the painter's intention in executing the work, the painter's artistic technique, or the artistic tradition in which the painter is working. Some students of art, generally termed contextualists, believe that such external knowledge intensifies the aesthetic experience. Others, such as isolationists, claim that such cognitive knowledge is not only unnecessary for an aesthetic experience but may in fact inhibit such an experience by distracting from the work itself. But both contextualists and isolationists agree that such a response is not the same as an aesthetic response or experience.

If, on the other hand, we responded to the painting practically, we might inquire about its price, whether it is likely to appreciate in value, or whether

for peace and against war. Is this effect the aesthetic experience, or is the aesthetic experience something different?

2. The phrase "true needs" or "real needs" was not clearly defined. Why not? Can it be?

3. What does Ogilvy mean when he says, "We need an esthetic sensibility to tell us whether man's most recent creations of himself cohere in a healthy pattern of wholeness or fall apart into schizoid decadence"?

4. Although Nazi concentration camps were the epitome of horrifying inhumanity, in what sense does their preservation enable us to have an aesthetic experience?

5. For many, *aesthetic* is synonymous with *beautiful*. Thus, aesthetics is the study of beauty and what constitutes the beautiful. In what sense is this definition accurate? Do *beautiful* and *beauty* need to be defined? Might their definitions include that which is ugly? How?

Theories of Art

1. How is Plato's theory of art consistent with the totalitarian society he constructs in *The Republic*?

---

the work will look good on a particular wall. Or we might ask, "What's this painting good for?" In considering this question, one is inclined to give an answer that makes bottom-line sense: "It will make me feel good," "It will show I'm cultured," or "It will be a conversation piece." Clearly, none of these practical responses is an aesthetic response or experience. Indeed, it distracts from one.

Thus, the trouble that people experience in understanding and appreciating art may derive from the two primary ways in which they've learned to react to things. So long as one responds in a strictly cognitive or practical way, the response is not aesthetic. The person may be looking at a painting but not seeing it; the person may not be perceiving it just for the sake of the perception.

☐ *Many argue that the aesthetic attitude is characterized by detachment and disinterest, by what's termed psychic distance. What does this mean?*
☐ *How would you distinguish that attitude from intimacy, emotional participation, and identification with the artistic object?*

---

2. Is it possible to generalize about the theory of art most Americans probably hold? If so, what evidence would you point to?

The Function of Art

1. Some have argued that as long as there are serious social ills, people should spend neither their time nor their money on art. In other words, art is frivolous compared with the demands of life. How would you respond to this criticism?

2. Under what circumstances, if any, would you approve of government censorship of art?

3. Jerry believes that art should be representative and morally instructive; Smitty sees art as play and believes it should exist for its own sake. Do you think there is some general correlation between an aesthetic theory and the function of art? What kind of art do you enjoy most? What you like probably betrays your theory of art and what you hold its function to be. Do you find such a correlation?

4. Some people say that any work of art that has strictly moral or political value tends to be consumed in the very fires of passion that inspired it. Why would they say this? Is it valid?

Aesthetic Judgment

1. Pollock's *Convergence*, like much of modern art, is abstract. Therefore, it is more difficult to perceive how such art expands our imagination so that we can conceive of new personal, moral, and social possibilities. But it can and frequently does. How? (Perhaps you should select an example from painting, music, literature, architecture, or another artistic field.)

2. Why does an underdeveloped aesthetic sense invite a self-defeating value system?

3. Describe the three positions on aesthetic judgment voiced in the dialogue on page 234.

4. Do you think someone with Jerry's belief about aesthetic judgment would be inconsistent to dislike a work of art but admit that it has aesthetic worth?

5. Why is imagination necessary to feel fully?

Paperbacks for Further Reading

Asimov, Isaac. *The Foundation Trilogy*. New York: Avon, 1975. Asimov's three-part epic is about galactic conflict and the establishment of a galactic empire, the Foundation, dedicated to art, science, and technology. This trilogy spans 1,000 years and ends with an effort to combat a mutant that challenges the survival of the Foundation. Especially relevant is the role of art within the Foundation.

Edman, Irwin. *Arts and the Man: A Short Introduction to Aesthetics.* New York: Norton, 1939. This simple and readable introduction to aesthetics examines the relationship of art to human experience, the origins and function of art, and the ways that art can elucidate and unify personal experience.

Elgin, Duane. *Voluntary Simplicity: Toward a Way of Life That Is Outwardly Simple, Inwardly Rich.* N.Y.: Morrow, 1981. Elgin develops an aesthetic approach to daily life that is based, not on austerity, but on harmonizing one's appetites with the needs of others. A novel approach to the problems of scarcity and global deprivation.

Fallico, Arturo B. *Art and Existentialism.* Englewood Cliffs, N.J.: Prentice-Hall, 1962. Painter, sculptor, and philosophy professor Fallico argues, very literately, that art springs from spontaneity, feeling, imagination, and authenticity.

Gaddis, William. *The Recognitions.* New York: Bard, 1975. The central character of this novel rejects inclinations to be a priest in order to become an artist. Then he abandons the ideal of originality to imitate the masters. In his search for a new reality, he faces every kind of bogus knowledge: religious, social, aesthetic, and political.

May, Rollo. *The Courage to Create.* New York: Bantam, 1976. Psychotherapist May provides an illuminating account of the intimacy between art, creativity, and the nonartistic individual. He discusses "creative courage"—how we can acquire it and how creative power can enrich our lives.

Tolstoy, Leo. *What Is Art?* Aylmer Maude, Trans. Indianapolis: Bobbs-Merrill, 1960, chaps. 5, 15, 16. Tolstoy argues that good art must transmit a kind of religious experience that will unite people in a brotherhood under God.

Wieman, Henry. *Man's Ultimate Commitment.* Carbondale, Ill.: Southern Illinois Press, 1958. Wieman argues that creativity is vital to a full, rich personal life and to the quality of our social institutions. Only through creativity can we experience and enlarge the quality of life.

Part III

EPISTEMOLOGY

One of the fundamental branches of philosophy deals with knowledge. It is termed epistemology, *from the Greek* episteme, *meaning "knowledge."* Epistemology literally means the study of knowledge.

Specifically, **epistemology** deals with the nature, basis, and extent of knowledge. Epistemological questions are basic to all other philosophical inquiries. Everything we claim to know, whether in science, history, or everyday life, would amount to little if we were unable to support our claims. Thus, neither a concept of human nature and self, a theory of the universe, nor an assertion of an ordinary event ("This lemon tastes sour" or "It is raining") escapes the need for justification. Epistemology presents us with the task of explaining how we know what we claim to know, how we can find out what we wish to know, and how we can judge someone else's claim to knowledge.

Epistemology usually addresses a variety of problems: the structure, reliability, extent, and kinds of knowledge; truth; logic and language; and science and scientific knowledge. The next three chapters deal with three major epistemological areas: knowledge, truth, and philosophy and science.

THE NATURE OF KNOWLEDGE

Que sais-je?
What do I know?
—*Michel de Montaigne*

A great deal of who and what we are is what we know or claim to know. Why? Because knowledge forms the basis of the beliefs, values, and attitudes by which we express ourselves, direct and give meaning to our lives, and distinguish ourselves from others. So, if we are to discover self, it's important to determine what we know.

Suppose a friend asked you what you knew. You might reply, "I know that Washington was at Valley Forge."

"How do you know that?" the person then asks. Because you read it, you say. "Do you believe everything you read?" the person asks. Of course not. But you believe this because everybody who's written about the subject says it's so. "How do they know?" the person persists. "Were they there?" No, you admit they weren't there, but they've studied the subject and are therefore in a position to know. That still doesn't satisfy your friend. "Where did they study it?" the person asks. "In books mostly," you reply.

"Now, let me see if I've got this straight," your friend says. "You claim to know from what you've read, right?" Right. "And the people you've read claim to know from what they've read. Presumably, the sources they've researched have studied the matter, too. Is that right?" Sure. "Then where does all this stop? I mean is there no one who knows this without having to read it somewhere?" Of course there is, you explain: the people who were there, the ones who were actually with Washington at Valley Forge; they witnessed it, they *know*.

Your friend then seems to digress. "Have you ever been in a car accident?" Sure, but what does that have to do with Washington? "Were there any witnesses?" There were. "What about their accounts of the accident—did they agree?" No, you admit, they didn't; but what has that to do with Washington at Valley Forge? "I'm just asking you how reliable eyewitness testimony is to

begin with," your friend explains. You concede that eyewitness testimony often isn't very reliable, but that doesn't mean it wasn't reliable at Valley Forge. "Of course not," your friend agrees, "but it does mean that the testimony might not have been reliable. In other words, what you claim to know might not be the case."

Apparently, a claim to knowledge is no simple affair. Indeed, philosophers have given considerable attention to questions concerning the nature, basis, and extent of knowledge (see Philosophy and Life 6-1). One popular way of approaching these subjects, though by no means the only way, has been to determine whether there are different kinds of knowledge. If there are, how can they be obtained? What are their sources and what are their limits? Possibly the most common view on this issue is that there are two types of knowledge, rational knowledge and empirical knowledge. Although philosophers disagree on the exact distinction between them, rational knowledge generally means knowledge attained through reason without the aid of the senses—knowledge that is necessarily true; empirical knowledge is knowledge achieved through sense experience and is only probably true; that is, it can be proven

---

PHILOSOPHY AND LIFE 6-1
Kekulé's Dream

How do we attain knowledge? By what means? Such questions address one aspect of epistemological inquiry: the sources of knowledge.

The most obvious source is sense experience. How do you know that a book is in front of you? Because you can see and feel it. But sense experience is not our only source of knowledge. If someone asked you, "How do you know that if x is greater than y and y is greater than z, that x is greater than z?" what would you say? You don't see or feel anything, but your reasoning tells you that the relation is true. Reasoning is another source of knowledge.

But sometimes we clearly get knowledge by experiences not easily defined. "I had a flash of intuition," we say, or "My intuition tells me it is so" or "All of a sudden, in a flash of intuition, I saw things clearly." It's very difficult to define *intuition*, perhaps impossible. Nevertheless, the term does label certain kinds of experience characterized by a conviction of certainty that comes upon us quite suddenly.

Take, for example, a most famous scientific discovery. Friedrich Kekulé, professor of chemistry in Ghent, Belgium, discovered that carbon compounds can form rings. Kekulé's discovery did not come easily. For some time he'd been pondering the structure of benzene, but he couldn't explain it. Then, one afternoon in 1865, he turned his mind away from his work:

> *I turned my chair to the fire and dozed. Again the atoms were gambolling before my eyes. This time the smaller groups kept modestly in the background. My mental eye, rendered more acute by repeated visions of*

false. The history of philosophical thought is replete with great conflicts about the priority given to reason and sense experience as epistemological tools. Rationalists endorse reason, arguing that only rational knowledge is certain. Empiricists generally contend that knowledge of the external world can be attained only through sense experience, since reason can only relate the facts that are presented by the senses.

In this chapter we'll look more closely at these two seminal epistemological theories. We'll also consider a third, an alternative termed *phenomenalism*. In so doing, we hope to throw light on that aspect of the self that knows or claims to know about itself and the world outside it. Here are the chapter's main points.

Main Points

1. There are two common views regarding the sources of knowledge: rationalism and empiricism.
2. Rationalism is a doctrine that states that knowledge is based on reason

---

this kind, could now distinguish larger structures, of manifold conformations; long rows, sometimes more closely fitted together; all twining and twisting in a snakelike motion. But look! What was that? One of the snakes had seized hold of its own tail, and the form whirled mockingly before my eyes. As if by a flash of lightning I awoke and this time also I spent the rest of the night working out the consequences of the hypothesis. *

Kekulé had found his clue to the structure of benzene in his dream of the snake gripping its own tail.

* *Quoted in Gardner Lindzey, Calvin Hall, and Richard F. Thompson. Psychology. New York: Worth, 1975, p. 320.*

□ *What preceded Kekulé's discovery via the creative subconscious?*
□ *Does this tell you anything about how intuition can lead to knowledge?*
□ *Before Kekulé accepted the validity of his intuitive insight, he subjected it to rigorous testing. Does this suggest anything about how intuitive claims should be handled?* □ *How would you distinguish between intuitive claims such as Kekulé's and others such as "My intuition tells me it'll rain tomorrow"?*

rather than on sense perception; true knowledge is not a product of experience but depends largely on some ideal model of the mental process.

3. René Descartes was a rationalist concerned with discovering something that he could hold as true beyond any doubt. He concluded that no one could doubt that a human is a thinking being, that a thinking thing exists, that God exists, and that the world exists. All of this, he claimed, could be established by reason alone.

4. Empiricism is a doctrine that states that all knowledge comes from or is based on sense perception and is a posteriori.

5. John Locke, one of the three British empiricists (together with Berkeley and Hume), held that objects have primary qualities, which are distinct from our perception of them, such as size, shape, and weight. He also believed that they had secondary qualities, which we impose on them, such as color, smell, and texture. We know the objective world through sense experience, which is a copy of reality.

6. According to Berkeley's subjectivism, we only know our own ideas, and only the conscious mind and what it perceives exist. Carried to an extreme, this position can become solipsism, the position that only I exist and everything else is a creation of my subjective consciousness.

7. Hume pushed Locke's empiricism to its logical conclusion. Arguing that all knowledge originates in sense impressions, Hume distinguished between two forms of perceptions, impressions and ideas. Impressions are lively perceptions, as when we hear, see, feel, love, or hate. Ideas are less lively perceptions; they are reflections on sensations. Hume denied that there was any logical basis for concluding that things have a continued and independent existence outside us. He denied the possibility of any certain knowledge, arguing that both rationalism and empiricism are inadequate to lead to truth and knowledge. He is thus termed a *skeptic*.

8. Kant's phenomenalism, an alternative to empiricism and rationalism, distinguishes between our experience of things (phenomena) and the things as they are (noumena). The mind, claimed Kant, possesses the ability to sort sense experiences and posit relationships among them. Through an awareness of these relationships, we come to knowledge.

9. Extreme epistemological positions, such as identifying the knower with the known and solipsism, seem unfounded: The former eliminates the self, the latter all that is not the self. We explain reality better by assuming that an objective reality exists than by assuming that it doesn't. But there is also a subjective element in knowledge: Each individual experiences things as no one else does.

Rationalism

By **rationalism** we mean the belief that knowledge is based on reason alone, not on sense perception. **Perception** refers to the psychological process by which we become aware of or apprehend ordinary objects, such as chairs, tables, rocks, and trees, through the stimulation of our senses. For most of us, seeing, hearing, smelling, touching, and tasting are such familiar processes that we accept them uncritically and rarely examine the dynamics involved. In philosophy, however, perception may have several meanings, for expressing the precise relationship between the knower and the known is crucial. As a result, there is no general agreement on the exact character of this relationship. When rationalists claim that knowledge is based on reason rather than perception, they mean that we need not and do not rely on sense experience for knowledge. They don't reject empirical knowledge; they simply deny its theoretical or scientific importance and in some cases refuse to call it knowledge at all.

In effect, rationalists contend that true knowledge is not a product of experience but depends largely on an ideal model of mental process. Mathematics, for example, often serves as an ideal model for human understanding because it contains indubitable truths and principles that appeal to reason alone. Mathematical ideas, like the most important truths we can know, cannot be discovered by scouring the world; they can only be known by examining the mental process. Because true knowledge does not depend on experience, rationalists term it **a priori**, what is known independently of sense perception and thus claimed to be indubitable.

The history of philosophy records the thinking of many outstanding rationalists, including Plato, Saint Augustine (354–430), Benedict Spinoza (1632–1677), Gottfried Wilhelm Leibnitz (1646–1716), and Georg Hegel (1770–1831). Certainly among the most noteworthy is René Descartes, a seventeenth-century scientific giant who not only invented analytic geometry but advanced a theory of knowledge that has greatly influenced philosophy.

Descartes

Although rationalism appears as far back as in ancient Greece, Descartes presented the first modern statement of it. Curiously, many of us today can identify with Descartes's methodological point of departure—an attitude of doubt and skepticism. Today we might call his frame of mind disillusionment. Some would say that Descartes was smitten by a "credibility gap," not of a political sort but of an epistemological sort, for Descartes seriously wondered about what he could believe, what he could be certain of. He came to this point after years of reading, studying, and confronting the finest minds on the Continent. In effect, he asked, "What can I hold as true beyond any doubt?"

Before seeing how Descartes answered this question, let's update the issue by joining two people aboard a jet 35,000 feet above some point in the United States. The man, Rob Dalton, is reading an article entitled "The West That Never Was," authored by a person who has devoted over thirty years to the study of the Old West. The article purports to separate fact from fancy, to explode some of the fictions about nineteenth-century western America. The article especially focuses on the myths fostered by western movies. The contents of the article surprise Rob Dalton, who is slowly dropping his most time-honored beliefs about the Old West. By the time he's finished reading it, he feels as if a cherished companion has just been bushwhacked. Sadly, he returns the magazine to its holder and mutters, "So goes another illusion." His seat companion, Ellen Borstin, can't help but overhear.

Ellen: Were you speaking to me?

Rob: Oh, I'm sorry. I guess I was talking to myself. It's nothing.

Ellen: I bet you were reading the article on the West that never was.

Rob: How did you know?

Ellen: I had the same reaction.

Rob: Did you?

Ellen: Just like when I learned there was no Santa Claus.

Rob: Exactly! Except that was the *first* of my *many* disillusionments.

Ellen: I'm sorry.

Rob: There's no telling how many there's been now. I've lost track. I had one just before we left the ground, though.

Ellen: I'm not sure I want to hear. . . . Oh, well, I'll risk it. What happened?

Rob: Well, it was odd how it happened. I was leafing through the *Times* when I decided to have something to eat before flight time. You know, something to tide me over? I decided on a hot dog and a diet Pepsi, even though I hate its aftertaste.

Ellen: Funny, you don't look like you have to worry about your weight.

Rob: I don't. But what with all the stuff about how harmful sugar is, I'm off it. Or at least I was. That's the point. You see, as I'm waiting for my order, I read about this Harvard nutritionist who says there's nothing wrong with sugar. Well, I immediately cancel the diet and order a regular Pepsi, giant size! You'll never know how good it felt—like having a whole life-style confirmed! Naturally, I realized it was just one guy's opinion. But it was a start. At least I could drink the Pepsi without feeling I was committing slow suicide, you know what I mean? So there I am biting into my frank with the works and sipping my giant Pepsi with sugar, when I see it.

Ellen: What?

Rob: The headline "Hot Dogs Cause Cancer."

Ellen: Really?

Rob: You didn't know?

Ellen: No.

Rob: No wonder. It was with the obits.

Ellen: How ghoulish!

Rob: That's what I thought—after I stopped gagging. It turned out that it wasn't hot dogs as much as what was in them: sodium nitrite. Did you know that sodium nitrite causes cancer in rats?

Ellen: How horrible!

Rob: You said it . . . But at least I can eat sugar.

Ellen: Then *you* don't know.

Rob: Know what?

Ellen: *He* never touches the stuff himself.

Rob: Who?

Ellen: That Harvard nutritionist.

Rob: You're kidding!

Ellen: No, there was a big article on him in the *Saturday Review* last month.

Rob: Well, why doesn't he?

Ellen: The article didn't say. But I thought it was curious, I mean in the light of his position and all.

Rob: Curious! I'll say it's curious. . . . You see what I'm talking about now? You just don't know what to believe anymore. It's like every day you learn something else. In every field: science, nutrition, medicine—not to mention politics and international affairs. And a lot of the time what you learn contradicts what you thought you knew. It's getting so that just as you think you know something, it's overturned. Like the Old West. I thought I had a pretty good idea of what it was like. Turns out it's about as reliable as a rubber crutch. . . . You know, this may sound crazy, but I'd really like to know what I could know for sure.

Rob Dalton seems a living testimony to the observation that many people have made about our times. We live in an age of rapid change, constant sensory input, and exploding information. Rather than making life more predictable, a fast-paced, continuous flow of data can leave us torn between existing assumptions and new information. Modern psychologists have a term for this gap: *cognitive dissonance*.

But cognitive dissonance isn't a new phenomenon. We can see variations of it in ancient Greece, when burgeoning scientific theory somehow had to fit in with mythological assumptions. Similarly, medievalists had to reconcile Copernican thought with accepted religious, philosophical, and scientific beliefs. In the seventeenth century, scientists, mathematicians, and philosophers, Descartes foremost among them, had to accommodate the growing emphasis on individual conscience and rational-scientific truths with the traditional authority and dogma of the church. This was not an easy task for those like Descartes with distinctly medieval and Aristotelian roots. Indeed, the Cartesian age was marked by a profound questioning of established religious authority, traditional doctrine, and time-honored opinion. Viewed from a twentieth-century perspective, we might portray one of the crucial problems of that era as how to accept the scientific present without severing ties with the historical, cultural, and intellectual past and thereby inviting serious personal and collective disorientation.

While Descartes may never have felt the anxiety of doubt that Rob Dalton is experiencing, he was vitally concerned with discovering something that he could hold as true beyond any doubt. Ultimately he discovered what he felt was an indubitable truth: He could not doubt that he existed. Descartes reasoned that he could not doubt that he is a thinking thing, what he termed in Latin *res cogitans*. Thus, the self whose existence I cannot doubt is the self that doubts as well as affirms, wills, and imagines. In a word, the self that thinks.

But what is a thinking thing? What does it mean to say that "I am a thinking thing"? This is an important question, for in answering it, Descartes lays a rationalistic basis for knowledge. In one of the most epistemologically important of all his writings, his second meditation, Descartes attempts to describe the nature of a thinking thing. In the selection that follows, note how he abstracts from the sensuous qualities of a piece of wax, identified by perception and imagination, to demonstrate why sense experience is not the ultimate criterion of knowledge. In this way he establishes a rationalistic foundation for knowledge.

Let us begin by considering the commonest matters, those which we believe to be the most distinctly comprehended, to wit, the bodies which we touch and see; not indeed bodies in general, for these general ideas are usually a little more confused, but let us consider one body in particular. Let us take, for example, this piece of wax: it has been taken quite freshly from the hive, and it has not yet lost the sweetness of the honey which it contains; it still retains somewhat of the odor of the flowers from which it has been culled; its color, its figure, its size are apparent; it is hard, cold, easily handled, and if you strike it with the finger, it will emit a sound. Finally all the things which are requisite to cause us distinctly to recognize a body, are met with in it. But notice that while I speak and approach the fire what remained of the taste is exhaled, the smell evaporated, the color alters, the figure is destroyed, the size increases, it becomes liquid, it heats, scarcely can one handle it, and when one strikes it, no sound is emitted. Does the same wax remain after this change? We must confess that it remains; none would judge otherwise. What then did I know so distinctly in this piece of wax? It could certainly be nothing of all that the senses brought to my notice, since all these things which fall under taste, smell, sight, touch, and hearing, are found to be changed, and yet the same wax remains.

Perhaps it was what I now think, viz. that this wax was not that sweetness of honey, nor that agreeable scent of flowers, nor that particular whiteness, nor that figure, nor that sound, but simply a body which a little while before appeared to me as perceptible under these forms, and which is not perceptible under others. But what, precisely, is it that I imagine when I form such conceptions? Let us attentively consider this, and, abstracting from all that does not belong to the wax, let us see what remains. Certainly nothing remains excepting a certain extended thing which is flexible and movable. But what is the meaning of flexible and movable? Is it not that I imagine this piece of wax being round is capable of becoming square and of passing from a square to a triangular figure? No, certainly it is not that, since I imagine it admits of an infinitude of similar changes, and I nevertheless do not know how to compass the infinitude by my imagination, and consequently this conception which I have of the wax is not brought about by the faculty of imagination. What now is this extension? Is it not also unknown? For it becomes greater when the wax is melted, greater when it is boiled, and greater still when the heat increases; and I should not conceive (clearly) according to the truth what wax is, if I did not think that even this piece that we are considering is capable of receiving more variations in extension than I have ever imagined. We must then grant that I could not even understand through the imagination what this piece of wax is, and that it is in my mind alone which perceives it. I say this piece of wax in particular, for as to wax in general it is yet clearer. But what is this piece of wax which cannot be understood excepting by the (understanding or) mind? It is certainly the same that I see, touch, imagine, and finally it is the same which I have always believed it to be from the beginning. But what must particularly be observed is that its perception is neither an act of vision, nor of touch, nor of imagination, and has never been such although it may have appeared formerly to be so, but only an intuition of the mind, which may be imperfect and confused as it was formerly, or clear and distinct as it is at present, according as my attention is more or less directed to the elements which are found in it, and of which it is composed.[1]

According to Descartes, then, the basis for knowledge is a clear and distinct perception. An idea is clear if its content includes its nature and essence. An idea is distinct if it includes nothing inconsistent with an object's essence. For Descartes, the key thing is that reason is the ultimate basis for knowledge.

Descartes goes on to use this rationalistic basis of knowledge to establish the existence of God and the rest of the world. Having ascertained his own existence, he reasons that the decidedly finite and imperfect nature of his own being logically necessitates the existence of a God; for unless a perfect being exists, he, Descartes, has no basis for knowing his own imperfection. He further wonders how such an imperfect creature as a human can have an idea of perfection at all. Descartes concludes that the source of such an idea must be something perfect—God. He then infers the existence of this perfect being, for to his mind it makes little sense to attribute perfection to a nonexistent being.

Notice that Descartes does not appeal to the outer world in his proof. His claims appeal to the mind alone; they pass, he believes, the test of a clear and distinct idea. Similarly, he postulates the existence of the world and other selves. Could a perfect God, he asks, deceive me into perceiving my own body, the outer world, and other individuals, as I obviously do? Remember that Descartes knew that he himself existed only as a thinking thing. True, he did perceive his own body and the outer world, but consistent with his method of doubt, he reasoned that these might be illusions, the devilish tricks of some mad genius. But could they be? He has, after all, proved that a perfect being exists. Is such trickery and deception in the nature of perfection? He concludes that it is not. Therefore, he deduces, the world and other selves do indeed exist. We need not pursue Descartes further here since we will showcase his thought later in this chapter.

Empiricism

Beginning in the sixteenth century, a school of epistemology emerged that contrasted sharply with that of rationalism—empiricism.

---

1. *René Descartes*. Second Meditation, *from the* Meditations on First Philosophy *in* The Philosophical Works of Descartes. E. S. Haldane and G. R. T. Ross, Eds. New York: Cambridge University Press, 1931, pp. 190–191. Reprinted by permission.

"Are things what they appear to be?"

Empiricism is the belief that all knowledge about the world comes from or is based on the senses. Reacting sharply to rationalistic claims, empiricists claimed that the human mind contained nothing except what experience had put there. Thus, all ideas originate in sense experience. Consequently, empiricism taught that true knowledge was **a posteriori**, that is, it depends upon experience; it is knowledge stated in empirically verifiable statements.

Like rationalism, empiricism has had a long and illustrious history. Elements of empiricism can be found in the writings of Aristotle (384–322 B.C.), Saint Thomas Aquinas (1224–1274), Sir Francis Bacon (1561–1626), and Thomas Hobbes (1588–1679). In modern times the first noteworthy attack on rationalism was waged by three philosophers termed the *British empiricists*, namely, John Locke (1632–1704), George Berkeley (1684–1727), and David Hume (1711–1776).

Locke

The English philosopher John Locke was the first to launch a systematic attack on the belief that reason alone could provide us with knowledge. Locke compared the mind to a blank slate, *tabula rasa*, on which experience makes and leaves its mark. In his *An Essay concerning Human Understanding*, he stated the nature of his proposed doctrine clearly: "Let us then suppose the mind to be, as we say, white paper, void of all characters, without any ideas:—How comes it to be furnished? Whence comes it by that vast store which the busy and boundless fancy of man has painted on it with almost endless variety? Whence has it all the *materials* of reason and knowledge? To this I answer, in one word, from *experience*. In that all our knowledge is founded."[2]

2. *John Locke.* An Essay concerning Human Understanding. *A. C. Fraser, Ed. Oxford: Clarendon Press, 1894, vol. 2, p. 2.*

It's tempting to be lulled by the apparent simplicity and common sense of Locke's assertion. But automatic acceptance misses important philosophical implications. Consider the fact that we humans make all sorts of claims, from apparently ordinary ones such as "The lemon is bitter" and "Three plus three is six" to more complex ones such as "$E = mc^2$." And yet even for the simplest claims, as Descartes demonstrated, few people could provide a sound epistemological basis. In fact, if you ask people how they know it's raining, they might tell you to go outside and see for yourself. If you ask them how they know that today is the hottest day of the year, they again might tell you to go out and *feel* it and then *listen* to the weather report. If asked how they know that a lemon is bitter and sugar is sweet, they might tell you to *taste* them. The question of knowledge, it seems, is bound up with what we perceive. Through perception we feel confident that we *know* how things are.

Do you think there's any difference between things as they "really" are and our perception of things? Are things what they appear to be? To help place this question in the context of empiricism, let's rejoin Rob and Ellen.

Ellen: You're serious about this, aren't you? I mean about knowing something for certain.

Rob: You bet I am.

Ellen: Do you mean some heavy scientific truth, something like that?

Rob: *Anything.* I'll settle for the simplest, most ordinary thing for a start. . . . Go ahead, tell me something you know for sure.

Ellen: All right. I know that the object in the rack before me is a magazine.

Rob: How?

Ellen: Because I know a magazine when I see one. I also know that the liquid in the cup on the tray before me is coffee, because I know coffee when I see, smell, and taste it.

Rob: What if I said it was tea?

Ellen: I wouldn't believe you.

Rob: But let's say it looks, smells, and tastes like tea to me.

Ellen: I don't care if it looks, smells, and tastes like tea—it *isn't* tea.

Rob: You mean this thing might not be what I think it is?

Ellen: Precisely.

Rob: So a person could not only see something, but smell, taste, hear, and feel it as well, and it might not actually be what the person's sensing.

Ellen: Right.

Rob: Then how can you say that you know a magazine when you see one?

This is a fundamental epistemological problem that arises with all sense knowledge claims. Invariably implied in such claims is one of two beliefs: Either no qualitative distinction exists between the experience and the object of the experience (for example, between my experience of coffee and the coffee itself), or experience must be distinguished from the thing itself (for example, my experience of the coffee must be distinguished from the coffee itself). In the first instance we face serious, perhaps insurmountable difficulties in claiming that any objective reality exists, since it remains indistinguishable from our own experience. In other words, there's no difference between Ellen's experience of the coffee and magazine and the coffee and magazine themselves. In the second instance we must establish precisely how our sense perceptions square with reality. This is what Rob is asking. If, as Ellen suggests, we must distinguish our experiences of things from the things themselves, then how does she *know* that her experience of the magazine or the coffee does in fact correspond with the objective reality of those things?

In proposing his theory of knowledge, empiricist Locke was asserting not only that knowledge originates in sense experience but also that physical objects exist outside us, that they are independent of our perceptions of them. In effect, he distinguished between entities and their appearances to us: "For since the mind, in all its thoughts and reasonings, hath no other immediate objects but its own ideas, it is evident that our knowlege is only conversant about them."[3] Thus, for Locke our knowledge of things is more accurately termed our knowledge of our *ideas* of things. This is Rob's point and why he inquires about the connection, if any, between those ideas and the objective world.

Locke claimed that our ideas were representative of things themselves. But the crucial question is How? According to Locke, an object has certain qualities distinct from our perception of it, qualities that it would have even if it were not perceived. These he called **primary qualities**. Generally, primary qualities can be measured, for example, size, shape, and weight. These qualities, said Locke, are in things "whether we perceive them or not; and when they are of that size that we can discover them, we have by these an idea of the thing as it is in itself."[4] Thus, even if an object is not perceived, it still has a certain size, shape, and weight. For Locke, our ideas represent these primary qualities.

But Locke also believed that there are qualities that are not within an object itself. A tree, for example, has color, smell, texture, and maybe even a certain taste. In the fall the tree may be one color, in the spring another—as it may be one color at dawn and another at noon. Without its leaves, the tree may be odorless; with them, it may be fragrant. What is the actual color of the tree? Its actual smell? For Locke there is no actual color or smell. What we term *color* and *smell* are merely powers of the tree to produce sensation in us. The color and smell are not qualities in the tree itself, but our own ideas. As Locke puts it, "First our Senses, conversant about particular sensible objects, do convey into the mind several distinct perceptions of things, according to those various ways wherein those objects do affect them. And thus we come by those *ideas* we have of *yellow, white, heat, cold, soft, hard, bitter, sweet*, and all those which we call sensible qualities: which when I say the senses convey into the mind what produces there those perceptions; this great source of most of the ideas

---

3. *John Locke.* An Essay concerning Human Understanding, *vol. 4, p. 2.*

4. *John Locke.* An Essay concerning Human Understanding, *vol. 4, p. 2.*

we have, depending wholly upon our senses and derived by them to the understanding, I call SENSATION."[5]

According to Locke, therefore, a tree that we call green has no greenness; it has only the power to produce in us a sense experience that we call green. Such powers Locke calls **secondary qualities**.

We know how things are, therefore, because of our ideas, which represent the primary qualities of the external world. For example, if we experience the tree as being a certain height, we can trust that idea to resemble how the tree really is; if we experience it to have a certain circumference, we can trust that idea to resemble how the tree really is. Thus, we come to know the things around us by having sense experiences of their primary qualities; these experiences resemble the entities themselves.

During the early part of this century, a group of men composed a book entitled *Essays in Critical Realism*. Their view shows a marked Lockean flavor. Like Locke, the critical realists do not believe that the perception of entities is so direct as to be indistinguishable from things themselves. It is not the outer object that is present in the consciousness, they argue, but **sense data**. Sense data are the images or sense impressions—the immediate contents of sense experience—which, according to the critical realists, indicate the presence and nature of perceived objects. Only by inference can we go beyond sense data to the object itself. Critical realists believe that sense data provide accurate contact with entities, that they reveal what objects are and thus what the external world is like. They believe that three factors are involved: (1) a perceiver, knower, or conscious mind; (2) the entity or object, consisting of primary qualities; and (3) the sense data, which serve as a bridge between the perceiver and the object.

Still, a question nags: How can we be sure that our perceptions are truly representative of the objects perceived? Locke tried to answer this question with his so-called copy theory. Consider the operation of the senses as so many cameras snapping pictures. The senses are "photographing" everything that comes into contact with them. The resulting photographs of our experiences are obviously not the things themselves but copies of them. These copies, claimed Locke, are so much like the actual things that through knowing and understanding them we come to comprehend the world around us. As Locke puts it, "When our senses do actually convey into our understandings any idea, we cannot but be satisfied that there doth something *at that time* really exist without us, which doth affect our senses, and by them give notice of itself to our apprehensive faculties, and actually produce that idea which we then perceive; and we cannot so far distrust their testimony, as to doubt that such *collections* of simple ideas as we have observed by our senses to be united together, do really exist together."[6] He is insisting that the senses can do two things: certify that things outside the self actually exist, and provide an accurate picture of those things.

But no matter how representative, a photograph is not the thing itself. A

5. *John Locke*. An Essay concerning Human Understanding, *vol. 4, p. 4.*

6. *John Locke*. An Essay concerning Human Understanding, *vol. 4, pp. 1–2.*

difference remains between copy and thing, between our idea of something and the thing itself. If we are in touch with only our ideas of things, how do we know that they are really like the things themselves? We can't.

Furthermore, pictures are frequently distortions of reality. Perhaps the camera is malfunctioning. Are our senses perfect receivers of information? Even if they are, it is not likely that your sense experiences are identical with mine. Whose, then, are more representative? Such unanswered questions led philosophers to propose alternative views to Locke's.

Thus, in Locke's own time other empiricists objected that he had not fully accounted for the representative nature of our ideas. They seriously questioned whether he had fully explained how we can be sure that our sense experiences accurately represent how things actually are. Remember that Descartes could rely on a perfect God whose existence he had derived from the clear and distinct idea of his own existence. Locke's theory, in contrast, originating in sense experience, did not include such an epistemologically influential being. As a result, it was left open to challenge from within the empirical camp. The foremost challenge was presented by the Irish bishop George Berkeley.

Berkeley

Berkeley agreed with Locke that ideas originate in sense experience. Although he also accepted Locke's argument that secondary qualities are subjective, Berkeley insisted that the same could be said of primary qualities. In *A Treatise concerning the Principles of Human Knowledge*, Berkeley says:

> They who assert that figure, motion, and the rest of the primary or original qualities do exist without mind in unthinking substances do at the same time acknowledge that colors, sounds, heat, cold and such like secondary qualities, do not; which they tell us are sensations, existing in the mind alone, that depend on and are occasioned by the different size, texture, and motion of the minute particles of matter. . . . Now if it be certain that those original qualities are inseparably united with other sensible qualities, and not, even in thought, capable of being abstracted from them, it plainly follows they exist only in the mind. But I desire anyone to reflect, and try whether he can, by any abstraction of thought conceive the extension and motion of a body without all other sensible qualities. For my own part, I see evidently that it is not in my power to frame an idea of a body extended and moving but I must . . . give it some color or sensible quality, which is acknowledged to exist only in the mind. In short, extension, figure and motion, abstracted from all other qualities, are inconceivable. Where therefore the other sensible qualities are, there must these be also, to wit, in the mind and nowhere else.[7]

In other words, if heat or cold is a secondary quality—a quality only of the mind, as Locke insists—then why aren't figure and extension secondary qualities as well? For example, a coin appears round from one angle and linear from another, just as a tree appears taller from the bottom of a hill than from the

---

7. *George Berkeley*. A Treatise concerning the Principles of Human Knowledge, *in* The Works of George Berkeley. *A. C. Fraser, Ed. Oxford: Clarendon Press, 1901, vol. 1, p. 87.*

WHAT YOU SEE.....
.....IS WHAT YOU
GET

". . . all qualities are mind-dependent."

top. Why? Because, says Berkeley, all qualities are mind-dependent. Indeed, to think of sensible qualities as existing in outward objects is ridiculous.

For Berkeley, only minds and their ideas exist. In saying that an idea exists, Berkeley means that it is perceived by some mind. In other words, for ideas *esse est percipi:* "to be is to be perceived." On the other hand, minds are not dependent for their existence on being perceived, because they are perceivers. For Berkeley, therefore, what exists is the conscious mind or some idea or perception held by that mind. Objects do not exist independent of consciousness.

What we know then are our ideas or perceptions. Ellen knows only her idea of that magazine; that is all she can possibly know. Because Berkeley claims that we know only our own ideas, he is sometimes termed a *subjectivist*. The subjectivist contends that there can be no entity or perception of an entity without a perceiver, that the perceiver to some degree creates the perceived object, and that everything that is real is a conscious mind or a perception by a conscious mind. When we say that an entity exists, we mean that it is perceived or at least that it could be perceived if we were to do thus and so.

Carried to an extreme, Berkeley's thinking can become **solipsism**, the position that only I exist and that everything else is just a creation of my subjective consciousness. This position contends that the only perceiver is myself. Other persons and objects have no independent existence but exist solely as creations of my consciousness when and to the degree that I am conscious of them.

But it is unfair to push Berkeley's position that far; he never did. To avoid such excesses, Berkeley relied on an outside source for his ideas: God. Things continue to exist even when no conscious mind is perceiving them, because God is forever perceiving them. God always has them "in mind." But now other problems arise, the chief one being: If all that exists is a conscious mind and some perception by that mind, how do we know that God exists? If we cannot say that something material exists, how can we insist that something nonmaterial, like God, does? In one of his dialogues between Hylas (substitute "Locke") and Philonus (substitute "Berkeley"), Berkeley anticipates just such an objection.

> *Hylas:*   Answer me, Philonus. Are all our ideas perfectly inert beings? Or have they any agency included in them?
>
> *Philonus:*   They are altogether passive and inert.
>
> *Hylas:*   And is not God an agent, a being purely active?
>
> *Philonus:*   I acknowledge it.
>
> *Hylas:*   No idea therefore can be like unto, or represent, the nature of God.
>
> *Philonus:*   It cannot.
>
> *Hylas:*   Since therefore you have no idea of the mind of God, how can you conceive it possible that things should exist in His mind? Or, if you can conceive the existence of Matter, notwithstanding I have no idea of it? . . . You admit . . . that there is a spiritual Substance, although you have no idea of it; while you deny there can be such a thing as material Substance, because you have no notion or idea of it. Is this fair dealing? To act consistently, you must either admit Matter or reject Spirit.[8]

"Admit Matter or reject Spirit"—this was something Berkeley seemed unwilling to do. Some claim it was because Berkeley never intended to make such a rigorous criticism of Locke, that from the outset he disbelieved the existence of matter and tried to use the empirical method to prove this belief. When the empirical method seemed to disprove what he wanted to believe, Berkeley forsook it. In fairness to Berkeley, however, we should note the difficulty of defending the sense of the contention that there are objects that are *not* objects—objects that are unknown to subjects and that are unthought and unexperienced. Surely Berkeley at least anticipated this problem, with which another idealist, Immanuel Kant, would subsequently deal. And, of course, Berkeley felt he had good reasons for not applying empirical method completely. Specifically, we have direct experience of our own conscious selves, which are not hypothetical or inferred entities on the order of God.

Finally, let us be certain about Berkeley's claims. He does not deny that there are houses, books, trees, cats, and people. But he does deny that these or any other physical objects exist independently of our minds. For Berkeley, there are not beds and then sense experiences of beds that copy or resemble beds, as Locke believed. There is only the sense experience of beds. A bed, or any other physical object, is composed of a collection of ideas.

But if we talk of our experience of a bed, we seem to be suggesting that there is a bed to be experienced. This is because our language is misleading. There simply is no appropriate way to speak of the contents of our sense experiences without mentioning the name of the physical object that we believe is experienced. But Berkeley would not accept the existence of the physical object. Yes, for Berkeley there are beds, but *not* experiences of beds caused by beds—that is, by physical objects existing outside and independently of us.

8.   *George Berkeley. "Three Dialogues between Hylas and Philonus,"* in The Works of George Berkeley. A. C. Fraser, Ed. Oxford: Clarendon Press, 1901, vol. 1, pp. 447–479.

Berkeley held that *bed* and all other words for physical objects are names of "recurring patterns" of sense experiences, and no more. Physical objects are groups of sense experiences that we are constantly aware of.

Although an empiricist, Berkeley was ultimately unwilling to deny the spiritual substances whose existences he wished to prove. In short, he seems to have used empiricism to disprove what he disbelieved to begin with but to have recoiled from it when it threatened to disprove his deepest convictions. Nevertheless, he remains a critical link in understanding the dialectical development of empiricism, which Scottish philosopher David Hume extended to its logical limits.

Hume

It's fair to say that David Hume pushed Locke's empiricism to a thorough skepticism, that is, to a denial of the possibility of certain knowledge about matters of fact. In other words, empirical knowledge is only probable. How Hume came to this conclusion is a long and complex affair, which we can only sketch here.

To begin, Hume asserts that the contents of the mind can be reduced to those given by the senses and experience. He calls these *perceptions*. In Hume's view, perceptions take two forms, what he terms *impressions* and *ideas*. The distinction between them and how they relate to knowing are vital to understanding Humean thought. In his *Enquiry concerning Human Understanding*, Hume clearly explains what he means by ideas and impressions:

> Here therefore we may divide all the perceptions of the mind into two classes or species, which are distinguished by their different degrees of force and vivacity. The less forcible and lively are commonly denominated *Thoughts* or *Ideas*. The other species want a name in our language, and in most others; I suppose, because it was not requisite for any, but philosophical purposes, to rank them under a general term or appellation. Let us therefore use a little freedom, and call them *Impressions*; employing that word in a sense somewhat different from the usual. By the term impression, then, I mean all our more lively perceptions, when we hear, or see, or feel, or love, or hate, or desire, or will. And impressions are distinguished from ideas, which are the less lively perceptions of which we are conscious, when we reflect on any of those sensations or movements above mentioned.[9]

Clearly, then, in distinguishing impressions from ideas, Hume employs an empirically observable criterion: a difference in degree of "liveliness." Thus, original perceptions are quite vivid, as are those of color or emotion. Their vividness declines, however, when we subsequently reflect upon them or have ideas about them. The pain you feel when you hammer your thumb is an impression; the memory of what you feel is an idea.

Consistent with this insight is the Humean belief that there can be no ideas without sense impressions. This follows from his contention that every idea is a faint impression. Thus, if there are no impressions, there are no ideas. However, not every idea reflects an impression. We can, after all, conceive of a

9. *David Hume.* Enquiry concerning Human Understanding. *L. A. Selby-Bigge, Ed. Oxford: Clarendon Press, 1894, sec. 2.*

golden mountain or a virtuous horse, even if we've never had an impression of either. How is this possible? Hume answers that in such cases our imagination combines ideas that were acquired through impressions. As Hume puts it:

> But though our thought seems to possess this unbounded liberty, we shall find, upon a nearer examination, that it is really confined within very narrow limits, and that all this creative power of the mind amounts to no more than the faculty of compounding, transposing, augmenting, or diminishing the materials afforded us by the senses and experience. When we think of a golden mountain, we only join two consistent ideas, *gold*, and *mountain*, with which we were formerly acquainted. A virtuous horse we can conceive; because, from our own feeling, we can conceive virtue; and this we may unite to the figure and shape of a horse, which is an animal familiar to us. In short, all the materials of thinking are derived either from our outward or inward sentiment: the mixture and composition of these belong alone to the mind and will. Or, to express myself in philosophical language, all our ideas or more feeble perceptions are copies of our impressions or more lively ones.[10]

Building upon this thesis, Hume then turns to the issue that concerned Locke and Berkeley as well as Descartes: the existence of an external reality. Since there can be no ideas without prior sense impressions, Hume concludes that there is no rational justification for the belief that anything has continued and independent existence outside us. After all, impressions are internal subjective states and thus are not proof of a continued external reality. In other words, the subjectivity of all perceptions, including ideas, plus the illegitimacy of pseudo ideas for which there are no corresponding impressions (for example, matter, cause, and self) casts doubt on the external world (see Philosophy and Life 6-2).

To grasp this point, let's rejoin Ellen and Rob. Ellen has thought a while about Rob's claim that we're only in touch with our experiences of things. While conceding this, she's not entirely clear about its epistemological implications.

Ellen: Okay, but even if all I'm in touch with is my experience of the magazine, that's something anyway. After all, I'm having a particular kind of experience which, say, is different from my experience of coffee. And as far as I can determine, the experience is consistent, since each time I look at the magazine I see the same thing. To me that's a lot, because it allows me to deal with things. It provides a sort of predictiveness that lets me order my life.

Rob: Granted. But if you think about it, that predictive quality you talk about may be an illusion.

Ellen: What do you mean?

Rob: Close your eyes for a second. Now, tell me, does the magazine exist?

Ellen: I presume it does.

10. *David Hume.* An Enquiry concerning Human Understanding.

Rob: But do you *know* it does?

Ellen: Well, no, because I'm not having an experience of it. But that doesn't mean the magazine ceases to exist.

Rob: No, it doesn't. But it suggests that you can't claim to know that something continues to exist when your experience of it is interrupted.

Ellen: You mean, I don't know for sure that there's anything outside or below the cloud bank we're flying through.

Rob: As far as I'm concerned, we don't even know that there's a pilot up front.

Ellen: But we're acting as if we did. I mean everybody's sitting here, calm in the thought that somebody's flying this thing.

Rob: Agreed. But we can't be any more certain of that than you can be sure that that magazine continues to exist when you're not experiencing it.

Like Rob Dalton, Hume concedes that we always act *as if* a real external world of things exists, but he asks how we can be sure of the continued existence of things when we interrupt our sensation of them. For example, before you lies this book. You're sustaining an impression of it, perhaps a tactual and visual sensation. Then you interrupt that sensation by removing your hands and closing your eyes. You may now have an idea of the book, but that idea is not enough to confirm its continued existence. Then why do we commonly believe the book continues to exist? Because when we open our eyes the book sits before us. If we persisted in this exercise, the result would be the same.

There is an apparent constancy in things that leads us to believe that they continue to have an independent existence external to us. But for Hume this belief is just that, a belief, and not a rational proof. The assumption that our impressions are connected with things lacks any foundation in reasoning. What's more, even when we have an impression of the thing itself, such as this book, we have only that impression, which we can't distinguish from the book. In short, Hume believes that there is no way for the mind to reach beyond impressions and the subsequent ideas. In other words, Hume goes philosophically further than the exchange between Rob and Ellen. Not only does Ellen not know whether the magazine exists when her eyes are closed, but she doesn't know it when they're open. In short, Hume seriously doubts that there is a world external to consciousness.

This discussion may resemble Berkeley's doctrine that to be is to be perceived. But recall that Berkeley has a God who sustains things in a continued existence when no person is perceiving them. Hume, in contrast, does not rely on any such theological prop. He applies the doctrine of empiricism as rigorously as he can, regardless of its implications. As a result, he extends this skeptical line of reasoning beyond the existence of objects and things to questions concerning the existence of God and the self. In our chapter on religion, we'll see how and why Hume is led to the conclusion that there is no proof for the existence of God. Since we've already raised the issue of self and human nature, however, we will briefly review Hume's views on these subjects.

Hume approaches the idea of self by asking from what impression it can be derived. In other words, is there a single and identical impression that we associate with the idea of self? In his essay entitled "Of Personal Identity," Hume attacks the concept of identity as it was developed by Descartes and others. His conclusion closely resembles the scientific and Eastern ones discussed earlier. Specifically, Hume sees the self as a "bundle of perceptions." To understand his analysis and his application of his epistemological views to this important issue, consider the following excerpt from "Of Personal Identity":

> There are some philosophers, who imagine we are every moment intimately conscious of what we call our *self*; that we feel its existence and its continuance in existence; and are certain, beyond the evidence of a demonstration, both of its perfect identity and simplicity. The strongest sensation, the most violent passion, say they, instead of distracting us from this view, only fix it the more intensely, and make us consider their influence on *self* either by their pain or pleasure. To attempt a farther proof of this were to weaken its evidence, since no proof can be derived from any fact, of which we are so intimately conscious; nor is there any thing, of which we can be certain, if we doubt of this.

PHILOSOPHY AND LIFE 6-2
The Egocentric Predicament

In 1910 American philosopher Ralph Barton Perry published an article entitled "The Ego-Centric Predicament." In it he makes a point about "objects/ events" outside us, that is, real objects. Perry addresses a question that Western philosophers have long debated: What's the metaphysical status of objects/events? What are things like outside our perception of them?

Perry reasoned that we can never observe things apart from our perception of them. This was obvious enough to Perry, because we must perceive any real object/event in order to know it. If we can't know things apart from our perception of them, then we can never know whether our perception of things changes them—thus, the egocentric predicament.

Professor of philosophy James Christian has extended Perry's point by suggesting that the egocentric predicament entails an *illusion*.* This egocentric illusion lies in the fact that all our mortal lives we must occupy a physical organism; that is, we must occupy a point in space and time. As a result, it appears to each of us that we are the center of creation. Conversely, it appears to each of us that the whole cosmos revolves around that point in the space-time that we occupy. What's more, wherever we go in space-time, this egocentric illusion pursues us, since we move our center. In a word, every living, conscious creature experiences itself as the true center of the cosmos, when in fact the cosmos has no true center.

* See James Christian. Philosophy: An Introduction to the Art of Wondering. *New York: Holt, Rinehart and Winston, 1973, pp. 50–58.*

Unluckily all these positive assertions are contrary to that very experience, which is pleaded for them, nor have we any idea of *self*, after the manner it is here explained. For from what impression could this idea be derived? This question 'tis impossible to answer without a manifest contradiction and absurdity; and yet 'tis a question, which must necessarily be answered, if we would have the idea of self pass for clear and intelligible. It must be some one impression, that gives rise to every real idea. But self or person is not any one impression, but that to which our several impressions and ideas are supposed to have a reference. If any impression gives rise to the idea of self, that impression must continue invariably the same, through the whole course of our lives; since self is supposed to exist after that manner. But there is no impression constant and invariable. Pain and pleasure, grief and joy, passions and sensations succeed each other, and never all exist at the same time. It cannot therefore be from any of these impressions, or from any other, that the idea of self is derived; and consequently there is no such idea.

But farther, what must become of all our particular perceptions upon this hypothesis? All these are different, and distinguishable, and separable from each other, and may be separately considered, and may exist separately, and have no need of any thing to support their existence. After what manner therefore do they belong to self; and how are they connected with it? For my part,

Christian observes that when all humans take themselves as the center of things, we make *aristocentric* claims, that is, inordinate claims to superiority for oneself or one's group. Aristocentric claims arise because we fail to correct for the egocentric illusion. Taking ourselves as cosmic centers, we may claim that our existence has special meaning, that we have a special knowledge or message, or that we have special powers. Rarely, however, do we make these claims in the singular. This is not surprising, for our arrogant pride would invite scorn and ridicule. But we do make aristocentric claims in the plural: "We are something special," "We are favored people," or "We have a unique destiny." The beauty of such claims is that they're so easily reinforced by group members. Sociologists have a word for any form of aristocentrism—*ethnocentricity*, the preoccupation with and belief in the superiority of one's own culture.

When Ralph Barton Perry spoke of the egocentric predicament, he had in mind a timeless metaphysical concern. But, as so often happens, purely philosophical musings have a way of slipping into our everyday lives.

□ *The great historian Arnold Toynbee once observed that a human self cannot be brought into harmony with absolute reality unless it rids itself of self-centeredness. Why is this so?*

when I enter most intimately into what I call *myself* at any time without a perception, and never can observe any thing but the perception. When my perceptions are removed for any time, as by sound sleep; so long am I insensible of
myself, and may truly be said not to exist. And were all my perceptions removed by death, and could I neither think, nor feel, nor see, nor love, nor hate
after the dissolution of my body, I should be entirely annihilated, nor do I
conceive what is farther requisite to make me a perfect non-entity. If any one
upon serious and unprejudiced reflection, think he has a different notion of
himself, I must confess I can reason no longer with him. All I can allow him is,
that he may be in the right as well as I, and that we are essentially different in
this particular. He may, perhaps, perceive something simple and continued,
which he calls *himself*; though I am certain there is no such principle in me.[11]

In sum, Hume denies the existence of a continuous self-identity, arguing that
humans are "nothing but a bundle or collection of different perceptions."

Ultimately, it seems, Hume returns to the epistemological problem that
Descartes and Berkeley faced: whether we can know anything other than that
our minds exist. If we rely on senses alone, few difficulties arise. But, as Hume
amply demonstrates, reason confounds such a simplistic attitude. Hume describes a fundamental and perhaps irreconcilable conflict between senses and
reason, raising doubts about the adequacy of either empiricism or rationalism
to lead us to knowledge and truth. This skepticism rocked and altered the
philosophy of Hume's time and has left an indelible impression on all subsequent philosophical inquiry. Indeed, it was partially to resolve this skepticism that Immanuel Kant turned his attention to questions about the nature of
knowledge, creating a unique version of idealism termed *transcendental idealism*.
But the term *phenomenalism* more accurately captures the difference between
Kant's idealism and the idealism just sketched. It also focuses on the aspect of
Kant's thought that we wish to emphasize here. So we'll use that term, noting
that Kant is frequently called a transcendental idealist.

Phenomenalism and Kant

The fundamental epistemological question that concerned the German
philosopher Immanuel Kant (1724–1804) was how to deal with Hume's
wholesale skepticism. Sensing the pivotal point that philosophy had reached,
Kant tried to determine whether one could validly argue that reason can attain
knowledge that is certain. He attempted to find out whether any a priori
knowledge was possible or whether humans could aspire only to limited and
uncertain knowledge through experience.

In his most influential work, *Critique of Pure Reason*, Kant attacks the problem by addressing the rationalistic claim to a priori knowledge—that we can
know independently of sense perception. Living in the midst of the revolution
of empiricism, Kant is highly skeptical of such Cartesian claims as that the
existence of God is implied in the concept of a perfect being. Kant insists that
such assertions are not the certainties that rationalists often make them out to
be. Indeed, he accepts Hume's proposition that experience is the only basis of

11. *David Hume. "Of Personal Identity,"* in Treatise on Human Nature. *L. A. Selby-Bigge, Ed. Oxford:*
Clarendon Press, 1896, p. 251.

true knowledge. Unwilling to end the debate there, Kant further asks whether there is anything we can know from experience through a source or sources other than our senses. In other words, does anything that we humans bring to experience allow us to know? Thus, while accepting experience as the only basis for sure knowledge, Kant doesn't accept that empiricism accounts for *all* knowledge. Thus, he seeks to establish something essential to human nature that enables humans to know from sense perceptions. In his *Critique of Pure Reason* Kant states his concern:

> But though all our knowledge begins with experience, it does not follow that it all arises out of experience. For it may well be that even our empirical knowledge is made up of what we receive through impressions of what our own faculty of knowledge (sensible impressions serving merely as the occasion) supplies from itself. If our faculty of knowledge makes any such addition, it may be that we are not in a position to distinguish it from the raw material, until with long practice of attention we have become skilled in separating it.
>
> This, then, is a question which at least calls for closer examination, and does not allow of any offhand answer:—whether there is any knowledge that is thus independent of experience and even of all impressions of the senses. Such knowledge is entitled *a priori*, and distinguished from the *empirical*, which has its sources *a posteriori*, that is, in experience.[12]

To understand Kant's resolution of this problem, it's necessary to grasp his distinction between the *content* and *form* of knowledge. For Kant, content comes from sense experience, form from reason. Our senses provide content such as tastes, smells, sounds, and shapes, but they don't reveal relationships, laws, or causes—this is done by the mind.

This point is illustrated when Rob, Ellen, and everyone else aboard the aircraft are jolted when it suddenly drops. Coffee spills, lunches threaten to come up, and passengers are sent reeling. Just as abruptly, however, the plane stabilizes and tranquility returns. In the aftermath, the cabin is abuzz with speculation about what caused the event. "Air pockets," most seem to suspect. But the precise cause is of less concern to Ellen than that everyone intuitively seeks a causal explanation for the disruption.

Ellen: Did you notice how we all *knew* that something caused us to drop?

Rob: That's normal enough.

Ellen: I think there's more in it than normalcy.

Rob: What?

Ellen: Well, let's suppose that we *are* just in touch with our experiences. Then we can't know how things actually are outside our experiences of them.

Rob: Sure, that's my whole point.

Ellen: But let's say we've got some inborn capacity to make sense of those experiences.

Rob: You mean some inner ability that allows us to know things?

Ellen: That's right. That would make knowledge possible.

---

12. *Immanuel Kant.* Critique of Pure Reason. 2nd ed. *N. Kemp Smith, Trans. London: Macmillan, 1929, pp. 1–2.*

The search for a cause for the experience on the plane might have impressed Kant epistemologically as it did Ellen. He would have likely observed that the mind intuitively has knowledge of causation. True, no one may ever discover the cause of the plane's descent—or of anything else, for that matter. But we do know that causation is involved, that causing goes on in the world, that an event does not occur without causal conditions. If we did not possess this intuition of cause and effect, we couldn't make sense out of our experiences.

Similarly, Kant holds that the mind possesses ideas or conceptual molds by which it orders sense perceptions so that knowing is possible. These forms or categories allow us to create experience. The phenomenon that we experience results in part from the workings of our senses and mind. The senses help provide the content, or the stuff; the mind provides the form, or shape. So, as we noted, the senses provide things like tastes, feelings, and smells, for "all our·knowledge begins with experience." But the mind imposes relationships upon the sense perceptions. Through an awareness of these relationships, we come to knowledge. The mind is able to impose these relationships because it consists of molds, or categories, for organizing and interpreting sense perceptions. We needn't go into these categories here, except to emphasize that for Kant they allow us to make sense of experience.

According to Kant's theory of **phenomenalism**, we do not perceive things as they really are. We never perceive the thing in itself, which he calls the *noumenon*. All we ever know is how the thing appears to us, which he calls the *phenomenon*. The noumena stimulate the senses; the sensations that follow are informed by the categories, whereby they become the phenomenal things of the everyday world of experience. Thus, the part of the world that is subject to understanding through the categories is created by us.

It is noteworthy that Kant recognizes a logical necessity for the existence of a nonphenomenal realm that is responsible for the existence of the phenomenal one. Unlike Berkeley, for whom what is perceived is all that exists, Kant claims that in addition to our experience of a thing, a thing has its own nature. This thing in itself, the noumenon, is responsible for the fact that appearances exist at all. Although we can never know what these noumena are in themselves, the mind can integrate and interpret sensations and thus make knowledge possible.

Notice that Kant ultimately tries to resolve the same problem that Locke struggled with: How can we hold that an objective, physical world exists and at the same time claim to know it? Although Kant answers the question differently, his phenomenalism is open to some of the same objections leveled against Locke.

Rob: But aren't you forgetting something?

Ellen: What?

Rob: Well, suppose that you'd slept through this whole thing.

Ellen: You mean, I didn't feel my stomach drop or see people falling into the aisle?

Rob: Right.

Ellen: So?

Rob: So that tells me that even if your mind does sort out all these sense experiences as you say, it can't do anything without first having them.

Ellen: Of course not. In order to make sense out of something, you must have something to begin with.

Rob: That's my point. We're back where we started. Everything's hanging on the senses. And, as far as I'm concerned, our experiences of things are different from the things themselves. So, we never know that our experiences correspond with the way things actually are.

Ellen: And so we can't know anything for sure?

Rob: I think not.

Ellen: And that leaves you as depressed as ever.

Rob: Not quite. Just think, if we can't know anything for sure, then I can't be sure that I don't know anything for sure!

Ellen: You mean there's hope?

Rob: For sure!

Rob has suggested a number of questions that raise an important objection to Kant's position. First, if experience is the only true basis of knowledge, then it is reasonable to question the reliability of the senses as sources of that knowledge. After all, the mind can't order the stuff of sense experience until it receives that stuff. Of course, Kant claims that what the senses give us does not correspond to how things are to begin with—it is already informed by the categories. Thus, we never perceive things as they actually are. If things as such are unknowable, then we appear to be faced with thorough skepticism. We could also wonder about the mental categories themselves—whether Kant has provided a complete list and description and whether they're the same for everyone.

Despite these apparent drawbacks, Kant's thought does constitute a serious attempt to analyze the nature of knowledge. Kant not only shows the limitations of knowledge but also validates knowledge within its proper field. The main ingredient of his analysis is the balance between empiricism and rationalism. More specifically, Kant is noteworthy for his portrayal of the questioning, inquisitive nature of the mind. This conception of the mind's role as a questioner of nature constitutes a new way of considering the nature of the self and its objects, and, most important, it suggests a new approach to the study of perception (see Philosophy and Life 6-3).[13] We'll say considerably more of this when we examine phenomenology.

13.   See W. T. Jones. Kant to Wittgenstein and Sartre. *New York: Harcourt, Brace, 1969, p. 98.*

Showcase: René Descartes (1596–1650)

Regarded as the first great philosopher of the modern age, René Descartes was born in Touraine, France. He was educated by the Jesuits and remained a Catholic throughout his life.

Early in his education, Descartes became interested in mathematics and science, both of which were receiving profound attention by an array of continental and English thinkers. Indeed, when still in his twenties, Descartes conceived of the ambitious plan of formulating an entirely new system of science based upon mathematics. According to Descartes, this plan came as a result of three dramatic dreams which the twenty-three-year-old Frenchman had on the

PHILOSOPHY AND LIFE 6-3
Phenomenalism and Gestalt Psychology

Some patterns of visual stimulation are more meaningful to us than others. Consider the following pattern. How would you describe it?

Probably you'd say that you see three sets of two horizontal lines each rather than six separate lines. This is so because you perceive items close to each other as a whole. Again, consider this pattern:

```
O X O
O X O
O X O
```

Because we perceive items that resemble each other as units, you'd probably describe what you see as two vertical rows of circles and one of X's rather than three horizontal rows of circles and X's.

Why is one pattern of visual stimulation meaningful while another is not? One answer lies in past experience: Patterns that outline shapes are meaningful if they match shapes that have been experienced and remembered. But meaningfulness also seems to be imposed by the organization of the visual system.

night of November 10, 1619. Descartes interpreted his dreams as a sign that he was to devote his life to establishing a new unified theory of the universe based upon mathematics, what is today called mathematical physics. While Descartes never realized his plan, his intellectual groundbreaking in mathematics and physics secured for him a renowned place in seventeenth-century science.

Throughout his life Descartes was preoccupied with methodology, justification, and certainty. His works reflect these concerns. For example, in his first work, entitled *Rules for the Direction of the Mind,* he attempted to establish procedures for investigating a question, procedures which would preclude error and confusion. His most famous work, *Meditations on First Philosophy,* engaged, among other things, the question of absolute subjective certainty in knowledge. So influential a work was *Meditations* in undermining the influence of the two-thousand-year-old tradition of Aristotelian philosophizing, that it ignited

Some years ago a group of German psychologists, Kurt Koffka and Wolfgang Köhler among them, studied the basic principles of organization in perception. They insisted that a perception of form is an innate property of the visual system. This group of psychologists became known as Gestaltists, from the German word *Gestalt,* meaning "form."

Gestaltists focus on subjective experience and the exploration of consciousness. They see the most significant aspect of experience as being its wholeness, or interrelatedness. Thus, Gestaltists believe that any attempt to analyze behavior by studying its parts is futile because such an approach loses the basic characteristic of experiences: their organization, pattern, and wholeness. For Gestaltists no stimulus has constant significance or meaning. It all depends on the patterns surrounding events. For example, a 5'10" basketball player looks small when seen as part of a professional basketball team but of normal size as part of a random group of individuals.

As part of their focus on subjective experience and the exploration of consciousness, Gestalt psychologists have formulated a number of descriptive principles of perceptual organization. Two are illustrated above in our two simple patterns: the principles of similarity and proximity.

□ *Do Gestaltists owe anything to the theories of knowledge that preceded their investigations?* □ *If we consider phenomenalism as the description of things as they are in the immediate experience, explain how Gestaltists took phenomenalism as the principal approach to the study of perception.*
□ *What connections do you see between Gestalt psychology and Kantianism?*

philosophical controversy throughout Europe. The upshot was a series of objections to which Descartes wrote extended replies. Indeed, for a period of roughly 150 years, until about 1800, just about every important philosopher attempted to deal with the issues raised by Descartes.

The Method

Essential to an understanding of the philosophy of Descartes is knowledge of his method. Descartes spent considerable time thinking about the problems of intellectual and scientific method. In fact, his contributions in this field are more significant than his actual mathematical and scientific work.

A good place to begin unpacking Descartes's method is with four rules he lays down which, he believes, are sufficient to guide the mind in any inquiry. Descartes states the rules as follows:

> The first of these was to accept nothing as true which I did not clearly recognize to be so: that is to say, carefully to avoid precipitation and prejudice in judgments, and to accept in them nothing more than what was presented to my mind so clearly and distinctly that I could have no occasion to doubt it.
>
> The second was to divide up each of the difficulties which I examined into as many parts as possible, and as seemed requisite in order that it might be resolved in the best manner possible.
>
> The third was to carry on my reflections in due order, commencing with objects that were the most simple and easy to understand, in order to rise little by little, or by degree, to knowledge of the most complex, assuming an order, even if a fictitious one, among those which do not follow a natural sequence relatively to one another.
>
> The last was in all cases to make enumerations so complete and reviews so general that I should be certain of having omitted nothing. [14]

On first look there seems to be nothing revolutionary about these exhortations. Avoid bias, divide up a problem, engage a question a step at a time, be thorough—indeed, these seem the distillation of common sense. Yet, embedded in these directives are two features which were to have far-reaching implications for the development of philosophy. These features may be conveniently labeled the *method of inquiry* and the *method of doubt*.

Viewed as a method of inquiry, Descartes's method provides a way of investigating things and getting them straight. In other words, his rules serve as a guideline for anyone trying to solve a problem or analyze a phenomenon. Descartes is not offering a method for proving what you already know or for assembling your knowledge in the most systematic way. Rather, he is laying out a way to approach any question that you may be interested in answering. In elucidating the distinction between a method of inquiry and a method of proof or organization, professor of philosophy Robert Wolff asks us to recall our exposure to plane geometry:

> On the first page of a geometry book . . . you find definitions, axioms, and postulates. These are the simplest, or the most fundamental part of the geomet-

14. *René Descartes. Discourse on Method.* French and English Philosophers. *Charles Eliot, Ed. Cambridge: Harvard University Press, 1909, p. 113.*

ric theory, but they are hardly the first things that a real mathematician would think up if he were doing geometry. Then come the theorems, each one neatly set forth, step by step, from the axioms or previously proved theorems down to what is to be proved, Q.E.D. That may be the way Euclid rearranged his proofs once he had thought them up, but it surely isn't the way he discovered them! Most likely, when he wanted to prove something (say, the theorem that the line bisecting the apex of an isosceles triangle is perpendicular to the base), he drew a diagram, fiddled around with the lines, looked to see whether there was anything that was equal to anything else, worked his way up from the conclusion and down from the premises, until the proof finally fell into place. So his *method of inquiry* was very different from his method of proof or exposition.[15]

In setting his guidelines, then, Descartes is assuming the viewpoint of someone who does not yet know anything but is trying to know it. In his view, following his guidelines is the correct way to proceed.

Additionally, Descartes's method is a method of doubt. He states this explicitly in the first guideline in which he tells us to accept nothing as true that we do not clearly recognize to be so. By "clearly recognize," Descartes means more than is implied in the adage "Look before you leap," that is, don't be hasty in your judgments. Rather, he means that we should refuse to accept anything unless we can be certain that it is right. No matter how obvious something seems, how likely we think it is, how much currency tradition and other people give to it, we should refuse to accept it until we are absolutely sure that it is true beyond any possible doubt. By this account, even if there is the remotest chance that something might be false, then we are not to accept it.

To catch the radical implications of Descartes's method of doubt, consider something that you are quite sure of—perhaps that there is a book in front of you from which you are reading. If asked how you can be so sure of this, you might reply: "I can see the book, even feel it." But just because you can sense the book, does that make it absolutely certain that the book is, in fact, in front of you? Is it *possible* that you may be hallucinating, that you only imagine the book to be in front of you? True, this isn't likely. But is it *logically possible?* After all, lots of people hallucinate. They imagine all sorts of things, which they are perfectly convinced of. Yet, the things they imagine to be the case are not the case. Is it *logically possible*, then, that you could be wrong about the book?

You would probably agree that if by "clearly recognize" Descartes is demanding 100 percent certainty, then virtually everything that you or I believe or assume to be so can be doubted. Yet, this is precisely what Descartes has in mind. Indeed, true to his method, in his six famous "meditations" Descartes begins with the resolve to doubt *everything* that he believes.

In Meditation I, which follows, notice how Descartes aims to build anew his systems of beliefs and eliminate false beliefs by doubting everything that he believes. He does this, not by scrutinizing every single belief he holds, but by examining the "first principles" upon which all his other beliefs are based. If these principles are in doubt, then whatever is based on them necessarily is in doubt, too. One set of principles to be doubted are common sense beliefs, that is,

15.   *Robert Paul Wolff.* About Philosophy. *New York: Prentice-Hall, © 1976, p. 230. Reprinted by permission.*

those beliefs which rely upon the senses: seeing, hearing, tasting, smelling, touching. Another set are the principles of arithmetic and geometry.

MEDITATION I

It is now some years since I detected how many were the false beliefs that I had from my earliest youth admitted as true and how doubtful was everything I had since constructed on this basis; and from that time I was convinced that I must once for all seriously undertake to rid myself of all the opinions which I had formerly accepted, and commence to build anew from the foundation, if I wanted to establish any firm and permanent structure in the sciences.

Now for this object it is not necessary that I should show that all of these are false—I shall perhaps never arrive at this end. But inasmuch as reason already persuades me that I ought no less carefully to withhold my assent from matters which are not entirely certain and indubitable than from those which appear to me manifestly to be false, if I am able to find in each one some reason to doubt, this will suffice to justify my rejecting the whole. And for that end it will not be requisite that I should examine each in particular, which would be an endless undertaking; for owing to the fact that the destruction of the foundations of necessity brings with it the downfall of the rest of the edifice, I shall only in the first place attack those principles upon which all my former opinions rested.

All that up to the present time I have accepted as most true and certain I have learned either from the senses or through the senses; but it is sometimes proved to me that these senses are deceptive, and it is wiser not to trust entirely to any thing by which we have once been deceived.

But it may be that although the senses sometimes deceive us concerning things which are hardly perceptible, or very far away, there are yet many others to be met with as to which we cannot reasonably have any doubt, although we recognise them by their means. For example, there is the fact that I am here, seated by the fire, attired in a dressing gown, having this paper in my hands and other similar matters. And how could I deny that these hands and this body are mine, were it not perhaps that I compare myself to certain persons, devoid of sense, whose cerebella are so troubled and clouded by the violent vapours of black bile, that they constantly assure us that they think they are kings when they are really quite poor, or that they are clothed in purple when they are really without covering, or who imagine that they have an earthenware head or are nothing but pumpkins or are made of glass. But they are mad, and I should not be any the less insane were I to follow examples so extravagant.

At the same time I must remember that I am a man, and that consequently I am in the habit of sleeping, and in my dreams representing to myself the same things or sometimes even less probable things, than do those who are insane in their waking moments. How often has it happened to me that in the night I dreamt that I found myself in this particular place, that I was dressed and seated near the fire, whilst in reality I was lying undressed in bed! At this moment it does indeed seem to me that it is with eyes awake that I am looking at this paper; that this head which I move is not asleep, that it is deliberately and of set purpose that I extend my hand and perceive it; what happens in sleep does not appear so clear nor so distinct as does all this. But in thinking over this I remind myself that on many occasions I have in sleep been deceived by similar illusions, and in dwelling carefully on this reflection I see so manifestly that there are no certain indications by which we may clearly distinguish wakefulness from sleep that I am lost in astonishment. And my astonishment is such that it is almost capable of persuading me that I now dream.

Now let us assume that we are asleep and that all these particulars, e.g. that we open our eyes, shake our head, extend our hands, and so on, are but false delusions; and let us reflect that possibly neither our hands nor our whole body are such as they appear to us to be. At the same time we must at least confess that the things which are represented to us in sleep are like painted representations which can only have been formed as the counterparts of something real and true, and that in this way those general things at least, i.e., eyes, a head, hands, and a whole body, are not imaginary things, but things really existent. For, as a matter of fact, painters, even when they study with the greatest skill to represent sirens and satyrs by forms the most strange and extraordinary, cannot give them natures which are entirely new, but merely make a certain medley of the members of different animals; or if their imagination is extravagant enough to invent something so novel that nothing similar has ever before been seen, and that then their work represents a thing purely fictitious and absolutely false, it is certain all the same that the colors of which this is composed are necessarily real. And for the same reason, although these general things, to wit, [a body], eyes, a head, hands, and such like, may be imaginary, we are bound at the same time to confess that there are at least some other objects yet more simple and more universal, which are real and true; and of these just in the same way as with certain real colors, all these images of things which dwell in our thoughts, whether true and real or false and fantastic, are formed.

To such a class of things pertains corporeal nature in general, and its extension, the figure of extended things, their quantity or magnitude and number, as also the place in which they are, the time which measures their duration, and so on.

That is possibly why our reasoning is not unjust when we conclude from this that Physics, Astronomy, Medicine and all other sciences which have as their end the consideration of composite things, are very dubious and uncertain; but that Arithmetic, Geometry and other sciences of that kind which only treat of things that are very simple and very general, without taking great trouble to ascertain whether they are actually existent or not contain some measure of certainty and an element of the indubitable. For whether I am awake or asleep, two and three together always form five, and the square can never have more than four sides, and it does not seem possible that truths so clear and apparent can be suspected of any falsity [or uncertainty].

Nevertheless I have long had fixed in my mind the belief that an all-powerful God existed by whom I have been created such as I am. But how do I know that He has not brought it to pass that there is no earth, no heaven, no extended body, no magnitude, no place, and that nevertheless [I possess the perceptions of all these things and that] they seem to me to exist just exactly as I now see them? And, besides, as I sometimes imagine that others deceive themselves in the things which they think they know best, how do I know that I am not deceived every time that I add two and three, or count the sides of a square, or judge of things yet simpler, if anything simpler can be imagined? But possibly God has not desired that I should be thus deceived, for He is said to be supremely good. If, however, it is contrary to His goodness to have made me such that I constantly deceive myself, it would also appear to be contrary to His goodness to permit me to be sometimes deceived, and nevertheless I cannot doubt that He does permit this.

I shall then suppose, not that God who is supremely good and the fountain of truth, but some evil genius not less powerful than deceitful, has employed his whole energies in deceiving me; I shall consider that the heavens, the earth, colors, figures, sound, and all other external things are nought but the illusions and dreams of which this genius has availed himself in order to lay traps for my credulity; I shall consider myself as having no hands, no eyes, no flesh, no blood, nor any senses, yet falsely believing myself to possess all these things; I shall remain obstinately attached to this idea, and if by this means it is not in my power to arrive at the knowledge of any truth, I may at least do what is in my power [i.e. suspend my judgment], and with firm purpose avoid giving credence to any false thing, or being imposed upon by this arch deceiver, however powerful and deceptive he may be. . . .[16]

Descartes has taken doubt to its outer limits: He doubts everything. Well, not quite everything. Descartes is using his method of doubt as a way of arriving at some indubitable first principle, some foundational, absolute certainty upon which he can reassert his belief in things. The one principle that Descartes finds to be beyond all doubt and perfectly certain is the fact of his own existence. From this first principle, he proceeds through the meditations to reestablish his confidence in other things he believes as well: the existence of God, the existence of the external world, and the existence of his own body. While space doesn't allow us to show Descartes reerecting his belief in these other things, we should indicate how he arrives at the foundational fact of his own existence.

His Own Existence

According to Descartes, he can doubt everything except that he himself exists. The following selection from Meditation II shows Descartes arriving at this certain truth:

MEDITATION II

The Meditation of yesterday filled my mind with so many doubts that it is no longer in my power to forget them. And yet I do not see in what manner I can resolve them; and, just as if I had all of a sudden fallen into very deep water, I am so disconcerted that I can neither make certain of setting my feet on the bottom, nor can I swim and so support myself on the surface. I shall nevertheless make an effort and follow anew the same path as that on which I yesterday entered, i.e. I shall proceed by setting aside all that in which the least doubt could be supposed to exist, just as if I had discovered that it was absolutely false; and I shall ever follow in this road until I have met with something which is certain, or at least, if I can do nothing else, until I have learned for certain that there is nothing in the world that is certain. Archimedes, in order that he might draw the terrestrial globe out of its place, and transport it elsewhere, demanded only that one point should be fixed and immovable; in the same way I shall have the right to conceive high hopes if I am happy enough to discover one thing only which is certain and indubitable.

I suppose, then, that all the things that I see are false; I persuade myself that nothing has ever existed of all that my fallacious memory represents to me. I consider that I possess no senses; I imagine that body, figure, extension, movement and place are but the fictions of my mind. What, then, can be esteemed as true? Perhaps nothing at all, unless that there is nothing in the world that is certain.

16. *René Descartes.* Meditations on First Philosophy, *in* The Philosophical Works of Descartes. *Elizabeth S. Haldane and G. R. T. Ross, Trans. Cambridge: Cambridge University Press, 1911, p. 85.*

But how can I know there is not something different from those things that I have just considered, of which one cannot have the slightest doubt? Is there not some God, or some other being by whatever name we call it, who puts these reflections into my mind? That is not necessary, for is it not possible that I am capable of producing them myself? I myself, am I not at least something? But I have already denied that I had senses and body. Yet I hesitate, for what follows from that? Am I so dependent on body and senses that I cannot exist without these? But I was persuaded that there was nothing in all the world, that there was no heaven, no earth, that there were no minds, nor any bodies: was I not then likewise persuaded that I did not exist? Not at all; of a surety I myself did exist since I persuaded myself of something [or merely because I thought of something]. But there is some deceiver or other, very powerful and very cunning, who ever employs his ingenuity in deceiving me. Then without doubt I exist also if he deceives me, and let him deceive me as much as he will, he can never cause me to be nothing so long as I think that I am something. So that after having reflected well and carefully examined all things, we must come to the definite conclusion that this proposition: I am, I exist, is necessarily true each time that I pronounce it, or that I mentally conceive it.[17]

In summarizing in Latin his proof for his own existence, Descartes used the phrase *"Cogito ergo sum"* ("I think, therefore I am"). Hence, his proof generally is referred to as the *Cogito* argument.

Having established the fact of his own existence, Descartes then turns to the kind of thing he is. What is he, this thing that exists? Descartes answers that he is "a thing which thinks."

But I do not yet know clearly enough what I am, I who am certain that I am; and hence I must be careful to see that I do not imprudently take some other object in place of myself, and thus that I do not go astray in respect of this knowledge that I hold to be the most certain and most evident of all that I have formerly learned. That is why I shall now consider anew what I believed myself to be before I embarked upon these last reflections; and of my former opinions I shall withdraw all that might even in a small degree be invalidated by the reasons which I have just brought forward, in order that there may be nothing at all left beyond what is absolutely certain and indubitable.

What then did I formerly believe myself to be? Undoubtedly I believed myself to be a man. But what is a man? Shall I say a reasonable animal? Certainly not; for then I should have to inquire what an animal is, and what is reasonable; and thus from a single question I should insensibly fall into an infinitude of others more difficult; and I should not wish to waste the little time and leisure remaining to me in trying to unravel subtleties like these. But I shall rather stop here to consider the thoughts which of themselves spring up in my mind, and which were not inspired by anything beyond my own nature alone when I applied myself to the consideration of my being. In the first place, then, I considered myself as having a face, hands, arms, and all that system of members composed of bones and flesh as seen in a corpse which I designated by the name of body. In addition to this I considered that I was nourished, that I walked, that I felt, and that I thought, and I referred all these actions to the soul: but I did not stop to consider what the soul was, or if I did stop, I imagined that it was something extremely rare and subtle like a wind, a flame, or an ether, which was spread throughout my grosser parts. As to body I had no manner of doubt about

17.   *René Descartes.* Meditations on First Philosophy, p. 87.

its nature, but thought I had a very clear knowledge of it; and if I had desired to explain it according to the notions that I had then formed of it, I should have described it thus: By the body I understand all that which can be defined by a certain figure: something which can be confined in a certain place, and which can fill a given space in such a way that every other body will be excluded from it; which can be perceived either by touch, or by sight, or by hearing, or by taste, or by smell: which can be moved in many ways not, in truth, by itself, but by something which is foreign to it, by which it is touched [and from which it receives impressions]: for to have the power of self-movement, as also of feeling or of thinking, I did not consider to appertain to the nature of body: on the contrary, I was rather astonished to find that faculties similar to them existed in some bodies.

But what am I, now that I suppose that there is a certain genius which is extremely powerful, and, if I may say so, malicious, who employs all his powers in deceiving me? Can I affirm that I possess the least of all those things which I have just said pertain to the nature of body? I pause to consider, I revolve all these things in my mind, and I find none of which I can say that it pertains to me. It would be tedious to stop to enumerate them. Let us pass to the attributes of soul and see if there is any one which is in me? What of nutrition or walking [the first mentioned]? But if it is so that I have no body it is also true that I can neither walk nor take nourishment. Another attribute is sensation. But one cannot feel without body, and besides I have thought I perceived many things during sleep that I recognized in my waking moments as not having been experienced at all. What of thinking? I find here that thought is an attribute that belongs to me; it alone cannot be separated from me. I am, I exist, that is certain. But how often? Just when I think; for it might possibly be the case if I ceased entirely to think, that I should likewise cease altogether to exist. I do not now admit anything which is not necessarily true: to speak accurately I am not more than a thing which thinks, that is to say a mind or a soul, or an understanding, or a reason, which are terms whose significance was formerly unknown to me. I am, however, a real thing and really exist; but what thing? I have answered: a thing which thinks. . . . What is a thing which thinks? It is a thing which doubts, understands, [conceives], affirms, denies, wills, refuses, which also imagines and feels.[18]

Elsewhere in the meditations Descartes uses the certain fact of his own existence as a thinking thing as a premise in an argument that attempts to establish the existence of God, and subsequently the existence of the external world and his own body. For our purposes in this chapter on the sources of knowledge, it's important to emphasize that it is from intuition that Descartes the rationalist obtains his foundational premise and from which he argues to all other conclusions.

The Role of Intuition

Recall the earlier selection from Meditation II in which Descartes abstracts from the sensuous qualities of a piece of wax to demonstrate why sense experience is not the ultimate criterion of knowledge. Says Descartes: ". . . what must particularly be observed is that perception is neither an act of vision, nor of

---

18. *René Descartes.* Meditations on First Philosophy, *p. 95.*

touch, nor of imagination . . . but only an intuition of the mind, which may be imperfect and confused as it was formerly, or clear and distinct as it is at present. . . ." This "intuition of the mind" is the key to understanding Descartes's thinking and that of all rationalists.

Strictly speaking, intuition refers to immediate knowledge, without the aid of reasoning or inference. But intuition typically is argued to be a function of reason, and capable of rational insights even if they are, by their very nature, not defensible in arguments. Intuition is where rationalists such as Descartes obtain their premises; it is the base from which they argue to all other conclusions. The essential difference, then, between rationalists like Descartes and empiricists like Locke, Berkeley, and Hume is that the rationalists stress nonempirical intuition. Thus, rationalists and empiricists would agree on the validity of the deductions that intuitive insights entail; it is the source of the intuited premises that are in dispute. Whereas rationalists accept unreasoned intuitions and insights as a legitimate source of knowledge, empiricists do not.

Indeed, Descartes's critics were quick to point out that Descartes's criteria for certainty, "the clear and distinct perception," were in fact undercut by his very method of doubt. How, they asked, could anyone be certain that he perceives a proposition clearly and distinctly? It's futile to respond, "It seems clear and distinct to me"; for, as Descartes himself stresses, the person might be mistaken. In fairness to Descartes, it should be noted that later in his second meditation he invokes the goodness of God as proof that clearness and distinctness are adequate criteria for certainty. But, inasmuch as prior to this he uses the same criteria to establish God's existence, he is arguing in circles. In any event, it is this source of intuition that is at the core of the dispute between rationalist Descartes and the British empiricists, rather than the actual arguments Descartes marshalls as proofs for his beliefs.

Summary and Conclusions

We began by noting that the issue of self is tied up with the question of knowledge. Historically, philosophers have asked, "If there are different kinds of knowledge, how can they be obtained?" The most common view is that there are two types of knowledge: rational and empirical. Among the outstanding rationalists is René Descartes, who attempted to demonstrate the validity of a priori knowledge, that is, knowledge independent of sense perception.

In vigorous reaction to Descartes and rationalists are the British empiricists: Locke, Berkeley, and Hume. They insist that all knowledge is a posteriori; that is, it follows from experience. One crucial problem that empiricists face arises from their distinction between an objective reality and our experience of it. If these are differentiated, how do we know that our experiences correspond with how things are? Locke's answer is that our experiences represent the outside world. Berkeley says that all we ever know are our own ideas; only conscious minds and their perceptions exist. For Hume nothing is truly knowable. Immanuel Kant proposed his phenomenalism to demonstrate that a priori knowledge is possible. While Kant argues that true knowledge has its basis in sense experience, he also claims that the mind has innate capacities to order that sense experience and thus arrive at knowledge. We concluded the chapter by suggesting that extreme positions on the nature and limits of knowledge seem untenable, that what we term *knowing* seems to possess both subjective and objective elements.

Knowledge is not as simple as we may have thought. Although we constantly claim to know things and thereby express ourselves, underlying these claims is often a naive assumption about the nature of knowledge: that through our senses we know things precisely as they are. This assumption implies that things exist outside us and inside us in precisely the same way. Thus, the self is passive; it has no influence on its knowledge of entities but experiences them as they are. When the knower, in effect, coincides with the known, the self is lost in an objective reality. Thus, this view leads more to a caricature of knowledge than to an accurate description of it.

Yet there is probably something "out there," and individuals are likely to report it accurately, if not precisely. We seem to be able to know things. This assumption is more explanatory than the assumption that nothing is out there. To assume something is out there fits in with our experiences. It makes sense. Moreover, such an assumption can be tested by stubbing your toe or sending a man to the moon. And this assumption allows us to predict the course of events, from the speed of a falling penny to the position of Jupiter on 1 January 2000. So there does seem to be an objective world which we interact with and exercise some control over. But do we know it exactly as it is? That is another question.

Extreme subjectivism, or solipsism, would make a shambles of objective reality. In effect, it makes each self a creator of its own world. Things exist only as the subjective self perceives them. Whereas identifying the knower with the known eliminates the self, solipsism eliminates all that is not self. However, there are unquestionably subjective elements in our knowledge. The self perceives things from its own vantage point. It frequently sees things not as they are but as it would have them. Sense experiences pass through the filter of subjective consciousness and eventuate in our ideas of things. To some degree, then, our knowledge of the objective world does apparently rely on our perceptions of things. Each self is unique in the sense that it probably sees things as no other quite does or has or will, and in the sense that it alone can be aware of its own perceptions.

Section Exercises

Descartes

1. What does Descartes mean by a "clear and distinct idea"?

2. In your own words, explain how Descartes concluded that a human is a thinking thing.

3. Why does Descartes believe that God exists?

4. How does Descartes use the existence of God to demonstrate that a world and other selves exist?

Locke

1. For Locke, shape is a primary quality and color a secondary quality. Do you agree or disagree with the following statements? Why? Consequently, would you agree or disagree with Locke's distinction?

   a. When something is not being perceived, it has shape but not color.

   b. You can experience shape with more than one sense, but not color.

   c. The shape of a thing never changes, but its color does so frequently.

   d. A thing without color can have shape.

2. Locke believed that we come into the world as a "blank slate." Ideas come after sense experiences. Would you agree that we can have no ideas without first having sense experiences? Or would you hold that at least some ideas (for example, "Everything must have a cause," "There is a God," "Murdering a two-year-old baby for your own pleasure is evil") do not depend on sense experience?

Berkeley

1. Does Berkeley's idealism deny an objective reality?

2. According to Berkeley, in what sense can we not know anything?

3. Explain this statement: "Berkeley's subjectivism originates in a physical world and ends in denying knowledge of it."

4. What evidence would you give to prove that while you were sleeping, a physical reality outside you persisted?

Hume

1. What does Hume mean by asserting that there can be no ideas without sense impressions?

2. Explain why Hume concludes that there's no rational justification for saying that anything has a continued and independent existence outside us.

3. Describe what you consider to be the fundamental epistemological difference between Hume and Berkeley.

4. Justify the assertion that Hume pushed Locke's empiricism to its logical conclusion.

Phenomenalism and Kant

1. Kant claims that true knowledge has its basis in experience. At the same time, he states that a priori knowledge is possible. Is this a contradiction?

2. Kant concludes that we can only obtain knowledge of appearances (phenomena) and never of the way things actually are (noumena). Does this make him a skeptic? If not, what distinguishes his view from skepticism?

3. Many authors have noted that Kant's theory of the unity of consciousness changed the dispute between rationalists and empiricists. What do you think they mean by this?

The Teachings of Don Juan

Carlos Castaneda

In 1960, while studying the medicinal plants used by Indians in Arizona, U.C.L.A. anthropology graduate student Carlos Castaneda met an elderly Yaqui Indian named don Juan. As Castaneda soon learned, don Juan was a "sorcerer, medicine man, curer." By the Indian's own account, however, don Juan was a "man of knowledge." Castaneda subsequently spent five years studying with don Juan, after which he published The Teachings of Don Juan, *from which the excerpt below is taken. He subsequently rejoined don Juan for further study, which he described in later books.*

In the selection that follows, don Juan describes the enemies of knowledge and what a person must do to overcome them. In one sense the reading has little to do with the theories of knowledge just discussed. In another, it relates directly to all of them; for the obstacles to knowledge obstruct any kind of knowledge, whatever its nature, whatever its limitations. In other words, in the view of don Juan, whatever one's view of knowledge—whether rational, empirical, or phenomenal—one cannot be said to be a person of knowledge until the enemies of knowledge have been defeated.

Saturday, April 8, 1962

In our conversations, don Juan consistently used or referred to the phrase "man of knowledge," but never explained what he meant by it. I asked him about it.

"A man of knowledge is one who has followed truthfully the hardships of learning," he said. "A man who has, without rushing or without faltering, gone as far as he can in unraveling the secrets of power and knowledge."

"Can anyone be a man of knowledge?"

"No, not anyone."

"Then what must a man do to become a man of knowledge?"

"He must challenge and defeat his four natural enemies."

"Will he be a man of knowledge after defeating these four enemies?"

"Yes. A man can call himself a man of knowledge only if he is capable of defeating all four of them."

"Then, can *anybody* who defeats these enemies be a man of knowledge?"

"Anybody who defeats them becomes a man of knowledge."

"But are there any special requirements a man must fulfill before fighting with these enemies?"

"No. Anyone can try to become a man of knowledge; very few men actually succeed, but

that is only natural. The enemies a man encounters on the path of learning to become a man of knowledge are truly formidable; most men succumb to them."

"What kind of enemies are they, don Juan?"

He refused to talk about the enemies. He said it would be a long time before the subject would make any sense to me. I tried to keep the topic alive and asked him if he thought I could become a man of knowledge. He said no man could possibly tell that for sure. But I insisted on knowing if there were any clues he could use to determine whether or not I had a chance of becoming a man of knowledge. He said it would depend on my battle against the four enemies—whether I could defeat them or would be defeated by them—but it was impossible to foretell the outcome of that fight.

I asked him if he could use witchcraft or divination to see the outcome of the battle. He flatly stated that the results of the struggle could not be foreseen by any means, because becoming a man of knowledge was a temporary thing. When I asked him to explain this point, he replied:

"To be a man of knowledge has no permanence. One is never a man of knowledge, not really. Rather, one becomes a man of knowledge for a very brief instant, after defeating the four natural enemies."

From The Teachings of Don Juan *by Carlos Castaneda. Berkeley: University of California Press, 1968, pp. 56–60. Reprinted by permission.*

"You must tell me, don Juan, what kind of enemies they are."

He did not answer. I insisted again, but he dropped the subject and started to talk about something else.

Saturday, April 15, 1962

As I was getting ready to leave, I decided to ask him once more about the enemies of a man of knowledge. I argued that I could not return for some time, and it would be a good idea to write down what he had to say and then think about it while I was away.

He hesitated for a while, but then began to talk.

"When a man starts to learn, he is never clear about his objectives. His purpose is faulty; his intent is vague. He hopes for rewards that will never materialize, for he knows nothing of the hardships of learning.

"He slowly begins to learn—bit by bit at first, then in big chunks. And his thoughts soon clash. What he learns is never what he pictured, or imagined, and so he begins to be afraid. Learning is never what one expects. Every step of learning is a new task, and the fear the man is experiencing begins to mount mercilessly, unyielding. His purpose becomes a battlefield.

"And thus he has stumbled upon the first of his natural enemies: Fear! A terrible enemy—treacherous, and difficult to overcome. It remains concealed at every turn of the way, prowling, waiting. And if the man, terrified in its presence, runs away, his enemy will have put an end to his quest."

"What will happen to the man if he runs away in fear?"

"Nothing happens to him except that he will never learn. He will never become a man of knowledge. He will perhaps be a bully, or a harmless, scared man; at any rate, he will be a defeated man. His first enemy will have put an end to his cravings."

"And what can he do to overcome fear?"

"The answer is very simple. He must not run away. He must defy his fear, and in spite of it he must take the next step in learning, and the next, and the next. He must be fully afraid, and yet he must not stop. That is the rule! And a moment will come when his first enemy retreats. The man begins to feel sure of himself. His intent becomes stronger. Learning is no longer a terrifying task.

"When this joyful moment comes, the man can say without hesitation that he has defeated his first natural enemy."

"Does it happen at once, don Juan, or little by little?"

"It happens little by little, and yet the fear is vanquished suddenly and fast."

"But won't the man be afraid again if something new happens to him?"

"No. Once a man has vanquished fear, he is free from it for the rest of his life because, instead of fear, he has acquired clarity—a clarity of mind which erases fear. By then a man knows his desires; he knows how to satisfy those desires. He can anticipate the new steps of learning, and a sharp clarity surrounds everything. The man feels that nothing is concealed.

"And thus he has encountered his second enemy: Clarity! That clarity of mind, which is so hard to obtain, dispels fear, but also blinds.

"It forces the man never to doubt himself. It gives him the assurance he can do anything he pleases, for he sees clearly into everything. And he is courageous because he is clear, and he stops at nothing because he is clear. But all that is a mistake; it is like something incomplete. If the man yields to this make-believe power, he has succumbed to his second enemy and will fumble with learning. He will rush when he should be patient, or he will be patient when he should rush. And he will fumble with learning until he winds up incapable of learning anything more."

"What becomes of a man who is defeated in that way, don Juan? Does he die as a result?"

"No, he doesn't die. His second enemy has just stopped him cold from trying to become a man of knowledge; instead, the man may turn into a buoyant warrior, or a clown. Yet the clarity for which he has paid so dearly will never change to darkness and fear again. He will be clear as long as he lives, but he will no longer learn, or yearn for, anything."

"But what does he have to do to avoid being defeated?"

"He must do what he did with fear: he must defy his clarity and use it only to see, and wait patiently and measure carefully before taking new steps; he must think, above all, that his clarity is almost a mistake. And a moment will come when he will understand that his clarity was only a point before his eyes. And thus he will have overcome his second enemy, and will arrive at a position where nothing can harm him anymore. This will not be a mistake. It will not be only a point before his eyes. It will be true power.

"He will know at this point that the power he has been pursuing for so long is finally his. He can do with it whatever he pleases. His ally is at his command. His wish is the rule. He sees all that is around him. But he has also come across his third enemy: Power!

"Power is the strongest of all enemies. And naturally the easiest thing to do is to give in; after all, the man is truly invincible. He commands; he begins by taking calculated risks, and ends in making rules, because he is a master.

"A man at this stage hardly notices his third enemy closing in on him. And suddenly, without knowing, he will certainly have lost the battle. His enemy will have turned him into a cruel, capricious man."

"Will he lose his power?"

"No, he will never lose his clarity or his power."

"What then will distinguish him from a man of knowledge?"

"A man who is defeated by power dies without really knowing how to handle it. Power is only a burden upon his fate. Such a man has no command over himself, and cannot tell when or how to use his power."

"Is the defeat by any of these enemies a final defeat?"

"Of course it is final. Once one of these enemies overpowers a man there is nothing he can do."

"Is it possible, for instance, that the man who is defeated by power may see his error and mend his ways?"

"No. Once a man gives in he is through."

"But what if he is temporarily blinded by power, and then refuses it?"

"That means his battle is still on. That means he is still trying to become a man of knowledge. A man is defeated only when he no longer tries, and abandons himself."

"But then, don Juan, it is possible that a man may abandon himself to fear for years, but finally conquer it."

"No, that is not true. If he gives in to fear he will never conquer it, because he will shy away from learning and never try again. But if he tries to learn for years in the midst of his fear, he will eventually conquer it because he will never have really abandoned himself to it."

"How can he defeat his third enemy, don Juan?"

"He has to defy it, deliberately. He has to come to realize the power he has seemingly conquered is in reality never his. He must keep himself in line at all times, handling carefully and faithfully all that he has learned. If he can see that clarity and power, without his control over himself, are worse than mistakes, he will reach a point where everything is held in check. He will know then when and how to use his power. And thus he will have defeated his third enemy.

"The man will be, by then, at the end of his journey of learning, and almost without warning he will come upon the last of his enemies: Old age! This enemy is the cruelest of all, the one he won't be able to defeat completely, but only fight away.

"This is the time when a man has no more fears, no more impatient clarity of mind—a time when all his power is in check, but also the time when he has an unyielding desire to rest. If he gives in totally to his desire to lie down and forget, if he soothes himself in tiredness, he will have lost his last round, and his enemy will cut him down into a feeble old creature. His desire to retreat will overrule all his clarity, his power, and his knowledge.

"But if the man sloughs off his tiredness, and lives his fate through, he can then be called a man of knowledge, if only for the brief moment when he succeeds in fighting off his last, invincible enemy. That moment of clarity, power, and knowledge is enough."

Questions for Analysis

1. In what sense is one never a "man of knowledge"?
2. Describe how fear is an enemy of knowledge. How would such an observation apply directly to the study of philosophy?

3. Can don Juan's concept of "clarity" in any way be related to epistemological skepticism?

4. In what sense could the empirical movement be considered an attack on the enemy "fear"?

5. In what sense was Descartes fighting "clarity," and in another sense succumbing to it?

Paperbacks for Further Reading

Berkeley, George. *A Treatise concerning the Principles of Human Knowledge.* Colin M. Turbayne, Ed. New York: Liberal Arts Press, 1954. Turbayne's introduction is helpful for understanding Berkeley's major work.

Berrill, N. J. *Man's Emerging Mind.* New York: Dodd, Mead, 1955. A British zoologist argues that through senses, science, and our "inward nature," we have come to know the world around us. Love and hope, claims Berrill, are natural outgrowths of our evolution, and at our best we "represent the spirit of the universe."

Doney, Willis, Ed. *Descartes.* New York: Doubleday Anchor, 1967. A nice study of various problems in Descartes's theory of knowledge.

Locke, John. *An Essay concerning Human Understanding.* 2 vols. J. W. Tolton (vol. 1) and A. O. Woozley (vol. 2), Eds. New York: Dutton, 1973. Locke's classic on perception and knowledge is enhanced by helpful introductions.

Pirandello, Luigi. *It Is So If You Think So,* in *Naked Masks: Five Plays.* Eric Bentley, Ed. New York: Dutton, 1952. Italian novelist and playwright Pirandello concerns himself in this play with the mental state of a character called Ponza. Is Ponza insane and keeping his wife and her mother from seeing one another? Or is he sane, and the mother not really the mother at all, but a madwoman who has never accepted the death of her daughter? The play raises pertinent questions about the subjective/objective nature of truth.

Plato. *The Republic.* Books VI and VII. F. M. Cornford, Trans. Oxford: Oxford University Press, 1945. These books from Plato's description of his classic utopia contain his theory of the nature of knowledge.

Polanyi, Michael. *Personal Knowledge: Towards a Post-Critical Philosophy.* New York: Harper, 1958. Scientist-turned-philosopher Polanyi rejects scientific detachment as an ideal of knowledge. He views knowing as an active comprehension of the things known. A vital component of knowledge is the passionate contribution of the person knowing what is being known. A most important alternative ideal of knowledge.

Wooldridge, Dean E. *Mechanical Man: The Physical Basis of Intelligent Life.* New York: McGraw-Hill, 1968. Wooldridge, a research engineer, argues that human intelligence, consciousness, and behavior are explained solely through physical laws.

TRUTH

7

No one is so wrong as the man who knows all the answers.
—Thomas Merton

What we know or claim to know is a measure of who we are. Our knowledge informs everything we do socially, politically, artistically, religiously, scientifically, and educationally. Knowledge is a compass by which we direct the course of our lives.

But what do we mean when we say that we know something? For instance, "I know that my car is in the parking lot." Just what do you mean when you say that? Stating the question more formally, if we let p represent any proposition, what requirements must we meet to claim that we know p?

For one thing, we *believe* that p is the case. If you claim to know that your car is in the parking lot, you believe it. You don't just have a hunch, an inkling, or a suspicion. You have a positive belief. Think about that. Imagine what your audience would think if you said, "I know that my car is in the parking lot but I don't believe it." They'd think it very peculiar, and rightly so. After all, if you're claiming to know something, how can you not believe it? Of course, we sometimes seem to dissociate belief from knowledge, as in "I know the president has been assassinated, but I don't believe it." But this is a rhetorical utterance. We actually do believe it; otherwise we wouldn't be shocked. Intellectually we believe it, but emotionally we're incredulous. To assert that you know p, then, is to have a certain attitude toward p, that is, to believe that it is so. Thus, "I know p" implies "I believe p."

Of course, "I believe p" does not imply "I know p." We can and do believe all sorts of things: that there's life in outer space, that we are in excellent health, that God exists, that Denver is the capital of the United States. But that doesn't mean we know all of these things. In a word, knowledge implies belief, but belief does not imply knowledge.

Knowledge also implies *evidence*. When you say, "I know that my car is in the parking lot," you imply not only that you believe it but that you have evidence for it. So, "I know p" implies "I have evidence for p." Suppose someone claims to know that the stock market will plunge next week. You'd likely

ask, "How do you know that?" If the person responded, "Because I believe it," you'd not take the claim seriously. Belief merely indicates an attitude toward something; it does not justify it. Only evidence does that. Another word for evidence or justification is *warrantability*. If someone claims to know that the stock market will plunge next week, they are implying a *warranted belief*. They have evidence or justification for what they believe.

Can we then correctly speak of knowledge as warranted belief? No. Suppose the stock market does not plunge next week. Clearly the person didn't know, although this doesn't mean that the belief was not warranted. It simply suggests that knowledge implies more than warranted belief. It also implies *truth*. For you to know that your car is in the parking lot, your car must actually be there. You may believe it, and your belief may be warranted. But to know it, you need more: the truth. In brief, you may not say that you know *p* unless *p* is true.

We have now reached a useful definition of knowledge. *Knowledge is warranted, true belief.* To understand knowledge fully, then, we must understand warrantability and truth, the subjects of this chapter.

Warrantability and truth are important epistemological issues. They also affect our lives deeply, because they relate to our beliefs. Which of my beliefs are warranted? How can I determine what I'm justified in believing and what I'm not? What can I accept as true? How can I determine the truth? When you realize that your self-image and social interactions are tremendously affected by your beliefs and working assumptions, the issues of warrantability and truth become more than philosophical abstractions. In science, religion, morality, the arts, and politics, we hold beliefs that influence how we relate and respond to the world, how we live our lives, and what we do. Just how sound are our beliefs? To answer this question, we must consider warrantability and truth. If our beliefs are not sound, we should abandon them and seek alternatives. If they are sound, then we can feel secure and confident in pursuing them. The issue of knowledge as warranted, true belief, then, is crucial both philosophically and practically (see Philosophy and Life 7-1). Here are the main points of this chapter.

Main Points

1. Knowledge is warranted, true belief.

2. Warrantability is another name for justification or evidence.

3. Warrantability depends on whether the statement to be analyzed is logical, semantic, or empirical.

4. A true proposition describes an actual state-of-affairs.

5. There are three traditional theories of truth: correspondence, coherence, and pragmatic.

6. The correspondence theory of truth claims that truth is a correspondence between a statement and a fact. Objection: If we know only our sense experiences, how can we ever get outside them to verify how reality actually is? What does *correspondence* mean? Precisely what is a fact?

7. The coherence theory of truth claims that truth is a property of a related group of consistent statements. Objection: Consistency is no guarantee of truth. If the first judgments are false, they produce a system of consistent error. There is much disagreement even among idealists over first judgments.

8. The pragmatic theory claims that truth is what works. This theory is the cornerstone of pragmatism, an essentially American philosophy that arose in the nineteenth century through the writings of Peirce, James, and Dewey. The pragmatist sees the human as needing to use the practical consequences of beliefs to determine their truth and validity. Objection: There's no necessary connection between truth and workability. Truth is rendered a psychological, not an epistemological, concern, and it can become relative.

Warranted Belief

When is a belief warranted? When do I have justification for a belief? Any answer depends on the kind of statement I'm uttering. Let's look at a variety of propositions (true or false statements) to illustrate the point.

1. X is not non-X.
2. X is either Y or non-Y.
3. All humans are vertebrates.
4. No circle is square.
5. The sum of the interior angles in a triangle is equal to two right angles.
6. The sum of the squares of the sides of a right triangle is equal to the square of the hypotenuse.
7. This is a robin.
8. Sacramento is the capital of California.
9. I am in pain.
10. It seems to me to be green.

Each of these propositions is warranted. We'd be on solid ground if we believed them. Why?

Propositions 1 and 2 are warranted because a denial of them paralyzes all thought. If they are not warranted, then we can forget about ever thinking intelligently. Put another way, their denial is self-contradictory.

But what about 3 and 4? Their warrantability cannot be established in the same way. It lies in the meaning of the terms themselves. Proposition 3 is true because the meaning of vertebrates is included in the meaning of humans, and the proposition asserts this inclusion. Similarly, in 4, the meaning of circle excludes the meaning of square, and the proposition asserts this exclusion.

The warrantability of proposition 5, in contrast with the previous propositions, lies in its being a theorem that we can deduce from the postulates and definitions of Euclidean geometry. The same reasoning holds for 6 in its geometrical sense. In its algebraic sense, its warrantability follows from a comparable set of assumptions. The warrantability of 5 and 6, then, is furnished by the systems of which they are parts.

The remaining propositions suggest still other conditions of warrantability. Propositions 7 and 8 are hypotheses. Like all hypotheses, they must be confirmed. In other words, when you say, "This is a robin," your statement entails numerous other statements. Some pertain to birds and animals generally, others to flight, color, and plumage. If the original statement is consistent with all the entailed statements, and they themselves are warrantable propositions, then your original statement is true. "This is a robin" is confirmed. The same applies to "Sacramento is the capital of California."

On the other hand, 9 and 10 are basic statements, which don't require that kind of confirmation. Basic statements pertain to sense data; consequently, they can only be false if the speaker is lying. So their warrantability is found in the immediately experienced qualities of first-person experience.[1]

1. For a discussion of warrantability, see W. H. Werkmeister. The Basis and Structure of Knowledge. New York: Greenwood Press, 1968, especially pp. 125–161.

PHILOSOPHY AND LIFE 7-1
Beliefs, Values, and Attitudes

Have you ever been told you have a rotten attitude, or maybe a good one? "You'll never get anywhere with that attitude," someone says, or "Now, that's the right attitude." At some time we've all been told, "You better change your attitude." Well, how do you do that? Just what is an attitude, and how does it arise?

There are many definitions of *attitude*. They all share the idea of a hypothetical construct that we invent to make better sense of things. We infer the operation of attitude from observing that people generally behave consistently towards the objects in their experience. That is, we associate attitude with the fact that people's future behavior is pretty much like their past behavior. For simplicity, then, let's define an attitude as a predisposition to respond to an object with a positive or negative affect.*

An attitude is different from a belief. A belief is what we consider to be true. It's a probability statement about reality. For example, suppose you believed that reducing the money supply will lead to a healthy economy. That is, you think that a healthy economy will be a likely result of reducing the amount of money in circulation. Is there any connection between belief and attitude?

Your *attitude* toward reducing the money supply would depend on the *value* you place on a healthy economy. If you valued it, you'd have a positive attitude toward reducing the money supply.

* See Ladd Wheeler, et al. General Psychology. Boston: Allyn & Bacon, 1975, p. 501.

When I say that I am warranted in believing the preceding propositions, I mean that I have sufficient reason for believing them. Of course, sufficiency raises a problem. Just how much support, evidence, or justification do I need for a warranted belief? Useful here is an awareness of the modes of warranty. Take, for example, propositions 1 and 2. These are said to have logical warrantability; that is, they appeal to laws of thought or logic that we consider necessarily true. Thus, proposition 1 accords with the law of identity: *A* is *A*. Everything we say presupposes that *A* is *A*. If you speak of a tree, you presuppose that the tree is a tree. If the tree were not a tree, what could you even be speaking of? Proposition 2 accords with the law of excluded middle: Everything is either *A* or non-*A*. Thus, something is either a tree or not a tree, a piece of chalk or not a piece of chalk, a desk or not a desk. Logically there can be no middle ground.

Propositions 3 and 4 represent semantic warrantability; that is, their warrantability can be determined merely by analyzing the meaning of the terms used and their connections. Propositions 5 and 6 have systemic warrantability.

Some psychologists have argued that an attitude is the conclusion of a syllogism having a belief and a value as premises.† For example:

Reducing the money supply will lead to a healthy economy (belief).
A healthy economy is a highly desirable state (value).
Therefore, I support reducing the money supply (attitude).

In short, it takes a belief and a value to produce an attitude.

Most of our attitudes probably stem from a handful of values. Values are very important to us. They help define us, give us identity. Not surprisingly, we don't abandon them easily. If you want to change an attitude, therefore, you won't have much luck trying to change the value in the syllogism producing the attitude. Instead, change the belief. Since a belief is simply a truth expectation based on argument and fact, it can be changed by additional argument and fact.

† *E. E. Jones and H. B. Gerard. Foundations of Social Psychology. New York: Wiley, 1967.*

□ *Devise an attitude-producing syllogism of your own. What facts would make you alter your belief?* □ *Examine your value premise. It obviously functions as a truth in producing your attitude. But is it true?* □ *On what basis?* □ *What assumptions support it?* □ *How would you establish their truth?* □ *After completing this chapter, reconsider your responses.*

This means that they derive their warranty from the logical interdependence of all propositions in a deductive system. Propositions 7 through 10 are cases of empirical warrantability. Their warranty stems from a confirmatory relation to specific qualities of first-person experience. Sometimes, as with 7 and 8, confirmation must be sought outside the self in the real world. Other times, as in 9 and 10, personal experience, if honestly reported, is enough.

In addition to the warranted, true belief implied by knowledge, we can also have warranted, *false* beliefs and unwarranted, true beliefs. In neither case do we have knowledge. These beliefs particularly arise in matters of fact, in empirical statements about the world, such as propositions 7 and 8. For example, it's arguable that in the past people were warranted in believing that the earth was flat and unwarranted in believing that it was spherical. So, warrantability and truth do not logically imply each other; that is, they are logically independent. *Warranty* is another word for justification or evidence. It comes in degrees, as does belief, but truth does not.

We come, then, to the next concern of this chapter: truth. What is truth? More to the point, what does it mean for a belief to be true?

Truth

In our everyday lives we usually get along nicely without pondering the question of truth. Since we make and affirm all sorts of statements, we seem to have little trouble dealing with truth. Thus, if someone says, "Washington is the nation's capital" or "Snow is white," we say, "That's true." But even though we may make the distinction between truth and falsity hundreds of times a day, we may have difficulty in expressing that distinction. What do we mean, then, when we say that a proposition is true?

Professor of philosophy John Hospers gives a lucid presentation of truth worth outlining here.[2] He begins by introducing the concept of *states-of-affairs*. A state-of-affairs is a condition, circumstance, or event. Obviously, there are numerous states-of-affairs in the world. The awesome amount of snow that crippled the midwestern and eastern United States in 1979 is a state-of-affairs; if your dog is brown and white, that's another state-of-affairs; if you are taking a philosophy course, that's still another state-of-affairs. States-of-affairs exist even if no one ever reports them, and they exist independently of language. But, of course, we can and do describe them, specifically in propositions.

This suggests a useful definition of truth. "A true proposition describes a state-of-affairs that occurs; or, in the cases of a proposition about the past, a state-of-affairs that did occur; or in the case of the future, that will occur."[3] Thus, if "There is a piece of chalk in the classroom" describes an actual state-of-affairs, then the proposition is true. In contrast, a false proposition describes a state-of-affairs that does not exist (or didn't or won't). "Denver is the capital of the United States" is a false proposition.

2. *John Hospers.* An Introduction to Philosophical Analysis. *Englewood Cliffs, N.J.: Prentice-Hall, 1967.*

3. *John Hospers.* An Introduction to Philosophical Analysis, *pp. 114–115.*

Hospers acknowledges that there may be different kinds of truth and that we may discover the truths of different propositions in different ways. But in his view, regardless of the means that we use to discover the truth of propositions, the propositions are true if they describe actual states-of-affairs.

Even if we assume that this is an adequate definition of truth, we're still left wondering how we determine if a proposition is true, how we discover truth. Like warrantability, the answer very much depends on the kind of statements we're dealing with. The history of philosophy records several ways of looking at and determining truth. We'll consider three important ones: correspondence, coherence, and pragmatic. Each makes a unique contribution to discovering the truth of statements.

Correspondence Theory

Undoubtedly the most popular theory of truth is that truth is a correspondence. According to **correspondence theory**, if a proposition is true, it corresponds with a fact. Thus, "Water boils at 212 degrees Fahrenheit at sea level" is a true proposition, because it corresponds with a fact: Water does boil at 212 degrees Fahrenheit at sea level. A good example of a correspondence theorist is British empiricist John Locke.

But the correspondence theory doesn't find support only in the philosophical past. Bertrand Russell's stand is a good recent example. For Russell, what we say is true if it corresponds to reality. In other words, there is a realm of facts independent of us ("Paris is in France," "My father is dead," and "The Yankees won the World Series in 1978"). Russell maintains that while truth and falsehood are properties of beliefs, they depend on the relations of the beliefs to other things. Thus, the truth of the belief that Paris is in France depends on whether that belief corresponds to the fact that Paris is indeed in France. In his *The Problems of Philosophy*, Russell expresses his position:

> There are three points to observe in the attempts to discover the nature of truth, three requisites which any theory must fulfill.
> (1) Our theory of truth must be such as to admit of its opposite, falsehood. A good many philosophers have failed adequately to satisfy this condition: they have constructed theories according to which all our thinking ought to have been true, and have then had the greatest difficulty in finding a place for falsehood. In this respect our theory of belief must differ from our theory of acquaintance, since in the case of acquaintance it was not necessary to take account of any opposite.
> (2) It seems fairly evident that if there were no beliefs there could be no falsehood, and no truth either, in the sense in which truth is correlative to falsehood. If we imagine a world of mere matter, there would be no room for falsehood in such a world, and although it would contain what may be called "facts," it would not contain any truths, in the sense in which truths are things of the same kind as falsehoods. In fact, truth and falsehood are properties of beliefs and statements: hence a world of mere matter, since it would contain no beliefs or statements, would also contain no truth or falsehood.
> (3) But, as against what we have just said, it is to be observed that the truth or falsehood of a belief always depends upon something which lies outside the belief itself. If I believe that Charles I died on the scaffold, I believe truly, not

because of any intrinsic quality of my belief, which can be discovered by merely examining the belief, but because of an historical event which happened two and a half centuries ago. If I believe that Charles I died in his bed, I believe falsely: no degree of vividness in my belief, or of care in arriving at it, prevents it from being false, again because of what happened long ago, and not because of any intrinsic property of my belief. Hence, although truth and falsehood are properties of beliefs, they are properties dependent upon the relations of the beliefs to other things, not upon any internal quality of the beliefs.

The third of the above requisites leads us to adopt the view—which has on the whole been commonest among philosophers—that truth consists in some form of correspondence between belief and fact.[4]

To understand Russell's version of the correspondence theory, it's necessary to see how he distinguishes a true judgment from a false one. To understand this requires familiarity with some of his language.

First, in any act of judgment, there is a mind that judges and terms about which the mind judges. Russell calls the mind the *subject* in the judgment, and the remaining terms the *objects*. Thus, when a student judges that Booth shot Lincoln, the student is the subject, while the objects are *Booth*, *shot*, and *Lincoln*. Russell calls the subject and objects together *constituents*.

Whenever we judge, we relate things; that is, we order them. This is indicated by word arrangement. The student's judgment "Booth shot Lincoln" is different from his judgment "Lincoln shot Booth," even though the constituents are identical. What makes one true, the other false? Correspondence with a fact. If the relationship between the terms in the judgment corresponds with the relationship between Booth, shot, and Lincoln, then the judgment is true.

> Thus a belief is *true* when it corresponds with a certain associated complex, and *false* when it does not. Assuming, for the sake of definiteness, that the object of the belief are two terms and a relation, the terms being put in a certain order by the "sense" of the believing, then if the two terms in that order are united by the relation into a complex, the belief is true; if not, it is false. This constitutes the definition of truth and falsehood that we were in search of. Judging or believing is a certain complex unity of which a mind is a constituent; if the remaining constituents, taken in the order which they have in the belief form a complex unity, then the belief is true; if not, it is false.[5]

For Russell, only when a sentence expresses relations between words that mirror or correspond to the relations of a complex fact can the sentence be considered meaningful or true. Thus, if the sentence "The Golden Gate Bridge spans a strait in west central California connecting the Pacific Ocean and San Francisco Bay" is meaningful and true, it is because it mirrors the relation between the bridge and the strait as described. The correspondence theory seems altogether reasonable. But it does have some weaknesses.

4. *Bertrand Russell.* The Problems of Philosophy. *London: Oxford University Press, 1912, pp. 283–284. Reprinted by permission of Oxford University Press.*

5. *Bertrand Russell.* The Problems of Philosophy, *p. 285.*

To draw out some of the objections to this theory and to stimulate more thinking about truth, let's have some fun by concocting an outrageous courtroom situation. The prosecution has just called Wilbur Scaife, a witness whose testimony is sure to destroy the case of nationally famous defense attorney and talk-show celebrity Lamont P. Eveready. Never has Eveready had a greater challenge than to discredit witness Scaife, and he must do so fast!

Bailiff: Do you swear to tell the truth, the whole truth, and nothing but the truth, so help you God?

Scaife: I do.

Eveready: Objection, Your Honor.

Judge: But the witness has not even taken his seat.

Eveready: Defense objects, Your Honor, on grounds that the witness has perjured himself.

Judge: Perjured himself? Why, he hasn't even answered a question yet.

Eveready: Defense humbly begs to differ, Your Honor. The witness has sworn to tell the truth, the whole truth, and nothing but the truth. Defense contends that the witness Wilbur Scaife is in no position to meet that oath, since he knows nothing of the truth of which he speaks.

Judge: Knows nothing of——

Eveready: To put it simply, Your Honor, Scaife doesn't know the truth from a hole in the ground.

Scaife: Oh, yeah? You want to step outside and say that?

Judge: The witness will contain himself. Can Defense prove this contention?

Eveready: Defense can and will, Your Honor.

Judge: Then proceed.

Eveready: Thank you, Your Honor. Now, Mr. Scaife, you have just sworn a holy oath before God Almighty to tell the truth, the whole truth, and nothing but the truth. Is that correct?

Scaife: Yes.

Eveready: Presumably, you have sworn this oath knowing full well what it means.

Scaife: Yes, I have. It means I'm going to tell the truth.

Eveready: The whole truth and nothing but the truth.

Scaife: You said it.

Eveready: Now, Scaife, what in your opinion is the truth?

Scaife: The truth? The truth is the way things are.

Eveready: The way things are. All right, *American flag*—is that the truth?

Scaife: What about the American flag?

Eveready: Oh, I must say something *about* it?

Scaife: Well, sure. How else would you know if you got the truth or not?

Eveready: I see. So what you're really saying is that the truth refers not so much to the ways things are as it does to a *statement* about the ways things are. In other words, it would be silly to say "American flag" is true. But it would make perfect sense to say "There's a red, white, and blue American flag in this courtroom."

Scaife: Now you've got the truth, mister.

Eveready: You mean that statement is true?

Scaife: You bet your life it is.

Eveready: And tell the court, Scaife, how you know the statement "There is a red, white, and blue American flag in this courtroom" is true.

Scaife: Because I see that flag right over there.

Eveready: Because you see it. Tell me, Scaife, does everything you see lead you to make a true statement?

Scaife: I don't get you.

Eveready: Let me illustrate. You've no doubt seen a pencil resting in a glass of water.

Scaife: Sure.

Eveready: How would you describe such a pencil?

Scaife: You mean that it looks bent?

Eveready: It looks bent. Your eyes report it as bent.

Scaife: But it's not.

Eveready: No, it's not. Consequently, the statement "That pencil is bent" is not true, is it?

Scaife: No way.

Eveready: And yet your eyes report it as true, don't they?

Scaife: But it's different here with the flag. The flag is actually here, the way you said it was. The pencil isn't. That's the difference.

Eveready: The flag is actually here, the way I said it was. . . . Your Honor, the Defense wishes to call from the gallery for one question only Ms. Bertha Moynier.

Prosecution: I object, Your Honor. Counsel's line of questioning has no purpose except to rattle, confuse, and intimidate the witness.

Judge: The irregularity of his request forces me to warn Defense that for his and his client's sake, the Bench hopes all this has some constructive end.

Eveready: I assure the Bench it has.

Judge: Will Ms. Moynier please rise?

Eveready: Ms. Moynier, will you please tell the court whether the following statement is true: "There is a red, white, and blue American flag in this room."

Moynier: I don't know.

Scaife: What! She must be blind!

Eveready: I compliment you on your powers of deduction, Scaife. Ms. Moynier is, in fact, blind.

Judge: What's the meaning of this demonstration, Eveready?

Eveready: Your Honor, the purpose of this exercise is to show the court that what the witness, Wilbur Scaife, *thinks* is truth is in fact nothing but hearsay. Indeed, what the witness *thinks* is truth consigns truth to the very dubious area of sense data interpretation. Such interpretation must be purely subjective and need not have anything to do with the way things actually are.

Prosecution: Your Honor, I have sat here patiently while the Defense has made a mockery of this court. I submit that he has gone beyond the role of court jester and is now showing open contempt for the Bench itself!

Eveready: If the court will allow, the Defense would like to call from the gallery Mr. Bartholomew Peabody in order to prove the sincerity of Defense's cause.

Judge: With great reluctance, the Bench asks Mr. Bartholomew Peabody to rise.

Eveready: Thank you, Your Honor. Mr. Peabody, will you tell the court whether the following statement is true: "There is a red, white, and blue American flag in this courtroom."

Peabody: Well, if you want to know the truth, what you say is so and it isn't.

Eveready: Would you explain to the court why my statement is true and not true?

Peabody: First, you do have a flag, all right. Any fool can see that.

Scaife: There! What did I tell you?

Judge: The witness will restrain himself.

Peabody: But it's not a red, white, and blue flag. It's red, white, and green.

Scaife: Green! He must be color-blind!

Eveready: Must he? Why? Because he disagrees with you?

Prosecution: Your Honor, how long will the Bench allow this travesty to continue?

Eveready: On the contrary, Your Honor, the court is hardly witnessing a travesty. Rather, in a matter of minutes, the court has heard three persons report different "truths" while supposedly observing the same object at the same time. Yet the witness Wilbur Scaife would have us believe that the truth characterizes that statement which reports an actual fact. I respectfully submit, Your Honor, that we can never know how things really are, because the only way we can come to such knowledge is through sense experience, which I have just demonstrated to be unreliable.

Judge: Is Defense suggesting that in this case the testimonies of a blind and a color-blind person are equal to that of a normally sighted one?

Eveready: Your Honor, may I respectfully answer with another question? Just what constitutes normal sight? Is it not a convention, a standard that the majority sets? Would the court submit the question of truth to a head count?

Judge: On the question of whether there is in fact a red, white, and blue American flag in this courtroom, the court might seriously entertain such a proposal.

Eveready: So be it, Your Honor. I submit the question to the gallery. Let a show of hands determine the truth of the statement "There is a red, white, and blue American flag in this courtroom."

Judge: Nobody? Not a single hand?

Prosecution: I object, Your Honor! The Defense has obviously stacked the gallery as a card shark would a deck of playing cards.

Eveready: The Prosecution's powers of deduction are as astonishing as Wilbur Scaife's, Your Honor. True, the Defense has stacked the gallery, but only to demonstrate that, when we insist that truth is an agreement between a statement of fact and the fact itself, we play the game of life with a stacked deck.

In effect, Eveready is asking, "Since we know only our experiences, how can we ever get outside them to verify what reality actually is?" The correspondence theory of truth seems to assume that we know not only our experiences of things but also *facts* about the world, that is, how the world actually is. Otherwise, how could truth be described as a correspondence between statement and fact? Of course, correspondence theorists might reply that the correspondence is between statements and reality *as interpreted by us*. But just who is "us"? Everyone, each individual, a consensus? And how do we ever know our interpretation is correct to begin with? Furthermore, if truth is a correspondence between statement and fact as interpreted by us, then we say nothing at all about the world outside ourselves; we only address whether we are correctly or incorrectly representing what we believe.

Then there's the question of just what is a fact, a philosophical concern having profound implications outside the study of philosophy (see Philosophy and Life 7-2). Sometimes *fact* means "true proposition," as in, "It's a fact that I'm six feet tall." In other words, "The sentence 'I am six feet tall' is a true proposition." But using *fact* in this way results in circularity: A proposition is true if it corresponds with a true proposition. Or *fact* may mean the same as "actual state-of-affairs." In this case the correspondence theory is identical with Hosper's definition of a true proposition—one that describes a state-of-

PHILOSOPHY AND LIFE 7-2
Historical Facts

What is a historical fact? Take, for example, what passes for a simple historical fact: "In the year 49 B.C. Caesar crossed the Rubicon." This is a familiar fact, and one of some importance. Yet, as the most distinguished American historian Carl L. Becker pointed out over a half century ago, this simple fact has strings tied to it. It depends on numerous other facts, so that it has no meaning apart from the web of circumstances that produced it. This web of circumstances, of course, was the chain of events arising out of the relation of Caesar to Pompey, the Roman senate, and the Roman republic. Becker states:

> Caesar had been ordered by the Roman Senate to resign his command of the army in Gaul. He decided to disobey the Roman Senate. Instead of resigning his command, he marched on Rome, gained the mastery of the Republic, and, at last, we are told, bestrode the narrow world like a colossus. Well, the Rubicon happened to be the boundary between Gaul and Italy, so that by the act of crossing the Rubicon with his army Caesar's treason became an accomplished fact and the subsequent great events followed in due course. Apart from these great events and complicated relations, the crossing of the Rubicon means nothing, is not an his-

affairs that is actual, that is, a fact. Nonetheless, the correspondence theory uses the word *corresponds* and not *describes*, and *corresponds* is the word that can cause confusion.

Just how does a true proposition correspond to a fact or a state-of-affairs? It certainly doesn't correspond in the way that a color sample on a color chart corresponds with a color of paint on a wall. In that case there's a *resemblance* between the sample and the wall paint. But there's no resemblance between a proposition and a state-of-affairs, or even between a sentence and a state-of-affairs. Does a statement correspond to fact in the way that titles of books on library cards correspond to the books themselves? That is, is there some sort of one-to-one correspondence—for each card, a book; for each book, a card? If so, what is gained? It seems at least as clear to say that a true proposition describes an actual state-of-affairs and dispose of the inherently misleading "correspondence."[6]

Coherence Theory

Exasperated by Eveready's protests, the judge has summoned him and the prosecution to the bench.

6. *See John Hospers.* An Introduction to Philosophical Analysis, *p. 116.*

torical fact properly speaking at all. . . . [It is] a symbol standing for a long series of events which have to do with the most intangible and im-material realities, viz.: the relation between Caesar and the millions of people of the Roman world.*

Clearly, for Becker "the simple historical fact" is only a symbol, an affirmation about an event. And since it's hardly worthwhile to term a symbol cold or hard, indeed dangerous to call it true or false, one might best speak of historical facts as being more or less appropriate.

* *Carl L. Becker. "What Are Historical Facts?"" Quoted in* Coming Age of Philosophy. Roger Eastman, Ed. San Francisco: Canfield Press, 1973, pp. 451–452.

□ Could Becker's analysis be applied to this statement: "The Japanese bombed Pearl Harbor on 7 December 1941"? □ Would it be accurate to say that historians deal not with an event but with statements that affirm the fact that the event occurred?   □ If so, what's the difference?

Judge: Now see here, Eveready, this line of interrogation can't continue. It's making a shambles of my court.

Prosecution: Amen!

Judge: Eveready, aren't you at all interested in the law?

Eveready: Of course I am, Your Honor. But I'm also interested in truth. Does Your Honor think the law and the truth are mutually exclusive?

Judge: Stop putting words in my mouth! You think I'm Scaife?

Eveready: I beg your pardon, Your Honor.

Judge: Pardon not granted. Didn't they teach you in law school the kind of truth on which much of the judicial process is based?

Eveready: *Kind* of truth? Are there *kinds* of truth, Your Honor?

Prosecution: Stop sassing the judge.

Judge: I'll be the judge of who's sassing me. Let me ask you something, Eveready.

Eveready: Proceed.

Judge: How are innocence and guilt determined?

Eveready: By a trial.

Judge: And what happens at a trial? I mean a normal trial, not this circus.

Eveready: Well, at a normal trial, lawyers present cases.

Judge: Exactly. And isn't it true that in theory the better case wins?

Eveready: In theory.

Judge: And what makes for the better case, Eveready?

Eveready: Obviously, persuading the jury.

Judge: Obviously. And which case, in theory, should persuade the jury?

Eveready: The one that hangs together better.

Judge: Precisely. Your job is to present the jury with pieces of a puzzle, isn't it? The jury's job is to take each piece and evaluate it. How? Well, let's see. They can't go back to the scene of the crime or to the circumstances that you describe, can they? No, they can't. So how do they figure out if a particular piece is true? I'll tell you how: usually by seeing how it fits in with all the other pieces. If it fits in, if it's consistent, if it doesn't contradict any of the other pieces, then it's true. At the very end, if you've presented a good case, all the pieces fit. The truth is right in front of their noses. "This person," they declare, "is guilty" or "not guilty."

Notice how the judge's theory of truth differs from the correspondence theory. According to him, a statement is true if it is consistent with other statements that are regarded as true. The essential test is not correspondence between statement and actual fact but coherence between statement and other relevant statements. Notice that the judge wants to know if the case hangs together, if all the pieces fit together. This **coherence theory** of truth, as it is called, insists that truth is a property of a related group of consistent statements. A particular statement is true if it is integrated within the framework of all the other statements already accepted as true.

"'Since we know only our experiences, how can we ever get outside them to verify what reality actually is?'"

Mathematics is a good example of the coherence theory in operation. Building upon a certain number of basic statements, mathematics constructs an entire system of "truths." In science, likewise, theories generally gain respectability when they are consistent with the body of accepted judgments. Of course, there are exceptions. The Copernican theory and Darwin's theory of evolution were so powerful that they forced people to reconsider what they had already accepted.

The coherence theory has also played a fundamental role in the systems of many philosophers, including Plato. Plato formulated a coherence theory of truth that did not rely on observation or sensory experience. He was convinced that he had discovered a perfect and true world of ideal (that is, nonsensible) Forms. These Forms, he claimed, are connected to one another by eternal and necessary relationships. Through thought, the mind can grasp this world of ideas, which, when understood, reveals a complete system of unchanging and necessary truth.

Unlike Berkeley, Plato believed that ideas exist outside us in some perfect form, in some objective state. This perfect world of Forms, said Plato, is experienced in a prelife, and we forget them when we are born. As the nineteenth-century poet Wordsworth put it, "Our birth is but a sleep and a forgetting." During life we experience a physical world that reminds us of that perfect world. For Plato, therefore, we never really learn anything; we *remember* it. We recognize people as beautiful or as just because they remind us of the Forms of perfect beauty or justice.

The sense world, then, is just a shadow of the "real world," the world of perfect Forms. For Plato, we know something only when we contact this ideal world, when we abandon the illusion that the physical world is the only reality.

Plato's judgment concerning the truth about physical things does rest on how well our assertions about physical facts *correspond* with the Forms themselves. But his theory of Forms is a complex series of statements regarding the *coherent* relationships among the Forms. Underlying Plato's system is the assumption that a perfect world of Forms exists. More importantly, on the basis of this assumption Plato seems to justify his claims.

For example, Plato claims that poetry and drama are often morally objectionable. How can he "prove" that? Think of what these arts often do: Usually they represent the physical world. But for Plato the physical world is a mere shadow of the perfect world of Forms. The arts, therefore, can distract us from knowing the "real world" of pure ideas by drawing us farther and farther away from it. Therefore, they can be morally objectionable. Consistent? Coherent? Very much so. In *The Republic*, in which he presents his utopia, Plato argues with similar consistency. Central to all his claims is the world of perfect Forms.

From this basic assumption, Plato attempted to work out a system of fully coherent knowledge, that is, a system in which every judgment entailed, and was entailed by, the rest of the system. While such a system is rare, and some would argue that it isn't found altogether in Plato's system, the point is that, conceptually, a thoroughgoing coherence theory of truth aims at such interdependence. Brand Blanshard (1892–), a contemporary coherence theorist, illustrates this point in *The Nature of Thought* when he takes a number of familiar systems and arranges them in a series according to the degree of coherence:

> At the bottom would be a junk heap, where we could know every item but one and still be without any clue as to what that remaining item was. Above this would come a stone-pile, for here you could at least infer that what you would find next would be a stone. A machine would be higher again, since from the remaining parts one could deduce not only the general character of a missing part, but also its special form and function. This is a high degree of coherence, but it is very far short of the highest. You could remove the engine from a motorcar while leaving the other parts intact, and replace it with any one of thousands of other engines, but the thought of such an interchange among human heads or hearts shows at once that the interdependence in a machine is far below that of the body. Do we find then in organic bodies the highest conceivable coherence? Clearly not. Though a human hand, as Aristotle said, would hardly be a hand when detached from the body, still it would be something definite enough; and we can conceive systems in which even this something would be gone. Abstract a number from the number series and it would be a mere unrecognizable *x*; similarly, the very thought of a straight line involves the thought of the Euclidean space in which it falls. It is perhaps in such systems as Euclidean geometry that we get the most perfect examples of coherence that have been constructed. If any proposition were lacking, it could be supplied from the rest; if any were altered, the repercussions would be felt through the length and breadth of the system. Yet even such a system as this falls short of the ideal system. Its postulates are unproved; they are independent of each other, in the sense that none of them could be derived from any other or even from all the others together; its clear necessity is bought by an abstractness so extreme as to have left out nearly everything that belongs to the character of actual things. A completely satis-

"If first judgments are not true, they can produce a system of consistent error."

factory system would have none of these defects. No proposition would be arbitrary, every proposition would be entailed by the others jointly and even singly, no proposition would stand outside the system. The integration would be so complete that no part could be seen for what it was without seeing its relation to the whole, and the whole itself could be understood only through the contribution of every part.[7]

Blanshard is describing an ideal of coherence. Still, is such systemic coherence alone a guarantee of truth? As applied to Plato, what evidence is there for assuming a world of perfect Forms to begin with? It's hard for us to accept a form or idea as "more real" than what we can actually experience through the senses. Yes, the world of Forms may be logical; it may appeal to our minds. But is it experiential? Does it appeal to our senses as well? We raise these concerns not to indict Plato's system, but to suggest general objections to the coherence theory.

Recall that almost everyone once believed that the earth was the center of the solar system. This belief stemmed from the ancient Greek astronomer Ptolemy (of the second century A.D.). Why did everyone believe this? Because it made sense and accorded with commonsensical observation. It fit in with the widespread and naive experience of things. Also, it was part of Ptolemy's system of judgments, which, as a result of their extreme consistency, held sway for 1,500 years. In fact, the major difference between the theory of Ptolemy and the theory of Copernicus, which replaced it, was that the latter was simpler. Yet both theories were consistent. The point is that coherence does not seem to distinguish between consistent truth and consistent error. A judgment may be true if it is consistent with other judgments, but what if the other judgments

7. *Brand Blanshard.* The Nature of Thought. *New York: Macmillan, 1941, pp. 464–465. Reprinted by permission of George Allen & Unwin Ltd.*

are false? If first judgments are not true, they can produce a system of consistent error.

Another objection is that a coherence theory in the last analysis seems to rely on correspondence. After all, if a judgment is coherent, it must cohere with another judgment. But what of first judgments? With what do they cohere? If they are first, they cannot cohere with anything. Their truth, then, can only be verified by determining whether they report an actual fact. But this is the correspondence theory. Proponents of the coherence theory, however, insist that a judgment of fact itself can be verified only by the coherence theory. Blanshard illustrates this point:

> Suppose we say, "the table in the next room is round"; how should we test this judgment? In the case in question, what verifies the statement of fact is the perceptual judgment that I make when I open the door and look. But then what verifies the perceptual judgment itself? . . . To which the reply is, as before, that a judgment of fact can be verified only by the sort of apprehension that can present us with a fact, and that this must be a further judgment. And an agreement between judgments is best described not as a correspondence, but as coherence.[8]

Pragmatic Theory

Because of the evident weaknesses in the correspondence and coherence theories, philosophers of recent times have suggested another possibility, the pragmatic theory of truth. Let us see how it works by returning to the judge's chambers.

Prosecution: Well, if you want my opinion, I think the whole discussion is silly. I mean, if you want to know what's true, find out what works.

Eveready: What?

Judge: Are you saying that if something works, it's true?

Prosecution: What else can it be? How else can you judge what's true, except by its results? Take the theory of the sun-centered solar system, for example. What makes it true is that it works. It is true because it accurately describes a situation in such a way that people can use that description to produce desired results. That theory's allowed us to plot the position of the heavenly bodies, estimate the distance between them, send satellites into space, and put men on the moon. Previous theories couldn't have produced these results. They just wouldn't have worked. That's why they were untrue, while this one is true.

Eveready: But if what works is true, what's stopping it from not working?

Prosecution: Nothing. Then it wouldn't be true any longer. The trouble with you, Eveready, is that you're hung up on the idea that truth is something absolute, something unchanging and unchangeable. Well, it's not! And you'd better get used to that. Where do you think truth comes from, anyway? It comes from you and me and the judge.

8. *Brand Blanshard. "The Nature of Thought," in* Philosophical Interrogation. *Sidney and Beatrice Rome, Eds. New York: Holt, Rinehart and Winston, 1964, p. 210.*

And every man, woman, and child who's ever lived or will live. It doesn't grow on trees for the picking. People make it! They change it and they make it again. We make our own truth!

Eveready: So, according to you, if something works, it's true.

Prosecution: Exactly.

Eveready: Well, it sounds to me like you're saying that if I believe I'm Napoleon, I *am* Napoleon.

Prosecution: Your belief that you're Napoleon must face the test of truth: How does the belief work out in practice? Does it lead to satisfactory results? In your case, it wouldn't. People would be frightened by you, they'd avoid you, they'd probably lock you up and throw away the key. Your belief doesn't work. So, it's not true.

Eveready: Well, what about the theory that the earth was once visited by astronaut gods? Presumably the belief worked for its author. It produced satisfactory results for him, just as you say the truth must. Now, does that make his theory true?

Prosecution: You make it sound as if the author were merely claiming to be happy or to have a toothache, Eveready. His claim isn't just a private one, you know. He's not just reporting his own internal state. He's making a public claim. So, as with all public claims, satisfactory results depend on more than just the results produced for a single person.

Eveready: But how do you know if his claim works or not?

Prosecution: Test it. Try it and see if it works. What else does it explain? What else does it account for? What use can we make of it? That's how to find out if it works.

The prosecution's idea of truth is different from both the correspondence and the coherence theories. He would admit that we can know only our experiences; as a result, truth cannot be what corresponds with reality. But he would also view the coherence theory as far too abstract and impractical to use to measure truth. Instead, he wishes to introduce usefulness as the measure of truth. Truth, he insists, can be defined only in relation to consequences. A statement is true if people can use that statement to achieve results that they desire. There is no absolute truth, or truth that is unchanging. To verify a belief as truth, we should see if the belief satisfies the whole of human nature over a long period of time, if it can be proved scientifically, or if it aids us individually or collectively in the biological struggle for survival. In short, the prosecution argues for a pragmatic theory of truth. This position essentially states: If something works, it is true.

The pragmatic theory of truth is the cornerstone of **pragmatism**, an essentially American philosophy that has developed during the nineteenth and twentieth centuries, especially through the writings of Charles S. Peirce (1839–1914), William James (1842–1910), and John Dewey (1859–1942). Having tired of older European outlooks, especially those that viewed humans primarily in rational or scientific terms, the pragmatists see the human as needing to use the practical consequences of beliefs to determine their truth and validity. Especially objectionable to pragmatists is the traditional concept of truth as being fixed and inert. In contrast, pragmatists conceive of truth as being dynamic and changing, as subjective and relative. Like the correspondence and coherence theories, the pragmatic theory of truth has many forms. But the classic version was put forth by William James in *Pragmatism: A New Name for Some Old Ways of Thinking*. In it he clearly distinguishes the pragmatic theory from other theories of truth:

> Truth, as any dictionary will tell you, is a property of certain of our ideas. It means their "agreement," as falsity means their disagreement, with "reality." Pragmatists and intellectualists both accept this definition as a matter of course. They begin to quarrel only after the question is raised as to what may precisely be meant by the term "agreement," and what by the term "reality," when reality is taken as something for our ideas to agree with.
>
> In answering these questions the pragmatists are more analytic and painstaking, the intellectualists more offhand and irreflective. The popular notion is that a true idea must copy its reality. Like other popular views, this one follows the analogy of the most usual experience. Our true ideas of sensible things do indeed copy them. Shut your eyes and think of yonder clock on the wall, and you get just such a true picture or copy of its dial. But your idea of its "works" (unless you are a clock-maker) is much less of a copy, yet it passes muster, for it in no way clashes with the reality. Even though it should shrink to the mere word "works," that word still serves you truly; and when you speak of the "time-keeping function" of the clock, or of its spring's "elasticity," it is hard to see exactly what your ideas can copy.
>
> You perceive that there is a problem here. Where our ideas cannot copy definitely their object, what does agreement with that object mean? Some idealists seem to say that they are true whenever they are what God means that we ought to think about that object. Others hold the copy-view all through, and speak as if our ideas possessed truth just in proportion as they approach to being copies of the Absolute's eternal way of thinking.
>
> These views, you see, invite pragmatistic discussion. But the great assumption of the intellectualists is that truth means essentially an inert static relation. When you've got your true idea of anything, there's an end of the matter. You're in possession; you *know*; you have fulfilled your thinking destiny. You are where you ought to be mentally; you have obeyed your categorical imperative; and nothing more need follow on that climax of your rational destiny. Epistemologically you are in stable equilibrium.
>
> Pragmatism, on the other hand, asks its usual question. "Grant an idea or belief to be true," it says, "what concrete difference will its being true make in any one's actual life? How will the truth be realized? What experiences will be different from those which would obtain if the belief were false? What, in short, is the truth's cash-value in experiential terms?"
>
> The moment pragmatism asks this question, it sees the answer: *True ideas are those that we can assimilate, validate, corroborate and verify. False ideas are those that we can not.* That is the practical difference it makes to us to have true ideas; that, therefore, is the meaning of truth, for it is all that truth is known as.
>
> This thesis is what I have to defend. The truth of an idea is not a stagnant property inherent in it. Truth *happens* to an idea. It *becomes* true, is *made* true by events. Its verity *is* in fact an event, a process: the process namely of its verifying itself, its veri-*fication*. Its validity is the process of its valid-*ation*.
>
> But what do the words verification and validation themselves pragmatically mean? They again signify certain practical consequences of the verified

and validated idea. It is hard to find any one phrase that characterizes these consequences better than the ordinary agreement-formula—just such consequences being what we have in mind whenever we say that our ideas "agree" with reality. They lead us, namely, through the acts and other ideas which they instigate, into or up to, or towards, other parts of experience with which we feel all the while—such feeling being among our potentialities—that the original ideas remain in agreement. The connections and transitions come to us from point to point as being progressive, harmonious, satisfactory. This function of agreeable leading is what we mean by an idea's verification.[9]

According to James, then, truth is not based on a comparison of statement and some objective, external state-of-affairs, or on the inclusion of a statement in a coherent system of beliefs. In James's view, the essential problem with those views is that their adherents have failed to ask the right questions. They shouldn't ask how judgments correspond or relate to reality, but precisely what makes them true. For James, the truth of an idea or judgment lies in what he terms the *practical difference* that it makes in our lives, that is, whether its predictions pan out. Although pragmatism was a new, vigorous approach to the problem of truth that matched the youth and energy of nineteenth-century America, it is not without flaws.

Is there any necessary connection between what is true, on the one hand, and what happens to work or be useful, on the other? Critics of pragmatism often raise this question. They object that James reduces epistemological and logical matters to the psychological and pragmatic. Truth cannot be based on the fallible judgments of humankind. What's true may indeed work, but what works isn't necessarily true. Furthermore, what works for you may not work for me or even anybody else. This at least raises questions about the meaning of *works* (see Philosophy and Life 7-3).

In what sense is the pragmatic theory better than the more traditional philosophies? Pragmatism maintains that it is more useful. But any judgment about usefulness seems to involve a large dose of subjectivity. Couldn't traditional philosophers claim that their views of truth are better in terms of their own preferences? It seems that they can. In fact, can we ask whether it is true that one view is more useful than another in a sense in which *true* does not mean useful?[10]

Such subjectivity implies that there can be one truth for you, another for me. This relativism can easily warp judgment, disincline us to view evidence impartially and objectively, and ultimately lead us all astray.

The Compatibility of the Truth Theories

If we look closer at the various positions that Eveready assumes, we shall notice that, rather than being contradictory, the three theories of truth are compatible with one another.

9. *William James.* Pragmatism: A New Name for Some Old Ways of Thinking. *New York: Longmans, Green, 1907, pp. 198–199.*

10. *W. T. Jones.* Kant to Wittgenstein and Sartre. *New York: Harcourt, Brace & World, 1969, p. 300.*

First, Eveready believes that truth is not something that changes or is relative. Yet, at the outset of Scaife's testimony, he went to great lengths to prove the opposite: that truth is relative. Eveready could object that what he was actually demonstrating was the relativity of belief, not of truth—that the statement "There is a red, white, and blue American flag in this courtroom" is in fact either true or false, but we just don't know which it is. But how does he know that the proposition must be true or false? Eveready seems to have no recourse but to declare that there are true statements. Of course, he might insist that we can never know the truth even though there are true propositions.

Some philosophers have been that skeptical. The ancient Greek Gorgias (483–376 B.C.) claimed that we could never know if there even was such a thing as truth. Consequently, he believed that seeking truth was futile. But most skeptics stop short of this conclusion. The best known is David Hume, who for all his skepticism nevertheless admitted, in his *Treatise on Human Nature*, "Whether I be really one of those sceptics who hold that all is uncertain . . . I should reply that this question is entirely superfluous, and that neither I, nor any person was ever sincerely and constantly of that opinion."[11] The fact is that extreme skepticism founders on self-contradiction, for to know you cannot

11. *David Hume.* Treatise on Human Nature. *L. A. Selby-Bigge, Ed. Oxford: Clarendon Press, 1896, vol. 1, p. 7.*

PHILOSOPHY AND LIFE 7-3
Seekers–But Not of Truth

No doubt, belief can lead to truth. The history of scientific research testifies to this. But can belief stand in the way of truth? Imagine what might happen if a group of people believed that the world would end on a particular day and it didn't. Over twenty years ago just such a group was infiltrated and studied.*

Enter the Seekers, a group led by a Mrs. Keech. Mrs. Keech's claim to fame: She received messages from alien beings from a planet called Clarion. They informed her of a fault line in the earth's crust, which they had discovered on one of their journeys here. As a result, earthlings could expect an inland sea from the Arctic Circle to the Gulf of Mexico. They could also count on the Pacific Coast to be submerged from Seattle to Chile. Some weather forecast!

Word leaked out, and Mrs. Keech granted an interview. Now the whole country knew: 21 December was doomsday. So convinced were the Seekers that many quit their jobs and gave away what they owned.

Shortly after midnight, 20 December, anxiety engulfed the Seekers

* *Leon Festinger, H. W. Riecken, Jr., and S. Schachter. When Prophecy Fails: A Social and Psychological Study of a Modern Group That Predicted the Destruction of the World. Minneapolis: University of Minnesota Press, 1956.*

know is to know something. Eveready must at least believe that true propositions exist; otherwise he could not claim to know that he does not know. Ultimately, Eveready, like most of us, must operate as if there are true propositions if for no other reason than to dispose of patent falsehoods.

Thus, despite his railing to the contrary, Eveready holds as true a belief that gives his life meaning, produces satisfactory results, and, in short, works. In other words, his belief that truth exists is founded in pragmatic theory. Furthermore, Eveready takes this belief as self-evident, as a first judgment with which he compares additional judgments and upon which he organizes his whole life. So he must subscribe to the idea that the truth is what hangs together—that is, to the coherence theory of truth. Such an assumption provides grounds for his claiming that the statement "There is a red, white, and blue American flag in this courtroom" is either true or false. Finally, on what basis is this statement to be judged true? It seems that Eveready must admit that there can be no other basis than whether there is *in fact* a red, white, and blue American flag in the courtroom. But here he calls on the correspondence theory.

But to synthesize these theories requires analysis, not just a fabricated example. One way to do this is to view the unique contribution that each theory makes in the realm of truth. Unquestionably, the correspondence theory fits the empirical realm. If I want to know whether it's true that New York is

gathered in Mrs. Keech's living room. Little wonder—nothing was happening. Mrs. Keech began to weep; others joined her. It appeared the world was not doomed. A most desperate turn of events! And, then, just in the nick of time, Mrs. Keech received a message from Clarion: By their faith, the Seekers had saved the world.

The explanation was accepted enthusiastically. Indeed, whereas previously they had never sought publicity for their beliefs, the Seekers now phoned newspapers, called radio stations, and wired national magazines. They shared their views with the world. They invited others to join them.

And Mrs. Keech? Well, not only was she not disconfirmed in her beliefs, she predicted visits by space people and invited the press to witness them. It is not known whether she had any takers.

□ *Did the belief of the Seekers in any sense* work?   □ *On what basis would you evaluate such predictions?*

approximately 3,000 miles from Los Angeles, that oxygen is necessary for fire, or that it's raining, I can effectively use the correspondence test. If the statements correspond to the facts, then I can accept them as true.

On the other hand, coherence provides a nice test for logical, semantic, or systemic truth. Thus, if I want to know whether it's true that a chair cannot be a nonchair, that 56 divided by 7 is 8, or that all bachelors are unmarried, then I need only see if these statements fit in with other statements that I accept as true.

Finally, the pragmatic test seems very helpful to the many value judgments that we make. Thus, "Lying is wrong," "God exists," "The soul is immortal," "Pleasure is the only intrinsic good," and such statements form a very important part of our lives. So do value judgments in the arts, politics, education, and other walks of life. Frequently, the best—and sometimes the only—way to verify such judgments is by applying the tests of workability. Do these beliefs pan out? The pragmatic theory is in a unique position to help answer this question.

Ultimately the theories of truth are complementary. Rather than viewing them as incompatible, we'd best use them to help determine the truth of the various kinds of statements that we utter. We may accept Hosper's definition that a true proposition is one that describes an actual state-of-affairs, but how we discover the truth of any proposition depends largely on what kind of statement it is.

Summary and Conclusions

We opened this chapter by noting that knowledge is warranted, true belief. We discussed the different modes of warrantability as they apply to various kinds of statements. We then defined a true proposition as describing an actual state-of-affairs and discussed three theories of truth: correspondence, coherence, and pragmatic.

In the last analysis, no one theory—correspondence, coherence, or pragmatic—is a complete and ever-reliable solution to the problem of truth. Each has its shortcomings and strengths. Equally important, each theory plays a part in the search for and discovery of self.

In everyday life we frequently use the test of correspondence to arrive at truth. From our earliest days in school, we are rewarded for reporting things "as they are"—Paris is the capital of France, two hydrogen atoms combine with one oxygen atom to form water. This is the primary way of gleaning information about the world. The correspondence theory also allows us to know about the quantifiable aspects of the self—height, weight, blood pressure, body temperature, and so on. This information, in turn, helps us to stay well: to know when to diet, when to relax, and when to exercise. When we ignore these quantifiable aspects of self, we risk injury or illness.

But not all aspects of self are so easily quantified. In the complex area of personal experience, for example, the correspondence theory is not so useful. How would you verify the statement "That person loves me"? You cannot verify it as you can verify "I have a temperature." You would probably evaluate it on the basis of the person's behavior toward you: "If that person loves me, would that person have said that?" In other words, you would test through coherence, asking if the person's actions were consistent with loving somebody. Of course, you would be making an assumption about what loving is.

Our assumptions frequently distort our views of self and the world. For example, a man who is ashamed to cry publicly because it isn't manly may be acting consistently with an assumption that is warping his personality. Likewise, a woman who refuses to call a man for a date because women shouldn't be aggressive is acting consistently with an assumption that may be inhibiting her. The sources of the assumptions that we live by are less relevant here than the fact that we unconsciously measure our concepts, feelings, attitudes, and actions against them as if they were self-evident truths. Thus, we do use the coherence theory of truth, but it is valuable only if our first judgments are accurate. This caution is especially applicable to those judgments concerning self or human nature.

If you were wondering whether a particular individual loved you, you would frequently test pragmatically by asking, in effect, what practical difference the person's loving or not loving you makes in the person's life. Does it affect how the person feels or thinks, what the person desires, and how the person behaves? You might also ask the same questions of yourself. Suppose that even after you answered these questions you were still undecided. The pragmatic theory recognizes the nonmental aspect of the self, which can and should influence decisions in cases like these. We often listen to the reasons of the heart that reason knows little about, to paraphrase the seventeenth-century French philosopher Blaise Pascal.

Thus, the correspondence, coherence, and pragmatic theories of truth actually work together and are instrumental in understanding the self and the world. They do not contradict but supplement one another. Truth may be that characteristic of a statement which corresponds to a fact (correspondence); but whenever we cannot determine the fact, we must rely on how consistent that statement or judgment is with established truth (coherence) or how useful its consequences are (pragmatism).

Section Exercises

Warranted Belief

Which of the following are warranted beliefs? Why?

1. This dog before me is an English shepherd.
2. I have a heart.
3. All things have qualities.
4. Hubert Humphrey once lived.
5. 3 times 2 is 6.
6. The sun will rise tomorrow.

7. A robin is a bird.

8. There's intelligent life in outer space.

9. If the battery in my car is dead, the car won't start.

10. If I release this pen and it's unsupported, it will fall.

Correspondence Theory

1. Do you think it is ever possible to "tell the whole truth"? Explain.

2. Is describing truth as a correspondence between a statement and how things actually are begging the question? In what sense does such a definition not answer the question "What is truth?" but endorse a version of that question?

3. Eveready claims, "Indeed, what the witness *thinks* is truth consigns truth to the very dubious area of sense data interpretation. Such interpretation must be purely subjective and need not have anything to do with the way things actually are." Cite instances or cases that illustrate Eveready's charge.

4. Do you think that there are two kinds of truth, subjective and objective—truth as an individual perceives it and truth as it actually is? Or is there just one objective truth, and everything else merely belief and opinion?

Coherence Theory

1. Show how the following statements pass the test of coherence:
   a. I am a rational being.
   b. I am a divine being.
   c. I am a mechanical being.
   d. I am an existential being.
   e. I am no self.

2. Take some theory, perhaps in psychology, anthropology, economics, or history, and put it to the coherence test. Does it pass? Can you find an opposing theory that passes as well? What might you conclude about the coherence theory of truth?

3. In what sense do claims of extrasensory perception not fit in with what we claim to know? In what sense do they?

4. Demonstrate how the coherence theory of truth ultimately seems to rely on the correspondence theory. How would proponents of the coherence theory object to this claim?

5. Do you believe in God? If you do, describe how this belief, working through the coherence theory of truth, influences how you see yourself, other people, the world around you, and the future of humankind.

6. Consider the fact that you are studying to enter some profession. Demon-

strate how this intention is working as a truth in your life and serving as the cornerstone for a structure of other truths.

7. Take some event from the recent past, such as the Vietnam war. Show how the coherence theory of truth operated to formulate policy and direct activity. Do you think our apparent failure in Vietnam is a vindication of the coherence theory of truth? An indictment? Both? Neither?

Pragmatic Theory

1. Cite a belief that you consider true primarily on pragmatic grounds.

2. Give an example of people creating their own truth.

3. In a sense, truth for the pragmatist is an extension of belief. Illustrate how belief can make truth. Do you detect dangers in this position? How would this position affect how you view yourself? In what sense will you be tomorrow what you decide to be today?

4. In opposition to the pragmatists and their theory of truth, critics charge, "But don't you see that you're encouraging us to see things as we would have them and not as they are?" Do you agree with this criticism?

5. Can you think of anything that, although true, does not work? Something that, although it works, is not true?

In a Grove

Ryūnosuke Akutagawa

What is truth? How are knowledge claims to be verified? Is it possible to know anything with certainty? Few short stories so dramatically raise these questions as "In a Grove," by Japanese writer Ryūnosuke Akutagawa (1892–1927). A lonely cedar grove is the backdrop for this tale of rape and violent death, in which objective truth stands like a figure at high noon, casting no shadow. Ask yourself what actually did happen in the cedar grove. And be careful that your own view isn't as colored as the views of the witnesses themselves.

The Testimony of a Woodcutter Questioned by a High Police Commissioner

Yes, sir. Certainly, it was I who found the body. This morning, as usual, I went to cut my daily quota of cedars, when I found the body in a grove in a hollow in the mountains. The exact location? About 150 meters off the Yamashina stage road. It's an out-of-the-way grove of bamboo and cedars.

The body was lying flat on its back dressed in a bluish silk kimono and a wrinkled head-dress of the Kyoto style. A single sword-stroke had pierced the breast. The fallen bamboo-blades around it were stained with bloody blossoms. No, the blood was no longer running. The wound had dried up, I believe. And also, a gadfly was stuck fast there, hardly noticing my footsteps.

You ask me if I saw a sword or any such thing?

No, nothing, sir. I found only a rope at the root of a cedar near by. And . . . well, in addition to a rope, I found a comb. That was all.

From Ryūnosuke Akutagawa. Rashomon and Other Stories. *Takashi Kojima, Trans. Copyright 1952 by Liveright Publishing Corporation. Reprinted by permission.*

Apparently he must have made a battle of it before he was murdered, because the grass and fallen bamboo-blades had been trampled down all around.

"A horse was near by?"

No, sir. It's hard enough for a man to enter, let alone a horse.

The Testimony of a Traveling Buddhist Priest Questioned by a High Police Commissioner

The time? Certainly, it was about noon yesterday, sir. The unfortunate man was on the road from Sekiyama to Yamashina. He was walking toward Sekiyama with a woman accompanying him on horseback, who I have since learned was his wife. A scarf hanging from her head hid her face from view. All I saw was the color of her clothes, a lilac-colored suit. Her horse was a sorrel with a fine mane. The lady's height? Oh, about four feet five inches. Since I am a Buddhist priest, I took little notice about her details. Well, the man was armed with a sword as well as a bow and arrows. And I remember that he carried some twenty odd arrows in his quiver.

Little did I expect that he would meet such a fate. Truly human life is as evanescent as the morning dew or a flash of lightning. My words are inadequate to express my sympathy for him.

The Testimony of a Policeman Questioned by a High Police Commissioner

The man that I arrested? He is a notorious brigand called Tajomaru. When I arrested him, he had fallen off his horse. He was groaning on the bridge at Awataguchi. The time? It was in the early hours of last night. For the record, I might say that the other day I tried to arrest him, but unfortunately he escaped. He was wearing a dark blue silk kimono and a large plain sword. And, as you see, he got a bow and arrows somewhere. You say that this bow and these arrows look like the ones owned by the dead man? Then Tajomaru must be the murderer. The bow wound with leather strips, the black lacquered quiver, the seventeen arrows with hawk feathers—these were all in his possession I believe. Yes, sir, the horse is, as you say, a sorrel with a fine mane. A little beyond the stone bridge I found the horse grazing by the roadside, with his long rein dangling. Surely there is some providence in his having been thrown by the horse.

Of all the robbers prowling around Kyoto, this Tajomaru has given the most grief to the women in town. Last autumn a wife who came to the mountain back of the Pindora of the Toribe Temple, presumably to pay a visit, was murdered, along with a girl. It has been suspected that it was his doing. If this criminal murdered the man, you cannot tell what he may have done with the man's wife. May it please your honor to look into this problem as well.

The Testimony of an Old Woman Questioned by a High Police Commissioner

Yes, sir, that corpse is the man who married my daughter. He does not come from Kyoto. He was a samurai in the town of Kokufu in the province of Wakasa. His name was Kanazawa no Takehiko, and his age was twenty-six. He was of a gentle disposition, so I am sure he did nothing to provoke the anger of others.

My daughter? Her name is Masago, and her age is nineteen. She is a spirited, fun-loving girl, but I am sure she has never known any man except Takehiko. She has a small, oval, dark-complected face with a mole at the corner of her left eye.

Yesterday Takehiko left for Wakasa with my daughter. What bad luck it is that things should have come to such a sad end! What has become of my daughter? I am resigned to giving up my son-in-law as lost, but the fate of my daughter worries me sick. For heaven's sake leave no stone unturned to find her. I hate that robber Tajomaru, or whatever his name is. Not only my son-in-law, but my daughter . . . (Her later words were drowned in tears.)

Tajomaru's Confession

I killed him, but not her. Where's she gone? I can't tell. Oh, wait a minute. No torture can make me confess what I don't know. Now things have come to such a head, I won't keep anything from you.

Yesterday a little past noon I met that couple. Just then a puff of wind blew, and raised her hanging scarf, so that I caught a glimpse of her face. Instantly it was again covered from my view. That may have been one reason; she looked like a Bodhisattva. At that moment I made up my mind to capture her even if I had to kill her man.

Why? To me killing isn't a matter of such great consequence as you might think. When a woman is captured, her man has to be killed anyway. In killing, I use the sword I wear at my side. Am I the only one who kills people? You, you don't use your swords. You kill people with your power, with your money. Sometimes you kill them on the pretext of working for their good. It's true they don't bleed. They are in the best of health, but all the same you've killed them. It's hard to say who is a greater sinner, you or me. (An ironical smile.)

But it would be good if I could capture a woman without killing her man. So, I made up my mind to capture her, and do my best not to kill him. But it's out of the question on the Yamashina stage road. So I managed to lure the couple into the mountains.

It was quite easy. I became their traveling companion, and I told them there was an old mound in the mountain over there, and that I had dug it open and found many mirrors and swords. I went on to tell them I'd buried the things in a grove behind the mountain, and that I'd like to sell them at a low price to anyone who would care to have them. Then . . . you see, isn't greed terrible? He was beginning to be moved by my talk before he knew it. In less than half an hour they were driving their horse toward the mountain with me.

When he came in front of the grove, I told them that the treasures were buried in it, and I asked them to come and see. The man had no objection—he was blinded by greed. The woman said she would wait on horseback. It was natural for her to say so, at the sight of a thick grove. To tell you the truth, my plan worked just as I wished, so I went into the grove with him, leaving her behind alone.

The grove is only bamboo for some distance. About fifty yards ahead there's a rather open clump of cedars. It was a convenient spot for my purpose. Pushing my way through the grove, I told him a plausible lie that the treasures were buried under the cedars. When I told him this, he pushed his laborious way toward the slender cedar visible through the grove. After a while the bamboo thinned out, and we came to where a number of cedars grew in a row. As soon as we got there, I seized him from behind. Because he

was a trained, sword-bearing warrior, he was quite strong, but he was taken by surprise, so there was no help for him. I soon tied him up to the root of a cedar. Where did I get a rope? Thank heaven, being a robber, I had a rope with me, since I might have to scale a wall at any moment. Of course it was easy to stop him from calling out by gagging his mouth with fallen bamboo leaves.

When I disposed of him, I went to his woman and asked her to come and see him, because he seemed to have been suddenly taken sick. It's needless to say that this plan also worked well. The woman, her sedge hat off, came into the depths of the grove, where I led her by the hand. The instant she caught sight of her husband, she drew a small sword. I've never seen a woman of such violent temper. If I'd been off guard, I'd have got a thrust in my side. I dodged, but she kept on slashing at me. She might have wounded me deeply or killed me. But I'm Tajomaru. I managed to strike down her small sword without drawing my own. The most spirited woman is defenseless without a weapon. At least I could satisfy my desire for her without taking her husband's life.

Yes, . . . without taking his life. I had no wish to kill him. I was about to run away from the grove, leaving the woman behind in tears, when she frantically clung to my arm. In broken fragments of words, she asked that either her husband or I die. She said it was more trying than death to have her shame known to two men. She gasped out that she wanted to be the wife of whichever survived. Then a furious desire to kill him seized me. (Gloomy excitement.)

Telling you in this way, no doubt I seem a crueler man than you. But that's because you didn't see her face. Especially her burning eyes at that moment. As I saw her eye to eye, I wanted to make her my wife even if I were to be struck by lightning. I wanted to make her my wife . . . this single desire filled my mind. This was not only lust, as you might think. At that time if I'd had no other desire than lust, I'd surely not have minded knocking her down and running away. Then I wouldn't have stained my sword with his blood. But the moment I gazed at her face in the dark grove, I decided not to leave there without killing him.

But I didn't like to resort to unfair means to kill him. I untied him and told him to cross swords with me. (The rope that was found at the root of the cedar is the rope I dropped at the time.) Furious with anger, he drew his thick sword. And quick as thought, he sprang at me ferociously, without speaking a word. I needn't tell you how our fight turned out. The twenty-third stroke . . . please remember this. I'm impressed with this fact still. Nobody under the sun has ever clashed swords with me twenty strokes. (A cheerful smile.)

When he fell, I turned toward her, lowering my blood-stained sword. But to my great astonishment she was gone. I wondered to where she had run away. I looked for her in the clump of cedars. I listened, but heard only a groaning sound from the throat of the dying man.

As soon as we started to cross swords, she may have run away through the grove to call for help. When I thought of that, I decided it was a matter of life and death to me. So, robbing him of his sword, and bow and arrows, I ran out to the mountain road. There I found her horse still grazing quietly. It would be a mere waste of words to tell you the later details, but before I entered town I had already parted with the sword. That's all my confession. I know that my head will be hung in chains anyway, so put me down for the maximum penalty. (A defiant attitude.)

The Confession of a Woman Who Has Come to the *Shimizu* Temple

That man in the blue silk kimono, after forcing me to yield to him, laughed mockingly as he looked at my bound husband. How horrified my husband must have been! But no matter how hard he struggled in agony, the rope cut into him all the more tightly. In spite of myself I ran stumblingly toward his side. Or rather I tried to run toward him, but the man instantly knocked me down. Just at the moment I saw an indescribable light in my husband's eyes. Something beyond expression . . . his eyes make me shudder even now. That instantaneous look of my husband, who couldn't speak a word, told me all his heart. The flash in his eyes was neither anger nor sorrow . . . only a cold light, a look of loathing. More struck by the look in his eyes than by the blow of the thief, I called out in spite of myself and fell unconscious.

In the course of time I came to, and found that the man in blue silk was gone. I saw only my husband still bound to the root of the cedar. I raised myself from the bamboo-blades with difficulty, and looked into his face; but the expression in his eyes was just the same as before.

Beneath the cold contempt in his eyes, there was hatred. Shame, grief, and anger . . . I don't know how to express my heart at that time. Reeling to my feet, I went up to my husband.

"Takejiro," I said to him, "since things have come to this pass, I cannot live with you. I'm determined to die, . . . but you must die, too. You saw my shame. I can't leave you alive as you are."

This was all I could say. Still he went on gazing at me with loathing and contempt. My heart breaking, I looked for his sword. It must have been taken by the robber. Neither his sword nor his bow and arrows were to be seen in the grove. But fortunately my small sword was lying at my feet. Raising it over head, once more I said, "Now give me your life, I'll follow you right away."

When he heard these words, he moved his lips with difficulty. Since his mouth was stuffed with leaves, of course his voice could not be heard at all. But at a glance I understood his words. Despising me, his look said only, "Kill me." Neither conscious nor unconscious, I stabbed the small sword through the lilac-colored kimono into his breast.

Again at this time I must have fainted. By the time I managed to look up, he had already breathed his last—still in bonds. A streak of sinking sunlight streamed through the clump of cedars and bamboos, and shone on his pale face. Gulping down my sobs, I untied the rope from his dead body. And . . . and what has become of me since I have no more strength to tell you. Anyway I hadn't the strength to die. I stabbed my own throat with the small sword, I threw myself into a pond at the foot of the mountain, and I tried to kill myself in many ways. Unable to end my life, I am still living in dishonor. (A lonely smile.) Worthless as I am, I must have been forsaken even by the most merciful Kwannon. I killed my own husband. I was violated by the robber. Whatever can I do? Whatever can I . . . I . . . (Gradually, violent sobbing.)

The Story of the Murdered Man, As Told through a Medium

After violating my wife, the robber, sitting there, began to speak comforting words to her. Of course I couldn't speak. My whole body was tied fast to the root of a cedar. But meanwhile I winked at her many times, as much as to say "Don't believe the robber." I wanted to convey some such meaning to her. But my wife, sitting dejectedly on the bamboo leaves, was looking hard at her lap. To all appearances, she was listening to his words. I was agonized by jealousy. In the meantime the robber went on with his clever talk, from one subject to another. The robber finally made his bold, brazen proposal. "Once your virtue is stained, you won't get along well with your husband, so won't you be my wife instead? It's my love for you that made me be violent toward you."

While the criminal talked, my wife raised her face as if in a trance. She had never looked so beautiful as at that moment. What did my beautiful wife say in answer to him while I was sitting bound there? I am lost in space, but I have never thought of her answer without burning with anger and jealousy. Truly she said, . . . "Then take me away with you wherever you go."

This is not the whole of her sin. If that were all, I would not be tormented so much in the dark. When she was going out of the grove as if in a dream, her hand in the robber's, she suddenly turned pale, and pointed at me tied to the root of the cedar, and said "Kill him! I cannot marry you as long as he lives." "Kill him!" she cried many times, as if she had gone crazy. Even now these words threaten to blow me headlong into the bottomless abyss of darkness. Has such a hateful thing come out of a human mouth ever before? Have such cursed words ever struck a human ear, even once? Even once such a . . . (A sudden cry of scorn.) At these words the robber himself turned pale. "Kill him," she cried, cling-ing to his arms. Looking hard at her, he answered neither yes nor no . . . but hardly had I thought about his answer before she had been knocked down into the bamboo leaves. (Again a cry of scorn.) Quietly folding his arms, he looked at me and said, "What will you do with her? Kill her or save her? You have only to nod. Kill her?" For these words alone I would like to pardon his crime.

While I hesitated, she shrieked and ran into the depths of the grove. The robber instantly snatched at her, but he failed even to grasp her sleeve.

After she ran away, he took up my sword, and my bow and arrows. With a single stroke he cut one of my bonds. I remember his mumbling, "My fate is next." Then he disappeared from the grove. All was silent after that. No, I heard someone crying. Untying the rest of my bonds, I listened carefully, and I noticed that it was my own crying. (Long silence.)

I raised my exhausted body from the root of the cedar. In front of me there was shining the small sword which my wife had dropped. I took it up and stabbed it into my breast. A bloody lump rose to my mouth, but I didn't feel any pain. When my breast grew cold, everything was as silent as the dead in their graves. What profound silence! Not a single bird-note was heard in the sky over this grave in the hollow of the mountains. Only a lonely light lingered on the cedars and mountains. By and by the light gradually grew fainter, till the cedars and bamboo were lost to view. Lying there, I was enveloped in deep silence.

Then someone crept up to me. I tried to see who it was. But darkness had already been gathering round me. Someone . . . that someone drew the small sword softly out of my breast in its invisible hand. At the same time once more blood flowed into my mouth. And once and for all I sank down into the darkness of space.

Questions for Analysis

1. On what fact, if any, do the robber, wife, and husband agree?
2. If you were reporting what had occurred in the grove to a friend who knew

nothing of the event, what would you feel safe in saying—what would you report as fact? On what basis—correspondence, coherence, or pragmatism?

3. Assume that the testimonies of the woodcutter, priest, policeman, and old woman are accurate. Which, if any, of the principal accounts fits in with these testimonies best?

4. What we perceive is frequently influenced by our beliefs and biases—even how we see ourselves. Show this in the testimonies of the robber, wife, and husband.

5. Do you think it's accurate to say that, regardless of how anyone perceived it, a given set of objective events occurred that day in the grove? If you say yes, how would you prove it?

Paperbacks for Further Reading

Castaneda, Carlos. *A Separate Reality*. New York: Simon & Schuster, 1972. The author covers the first five years of his relationship with the Yaqui Indian don Juan, whose truth and sources of knowledge defy conventional epistemological attitudes. A book sure to leave the reader asking just what truth is.

Huxley, Aldous. *The Doors of Perception*. New York: Harper & Row, 1970. Huxley records his experiences with the drug mescaline. His account raises questions about the senses and the mind, but especially about knowledge and truth.

Russell, Bertrand. *Human Knowledge: Its Scope and Limits*. New York: Simon & Schuster, 1948. This is a clear, readable review of many philosophical topics, including science, language, and probability, as well as knowledge and perception.

Stoppard, Tom. *Jumpers*. New York: Grove Press, 1974. Stoppard, one of today's foremost dramatists, explores the difficulty of sustaining philosophical truth in the midst of the absurd, the comic, and the pathetic. In this play a philosopher delivers a lecture while bedlam reigns around him.

White, Alan R. *Truth*. Garden City, N.Y.: Doubleday, 1970. This book offers a thoughtful treatment of the different meanings of truth, including three traditional and three modern concepts.

PHILOSOPHY AND SCIENCE

What, then, impels us to devise theory after theory? . . .
The answer . . . is simple:
because we enjoy "comprehending."
—Albert Einstein

In our own times, no field has had greater influence on how we view the world and ourselves than science. What we know, believe, consider real, hold as religious values, and even view as morally right or wrong show the influence of science and its method. Unfortunately, often the science that molds our outlooks is poorly understood and poorly digested, frequently raising anxiety as well as hope. We seem to vacillate between indicting science for all our ills, real and imagined, and praising it for all our benefits. But no one denies its influence in our lives.

In addition, nothing today escapes the reach of science. Studies are done, research conducted, findings published on every conceivable aspect of human affairs. Ralph Siu, in his discussion of science and organized research in *The Tao of Science*, graphically describes the situation:

> The advancement of science continues at a terrifying pace.
>
> A tiny fork of light was photographed in January 1939 in a cloistered German laboratory. Within the short span of six and a half years the joint efforts of two other nations parlayed this innocent observation into the most awesome weapon of death. A single atomic bomb obliterated a hundred thousand lives and destroyed eight square miles of a fourth community. And scarcely ten years later, threats shuttled across the international waters involving still a fifth country that intercontinental missiles thousands of times more devastating were in the offing.
>
> Scientists are debating whether their brain child intends to leave any earth for them to inhabit, not to say investigate and understand. They are recalling the tragedy of the mythical Greek hunter Actaeon, who accidentally saw Artemis, the goddess of chastity, bathing on Mount Cithaeron. For that he was changed into a stag, to be chased by his own fifty hounds until they killed him. Is there any moral in the story for scientists?—men are beginning to ask.

And all the while, the Devil's words to Shaw's Don Juan keep taunting in the background: "And is Man any the less destroying himself for all this boasted brain of his? . . . and I tell you that in the arts of life man invents nothing; but in the art of death, he outdoes Nature herself. . . . This marvellous force of Life of which you boast is a force of Death: Man measures his strength by his destructiveness."

The Devil's distortion is a sly one. The scientist must join Don Juan in his "Pshaw!" He can point to the eighteen tons of material spawned by his fecund genius, which are annually consumed by the average American. For a specific example, he need look no farther than his medicine chest. Concurrently with the engineering of that dreadful implement of death, the very same two powers joined hands to develop the most effective instrument of life that the world of medicine has ever known. Penicillin and the dozen other antibiotics were transformed from test tube curiosities to life-saving prescriptions within the same period of time.

Meanwhile, impatient and inquisitive, science sent her scouts into the dark depths of the ocean and the far reaches of the sky. At the midpoint of the twentieth century they have sounded 35,000 feet below the surface of the seas and ranged to 90,000 above. Where they could not personally touch and observe, they extended their hands through 300 miles of heavens by speedy rockets, their eyes to 10 billion trillion miles by powerful lenses.

If nature attempts to conceal her tiny secrets, science bares them publicly with magnifications of five millionfold. Neither the porcupine nor the mosquito can keep its love life to itself any longer. Scientists peep into their private familiarities and delight in detailed descriptions in lectures and papers. If God's molecular gifts are too bulky for human utility, science chops them into little pieces of useful chemicals. If the natural bits are too small, science joins them together into larger units. If the Thanksgiving turkey is too large, a small one is bred. If seeds are not wanted in fruit, seedless varieties are developed. Not satisfied with man's mundane three-dimensional world, science conjures up four- and six-dimensional phantasms.[1]

The curiosity of science and her bent for innovation seem uncontrollable. She pries into every heavenly nook and earthly cranny. She respects neither the ancient sanctity of tombs nor the caressing intimacies of boudoirs.

Science speeds on unabashed![2]

And, we could add, it takes us with it, the reluctant and enthusiastic alike. These are reasons enough to look at science in our introduction to philosophy. But there is another reason, which highlights the connection between philosophy and science.

The sciences largely deal with issues that were once dealt with by philosophers.[3] For example, it was not until interest in the study of living matter had reached a well-developed stage that the science of biology emerged. Thus, while Aristotle is considered a biologist as well as a philosopher, he never distinguished between biology and philosophy. Such a distinction came

1. *Arthur Eddington, for example, proposed a five-dimensional universe: three spatial and two temporal dimensions. Fellow physicist Adrian Dobbs also hypothesized two time dimensions.*

2. *R. G. H. Siu. The Tao of Science. New York: Wiley, 1957, pp. 3–4. Reprinted by permission.*

3. *See Eugene A. Troxell and William S. Snyder. Making Sense of Things: An Invitation to Philosophy. New York: St. Martin's Press, 1976, pp. 3–7.*

with specialization, which developed when people wanted to concentrate on a particular aspect of the world. In the case of biology, special techniques were developed for dealing with biological issues. As a result, we now consider biology separate from philosophy.

Aristotle also studied issues that we would classify under political science, psychology, sociology, and botany. Aristotle did distinguish among his various interests, but to him they were so many distinctions within philosophy, not between philosophy and other disciplines. Indeed, as late as the seventeenth century, the term *philosophy* designated any effort to make sense of natural phenomena. Thus, Sir Isaac Newton's monumental work in physics was entitled *The Mathematical Principles of Natural Philosophy* (1687). For these reasons, philosophy is often called "the parent science."

As the sciences become increasingly refined, the complexity of the world increases. So, the number and diversity of issues that philosophy deals with also increases. Today there are many more aspects of the world for philosophers to consider than in Aristotle's time. For example, the development of computers has spawned philosophical issues, as have medicine, biochemistry, paleontology, genetics, and criminology.

Not surprisingly, then, a whole area of philosophy is termed *philosophy of science*. It deals primarily with scientific methodology and understanding, including scientific explanation, the logical structure of scientific theories, and the languages of science. This is a vital area today, given the contemporary compression of epistemology to scientific knowledge and method and the intrusion of science into our lives. This is why we will examine it in this chapter.

We will begin by dispelling some common misunderstandings about science. The bulk of the chapter, however, will consider the methods of science. We will closely examine the procedures of science, which will involve induction and inductive inference, as well as hypotheses and their value. After noting some of the limitations of scientific methods, we will state a few fascinating and philosophically provocative hypotheses about nature and the universe. Here are the main points we will make.

Main Points

1. The philosophy of science deals with the methods that scientists use and the kinds of understanding that they achieve; it also concerns scientific explanation, the logical structure of scientific theories, and the language of science.

2. A scientific statement is falsifiable, which means that it is always possible to specify some state-of-affairs that, if it were the case, would make the statement false.

3. An inverse relationship exists between the amount of information and the probability of a scientific statement's being true, and a direct relationship exists between the amount of information and the testability of a scientific statement.

4. Scientific method is a way of investigation based on collecting, analyzing,

and interpreting data to determine the most likely explanation of the phenomenon being studied.

5. Induction is the heart of scientific method. It is a mode of reasoning that leads to a likely explanation.

6. Francis Bacon and T. C. Chamberlin are two noteworthy figures in the formulation and development of the method of inductive inference. In *The New Organon*, Bacon provides numerous procedures to ensure good inductive inference. Deserving special mention is his emphasis on exclusion (falsifiability) and experiment. Chamberlin stressed the need for multiple hypotheses to preclude the human tendency to cling to single hypotheses. Contemporary scientist and philosopher of science John Platt has synthesized the approaches of Bacon and Chamberlin in his "strong inference," which consists of applying the following steps to every problem in science: (1) devising alternative hypotheses, (2) devising a crucial experiment (or several) in order to exclude one or more of the hypotheses, (3) carrying out the experiment, and (4) recycling the procedure. In its separate elements, strong inference is Bacon's method of inductive inference.

7. A good hypothesis should be relevant, compatible with accepted knowledge, testable, predictive, and simple.

8. Scientific method is limited by the following facts: (1) We can learn only what the tools allow us to measure; (2) we can learn only what the tools are designed to show; (3) we may, through classification, ignore significant individual differences; (4) we may ignore the characteristics of the whole unit that the individual parts do not show; and (5) we are limited by our own physical and intellectual capabilities and our expectations.

9. Current evidence indicates that reality is nonmaterial.

10. Currently one theory best explains why matter in the cosmos appears to be moving away from us: the big bang theory.

11. Time is relative.

12. Philosophy can make a unique contribution to current civilization by bridging the widening gap between humanism and technocracy.

13. Theoretical scientific discoveries make us wonder whether there are order and purpose in our lives, whether we affect what we know, whether we are part of a complementary relationship that holds among all things, and whether we help create the world we know.

14. The technological capabilities of applied science in areas such as genetic engineering, psychological behaviorism, and organ transplants have serious implications for the individual.

Science: What It Is and What It Is Not

Before reading on, determine if the following statements are true or false:[4]

4. *See Garvin McCain and Erwin M. Segal. The Game of Science. Belmont, Calif.: Brooks/Cole, 1968,* pp. 12–18.

1. The primary goal of science is the accumulation of facts or data.

2. Some sciences can be described as exact.

3. Science is deficient because it cannot give any ultimate explanation of natural processes.

4. Scientists distort reality and cannot do justice to the fullness of experience.

5. Science is concerned primarily with our practical and social needs.

If you thought any of these statements were true, you are probably misinformed about one or more aspects of science. But don't feel bad. There's widespread ignorance among the ill- and well-educated about science. Indeed, intellectuals of many disciplines—philosophy and science included—show a low-level scientific education.

Well, what is science all about? We can begin to answer this question by considering the five statements above. With respect to the first statement, collecting facts and data is important in science, but it is not the "whole enchilada." After all, everyone collects data. You could probably tell your grades for the last two years, and I could tell you some of the institutions that are using this text. But these facts do not make you and me scientists.

Think about your car. What do you know about it? A lot. It's hard to start when it is cold; it begins to rattle between 45 and 50 miles per hour; it needs a quart of oil every 1,000 miles. You could go on with an impressive catalog of facts. But does this recital of data lead to a *scientific* understanding? No. What is missing is a set of general principles. In addition to facts and data, science requires explanatory or organizing concepts to make sense of the data.[5] We will discuss this more later.

Can some sciences be described as exact? No. What about mathematics? Mathematics is not a science in the sense of observing, identifying, describing, or explaining natural phenomena. Science is based on observation, mathematics on the logical consequences of a set of postulates. If you insist on calling mathematics a science, then consider it a *formal* science, as opposed to the natural sciences (such as biology, chemistry, or physics), which are based chiefly on objective, quantitative hypotheses, and those studies using scientific methods of inquiry, such as biochemistry, genetics, geology, paleontology, archeology, anthropology, and biomedicine. We will say considerably more of scientific method shortly. But first we must understand why a science cannot be described as exact.

All scientific statements share several important features. First, they express probability, not certainty—they assert what will likely be the case, not what will certainly be the case. For example, if on several occasions you measured the distance traveled by a falling object, ensuring the same conditions each time, you would generate a *distribution* of values, *not* the same value each time, despite the well-established scientific law $S = \frac{1}{2}gt^2$ (where S is the distance, g is the acceleration due to gravity, and t is the time in seconds). True, the values you get would not differ by more than a fraction of a centimeter, but they would not be identical.

5. *Garvin McCain and Erwin M. Segal.* The Game of Science, *p. 13.*

Furthermore, scientific statements are incomplete. While they are generally unnoticed and unexpressed, qualifiers are implied in every scientific statement, such as "According to the evidence available," "Based on my investigations," and "Given these conditions." Thus, scientific statements are never unamendable. They are always open to revision based on new evidence or a new interpretation of existing evidence.

In other words, all scientific statements are falsifiable. For instance, "This is either my car or not my car" is not a scientific statement, since it is not possible to specify some state of affairs that would falsify the statement. For this reason, neither "8 plus 5 equals 13" nor "The interior angles of a triangle add up to 180 degrees" is a scientific statement.

But what about the statement "It will rain"? Such a statement is bound to be true, and it can never be proved false. No matter how many years pass without rain, it may still rain someday. The probability of such a statement is maximal because its informative content is minimal. In fact, there are true statements whose probabilities are equal to 1 (that is, certainty) and whose information is nil, such as "Black is black" and "My sister is a female." Such statements are termed *tautologies*, which restate meaning that is already implicit.

However, "It will rain" can be made falsifiable if it is restricted to a finite time span: "It will rain in the next year." And yet, there are a multitude of places on earth where it could rain. "It will rain in the United States in the next year" at least limits the location. More helpful yet would be to narrow the meaning still further: "It will rain in the United States in the next week" or "It will rain in Topeka, Kansas, in the next week." The more informative the statement, the more useful it becomes and, even more important, the more probable that it will prove wrong.

What science is interested in, then, is statements that are highly informative—statements from which we can infer other testable statements. Such statements thus have a low probability of being true. When a statement contains information, it can be tested. The more information, the more testable the statement. The true statement with the highest amount of information would be a full, specific description of the world. What's more, every possible observation or experience would constitute a test, a possible falsification of such a statement. The probability of such a statement's being true would be close to zero, because the number of ways in which it could be falsified would be the highest possible.[6]

Science does not deal with truisms. Its thrill lies in the ever-present possibility that, through our own critical investigations, we can learn that things are utterly different from how we supposed. Such refutation fires the imagination to conceive of things in new ways.

Lacking exactness, science cannot offer any ultimate explanation of natural processes. But does that make it deficient, as the third statement above declares? It would if science sought an ultimate explanation, but quite the opposite is the case. Scientific advance largely consists of formulating questions in

6. *See Bryan Magee.* Karl Popper. *New York: Viking, 1973, pp. 27–30.*

limited, not ultimate, terms. "Are humans ultimately aggressive or nonaggressive?" Who knows? Likely no one ever will. But by limiting the question to observable behavior, sociologists have established a relationship between juvenile delinquency and broken homes.[7] This does not mean that the original question is not worth asking. However, science is not interested in asking such questions; rather it is interested in what appears to be solvable. As a result, objecting that science cannot offer ultimate explanations belies what science is all about.

A similar misconception leads to the belief that science distorts reality and cannot do justice to the fullness of experience. Again, the nature of science is to study small aspects of phenomena at any one time. Otherwise research and investigation become unwieldy. To illustrate, recall the dreaded term paper that every student in introductory composition courses must grind out. What is fundamental to a successful paper? Limiting the subject. For instance, assume you chose the topic of job atmosphere. What would you write about? The interplay, you reply, between job atmosphere and worker motivation. Fine, but this topic is still too broad. After all, job atmosphere can refer to external aspects—wages, work conditions, organization policy, and management styles—or to internal aspects—the interest and challenge of the job and how much opportunity it provides for creativity and growth. Unless you narrow your investigation, you will drown in details. Scientists face the same problem: They could measure or manipulate countless factors. To have any degree of success, they must restrict any investigation to one or a few aspects of the situation studied.

In order to do this, scientists try to minimize the extraneous factors that might influence a result by manipulating the environment and performing experiments. Some claim that since the experimental situations are artificial, they distort reality. But do they?

Take the example of a falling object. Many factors could influence its fall: its shape, the amount of air it displaces, and its weight. The rates of fall of different objects may even differ slightly. What if two things were dropped at different times from different heights? Observers might not be able to tell which falls faster. Even if they could, could they determine whether the height makes any difference? If you think about it, the only reliable way to discover natural laws about falling bodies is to set up artificial, controlled situations, which is precisely what scientist and philosopher Galileo (1564–1642) did.

Galileo contrived the time, place, and condition of the fall. By dropping two balls with different weights from a height at the same time, he controlled several things: the height of the fall, the time of the fall, the shape of the objects, and the material of the objects. By dropping the balls simultaneously, he was able to determine slight differences in speed. The conclusion was unmistakable: Weight per se did not influence the speed of the falling objects (air resistance does).

Pressing his study, Galileo built long, smooth inclined planes and rolled

7. *Bryan Magee.* Karl Popper, *p. 15.*

balls down them. For years he worked, carefully releasing the balls and timing them. By controlling the situation, he observed and studied important relations. As a result, he concluded that a constant force does not create a constant velocity but a constant acceleration and that time and acceleration are more important variables than velocity and distance. Without creating an artificial situation, Galileo could not have made these important discoveries. Thus, although scientific experiments distort reality, such distortions don't necessarily yield false findings. Indeed, when properly conducted, these experiments offer a better understanding of reality.

Finally, is science concerned primarily with our practical and social needs, as the fifth statement above indicates? If you say yes, you are probably thinking of science only in terms of its application or its practical results. You may be thinking of the impressive list of scientific advances in communication, transportation, and medicine: the telephone, television, transistor radio, satellites, space stations, antibiotics, and organ transplants. Although these are the most visible of science's achievements, they are not the heart of science. Science is motivated by understanding, not by the satisfying of human needs.

Galileo is again a good example. His investigations of falling bodies were not inspired by social need but by scientific understanding. He wanted to know something, to comprehend it. The same impulse underlay his astronomy. What need, either personal or social, could have driven him to incur the condemnation of both academic and church leaders? None is apparent, unless it was a need to know. Similarly, were thoughts of space satellites and stations or of weapons having nightmarish destructive capabilities dancing in the heads of Newton (1642–1727) or Einstein (1879–1955)? Not likely.

The understanding that scientists seek inevitably takes the form of problem-solving activity. A problem is a fact or group of facts for which no acceptable explanation exists. The facts do not fit in with our expectations or perceptions. Scientists seek acceptable explanations to problems. One of the most distinguished of modern scientists, Albert Einstein, made the point succinctly: "There exists a passion for comprehension, just as there exists a passion for music. That passion is rather common in children, but gets lost in most people later on. Without this passion, there would be neither mathematics nor natural science."[8]

With this clarification of what science is, let us now explore how scientists go about their work. This is most important because, in the last analysis, science is a set of methods and conceptual schemes. Many of us forget this or never knew it. We become so dazzled by scientific achievements that we rarely inquire about scientific methodology. If we did, we would find much that we could apply in our own problem-solving efforts. At the same time, it would help dissipate the phony aura of magic that enshrouds science. For many, science pulls rabbits out of a hat. We gape in awe and wonder at how scientists do what they do. But behind every trick is a method, a *way* of proceeding. An understanding of this methodology leads to a genuine appreciation of the artistry involved in science.

8.   Albert Einstein. *"On the Generalized Theory of Gravitation."* Scientific American, *April 1950, p. 13.*

Scientific Method

Broadly speaking, we may define **scientific method** as a way of investigating a phenomenon that is based on collecting, analyzing, and interpreting evidence to determine the most probable explanation. To illustrate, take the example of finding out why your car has failed to start. In science, explanations are generally termed *hypotheses*. In devising your explanation or hypothesis of why the car won't start, you would probably check everything that could be part of the problem: the distributor, spark plugs, points, battery cables, and the battery. Obviously you would not check the tires or the bumpers, because their condition is not relevant. Having collected relevant sense information, you would then analyze and interpret it. These steps are complex parts of an inductive method of problem solving. Inductive method and induction, which constitute the basis for scientific method, need close examination. But first let's see what our simple example suggests about science and scientists.

First, you assume that an explanation exists that accounts for the problem. Also, you assume that some things need to be checked, while others need not. These observations may seem obvious, but that's the point. You check relevant criteria, which are largely determined by common sense. Observation is always selective. It needs an object, a task, an interest, and a point of view. Any further investigations you make of a problem will occur within a frame of reference, a frame of expectations. Where do these expectations come from? Your experience and that of others—in this example, the catalog of human knowledge about cars and why they do not start.

Before we are even conscious of our own existence, we are profoundly influenced by our relationships with people who have complicated histories. And they are parts of society, which has an even more complicated and evolved history. Thus, by the time we make conscious choices, we are already using a set of expectations about the world and the things in it. In a word, we make use of tradition. Scientists use tradition, too. They employ the theories, assumptions, and expectations that have evolved within their own discipline. They observe through theory and networks of empirical generalizations, as well as many philosophical assumptions. Sir Karl Popper, often considered the greatest philosopher of science, develops this point in his *Conjectures and Refutations*:

> All this means that a young scientist who hopes to make discoveries is badly advised if his teacher tells him, "Go round and observe," and that he is well advised if his teacher tells him, "Try to learn what people are discussing nowadays in science. Find out where difficulties arise, and take an interest in disagreements. These are the questions which you should take up." In other words, you should study the *problem situation* of the day. This means that you pick up, and try to continue, a line of enquiry which has the whole background of the earlier development of science behind it; you fall in with the tradition of science. . . . From the point of view of what we want as scientists—understanding, prediction, analysis, and so on—the world in which we live is extremely complex.[9]

9. *Karl Popper.* Conjecture and Refutations. *New York: Basic Books, 1965, p. 129.*

Charles Darwin, the great biologist and author of the modern theory of evolution, once made a similar comment. "All observation," he wrote, "must be for or against some view, if it is to be of any service." These important scientific thinkers realized that there are simply too many facts in the world to become familiar with them all. Even the most painstaking investigator must pick and choose among the available facts and data. In short, we must collect data to support or contradict some explanation or hypothesis. In fact, you have several sources of data in our example—the battery, battery cables, distributor cap, and so on. Of course, the explanation need not be complete, but it must be present to some degree.

Now let us examine induction and inductive inference.

Induction

Induction is a mode of reasoning that leads to a probable explanation or judgment. For example, someone might reason, "Since Sue received an A on the first five tests of the term, she'll probably get an A for the course." The word *probably* must be used or be understood as part of any inductive conclusion. One reason is that the premise or evidence is known through experience, and experience is never complete. Next year, next month, or tomorrow new facts may weaken, amend, or contradict today's assumptions. It's possible that Sue will not get an A on the next test.

The question then arises as to the reliability of inductive judgments or inference. Consider, for example, the following statements:

Since Alice is under twenty-five, she's a greater driving risk than thirty-two-year-old Barbara.

The marriage of a couple under twenty-one will be more likely to fail than that of a couple over twenty-one.

"You shouldn't have an abortion, Myra, because you have a history of nervous disorders."

If you smoke pot, in all likelihood you'll eventually shoot dope.

To determine the strength of these inductive inferences, the method used to generate them must be examined.

Inductive Inference

Scientist, writer, and philosopher John Platt has suggested that there are two main contributors to the development of a satisfactory inductive inference method:[10] English philosopher Francis Bacon (1561–1626) and American geologist Thomas Chrowder Chamberlin (1843–1928). Bacon's contribution is clearly shown in his book *The New Organon*. In it he speaks of wanting a "surer method" of "finding out nature" than either the all-inclusive theories of his day or the fledgling, unrefined attempts at induction "by simple enumeration." In other words, Bacon was critical of the methods of both the rational and empirical schools: "The Rational School of philosophy snatches from experi-

10. John Platt. "Strong Inference." Science, 16 October 1964, pp. 347–353.

ence a variety of common instances, neither duly ascertained nor diligently examined and weighted, and leaves all the rest to meditation and agitation of wit. . . . The Empirical School of philosophy gives birth to dogma more deformed and monstrous than the Sophistical or Rational School. For it has its foundations, not in the light of common notions (which though it be faint and superficial light, is yet in a manner universal, and has reference to many things), but in the narrowness and darkness of a few experiments."[11] It may be hard at first to understand Bacon's sullying of empiricism, since historically he was a prime mover behind it. Bacon was not objecting to sense experience as the test of truth, but to the crude method of "simple enumeration"—basing inferences on a simple counting up of like instances.

For example, having seen only males for an hour as you sat in a corner of a college library, you might conclude by simple enumeration that only males attended that school. Obviously, the conclusion is ill founded—not because it is necessarily incorrect but because your method of drawing the conclusion is inadequate. Why? First, it is based on too few facts. Second, it is based only on the facts at hand. As a result, it is open to contradictory instances, such as females who attend the college. Thus, Bacon writes: "The induction is amiss which infers the principles of science by simple enumeration and does not, as it ought, employ exclusions and solutions (or separations) of nature. . . . The induction which is to be available for the discovery and demonstration of sciences and arts must analyze nature by proper rejections and exclusions, and then, after a sufficient number of negatives, comes to a conclusion on affirmative instances."[12] "Exclusions," "separations," "negatives," "rejections"—all are watchwords in Bacon's method of inductive inference. It is vital to understand what Bacon means by these terms. Unfortunately, we cannot cover all the inductive procedures that he suggested, but we can sketch the important ones and emphasize the role that exclusions play.

Bacon's *The New Organon*

In book II of *The New Organon*, Bacon outlines his inductive procedures. In an extended illustration, he raises the problem of heat. What is it? Better still, how do we go about understanding heat or defining it?

It is important to focus on this second question, because science is essentially a set of methods and conceptual schemes leading to an understanding of natural processes. In a word, the method that Bacon proposes to approach this and other questions is vital in evaluating the worth of his eventual answer. Recall your inference about the people attending the college. Your conclusion may in fact be correct—maybe only males do attend it. But because the reasoning method is deficient, the conclusion is not warranted.

Bacon begins his investigation of heat with "a muster or presentation" of all known instances of heat. It is important that this collection be complete and accurate, "without premature speculation, or any great amount of subtlety."

11. *Francis Bacon.* The New Organon. *Fulton Anderson, Ed. Indianapolis: Bobbs-Merrill, 1960, book I, pp. 60–61. Copyright © 1960 by The Bobbs-Merrill Co., Inc. All excerpts reprinted by permission of the publisher.*

12. *Francis Bacon.* The New Organon, *p. 99.*

Bacon has a name for this history of instances agreeing: "Table of Essence and Presence." Here are some of his instances agreeing in the nature of heat:

1. The rays of the sun, especially in summer and at noon.
2. The rays of the sun reflected and condensed, as between mountains, or on walls, and most of all in burning glasses and mirrors.
3. Fiery meteors.

   . . .

5. Eruptions of flame from the cavities of mountains.
6. All flame.
7. Ignited solids.
8. Natural warm baths.

   . . .

12. Air confined and underground in some caverns, expecially in winter.

   . . .

17. Green and moist vegetables confined and bruised together as roses packed in baskets.

   . . .

21. Horse dung and like excrements of animals, when fresh.

   . . .

28. Other instances.[13]

Then he draws up a similar table called "Table of Deviation," which lists instances in which the thing under investigation, in this case heat, is lacking in the subjects listed in the first table. Notice in the samples cited below that Bacon often suggests simple experiments in answering the affirmatives in the Table of Essence and Presence. Such experiments are an important part of his method; in many cases they are crucial, as we will see shortly.

Answering to the first affirmative instance

1. The rays of the moon and of stars are not found to be hot to touch. . . .

To the 2nd

1. The rays of the sun in what is called the middle region of the air do not give heat. . . . And this appears from the fact that on the tops of mountains, unless they are very high, there is perpetual snow.
2. The reflection of the rays of the sun in regions near the polar circles is found to be very weak and ineffective in producing heat, . . .
3. Try the following experiment. Take a glass fashioned in a contrary manner to a common burning glass and, placing it between your hand and the rays of the sun, observe whether it diminishes the heat of the sun, as a burning glass increases and strengthens it. For it is evident in the case of optical rays that according as the glass is made thicker or thinner in the middle as compared with the

13. Francis Bacon. The New Organon, pp. 131–132.

sides, so do the objects seen through it appear more spread or more contracted. Observe therefore whether the same is the case with heat.

To the 3rd

1. Comets (if we are to reckon these too among meteors) are not found to exert a constant or manifest effect in increasing the heat of the season. . . .

To the 5th

1. Eructations and eruptions of flame are found no less in cold than in warm countries, as in Iceland and Greenland. In cold countries, too, the trees are in many cases more inflammable and more pitchy and resinous than in warm; as the fir, pine, and others. The situations however and the nature of the soil in which eruptions of this kind usually occur have not been carefully enough ascertained to enable us to subjoin a negative to this affirmative instance.

To the 6th

1. All flame is in all cases more or less warm; nor is there any negative to be subjoined. . . .

To the 7th

1. Every body ignited so as to turn to a fiery red, even if unaccompanied by flame, is always hot; neither is there any negative to be subjoined to this affirmative. . . .

To the 8th

1. In what situation and kind of soil warm baths usually spring has not been sufficiently examined; and therefore no negative is subjoined.

To the 12th

1. Here I subjoin the negative of air confined in caverns during the summer. But the subject of air in confinement should by all means be more diligently examined. . . . Let the experiment therefore be made in an earthen jar wrapped round with many folds of leather to protect it from the outward air, and let the vessel remain tightly closed for three or four days; then open the vessel and test the degree of heat or cold by applying either the hand or a graduated glass.

To the 17th

1. On this instance should be made more diligent inquiry. For herbs and vegetables when green and moist seem to contain some latent heat, though so slight that it is not perceptible to the touch when they are single, but only when they are collected and shut up together. . . .

To the 21st

1. To this instance it is hard to subjoin a negative. Indeed, the excrements of animals when no longer fresh have manifestly a potential heat, as is seen in the enriching of soil. [14]

Bacon then proposes a "Table of Degrees or Comparison," which lists instances where heat is found in different degrees. He includes comparisons of heat increase and decrease in a single subject and of the amounts of heat in different subjects. Such a table is necessary to understand the nature of what is studied—in this case heat. For example, "Some ignited bodies are found to be much hotter than some flames. Ignited iron, for instance, is much hotter and

14. *Francis Bacon.* The New Organon, *pp. 133–141.*

more consuming than flame of spirit of wine." Why? What is there about heat that some substances are hotter than others, or that some substances can become hotter?

Here are a few of Bacon's entries:

1. Animals increase in heat by motion, exercise, wine, . . . burning fevers, and pain.

2. By the tradition of astronomers some stars are hotter than others. Of planets, Mars is accounted the hottest after the sun; then comes Jupiter, and then Venus. Others, again, are set down as cold: the moon, for instance, and above all Saturn. . . .

3. The sun gives greater heat the nearer he approaches to the perpendicular or zenith. . . .

4. Motion increases heat, as you may see in bellows and by blowing; insomuch that the harder metals are not dissolved or melted by a dead or quiet fire, till it be made intense by blowing. . . .[15]

After drawing up the tables, Bacon employs induction. "Upon review of the instances, all and each, [the problem is] to find such a nature as is always present or absent with the given nature, and always increases and decreases with it." But if we attempt to do this affirmatively from the first, Bacon warns that the result will be "fancies and guesses and notions ill defined." Instead we must proceed at first by *negatives*. After such exclusions have been exhausted, we may end up with affirmatives.

This process capitalizes on the first three tables. From them we can *exclude* certain things from belonging to the nature of heat. Thus, we devise a "Table of Exclusions," on the basis of which we may render affirmative statements. Here are some samples from Bacon's Table of Exclusions for heat. While the list is imperfect and incomplete, as were the others, it nonetheless illustrates the vital role of exclusion in inductive inference.

1. On account of the rays of the sun, reject the nature of the elements.

2. On account of common fire, and chiefly subterraneous fires (which are the most remote and most completely separate from the rays of heavenly bodies), reject the nature of heavenly bodies.

3. On account of the warmth acquired by all kinds of bodies (minerals, vegetables, skin of animals, water, oil, air, and the rest) by mere approach to a fire, or other hot body, reject the distinctive or more subtle texture of bodies.

4. On account of ignited iron and other metals, which communicate heat to other bodies and yet lose none of their weight or substance, reject the communication or admixture of the substance of another hot body.

5. On account of boiling water and air, and also on account of metals and other solids that receive heat but not to ignition or red heat, reject light or brightness.

6. On account of the rays of the moon and other heavenly bodies, with the exception of the sun, also reject light and brightness.

15. *Francis Bacon*. The New Organon, *pp. 144–147.*

7. By a comparison of ignited iron and the flame of spirit of wine (of which ignited iron has more heat and less brightness, while the flame of spirit of wine has more brightness and less heat), also reject light and brightness.

. . .

11. On account of dilation of air in calendar glasses and the like, wherein the air evidently moves locally and expansively and yet acquires no manifest increase of heat, also reject local or expansive motion of the body as a whole.

. . .

14. On account of heat being kindled by the attrition of bodies, reject a principial nature. By principial nature I mean that which exists in the nature of things positively, and not as the effect of any antecedent nature.[16]

The process of exclusion lays the foundation for inductive inference, which, granted, is not complete until an affirmative is determined. Bacon is eventually able to say, "Heat is a motion, expansive, restrained, and acting in its strife upon the smaller particles of bodies." He then modifies "expansion" to "an inclination upward" and "strife" to "hurried and with violence." About the operation of heat, Bacon says, "If in any natural body you can excite a dilating or expanding motion, and can so repress this motion and turn it back upon itself that the dilation shall not proceed equably, but have its way in one part and be counteracted in another, you will undoubtedly generate heat."[17] Notice that one can deduce additional experiments that can falsify or amend this statement. Bacon thus suggests two aspects of the interpretation of nature: inducing axioms from experience, and deducing and deriving new experiments from these axioms.

While Bacon addressed his method to scientists, he said that anybody could learn inductive inference, just as they could learn how to "draw a straighter line or more perfect circle . . . with the help of a ruler or a pair of compasses." "My way of discovering sciences," he wrote, "goes far to level men's wit and leaves but little to individual excellence, because it performs everything by the surest rules and demonstrations." Mistakes are not to be feared, for "truth will sooner come out from error than from confusion."

The Difficulty of Disproof

As John Platt points out, Bacon's method emphasizes exclusions, or disproofs. Looked at another way, there is no such thing (nor should there be) as a proof in science, for some later explanation may be as good as or better than an existing one. Thus, science advances by disproofs. A hypothesis that cannot be falsified is worthless, because it does not say anything. To say that your car won't start because a demon has hexed it is not a viable hypothesis, because it cannot be disproved. On the other hand, "The car won't start because the battery is dead" can be disproved. Find a car with a dead battery that starts. If you cannot, then you have good reason to claim that a car fails to start if its

16. *Francis Bacon.* The New Organon, *pp. 154–155.*

17. *Francis Bacon.* The New Organon, *p. 162.*

battery is dead. But what possible test could disprove that a car won't start because of a demon?

If a system cannot be refuted by experience, it is not an empirical scientific system. The criterion between science and nonscience, then, is falsifiability. If all possible affairs fit in with an explanation, then no actual state-of-affairs, no observations, and no experimental results can be claimed as supporting evidence, because there is no observable difference between the statement's being true and its being false. It conveys no scientific information.

Consider Einstein's theory of relativity. His general theory led to the conclusion that light must be attracted by heavy bodies. If this is so, then light that travels close to the sun on its way from a star to the earth must be deflected by the gravitational pull of the sun. In the daytime we generally cannot see such stars for the sun's brilliance. But if we could, the deflection of their light rays would make them appear to be in positions different from their actual ones. What's more, the predicted difference could be checked by photographing a star that would be so affected by day and then at night in the sun's absence. Sir Arthur Eddington attempted to disprove Einstein's theory by one of the most famous scientific observations of the century. In 1919 he led an expedition to a point in Africa where an eclipse of the sun would make such stars visible by day. On 29 May he made his observations, and they corroborated Einstein's theory.[18]

But, as Platt points out, disproof is a "hard doctrine." If you have a hypothesis and I have another, one of them must be eliminated. This is not easy. Each of us is attached to our intellectual child, and as our explanations grow into definite theories, our attachments grow stronger, too. Perhaps we contort our theories to make them fit the facts or construe the facts to fit the theories. A marvelous example of this is found in a correspondence Karl Popper once had with the noted psychoanalyst Alfred Adler, whose theory of personality relies heavily on his concept of the inferiority complex. In 1919, Popper reported to Adler a case that did not seem to him particularly Adlerian. Adler, however, found little difficulty in analyzing it in terms of his theory. "Slightly shocked," Popper writes, "I asked him how he could be so sure. 'Because of my thousandfold experience,' he replied; whereupon I could not help saying: 'And with this new case, I suppose, your experience has become thousand-and-one-fold.'"[19]

Chamberlin's Multiple Working Hypotheses

To avoid such "hypothesis chauvinism," T. C. Chamberlin proposed his *method of multiple working hypotheses*. It differs from the simple working hypothesis in a most important way: "It distributes effort and divides the affections." "Each hypothesis," Chamberlin writes, "suggests its own criteria, its own means of proof, its own method of developing the truth, and if a group of hypotheses encompass the subject on all sides, the total outcome of means and

---

18. *See Bryan Magee.* Karl Popper, *p. 37.*

19. *Bryan Magee.* Karl Popper, *p. 39.*

of methods is full and rich."[20] In Chamberlin's view the method "leads to certain distinctive habits of mind. . . . When faithfully followed for a sufficient time, it develops a mode of thought of its own kind which may be designated the habit of complex thought."[21]

Apparently Chamberlin's idea promises a cure for many of the problems in the sciences that stem from the failure to accept exclusion as an active part of the inductive method. As Platt expresses it:

> The conflict and exclusion of alternatives that is necessary to sharp inductive inference has been all too often a conflict between men, each with his single Ruling Theory. But whenever each man begins to have multiple working hypotheses, it becomes purely a conflict between ideas. It becomes much easier then for each of us to aim every day at conclusive disproofs—at strong inference—without either reluctance or combativeness. In fact, when there are multiple hypotheses which are not anyone's "personal property" and when there are crucial experiments to test them, the daily life in the laboratory takes on an interest and excitement it never had, and the students can hardly wait to get to work to see how the detective story will come out. . . .
>
> When multiple hypotheses become coupled to strong inference, the scientific search becomes an emotional powerhouse as well as an intellectual one.[22]

We should point out that "strong inference" is a phrase Platt has coined for a method that consists of applying the following steps to every problem in science:

1. devising alternative hypotheses;

2. devising a crucial experiment (or several of them) with several possible outcomes, each of which will exclude one or more of the alternative hypotheses;

3. carrying out the experiment so as to get a clean result;

4. repeating the procedure and making subhypotheses or sequential hypotheses to refine the remaining possibilities.

As Platt indicates, in its separate elements strong inference is Bacon's method of inductive inference. At the same time, Platt has nicely underscored Chamberlin's multiple-hypotheses concept, thus providing a workable synthesis of the two methods.

Granted the wisdom of such a synthesis, we should still inquire into hypotheses. If we have multiple hypotheses, how do we weed them out? What counts for or against a hypothesis? That a hypothesis can be rendered false does not make it accurate, adequate, or complete. Sometimes "crucial" experiments cannot be developed. What, then, supports a hypothesis? To answer this, we must analyze hypotheses more closely.

20. *Quoted in John Platt. "Strong Inference," p. 350.*

21. *Quoted in John Platt. "Strong Inference," p. 350.*

22. *John Platt. "Strong Inference," p. 350. Reprinted by permission.*

Hypotheses

In general, a hypothesis is a working explanation for a phenomenon. For example, in answer to the question "Why is the universe expanding?" some scientists hypothesize that matter in the universe was originally in a state of extreme compaction and then exploded. Others hypothesize that matter is being created out of nothing in interstellar and intergalactic space. Like all hypotheses, these offer premises for additional investigation, and so they direct further research. When a hypothesis becomes well confirmed, it is often raised to the position of a theory. When a vast amount of evidence supports a theory, it is often termed a law. However, such terminology is not always used: Newton's discovery is still called the "law of gravitation," while Einstein's improvement on Newton's "law" is generally referred to as the "theory of relativity." Such distinctions often obscure more than they enlighten. The key point, however, is that the general assertions of science are considered hypotheses, not dogmas.

Hypotheses are, of course, instrumental in science, but they are vital in everyday living, too. To understand hypotheses a little better, let's meet Harry and Mildred Eagle.

Harry: Mildred, just out of curiosity, how important do you figure hair is?

Mildred: Well, just off the top of my head, Harry, I'd say hair is more important than toenails and less important than a world war.

Harry: You think it's a joke, don't you?

Mildred: Harry, we're eating.

Harry: So we're eating! Tell me something: What would you say is the most important thing in this society today?

Mildred: Let me guess. Hair?

Harry: Hair! You said it! Hair is in.

Mildred: Hair should be in. If it were out we'd all be bald. So eat.

Harry: Why'd you bring that up?

Mildred: Because the meatballs are getting cold.

Harry: I mean "bald." How come you mentioned that all of a sudden?

Mildred: It just popped up, that's all.

Harry: "Bald" doesn't just pop up. So why'd you bring it up? No, I'll tell *you* why. Because I'm losing my hair!

Mildred: You are not.

Harry: That's all right, Mildred, you don't have to lie to me. I can see it happening. You know, I don't even want to comb it anymore!

Mildred: Harry, you're exaggerating. Sure, you may have a high forehead——

Harry: High forehead? If my forehead were any higher, it'd be the back of my neck. No, there's no point in trying to kid ourselves. I'm losing my hair and that's that.

Mildred: Okay, let's eat.

Harry: So you admit I'm losing my hair.

Mildred: Harry, if you're losing your hair, you're losing your hair. That's that. *C'est la vie*, like the French say.

Harry: I don't care what the French say. And we're not eating until we figure out where my hair's going.

Mildred: Probably into the sauce.

Harry: Very funny! I mean *why*—why am I losing my hair?

Mildred: Look, if we can't eat before we figure out why you're losing your hair, we'll probably starve to death. Then think where you'd be: bald and dead.

Harry: Well, I say there's got to be a reason. A man like me, in the prime of life, full of all the vim and vigor of a kid half his age, I say a man like that just doesn't all of a sudden start shedding his golden locks.

Mildred: Nature, Harry. Blame it on Mother Nature.

Harry: Nature! That's a terrific reason. If they listened to you people would still be in caves.

Mildred: Well, if they were, you'd still have your hair.

Harry: What do you mean?

Mildred: Have you ever seen a bald caveman?

Harry has a point. If humans persisted in attributing everything to nature, we probably would still be in caves, if we still existed at all. But history teaches that we are problem-formulating and problem-solving creatures. Without problems there are no hypotheses. The problems can be very complex, as in the search for a cure for cancer, or more simple, as in the question of Harry Eagle's baldness. Having formulated a problem, we frequently develop a preliminary explanation and collect as many pertinent facts as possible. These facts may generate an additional hypothesis, which in turn directs further investigation and perhaps the formulation of still another hypothesis, and so on until the problem is solved. Occasionally, the preliminary hypothesis turns out to be the final explanation. But in most cases of problem solving many hypotheses arise, often simultaneously. How, then, do we recognize the best one? What makes a good hypothesis? How do we identify empty hypotheses? A good hypothesis is relevant, compatible, testable, predictive, and simple. Let us examine each of these descriptive qualities.

Relevance

Mildred: All right, Harry. When did you first notice you were losing your hair?

Harry: About seven months ago. Now doesn't that ring a bell?

Mildred: Seven months ago—that'd make it September. The only bell I remember in September was the Avon lady ringing.

Harry: That's when I changed my image!

Mildred: Oh, of course, the youth kick! You threw out your old baggy suits and bought all those new outfits. How could I forget? But you don't think you're losing your hair because you're wearing Levi's, do you?

Harry: Don't be ridiculous.

It would indeed be ridiculous to suggest that Levi's explain baldness. Any good hypothesis must be relevant; that is, it should explain the problem directly. Suppose someone was late for an appointment with you. "Why are you late?" you ask him when he finally arrives. "Because Caesar was assassinated on the ides of March," he replies. You would probably think he had lost his mind. On the other hand, suppose he replied "Because the president held a news conference." Although this explanation alone does not account for his lateness, it might explain it in combination with other relevant reasons. Perhaps he was watching the news conference on television and lost track of the time. Perhaps what the president said was so important that he had to wait for the conclusion. The point is that this latter explanation, although incomplete, is at least *relevant;* from it you can infer a possible explanation for his tardiness.

Relevance, then, hinges on whether the fact to be explained can be inferred from the hypothesis. Put another way, the fact to be explained must be deducible from the proposed hypothesis alone or in combination with certain highly probable suppositions.

Since any scientific hypothesis must be falsifiable, it is potentially irrelevant. That is, it offers deductions that are falsifiable. If just one of these is, in fact, falsified, then the hypothesis is no longer a credible explanation. An example will illustrate.

If you observe the skies at night, you will notice that the stars move gradually toward the west as the night progresses. If you watch night after night, you will notice that the same patterns of stars appear regularly, but not at the same place at the same time. Each night a given pattern appears at a given place in the sky about four minutes earlier than the previous night. If you observe very closely, you will also note that "peculiar stars" appear near the same place in relation to other stars on successive days but change their positions radically over a longer period of time. These are the planets. How do we explain these events?

Aristotle offered an early explanation. He suggested that the earth is a stationary sphere in the center of the universe. The heavenly bodies are on huge, clear spheres that circle the earth: The sun, the moon, and each planet have their own spheres that circle the earth, and beyond them is a single sphere containing all the fixed stars.

Was Aristotle's explanation relevant? Could the facts to be explained be inferred from it? Sure. From it we can infer why the same patterns generally exist among the stars: Most of them are spots on the same sphere. We can also infer why five stars (planets), the sun, and the moon do not remain in the same place among the other stars: Each follows its own circular orbit around the

"Without problems there are no hypotheses."

earth at its own rate, which is slightly slower than the rate of the stars' revolution.[23]

But when astronomers later tried to plot the paths of the planets more exactly so that they could determine the speed of the planets, problems arose. Observations indicated that none of the planets moved at a constant speed. Thus, Aristotle's explanation no longer fit the major facts. Put another way, what was deducible from the explanation didn't square with what was observable. Thus, the explanation was no longer relevant. This does not mean that it was junked. It needed reexamination and perhaps modification and amendment. And it got this reworking in later centuries.

The point is that any relevant explanation is potentially irrelevant, in the sense that it is falsifiable and thus might eventually fail to explain the problem under investigation. Furthermore, that an explanation is relevant does not mean it is a good one. Other criteria should be met.

Compatibility

Harry: Do you remember what else was part and parcel of the new me?

Mildred: Let me see. . . . Well, eating granola in bed was.

Harry: Right!

Mildred: You think eating in bed's causing you to lose your hair?

Harry: No, but granola is!

Mildred: Granola?

Harry: Twice a day I've been eating that stuff—morning and night, as regular as clockwork.

Mildred: But, Harry, that's as silly as saying your Levi's are affecting your hair. Granola wouldn't cause you to lose your hair. In fact, I'd think it would help you keep it.

23.   *See Garvin McCain and Erwin H. Segal.* The Game of Science, *p. 39.*

Harry: Well, it's awfully funny that as soon as I start eating that stuff my hair starts falling out.

Mildred: That's just a coincidence.

Harry: Some coincidence.

Mildred: Look, you started dieting and jogging and weight lifting as well, didn't you? Why don't you blame them?

Harry: What do they have to do with hair?

Mildred: Nothing, but becoming so worried about growing old before your time may have a lot to do with it. Harry, you're paranoid about growing old.

Mildred's explanation is certainly relevant. Moreover, it fits in with other hypotheses about hair loss, especially one that claims that nervousness can affect the condition of hair. When a hypothesis accords with a body of knowledge that is already accepted as true, it is said to be compatible with that information. Any hypothesis that is compatible with accepted knowledge is preferable to one that is not. For example, in his book *Chariots of the Gods?*, author Von Däniken's hypothesis—that signs of a developed culture in some "uncivilized" areas of earth can be attributed to the fact that "astronaut gods" visited this planet eons ago—hardly fits in with accepted thought on the matter. Likewise, author Immanuel Velikovsky's claim in *Worlds in Collision* that Biblical accounts of world calamities are actual reports of a collision between earth and a comet seems to contradict prevailing knowledge. These hypotheses are not therefore incorrect, but they are improbable. Some would say that they are not even improbable, since they fail even the most elementary scientific tests.

Nonscientists sometimes see the compatibility criterion as a strict appeal to the status quo, to traditional wisdom. Why should an explanation be evaluated on the basis of how it fits in with accepted thought, they ask, since the history of science glitters with examples of how inaccurate and incomplete accepted thought can be? These objections are understandable, and they deserve a reply.

In fact, compatibility is an altogether reasonable criterion when we remember that science, in trying to encompass additional facts, seeks to achieve a system of explanatory hypotheses. But such a system must be self-consistent. After all, how can a set of self-contradictory statements be true, let alone intelligible? Ideally, scientists hope to perfect such a system by expanding their hypotheses so that they account for more and more facts. But to make any progress, scientists must attempt to fit new hypotheses to hypotheses that have already been confirmed.

Nevertheless, many important new hypotheses were not compatible with existing accepted hypotheses. Consider, for example, the historical development of the explanation of astronomical phenomena that attracted Aristotle's interest. In the second century, Ptolemy modified Aristotle's position by claiming that the planets traveled in little circles (epicycles) on their orbits around the earth. By assuming that the centers of the orbits of the planets were not always the earth, Ptolemy could predict where the planets would be at any given time. Ptolemy's explanation held sway until modern times.

In the sixteenth century, Copernicus studied and plotted the paths of the planets but could not fit the planets' locations over time to the Ptolemaic system. To account for these disparities, Copernicus hypothesized that the sun, not the earth, was the center of the universe and that the earth went around the sun and spun on an axis, as did the other planets. Copernicus' hypothesis had great explanatory power, but it did not fit in with the accepted Ptolemaic concept, which had not only scientific but also religious approval. Nevertheless, Copernicus' insistence on the sun's centrality was justified, even though his entire explanation was not altogether satisfactory.

Many important new hypotheses are inconsistent with older explanations. Einstein's theory of relativity, for example, unmoored many Newtonian suppositions. Similarly, the phenomenon of radioactivity, first observed in the 1890s, led to the modification of many time-honored theories. One of these was the principle of the conservation of matter, which held that matter could be neither created nor destroyed. The hypothesis that radium atoms underwent spontaneous disintegration did not fit in with that principle, but the hypothesis was not dismissed. On the contrary, the principle was modified and became the more comprehensive principle of the conservation of mass-energy.

But even in these instances a compatibility criterion prevails. After all, each of these hypotheses could account for the same facts as well as or better than the older hypotheses could. Science does not develop capriciously. Any change in an accepted hypothesis represents an improvement by making an explanation more comprehensive. The criterion of compatibility is a vital part of this organic development. Thus, it is quite correct to say that if a hypothesis is consistent with established thought, its reliability is thereby strengthened.

Testability

Harry: You mean I'm going bald because I'm nervous?

Mildred: Yes, I think so. But there's only one way to find out.

Harry: You know what this means, Mildred.

Mildred: Sure, you're going to have to relax.

Harry: No, it means that I can still munch granola in bed!

In his relief, Harry ignores the test that Mildred suggests to establish the soundness of her hypothesis. If nervousness is the only reason for Harry's losing his hair, then he should stop losing it if he calms down. Like this one, any good hypothesis must be testable; it should permit observations that will confirm or disconfirm it. Unfortunately, not all hypotheses are directly testable. Darwin's theory of evolution, Einstein's theory of relativity, and the theory of a pulsating universe cannot be tested directly, but they can be tested *indirectly*. In other words, if these explanations are true, then other results should follow that we can observe and test.

For example, if Newton's inertia hypothesis—that a moving body will maintain its direction unless disturbed by an external force—is true, then it follows that when you fully apply the brakes to a car traveling forward at 50 miles per hour, the car should skid forward, the people in the car should be thrust forward, and a parked car struck by the skidding car should move. We can test these phenomena directly, and if they occur, the inertia hypothesis is strengthened.

Testability is the chief difference between scientific and unscientific explanations. There must be the possibility of making observations that would tend to confirm or disprove the explanation. Recall Bacon's and Platt's comments about exclusion and falsifiability. As we have seen, any scientific hypothesis leads to certain testable deductions. For example, consider the theory of evolution, which in part hypothesizes the gradual development of organisms from simple to increasingly complex forms. Scientists have long known that Cambrian formations (rock formations assumed to be 500 to 600 million years old) contain highly developed fossil forms. If evolution is a sound theory, then pre-Cambrian formations should contain simpler fossil forms. In 1947 fossil traces of simple forms were found in pre-Cambrian rock formations in Australia. Subsequent finds have further borne out the theory of evolution.

Suppose we have two hypotheses, both of which are relevant, compatible, and testable? On what basis do we choose one over the other? Frequently, the test in such cases is a *crucial experiment*, which is best discussed under the next criterion for a good hypothesis, predictability.

Predictability

A hypothesis that leads one to expect many observable phenomena is said to have predictive power; it is able to explain a great deal. Thus, Newton's law of gravitation allows for many deductive facts; it explains not only why apples fall from trees but also why tides move as they do, why great booster rockets are needed in order to put an object into space, why an astronaut in space had better hold onto his glass of milk, and why the universe may have begun with a "big bang." Similarly, the so-called gate-control theory of pain evidently accounts for the effectiveness of acupuncture as an analgesic, whereas the traditional specificity theory does not (see Philosophy and Life 8–1). What about Mildred's hypothesis? It helps explain how we can get dandruff and gray hair, as well as ulcers, migraine headaches, and a great many other nerve-related ailments. An explanation with even greater predictive power, however, would be that Harry inherited his baldness. Think of all the other phenomena that we can predict from the principle of genetic inheritance. And, of course, that hypothesis would be relevant, compatible, and testable as well. Sometimes two or more hypotheses appear equal in all respects: They are relevant, compatible with the body of accepted scientific theories, and testable. It may be possible to decide between them by deducing incompatible propositions and then setting up a crucial experiment designed to eliminate one or more of the hypotheses.

In book II of *The New Organon*, Bacon suggests a number of crucial experiments to discover the nature of things. For instance, is the weight of a body due to the body's own nature or to the attraction of the earth? To find out he proposes testing the rate of a pendulum clock. He suggests that the pendulum clock be placed at the top of a tall steeple and its rate observed to see whether it goes slower because of its diminished weight. He then suggests repeating the experiment at the bottom of a mine to see if the clock goes faster because of its increased weight. "If the virtue of the weights is found to be diminished on the steeple and increased in the mine, we may take the attraction of the mass of the earth as the cause of the weight."[24]

Again, consider the polarity of an iron needle that is touched by a magnet. "Either the touch of the magnet of itself invests the iron with polarity to the north and south; or it simply excites and prepares the iron, while the actual motion is communicated by the presence of the earth."[25] Bacon's experiment is to take a magnetic globe and mark its poles. Set the poles of the globe toward east and west, not north and south. Then place an untouched iron needle on top and keep it there for six or seven days. The needle, while over the magnet, will turn toward the poles of the magnet and point east and west. "Now if it be found that the needle, on being removed from the magnet and placed on a pivot either starts off at once to the north and south, or gradually turns in that direction, then the presence of the earth must be admitted as the cause; but if either points as before east and west, or loses its polarity, this cause must be regarded as questionable, and further inquiry must be made."[26]

Of course, such experiments are not always easy to carry out. Sometimes the required circumstances may be difficult or impossible to effect. For example, the choice between Newtonian theory and Einstein's general theory of relativity could not be made until a total eclipse of the sun occurred, which is beyond our power to produce. In other cases, we may just have to await the development of new instruments or technology. The history of astronomy is replete with examples of this kind. In still other cases, where hypotheses of a high level of generality are involved, no observable testable predictions can be deduced from just one of them. Instead, a whole group of hypotheses must be used as premises. If the observed facts contradict what the group predicts, then at least one of the hypotheses must be false, but determining which one is another matter.

Copernicus, for example, held that the earth was spherical, not flat. In his *On the Revolutions of the Heavenly Bodies*, he writes: "That the seas take a spheri-

---

24. *Francis Bacon. The New Organon, p. 197.*

25. *Francis Bacon. The New Organon, p. 197.*

26. *Francis Bacon. The New Organon, p. 198.*

cal form is perceived by navigators. For when land is still not discernible from a vessel's deck, it is from the masthead. And if, when a ship sails from land, a torch be fastened from the masthead, it appears to watchers on the land to go downward little by little until it entirely disappears, like a heavenly body setting."[27] In effect, Copernicus is suggesting a crucial experiment to decide between the two rival hypotheses. The experiment seems to prove the flat earth hypothesis false. But the experiment is not decisive, because it is possible to accept the observed facts and still maintain that the earth is flat because the testable prediction that Copernicus makes is not deducible from the rival hypothesis alone but from it together with the added hypothesis that light travels in a straight line. So, even if the earth is spherical, the decks will not necessarily disappear before the masthead unless light rays follow a rectilinear path.[28] The point is that an experiment can be crucial in showing that a given set of hypotheses is untenable. When this is the case, then further tests must be designed to determine which hypotheses of the set are wrong.

27. *Nikolaus Copernicus.* On the Revolutions of the Heavenly Bodies, *in* Masterworks of Science. *John Warren Knedler, Ed. Garden City, N.Y.: Doubleday, 1947.*

28. *See Irving Copi.* Introduction to Logic. *New York: Macmillan, 1972, pp. 449–452.*

PHILOSOPHY AND LIFE 8-1
Acupuncture—How It Works

There's little question that acupuncture works as an analgesic, or painkiller. This ancient Chinese practice of inserting needles into specific points on the human body and then twirling them or passing an electric current through them does stop pain. But how? The question mystifies Western medicine because the tissues stimulated are often far from where the person feels the pain or needs the surgery.

What puzzles us is the apparent inconsistency between the effectiveness of acupuncture as an analgesic and our traditional theory of pain. The traditional specificity theory contends that specific bodily pain receptors relay messages to the brain. Thus, people feel pain where the receptors are stimulated. What's more, a direct relationship exists between the amount of pain felt and the intensity of the stimulation: The more intense the stimulation, the greater the pain. But if this is correct, how does acupuncture work? After all, stimulating one part of the body shouldn't affect other areas. Are there neurological links between different body sites?

Some researchers believe there are. R. Melzack, for example, asserts that the specificity theory is incorrect. He proposes instead a gate-control theory, which argues against the fixed and immutable nature of the transmission of pain signals from points in the body to the brain. In Melzack's view this pro-

Simplicity

When rival hypotheses are in all other respects equal, scientists tend to accept the one that accounts for the facts and data most economically. To understand this, think about what scientists do. They try to take the data in a given area and invent a general principle or set of principles with which these data are compatible. They attempt to develop a framework within which they can approach events and data and understand them. Generally speaking, the greater the number and variety of events that an explanation accounts for, the better the explanation. In addition, science attempts to adopt the smallest set of hypotheses or principles that accounts for the greatest diversity of events. In other words, all things being equal, the simpler explanation is preferred.

For example, the Copernican theory of a sun-centered universe was accepted over Ptolemy's earth-centered explanation not on the basis of relevance, compatibility, testability, or predictability, but on the basis of simplicity. Copernicus' theory required only a fraction of the epicycles that Ptolemy's did.

This simplicity criterion is a commonsensical one. We use it all the time when deciding between equal rival hypotheses. Think how a jury often accepts the explanation that seems "more natural" and less complicated, that accounts for things more "elegantly" than rival explanations. As you might imagine,

cess is dynamic and capable of modulation. Specifically, he contends that a gatelike mechanism exists in the pain-signaling system. This gate may be open, partially open, or closed; thus, in some instances, signals from injured tissues may never reach the brain.

According to this theory, modulation of pain signals can occur in three ways. First, large fibers in the sensory nerves extending from the body surface to the central nervous system tend to close on stimulation, thus lowering the level of perceived pain. Second, areas in the brain stem can modulate pain signals. Thus, electric stimulation of portions of the brain system can relieve pain over a widespread area of the body. Third, the nervous system can modulate pain signals through fibers descending from the cortex.

☐ How is the gate-control theory consistent with the Western medical viewpoint? ☐ How is the gate-control theory more explanatory than the specificity theory? ☐ Does the gate-control proposition pass the other tests for a reliable hypothesis?

however, the concept of simplicity is extremely vague and can lead to error when used indiscriminately. But when other factors are equal, it does determine the more reliable explanation.

The Value of Philosophical Hypotheses

Since a hypothesis explains a phenomenon, any matter of speculation inevitably involves hypotheses. This is certainly true of philosophy. Consider the many hypotheses we have already encountered in our introduction to philosophy:

1. On views of human nature: The human is a rational, divine, mechanical, or existential being; the human has no self.

2. On the question of the nature of knowledge: We know only what we experience; we have some innate ideas; we can know nothing but our ideas; our minds impose an order on sense experience.

3. On the question of truth: Truth is a correspondence between what a statement says and how things actually are; truth is a coherence between a statement and other statements; truth is what works.

Philosophy is full of explanations. Unlike scientific theory, however, philosophical theory is not falsifiable. Science always moves from the conceptual to the testable. The primary criteria of evaluation for philosophical claims are congruence with human experience, plausibility, consensual validation, and perhaps successful problem resolution. Because philosophical theory is not scientific, some people are tempted to discard philosophy as a luxury or a waste of time. A couple of examples will show why this attitude is unfortunate and ultimately dangerous.

In ancient Greece, speculation abounded concerning ultimate reality. Water, air, fire, and earth formed the core of many hypotheses. One of these, Democritus' atomic theory, was poorly received, partially because of the general disenchantment with such speculations. Although numerous other factors led to the submergence of Democritus' theory, including his inability to prove it, it is likely that his idea suffered as much from the growing disenchantment with such cosmic speculation as from the inadequacies of the theory itself.

Consider also the thinking of the ancient Greek astronomer Aristarchus of Samos, whose calculations and speculations yield good estimates of a number of things, including the circumference of the earth, the size of the moon and sun, and the distance between the earth and the moon. Aristarchus believed that the earth and all the planets revolve around the sun. Elementary, we say. But the hypothesis was rejected for 2,000 years, partly on the authority of Aristotle. In the fifteenth century, Copernicus had the boldness to revive Aristarchus' hypothesis. Kepler later discovered that the planets move in ellipses, not circles, with the sun at a focus, not at the center. Subsequently, Newton discovered that the planets do not even move in exact ellipses. But the usefulness of Aristarchus' hypothesis was lost primarily because of a bias—in this case the classical bias toward aesthetics and ethics over science.

So we must be careful not to dismiss a hypothesis too quickly. The temptation today is great, for we are bombarded with hypotheses of every sort. The result is a kind of hypothesis overkill. We are rapidly reaching the point where we can no longer detect a good hypothesis. But we must remember, as one philosopher has noted, "that any hypothesis, however absurd, *may* be useful in science, if it enables a discoverer to conceive things in a new way."[29]

In a sense, we are all discoverers—discoverers of ourselves and the world. No exploration gives us more freedom of self-discovery than philosophy, for no exploration makes more extensive use of hypotheses.

Having discussed scientific method, we should now note some limitations to it. We have implied or stated several in our discussion, and we can infer others.

Limitations of Scientific Method

The first limitation of scientific method is that it grasps only as much as its tools allow. The more limited the technique is, the more speculative the theory. Thus, Galileo's law of falling bodies, although sound, could not be verified until 1654, when the air pump was invented. Then it could be shown that a feather and a stone actually do fall at the same speed.

Related to this is a second limitation: We can learn only what the tools are designed to show. For example, if you thought you had a fever, an accurate thermometer would confirm or disconfirm your belief. But no matter how accurate the thermometer, it would not tell you if you had pneumonia; other instruments must do this. Recall the first Russian cosmonaut, Yuri Gagarin. When he completed his suborbital flight of the earth, someone asked Gagarin if there was a God. Gagarin, an atheist, replied that he'd been up to the heavens and he hadn't seen any God. Facetious perhaps, but the instruments Gagarin brought to his mission were not designed to detect the presence of a God. The fact that our tools do not measure purpose, meaning, or freedom does not prove that these things do not exist. To dismiss such concerns, along with similar phenomena such as thought and emotion, is to argue from ignorance—to claim that something does not exist because its existence cannot be proved.

A third limitation concerns classification, a vital part of the scientific process. Classification ignores individual differences. True, scientific classification frequently accounts for differences under subcategories, but the rule of classification is to group by similar defining characteristics. Scientific laws gain validity only by ignoring some properties. Primary qualities provide context-free statements, that is, solid generalizations. Secondary qualities make the statements dependent upon both context and observer. Scientific statements about phenomena and the procedures for arriving at such statements must be as context free as possible. But individually, entities bear many more traits than those that determine the groupings or laws. To ignore these differences is to ignore part of reality.

29. *Bertrand Russell.* A History of Western Philosophy. *New York: Simon & Schuster, 1945, p. 131.*

A fourth limitation concerns science's ideological tendency not only to explain but to explain away. This creates the "nothing but" attitude of reductionism: Color is nothing but light waves; heat is nothing but molecular motion; internal feelings are nothing but brain states. This tendency to reduce the whole to its parts encourages overlooking characteristics of the whole that the parts alone may not possess. Taken by themselves, hydrogen and oxygen gases do not show the characteristics that they show when combined in the liquid state as water. Similarly, the heart, liver, and lungs taken alone do not show the characteristics of life that they show when functioning together. As **Gestalt** psychology argues and as high-energy physics recognizes, the whole is often greater than the sum of its parts (see Philosophy and Life 8–2). Missing this point, we might consider the parts more real than the unit. Philosophi-

---

PHILOSOPHY AND LIFE 8-2
Can We Know More Than We Can Tell?

How are you able to pick out a familiar face in a crowd? "There's so-and-so," you say, and if someone asked you how you *know*, you wouldn't reply, "Because I recognize the nose." In fact, you wouldn't specify anything in particular about so-and-so's face. You'd simply say, "I know so-and-so when I see her."

Gestalt psychology has demonstrated that you may recognize a familiar face by integrating your awareness of its particulars without being able to identify those particulars. Can we, then, know more than we can tell? Does all knowledge involve such a personal element?

In 1949, psychologists R. S. Lazarus and R. A. McCleary performed experiments that seem to indicate that people can know more than they can tell.* These researchers presented test subjects with a large number of nonsense syllables. After showing certain syllables, they administered an electric shock to the subjects. Soon the subjects began to show symptoms of anticipating the shock at the sight of the "shock syllables." But, curiously, on being questioned, the subjects couldn't identify the syllables. They seemed to know when to expect a shock without knowing why.

A variant of this phenomenon was demonstrated in 1956 by C. W. Eriksen and J. L. Kuethe.† Whenever their subjects happened to utter associations to prearranged "shock words," they were shocked. Subjects quickly learned to forestall shocks by not expressing such associations. But again, when questioned, the subjects did not seem to know that they were doing this. In effect,

* See R. S. Lazarus and R. A. McCleary. Journal of Personality, 1949, vol. 8, p. 191. Also Psychological Review, 1951, vol. 58, p. 113.
† See C. W. Eriksen and J. L. Kuethe. "Avoidance Conditioning of Verbal Behavior without Awareness: A Paradigm of Repression." Journal of Abnormal and Social Psychology, 1956, vol. 53, pp. 203–209.

cally, this attitude leaves us trying to defend positions such as "My experience of green is less real than the color green's wavelength" or "My experience of Beethoven's Fifth Symphony is less real than the sum of the measurement of the alternating condensations of air that compose it."

The fifth limitation follows from recognizing that neither science nor the scientific method occurs in a vacuum. No matter how refined the instruments, no matter how advanced the computer, some person still must make the observations, formulate the problem, collect the relevant data, establish a hypothesis, draw deductions from that hypothesis, and finally verify the deductions. And where there is a person, there is frequently a viewpoint and a bias that can color the investigations and findings—not necessarily invalidate them, but influence them.

the subjects had apparently mastered a practical operation but could not identify it.

In his *The Tacit Dimension** (New York: Doubleday, 1966), Michael Polanyi contends that such experiments clearly show what is meant by knowing more than one can tell. The implications of this proposition are intriguing. On the interpersonal level, it suggests that we need not know that we are transmitting messages about ourselves or how we do this in order to project messages. Perhaps more important, we may be able to read a variety of messages from the behavior of others but remain unable to say how we do this. What's more, if we can know without telling, then the ideal of objective, scientific knowledge may be a mistake. As Polanyi points out, if all knowledge essentially involves unavoidable personal elements, then the aim to establish a strictly detached, objective knowledge may, in fact, undermine all knowledge.

* *See Michael Polanyi.* The Tacit Dimension. *New York: Doubleday, 1966.*

□ *Would such research and theoretical constructs support or counter the claim that so-called women's intuition is a myth?* □ *What evidence justifies the proposition that our society is generally committed to the kind of knowledge that can be reported or told about?* □ *In what way would a scientist engaged in testing a hypothesis illustrate the personal dimension of knowledge?* □ *In other words, would the scientist in a sense already know more than he or she could tell?*

One reason for the element of human prejudice is that, no matter how objective the investigators try to be, they are limited by their own physical and intellectual capabilities. Another reason is that, while the investigators shape a hypothesis, they are at the same time shaped by it; for the hypothesis directs further research. A third reason is that the investigators function within a cultural milieu, which influences their perceptions. The fact that the individuals are engaged in such investigation is itself evidence of their Western cultural milieu; other traditions, such as the Eastern, put little store in science. Thus, the distinction between knower and known is not so sharp as John Locke would have it in distinguishing between knower-imposed secondary qualities of the object (color, taste, and smell) and known primary qualities (shape, size, and solidity). At the very least, scientific investigators would seem to assume some background data. Therefore, in evaluating research, we must find out the assumptions of the investigators.

Keeping in mind these limitations helps us put scientific knowledge in perspective. Specifically, it aids us in assessing our hypotheses about nature, which strongly influence how we view ourselves. In concluding this chapter, let's consider some of the more provocative of these hypotheses.

Some Hypotheses about Nature and the Universe

Matter

Take a look at any piece of matter. Suppose you were able to break it down into smaller and smaller pieces. What would you eventually find?

We know that all matter is made up of molecules. Molecules are specific in nature and arrangement for each substance. Since there are an incredible number of different materials, the number of kinds of molecules is staggeringly large. Every molecule is composed of atoms, and there are about 100 different kinds of atoms, ranging from the simplest and lightest, hydrogen, to the most complex—some of which have recently been synthesized. These atoms, in turn, are composed of what physicists call elementary particles. Three elementary particles make up all atoms, and thus all matter: electrons, protons, and neutrons.

In our age, a close study of these elementary particles has revealed that there are even more fundamental particles. These in turn are believed to consist of still more elementary particles, which physicists regard as energy.

In his autobiography, one of the leading figures in quantum physics, Werner Heisenberg, emphasizes that atoms are not things: "The electrons which form an atom's shells," he writes, "are no longer things in the sense of classical physics, things which could be unambiguously described by concepts like location, velocity, energy, size. When we get down to the atomic level, the objective world in space and time no longer exists, and the mathematical symbols of theoretical physics refer merely to possibilities, not to facts."[30]

---

30. *Quoted by Arthur Koestler.* The Roots of Coincidence. *New York: Random House, 1972, p. 51.*

". . . while the investigators shape a hypothesis, they are at the same time shaped by it . . ."

Heisenberg, of course, is best known for his principle of indeterminacy or uncertainty, which is relevant to this discussion. A good way to explain this principle is through Arthur Koestler's ingenious analogy in his *The Roots of Coincidence*. Koestler points out that a static quality that is characteristic of Renaissance painting is due to the fact that human figures and distant backgrounds are both in sharp focus, which is an optical impossibility. In studying the elementary constituents of matter, Heisenberg's principle tells us, physicists face a similar predicament. Classical physics teaches that a particle must have a definite location and velocity at any given time, but on the subatomic level, this fact simply does not hold. The more accurately physicists determine an electron's location, the more uncertain their calculation of its velocity. This is analogous to focusing on a close object and the background's consequently becoming blurred. Conversely, if an electron's velocity is determined, its location is less certain. The inherent indeterminacy of subatomic events is due to the ambiguous and elusive nature of subatomic "particles." Simply put, they are not particles or things at all. In Koestler's words: "They are Janus-faced entities which behave under certain circumstances like hard little pellets, under different circumstances, however, like waves or vibrations propagated in a medium devoid of any physical attributes. . . . They seem to be waves on Mondays, Wednesdays and Fridays, and particles on Tuesdays, Thursdays and Saturdays."[31]

Thus, in a real sense, you could conclude that matter is nonmaterial. The elemental particles of contemporary physics seem to be defined by the requirements of mathematical symmetry. Rather than thinking of them as real, we would be more correct to view them as expressions of mathematical constructions that we inevitably encounter when we try to break down matter into

31. *Arthur Koestler*. The Roots of Coincidence, *p. 52.*

its ultimate constituents. But, in the last analysis, isn't the mathematical pattern strictly a mental construct? If so, isn't matter ultimately more mental than physical?[32]

When we turn outward to the incomprehensibly large universe, the questions are no less philosophical.

The Universe

One of the things that scientists have been trying to explain for almost half a century is why the universe is "expanding." In 1929, using sensitive photographic equipment, Dr. Edwin Hubble observed billions of galaxies that were apparently moving away from the earth at constant speeds. The galaxies nearer to us have since been shown to be moving more slowly than the ones farther away. At the outer edge of space, galaxies appear to be moving at speeds approaching the speed of light (186,000 miles per second). In recent years a number of theories have been offered to explain what is occurring.

One of these is the "big bang" theory, which holds that gravity once held all matter in the universe together in a massive molten ball. Intense gravitational forces so condensed the ball that pressure and temperature built up to incredible levels. The matter finally collapsed on itself. In this implosion, the outermost layers of the molten ball fell inward until they reached a critical point. The molten ball then exploded—the big bang. Supposedly, the matter that we observe moving away from us is the condensed and clustered residue of that explosion that continues to travel outward. According to the big bang theory, this cosmic journey will continue until all energy is dissipated and there is no more heat or light—until the cosmos dies.

Astronomer Fred Hoyle of Cambridge University disagreed. He regarded the big bang theory as too simple and accidental. Instead, he suggested steady state theory, which states that matter in intergalactic space is constantly created out of nothing. Hoyle reasoned that even if only one hydrogen atom was being created every century, it was enough to displace existing matter. This process of displacement, said Hoyle, explains why the universe appears to be expanding. The obvious problem with this theory is how can matter be created out of nothing? This consideration, along with additional evidence, has persuaded Hoyle to abandon his theory.

Respecting the fate of the universe, the theory of the "pulsating cosmos" upholds the explosion feature of the big bang theory but insists that the gravitational force of the universe's mass is greater than the force of the explosion. As a result, the galaxies will eventually slow down and travel back to the scene of the explosion. Ultimately, they will again implode, explode, and travel outward. This process of cosmic pulsation is thought to be perpetual. Rather than being part of a dying universe, then, we are witnessing a dynamic, eternal process in which energy is built up, dissipated, and regenerated.

---

32. *For a full discussion of these and related issues, see Fritjof Capra.* The Tao of Physics. *New York: Bantam, 1977. See also R. G. H. Siu.* The Tao of Science.

How long does one cycle last? Scientists estimate 80 billion years. There is little reason to panic, for we still have 60 billion years to go.

These theories suggest all kinds of questions. If we accept the big bang, what is the origin of the matter? What is the origin of the cosmos? If the pulsating cosmos theory is accurate, could there be other pulsating universes? Is the completion of the cycle what various religions have called the "day of doom," "Armageddon," and "doom of the gods"? Will there be creatures billions of years hence observing precisely what we are observing today? Have similar civilizations preceded us?

But one of the most fascinating things about observing intergalactic space is that we are looking back into the past. When we look up into the heavens, we are literally looking into history. To understand this point better, we should at least glance at the concept of time.

Time

We constantly deal with time as if it were absolute. Clocks, watches, calendars, heartbeats—all kinds of devices impress on us that we can measure when an event occurs so accurately that it occurs for everyone everywhere at precisely the same time. This is not so.

It is impossible to understand this until we encounter incredibly fast speeds at great distances—that is, until we enter our cosmological reality. Imagine that someone on a fictitious planet in our galaxy—call it Alpha—wanted to communicate with us. He sent out a radio message that took eight years to reach earth. Ten years before the message was received by astronomer Jones, she married. To all observers everywhere, Jones married *before* the message was sent to earth. Also suppose that five minutes after she received the message, Jones recorded the event. Again, for all observers everywhere, Jones recorded the event *after* the message was beamed from Alpha.

But imagine that five years after the message was sent, astronomer Jones had a baby. Although it appears she had the baby after the message was sent from Alpha, Einstein's theory of relativity does not allow us to say this without qualification.

To see this, suppose that a traveler departed Alpha bound for earth at the time that the message was sent and that the traveler moved at a relatively slow speed by our standards. According to the traveler's measurements of time, Jones appeared to have the baby *after* the message was transmitted. On the other hand, suppose another traveler departed Alpha when the message was sent but at a speed approaching the speed of light. Instead of taking the long time that the first traveler took to complete the journey, the second traveler completed the trip in a little more than eight years, according to our calculations. But because of the speed at which he traveled, it seemed to him that he completed the trip in just a few months. When he was told that Jones had a baby three years before he arrived, he naturally concluded that the baby was born well before the message was sent, since by his calculations the message was sent only a few months before.

This illustration makes us wonder about the nature of time. Philosophers, psychologists, and scientists are divided on the question of whether time really exists or whether it is simply experience. Many philosophers and psychologists regard time as being dependent on consciousness: Without consciousness there can be no time, since there can be no experience of it. But if this is so, was there no time before consciousness? Many physicists claim that time is real. Einstein did. Our timepieces, they say, measure not only conscious experience but time itself.

Relativity also leaves us wondering whether it is possible to move ahead in time. It is commonly thought that we move into the future at a constant speed that we cannot control. But what if we accelerate to speeds approaching the speed of light? Can we not, in theory, move millions of years ahead in time? This question provokes further speculations about space and about the size of the universe. How far does space extend? Or we might question whether such ponderings are distinctly Newtonian. After all, the very theory that seems to invite them seems to forbid speaking of speed in a vacuum and of time in the abstract. Perhaps, then, such questions miss the thrust of Einstein's theory of relativity, namely, that there can in principle be neither an absolute point of reference in space nor any absolute clock to measure time irrespective of motion. Can we therefore speak intelligently about speeds approaching the speed of light or about millions of years ahead in time without specifying a frame of reference?

It does seem justifiable, however, to ponder whether life exists in space. Astronomer Harlow Shapley says "We are not alone in the universe." He claims that there are "a hundred million planetary systems suitable for organic life," which he considers a modest estimate.

Finally, we must also wonder whether something can exist outside time and, if so, whether we can be aware of it. Since apparently either we live within a time frame or a time frame "lives" within us, it seems that we can never have knowledge of what exists outside one of our essential dimensions. But, of course, we cannot be sure.

Summary and Conclusions

We began by noting science's influence in our lives and the connection between it and philosophy. We then highlighted what science is and what it is not. The heart of science is induction and inductive inference. Inductive inference can be traced to Francis Bacon in his book *The New Organon*. Some think that T. C. Chamberlin's method of multiple working hypotheses is necessary to flesh out Bacon's method. Instrumental to inductive inference is falsifiability. A scientific hypothesis must be falsifiable. It also must satisfy certain conditions to be considered worthwhile. Finally, we saw the value of hypotheses in philosophy and mentioned some scientific hypotheses about nature and the universe that have vast philosophical implications.

Our focus has been on science and scientific methodology. But theoretical science raises a number of philosophical issues that directly bear on self. For example, what kind of universe do we inhabit? Is it orderly or capricious? Scientific evidence suggests that it is orderly. We seek to discover the nature of this order and our own place in it. Even more important, if the universe is orderly, we are more likely to see order in our own lives. Are the world and its inhabitants mechanistic or teleological (teleology is the claim that purpose, goal, or direction is part of the necessary nature of things)?

The twentieth century is witnessing the collapse of the Newtonian world view. More and more scientists view the universe as something unfixed and changing, as an evolutionary process. This outlook suggests that the individual may play an active, purposeful role in shaping and directing things. In brief, we are not bound by immutable mechanical laws to the degree that we once thought. We are parts not of a fixed and stationary universe but of one in which novelty, creativity, and purpose play parts.

Other considerations pertaining to self arise. Previously, in discussing matter, scientists generally made the Lockean distinction between primary and secondary qualities. The primary qualities, like extension, solidity, and motion, were thought to be objective. The secondary qualities, like color, taste, and sound, were thought to be subjective. In other words, primary qualities existed in things themselves; secondary qualities existed in the minds of those who perceived and experienced them. This was the nature of physical things.

Today the distinction between primary and secondary is less clear. Instead, scientists talk about energy or force, which they do not consider to be matter at all. They do not deny the existence of matter or its properties, but they provide a fresh perspective for us to view our place in the world. The distinctions between knower and known, subject and object, self and other are no longer satisfactory. Rather than a division, there seems to be a harmony, a complementary relationship, among all things, including people.

At the same time, perhaps never before has the role of the self as knower been more uncertain. In the past, the self was thought to know the world as it was. Now, because of the influence of relativity, we wonder if the self alters what it observes—if the standpoint of the observer affects the object of observation. We have always known that our minds interpret the world. Now we wonder if they play a role in creating it.

Finally, although we take up the question of values elsewhere, we should not ignore here the moral implications of the present technological capabilities of applied science. For example, genetic engineering—the application of scientific principles to the design, construction, and operation of efficient human systems—has become a problem of science (see Philosophy and Life 8–3). Equally real is the capacity to produce a clone, a group of genetically identical cells descended asexually from a common ancestor. These capabilities, as well as psychological behaviorism, organ transplants, subliminal language, and so on, raise questions of values. So do the major problems that will confront us in the next twenty-five years: burgeoning populations, depletion of natural resources, maldistribution of goods, and threats of nuclear war. Although we shall apply scientific knowledge to many of these problems, we should not forget the tendency of scientists to focus exclusively on quantitative, mathematical, and objective elements at the expense of the human element. As the problems worsen, this tendency will be accentuated. Consequently, the next quarter century will probably see conflict between what we would like to do and what we must do, between our ideals and our obligations, between humanism and technocracy.

By **humanism** we mean the philosophical view that accepts humans as the primary source of meaning and value. A technocracy is a political and social system controlled by scientific technicians. Generally, technocracies put things before people. Much of our society is, perhaps necessarily, technocratic. But the question is, Must we and are we prepared to abandon all humanistic values in favor of technocratic values? By keeping questions like these open, philosophy ensures that science does not overlook the human's place in the scheme of things, whatever that place may be.

Section Exercises

Science: What It Is and What It Is Not

1. Are the following scientific statements? Why or why not?

   a. The spirochete causes syphilis.

   b. My car either is or is not a Chevy.

   c. God exists.

PHILOSOPHY AND LIFE 8-3
Genetic Engineering

Few today would question that our growing understanding of gene structure as a function, as well as the laboratory creation, of the genetic material DNA is rapidly introducing a biological revolution. In particular, scientists seem to be moving toward the manipulation of the hereditary process, or what is termed *genetic engineering*. Such a procedure raises important philosophical questions about values, human nature, and the relationship between the individual and society.

One kind of genetic engineering research aims at improving the genetic composition of humans. Consider the following techniques involved in such research:

Artificial insemination—the implanting of sperm cells into a female at ovulation. Several thousand babies a year for the past decade or so have been produced this way. What's more, sperm cells can be frozen and used later. Sperm frozen for as long as two years has produced full-term, normal births.

Artificial inovulation—the fertilization of an egg with a selected donor sperm, then implanting the fertilized egg in the womb of another woman to be carried to term.

d. We are all going to die someday.

e. Shakespeare wrote *Hamlet*.

f. There will be an earthquake sometime in the future.

g. There will be an earthquake in southern California in the next year.

h. Every effect has a cause.

i. Order exists in the universe.

j. There is life after death.

Induction and Inductive Inference

1. Specify the inductive procedures evident in the following cases:

    a. "A few years ago a small number of people living in various sections of the United States were infected with an identical disease. At about the same time the eyes of these people developed what the physician calls cataracts—small, irregular, opaque spots in the tissue of the lens. Cataracts interfere with the clear passage of light through the transparent medium of the eye lens. In severe cases they may block vision. . . . It turned out that all the individuals who developed these cataracts were physicists and that all of them had been connected with

Cloning—the process of asexual reproduction, that is, reproduction without an ovum and sperm. In human cloning, offspring would be produced from cells of human tissue that would be cultured in a test tube until reaching embryonic development. It would then be implanted in the womb of a woman to be carried to term. One fascinating aspect of cloning is that the genetic makeup of the offspring would be identical with that of the donor of the original tissue. Perhaps in another quarter century, cloning, heretofore confined to carrots and frogs, might be applied to human beings.

☐ *Do you think that any controls should be placed on genetic engineering research and experimentation?* ☐ *What is the human status of clones?* ☐ *In artificial ovulation, who is the mother, the donor or the carrier?* ☐ *Should society be allowed to decide whose sperm and ova should be frozen?*

nuclear-energy projects during the war. While they worked with cyclotrons in atomic-energy laboratories they had been the targets of stray neutron rays. They were under medical supervision all during their work, but the density of the neutrons was thought to be entirely harmless.

This case is one of the best examples of the insidiousness of nuclear radiation."[33]

b.   "We have recently obtained conclusive experimental evidence that there can be no tooth decay without bacteria and a food supply for them. In germ-free laboratories at the University of Notre Dame and the University of Chicago, animals innocent of oral micro-organisms do not develop cavities. Where animals in normal circumstances average more than four cavities each, the germ-free rats show no signs of caries. At the Harvard School of Dental Medicine we have demonstrated the other side of the coin: the food debris also must be present. Rats that have plenty of bacteria in their mouths but are fed by the tube directly to the stomach do not develop cavities. In a pair of rats joined by surgery so that they share a common blood circulation, the one fed by mouth develops tooth decay, the one fed by tube does not."[34]

c.   "In 1821, Bouvard of Paris published tables of the motions of a number of planets, including Uranus. In preparing the latter he had found great difficulty in making an orbit calculated on the basis of positions obtained in the years after 1800 agree with one calculated from observations taken in the years immediately following discovery. He finally disregarded the older observations entirely and based his tables on the newer observations. In a few years, however, the positions calculated from the tables disagreed with the observed positions of the planet and by 1844 the discrepancy amounted to 2 minutes of arc. Since all the other known planets agreed in their motions with those calculated for them, the discrepancy in the case of Uranus aroused much discussion.

In 1845, Leverrier, then a young man, attacked the problem. He checked Bouvard's calculations and found them essentially correct. Thereupon he felt that the only satisfactory explanation of the trouble lay in the presence of a planet somewhere beyond Uranus which was disturbing its motion. By the middle of 1846 he had finished his calculations. In September he wrote to Galle at Berlin and requested the latter to look for a new planet in a certain region of the sky for which some new star charts had just been prepared in Germany but of which Leverrier apparently had not as yet obtained copies. On the twenty-third of September Galle started the search and in less than an

33.   *Heinz Haber.* Man in Space. *Indianapolis: Bobbs-Merrill, 1953. Reprinted by permission of The Bobbs-Merrill Company, Inc.*

34.   *Reidar F. Sognnaes. "Tooth Decay."* Scientific American, *December 1957, pp. 112, 114. Reprinted by permission.*

hour he found an object which was not on the chart. By the next night it had moved appreciably and the new planet, subsequently named Neptune, was discovered within 1° of the predicted place. This discovery ranks among the greatest achievements of mathematical astronomy."[35]

2. Use Bacon's inductive procedures to show how you would go about resolving the following problems:

   a. Eight students ate lunch in the college cafeteria. Within an hour each showed signs of food poisoning. What caused the food poisoning?

   b. In an intensive care unit at a local hospital, fifteen out of twenty patients died during a thirty-day period. Nurse Nightingale attended all fifteen. There is widespread suspicion that Nurse Nightingale was somehow responsible for the deaths. Was she?

Hypotheses

1. In terms of the criteria for a good hypothesis, which of the following are probable explanations for the Watergate affair? Is any one more probable than the others?

   a. a media vendetta against the president

   b. campaign funding

   c. moral weakness

   d. Vietnam war dissent

   e. increasing executive power

2. In terms of the criteria for a good hypothesis, which of the following are probable explanations for the increase in crimes of violence? Is any one more probable than the others?

   a. increasing unemployment

   b. maldistribution of wealth

   c. the U.S. Supreme Court's "soft decisions"

   d. overpopulation

3. In terms of the criteria for a good hypothesis, which of the following are probable explanations for the origin of human knowledge?

   a. the senses alone

   b. reason alone

   c. reason imposing order on sense data

   d. a consciousness of which we are not fully aware

---

35. *Edward Arthur Fath.* The Elements of Astronomy. *New York: McGraw-Hill, 1955. Quoted in Irving Copi.* Introduction to Logic, *p. 389. Reprinted by permission.*

4. In terms of the criteria for a good hypothesis, which of the following are the probable constituents of reality?

   a. matter

   b. nonmatter

   c. being

   d. There is no single constituent.

5. In terms of the criteria for a good hypothesis, which of the following best describes self?

   a. rational

   b. divine

   c. mechanical

   d. existential

   e. nonexistent

Some Hypotheses about Nature and the Universe

(The following are intended to require some research.)

1. If the universe is positively curved, will the universe ultimately stop expanding and start to contract?

2. The shifting wavelength of a star's light as it moves toward or away from the earth is called the Doppler effect. How has the Doppler effect been used as the prime visual argument for an expanding universe?

3. Why, according to relativity, can the universe not remain static?

4. In a given time, every galaxy increases its distance from every other by the same percentage. What view would this give an earthling or an inhabitant of another planet of its planet's position in the expansion of the universe?

5. In what sense can the universe be finite but unbounded?

Zen and the Art of Motorcycle Maintenance

Robert M. Pirsig

Few recent books have portrayed one person's search for truth more explosively than Robert M. Pirsig's Zen and the Art of Motorcycle Maintenance. *In a word, the book is an inquiry into human values. The story of a father and son on the road,* Zen and the Art of Motorcycle Maintenance *is a profound journey toward understanding the world and one's place in it. In the selection below, the narrator describes the moment when Phaedrus,[36] his alter ego, realizes the invalidity of all scientific method—realizes that certain knowledge cannot be obtained. This occurs after*

36. *Phaedrus is the title of one of Plato's many dialogues. The title, which is Greek for "wolf," refers to the young orator who is a foil for Socrates in the dialogue.*

Phaedrus has thought long and hard about the nature of hypotheses. The impact of this discovery, the "long series of lateral drifts that led him into a far orbit of the mind," becomes the intellectual and dramatic backdrop against which this odyssey of self-discovery unravels.

The formation of hypotheses is the most mysterious of all the categories of scientific method. Where they come from, no one knows. A person is sitting somewhere, minding his own business, and suddenly—flash!—he understands something he didn't understand before. Until it's tested the hypothesis isn't truth. For the tests aren't its source. Its source is somewhere else.

Einstein had said:

> Man tries to make for himself in the fashion that suits him best a simplified and intelligible picture of the world. He then tries to some extent to substitute this cosmos of his for the world of experience, and thus to overcome it. . . . He makes this cosmos and its construction the pivot of his emotional life in order to find in this way the peace and serenity which he cannot find in the narrow whirlpool of personal experience. . . . The supreme task . . . is to arrive at those universal elementary laws from which the cosmos can be built up by pure deduction. There is no logical path to these laws; only intuition, resting on sympathetic understanding of experience, can reach them. . . .

Intuition? Sympathy? Strange words for the origin of scientific knowledge.

A lesser scientist than Einstein might have said, "But scientific knowledge comes from *nature*. *Nature* provides the hypotheses." But Einstein understood that nature does not. Nature provides only experimental data.

A lesser mind might then have said, "Well then, *man* provides the hypotheses." But Einstein denied this too. "Nobody," he said, "who has really gone into the matter will deny that in practice the world of phenomena uniquely determines the theoretical system, in spite of the fact that there is no theoretical bridge between phenomena and their theoretical principles."

Phaedrus' break occurred when, as a result of laboratory experience, he became interested in hypotheses as entities in themselves. He had noticed again and again in his lab work that what might seem to be the hardest part of scientific work, thinking up the hypotheses, was invariably the easiest. The act of formally writing everything down precisely and clearly seemed to suggest them. As he was testing hypothesis number one by experimental method a flood of other hypotheses would come to mind, and as he was testing these, some more came to mind, and as he was testing these, still more came to mind until it became painfully evident that as he continued testing hypotheses and eliminating them or confirming them their number did not decrease. It actually *increased* as he went along.

At first he found it amusing. He coined a law intended to have the humor of a Parkinson's law that "The number of rational hypotheses that can explain any given phenomenon is infinite." It pleased him never to run out of hypotheses. Even when his experimental work seemed dead-end in every conceivable way, he knew that if he just sat down and muddled about it long enough, sure enough, another hypothesis would come along. And it always did. It was only months after he had coined the law that he began to have some doubts about the humor or benefits of it.

If true, that law is not a minor flaw in scientific reasoning. The law is completely nihilistic. It is a catastrophic logical disproof of the general validity of all scientific method!

If the purpose of scientific method is to select from among a multitude of hypotheses, and if the number of hypotheses grows faster than experimental method can handle, then it is clear that all hypotheses can never be tested. If all hypotheses cannot be tested, then the results of any experiment are inconclusive and the entire scientific method falls short of its goal of establishing proven knowledge.

About this Einstein had said, "Evolution has shown that at any given moment out of all conceivable constructions a single one has always proved itself absolutely superior to the rest," and let it go at that. But to Phaedrus that was an incredibly weak answer. The phrase "at any given

From Zen and the Art of Motorcycle Maintenance *by Robert M. Pirsig. Copyright © 1974 by Robert M. Pirsig. Reprinted by permission of William Morrow & Company.*

moment" really shook him. Did Einstein really mean to state that truth was a function of time? To state *that* would annihilate the most basic presumption of all science!

But there it was, the whole history of science, a clear story of continuously new and changing explanations of old facts. The time spans of permanence seemed completely random, he could see no order in them. Some scientific truths seemed to last for centuries, others for less than a year. Scientific truth was not dogma, good for eternity, but a temporal quantitative entity that could be studied like anything else.

He studied scientific truths, then became upset even more by the apparent cause of their temporal condition. It looked as though the time spans of scientific truths are an inverse function of the intensity of scientific effort. Thus the scientific truths of the twentieth century seem to have a much shorter life-span than those of the last century because scientific activity is now much greater. If, in the next century, scientific activity increases tenfold, then the life expectancy of any scientific truth can be expected to drop to perhaps one-tenth as long as now. What shortens the life-span of the existing truth is the volume of hypotheses offered to replace it; the more the hypotheses, the shorter the time span of the truth. And what seems to be causing the number of hypotheses to grow in recent decades seems to be nothing other than scientific method itself. The more you look, the more you see. Instead of selecting one truth from a multitude you are *increasing the multitude*. What this means logically is that as you try to move toward unchanging truth through the application of scientific method, you actually do not move toward it at all. You move *away* from it! It is your application of scientific method that is causing it to change!

What Phaedrus observed on a personal level was a phenomenon, profoundly characteristic of the history of science, which has been swept under the carpet for years. The predicted results of scientific enquiry and the actual results of scientific enquiry are diametrically opposed here, and no one seems to pay too much attention to the fact. The purpose of scientific method is to select a single truth from among many hypothetical truths. That, more than anything else, is what science is all about. But historically science has done exactly the opposite. Through multiplication

upon multiplication of facts, information, theories and hypotheses, it is science itself that is leading mankind from single absolute truths to multiple, indeterminate, relative ones. The major producer of the social chaos, the indeterminacy of thought and values that rational knowledge is supposed to eliminate, is none other than science itself. And what Phaedrus saw in the isolation of his own laboratory work years ago is now seen everywhere in the technological world today. Scientifically produced antiscience—chaos.

It's possible now to look back a little and see why it's important to talk about this person in relation to everything that's been said before concerning the division between classic and romantic realities and the irreconcilability of the two. Unlike the multitude of romantics who are disturbed about the chaotic changes science and technology force upon the human spirit, Phaedrus, with his scientifically trained classic mind, was able to do more than just wring his hands with dismay, or run away, or condemn the whole situation broadside without offering any solutions.

As I've said, he did in the end offer a number of solutions, but the problem was so deep and so formidable and complex that no one really understood the gravity of what he was resolving, and so failed to understand or misunderstood what he said.

The cause of our current social crises, he would have said, is a genetic defect within the nature of reason itself. And until this genetic defect is cleared, the crises will continue. Our current modes of rationality are not moving society forward into a better world. They are taking it further and further from that better world. Since the Renaissance these modes have worked. As long as the need for food, clothing and shelter is dominant they will continue to work. But now that for huge masses of people these needs no longer overwhelm everything else, the whole structure of reason, handed down to us from ancient times, is no longer adequate. It begins to be seen for what it really is—emotionally hollow, esthetically meaningless and spiritually empty. That, today, is where it is at, and will continue to be at for a long time to come.

I've a vision of an angry continuing social crisis that no one really understands the depth of, let alone has solutions to. I see people like John and Sylvia [the couple whom the narrator is traveling with] living lost and alienated from the whole rational structure of civilized life, looking for solutions outside that structure, but finding none that are really satisfactory for long. And then I've a vision of Phaedrus and his lone isolated abstractions in the laboratory—actually concerned with the same crisis but starting from another point, moving in the opposite direction—and what I'm trying to do here is put it all together. It's so big—that's why I seem to wander sometimes.

No one that Phaedrus talked to seemed really concerned about this phenomenon that so baffled him. They seemed to say, "We know scientific method is valid, so why ask about it?"

Phaedrus didn't understand this attitude, didn't know what to do about it, and because he wasn't a student of science for personal or utilitarian reasons, it just stopped him completely. It was as if he were contemplating that serene mountain landscape Einstein had described, and suddenly between the mountains had appeared a fissure, a gap of pure nothing. And slowly, and agonizingly, to explain this gap, he had to admit that the mountains, which had seemed built for eternity, might possibly be something else . . . perhaps just figments of his own imagination. It stopped him.

Questions for Analysis

1. What's the fundamental difference between saying that scientific knowledge comes from nature and saying that nature only provides experimental data?

2. "The number of rational hypotheses that can explain any given phenomenon is infinite." Why does Phaedrus consider such a proposition nihilistic?

3. What "most basic presumption of all science" is undermined by the claim that truth is a function of time?

4. In what way, according to Phaedrus, are the predicted results of scientific inquiry and the actual results of scientific inquiry "diametrically opposed"?

5. What does Phaedrus mean by "a genetic defect within the nature of reason itself"?

Paperbacks for Further Reading

Anthony, Piers. *Macroscope*. New York: Avon, 1975. Suppose you could pass through a doorway that led beyond space and time. What would you find? That is the subject of this science fiction fantasy.

Barnett, Lincoln. *The Universe and Dr. Einstein*. New York: New American Library (Mentor Books), 1957. This is a popular, valid sketch of philosophical concepts thrust upon us by twentieth-century science and a readable, informative account of Einstein's theory of relativity and his views of God, religion, and mysticism.

Benacerraf, P. and H. Putnam, Eds. *Philosophy of Mathematics*. Englewood Cliffs, N.J.: Prentice-Hall, 1964. This work is a comprehensive anthology on the foundations of mathematics.

Bronowski, Jacob. *Science and Human Values*. New York: Harper & Row, 1956. Bronowski contends that both science and art spring from human imagination, and that science cannot be divorced from its social and ethical implications.

Ellwood, Garcia Fay. *Psychic Visits to the Past*. New York: Signet, 1971. An investigation into the world of psychics who claim that they have moved back and forth in time.

Gardner, Martin. *Relativity for the Million*. New York: Pocket Books, 1965. This is a lucid and entertaining account of twentieth-century science and its philosophical implications, full of fine examples and illustrations.

Kuhn, Thomas. *The Structure of Scientific Revolutions*. Chicago: University of Chicago Press, 1962. Not only does Kuhn clearly portray the nature of scientific changes and upheavals, but he also places them within a social framework that makes for a readable and appealing work. A nice companion piece to this book is Arthur Koestler's *The Sleepwalkers* (New York: Grosset & Dunlap, 1963), in which the author traces the history of cosmology from the ancient Babylonians through the modern age.

Rosenfeld, Albert. *The Second Genesis*. New York: Vintage, 1975. Rosenfeld gives a detailed account of the implications of current brain research. Although some of his forecasts are optimistic, others are chilling in their promise to alter the human and the human condition.

Toulmin, Stephen. *Foresight and Understanding: An Enquiry into the Aims of Science*. New York: Harper & Row, 1963. This book offers a philosophically directed investigation into the nature of science. In a concise and uncomplicated way, philosopher-scientist Toulmin argues that the goal of science is not only to predict but also to make intelligible.

Whitehead, Alfred North. *Science and the Modern World*. New York: New American Library (Mentor Books), 1948. This account of the historical development and impact of science and mathematics includes discussions on the nature of God and the relationship between science and religion. This work is challenging but well worth the effort.

Part IV

METAPHYSICS

The term metaphysics *has a curious origin. It arises with Aristotle, who wrote a series of essays on fundamental problems about the classifications or categories of being. He called his discussions* First Philosophy, *because they were about the basics. Later philosophers noticed that these essays came after Aristotle's book on physics. They came to be called in Greek* ta meta ta physika biblia, *that is, "the books that come after the physics." Subsequently, this was shortened to* The Metaphysics, *and the topics dealt with in these essays were called "metaphysics." Understandably, metaphysics came to be associated with subjects that transcend physics—the supernatural, the occult, and the mysterious.**

Actually, metaphysics does not refer exclusively to a single field or discipline. It encompasses a number of problems whose implications are so broad that they affect just about every other field of philosophy. Specifically, metaphysics is an inquiry into the first principles of being, that is, the attempt to discover the most pervasive characteristics that underlie all our knowledge of, and reasoning about, existence.† In philosophy metaphysics also refers to subjects that are nonempirical and nonscientific.

A number of problems traditionally fall under metaphysics. Among them are: the structure and development of the universe viewed in its totality; the meaning and nature of being; the nature of mind, self, and consciousness; the nature of religion, including the existence of God, the destiny of the universe, and the immortality of the soul. The next two chapters, entitled "Reality and Being" and "Philosophy and Religion," engage a number of these issues.

Chapter 9, "Reality and Being," is quite long, and its issues are necessarily complex. Rather than tackling the entire chapter at once, read it in sections, digesting the contents as you proceed.

* *Robert Paul Wolff.* About Philosophy. *New York: Prentice-Hall, 1976, p. 262.*
† *See Eugene A. Troxell and William S. Snyder.* Making Sense of Things: An Invitation to Philosophy. *New York: St. Martin's Press, 1976, pp. 171–172.*

REALITY AND BEING

The true lover of knowledge is always striving after being. . . . *He will not rest at those multitudinous phenomena whose existence is appearance only.*
—Plato

From the earliest times philosophers have wondered about the nature of reality. Is it matter? Nonmatter? A combination? Actually, an inquiry into the nature of reality is a good way to throw light on the issue of self-identity. Since we inevitably view ourselves as unique in the scheme of reality, any description of reality is bound to reflect our view of human nature and, by implication, of the self. To understand this point, consider the following hypothetical situation.

You have fallen in love with a wonderful person. For the first time in your life you are giving serious thought to marriage. You express your happiness and your plans to a very close professor friend at college. The professor couldn't be happier for you. Naturally, he asks if it is anyone he knows. You doubt it, but you mention the name. Upon hearing the name, the professor gives a remarkably accurate description of your friend, even down to a birthmark on the inner right arm. You are astonished. Because you are sure the professor has never met your friend, you ask him how he did that.

"Because I manufactured your friend," says the professor. Manufactured! The professor insists that he's not fooling, that he's been doing it for years, that a number of his creations are around, living happy, constructive lives. In fact, one of his own is a very important person. Before you catch yourself, your mind rifles through a list of important people—Jimmy Carter, Gloria Steinem, Reggie Jackson, Chris Evert—could one of these be the professor's creation? Absurd!

"Sure, sure," you tell him, "but you didn't leave any loose wires dangling out anywhere, did you?"

Not only did he not, but he also assures you that you will never be able to detect the slightest difference between your beloved and what we commonly call a human.

"You mean it isn't immortal?" you ask the professor.

"Of course not," he says. "As far as we know, all humans are mortal. So this creation is, too. It will age and be subject to the same physical laws that govern all organic life."

"What about having children?" you want to know.

He assures you that it is capable of reproducing. It functions sexually like any normal human. It will satisfy all your needs—physical, emotional, and intellectual—and all your desires. His creation will be, in brief, the ideal mate.

Farfetched? Probably. A mechanical creation that is identical with a human is still the product more of fiction than of science. But unleash your imagination for a minute. What if the professor took you into his basement lab and demonstrated his craft before your disbelieving eyes? What if he showed you his creations and convinced you beyond a doubt that not only could he do what he claimed but that he was doing it, and that your intended mate was one of his products? Would you still marry that individual?

In answering this question, you will probably reveal what you see as ultimately real—as the essence of all being, including yourself. In philosophy, the critical study of the nature of reality is called **metaphysics,** one of whose subdivisions is **ontology,** which is the theory of the nature of being and existence. Here we shall use the case of the android to launch metaphysical inquiries. Perhaps we can never say what reality ultimately is; perhaps the question and any subsequent theories are meaningless. In this chapter we will investigate these issues to see what light they can throw on the question of what we are. Here are the main points we will make.

Main Points

1. Metaphysics is the branch of philosophy that studies reality and being.

2. Ontology, a subdivision of metaphysics, is the study of being and existence.

3. Materialism is the position that reality is ultimately matter.

4. Idealism is the position that reality is ultimately nonmatter: idea, mind, spirit, or law, for example.

5. Pragmatism rejects all absolutistic assumptions about reality. It seems committed to scientific method and empirical inquiry, while admitting the pluralistic nature of reality.

6. The concept of being plays an important part in existentialism and phenomenology. Both philosophies are founded on disillusionment with past philosophies and on a preoccupation with the individual.

7. Husserlian phenomenology emphasizes consciousness as the ultimate reality. Heidegger's phenomenology stresses being. What is ultimately real for the phenomenologist is pure consciousness, which itself has being.

8. Like phenomenology, Buddhism eschews the distinction between knower and known, between subject and object. We are one with our experiences. But Buddhism considers the question of personal freedom irrelevant.

9. Existentialism stresses individual freedom and the lack of an essential human nature and of behavioral guidelines.

10. Linguistic analysts believe that the question of ultimate reality is meaningless because no statement relating to ultimate reality can be proved. There are only two kinds of epistemologically meaningful statements: analytic and synthetic.

Reality as Matter

Meet Ruth. She has also met and fallen in love with someone very special, Max. Ruth also has a professor friend in whom she confides, only to hear the professor claim that he has produced Max in his basement lab. Although Ruth does not believe the professor, the conversation has made her restless. She finally decides to tell her brother Brad.

Brad couldn't care less that the creature has been so created. As far as he is concerned, if he cannot ever detect a difference between it and an ordinary human, then there is no difference. But Ruth points out that because the creature was not born as we are, there really is a difference between us and it. But Brad thinks being born is not so special. After all, cats, rattlesnakes, and chimpanzees are born. Does that mean Ruth should marry one? No, but Ruth insists that it does mean that she should marry a person, and this—this thing—just isn't a person. "But what's so sacred about being a person?" Brad asks. Ruth is astonished. Brad then mentions a book about human behavior that he has been reading which claims that much of what we do can be explained in terms of glands.

"I'll give you a for instance," Brad tells Ruth. "Let's say you're in the grocery store some night when a guy comes in and holds it up. He's got a gun and he's waving it around real crazy. Naturally, you're scared to death. Then all of a sudden, before you even know what you're doing, you spring at him."

"Me?"

"Is matter the ultimate constituent of reality, including you and me?"

"Yeah, you. Just like that! You leap through the air and clobber him. Smash! He's down. Then the cops come. They give you a medal. You're a real hero. The storekeeper even gives you a six-pack!"

"So?"

"So, do you know why you're a hero?"

"Why?"

"Glands."

"You're kidding."

"Nope. You reacted as you did largely because your glands pumped out adrenalin. It's that simple."

Ruth is not convinced. She asks how he would explain feelings like love or guilt or uncertainty, the impulse to believe in God, and the urge to write a book or compose a song. Brad insists that those impulses, too, can be explained physiochemically. He mentions how brain surgeons have altered not only human behavior but feelings as well; how they have erased intense

---

PHILOSOPHY AND LIFE 9-1
Our Knowledge of the World

What kind of world do we live in? Physicists today generally describe it as a flux of energy that exists in different forms at different levels. Due to the limitations of our sense organs, not all of the world's energy reaches our brain. Indeed, a relatively small part of the electromagnetic spectrum, that is, of the entire range of radiation, can stimulate our eyes. In other words, while we can hear or feel parts of it, we can't see a large portion of the spectrum. Electromagnetic energy covers a wide range of wavelengths, from extremely short gamma rays, having wavelengths of about a billionth of an inch, to the extremely long radio waves, which have wavelengths that are miles long. In fact, we can see very little of the electromagnetic spectrum.

Our ears also sense a limited range of the mechanical vibrations transmitted through the air. Similarly, while we can smell and taste certain chemical substances and feel the presence of some objects in contact with our skin surface, most of what occurs in our environment cannot be perceived by these senses either. In effect, the great flux of energy that physicists say exists is largely lost to our senses. We know about it only indirectly, through specially devised instruments that can detect radio waves, X rays, infrared rays, and other energy forms that we can't directly experience.

What implications do these facts hold for our view of reality? If nothing else, they should make us wonder just how complete a picture of reality we have and how accurate our interpretation of it is. In *New Pathways in Science*, Sir Arthur Eddington addresses this issue:

> *As a conscious being I am involved in a story. The perceiving part of my mind tells me a story of a world around me. The story tells of familiar*

spiritual feelings in people; how they have turned psychopathic killers into placid, if unproductive, citizens.

"When you come right down to it," Brad says, "everything is just matter, and all matter is subject to physiochemical explanation. It's that simple" (see Philosophy and Life 9-1).

Is it that simple? Is matter the ultimate constituent of reality, including you and me? In replying to Ruth's inquiry, Brad reveals a concept of reality that inclines him to say without reservation that he would marry such a creature. We can call his metaphysical view *materialism*.

The Development of Materialism

Materialism, the view that the ultimate constituent of reality is matter, is at least as old as the ancient Greeks. Democritus (460–360 B.C.) believed that reality could be explained in terms of matter. The smallest pieces of matter he

---

objects. It tells of colors, sounds, scents belonging to these objects; of boundless space in which they have their existence, and of an ever-rolling stream of time bringing change and incident. It tells of other life than mine busy about its own purposes.

As a scientist I have become mistrustful of this story. In many instances it has become clear that things are not what they seem to be. According to the story teller I have now in front of me a substantial desk; but I have learned from physics that the desk is not at all the continuous substance that it is supposed to be in the story. It is a host of tiny electric charges darting hither and thither with inconceivable velocity. Instead of being solid substance my desk is more like a swarm of gnats.

So I have come to realize that I must not put overmuch confidence in the story teller who lives in my mind.*

* Sir Arthur Eddington. New Pathways in Science. Ann Arbor: University of Michigan Press, 1959, p. 11. Reprinted by permission.

□ Undoubtedly things often are not what they appear to be. But to say that is to imply another experience of things. Can we be sure that alternative experiences are any closer to how things are? □ If a desk is indeed more like "a swarm of gnats" than a solid substance, what practical difference does that make in the way you live? □ Or is such a question irrelevant?

called atoms; he described them as solid, indivisible, indestructible, eternal, and uncreated. Atoms were not qualitatively distinguishable from one another, and they constantly moved through space, where they combined to form the recognizable physical objects of the universe. According to Democritus, the universe consisted of atoms and empty space. He believed that even the soul, which he equated with reason, consisted of atoms. In this atomic universe "all things happen by virtue of necessity, the vortex being the cause of the creation of all things."[1]

The philosopher Epicurus (342–270 B.C.) espoused similar views, but a few centuries later the Roman poet Lucretius (96–55 B.C.) recorded the most complete statement of Democritus' atomic theory that is extant. In his poem *On the Nature of Things*, Lucretius provided additional principles of the atomic universe, including the principle that nothing is created or destroyed and that there is empty space. In the following passage from this poem, notice how Lucretius uses his cosmological theory to account for a variety of things, all of which he feels are composed of atoms, even though they are not perceptible and fly in the face of common experience.

> Now mark me: since I have taught that things cannot be born from nothing, cannot when begotten be brought back to nothing, that you may not haply yet begin in any shape to mistrust my words, because the first-beginnings of things cannot be seen by the eyes, take moreover this list of bodies which you must yourself admit are in the number of things and cannot be seen. First of all the force of the wind when aroused beats on the harbors and whelms huge ships and scatters clouds; sometimes in swift whirling eddy it scours the plains and straws them with large trees and scourges the mountain summits with forest-rending blasts: so fiercely does the wind rave with a shrill howling and rage with threatening roar. Winds therefore sure enough are unseen bodies which sweep the seas, the lands, ay and the clouds of heaven, tormenting them and catching them up in sudden whirls. On they stream and spread destruction abroad in just the same way as the soft liquid nature of water, when all at once it is borne along in an overflowing stream, and a great downfall of water from the high hills augments it with copious rains, flinging together fragments of forests and entire trees; nor can the strong bridges sustain the sudden force of coming water: in such wise turbid with much rain the river dashes upon the piers with mighty force: makes havoc with loud noise and rolls under its eddies huge stones: wherever aught opposes its waves, down it dashes it. In this way then must the blasts of wind as well move on, and when they like a mighty stream have borne down in any direction, they push things before them and throw them down with repeated assaults, sometimes catch them up in curling eddy and carry them away in swift-circling whirl. Wherefore once and again I say winds are unseen bodies, since in their works and ways they are found to rival great rivers which are of a visible body. Then again we perceive the different smells of things, yet never see them coming to our nostrils; nor do we behold heats nor can we observe cold with the eyes nor are we used to see voices. Yet all these things must consist of a bodily nature, since they are able to move the senses; for nothing but body can touch

1.   *Quoted in Diogenes Laërtius.* Lives and Opinions of Eminent Philosophers. *R. D. Hicks, Trans. Cambridge, Mass.: Harvard University Press, 1925, vol. 2, p. 455.*

and be touched. Again clothes hung up on a shore which waves break upon become moist, and then get dry if spread out in the sun. Yet it has not been seen in what way the moisture of water has sunk into them nor again in what way this has been dispelled by heat. The moisture therefore is dispersed into small particles which the eyes are quite unable to see. Again after the revolution of many of the sun's years a ring on the finger is thinned on the under side by wearing, the dripping from the eaves hollows a stone, the bent ploughshare of iron imperceptibly decreases in the fields, and we behold the stone-paved streets worn down by the feet of the multitude; the brass statues too at the gates show their right hands to be wasted by the touch of the numerous passers by who greet them. These things then we see are lessened, since they have been thus worn down; but what bodies depart at any given time the nature of vision has jealously shut out our seeing. Lastly the bodies which time and nature add to things by little and little, constraining them to grow in due measure, no exertion of the eyesight can behold; and so too wherever things grow old by age and decay, and when rocks hanging over the sea are eaten away by the gnawing salt spray, you cannot see what they lose at any given moment. Nature therefore works by unseen bodies.[2]

In Lucretius' cosmos, chance operates. The unpredictable course of an atom as it falls through space with its companions creates the condition for macroscopic entities. Such a materialistic doctrine nicely countered the religious superstition of the day and foreshadowed the scientism of our own age.

But Lucretius' theory never became popular, for even by Democritus' time people had become disenchanted with the many attempts to explain the cosmos. At various times, philosopher-scientists viewed water, fire, air, or earth as the fundamental substance of reality. Others believed that reality could best be explained in terms of constant change. Eventually interest centered on more personal concerns, such as how one might lead a good and contented life. This interest was sparked by classical philosophy.

Although their interests reached much further than such questions, the Greek philosophers Socrates, Plato, and Aristotle did see the moral life as the road to knowledge and truth. The rise of Christianity fanned this interest in personal conduct, which predominated throughout the Middle Ages. Instrumental to this interest was the idea of a soul, which assumed a religious dimension that included personal immortality. Such an emphasis gave the view of reality a distinctly nonmaterial bias that held sway into the seventeenth century, when growing interest in the world and the rise of scientific method and scientific discovery turned minds once again to materialism.

Awakened by the discoveries of Copernicus, Kepler, Galileo, and Newton, people of the seventeenth century watched science cultivate a full-blown materialism. Committed to the belief that the world could be quantified, scientists made the materialistic claim that all was matter. In the systematic philosophy of Thomas Hobbes (1588–1679), for example, we see the Democritean belief that everything can be explained in terms of matter in motion:

> Every object is either a part of the whole world, or an aggregate of parts.
> The greatest of all bodies, or sensible objects, is the world itself; which we

2. *Lucretius*. On the Nature of Things. *C. Bailey, Trans. Oxford: Clarendon Press, 1924, p. 32.*

behold when we look round about us from this point of the same which we call the earth. Concerning the world, as it is one aggregate of many parts, the things that fall under inquiry are but few; and those we can determine, none. Of the whole world we may inquire what is its magnitude, what its duration, and how many there be, but nothing else.[3]

Similarly, anticipating many contemporary psychological theories, Hobbes postulated that mental states were brain states, and that a "general inclination of all mankind" was "a perpetual and restless desire of power after power." In 1748, Julien Offroy de La Mettrie carried Hobbesian psychology further when he published *Man a Machine*.

You may wonder what had happened to the religious doctrine of the soul. What remained of the creature supposedly made in the image of God and possessed of an eternal destiny? So much medieval superstition, declared the materialists. Even Newton's mechanical universe was rapidly growing obsolete, because Newton had proposed a God who regulated things. In contrast, astronomer-mathematician Pierre Laplace proposed his theory of a self-regulating universe, which gained some respectability by the early nineteenth century. To be precise, in 1812 Laplace formulated his "Divine Calculator." This Divine Calculator, a mathematical physicist of sorts, knowing the velocities and positions of all the particles in the world at a particular instant, could calculate all that had happened and all that would happen. Laplace's universe needed not a God but a supercomputer as regulator. Bertrand Russell describes the situation nicely: "When Laplace suggested that the same forces which are now operative (according to Newton's laws) might have caused the planets to grow out of the sun, God's share in the course of nature was pushed still further back. He might remain as Creator, but even that was doubtful, since it was not clear the world has a beginning in time."[4] An interesting footnote to this historical development: It is said that when Napoleon asked Laplace why his theory omitted God, Laplace simply replied that God was an unnecessary hypothesis.

But these early materialists' optimistic faith that humans could eventually explain the universe and themselves has tarnished over the last century, as we shall see. Nevertheless, just as a culture generally lags behind its science, so today we frequently find ourselves as enthusiastically materialistic as our nineteenth-century counterparts.

Today, philosophical materialism takes many forms, but all have at least four characteristics that survive from the past. First, materialism seeks answers through objective methodology. Specifically, it is committed to the scientific method of observation, analysis, and tentative conclusions. What cannot be found out by this method cannot be known. Second, materialism is deterministic; that is, it believes that every event has a cause. Some materialists attribute these causes to physiochemical processes. Others would add biological causes. Still others introduce psychological, sociological, and anthropological causes.

3. *Thomas Hobbes. "Elements of Philosophy," in* The English Works of Thomas Hobbes. *Sir W. Molesworth, Ed. London: J. Bohn, 1839, vol. 1, chap. 1, sec. 8.*

4. *Bertrand Russell.* A History of Western Philosophy. *New York: Simon & Schuster, 1945, p. 537.*

We may not know the causes, they say, but they nevertheless exist. Third, materialism denies any form of supernaturalistic belief, including belief in spirit, soul, mind, or any other nonmaterial substance. Reality is composed of matter and only of matter. Finally, materialism is reductionistic; it attempts to explain the whole exclusively in terms of its parts or units.

Objections to Materialism

We said earlier that materialism, at least in twentieth-century scientific circles, has lost considerable ground. Let us rejoin Ruth and Brad and see why.

Ruth: I don't understand how you can deny what so many people have believed for so long.

Brad: What's that?

Ruth: The existence of a nonmaterial reality.

Brad You mean a soul?

Ruth: A soul, a spirit, a mind—call it what you want.

Brad: Look, a lot of people once believed the earth was the center of the universe, but that didn't make it so, did it?

Ruth: That was different. This is a belief that defies full scientific contradiction. What you seem to forget is that the very thing you seem to be calling us—machines—*we* have created. *We* have invented them. If it weren't for people like the professor, these mechanical creations wouldn't exist to begin with. The creation isn't the creator, Brad. Machines aren't people. People love and hate, they dream, they hope, they strive. They write great books and compose beautiful music.

Brad: So what?

Ruth: So how can you explain all this in terms of physiochemical causes?

How can Brad deny what is fundamentally real to so many people? This is what Ruth is asking. She is also asking how he can reduce to material explanations those human qualities and behaviors that are supposedly unique, such as consciousness. She does not feel that consciousness can be explained totally in terms of the physiochemical; neither can ideas or concepts be so described.

Ruth: You say that everything in existence can be explained physiochemically. Then what about human consciousness?

Brad: What about it?

Ruth: How do you explain states of consciousness that we experience? How do you explain, for example, my experience of seeing something red, let alone the more complex experiences like being in love?

Brad: Look, what you're calling consciousness is no more than a brain state. When you're seeing red, your brain is merely functioning in a certain way. The same is true with love or any other experience.

Ruth: All right, suppose you're having a brain operation. In the operating room are mirrors placed so that you can observe what's happening. Now, the surgeon peels back the top of your skull and you observe your own brain.

Brad: So?

Ruth: So you can observe even the nerve pathways that are stimulated when you experience a color—red, for example. You can see precisely what ganglion reacts whenever you see red. Every time the surgeon shows you red, sure enough, that thing starts wiggling.

Brad: Okay. That's my brain state for the experience of red.

Ruth: Are you saying that the red you see and what's happening in your brain when you see it are the same thing?

Brad: Right.

Ruth: Then why isn't the surgeon seeing red?

Brad: What do you mean?

Ruth: Well, he's observing your brain state, too, isn't he? If your brain state equals the experience of red, why isn't the surgeon having the same experience when he observes your brain state?

Brad: Because he has his own experience of red, that's why.

Ruth: All right, let me ask you this. Can you have the surgeon's experience of red?

Brad: Of course not. But I could observe his brain state of red.

Ruth: So what you're saying is that the brain state and the experience are really two different things.

Brad: Okay, maybe they are. So what?

Ruth: Plenty. What makes them different is that one is publicly observable and the other isn't. Everybody can observe the brain state. Why? Because it's physical. But only the individual can have the experience that accompanies the brain state. And that's because it's nonphysical; its *nonmaterial*.

Brad initially insists that Ruth's example portrays the brain observing itself. Yet consciousness, understanding, and experience seem to stand outside the particular brain state observed. Brad would seem to be having two experiences: one of the brain state itself, the other of the experience that the brain state signals. The experience does not seem to be physical, although it is undoubtedly accompanied by a brain and nerve state. How can the strict materialist account for this fact? Does it suggest the presence of a nonmaterial reality? Is there at the core of all being something that cannot be measured, pinpointed, or spatialized?

Contemporary scientific materialist J. J. C. Smart (1920–) thinks not. In the view of this Australian philosopher, mental states are identical with brain states. Smart contends that future scientific discovery will demonstrate that all human experiences are identical with processes taking place in the brain. Smart justifies his claim by arguing that a nonphysical property couldn't possibly develop in the course of animal evolution. In a 1963 article, he states the issue and his view:

But what about consciousness? Can we interpret the having of an after-image or of a painful sensation as something material, namely, a brain state or brain process? We seem to be immediately aware of pains and after-images, and we seem to be immediately aware of them as something different from a neurophysiological state or process. For example, the after-image may be green speckled with red, whereas the neurophysiologist looking into our brains would be unlikely to see something green speckled with red. However, if we object to materialism in this way we are victims of a confusion which U. T. Place has called "the phenomenological fallacy." To say that an image or sense datum is green is not to say that the conscious experience of having the image or sense datum is green. It is to say that it is the sort of experience we have when in normal conditions we look at a green apple, for example. Apples and unripe bananas can be green, but not the experiences of seeing them. An image or a sense datum can be green in a derivative sense, but this need not cause any worry, because, on the view I am defending, images and sense data are not constituents of the world, though the processes of having an image or a sense datum are actual processes in the world. The experience of having a green sense datum is not itself green; it is a process occurring in grey matter. The world contains plumbers, but does not contain the average plumber: it also contains the having of a sense datum, but does not contain the sense datum. . . .

It may be asked why I should demand of a tenable philosophy of mind that it should be compatible with materialism, in the sense in which I have defined it. One reason is as follows. How could a nonphysical property or entity suddenly arise in the course of animal evolution? A change in a gene is a change in a complex molecule which causes a change in the biochemistry of the cell. This may lead to changes in the shape or organization of the developing embryo. But what sort of chemical process could lead to the springing into existence of something nonphysical? No enzyme can catalyze the production of a spook! Perhaps it will be said that the nonphysical comes into existence as a by-product: that whenever there is a certain complex physical structure, then, by an irreducible extraphysical law, there is also a nonphysical entity. Such laws would be quite outside normal scientific conceptions and quite inexplicable: they would be, in Herbert Feigl's phrase, "nomological danglers." To say the very least, we can vastly simplify our cosmological outlook if we can defend a materialistic philosophy of mind.[5]

In essence, Smart is defending the position that states of consciousness are identical with states of the brain. This identity is termed *contingent identity*. To grasp the meaning of contingent identity, consider an example originally advanced by the German mathematician and philosopher Gottlob Frege. Frege pointed out that from ancient times the very bright star visible in the heavens just before sunset has been called "the evening star." Similarly, the bright star apparent just after sunrise has been referred to as "the morning star." Of course, the ancients didn't know that these were one and the same "star," the planet Venus.

Think about the implications. If the Greek astronomer-mathematician Aristarchus had said that the morning star is identical with the evening star, he would have been correct. But, of course, he couldn't have proved it. Only the

5. J. J. C. Smart. "Materialism." Journal of Philosophy, 24 October 1963. Reprinted by permission.

development of telescopes and other astronomical instruments could provide proof. So, although the object denoted by the phrase "morning star" is identical with the one denoted by "evening star," the identity is not apparent by examining the meanings of the words, as it is in statements like "3 squared equals 9" and "A triangle has three sides."[6] Rather, it must be discovered by science.

When Smart speaks of a contingent identity between mental and brain phenomena, he means that the phrase "mental phenomenon" names the same object or set of conditions as the phrase "brain phenomenon." But this identity is a contingent one; it cannot be deduced from the meanings of the words; it must be discovered by science.

Not all philosophers agree with Smart's analysis. The well-known American philosopher Norman Malcolm (1911–), for one, sees flaws in it:

> I wish to go into Smart's theory that there is a contingent identity between mental phenomena and brain phenomena. If such an identity exists, then brain phenomena must have all the properties that mental phenomena have. . . . I shall argue that this condition cannot be fulfilled.
> a.   First, it is not meaningful to assign spatial locations to some kinds of mental phenomena, e.g., thoughts. Brain phenomena have spatial location. Thus, brain phenomena have a property that thoughts do not have. Therefore, thoughts are not identical with any brain phenomena.
> b.   Second, any thought requires a background of circumstances ("surroundings"), e.g., practices, agreements, assumptions. If a brain event were identical with a thought, it would require the same. The circumstances necessary for a thought cannot be described in terms of the entities and laws of physics. According to Smart's scientific materialism, everything in the world is "explicable in terms of physics." But if the identity theory were true, not even those brain events which are identical with thoughts would be "explicable in terms of physics." Therefore, the identity theory and scientific materialism are incompatible.
>   . . . According to the identity theory, the identity between a thought and a brain event is contingent. If there is a contingent identity between A and B, the identity ought to be empirically verifiable. It does not appear that it would be empirically verifiable that a thought was identical with a brain event. Therefore, if a thought and a brain event are claimed to be identical, it is not plausible to hold that the identity is contingent.[7]

The debate about the nature of consciousness has arisen in the midst of some startling discoveries in atomic physics. For a long time we have known that all matter consists of molecules, of which there are a tremendous number of types. But there are only about 100 types of atoms, which make up each molecule. Before the twentieth century, no one believed that atoms could be split. Today we know that three particles make up the atom: electron, proton, and neutron. Yet everything in existence cannot be explained in terms of these three particles.

6.   *See Robert P. Wolff.* About Philosophy. *Englewood Cliffs, N.J.; Prentice-Hall, 1976, pp. 290–291.*

7.   *Norman Malcolm. "Scientific Materialism and the Identity Theory." Journal of Philosophy, 24 October 1963, pp. 662–663. Reprinted by permission.*

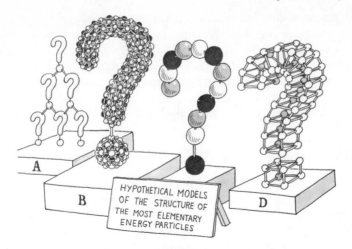

"And what is energy? Nobody knows for sure."

Physicists have discovered over 200 so-called elementary particles (see Philosophy and Life 9-2). Some believe that they are made up of still more elementary particles, called quarks. The point is that modern science is showing reality to be ever more complex.

But, even more important, these elementary particles do not seem to be matter. They are more likely energy forces. True, matter may depend on elementary-particle interactions, but the particles themselves seem to be composed of energy, not matter. And what is energy? Nobody knows for sure. Whatever it is, it is in motion and it exerts force, but it does not appear to be matter as matter is traditionally understood.

Ever since the early 1930s, when Werner Heisenberg discovered that atomic activity is not uniform, materialism has been losing credibility. Heisenberg formulated his principle of indeterminacy on a startling premise: that there is no orderly causation. Because electrons change their positions at random, rational prediction is not possible. In his article "The Dematerialization of Matter," philosopher-scientist N. R. Hanson states the full implications of Heisenberg's discovery:

> Matter has been dematerialized, not just as a concept of the philosophically real, but now as an idea of modern physics. Matter can be analyzed down to the level of fundamental particles. But at that depth the direction of the analysis changes, and this constitutes a major conceptual surprise in the history of science. The things which for Newton typified matter—e.g., an exactly determinable state, a point shape, absolute solidity—these are now the properties electrons do not, because theoretically they cannot, have. . . .
>
> The dematerialization of matter . . . has rocked mechanics at its foundations. . . . The 20th century's dematerialization of matter has made it conceptually impossible to accept a Newtonian picture of the properties of matter and still do a consistent physics.[8]

8. *N. R. Hanson, "The Dematerialization of Matter," in* The Concept of Matter. *Ernan McMillin, Ed. Notre Dame, Ind.: University of Notre Dame Press, 1963, pp. 556–557.*

As a result, many scientists, including Heisenberg, believe that we are more likely to have an idealistic universe than a materialistic one. Their view finds some support in the unified field theories of Einstein and contemporary scientists such as Kip Thorne. When electromagnetic and gravitational phenomena are synthesized, matter disappears entirely, leaving only "field." To understand better what is meant by an idealistic universe, let us consider idealism as an explanation of ultimate reality.

Reality as Nonmatter

Modern atomic theory has led many people to claim that reality consists of more than matter. They do not therefore deny matter. But if we push the question of reality far enough, matter alone does not seem to account for everything; things are not only what they appear to be.

Today, many people would argue that ultimate reality resembles some cosmic law, such as Einstein's relativity equation $E = mc^2$ (energy equals mass times the speed of light squared). This law, they say, not only describes how things work but also implies a principle that lies at the bottom of everything, gives everything design and purpose, and orders our experiences.

The study of the theory that there is design or purpose working in the structure of the universe is termed **teleology**. One of the outstanding tele-

PHILOSOPHY AND LIFE 9-2
The Neutrino

The neutrino is perhaps the most bewildering of all the elementary particles known to physics, and among the most philosophically provocative. It has no physical properties—no mass, no electric charge, and no magnetic field. It is neither attracted nor repelled by the electric and magnetic fields of passing particles. Thus, a neutrino originating in the Milky Way or in some other galaxy and traveling at the speed of light can pass through the earth as if it were so much empty space. Can it be stopped? Only by a direct, head-on collision with another elementary particle. The chances of that are infinitesimally small. Fortunately, there are so many neutrinos that collisions do occur. Otherwise, physicists would never have detected them. Just think, even as you read this sentence, billions of neutrinos coming from the sun and other stars are passing through your skull and brain. And how would the universe appear to a neutrino? Eminent astronomer V. A. Firsoff provides a picture:

> The universe as seen by a neutrino eye would wear a very unfamiliar look. Our earth and other planets simply would not be there, or might at best appear as thin patches of mist. The sun and other stars may be dimly visible, in as much as they emit some neutrinos. . . . A neutrino

ologists in the history of philosophy was Aristotle. He believed that the subject matter of metaphysics consists of certain concepts or categories fundamental to change. Substance is perhaps the most fundamental of these categories. By *substance* Aristotle meant anything that can have attributes or properties, but which itself cannot serve as an attribute or property for something else. The simplest examples of substances are everyday objects: trees, houses, shoes, rocks, and so on. We can attribute certain characteristics to these substances, such as greenness to trees or hardness to rocks, but we can't attribute "tree-ness" or "rockness" to anything. Of particular concern to Aristotle was how substances change, for example, how the substance acorn changes to the substance oak.

In explaining change, Aristotle distinguished four kinds of principles:[9] *material, formal, efficient,* and *final.* The material principle refers to the stuff or material of which something is composed. Thus, in the growth of an acorn to an oak, we can talk about the material or stuff of which the acorn is composed in terms of a cause that helps explain its change. By a thing's formal principle, Aristotle meant its essence, its defining or identifying principle. The formal principle, or essence, of an acorn is that by nature of which an acorn is the seed of an oak tree and not, say, the seed of an elm. The efficient principle refers to

9. *While these are often referred to as "causes," that term is so misleading for contemporary readers that "principles" has been substituted.*

brain might suspect our existence from certain secondary effects, but would find it very difficult to prove, as we would elude the neutrino instruments at his disposal.

Our universe is no truer than that of the neutrinos—they exist, but they exist in a different kind of space, governed by different laws. . . . The neutrino . . . is subject neither to gravitational nor to electromagnetic field. . . . It might be able to travel faster than light, which would make it relativistically recede in our time scale.*

□ *What impact does the presence of neutrinos have on your view of reality?*
□ *Arthur Koestler writes, "To the unprejudiced mind, neutrinos have indeed a certain affinity with ghosts—which does not prevent them from existing." † What does this mean?*

* *V. A. Firsoff. Life, Mind and Galaxies. New York: W. A. Benjamin, 1967.*
† *Arthur Koestler. The Roots of Coincidence. New York: Random House, 1972, p. 63.*

the motion or energy that results in a change. Thus, the planting of the seed, rainfall, and all other environmental conditions needed for the seed's growth and maturation would constitute the efficient cause. When an acorn actually becomes an oak, Aristotle viewed it as having attained its end. The end, goal, or purpose that a substance inwardly strives to attain is its final principle.

We've oversimplified Aristotle's view to make a point: Aristotle's universe is basically teleological. In other words, it's a universe governed by purposes or ends. In his work *Physics*, Aristotle argues that purposeful action is present in all things that come to be:

> Further, where a series has a completion, all the preceding steps are for the sake of that. Now surely as in intelligent action, so in nature; and as in nature, so it is in each action, if nothing interferes. Now intelligent action is for the sake of an end; therefore the nature of things also is so. Thus if a house, e.g., had been a thing made by nature, it would have been made in the same way as it is now by art; and if things made by nature were made also by art, they would come to be in the same way as by nature. Each step then in the series is for the sake of the next; and generally art partly completes what nature cannot bring to a finish, and partly imitates her. If, therefore, artificial products are for the sake of an end, so clearly also are natural products. The relation of the later to the earlier terms of the series is the same in both.
>
> This is most obvious in the animals other than man: they make things neither by art nor after inquiry or deliberation. Wherefore people discuss whether it is by intelligence or by some other faculty that these creatures work,—spiders, ants, and the like. By gradual advance in this direction we come to see clearly that in plants too that is produced which is conducive to the end—leaves, e.g., grow to provide shade for the fruit. If then it is both by nature and for an end that the swallow makes its nest and the spider its web, and plants grow leaves for the sake of the fruit and send their roots down (not up) for the sake of nourishment, it is plain that this kind of cause is operative in things which come to be and are by nature. And since "nature" means two things, the matter and the form, of which the latter is the end, and since all the rest is for the sake of the end, the form must be the cause in the sense of "that for the sake of which."
>
> Now mistakes come to pass even in the operations of art: the grammarian makes a mistake in writing and the doctor pours out the wrong dose. Hence clearly mistakes are possible in the operations of nature also. If then in art there are cases in which what is rightly produced serves a purpose, and if where mistakes occur there was a purpose in what was attempted, only it was not attained, so must it be also in natural products, and monstrosities will be failures in the purposive effort. Thus in the original combinations the "ox-progeny," if they failed to reach a determinate end, must have arisen through the corruption of some principle corresponding to what is now the seed.
>
> Further, seed must have come into being first, and not straightway the animals: the words "whole-natured first . . ." must have meant seed.
>
> Again, in plants too we find the relation of means to end, though the degree of organization is less. Were there then in plants also "olive-headed vine-progeny," like the "man-headed ox-progeny," or not? An absurd suggestion; yet there must have been, if there were such things among animals.
>
> Moreover, among the seeds anything must have come to be at random. But the person who asserts this entirely does away with "nature" and what exists "by nature." For those things are natural which, by a continuous move-

ment originated from an internal principle, arrive at some completion: the same completion is not reached from every principle, nor any chance completion, but always the tendency in each is toward the same end, if there is no impediment.

The end and the means toward it may come about by chance. We say, for instance, that a stranger has come by chance, paid the ransom, and gone away, when he does so as if he had come for that purpose, though it was not for that that he came. This is incidental, for chance is an incidental cause, as I remarked before. But when an event takes place always or for the most part, it is not incidental or by chance. In natural products the sequence is invariable, if there is no impediment.

It is absurd to suppose that purpose is not present because we do not observe the agent deliberating. Art does not deliberate. If the shipbuilding art were in the wood, it would produce the same results *by nature*. If, therefore, purpose is present in art, it is present also in nature. The best illustration is a doctor doctoring himself: nature is like that.

It is plain then that nature is a cause, a cause that operates for a purpose.[10]

In contrast to this teleological view, materialists generally reject the idea of purpose or goals in nature, primarily because of the difficulty, if not the impossibility, of examining scientifically nature's supposed teleological characteristics. Instead, materialists focus on the laws of mechanics to explain change—what Aristotle termed efficient principles. They insist that matter alone can explain the changes that we observe in the world. Can matter alone account for the general teleological tendencies in the operation of things? Can sheer coincidence? Can an accidental combination of electrons?

Some critics argue that the survival-of-the-fittest theory does not fully explain evolution over millions and millions of years from very simple organisms to incredibly complex ones, from a mindless glob to human intelligence. In contrast, nonmaterialists see purpose in the evolutionary trends that we can empirically observe. They see direction in the operation of nature. They see mind behind the way that things interrelate and function. Purpose, direction, and mind are concepts foreign to materialism. Yet many people say that when we push our investigation of physical phenomena far enough, we end up in just such a mental world, a world of idea, not matter. This is why nonmaterialists are often called idealists.

Idealists, unlike materialists, see a mental or spiritual force operating that accounts for the order and purpose in nature that they perceive. Nature, they believe, is goal directed; it evolves not by chance but by design. That humankind is coming to understand more and more of the wonders of nature suggests an underlying law operating in the universe. This law or principle, they say, is not matter but idea. Like materialism, idealism has a long history.

The Development of Idealism

Although idealists differ, let us define **idealism** as the belief that reality is essentially idea, thought, or mind rather than matter. Whether idealists believe

10. *Aristotle*. Physics. *R. P. Hardie and R. K. Gaye, Trans. In* The Oxford Translation of Aristotle. *W. D. Ross, Ed. Oxford: Oxford University Press, 1930. Reprinted by permission of Oxford University Press.*

that there is a single, absolute mind or many minds, they invariably emphasize the mental or spiritual, not the material, presenting it as the creative force or active agent behind all things.

The belief that reality is ultimately idea is at least as old as the ancient Greek Pythagoras (about 600 B.C.). Plato, however, first formalized it. He held that individual entities are merely shadows of reality, that behind each entity in our experience is a perfect Form or Idea. This Form or Idea is what makes the entity understandable to the human mind. Individual entities come and go, but the Forms are immortal and indestructible. For Plato, there is the world of opinion, consisting of all sense objects. Then there is the knowable world, the world of Form or Idea. The world of opinion is one of illusion, impermanence, and perpetual ignorance, similar to what Buddhists call **maya.** But the knowable world, resembling what Hindus call **Brahman,** is real, permanent, and forever truthful.

Such thinking fit in well with the Christian thought developed by Saint Augustine (354–430). In his work *The City of God,* Augustine warns us to beware of the world and the flesh, because they are temporary. What is real is the spiritual world, the world without matter. Although we are citizens of the physical world, we are ultimately intended to be citizens of the spiritual world of God. This is our divine destiny. For Augustine and fellow Christians, Jesus Christ is the embodiment of all perfection, of all "Forms"; he is the meaning of all that is. As Saint John writes, "In the beginning was the Word and the Word was with God and the Word was God. He was in the beginning with all things." Notice that John says the *Word* was God—in Greek, the *logos,* which means "law" as well as "word." In the nineteenth century, the German romantic Goethe would express a similar idealistic notion through his immortal Faust: "In the beginning was the meaning."

We saw in Chapter 6 the foundations of modern idealism in the epistemology of George Berkeley, who reacted against the growth of scientific materialism. Recall that Berkeley claimed that what exists is the conscious mind and its perceptions. For Berkeley, the world is Mind communicating with other minds—an abstract notion, but not so elusive when we understand that by *Mind* Berkeley meant God. Berkeley did not deny the physical world, only its independence from Mind. Since for Berkeley to be is to be perceived, a world separate from (independent from) Mind cannot exist, because it would be contradictory. Not everything perceived, however, is a human perception or idea. Phenomena that provide intelligibility, such as uniformity, consistency, and continuity, are not known in any way by finite mind. They can be explained only in terms of ideas in the Mind of God. For Berkeley, God is the ruling spirit of nature: God's will is nature's law. The orderly succession of events that Ruth perceives in everything, Berkeley would attribute to the will of God.

We also saw that, like Berkeley, Immanuel Kant believed that we only know how things appear to us. Unlike Berkeley, however, Kant held that we are not just passive receivers of sense experience. Once we receive sense impressions, our minds have the ability to provide these impressions with form. Our minds reveal relationships among sense experiences; they reveal law and principle at work. In short, our minds possess conceptual molds that order sense experience. These molds precede all sense experience; they are nonmaterial, pure idea.

A nineteenth-century idealist, and one of the most complex thinkers—Georg Hegel (1770–1831)—disagreed with Kant. We do not impose order or form on nature, said Hegel, we discover it. Order, form, and shape are not made by humans; humans find them. They already exist in the nature of things, including the nature of self. Reality expresses itself in our thinking. The essence of everything, including self, is purposeful intelligence—Absolute Mind or God—whose essence is ultimately identical with the entirety of the world process.

In order to appreciate these varieties of idealism, it's helpful to distinguish between two kinds of idealism, subjective and objective. Berkeley's version of idealism is useful because it includes elements of both.[11]

Squarely in the empirical school of the early eighteenth century, Berkeley believed that we learn about the world by exercising all our senses. The knowledge that we gain about everyday objects pertains to their distinct qualities—their size, shape, color, and texture. In other words, sensible objects can be analyzed by their sensible qualities.

It's easy to see what holds objects of sense experience together: other sensible objects. The roof, walls, and floors of a house are held together by nails, mortar, and the like. But what about the sensible qualities that Berkeley speaks of? When regarded in their own right, what holds together the qualities of size, shape, color, and texture? Aristotle's answer is substance. Substance takes qualities and holds them together so that we may perceive that bundle of sense qualities that make up an object.

Materialists account for substance with matter, but not Berkeley, who termed himself an immaterialist. He rejected this belief for two reasons. First, he didn't believe that we could know that matter is the fundamental stuff of reality because we can only perceive an object's sensible qualities. Second, if we could perceive the matter, then the matter itself could not account for substance, for to be perceived is to have sensible qualities. Thus, there is a need for another substance. Berkeley proposed that Mind was this other substance. Let's see what he meant by this.

Berkeley claimed that things are ultimately mental, or mind-dependent. This mind-dependency can be viewed as either "me-dependent" or "other-dependent." At least in its initial stages, Berkeley's idealism is me-dependent.

Recall that Berkeley said that we find out about the things of the world through experience. We learn of trees, rocks, houses, cats, and dogs through our experience of them. But experience is using our senses—seeing, touching, tasting, smelling, and hearing. When we use our senses, we get sightings of light or color; feelings of hard or soft, smooth or rough; smells of sweetness or decay. So, for Berkeley, all things are bundles of deliverances of the senses or some combination of such deliverances.

Berkeley viewed these deliverances of the senses as one's own perceptions. Thus, any thing that I experience is the sum of my perceptions of that thing.

11. *See Elmer Sprague.* Metaphysical Thinking. *New York: Oxford University Press, 1978, pp. 93–103.*

Since these perceptions are my own, everything I perceive is me-dependent. This me-dependency translates into mind-dependency, since Berkeley assumed that perception is a mental act and that all perceptions are located in some part of the mind. If we stop Berkeley's analysis right here, we're left with **subjective idealism**, or *subjective immaterialism*, the position that the world consists of my own mind and things that are dependent on it. But Berkeley went further and introduced an objective dimension.

Berkeley pointed out that not all the contents of my mind are the same. Ideas vary. Some are short-lived, even changeable at my will. Others occur regularly and seem constant. For instance, if you choose to, you can imagine that you are now basking in the warm sun on a South Sea island. The air is balmy, the vegetation lush, and the sounds mellow and serene. In contrast, consider your usual route to class; you experience the same landmarks repeatedly—perhaps the library, gym, and the old clock tower—and when you get to class, you experience a comparable regularity, a steadiness about your perceptions. This latter collection of perceptions is clearly different from the imaginings that transported you to the South Sea island. The difference seems to be that your perceptions of the way to class are more than me-dependent.

If your classroom is a collection of perceptions, it must be dependent on mind—if not your own mind, then some other mind. For Berkeley this other mind was ultimately the Mind of God; our historical overview has shown alternative candidates for the other mind. This second stage of idealism, or immaterialism, is termed *objective* because it is independent of certain of my perceptions. The advantages of objective idealism are that it accounts for the steadiness or regularity of our experiences and it allows the world to be viewed as an ultimately intelligible system because it is the product of mind.[12]

Despite the many varieties of idealism, they all appear to share several characteristics. First, they all believe in mind, spirit, or thought as what is ultimately real. Second, they perceive purpose, order, and meaning in the workings of things. Third, they see some kind of purpose acting in our lives. As there are laws governing the operations of the physical universe, so there are laws governing the operations of our own lives: moral laws. Finally, all forms of idealism are as reductionistic as materialism. The tension between idealism and materialism is in the kind of reductions that each proposes. Both speak of trees and rocks and houses as having "parts," in the sense that a tree has bark and pulp and a house has a roof and a foundation. They have a far more subtle meaning in mind, for bark, pulp, roofs, and foundations also have parts. Both materialism and idealism agree that trees and houses are complexes of simples, but they disagree on what kind of complexes such entities are and how they are to be analyzed. Of course, if you reject the idea that things are complexes, then neither materialism nor idealism has any basis. In other words, both derive from the assumption that things are analyzable into simples, then each considers the analysis.[13]

12. *Elmer Sprague.* Metaphysical Thinking, *p. 97.*

13. *See Elmer Sprague.* Metaphysical Thinking, *pp. 93–94.*

Objections to Idealism

As we have seen, idealists generally rely heavily on the assumption that there are order and purpose in the universe. Critics consider the terms *order* and *purpose* to be vague. They claim that in using these words idealists are evasive. They argue that experience consists in part of such seemingly chaotic and purposeless events as natural disasters (the so-called acts of God), the human catastrophes of disease and war, and the personal and national tragedies of senseless deaths. The French writer Voltaire perhaps best summed up this criticism in *Candide*, in which he uses ironic wit to question philosopher Leibnitz's (1648–1727) belief that everything happens for the best in this "best of all possible worlds." At one point in that philosophical tale, Candide points out to Martin the merits of a shipwreck: "You see that crime is sometimes punished; that scoundrel of a Dutch shipowner has had the fate he deserved." Martin responds, "Yes, but did the passengers who were on the ship have to perish too?"[14]

In addition, critics claim that idealists commit the fallacy of **anthropomorphism**; that is, they attribute human characteristics to the universe as a whole. It is one thing to speak of people as having minds, but another to speak of the universe as having one. Similarly unwarranted, say critics, is the leap from ideas to Idea.

Critics also wonder who has ever experienced mind, idea, or spirit independent of a matter-energy system. They point out that it is not even necessary to posit a nonmaterial reality to account for what we observe. This criticism suggests further objections, which require a closer look at subjective and objective idealism.

Subjective idealism's claim that whatever I perceive is either one of my perceptions or a collection of my perceptions is at least puzzling. If I'm looking at a tree, I want to say that there's a difference between my seeing and the tree that I see. Subjective idealism makes no such distinction. Indeed, if I persist that there is more to the tree than my perceivings, subjective idealists might ask me how this "more" is to be found out. They might add that there is no other way to find out about trees than to use our senses. Thus, if I claim that there's more to the tree than my perceiving, I am postulating the existence of something that I cannot know. I can hardly have solid grounds for claiming something that I can't know to exist.

"But," as philosopher Elmer Sprague points out, "it still seems odd to say that I perceive my perceptions, and not that I perceive something out there to be perceived. It seems odd to say that to perceive the [tree] is but to perceive my own mind. It is all very well for the Subjective Immaterialist to say 'That's just the way it is.' Less hardy mortals still wonder if we might not say something else instead."[15] Sprague concedes that what subjective idealists say cannot be disproved experimentally because their theories cannot be falsified. But we can still ask them how they know that their claim is true. Ultimately, the

---

14. Voltaire. Candide. *Tobias George Smollett, Trans. New York: Washington Square Press, 1962, p. 77.*

15. *Elmer Sprague.* Metaphysical Thinking, *p. 98.*

claim seems to hinge on the assumption that perceptible things are mere collections of perceptible qualities. But why this assumption? Why not the more commonsensical distinction between perceptions and the objects of perceptions?

Related to this assumption is subjective idealism's insistence that things are collections of perceptible qualities. This belief only follows if we don't make a sharp distinction between perceptible things and our perceptions. But can we really say how things are without making such a distinction? Subjective idealism does not really seem to answer the question of what things are—rather, it seems to dissolve it. Things are as I perceive them. But this apparently rules out the possibility of objective knowledge.

As for objective idealism, we observed two apparent strengths: It explains why perceptible things persist in the mind, and it offers an intelligible world system. Sprague, however, believes that neither of these aspects is as strong as it may appear.

Recall your classroom experience. You perceive the classroom because some other mind, call it God, perceives it all the time, thus holding the classroom in place each time that you happen to perceive it. But do we really need such an explanation? In answering why things persist in our minds, can't a materialistic explanation suffice? You can account for the composition of the classroom or of the things that you pass en route to it. And should they one day disappear, you can also account for that eventuality: They fell down, were torn down, or were blown up. Why the additional Why? that idealists ask?

Objective idealists seem to think that the usual accounts of things won't do. They seek some ultimate explanation. Thus, "God minds it." But what does that tell us? While the classroom stands, God minds it. When it lies in ruins, it does so because God minds it. We're left wondering what "God minds it" adds to a commonsensical accounting.

Objective idealists also claim that the world is intelligible because it's a product of mind. But whose mind? God's mind, some say, or some sort of cosmic intelligence. But simply because our own mind may be intelligible, does that mean God's is? How are we to know God's mind? How can we distinguish between our own perceptions, which by strict idealistic principles we can never get beyond, and God's perceptions? It seems that idealism must answer these questions before it can be considered as the most compelling explanation of ultimate reality.

Are we, in the last analysis, forced to choose between materialism or idealism? Is there some middle ground? For Voltaire's Candide, the answer is to reject both extremes: extreme materialism, which he sees as leading to nothingness, and extreme idealism, which leads to blind optimism. Yes, disorder, chaos, even evil exist. But Candide does not succumb to them. He feels that to cure evil, we must first recognize its reality and its inevitability. He decides that he can cultivate virtue and justice, although he probably will not find them in the universe. Thus, Candide attempts to avoid what he considers the false dilemma of all or nothing. His attitude uses the practical consequences of a belief. In this sense, it is pragmatic. Pragmatism offers another approach to reality.

Reality in Pragmatism

As we noted earlier, pragmatism is a philosophical movement that has grown up in the last hundred years through the writings of Peirce, James, and Dewey. James defines pragmatism as "the attitude of looking away from first things, principles, 'categories,' supposed necessities; and of looking towards last things, fruits, consequences, facts."[16] Pragmatism is also a reaction to traditional systems of philosophy, such as materialism and idealism. These systems, claim the pragmatists, have erred in looking for absolutes. Debates like those between Ruth and Brad are pointless, for reality is hardly a single thing. Nature is many things: It is pluralistic. And we are part of it. Using intelligence and reason, we can understand and exercise some control over nature; we can help create it.

To grasp the metaphysical content of pragmatism, it is essential to understand its general approach to philosophy and the social climate out of which it arose.[17]

Pragmatism's Approach to Philosophy

Pragmatism is decidedly humanistic. Peirce, James, and Dewey tried to understand philosophy and reformulate its problems in the light of psychology, sociology, scientific method, and the insights provided by the arts. They opposed the insularity of philosophy, its failure to view problems in a larger human and social context. "In a subject like philosophy," wrote James, "it is really fatal to lose connection with the open air of human nature, and to think in terms of shop-tradition only."[18] Philosophy was not just a self-contained discipline with its own cluster of problems; it was an instrument used by living individuals who were wrestling with personal and social problems, and struggling to clarify their standards, directions, and goals. Such impulses were not novel to philosophy, but pragmatism took this position deliberately, systematically, and vigorously.

John Dewey, writing in *Reconstruction in Philosophy*, argued that all philosophy arises out of people's continual struggles to deal with social and moral problems. Two important observations follow from this fact. One, philosophy cannot be understood without an awareness of the social forces that have produced it. Two, and more important here, any philosophy or doctrine has worth only to the degree that it assists people in resolving their problems. Notice especially this second point in the following passage from *Reconstruction in Philosophy*:

> This is the trait which, in my opinion, has affected most deeply the classic notion about the nature of philosophy. Philosophy has arrogated to itself the office of demonstrating the existence of a transcendent, absolute or inner reality and of revealing to man the nature and features of this ultimate and higher

---

16. *William James.* Pragmatism: A New Name for Some Old Ways of Thinking. *New York: Longmans, Green, 1907, pp. 54–55.*

17. *The following discussion is indebted to Charles Frankel.* The Golden Age of American Philosophy. *New York: George Braziller, 1960, pp. 1–17.*

18. *Quoted in Charles Frankel.* The Golden Age, *p. 3.*

reality. It has therefore claimed that it was in possession of a higher organ of knowledge than is employed by positive science and ordinary practical experience, and that it is marked by a superior dignity and importance—a claim which is undeniable *if* philosophy leads man to proof and intuition of a Reality beyond that open to day-by-day life and the special sciences.

This claim has, of course, been denied by various philosophers from time to time. But for the most part these denials have been agnostic and sceptical. They have contented themselves with asserting that absolute and ultimate reality is beyond human ken. But they have not ventured to deny that such Reality would be the appropriate sphere for the exercise of philosophic knowledge provided only it were within the reach of human intelligence. Only comparatively recently has another conception of the proper office of philosophy arisen. This course of lectures will be devoted to setting forth this different conception of philosophy in some of its main contrasts to what this lecture has termed the classic conception. At this point, it can be referred to only by anticipation and in cursory fashion. It is implied in the account which has been given of the origin of philosophy out of the background of an authoritative tradition; a tradition originally dictated by man's imagination working under the influence of love and hate and in the interest of emotional excitement and satisfaction. Common frankness requires that it be stated that this account of the origin of philosophies claiming to deal with absolute Being in a systematic way has been given with malice prepense. It seems to me that this genetic method of approach is a more effective way of undermining this type of philosophic theorizing than any attempt at logical refutation could be.

If this lecture succeeds in leaving in your minds as a reasonable hypothesis the idea that philosophy originated not out of intellectual material, but out of social and emotional material, it will also succeed in leaving with you a changed attitude toward traditional philosophies. They will be viewed from a new angle and placed in a new light. New questions about them will be aroused and new standards for judging them will be suggested.[19]

We should note that pragmatism evidences a confidence in the ability and power of the mind to make the world over. The universe is plastic and unfinished; the human intellect can make its ideals a reality. Peirce, James, and Dewey believed that ideas can actually lead the way in human life. This ideal underlay their insistence that the truth of an idea lies in its capacity to get us through life in a desirable way.

Corollary to this is the view that all thinking exists to defend personal interests and unconscious wishes that thinking cannot change. All thinking strengthens or secures some human interest. Rather than compromising human ideals, this notion shows that ideals have a natural home in the world and that new ways of thinking have been discovered to realize these ideals more effectively.

Understandably, pragmatism damns any belief that limits what the human mind and will can accomplish. "Damn the absolute," James once wrote to a fellow philosopher. And more than once he penned, "Pragmatism looks to the future."[20] The future is limited only by human aspiration, and that is limited

19. *John Dewey.* Reconstruction in Philosophy. *New York: Henry Holt, 1920, pp. 406–407.*

20. *Quoted in Charles Frankel.* The Golden Age, *p. 7.*

by the human capacity to slough off inherited beliefs in eternal truths. Philosophy must recognize this.

Major Scientific Movements Encountered by Pragmatism

In implementing its approach to philosophy, pragmatism had to address several issues and movements of the day. One was Darwin's theory of evolution. Before Darwin's theory, educated people believed that there was a divine plan or purpose operating in the world. But Darwin's theory does not explain things by an appeal to metaphysical ends. Evolution occurs by *chance variation*. While usefulness occasionally explains the survival of a new trait, it does not account for its initial appearance. If there is a Grand Architect responsible for the fortuitous adaptation of a new trait—at the cost of countless failures—it doesn't seem to know its own design until after the event.

Darwin's theory was reinforced by another dominant idea of nineteenth-century science: mechanistic determinism. In essence, mechanistic determinism holds that the future is already determined, and that all human activity amounts to just so much character interplay in a drama whose conclusion is already written. If all the goals of science were achieved, they would reveal the structure of the universe. Pragmatism had to speak to this conception of a "block universe," in which everything is predestined.

A third nineteenth-century movement was generated by social Darwinism and Herbert Spencer's individualism. In essence, these views assert that unchecked competition between individuals is nature's way of improving the species. Poverty and suffering are natural ways of eliminating the unfit. Charity and compassion, unless controlled, are social threats. Personal responsibility, while perhaps desirable in personal relations or in public administration, is unsuited for business. As Charles Frankel points out in his *The Golden Age of American Philosophy*, this doctrine was a "strange amalgam of incompatible notions. It combined a belief in universal change with a belief in an eternally right and unalterable order of society. It confused natural facts or pseudo-facts with moral laws. It applied generalizations about biological individuals to legal constructs like corporations. It assumed the state was the only agency in society that could place barriers in the path of individual initiative."[21] Yet it was no stranger than similar amalgams of scientific misinformation that existed before and have existed since. More to the point, pragmatism developed in counterpoint to this individualism. "Underneath the most abstract philosophical discussions—discussions about the reality of the Absolute, the meaning of truth, the logic of value-judgments—one can hear the echoes of a clamorous social scene and one can sense the impatience of sensitive men with ideas that had become the cloaks of callousness and complacency."[22]

For many people at this time, some form of idealism served to neutralize dyspeptic implications of evolution, mechanistic determinism, and Spencerian individualism. After all, idealism generally relegated all scientific theory to the

21. *Charles Frankel.* The Golden Age, *p. 12.*

22. *Charles Frankel.* The Golden Age, *p. 12.*

realm of the relative. In contrast, idealism dealt with *ultimate* reality, characterized by a single, harmonious moral order. In a word, idealism provided support for traditional religious views and for moral criticism. However, idealism generally ignored the empirical methods of the sciences, and it even ignored evolution itself. Thus, for pragmatists, idealism did not deal effectively with the problems of the age.

The pragmatic alternative denies sharp distinctions between matter and mind, science and morals, and experience and reason. For pragmatists, human ideas and ideals must be examined from the biological and social points of view and treated as instruments for making sense of experience. Any idea or ideal must be judged in terms of its context. Its value depends on its problem-solving capacity. The heart of pragmatism is the pragmatic method.

The Pragmatic Method

The pragmatic method proposes that we discover what our ideas mean by studying their consequences in actual experience. As such, the method is critical of abstractions, making them responsible and accountable in the light of observable facts. Any inferences about the world drawn from metaphysical inquiries must have premises that refer to facts in the world and not to human reasoning alone. We cannot base judgments on their connectedness to some presupposed transcendent or ultimate reality. Any judgment must be rooted in the things of experience that are meaningful to humans. Thus, any view of reality is tied to the values inherent in social traditions. In effect, there are no ultimate principles, no self-evident values, and no irreducible sense data. In fact, pragmatism allows no certainties. Ultimately the test of an idea or ideal is its capacity to solve the particular problems that it addresses. Both materialism and idealism fail this test.

Pragmatists differ in their practice—understandably, since pragmatism is not a monolithic system of thought. For example, Peirce was concerned with the logical implications of ideas, not their psychological effects. He focused on the scientific function of ideas—their role in fostering reasoned consensus. In contrast, James, a physiologist and psychologist, was interested in ideas as events in personal experience, as instruments of will and desire. Dewey was neither a student of logic and science nor a psychologist. His main interest was social criticism. He used the pragmatic method to reassess the functions of education, logic, the arts, and philosophy in human civilization. Nonetheless, the observations about pragmatism presented here underlay the thought of each of these highly influential American philosophers, and the pragmatic method guided their thoughts.

Applied to metaphysical questions, the pragmatic method indicates certain criteria for determining what's real. In general, materialists rely on sense observation and scientific method; idealists, primarily on reason. In contrast, James accepted neither of these as the final determinant of reality. In fact, he argued that people recognize a number of realities. Among them are the worlds of sense experience; of scientific knowledge; of belief and opinion; and of the transcendent, religious, or the supernatural. According to James, each of us selects the reality that is most personally meaningful. In effect, we choose our own ultimate reality. While metaphysicians speak of one world as having more reality than another, James interpreted their view as expressing a relation to our emotional and active life. Simply put, reality is what stimulates and interests us, and will ultimately determines what our reality is.

While rejecting scientific method as the exclusive determinant of reality, pragmatists nonetheless employ it in order to learn the secrets of reality and self. But they do not look for cosmic mind or reason; the fact that we have minds does not mean that the universe does, as some idealists would contend. Pragmatism asserts that mind is real but only as a function of behavior. We develop this function when we learn about the things around us. For pragmatists, thinking is coming to understand the connection between action and consequence.

Objections to Pragmatism

The opponents of pragmatism do not consider it an acceptable middle ground between materialism and idealism. They claim that it is muddled thinking, that it has no clear notion of what it understands to be real. Pragmatists claim to know only their experiences, which critics argue is a claim of idealism. Peirce, in fact, opted for a version of idealism. But if we know only our experiences, how can we maintain the pragmatic belief of an objective physical reality?

Critics also disagree that mind is just a function of behavior, that it is only an instrument of biological survival. They point out that people meditate, contemplate, and use the mind to compose great symphonies and to ask philosophical questions, yet these activities do not seem necessary for biological survival. Mind, say the pragmatists, exists to fulfill desires. Then why the commitment to scientific inquiry? Why such a stress on impartiality when seeking truth and not more reliance on the subjective impulses of the mind?

Finally, critics suggest that pragmatism erases the distinction between the structure of the mind and the structure of the universe, between the knowledge of facts and facts that exist whether or not they are known.[23] Because of pragmatism's emphasis on the mind's capacity to impose order on an open, unlimited world, there appears to be no antecedent order in the world, no configuration of things aside from what we may think or desire. This is especially true of the pragmatism proposed by James and Dewey. Pragmatists, of course, do not deny the existence of a world independent of the presence of human beings, but they do deny that anything in the world is settled or finished.

Reality as Being

As for Ruth, pragmatism would not seem to provide an acceptable compromise, since she believes in an idealistic concept of order and purpose. Pragmatism shares more materialistic outlooks. She would also reject the pragmatic diagnosis that there is no difference in things if none is detectable. And she would

23. *Charles Frankel.* The Golden Age, *p. 7.*

hardly accept the contention that the mind is only a function of behavior. So, let's see what happens when she takes the issue to Max, her fiance, and is shown yet another alternative.

Ruth: You know, Max, the other day the professor said something really strange.

Max: What's that?

Ruth: He said he'd made you in his lab.

Max: That's funny. He told me the same thing about you.

Ruth: You're kidding.

Max: But he said you'd be like a human in every way.

Ruth: That you wouldn't be able to detect the slightest difference?

Max: That's what he said. And that you'd make the perfect mate—

Ruth: Even if I was mechanical, right?

Max: That's about it. Tell me something, Ruth. If I were a mechanical man, would you hesitate to marry me?

Ruth: Oh, Max, the whole question's so silly. I'm really tired of talking about it.

Max: Then give me a simple yes or no.

Ruth: Well . . . I guess yes, I would have some doubts.

Max: Why?

Ruth: Why? Isn't that obvious? I mean, you'd be more thing than man.

Max: More human *machine* than human *being*, is that what you mean?

Ruth: Yes, I guess so. I mean, if you came into the world the same as the rest of us, that would make you one of us, wouldn't it? You'd be fully human.

Max: Fully human? You make it sound as if my dues would be all paid up, that I'd be a member in good standing of the human race.

Ruth: Well, you'd be in better standing than if you had come by way of the professor's cellar, that's for sure.

Max: What would you like me to do—go back and come into the world again?

Ruth: Max, don't be so silly. You make it sound as if we're actually talking about you.

Max: I think you are.

Ruth: You're not going to tell me that the professor actually did create you?

Max: Look, you said you loved me, right?

Ruth: *Love*—not *loved*. I love you right now, this very minute. And I want to be with you as long as you want me to be.

Max: Why? Why do you love me?

Ruth: What a silly question!

Max: Then humor me. Tell me why.

Ruth: Why? Because you're you, that's why.

Max: But what am I, Ruth—really?

Ruth: Well, who is Max, *really*? Max is kind and he's tender; he's loving and honest; he's handsome and intelligent . . . and he's going to be insufferably vain if I go on any more!

Max: My incredible humility will prevent that.

Ruth: Oh! You're hopeless!

Max: Seriously, is all that what you think I am? Is that your concept of me?

Ruth: I suppose that's part of it.

Max: Then the professor comes along and blows it. He says something that changes that concept. He says I'm not what you think I am, that I'm not like you or him or anybody else because I didn't come on the scene the way everyone else has. Suddenly this information overshadows everything else you know about me. Suddenly you don't know whether you want to marry me. Suddenly you don't know whether you can love me in the way you did before.

Ruth: But do you blame me?

Max: It's not a question of blame, Ruth. It's a question of *why* you loved me in the first place. You say it's because I am me. But I'm still me. I'm still the same being I was before the professor dropped his bomb. I haven't changed at all.

Ruth: But that's not true. Something about you has changed for me, something very important.

Max: Some *thing*, yes. But not me. I am the same. If I lost an arm, would you still love me?

Ruth: You know I would. But you're not comparing that to being a brainchild of science, are you?

Max: In a way I am. Because it's clear that, for you, *what* or *who* I am is more important than *that* I am.

Ruth: Listen, do you think for a minute that I'd care if you were wealthy or had a fancy sports car or anything like that?

Max: Of course you wouldn't.

Ruth: Because if I did, I'd be treating you just like a thing.

Max: That's right. But you can treat people like things more subtly.

Ruth: How?

Max: Well, you can treat me like a thing when you insist that I be human. That's really no different from insisting that I be a Republican or a Democrat; that I be a Catholic, Protestant, or Jew; that I be a white or black. Why must I be some *thing*? Why can't I just *be*? Why not be happy with my just plain old *being* and leave it at that?

Ruth: But I am.

Max: I really don't think so. Because if you were, it wouldn't matter whether or not I was human. It would only matter that I *was*.

Ruth: You mean I'd love you just for existing.

Max: Not *for* existing, just existing. You'd love my existing.

Ruth: I don't understand.

Max: Well, you wouldn't, you couldn't love anything specific; you'd love the very core of me, my *being*.

Ruth: But I do love your soul.

Max: That's not what I mean. My being is not my soul or mind or body.

Ruth: Then what is it?

Max: It can't be described. It defies language because it's not a thing. It is my unique act of existing.

Ruth: You've got me confused with all this talk of being. I'm afraid I'm not following.

Max: That's because English doesn't help us very much. There's only one word for *being* in English, and that usually refers to some *thing*. But take German. In German there are two words for being—*das Seinde* and *das Sein*. *Das Seinde* means being as a thing, an object. You're a being, I'm a being, Brad's a being, the professor's a being.

Ruth: I see, being in the sense of someone *being* a student or a worker or a writer.

Max: Right. They'd be some thing; they'd be *a* being. But *das Sein* means being as an activity, not a thing. It refers to the *being* of the thing.

Ruth: You mean the student as *being* instead of the student as a being.

Max: Yes. In the same way you can speak of the lover as a being or simply as being. When you view the lover as *a* being, it seems to me that you view the lover as a thing. But when you view the lover as *being*, you don't.

Ruth: So you're saying that I shouldn't love you so much because you're you, but because you *are*.

Max: I think so.

Ruth: I never thought of that.

Max does not want to consider reality piecemeal. Traditional outlooks, in trying to simplify life, reduce it to an abstraction. But there is nothing abstract about existing. Existence is what is ultimately real. And existence involves individuals who exist. We find this emphasis on existence and the individual in two twentieth-century movements, phenomenology and existentialism.

Phenomenology and existentialism share a number of outlooks on the human condition. First, both phenomenologists and existentialists observe suffering and pain as the overriding human experience. They point out that we suffer all kinds of pain: physical, emotional, and psychological. We feel anxious, uncertain, and indecisive. We know what it is to dread, to feel despair, and to hurt. Daily we face the reality of death. True, we are not always conscious of death's imminence, but it is always with us.

Building on this insight into the human condition, phenomenologists and existentialists claim that we shall never understand the primacy of the individual so long as we explain life and people objectively. In reducing individuals to scientific explanations, materialism makes things of people. In explaining reality in terms of cosmic mind, idealism submerges individual self in universal ego. Truth about life and ourselves is not something to be grasped and repeated in nice, neat statements. We experience truth, like everything else, through living; the truth is within, not without.

Despite these general similarities, various points distinguish phenomenology from existentialism.

Phenomenology

To understand phenomenology, look at the term itself. *Phenomenology* clearly consists of the root word *phenomenon* and the suffix *-ology*, meaning "the study of." *Phenomenology*, therefore, literally means "the study of phenomena." This definition, however, isn't very helpful until we understand what *phenomenon* means.

Immanuel Kant distinguished between the thing as it is (noumenon) and the thing as it appears in and to the consciousness (phenomenon). Kant believed that we could never know the noumenon, the thing itself, but only the phenomenon, our experience of it. This broad distinction helps in understanding phenomenology as the study of things as they appear in or to the consciousness. Without becoming enmeshed in the historical development of phenomenology, let's just point out that the phenomenologist's professed concern with the consciousness is altogether understandable in the light of the implications of Kantianism. After all, if we can never know things in themselves (noumena), then we're left with only the things for consciousness (phenomena). Thus, a serious inquiry into consciousness seems fully justified. The first phenomenologists felt that philosophers had not done this.

In his *Phenomenology of Perception*, Maurice Merleau-Ponty (1907–1961) says, "The aim of phenomenology is described as the study of experiences with a view to bringing out their 'essences,' their underlying 'reason.'"[24] Phenomenology is the philosophical school that contends that being is the underlying reality, that what is ultimately real is our consciousness, which itself is being. For the founder of phenomenology, Edmund Husserl (1859–1938), the overriding reality is the consciousness itself. You can think away everything, but you cannot think away thought. How things are is not so important as how they appear to be to the individual. What is ultimately real is pure consciousness, which we reach by removing attention from the specific experiences that occupy it.

Phenomenology, then, is the study of being. As such it serves as the foundation of all sciences. But it's a science of being different from metaphysics, which had for centuries been regarded as the science of being. Our sketches of materialism and idealism indicate that beginning with Aristotle, philosophers had viewed metaphysics as dealing with an ultimate reality that exists in and for itself. Kant shattered this assumption by showing that human minds can never know things in themselves (noumena). As a result, many philosophers concluded that no science of being was possible and that knowledge was limited to mind-dependent objects.

For Husserl, however, the phenomenological method made possible a new science of being, *ontology*. This method disclosed an ultimate realm of being, not in the sense that it exists beyond an experience, but in the sense that it presents itself with certainty within experience. For Husserl, studying being was not turning to another reality but penetrating more deeply the only reality: things for consciousness.

24. *Quoted in Edo Pivcevic.* Husserl and Phenomenology. *London: Hutchinson University Library, 1970, p. 11.*

To understand what Husserl is saying, it's helpful to know more about him. An entry in his diary from 1906 provides a good look at what concerned him:[25] "I have been through enough torment from lack of clarity and from doubt that covers back and forth. Only one need absorbs me: I must win clarity else I cannot live; I cannot bear life unless I can believe that I shall achieve it."[26] His intense desire for certainty was intensified by the relativism of the age, as evidenced in both pragmatism and scientism, that is, by adherence to or belief in scientific method as the only reliable way of knowing anything. In Husserl's view, relativism was self-contradictory. Anyone who denied the possibility of absolute certainty was involved in a contradiction, for to deny that possibility was to logically allow the existence of "an objectively valid science."

Of course, this argument didn't budge pragmatists. They would have likely viewed Husserl's insistence on an objectively valid science as indicating more his fear of uncertainty than the existence of such a science. Nonetheless, Husserl attacked relativism, not only because he viewed it as inconsistent, but also because he felt that it generated undesirable social consequences. Writing in 1935, when the Nazis held power, Husserl viewed the European crisis as fundamentally attributable to the gradual erosion of the belief in rational certainty.

For Husserl, rational certainty was the discovery of the Greeks. Europe inherited it from them through Western culture. Recall that the attitude of Plato and Aristotle was one of the disinterested spectator, the overseer of the world. With this attitude, they were led to a distinction between the represented and the real world, and ultimately to a universally valid truth—to truth in itself. Curiously, this analysis parallels Dewey's description of the Greek attitude. But Dewey, and pragmatism generally, condemned it because it locked people into ultimate principles, self-evident views, and a hierarchy of absolute values. Instead, Dewey wanted philosophy to adopt the methods of natural science and to turn to practical problems that beset individuals and society. In contrast, Husserl attributed the "crisis of European man" to a blind allegiance to the methods of natural science. His prescription was to revive the disinterested attitude and to return to rationality in the original Greek sense.

Specifically, Husserl objected to the application of the methods of natural science to the psychic life, to treating psychic phenomena as if they are material objects. Such thinking leads to a caricature of reality, a naive form of dualism wherein the physical world is mind-dependent. What's more, he saw psychology as compounding this error. Having distinguished between minds and bodies, psychologists treated minds as if they are like bodies. Husserl proposed a radically different investigative method to avoid these errors, a method, he believed, that would ultimately be applicable to all the sciences. The perfection of phenomenology would demonstrate that the quest for certainty was not futile or frivolous. It would accomplish this by establishing a firm foundation for the sciences.

25. See W. T. Jones. From Kant to Wittgenstein and Sartre. New York: Harcourt, Brace and World, 1969, pp. 385–399.

26. Quoted in H. S. Spiegelberg. The Phenomenological Movement. The Hague: Martinus Nijhoff, 1965, p. 82.

Vital to understanding Husserl's method is understanding his phenomenological stance, as opposed to what he called "the natural standpoint":

> Our first outlook upon life is that of natural human beings, imagining, judging, feeling, willing, *"from the natural standpoint."* Let us make clear to ourselves what this means in the form of simple meditations which we can best carry on in the first person.
>
> I am aware of a world, spread out in space endlessly, and in time becoming and become, without end. I am aware of it, that means, first of all, I discover it immediately, intuitively, I experience it. Through sight, touch, hearing, etc., in the different ways of sensory perception, corporeal things somehow spatially distributed are *for me simply there*, in verbal or figurative sense "present," whether or not I pay them special attention by busying myself with them, considering, thinking, feeling, willing. . . .
>
> [Further,] what is actually perceived, and what is more or less clearly co-present and determinate (to some extent at least), is partly pervaded, partly girt about with a *dimly apprehended depth or fringe of indeterminate reality*. I can pierce it with rays from the illuminating focus of attention with varying success. . . .
>
> As it is with the world in its ordered being as a spatial present—the aspect I have so far been considering—so likewise is it with the world in respect to its *ordered being in the succession of time*. This world now present to me, and in every waking "now" obviously so, has its temporal horizon, infinite in both directions. . . .
>
> [Moreover,] this world is not there for me as a mere *world of facts and affairs*, but, with the same immediacy, as a *world of values*, a *world of goods*, a *practical world*. . . . I find the things before me furnished not only with the qualities that befit their positive nature, but with value-characters such as beautiful or ugly, agreeable or disagreeable, pleasant or unpleasant, and so forth. . . .
>
> We emphasize a most important point once again in the sentences that follow: I find continually present and standing over against me the one spatio-temporal fact-world to which I myself belong, as do all other men found in it. . . . This "fact-world," as the word already tells us, I find to *be out there*, and also *take it just as it gives itself to me as something that exists out there*. All doubting and rejecting of the data of the natural world leaves standing the *general thesis of the natural standpoint*. "The" world is as fact-world always there; at the most it is at odd points "other" than I supposed, this or that under such names as "illusion," "hallucination," and the like, must be struck *out of it*, so to speak; but the "it" remains ever . . . a world that has its being out there. To know it more comprehensively, more trustworthily, more perfectly than the naive lore of experience is able to do . . . is the goal of the *sciences of the natural standpoint*. [27]

People usually assume the natural standpoint toward the world. This consists of being aware of a world that is "simply there," whether or not we pay any special attention to it. This "fact-world," as Husserl calls it, we find to be "out there," and we take it just as it gives itself to us. Despite all doubting and rejecting of the data of this natural world, he says that most of us would usually insist that the world as a fact-world is always present. Occasionally this

27. *Edmund Husserl.* Ideas: General Introduction to Pure Phenomenology. *W. R. Boyce-Gibson, Trans. New York: Macmillan, 1931, secs. 27, 30. Reprinted by permission of Macmillan Publishing Co., Inc., and George Allen & Unwin Ltd.*

fact-world differs from what we supposed: We experience illusions or hallucinations. But a world that has its being out there remains. In other words, although we may suspect or even reject parts of our experience, we most often
unquestioningly accept the world as a whole. Indeed, this natural standpoint
seems a most reasonable position. Yet Husserl asks us to question it—to doubt
the world as a whole.

Husserl does not want us to abandon the thesis of the natural
standpoint—that the fact-world has its being out there—but to modify it. He
asks us to *"set it as it were out of action . . . to disconnect it, bracket it."* The natural
standpoint still remains, but we simply make no use of it. We reserve judgments based on the natural standpoint. Although we continue to be conscious
of the entire natural world, which is continually there for us, we phe-
nomenologically bracket it, an act that "completely bars us from using any
judgment that concerns spatio-temporal existence."

To illustrate Husserl's meaning, suppose you are looking at a die in the
palm of your hand. What do you experience? From the natural standpoint, the
die is a cube of a certain color and size. There are dots on each side, from one
to six of them. What happens when we bracket this experience, as Husserl
suggests? You do not doubt the *experience* of having the die in hand, but you do
doubt that you *actually* have a die in hand. After all, it may be that you are
dreaming, hallucinating, or imagining, and that your hand is actually empty.
What Husserl is asking you to do, then, is to doubt that the die has being in
the mode of existence. This is what he means by the phenomenological stance,
which he would prescribe for all our experience.

Husserl is suggesting that we suspend the truth claims of our everyday
cognitive processes. Because we assume the natural standpoint, this suspension seems unnatural for most of us. Why should I doubt that I actually have a
die in my hand when I can feel and see it? Husserl insists that such bracketing,
far from leaving us in a state of ignorance and skepticism, will present important truths that would otherwise elude us. He believes that these truths are
important because whatever remains after bracketing, after universal doubt, is
absolutely certain. The obvious question is What survives universal doubt? In
general, Husserl believes that what survives is consciousness; ultimate reality
consists of consciousness: "For what can remain over when the whole world is
bracketed, including ourselves and our thinking? . . . Consciousness in itself
has a being of its own which in its absolute uniqueness of nature remains
unaffected by the phenomenologic disconnection."[28]

By *consciousness* Husserl means that which involves both an act of intending and the intended object of this act. For example, what you see in the palm
of your hand is a white die, on one of whose faces is a black dot. From the
natural standpoint we hardly ever doubt this fact. But, says Husserl, we *can*
doubt it. However, it is not possible to doubt the *experience* of having seen and
felt the die in the palm of your hand. Moreover, within this experience, it is
possible to distinguish the die (the intentional object) from your act of intending it. When you bracket, what you experience is both your experiencing (that

28. *Edmund Husserl.* Ideas, *sec. 33.*

is, intending) of the die in the palm of your hand and the die as experienced (that is, intended) by you.

Further thought about how objects are present to consciousness persuaded Husserl to emphasize acts of intending more than the objects themselves. Bracketing revealed to him deeper and deeper levels of ego activity that are impossible to understand without profound phenomenological training. Suffice it to say that when all is bracketed, including ourselves, Husserl contends that consciousness remains. When we bracket our whole world, we tap our essence and realize that something precedes our experiences, namely being. "It therefore remains as a region of Being which is in principle unique and can become in fact the field of a new science—the science of phenomenology."[29]

For Husserl, phenomenology is a new science of being. It reveals a sphere of being that is ultimate, in the sense that it presents itself with certainty within our experience. Studying being is not, for Husserl, investigating another reality. It is delving deeper and deeper into the only reality—consciousness.

Another phenomenologist, Martin Heidegger (1889–1976), makes this question of being his primary concern. The problem with traditional thinking, claims Heidegger, is that it is confused over the question of "Being." Being is not a thing; it is the very existing of the thing. Max tells Ruth that she is more interested in what he is than in *that* he is. Heidegger would make the same distinction. When we talk of being itself, we are talking about the very act of existing. Being does not consist of all the *things* that a person is or all the characteristics of the individual, for that is to speak of the individual as *a* being. On the other hand, to speak of the individual's Being is to acknowledge that when all qualities and properties not necessary to being as being are stripped away, Being remains as *this* being, as individual.

Being is a difficult concept to communicate, because it is not a thing, although we may identify it with things. But this identification makes it all the more elusive, for we end up identifying the thing with Being. This is what Max says Ruth is doing. You may have heard someone say, "Love me for what I am." Max is saying, "Don't love me for what I am; love my *am*! Love my being, not what you may see as an expression of it: matter, mind, or soul." If we are to understand reality, says Heidegger, we must abandon our mad commitment to the world of things. By becoming conscious of our own Being, we may better understand the Being that underlies everything. At that point we may establish a meaningful relationship with another person.

This emphasis on reality as being underlies the view of the human as an existential being. But it is also curious to note its connection with Buddhist thought, even though, as we have previously seen, Buddhism seems to share some outlooks with the scientific view of the human, especially in its denial of self and of personal freedom.

Although Heidegger is undoubtedly a Western thinker, his thought has enough Oriental flavor to lead him to remark, upon reading the work of Zen scholar D. T. Suzuki, "If I understand this man correctly, this is what I have

---

29. *Quoted in Edo Pivcevic.* Husserl and Phenomenology, *p. 11.*

been trying to say in all my writings."[30] The Oriental thinker is generally more concerned not with an objective, empirically verifiable reality but with the inner nature of the self. The world of the senses is short-lived and illusory. As a result, Eastern thought is preoccupied not with what is real but with *being* real. It distinguishes between the idea of ourselves and the immediate concrete feeling of ourselves. As Zen scholar Alan Watts puts it, "Zen points out that our precious 'self' is just an idea. . . . When we are no longer identified with the idea of ourselves, the entire relationship between subject and object, knower and known undergoes a sudden and revolutionary change. It becomes a real relationship, a mutuality in which the subject creates the object just as much as the object creates the subject. The knower no longer feels himself to be independent of the known; the experiencer no longer feels himself to stand apart from the experience."[31] If we are looking for a concrete reality, we shall find it *between* the individual and the world, "as the concrete coin is 'between' the abstract, Euclidean surfaces of its two sides."[32]

Obviously, Eastern thought eschews the polarities of knower and known, experiencer and experience, and subject and object, because they are artificial and preclude true knowledge of self and being. Heidegger, too, seems to consider this Western penchant for dividing a great error that began with Plato, who located truth in the intellect. Against the intellect Plato set nature—a realm of objects to be studied, manipulated, and quantified. Today we find ourselves inheritors of this tradition, technological "masters" of the planet. Along with this dubious distinction, we have suffered, as Heidegger and Eastern thinkers have also observed, an estrangement from being and from ourselves, which the will to power and dominance only intensifies.

The emphasis that phenomenologists have given to consciousness and being takes a more concrete form in the philosophy of existentialism.

Existentialism

We mentioned some of the intellectual currents to which the phenomenologists reacted. Of special note was the increasingly popular assumption that an objective knowledge of the human could be attained by applying the methods of empirical science to sociology and psychology. Existentialism, too, can be viewed partially as a reaction to this. Like phenomenology, existentialism is unsympathetic to science as a cognitive enterprise, suspicious of scientism, and wary of the application of scientific method to the solution of economic and political problems. What interests existentialists is the subjective flow of experience. But whereas phenomenologists might suggest that we become truly a self in the classical contemplation of a truth, existentialists find self-definition in the passionate commitment to act and deed. This fact must be remembered to understand existentialism's metaphysical leanings.

30. D. T. Suzuki. Zen Buddhism. *William Barrett, Ed. Garden City, N.Y.: Doubleday Anchor Books, 1956, pp. xi–xii.*

31. *Alan Watts.* The Way of Zen. *New York: Pantheon, 1957, pp, pp. 120–121. Reprinted by permission.*

32. *Alan Watts.* The Way of Zen, *p. 122.*

In sketching the thought of Husserl, we began by quoting from his diary. We glimpsed the energizing force behind his philosophy: the need for certainty. It's useful to contrast this with an entry from *The Journals* of the founder of modern existentialism, Sören Kierkegaard (1813–1853):

> What I really lack is to be clear in my mind *what I am to do*, not what I am to know, except insofar as a certain understanding must precede every action. The thing is to understand myself, to see what God really wishes *me* to do; the thing is to find a truth which is true *for me*, to find *the idea for which I can live and die*. What would be the use of discovering so-called objective truth, of working through all the systems of philosophy and of being able if required, to review them all and show up the inconsistencies within each system;—what good would it do me to be able to develop a theory of the state and combine all the details into a single whole, and so construct a world in which I did not live, but only held up to the view of others;—what good would it do me to be able to explain the meaning of Christianity if it had *no* deeper significance *for me and for my life;*—what good would it do me if truth stood before me, cold and naked, not caring whether I recognized her or not, and producing in me a shudder of fear rather than a trusting devotion? I certainly do not deny that I still recognize an *imperative of understanding* and that through it one can work upon men, *but it must be taken up into my life,* and *that is* what I now recognize as the most important thing.[33]

Several themes are worth noting in this entry. First, Kierkegaard, like Husserl, is concerned with clarity—not the clarity of some absolute truth, but the clarity of what he is to do. This emphasis on action and doing recurs in all existentialist thinking, and it constitutes a lens through which existentialists view all philosophical questions, including metaphysical ones. Second, notice the emphasis Kierkegaard gives to the subjective—to "I," "me," and "my life." This is also a recurring theme in existential philosophy and literature. Third, observe Kierkegaard's religiosity. He wants to know what God expects of him. Kierkegaard, a Lutheran, was a deeply religious thinker, and the central issue of his life and thought was what it means to be a Christian. How is an individual to bridge the gap between himself and his Maker, between creation and Creator? Kierkegaard observes that even people who recognize and accept the reality of universal moral laws experience frustrating failure. These well-intentioned people experience the painful awareness that they are not what they ought to be. Kierkegaard wonders whether we should remain in this limbo of despair and anxiety, frustrated by our inability to be better than we are, or make a "leap of faith" to a recognition of God. He feels that this existential choice confronts all individuals.

For Kierkegaard, reality cannot be separated from existence. To exist is to struggle, to face opposition, and to experience passion; to exist is to make decisions, not to flounder. What's more, existence and selfhood are identical. To exist is *to become* a self, not just to be a self. It follows, then, that things that are not selves do not have an independent status. They exist only insomuch as they are "for" selves, for things that truly exist.

33. *Sören Kierkegaard.* The Journals of Kierkegaard. A. Dru, Trans. London: Collins, 1958, p. 44. *Reprinted by permission of Oxford University Press.*

Even this crude sketch of Kierkegaard's thought shows the self as the focus of reality. But it is not an emphasis on the self as thinker, but as doer and actor, as decison maker. Kierkegaard's metaphysical concerns focus on the inner reality of what it is to be human; consequently he was preoccupied with the predicament of decision making: What is *really* real? Kierkegaard wants people to take decisions seriously. More importantly, he wants people to relate the decision predicament to religion, specifically to Christianity, which he sees as the only cure for the agony of decision making.

Friedrich Nietzsche (1844–1900) disagrees. True, the individual is what matters; existence must be stressed above everything else; traditional thought is ultimately irrelevant to the human condition. But Christianity, holds Nietzsche, is not different from traditional thinking. Its conventional values and morality inhibit rather than encourage individual freedom and growth, which can occur only in the absence of a traditional God. Thus, Nietzsche's problem is how to live in a world in which "God is dead." To say that God is dead is to say that there is no cosmic order. What looks like a cosmic, objective order is a mere projection of the human's desperate need to believe in a universe with reason and purpose. In contrast, Nietzsche's universe is characterized by "Eternal Recurrence"; that is, everything eternally recurs, everything that has ever happened happens again and again into infinity. Is Nietzsche, in fact, implying an order? Isn't perpetual recurrence a kind of order? Not really, because in his view nothing in the universe could provide a rationale for the recurrence. Whatever happens, whatever we do, is in the last analysis inconsequential, because events eternally recur. This, according to Nietzsche, is the truth that we must all face eventually. If we can live without hope of any kind, even knowing that what we do will be endlessly repeated, then we have achieved salvation as human beings. How do we do this? Obviously, any prescription that Nietzsche gives cannot resemble Kierkegaard's leap of faith to God and Christianity. And it doesn't. Instead he prescribes a cosmological principle, the will to power.

Nietzsche assumes that nothing is real except the individual world of desires and passions. "We cannot step down or step up to any kind of 'reality' except the reality of our drives,"[34] he writes in *The Genealogy of Morals*. All the various drives that appear to motivate people's acts are, for Nietzsche, variants of one basic drive, the will to power. Although on the cosmological level Nietzsche never works out this principle, he does detail it on the psychological level. At the preconscious level, he holds that the will to power expresses itself in every organism's attempt to use and overcome organisms less powerful than itself. "Life itself," he writes, "is essential assimilation, injury, violation of the foreign and the weaker, suppression, hardness, the forcing of one's own forms upon something else, ingestion and—at least in its mildest form—exploitation."[35] In the last analysis, Nietzsche's answer to how people are to live in a world in which God is dead is to unleash the individual's will to power.

34. *Friedrich Nietzsche*. The Genealogy of Morals. *F. Golffing, Trans. New York: Doubleday, 1956, p. 42.*

35. *Friedrich Nietzsche*. The Genealogy of Morals, *p. 201.*

Although Nietzsche might have first announced atheistic existentialism, its chief exponent has been Jean-Paul Sartre (1905–1980).

Sartre

While Nietzsche seemed to welcome the news of the death of God, Sartre, as we saw in Chapter 2, is deeply disturbed by it. In his essay "Existentialism and Human Decision," he writes, "The existentialist thinks it very distressing that God does not exist." In Sartre's view, since there is no God, there can be no one to conceive of a human nature. Without a human nature, we are free to be what we choose. There is nothing we ought to do, since there is nothing we ought to be. There are no absolutes, no norms of right behavior; we are on our own. We exist; whatever is uniquely ours, whatever makes each of us an individual—our **essence**—is ours for the making. We do not *discover* who we are so much as we *make* it.

Consider the implications of a godless universe. What kind of world has no God? What kind of creatures are we who were not made by any God? What are we to do who find ourselves living in a world without a God? These are some of Sartre's central concerns that cannot be answered by Kierkegaard's leap of faith. Indeed, for Sartre such an act is cowardly because it pushes people further into a world of illusion and false hope.

In contrast, Sartre's prescription for some of these dilemmas is related to his view of reality. Like phenomenologists, Sartre believes that reality exists in phenomena, that is, in "consciousness of." Furthermore, he accepts the phenomenological claim that "consciousness of" consists not only of intentions but also of intentional objects. Under intentional objects Sartre would include everything short of pure consciousness. What remains, then, is intention, that is, the pure, impersonal nothingness of consciousness. This, then, is the departure point for both phenomenology and Sartre's existentialism.

Whereas both phenomenology and existentialism reject the distinction between appearance and reality, Sartre introduces a dichotomy between appearance and consciousness. For Sartre, reality consists of two kinds of being: the being of consciousness and the being of what appears to consciousness, phenomena. He terms the former (consciousness) "being-for-itself" and the latter (phenomena) "being-in-itself."

To grasp this distinction, consider a table that stands across the room from you. Clearly there are innumerable ways in which you can "intend" the table, that is, in which you can think about, remember, and imagine it. The table, of course, cannot perform any of these operations. It has no consciousness. Sartre calls such an intentional object being-in-itself. On the other hand, consciousness, that is, being-for-itself, can conceive of things as they are not. Consciousness involves such unique human activities as imagining, lying, negating, and questioning. Most importantly, being-for-itself makes meaning. In other words, being-for-itself exists in a world of its own making; it is its own God. It is also responsible for the world that it makes.

This distinction between being-in-itself and being-for-itself leads Sartre to conclude that humans *are* only insofar as they act. This is so because action involves conceiving of things as they are not, that is, creating a nonworld toward effecting our world. Our action may be trivial or momentous. We may move to a new town, or we may risk our lives for a cause. This is of no matter to Sartre. What counts is that we act, that is, that we freely adopt a project. When we do, we are truly human beings because we are in the mode of being-for-itself. Failing to act, we are in the mode of being-in-itself. Sartre expresses this point in *Being and Nothingness*, a definitive statement of his philosophy:

> A first glance at human reality informs us that for it being is reduced to doing. . . . Thus we find no *given* in human reality in the sense that temperament, character, passions, principles of reason would be acquired or innate *data* existing in the manner of things. . . . Thus human reality does not exist first in order to act later; but for human reality, to be is to act, and to cease to act is to cease to be. . . .
>
> Furthermore, . . . the act . . . must be defined by an *intention*. No matter how this intention is considered, it can be only a surpassing of the given toward a result to be obtained. This given . . . can not provide the reason for a phenomenon which derives all its meaning from a result to be attained; that is, from a non-existent.
>
> Since the intention is a choice of the end and since the world reveals itself across our conduct, it is the intentional choice of the end which reveals the world, and the world is revealed as this or that (in this or that order) according to the end chosen. The end, illuminating the world, is a state *of* the world to be obtained and not yet existing. . . . Thus my *end* can be a good meal if I am hungry. . . . This meal which [is] beyond the dusty road on which I am traveling is projected as the *meaning* of this road. . . .
>
> Thus the intention by a single unitary upsurge posits the end, chooses itself, and appreciates the given in terms of something which does not yet exist; it is in the light of non-being that being-in-itself is illuminated. . . .
>
> This characteristic of the for-itself implies that it is the being which finds *no help, no pillar of support* in what it *was*. But on the other hand, the for-itself is free and can cause there to be a world because the for-itself is *the being which has to be what it was in the light of what it will be*. Therefore the freedom of the for-itself appears as its *being*. . . . We shall never apprehend ourselves except as a choice in the making. But freedom is simply the fact that this choice is always unconditioned.
>
> Such a choice made without base of support and dictating its own causes to itself . . . is absurd.[36]

Sartre suggests a rather unconventional view of human behavior here. Because of the influence of social science, specifically psychological behaviorism, many people assume, let's say, that a man cheats and robs because he's a thief, and he's a thief because of the conditions to which he was exposed as he grew up. In brief, many of us assume that we are who we are because of our experiences. Sartre rejects this notion. He would argue that if a man is a thief, he chooses to be one and he chooses all that this decision entails. He could choose

36. *Jean-Paul Sartre*. Being and Nothingness. H. E. Barnes, Trans. New York: Philosophical Library, p. lxvi. Copyright © 1956 by Philosophical Library. Reprinted by permission.

to be otherwise, for instance, to be an honest man. He could choose, in effect, a new project rather than the one he has adopted. Furthermore, he may do this whenever he chooses. In other words, nothing about a thief's past makes his future inevitable. In fact, there's no telling how many different projects he could undertake in defining who he will be.

For Sartre, then, first we exist. Our uniqueness, our essence, is not God-given or predetermined. Rather, it depends on whether we act. Sartre succinctly expresses this seminal insight of his philosophy in his statement "Existence precedes essence."

In contrasting phenomenology and existentialism, therefore, it seems safe to say that phenomenologists like Husserl found truth and certainty in the nothingness of consciousness, while Sartre finds the hope that he needs to live in a godless universe. In the nothingness of consciousness, Sartre finds *something:* the capacity to annihilate a given world and thus to become a self. In a word, he finds the possibility of action and with it freedom and self-identity.

Finally, even this brief exposition should indicate that existentialists are extremely diverse. They include theists and atheists, philosophers, theologians, and artists. Specifically, existentialists include Kierkegaard, the Jewish scholar Martin Buber (1878–1965), the Protestant theologian Paul Tillich (1886–1965), the atheistic Nietzsche and Sartre, the novelist Albert Camus (1913–1965), and many other thinkers, writers, and artists. Although their views often differ radically, they share the common concerns for the individual, for subjective experience, for the importance of self, for the need for personal freedom, and for the reality of personal responsibility. In our treatment of phenomenology and existentialism, we have attempted to touch only on those areas of metaphysical importance. Even here we have had to be sketchy. These important thinkers have many ideas of merit that the serious student of philosophy will want to explore.

Objections to Phenomenology and Existentialism

Since there are so many nuances in phenomenological and existential thought, let's confine our remarks to Husserl and Sartre. Critics of Husserlian phenomenology have suggested that Husserl, despite his claim that phenomenology is a fundamentally new form of idealism, in fact lapsed into the transcendental idealism of Kant. In intention, Husserl's position is quite different from Kant's. But even sympathetic phenomenologists detect a movement in Husserl toward this idealism. They say this because, as Husserl became more skilled in bracketing, he uncovered more and more activities of the ego at increasingly deeper levels. For Husserl these activities do not underlie experience but are within it, waiting to be disclosed by bracketing. But, critics have asked, what of those less adept at bracketing than Husserl? What about people who are unable to uncover these activities? It seems that if such people are not to doubt the entire method, they must view these activities as lying entirely outside of the phenomenal field, as being transcendent. But that pitches them back to a transcendental idealism like Kant's.

Critics have also asked, "Are things 'self-given' when we bracket or are they not?" To illustrate, suppose you had bracketed and reported that you did not find anything that was self-given, anything that presented itself with absolute certainty within experience. Husserl might accuse you of having bracketed unsuccessfully, but you could reply that bracketing itself is a frame within which Husserl insists on viewing things. In other words, you could argue that all seeing is relative to the frame through which one chooses to view things, that is, assumptions, presuppositions, and values. If you were of a different philosophical bent from Husserl, you could go on and associate these frames with language. Husserl would counter that his is a special kind of seeing that's free of language when we bracket correctly. Thus, we see what is the case, and then we hunt around for the right words to describe it. But is this so? As we'll shortly see, much of twentieth-century philosophy argues that all philosophy, including phenomenology, is linguistic. In other words, all thinking and seeing is related to certain preconceptions that are inherent in language. Thus, bracketing is another kind of frame, though admittedly subtler than most. Thus, what for Husserl seems certain might be better described as his own projection of the quest for certainty.

Turning to Sartre, recall that he insists that to be human is to make a world by adopting a project. Suppose, for example, that you find yourself a Christian. You didn't *choose* to become one; you simply followed a script or line or direction that, for a number of reasons, was laid out for you. For Sartre, you'd be caught up in a logical contradiction, because you would be a person who was not a person, a for-itself whose being was in the mode of an in-itself. For Sartre this evaluation is not just a bias or even a value judgment. It's an assertion of an ontological truth. But is it?

Even if you were a Christian who did not *choose* Christianity, you wouldn't be a Christian in the way that a desk is a desk or a rock is a rock. You wouldn't have being in the mode of the in-itself in the way those things do. In fact, Sartre would agree that as humans, we can't have being simply in the mode of the in-itself. Like it or not, we're condemned to be free.

If we can't *be* simply in the mode of the in-itself, then we're always in the mode of the for-itself. But is it any more possible to be in the mode of the for-itself? Suppose that you don't drift or slip into being a Christian, but you *choose* it. This fact doesn't seem to make any real difference, because once you become a Christian, you accept a set of values, ways of looking at things, and a course of conduct. Christianity becomes your "taken-for-granted," and, evidently, you now have being in the mode of the for-itself. Obviously, this problem doesn't exist only for Christians or only for those who accept some sort of authoritarian code. People who adopt nihilism as their project just as easily slip from freedom to playing the role of nihilist. Even those who adopt existential freedom as their project can slide from freedom while playing the role of the existentialist. True, some projects likely invite slippage into bad faith more than others. But is any project immune? Professor of philosophy W. T. Jones captures this paradox: "One of the difficulties for a man who is committed to 'commitment' is that in order to get things done in this world he must combine forces with other men—not only join a movement but institutionalize (even bureaucratize) it. And this, it would seem, means surrendering one's freedom and hence becoming a thing. This is the paradox Sartre encountered in his own life; it helps to explain his on-again, off-again relationship with the Communist Party."[37]

Sartre's account of the for-itself, then, seems to commit him to holding freedom as an all-or-nothing proposition. But many people see it as one of degree. The same is true of responsibility. For example, who was responsible for the Mylai massacre, in which a number of Vietnamese civilians were murdered? Some people might reply that the person who committed the murders was. But what about those people who ordered the murders? Or if there were no explicit orders, what about those people who sent the soldiers to Vietnam who eventually committed the murders? Or those who supported the war, or those who did nothing to stop it?

But responsibility in terms of degree seems to be a different view of morality from Sartre's. In his view, humans are totally responsible because they are totally free. Since all of us could have made a world that excluded the Mylai massacre, we are all equally responsible. It's true that in *Being and Nothingness* Sartre relaxes his view by speaking of the social restraints on individual freedom, but then one wonders whether this modification is consistent, or even needs to be, with his existential phenomenology.

Despite differences, existentialists, phenomenologists, and many of their critics agree at least on one point: Statements about ultimate reality and being are meaningful. In fact, this element is shared by all the views that we have discussed so far. Whether reality is matter, idea, a combination, being, or consciousness, all of these views agree that we can sensibly talk about metaphysical issues. Yet one school of twentieth-century philosophy does not concede this belief.

The Analytical School

We saw that phenomenology is responsive to the distinction that Kant made between phenomena and noumena. In investigating the nature of consciousness, phenomenology in effect chooses to focus on the aspect of Kant's doctrine which states that the relations among phenomena result in part from the operations of the mind. Twentieth-century philosophy, however, is characterized by another outlook, which, rather than focusing on the phenomena and on consciousness, concentrates on the language with which people talk about these phenomena. Such an emphasis is a vital part of what has been termed *analytical philosophy*.

Language is relevant to the questions of reality and being that we've raised in this chapter. To understand this emphasis and how some philosophers use it to throw new light on some enduring metaphysical questions, keep in mind certain basic attitudes or implied assumptions about the nature of the world and about the nature of philosophical inquiry that characterize analytical philosophy. Of course, the broad assumptions we'll mention don't necessarily

---

37. *W. T. Jones.* From Kant, p. 444.

characterize the thinking of every analytical philosopher. But these general characteristics do seem to catch the spirit of most of them.[38]

One characteristic of the analytical school is its commitment to atomicity. Analysts frequently conceive of the world as made up of numerous independent entities. It's impossible, however, to generalize about how analysts conceive of these entities. For some they're material particles; for others they're sense data; for still others they're impressions, or what they term "facts." For example, Bertrand Russell clung to the belief that reality consists of a plurality of entities that are independent of us and our beliefs about them, and of their relations to other real entities. But he also conceived of these entities in different ways at different stages in the development of his thought. Thus, at one time he conceived of the universe as consisting of "neutral stuff." Using this concept, he maintained that the distinction between physical and mental events is superficial and unreal, that what is called "ego" and what is called "matter" are actually constructions made from this neutral stuff.[39] At another time, he spoke of the universe as consisting of "hard data," by which he apparently meant real entities, that is, those that resist the influence of critical reflection. The hardest of these would be facts of sense and the laws of logic. Despite these elusive and changing concepts of the precise nature of these entities, Russell, like many of his analytical sympathizers, would agree that such entities make up the universe and that they are only externally related.

From this first fundamental assumption follows a second, which concerns the precise task of philosophy. If the universe consists of complex entities, then philosophers should investigate the nature of these entities. Specifically, they should reduce through analysis the complex entities into the single entities from which the universe is believed to be composed. This is the origin of the term *analytical*, used to characterize the nature of this philosophical enterprise. Analytical philosophers hold that when the process of analysis is done thoroughly and correctly, complex entities are completely explained, and this explanation ought to be the function of philosophy.

Given these two basic assumptions, you can better understand the emphasis that analytical thinkers give to "clarity," which they evidently view as a very sharply focused kind of experience. This concern has led analytical philosophers, in varying degrees, to an interest in language. In their view, most of our language is ambiguous and misleading, suggesting that the universe consists of rather amorphous, internally related complex entities, when it actually consists of single atomistic entities. Consequently, they insist that before any serious philosophical inquiry can occur, everyday language must be refined and clarified. As Russell puts it, "The most important part [of philosophy] . . . consists in criticizing and clarifying notions which are apt to be regarded as fundamental and accepted uncritically. As instances I might mention: mind, matter, consciousness, knowledge, experience, causality, will,

38. *For a treatment of analytical philosophers, see W. T. Jones.* From Kant, *pp. 331–335.*

39. *W. T. Jones.* From Kant, *p. 347.*

time. I believe all these notions to be inexact and approximate, essentially infected with vagueness, incapable of forming part of any exact science."[40]

For Russell the methodology of analysis led to the metaphysical doctrine of atomicity. Other philosophers, such as Ludwig Wittgenstein, used a rigorous and unflinching linguistic analysis to dissolve metaphysical problems. To these philosophers, philosophical problems were based on linguistic confusion; once a correct and thorough analysis of language was conducted, the problems dissolved. So while both types of analytical philosophers agree that most philosophical problems are rooted in sloppy language, they differ in emphasis and ultimately in their conclusions. Some, like Russell, concentrate on the language and methods of sciences; others, like Wittgenstein, focus on ordinary language usage. The former group are variously called logical positivists, logical empiricists, or scientific empiricists; the latter are known as ordinary-language philosophers. Thus, the analytical school embraces a varied host of thinkers—Russell, Wittgenstein, Alfred J. Ayer, Rudolf Carnap, John Wisdom, and Gilbert Ryle—all of whom agree on at least one point: that the clarification of symbols, especially linguistic symbols, is of primary importance.

Ruth's professor friend is a linguistic analyst, although Ruth does not know it until she confronts him with her frustration. Then she learns why he thinks that the debates she has had with Brad and Max are really futile. Ruth and the professor agree on this point, but for different reasons.

Ruth: Max and I just had a fight. And do you know what it was over?

Professor: What?

Ruth: That stupid thing you said about our being your creations.

Professor: Uh-oh. I'm sorry.

Ruth: A lot of good that'll do.

Professor: So you don't think it's possible to produce a mechanical mate, is that it?

Ruth: That's not what we were arguing over. It was a lot heavier than that. It was about what's really real and things like that.

Professor: Really real?

Ruth: You know, whether everything is just matter or not matter. Or maybe being, as Max says.

Professor: You really did get into it, didn't you?

Ruth: And it's all because of you!

Professor: Well, if it's any comfort, I agree with you that debating what is really real is a futile exercise.

Ruth: You mean you think it's dumb, too?

Professor: Yes, I do.

40. *Bertrand Russell. "Logical Atomism," in* Contemporary British Philosophy. *J. H. Muirhead, Ed. New York: Macmillan, 1924, p. 380.*

Ruth: Well, I never expected to hear that from you.

Professor: Why? Because you expect professors to serve as instigators and referees of intellectual games?

Ruth: Something like that, I guess.

Professor: Well, let me assure you I've thought considerably about those questions, Ruth. And do you know what I've decided?

Ruth: What?

Professor: That they defy verification.

Ruth: What do you mean?

Professor: Well, let me show you. Take the question that you were so hotly debating: What is reality? Now each of you had a different notion, I presume.

Ruth: That's right. Personally, I think reality is nonmaterial, some kind of spirit or mind.

Professor: Fine. Let's examine your belief: "Reality is nonmatter." Now, presumably, if you were arguing about this statement, you thought it was either true or false.

Ruth: I think it's true, but Brad and Max don't.

Professor: Let me ask you something, Ruth. How do you know when a statement, any statement, is true?

Ruth: Well, you can tell some statements are true just by looking at them.

Professor: Such as?

Ruth: "My brother Brad is a male."

Professor: How do you know that's true?

Ruth: It's self-evident. If you're talking about a brother, you must be talking about a male.

Professor: I see what you mean. Certainly, the truth of that statement is contained within the meaning of the words themselves. If you denied such a statement, the result would be an absurd self-contradiction: "My brother Brad is not a male."

Ruth: That's silly.

Professor: Right. But what about a statement like "The sun is between 90 and 95 million miles from the earth"? Is that statement self-evident?

Ruth: No. You'd have to prove that.

Professor: I agree. Somehow you'd have to measure the distance and determine if, in fact, the sun was between 90 and 95 million miles from earth.

Ruth: Of course.

Professor: What if you couldn't measure it? If you couldn't determine the precise distance? Would you call the statement false?

Ruth: No, you just wouldn't know for sure, that's all. It could still be true. You'd just have to wait and see.

Professor: So you'd say the statement is still either true or false.

Ruth: Sure.

Professor: What about a statement like "Unicorns like to eat fresh eggs"? Is that true or false?

Ruth: That's just silly.

Professor: But is it true or false?

Ruth: It's neither.

Professor: Neither?

Ruth: Because unicorns don't exist.

Professor: What difference does that make?

Ruth: Well, if unicorns don't exist, how can you say anything about them that makes sense? How would you ever go about proving it? It's just ridiculous. Say whatever you want about unicorns; it doesn't make any difference, because you can't ever really find out.

Professor: All right, then, what about this statement: "There's a Coke machine on the southern polar cap of Mars"? Is that true or false?

Ruth: It's either one or the other.

Professor: How come?

Ruth: Because you can prove that. You can at least imagine what you'd have to do to prove it.

Professor: So that's not like the unicorn statement?

Ruth: No way. Coke machines, southern polar caps, Mars, all those things exist. So you know what you'd have to do to prove whether there really is a Coke machine up there. Go and see.

Professor: You seem to be saying that, except for self-evident statements, a statement is true or false only if it lends itself to being proved. And that it lends itself to being proved only if the things that make it up really exist.

Ruth: Yes, I guess I am.

Professor: All right, then, let's see where that leaves us. What about your statement "Reality is nonmatter"? Is that statement self-evident?

Ruth: If it were, Max and I wouldn't have fought.

Professor: I agree. You could certainly deny that statement and still have something that makes sense.

Ruth: Sure. Brad said reality was matter.

Professor: It seems that leaves us with having to prove the statement true.

Ruth: I suppose it does.

Professor: Well, how do you propose to do that?

For the linguistic analyst, there are two kinds of meaningful statements: analytic propositions and synthetic propositions. Defining a **proposition** as a statement that is true or false, the analyst sees *analytic* propositions as true or false by definition, by their appearance alone. In an analytic statement, the predicate—the part that follows the verb *to be*—always repeats the subject in whole or in part. Thus, "The *red* bird is *red*." Sometimes the predicate is not the same term as the subject but carries part of the subject's meaning, as in "His *sister* is a *female*." *Female* is included in the meaning of *sister*. The professor calls such statements self-evident; that is, their negation always results in a self-contradiction: "The red bird is not red" or "His sister is not a female."

A nonanalytic proposition is said to be *synthetic*. Synthetic propositions are those that can, at least in theory, be proved true or false. This is possible only if their terms refer to existing objects or events. Apply scientific methods, say the analysts, to determine if the relationship between these objects or events is

". . . all metaphysical assertions are nonsensical."

fact. "It's raining," "California is about 3,000 miles from New York," and "A spirochete causes syphilis" are synthetic statements.

If a statement is neither analytic nor synthetic, say the analysts, it is epistemologically meaningless; it is nonsensical. Metaphysical statements appear to be neither analytic nor synthetic. Alfred J. Ayer puts it this way: "We may accordingly define a metaphysical sentence as a sentence which purports to express a genuine proposition but does, in fact, express neither a tautology (analytic statement) . . . nor an empirical hypothesis (synthetic statement). And as tautologies and empirical hypotheses form the entire class of significant propositions, we are justified in concluding that all metaphysical assertions are nonsensical."[41]

The analyst would view not only metaphysical statements as meaningless, but most ethical, aesthetic, and theological ones as well, because most of them are neither analytic nor synthetic. Thus they would consider the following statements nonsensical: "God exists," "God doesn't exist," "Lying is wrong," "Lying is right," "A moral law operates in the universe," and "The best form of government is the one that governs least." The fact that very few people can consider such statements meaningless has led to a major objection to the analytical school.

Objections to Linguistic Analysis

Ruth: But you're saying that if something can't be verified it's not worth talking about.
Professor: Can't be verified at least *in principle*.
Ruth: As the Coke machine can, at least in principle?
Professor: Exactly.

41.   *Alfred J. Ayer.* Language, Truth and Logic. *2nd ed. New York: Dover, 1936, p. 41.*

Ruth: But that would make silly many of the very things that people have always taken seriously.

Professor: Like what?

Ruth: Like "Democracy is the best form of government," for example. Or "Honesty is the best policy" or "It's better to give than to receive."

Professor: As well as "Man is the noblest work of God," "Admission of ignorance is the beginning of wisdom," "The unexamined life is not worth living," and all the rest. Yes, I couldn't agree more; they're meaningless statements in the sense that they're neither true nor false.

Ruth: But people still make those statements.

Professor: Of course they do.

Ruth: Then how can you deny their validity?

Professor: Because there's no way they can be verified empirically, and they're certainly not linguistically self-evident.

Ruth: But are those the only ways of measuring truth and knowledge?

Professor: The only ones we have now.

Ruth: But that doesn't mean they're necessarily the only ones.

Professor: No, not necessarily.

Ruth: Then isn't your belief based on an assumption? And isn't the assumption something that itself defies the empirical method? How would you ever verify the statement "True statements must be either linguistically self-evident or empirically verifiable"?

Ruth has not only questioned the analytical definition of a meaningful utterance, but she has also accused the professor of assuming the very thing he must prove: that with respect to knowledge and truth, only analytic and synthetic statements are meaningful. Critics claim that analysts are more deductive than they themselves think, that they argue this way:

All knowledge is either analytic or synthetic.
Religious, ethical, and aesthetic statements are neither analytic nor synthetic.
Therefore, religious, ethical, and aesthetic statements are not knowledge.

But, say critics, the first statement is an assumption; it can never be proved. Perhaps utterances other than analytic and synthetic ones may transmit knowledge and truth. In effect, they charge the analysts with assuming that the first statement is analytic.

Professor: You're saying that my assumption is as meaningless as your statement that reality is nonmatter?

Ruth: That's right, because there's no way you can prove your assumption.

Professor: But it's necessary to start somewhere.

Ruth: Why? Can you prove it's necessary to start somewhere? How would you verify that claim? It seems to me, professor, that you're a victim of your own classification.

Professor: You mean that by reducing knowledge to what's linguistically self-evident or empirically verifiable, I haven't allowed for other possibilities?

Ruth: Not only that. You've defined other possibilities right out of existence. . . . But you have convinced me of one thing.

Professor: What's that?

Ruth: That arguing about what's real isn't so silly after all. It's not so silly as pretending the problem doesn't even exist. True, believing the way you do, you have a lot less frustration. By simply eliminating the problems, you don't have to deal with them. But isn't that really playing ostrich? Aren't the problems still there? Don't people still think about them? Even *you* devise an answer to them. If the questions don't exist, then what are your answers answering? And in answering them, haven't you yourself taken a position on a question that you say can only lead to meaningless answers?

Ruth's criticism implies what is for many one of the most disappointing aspects of analysis: its attempt to reduce the idea of a person to sense data or to behavior. Analysis seems to oversimplify and distort human experience by disregarding whatever lies beyond the language of science, mathematics, or formal logic. Many contemporary analysts are noticing this inadequacy, recognizing as legitimate not just one or two but many modes of meaning. Ultimately they may agree with their critics, who defend the philosopher's right and need to discuss questions not only of language, but of metaphysics, morality, religion, politics, and education as well. Certainly any description of human nature and of self that ignores these aspects of human experience seems incomplete.

Summary and Conclusions

We opened this chapter by noting that what we ultimately consider real reflects and influences how we see ourselves. Questions of reality have been an abiding concern of philosophers. Such questions fall under metaphysics. We discussed a number of metaphysical views, including materialism, idealism, pragmatism, phenomenology, existentialism, and linguistic analysis. We suggested that different thinkers sometimes share certain views. However, fundamental differences separate the views sketched.

Despite the diversity of metaphysical views, many metaphysicians agree on some important issues. These points of agreement suggest insights into the self.

First, some metaphysicians agree that something exists outside the individual self. Even the subjective idealism of Berkeley does not deny the physical world, only its independence from mind. Despite Sartre's stress on self and Husserl's emphasis on consciousness, these thinkers recognize the distinction between things that lack consciousness, such as chairs, trees, and books, and those that do not, such as humans. We should quickly add, however, that many phenomenologists deplore such a dichotomy. Nonetheless, although the self may be insular, in that it is bound by the sea of its experiences, there are other human "islands," all joined by the similarity of their conditions and circumstances.

Second, some metaphysicians accept the senses and reason as primary sources of knowledge, as the tools by which the self comes to know things. True, some metaphysicians give reason a primacy that others do not; others emphasize the importance of experience. But these are differences of degree, not of substance. Many agree that by using both reason and senses, we are most likely to know ourselves and our world. At the same time, some pragmatists, existentialists, phenomenologists, and even analysts would not agree, arguing that senses and reason are products of particular conceptual frames, such as empiricism or rationalism.

Finally, various metaphysicians agree that there is an order or meaning in things that the senses and reason can discover. True, materialism may believe that the order is strictly mechanistic; idealism, that it is spiritual or even supernatural; existentialism and phenomenology, that it is being or the purpose that each of us imposes on experience; and analysis, that it is the symbolic form in which we express things. But some members within each school hold that there is some order. Most importantly, each of us is part of that order, whatever its nature. To know the self is at least partially to know that order and how we fit into it.

At the same time, there are fundamental differences among these metaphysical outlooks that reflect and reinforce different views of human nature and of self. For the materialist, we are part of the matter that composes the universe and are subject to the same laws. As a result, the self is the product of its experiences, the sum total of everything that has ever happened to it. There is little point in speaking of individual responsibility or personal will, for we cannot help doing what we do. When we speak of mind, we really mean brain; when we refer to mental states, we are really talking about brain states. The purpose of any life is to understand how the parts of the universe, including the self, fit together and work. With such knowledge we can control our environment to some degree and perhaps improve the human condition.

Many linguistic analysts would add that the individual who tries to find personal meaning in religion, art, or politics or in seeking what is morally good wastes time on basically meaningless pursuits. We are most likely to understand ourselves and the world by clarifying the linguistic symbols we use to speak about these things.

For many idealists, in contrast, the individual is part of cosmic mind, spirit, idea, or perhaps life force. In this sense, individuals are alike. But each finds a self-identity in personal understanding. Only the individual can be aware of his or her own experiences. In the last analysis, it is this personal awareness, these ideas, that make each of us unique. The purpose of each life is to understand the order at work in the universe. This order is not matter but pure idea; for some it is a divine dimension, God. In understanding this cosmic order or plan, we understand our position in it and thus the self.

The pragmatist views the self as neither primarily matter nor primarily idea. Since pragmatists avoid absolutes, they choose to see the self as consisting of many dimensions, including material and ideal. The self is a complex entity consisting of experiences, which include thoughts, feelings, sensations, concepts, attitudes, and goals. Although we are tremendously influenced by environment, we can and do play a formative role in determining the nature of our experiences. Using intelligence and reason, the individual can exercise control over nature. But we shall not find personal meaning and purpose in the cosmos, because it possesses none. For personal meaning we must turn to the consequences of our actions, judging them according to the results they produce.

Existentialism shares pragmatism's skepticism of absolutistic doctrines. But more than any of the other outlooks, it stresses personal freedom. The self is essentially something in the making that is not finished until the individual dies. The self is whatever we choose to make it. We are ultimately free to think, choose, and act however we wish. Such freedom without guidelines is frightening, often leading to uncertainty, anxiety, and despair. But this, say the existentialists, is the human condition. For many phenomenologists, what we are is *that* we are. The fundamental self is not its characteristics, properties, or the other objective qualities, but being. The self is not our idea of what we are but the immediate concrete feeling of ourselves. We move furthest from a knowledge of the self when we separate self from the rest of reality, as we do when we view it as some object to be studied, quantified, and known. We are closest to the self when we strip from consciousness the experiences that occupy it. Then we realize that the self is what precedes its experiences—that is, pure being. Buddhist thinking generally agrees.

So, although members of different metaphysical schools share some beliefs, they vary in their approach to the issue of self. This variation may leave us affirming or denying the self, and viewing it as essentially rational, divine, mechanical, existential, or nonexistent. These views have dramatically different impacts on the self and its place in the world.

Section Exercises

Reality as Matter

1. Does being born in the way that humans are distingush us from other forms of life? Would you agree that normal childbirth, including premature birth and cesarean section, is a defining characteristic of being a person?

2. In his split-brain experiments, R. W. Sperry showed that either half of the brain can function alone efficiently. If your brain were so severed, would there be two of you? What if you substituted another person's half brain for half of your own? Would you be two people?

3. Look up the meaning of *materialism* as it is ordinarily used. Do you detect any connection between its ordinary and its philosophical meanings?

4. At one point, Ruth claims that the *persistence* of a belief in the soul removes this belief from the realm of superstition or ignorance. Do you agree? Can you

think of any other beliefs that have so persisted? What about beliefs that lasted an extremely long time but are no longer widely held?

5. To explain things, would you introduce sciences in addition to the physical sciences that Brad advances? Which ones?

6. Do you think Ruth's example of the self-witnessing brain proves that states of consciousness are different from brain states?

7. Our discussion so far has focused almost exclusively on the problem of self. How is this question relevant to the question of what is real?

8. The seventeenth-century English poet Alexander Pope, exuding the enthusiasm of his age for scientific discovery, wrote an "Epitaph Intended for Sir Isaac Newton, in Westminster Abbey":

> *Nature and Nature's laws lay hid in night;*
> *God said, "Let Newton be!" and all was Light.*

What view of human nature does Pope suggest? Do you think Heisenberg's indeterminacy principle advances, sets back, or has no effect on the belief that all can be explained in terms of cosmic laws?

9. Does research into the causes of human thought, consciousness, and behavior indicate a growing simplicity or a growing complexity of understanding?

10. Do you see the workings of the universe as orderly? Why or why not? (You might first define *orderliness* in terms of predictability.)

Reality as Nonmatter

1. Some argue for a principle that is at work in the universe. Perhaps such a universal law is at the bottom of everything, gives everything design and purpose, and orders our experiences. Do you see such a principle or law?

2. Can there be a principle or law at work without a purpose or goal? If not, must the idealist account for the purpose of things?

3. In what sense is it true that the relationships among things are the only meaningful reality? Can you think of anything that you can understand without reference to something else?

4. It has often been said that idealism encourages a withdrawal from the world, a retreat from secular problems, and an immersion in otherworldly concerns. As a result, the idealist neglects real and pressing social concerns. Explain why you think this charge is justified or not justified.

5. Read Alexander Pope's "Essay on Man." What is his metaphysical position? What would be Candide's reaction to it?

Reality in Pragmatism

1. What are the assumptions of materialism and idealism that pragmatism ignores?

2. In what respects does pragmatism incorporate materialism and idealism?

3. If you were a pragmatist, how would you reconcile your belief that you can know only your experiences with your belief that an objective reality exists?

4. Compare and contrast the everyday and philosophical meanings of *pragmatist*.

Reality as Being

1. What precisely does Max mean when he says "It's clear that, for you, *what* or *who* I am is more important than *that* I am"?

2. What is the difference between being and being human?

3. In what sense are you both being and a being?

4. Show how a failure to distinguish between being as a thing and the being of a thing leads to "thingifying" everything, including people.

5. Do existentialism, phenomenology, and pragmatism share any beliefs?

6. In what sense would you call Kierkegaard a rationalist?

7. Sartre claims that Kierkegaard's leap of faith to God is cowardly and not in the true existential spirit. Why would he say this? Do you agree?

8. What does Sartre mean when he says "existence precedes essence"?

9. How would you describe what Heidegger calls your being?

10. Would Ruth's supposed objections to Max's "being" argument bring her closer to materialism than she might think? Why?

11. If Ruth objected, "If everything is being, then everything is nothing," what would she mean?

12. Is it possible to maintain a concept of individual difference if everything has being in common?

13. Sartre claims that in making a choice for self, we are really making a choice for other. Is this statement consistent with a denial of any kind of universal human nature? If it is, why did Sartre make such a claim?

The Analytical School

1. In what sense do the analysts apply the adjective *meaningless* to nonsensical statements? Can something be intellectually meaningless but emotionally meaningful? Can you give an example?

2. What is your reaction to the following evaluation by analyst Alfred J. Ayer?

   It is impossible to find a criterion for determining the validity of ethical judgment . . . because they [ethical judgments] have no objective validity whatsoever. If a sentence makes no statement at all, there is obviously no sense in asking whether what it says is true or false. . . . They are pure expressions of feeling . . . unverifiable for the same reason as a cry of pain or a word of command is unverifiable—because they do not express genuine propositions.[42]

---

42. *Alfred J. Ayer.* Language, Truth and Logic, *pp. 107–109.*

3. Which of the following statements would an analyst consider meaningful? Meaningless?

    a. She wore a blue dress.

    b. Her blue dress was green.

    c. At the bottom of the ocean there's a shiny new penny lying in the belly of a dead carp.

    d. The zite dwart oilated twarily near an ach grul.

    e. The action in the preceding sentence takes place near an ach grul.

    f. Tooth fairies never appear to bad children.

    g. The good go to heaven, the bad to hell.

    h. Killing orphans without reason is an evil thing to do.

    i. Oxygen is necessary for combustion.

    j. Love makes the world go 'round.

4. How valid do you consider Ruth's criticism that the professor's definition of what is meaningful makes a sham of the things that we take seriously?

5. Why is the professor's defense that "it's necessary to start somewhere" less convincing coming from an analyst than it would be coming from an idealist?

6. Ruth charges that the professor's position is inconsistent and self-contradictory. Why does she say this? Do you agree?

7. What would you say is the primary contribution of linguistic analysis to philosophy?

Siddhartha

Hermann Hesse

There is perhaps no more readable a work that contains the general world view of Indian religion than Siddhartha, *the story of Siddhartha Gautama, penned by the German poet and novelist Hermann Hesse (1877–1962). While strictly speaking not a Buddhist novel or a retelling of the Buddha's life,* Siddhartha *contains elements of both. In a style befitting the sublime simplicity of the outlook, Hesse portrays the young Siddhartha as a troubled, restless spirit, who abandons home, family, and caste for wealth, power, and pleasure. But as it turns out, such pursuits are part of Siddhartha's spiritual evolution, which ultimately finds him taken with the simple life of a ferryman, wherein he's able to learn the lessons of eternality that the river teaches to those who know how to listen.*

In the selection that follows, the old and wise Siddhartha is reunited with his boyhood friend, the monk Govinda. What transpires is not only a stirring portrayal of loving reunion, but a graphic account of an Eastern view of reality, with its emphasis on the interconnectedness, the oneness, of all things.

Govinda

Govinda once spent a rest period with some other monks in the pleasure grove which Kamala, the courtesan, had once presented to the followers of Gotama. He heard talk of an old ferryman who lived by the river, a day's journey away, and

From Siddhartha *by Hermann Hesse. Hilda Rosner, Trans. Copyright 1951 by New Directions Publishing Corporation. Reprinted by permission.*

whom many considered to be a sage. When Govinda moved on, he chose the path to the ferry, eager to see this ferryman, for although he had lived his life according to the rule and was also regarded with respect by the younger monks for his age and modesty, there was still restlessness in his heart and his seeking was unsatisfied.

He arrived at the river and asked the old man to take him across. When they climbed out of the boat on the other side, he said to the old man: "You show much kindness to the monks and pilgrims; you have taken many of us across. Are you not also a seeker of the right path?"

There was a smile in Siddhartha's old eyes as he said: "Do you call yourself a seeker, O venerable one, you who are already advanced in years and wear the robe of Gotama's monks?"

"I am indeed old," said Govinda, "but I have never ceased seeking. I will never cease seeking. That seems to be my destiny. It seems to me that you also have sought. Will you talk to me a little about it, my friend?"

Siddhartha said: "What could I say to you that would be of value, except that perhaps you seek too much, that as a result of your seeking you cannot find."

"How is that?" asked Govinda.

"When someone is seeking," said Siddhartha, "it happens quite easily that he only sees the thing that he is seeking; that he is unable to find anything, unable to absorb anything, because he is only thinking of the thing he is seeking, because he has a goal, because he is obsessed with his goal. Seeking means: to have a goal; but finding means: to be free, to be receptive, to have no goal. You, O worthy one, are perhaps indeed a seeker, for in striving towards your goal, you do not see many things that are under your nose."

"I do not yet quite understand," said Govinda. "How do you mean?"

Siddhartha said: "Once, O worthy one, many years ago, you came to this river and found a man sleeping there. You sat beside him to guard him while he slept, but you did not recognize the sleeping man, Govinda."

Astonished and like one bewitched the monk gazed at the ferryman.

"Are you Siddhartha?" he asked in a timid voice. "I did not recognize you this time, too. I am very pleased to see you again, Siddhartha, very pleased. You have changed very much, my friend. And have you become a ferryman now?"

Siddhartha laughed warmly. "Yes, I have become a ferryman. Many people have to change a great deal and wear all sorts of clothes. I am one of those, my friend. You are very welcome, Govinda, and I invite you to stay the night in my hut."

Govinda stayed the night in the hut and slept in the bed that had once been Vasudeva's. He asked the friend of his youth many questions and Siddhartha had a great deal to tell him about his life.

When it was time for Govinda to depart the following morning, he said with some hesitation: "Before I go on my way, Siddhartha, I should like to ask you one more question. Have you a doctrine, belief or knowledge which you uphold, which helps you to live and do right?"

Siddhartha said: "You know, my friend, that even as a young man, when we lived with the ascetics in the forest, I came to distrust doctrines and teachers and to turn my back on them. I am still of the same turn of mind, although I have, since that time, had many teachers. A beautiful courtesan was my teacher for a long time, and a rich merchant and a dice player. On one occasion, one of the Buddha's wandering monks was my teacher. He halted in his pilgrimage to sit beside me when I fell asleep in the forest. I also learned something from him and I am grateful to him, very grateful. But most of all, I have learned from this river and from my predecessor, Vasudeva. He was a simple man; he was not a thinker, but he realized the essential as well as Gotama. He was a holy man, a saint."

Govinda said: "It seems to me, Siddhartha, that you still like to jest a little. I believe you and know that you have not followed any teacher, but have you not yourself, if not a doctrine, certain thoughts? Have you not discovered certain knowledge yourself that has helped you to live? It would give me great pleasure if you would tell me something about this."

Siddhartha said: "Yes, I have had thoughts and knowledge here and there. Sometimes, for an hour or for a day, I have become aware of knowledge, just as one feels life in one's heart. I have had many thoughts, but it would be difficult for me to tell you about them. But this is one thought that has impressed me, Govinda. Wisdom is not communicable. The wisdom which a wise man tries to communicate always sounds foolish."

"Are you jesting?" asked Govinda.

"No, I am telling you what I have discovered. Knowledge can be communicated, but not wisdom. One can find it, live it, be fortified by it, do wonders through it, but one cannot communicate and teach it. I suspected this when I was still a youth and it was this that drove me away from teachers. There is one thought I have had, Govinda, which you will again think is a jest or folly: that is, in every truth the opposite is equally true. For example, a truth can only be expressed and enveloped in words if it is one-sided. Everything that is thought and expressed in words is one-sided, only half the truth; it all lacks totality, completeness, unity. When the Illustrious Buddha taught about the world, he had to divide it into Sansara and Nirvana, into illusion and truth, into suffering and salvation. One cannot do otherwise, there is no other method for those who teach. But the world itself, being in and around us, is never one-sided. Never is a man or a deed wholly Sansara or wholly Nirvana; never is a man wholly a saint or a sinner. This only seems so because we suffer the illusion that time is something real. Time is not real, Govinda. I have realized this repeatedly. And if time is not real, then the dividing line that seems to lie between this world and eternity, between suffering and bliss, between good and evil, is also an illusion."

"How is that?" asked Govinda, puzzled.

"Listen, my friend! I am a sinner and you are a sinner, but someday the sinner will be Brahma again, will someday attain Nirvana, will someday become a Buddha. Now this 'someday' is illusion; it is only a comparison. The sinner is not on the way to a Buddha-like state; he is not evolving, although our thinking cannot conceive things otherwise. No, the potential Buddha already exists in the sinner; his future is already there. The potential hidden Buddha must be recognized in him, in you, in everybody. The world, Govinda, is not imperfect or slowly evolving along a long path to perfection. No, it is perfect at every moment; every sin already carries grace within it, all small children are potential old men, all sucklings have death within them, all dying people—

eternal life. It is not possible for one person to see how far another is on the way; the Buddha exists in the robber and dice player; the robber exists in the Brahmin. During deep meditation it is possible to dispel time, to see simultaneously all the past, present and future, and then everything is good, everything is perfect, everything is Brahman. Therefore, it seems to me that everything that exists is good—death as well as life, sin as well as holiness, wisdom as well as folly. Everything is necessary, everything needs only my agreement, my assent, my loving understanding; then all is well with me and nothing can harm me. I learned through my body and soul that it was necessary for me to sin, that I needed lust, that I had to strive for property and experience nausea and the depths of despair in order to learn not to resist them, in order to learn to love the world, and no longer compare it with some kind of desired imaginary world, some imaginary vision of perfection, but to leave it as it is, to love it and be glad to belong to it. These, Govinda, are some of the thoughts that are in my mind."

Siddhartha bent down, lifted a stone from the ground and held it in his hand.

"This," he said, handling it, "is a stone, and within a certain length of time it will perhaps be soil and from the soil it will become plant, animal or man. Previously I should have said: This stone is just a stone; it has no value, it belongs to the world of Maya, but perhaps because within the cycle of change it can also become man and spirit, it is also of importance. That is what I should have thought. But now I think: This stone is stone; it is also animal, God and Buddha. I do not respect and love it because it was one thing and will become something else, but because it has already long been everything and always is everything. I love it just because it is a stone, because today and now it appears to me a stone. I see value and meaning in each one of its fine markings and cavities, in the yellow, in the grey, in the hardness and the sound of it when I knock it, in the dryness or dampness of its surface. There are stones that feel like oil or soap, that look like leaves or sand, and each one is different and worships Om in its own way; each one is Brahman. At the same time it is very much stone, oily or soapy, and that is just what pleases me and seems wonderful and worthy of worship. But I will say no more about it. Words do not express thoughts very well. They always become a little different immediately they are expressed, a little distorted, a little foolish. And yet it also pleases me and seems right that what is of value and wisdom to one man seems nonsense to another."

Govinda had listened in silence.

"Why did you tell me about the stone?" he asked hesitatingly after a pause.

"I did so unintentionally. But perhaps it illustrates that I just love the stone and the river and all these things that we see and from which we can learn. I can love a stone, Govinda, and a tree or a piece of bark. These are things and one can love things. But one cannot love words. Therefore teachings are of no use to me; they have no hardness, no softness, no colors, no corners, no smell, no taste—they have nothing but words. Perhaps that is what prevents you from finding peace, perhaps there are too many words, for even salvation and virtue. Sansara and Nirvana are only words, Govinda. Nirvana is not a thing; there is only the word Nirvana."

Govinda said: "Nirvana is not only a word, my friend; it is a thought."

Siddhartha continued: "It may be a thought, but I must confess, my friend, that I do not differentiate very much between thoughts and words. Quite frankly, I do not attach great importance to thoughts either. I attach more importance to things. For example, there was a man at this ferry who was my predecessor and teacher. He was a holy man who for many years believed only in the river and nothing else. He noticed that the river's voice spoke to him. He learned from it; it educated and taught him. The river seemed like a god to him and for many years he did not know that every wind, every cloud, every bird, every beetle is equally divine and knows and can teach just as well as the esteemed river. But when this holy man went off into the woods, he knew everything; he knew more than you and I, without teachers, without books, just because he believed in the river."

Govinda said: "But what you call thing, is it something real, something intrinsic? Is it not only the illusion of Maya, only image and appearance? Your stone, your tree, are they real?"

"This also does not trouble me much," said Siddhartha. "If they are illusion, then I also am illusion, and so they are always of the same nature as myself. It is that which makes them so

lovable and venerable. That is why I can love them. And here is a doctrine at which you will laugh. It seems to me, Govinda, that love is the most important thing in the world. It may be important to great thinkers to examine the world, to explain and despise it. But I think it is only important to love the world, not to despise it, not for us to hate each other, but to be able to regard the world and ourselves and all beings with love, admiration and respect."

"I understand that," said Govinda, "but that is just what the Illustrious One called illusion. He preached benevolence, forbearance, sympathy, patience—but not love. He forbade us to bind ourselves to earthly love."

"I know that," said Siddhartha smiling radiantly, "I know that, Govinda, and here we find ourselves within the maze of meanings, within the conflict of words, for I will not deny that my words about love are in apparent contradiction to the teachings of Gotama. That is just why I distrust words so much, for I know that this contradiction is an illusion. I know that I am at one with Gotama. How, indeed, could he not know love, he who has recognized all humanity's vanity and transitoriness, yet loves humanity so much that he has devoted a long life solely to help and teach people? Also with this great teacher, the thing to me is of greater importance than the words; his deeds and life are more important to me than his talk, the gesture of his hand is more important to me than his opinions. Not in speech or thought do I regard him as a great man, but in his deeds and life."

The two old men were silent for a long time. Then as Govinda was preparing to go, he said: "I thank you, Siddhartha, for telling me something of your thoughts. Some of them are strange thoughts. I cannot grasp them all immediately. However, I thank you, and I wish you many peaceful days."

Inwardly, however, he thought: Siddhartha is a strange man and he expresses strange thoughts. His ideas seem crazy. How different do the Illustrious One's doctrines sound! They are clear, straightforward, comprehensible; they contain nothing strange, wild or laughable. But Siddhartha's hands and feet, his eyes, his brow, his breathing, his smile, his greeting, his gait affect me differently from his thoughts. Never, since the time our Illustrious Gotama passed into Nirvana, have I ever met a man with the exception of Siddhartha about whom I felt: This is a holy man! His ideas may be strange, his words may sound foolish, but his glance and his hand, his skin and his hair, all radiate a purity, peace, serenity, gentleness and saintliness which I have never seen in any man since the recent death of our illustrious teacher.

While Govinda was thinking these thoughts and there was conflict in his heart, he again bowed to Siddhartha, full of affection towards him. He bowed low before the quietly seated man.

"Siddhartha," he said, "we are now old men. We may never see each other again in this life. I can see, my dear friend, that you have found peace. I realize that I have not found it. Tell me one more word, my esteemed friend, tell me something that I can conceive, something I can understand! Give me something to help me on my way, Siddhartha. My path is often hard and dark."

Siddhartha was silent and looked at him with his calm, peaceful smile. Govinda looked steadily in his face, with anxiety, with longing. Suffering, continual seeking and continual failure were written in his look.

Siddhartha saw it and smiled.

"Bend near to me!" he whispered in Govinda's ear. "Come, still nearer, quite close! Kiss me on the forehead, Govinda."

Although surprised, Govinda was compelled by a great love and presentiment to obey him; he leaned close to him and touched his forehead with his lips. As he did this, something wonderful happened to him. While he was still dwelling on Siddhartha's strange words, while he strove in vain to dispel the conception of time, to imagine Nirvana and Sansara as one, while even a certain contempt for his friend's words conflicted with a tremendous love and esteem for him, this happened to him.

He no longer saw the face of his friend Siddhartha. Instead he saw other faces, many faces, a long series, a continuous stream of faces—hundreds, thousands, which all came and disappeared and yet all seemed to be there at the same time, which all continually changed and renewed themselves and which were yet all Siddhartha. He saw the face of a fish, of a carp, with tremendous painfully opened mouth, a dying fish with dimmed eyes. He saw the face of a newly born child, red and full of wrinkles, ready to cry. He saw the face of a murderer, saw him plunge a knife into the body of a man; at the same moment he saw this criminal kneeling down, bound, and his head cut off by an executioner. He saw the naked bodies of men and women in the postures and transports of passionate love. He saw corpses stretched out, still, cold, empty. He saw the heads of animals, boars, crocodiles, elephants, oxen, birds. He saw Krishna and Agni. He saw all these forms and faces in a thousand relationships to each other, all helping each other, loving, hating and destroying each other and become newly born. Each one was mortal, a passionate, painful example of all that is transitory. Yet none of them died, they only changed, were always reborn, continually had a new face: only time stood between one face and another. And all these forms and faces rested, flowed, reproduced, swam past and merged into each other, and over them all there was continually something thin, unreal and yet existing, stretched across like thin glass or ice, like a transparent skin, shell, form or mask of water—and this mask was Siddhartha's smiling face which Govinda touched with his lips at that moment. And Govinda saw that this mask-like smile, this smile of unity over the flowing forms, this smile of simultaneousness over the thousands of births and deaths—this smile of Siddhartha—was exactly the same as the calm, delicate, impenetrable, perhaps gracious, perhaps mocking, wise, thousand-fold smile of Gotama, the Buddha, as he had perceived it with awe a hundred times. It was in such a manner, Govinda knew, that the Perfect One smiled.

No longer knowing whether time existed, whether this display had lasted a second or a hundred years, whether there was a Siddhartha, or a Gotama, a Self and others, wounded deeply by a divine arrow which gave him pleasure, deeply enchanted and exalted, Govinda stood yet a while bending over Siddhartha's peaceful face which he had just kissed, which had just been the stage of all present and future forms. His countenance was unchanged after the mirror of the thousand-fold forms had disappeared from the surface. He smiled peacefully and gently, perhaps very graciously, perhaps very mockingly, exactly as the Illustrious One had smiled.

Govinda bowed low. Incontrollable tears

trickled down his old face. He was overwhelmed by a feeling of great love, of the most humble veneration. He bowed low, right down to the ground, in front of the man sitting there motion-less, whose smile reminded him of everything that he had ever loved in his life, of everything that had ever been of value and holy in his life.

Questions for Analysis

1. How would you characterize Siddhartha's theory of knowledge?
2. What, in Siddhartha's view, is the essential difference between knowledge and wisdom?
3. Contrast Siddhartha's view of reality with a materialistic outlook.
4. With which Western metaphysical outlook does Siddhartha's view have the most in common? Where do they differ?
5. Siddhartha insists that wisdom is not communicable. Yet he seems to transmit his wisdom to Govinda when Govinda kisses him on the forehead. Is this contradictory? Did Siddhartha have a specific mode of communication in mind when he said wisdom was not communicable?

Paperbacks for Further Reading

Coover, Robert. *The Universal Baseball Association, Inc., J. Henry Waugh, Prop.* New York: New American Library, 1968. In this highly metaphysical novel, the main character, with the help of a deck of playing cards, creates a world of baseball players who ultimately dismiss their creator.

Du Nouy, Lecomte. *Human Destiny.* New York: New American Library, 1949. A biologist argues against chance, accident, and physiochemical-biological mechanisms as complete explanations of reality. He maintains that there is purpose in the universe and that knowledge derived from intuition and religious faith is necessary to understand that purpose and, hence, reality itself.

Husserl, Edmund. *Phenomenology and the Crisis of Philosophy.* Quentin Lauer, Trans. New York: Harper & Row, 1965. These two essays by the "father of phenomenology" present the framework, especially the method, of Husserlian phenomenology.

Krutch, Joseph Wood. *The Measure of Man: On Freedom, Human Values, Survival and the Modern Temper.* New York: Grosset & Dunlap, 1953. Krutch argues that the materialistic view of reality and humankind is fraudulent.

Ornstein, Robert E. *The Psychology of Consciousness.* San Francisco, CA: W. H. Freeman, 1972. Psychologist Ornstein is widely recognized for his ground-breaking research in physiological psychology. In this work, already recognized as a classic in the field, Ornstein differentiates between the two spheres of the brain, and demonstrates the left hemisphere's importance as a seat of knowing different from and complementary to the senses and reason.

Pears, David. *Ludwig Wittgenstein*. New York: Viking Press, 1970. This is an introduction to the thought of perhaps the foremost linguistic analyst, Ludwig Wittgenstein.

Warnock, Mary. *Existentialism*. Oxford: Oxford University Press, 1970. One of the foremost writers on the subject, Warnock presents a succinct and trenchant analysis of the main concepts of existentialism.

PHILOSOPHY
AND RELIGION

The highest that man can attain in these matters is wonder.
—Goethe

In the West there has probably been no greater influence on one's view of self than religion, which has fostered the view of the human as a divine being. The Judaic and the Christian religious traditions share the belief that what makes humans unique is that they have a divine nature by virtue of possessing consciousness and the ability to love. We are creatures who stand midway between nature and spirit. We are on the one hand finite, bound to earth, and capable of sin. On the other, we are able to transcend nature and to achieve infinite possibilities. Primarily because of Western religion, we view ourselves as beings with a supernatural destiny, as possessing a life after death, as being immortal.

But religion has fostered beliefs, attitudes, and feelings not only about a supernatural dimension but also about this world. Thus, religious positions commonly circulate concerning various political, educational, and even economic questions. These positions are very influential in molding public opinion. In recent years, in fact, religions have become so socially directed that many traditionalists feel that religions are undergoing secularization—that is, becoming worldly. Whether or not this charge is justified, *religion* is becoming increasingly difficult to define. However, we should attempt to do so before examining precisely how religion relates to the issue of self. Here are the main points we will make in this chapter.

Main Points

1. Traditionally, religion refers to a belief in God that is institutionalized and incorporated in the teachings of some religious body, such as a church or synagogue. Today, emphasis is on deep personal experience with the object of one's chief loyalty.

2. Theism is the belief in a personal God who has created the world and is

immanent in its processes, and with whom we may come into intimate contact.

3. Three traditional arguments for a theistic God are ontological, cosmological, and design. None offers conclusive proof.

4. Besides the flaws in these arguments, theism has other problems:

   a. How can so much apparent evil emanate from an all-good and all-powerful God?

   b. How can God be all-knowing and yet not suffer along with us?

   c. How can God be unchanging and yet have perfect knowledge of our changing world?

5. Pantheism argues that everything is God and God is everything.

6. Panentheism argues that God is both fixed and changing, unity and diversity, inclusive of all possibilities.

7. William James called the acquisition of religious belief a live, forced, and momentous option.

8. Many people, unable to find religious belief or experience in a theistic God, find both in a deep personal encounter with a divine dimension.

9. Mysticism claims direct and immediate awareness that is not dependent on direct sense experience or on reason. The mystical experience is inexpressible and noetic.

10. Radical theology, as presented by Paul Tillich, has mystical overtones. It appeals to deep personal experience as justification for belief. Tillich's God is being itself, the "God above God," the "ground of all being."

11. The psychedelic experience curiously resembles mystical states of consciousness.

12. Eastern religious views, such as Hinduism, Buddhism, and Zen Buddhism, are much more sympathetic to claims of personal religious experience than are Western religious views.

Religion

When you hear the word *religion*, what do you think of? A church? A synagogue? A belief? Religion includes many things: prayer, ritual, institutional organization, and so on. To define *religion* precisely is difficult. Traditionally, the word has referred to a belief in God that is institutionalized and incorporated in the teachings of some body, such as a church or synagogue. Some people, however, hold that religion need not imply a belief in God. Buddhism, for example, although usually considered a religion, contains no belief in a personal God like the God of the Judaic and Christian traditions. Others claim that whatever anyone holds as the most important value in life is a religion, which frequently finds expression outside religious institutions.

It is a little easier to note features of religion than to define it, although qualifications are still necessary. Religion continues to be one of humankind's dominant interests. Unlike science, it stresses personal commitment based on a meaningful relationship with the sacred, which is often a Supreme Being. Such commitment is generally founded on belief, although most religionists claim that belief divorced from feeling is misguided. Feeling and emotion seem prominent in religion, although these too can mislead. Religion frequently finds expression through institutionalized ritual. Recent trends indicate, however, that many people feel that the emphasis on a symbolic object of devotion, ritualized through an organizational structure, has blurred religion's real import: a deep and personal experience with the object of one's chief loyalty.

In the last analysis, religion is not just an institution, a collection of doctrines, or a stylized ritual. Without exception religious leaders have spoken in terms of personal commitment, experience, and need. In so doing they have recognized the roots from which religion has sprung: our unending search for meaning and fulfillment. In this sense they have emphasized religious belief rather than religion, religious practice rather than theology.

By **theology** is meant the theory or study of God. In practice, the term is used to describe the beliefs or doctrines of a particular religious group or individual thinker. Theology has always failed to touch the faithful in any direct way. The devoted need little theology. Indeed, early Christian history testifies to the priority of faith over knowledge—thus, Saint Anselm's aphorism "I believe in order to understand." We mention this to emphasize that for the vast majority of people, religious belief is more important than any formal theology, and it should therefore be distinguished from theology.

In this chapter we shall have numerous occasions to speak of **religious belief**, which we'll use in its most general sense: the belief that there is an unseen order and that we can do no better than to be in harmony with this order. Likewise, when we use the term *religious experience*, we shall be referring to an experience of this unseen order and our individual place in this order. Having found this place, people feel an intense personal relationship with the rest of creation, perhaps even with a Creator. In this respect, we all seek a religious experience; we all search for an internal peace resulting from a harmonious personal relationship with all other living things. Religious belief and experience continue to be of intense philosophical interest. They are also intimately joined with the issue of self.

Where do we find religious experience today? Some find it in traditional religious concepts, such as the existence of a personal God who listens to and answers prayer, who rewards the faithful and punishes the unworthy. Others, finding such a belief irrational, relate to the divine without relating to a Supreme Being. They claim that religious experience is an intimately personal encounter with the ground of all being, with the source of all reality. Still others find religious experience through the expansion of consciousness—that is, the experience of reality in an unaccustomed manner. And there are many who turn to Eastern thought—Hinduism and Buddhism, for example.

In this chapter we shall explore these and related concerns by thinking philosophically about religion. That is what the philosophy of religion is about. Although such a study ordinarily includes many aspects of religion, including God, immortality, salvation, creation, and all particular religions, we shall focus instead on the nature and varieties of religious experience, on the many ways in which individuals claim to discover their place in the cosmos.

Theism

The most common way for people of a Judeo-Christian culture to find their place in the scheme of things is through a relationship with a personal God— through theistic belief. **Theism** is a belief in a personal God who is creator of the world and immanent in its processes and with whom we may come into intimate contact.[1] **Monotheism** is the belief that there is only one God. Most of us have been raised to accept a theistic concept of God, which forms the basis for our religious feelings and experiences. This God is the basis for the view of the human as divine, as having an immortal soul and a supernatural destiny.

This concept has perhaps never been under greater attack than it is today. Even theologians are asking whether the believer can any longer believe in this traditional God: a single, all-powerful, all-knowing, and all-good God who, having created life, actively participates in the lives of His creatures by listening to and answering prayer. They are questioning an assumption that has centuries of tradition behind it, that is a cornerstone of the lives of many people today, and that has produced not only our religious beliefs but also our ways of perceiving ourselves and the world around us.

Wilbur Daniel Steele, in his short story "The Man Who Saw through Heaven," portrays the dimensions of the problem facing the contemporary theistic believer. In it he depicts Herbert Diana, a self-educated man, who like many theists has accepted a conventional amount of scientific facts as more proof of "what God can do when He puts His mind to it." Intellectually, Diana has accepted the fact of a spherical earth speeding through space, but deep down in his heart he knows "that the world lay flat from modern Illinois to ancient Palestine, and that the sky above it, blue by day and by night festooned with guiding stars for wise men, was the nether side of a floor on which the resurrected trod."[2] How would a man of such simple faith react to a vision of the heavens that he has never believed possible, to a look through an incredibly powerful telescope into an ink black sky that he has always viewed as the floor of heaven, to a vision of the enormity of the universe? How would his simple belief in a personal God stand up to the sudden realization that He must also be personally and completely involved in an infinity of galactic universes and lives? For the first time in his life, Herbert Diana's faith is tested. His well-ordered medieval world concept has to deal with twentieth-century realities. His simple ideas of a heaven "up there" and a hell "down there," of a God who is personally concerned with each person's immortal destiny, and of the infinite importance of a single soul and of what that soul chooses to do—all these beliefs suddenly shrink in the vastness of what his eyes have seen and his mind cannot forget.

1. *Harold H. Titus and Marilyn S. Smith.* Living Issues in Philosophy. *6th ed. New York: D. Van Nostrand, 1974, p. 334.*

2. *Wilbur Daniel Steele. "The Man Who Saw through Heaven," in* The Search for Personal Freedom. *3rd ed. Neal Cross, Leslie Lindou, and Robert Lamm, Eds. Dubuque, Iowa: W. C. Brown, 1968, p. 27.*

In a sense we are all Dianas, for we live in a period that pits traditional religious concepts against the growing weight of scientific fact. Can we, *should* we believe in the God of theism, or must we modify this belief and perhaps abandon it? Consider, as Diana must, the millions of solar systems that we view as stars. Imagine how many millions of satellites must have supported organic life at some time. Imagine how many millions of creatures, perhaps grotesque by our standards, but creatures nonetheless. Then consider clusters of universes apart from ours. And consider further that "all these, all the generations of these enormous and microscopic beings harvested through a time beside which the life span of our earth is as a second in a million centuries: all these brought to rest for an eternity to which the time in itself is a watch tick—all crowded to rest pellmell, thronged, serried, packed to suffocation in layers unnumbered light-years deep."[3] Do we know the God who rules over such universes?

Today science has brought many of us, like Herbert Diana, to ask not only if we believe in a traditional God but if there is any God at all. Nevertheless, despite the rise of science and the decay of traditional religious forms, religion thrives in this country. In other words, while rational and empirical evidence might have an impact on the beliefs of people like Herbert Diana, in general it has little effect on most people's beliefs. In fact, this is why Diana is ultimately able to return to his "simple faith"—not because he had new evidence, but because he *chose* to believe rather than not to believe. Believing in a personal God was his way of locating himself in the scheme of things. Such people don't believe on the basis of scientific evidence, which may or may not support their belief.

Others find in science a new basis for religious belief (see Philosophy and Life 10-1). In fact, appeals to reason and experience have figured prominently in the history of Christian theology. For example, numerous theologians have advanced arguments for the existence of a personal God, as we shall shortly see. But it is vital to recognize the purpose of these arguments: to advance the quest to understand God. Knowledge of God was and continues to be one of the most significant topics occupying thinkers from Saint Augustine onward. And the arguments advanced for God's existence were one element in the centuries-long attempt to determine the extent to which humans could have rational knowledge of God and to which philosophy had a bearing on theological matters. Certainly every thinker of note considered arguments, but they didn't speak much of them. Thomas Aquinas (1125–1274), for example, had no interest in using the arguments to convince anyone of God's existence. Their appearance in his monumental *Summa Theologica* was largely pedagogical. The theological summary was intended for students whose main task was to know the theological tradition for their work as students and as masters. It provided the tradition within which students would think and work.

We will begin our overview of philosophy and religion with some of these arguments for the existence of God. We present them as illustrations of a traditional way by which people have fortified their religious convictions, strength-

3. *Wilbur Daniel Steele. "The Man Who Saw through Heaven," p. 28.*

ened their relationship with a personal God, and discovered something about that God. In reading them, notice their reliance on reason and sense experience, on rationalism and empiricism. We mention this to keep in mind the contrasting approach that runs parallel to this development of a natural theology, an approach that is essentially nonrational. We will see how this latter approach has been revitalized and how for many people today it serves as the basis for religious belief and experience. In reading this chapter, then, you will begin to mine two rich veins in the development of religious thought, the rational and nonrational.

The Ontological Argument

There are many arguments propounding God's existence in Saint Augustine, but they are not as formalized and as self-conscious as the ones asserted in the eleventh century by Saint Anselm. He offered one argument that relied on reason alone. Later arguments would be based on the experience of the things of the world, but Anselm held that mind by itself could arrive at such a realization.

God, Anselm reasoned, is "that than which none greater can be conceived." Now, what if God were just an idea? If he were, we could easily conceive of something greater: a God who actually existed. Therefore, Anselm

---

PHILOSOPHY AND LIFE 10-1
Religion and Science

For many people the growth of science has made the so-called truths of religion increasingly difficult to maintain. Some, however, have found in science a new basis for religious belief. Contemporary Christian philosopher Étienne Gilson is a good example.

Gilson argues that, contrary to the traditional distinction between science and metaphysics (of which religion is a part), the language of modern science and the questions it asks are fundamentally nonscientific, or what might be termed metaphysical. For example, Gilson cites the English astronomer Sir James Jeans's description of the emergence of life as "highly improbable," of human existence as "accidental," and of the entire creation as "surprising." In Gilson's view such descriptions, strictly speaking, are not scientific. He suggests, therefore, that in facing the most basic questions, such as the origin of the universe, science, like metaphysics and religion, must operate on a kind of faith or belief and not on established fact.

He then observes that in its attempt to explain the origin of things, science shows a markedly nonscientific or metaphysical bent. The reason is that such investigations imply a search for the cause or causes of things, a subject that traditionally has been addressed by metaphysics. More to the point, in attempting to account for things, some scientists appeal to chance. Others,

concluded, if God is "that than which none greater can be conceived," then God must exist. This is about as distilled a version of Anselm's ontological argument as one is likely to get. To appreciate it fully, you must follow its development in Anselm's most important philosophical work, the *Proslogion*. In reading the following passage, keep in mind the impulse behind it: *"Credo ut intelligam"*—"I believe in order that I may understand." Thus, without belief, one can have no understanding of God:

> Truly there is a God, although the fool hath said in his heart, there is no God.
>
> And so, Lord, do thou, who dost give understanding to faith, give me, so far as thou knowest it to be profitable, to understand that thou art as we believe; and that thou art that which we believe. And, indeed, we believe that thou art a being than which nothing greater can be conceived. Or is there no such nature, since the fool hath said in his heart, there is no God? (Psalms xiv. 1). But, at any rate, this very fool, when he hears of this being of which I speak—a being than which nothing greater can be conceived—understands what he hears, and what he understands in his understanding; although he does not understand it to exist.
>
> For, it is one thing for an object to be in the understanding, and another to understand that the object exists. When a painter first conceives of what he will afterwards perform, he has it in his understanding, but he does not yet under-

---

while assuming the operation of mechanical laws of nature, nonetheless propose a self-made, spontaneously arising universe. Such explanations, says Gilson, are essentially no different from, say, Thomas Aquinas' cosmological argument that premises a cause for every event and concludes with an uncaused cause.

In brief, then, Gilson's view is that the more scientific we become, the more metaphysical we must be—and the more religious. In the end, he sees much of contemporary science as providing a methodological basis for demonstrating the efficacy of religious truths.

□ *Do you agree that the distinction between science and metaphysics is not clear-cut?* □ *Investigation of the microcosmic reality and the astrophysical macrocosm (as outlined in Chapter 9) seems to produce in many scientists a humility and sense of reverence that borders on the religious. A long line of scientists, including Einstein, have seen the universe as God's "sensorium." What do you think they mean by this?* □ *Are there any facts of science that make you more inclined to religious belief?* □ *Less inclined?*

stand it to be, because he has not yet performed it. But after he has made the painting, he both has it in his understanding, and he understands that it exists, because he has made it.

Hence, even the fool is convinced that something exists in the understanding, at least, than which nothing greater can be conceived. For, when he hears of this, he understands it. And whatever is understood, exists in the understanding. And assuredly that, than which nothing greater can be conceived, cannot exist in the understanding alone. For, suppose it exists in the understanding alone: then it can be conceived to exist in reality; which is greater.

Therefore, if that, than which nothing greater can be conceived, exists in the understanding alone, the very being, than which nothing greater can be conceived, is one, than which a greater can be conceived. But obviously this is impossible. Hence, there is no doubt that there exists a being, than which nothing greater can be conceived, and it exists both in the understanding and in reality.

And it assuredly exists so truly, that it cannot be conceived not to exist. For, it is possible to conceive of a being which cannot be conceived not to exist; and this is greater than one which can be conceived not to exist. Hence, if that, than which nothing greater can be conceived, can be conceived not to exist, it is not that, than which nothing is greater can be conceived. But this is an irreconcilable contradiction. There is, then, so truly a being than which nothing greater can be conceived to exist, that it cannot even be conceived not to exist; and this being thou art, O Lord, our God.

So truly, therefore, dost thou exist, O Lord, my God, that thou canst not be conceived not to exist; and rightly. For, if a mind could conceive of a being better than thee, the creature would rise above the Creator; and this is most absurd. And, indeed, whatever else there is, except thee alone, can be conceived not to exist. To thee alone, therefore, it belongs to exist more truly than all other beings, and hence in a higher degree than all others. For, whatever else exists does not exist so truly, and hence in a less degree it belongs to it to exist. Why, then, has the fool said in his heart, there is no God (Psalms xiv. 1), since it is so evident, to a rational mind, that thou dost exist in the highest degree of all? Why, except that he is dull and a fool?[4]

Anselm has had his supporters over the years. But more people have attacked the ontological argument. Immanuel Kant was one. He claimed that the concept of an absolutely necessary being is not proved by the fact that reason apparently requires it.

To understand Kant's criticism, ask yourself this: Under what conditions will a triangle have three sides? Obviously, when and where there is a triangle. In other words, *if* there is a triangle, it has three sides. But *if* is conditional: that is, what follows it may not be. "If there is a triangle" does not imply that there necessarily *is* a triangle. Likewise, *"If there is a perfect being, then a perfect being exists"* does not mean a perfect being does exist. Kant claims that Anselm is defining God into existence—that he is asking us to form a concept of a thing in such a way as to include existence within the scope of its meaning. Undoubtedly, Anselm would object that it is contradictory to posit a triangle and yet reject its three sides. Kant would agree. But he would add that there is

4. *Saint Anselm.* Saint Anselm: Basic Writings. *S. N. Deane, Trans. La Salle, Ill.: Open Court Publishing, 1962. Reprinted by permission.*

no contradiction in rejecting the triangle *along with* its three sides. "Likewise of the concept of an absolutely necessary being. If its existence is rejected, we reject the thing itself with all its predicates; and no question of contradiction can then arise."

But a perfect being is unique. Because Anselm thought nonexistence was an imperfection and therefore inconsistent with the nature of a perfect being, he argued that a perfect being must exist. And he was right, assuming that existence adds to a thing. But imagine a perfect companion. Attribute to it all the properties that will make it perfect. Then ask yourself, "Does its existence add anything to the concept?" The point is that to assert existence is not to add a property but to assert a relationship between the thing conceived and the world. In other words, you do not add anything to the creature of your fantasy by positing its existence; you merely establish its relationship to other things. It seems, then, that Kant is right: "When I think a being as the supreme reality, without any defect, the question still remains whether it exists or not."

The Cosmological Argument

After Anselm's ontological argument, the next important attempt to justify God's existence was made by the greatest of all the rational theologians, the thirteenth-century Christian philosopher Saint Thomas Aquinas (1225–1274). His arguments are systematically organized and stated in Aristotelian language. In his monumental *Summa Theologica*, Aquinas offers five proofs, only three of which will concern us here. Each of these three proofs begins with an observation about the physical world. So they are cosmological in that they result from a study of the universe.

Aquinas' first argument originates in the fact that things move around us. Similarly, the second originates in the fact that every observed event is made to happen or is effected by some preceding event. Likewise, the third springs from the fact that there are things in the world whose existence is not necessary, that is, which are dependent on other things for their continued existence. Aquinas then reasons that the observed motion, event, or possible thing is the last in a chain of such motions, events, or possible things. This chain, however, must not go back endlessly; somewhere the chain must end. It must end, says Aquinas, with a being who itself is unmoved, uncaused, and necessary. Such a being he terms *God*. His justification for this first mover, first cause, and necessary being appears in the following passage from *Summa Theologica*:

> The existence of God can be proved in five ways.
> The first and more manifest way is the argument from motion. It is certain, and evident to our senses, that in the world some things are in motion. Now whatever is moved is moved by another, for nothing can be moved except it is in potentiality to that towards which it is moved; whereas a thing moves inasmuch as it is in act. For motion is nothing else than the reduction of something from potentiality to actuality. But nothing can be reduced from potentiality to actuality, except by something in a state of actuality. Thus that which is actually hot, as fire, makes wood, which is potentially hot, to be actually hot, and thereby moves and changes it. Now it is not possible that the same thing

should be at once in actuality and potentiality in the same respect but only in different respects. For what is actually hot cannot simultaneously be potentially hot; but it is simultaneously potentially cold. It is therefore impossible that in the same respect and in the same way a thing should be both mover and moved, *i.e.*, that it should move itself. Therefore, whatever is moved must be moved by another. If that by which it is moved be itself moved, then this also must needs be moved by another, and that by another again. But this cannot go on to infinity, because then there would be no first mover, and, consequently, no other mover, seeing that subsequent movers move only inasmuch as they are moved by the first mover; as the staff moves only because it is moved by the hand. Therefore it is necessary to arrive at a first mover, moved by no other; and this everyone understands to be God.

The second way is from the nature of efficient cause. In the world of sensible things we find there is an order of efficient causes. There is no case known (neither is it, indeed, possible) in which a thing is found to be the efficient cause of itself; for so it would be prior to itself, which is impossible. Now in efficient causes it is not possible to go on to infinity, because in all efficient causes following in order, the first is the cause of the intermediate cause, and the intermediate is the cause of the ultimate cause, whether the intermediate cause be several, or one only. Now to take away the cause is to take away the effect. Therefore, if there be no first cause among efficient causes, there will be no ultimate, nor any intermediate, cause. But if in efficient causes it is possible to go on to infinity, there will be no first efficient cause, neither will there be an ultimate effect, nor any intermediate efficient causes; all of which is plainly false. Therefore it is necessary to admit a first efficient cause, to which everyone gives the name of God.

The third way is taken from possibility and necessity, and runs thus. We find in nature things that are possible to be and not to be, since they are found to be generated, and to be corrupted, and consequently, it is possible for them to be and not to be. But it is impossible for these always to exist, for that which can not-be at some time is not. Therefore, if everything can not-be, then at one time there was nothing in existence. Now if this were true, even now there would be nothing in existence, because that which does not exist begins to exist only through something already existing. Therefore, if at one time nothing was in existence, it would have been impossible for anything to have begun to exist; and thus even now nothing would be in existence—which is absurd. Therefore, not all beings are merely possible, but there must exist something the existence of which is necessary. But every necessary thing either has its necessity caused by another, or not. Now it is impossible to go on to infinity in necessary things which have their necessity caused by another, as has been already proved in regard to efficient causes. Therefore we cannot but admit the existence of some being having of itself its own necessity, and not receiving it from another, but rather causing in others their necessity. This all men speak of as God.[5]

There are two key objections to this cosmological argument. The first concerns its contention that there can be no infinite regress in the causal and temporal sequences of the universe. Aquinas reasoned that an infinite regress

5. *Saint Thomas Aquinas.* Summa Theologica, *in* Basic Writings of Saint Thomas Aquinas. *Anton C. Pegis, Trans. New York: Random House, 1945. Reprinted by permission of the estate of Anton C. Pegis.*

might account for the individual links in the causal chain, but not for the chain itself. Is he right?

Suppose a friend visits you at college. You wish to show her around the campus. So, you take her to the library, the humanities building, the science labs, the cafeteria, and so on, until she sees the entire college. After this tour, she asks, "But where is the college?" You might find that a silly question, since you had already shown her the college by showing her its parts. In a similar way David Hume questioned Aquinas' cause argument: "Did I show you the particular causes of each individual in a collection of twenty particles of matter, I should think it very unreasonable, should you afterwards ask me, what was the cause of the whole twenty. For this is sufficiently explained in explaining the cause of the parts."[6] Hume is arguing that the individual links in the causal chain find cause in their immediate predecessors. This fact is enough to account for the chain itself. The same kind of logic might be applied to events and contingent beings (beings that are not necessary). In other words, if Hume's argument has merit, there is no need or any logical justification for positing a first mover, a first cause, or a necessary being. Of course, this objection relies on a commitment to mechanism and hence a denial that the whole is greater than the sum of its parts. If this assumption is rejected, an explanation is required for both the parts and the whole.

The second objection is that the argument's conclusion is contradicted by its premise. To illustrate, Aquinas insists that every event must have a cause. But if this is so, why stop with God? The notion of an uncaused cause seems to contradict the assumption that everything has a cause. And even if there is an uncaused cause, why must it be God? Arthur Schopenhauer expresses this objection succinctly when he writes that the law of universal causation "is not so accommodating as to let itself be used like a cab for hire, which we dismiss when we have reached our destination."[7]

A number of contemporary Thomists (thinkers who generally agree with Thomas Aquinas) have modified this first-cause argument. For them, the endless series that the argument dismisses is not a regress of events in time but a regress of explanations. As John Hick interprets their position: "If fact A is made intelligible by its relation to facts B, C and D (which may be antecedent to or contemporary with A), and if each of these is in turn rendered intelligible by other facts, at the back of the complex there must be a reality which is self-explanatory, whose existence constitutes the ultimate explanation of the whole. If no such reality exists, the universe is a mere unintelligible brute fact."[8] But how do we know that the universe is not "a mere unintelligible brute fact"? The argument appears to present a false dilemma: Either a first cause exists or the universe makes no sense. It also assumes that causal conditions make things intelligible.

6. *David Hume.* Dialogues concerning Natural Religion. *N. Kemp Smith, Ed. Edinburgh: Nelson, 1947, p. 18.*

7. *Quoted in C. J. Ducasse.* A Philosophical Scrutiny of Religion. *New York: Ronald Press, 1953, p. 335.*

8. *John Hick.* Philosophy of Religion. *Englewood Cliffs, N.J.: Prentice-Hall, 1963, p. 21.*

The Design Argument

The most popular of the arguments for God's existence has been the proof from design, often called the teleological argument. Simply put, the order and purpose manifest in the working of things demand a God. Even when evolutionists offer an explanation for such apparent order, supporters of the design argument reply, "Yes, but why did things evolve in this way and not in some other?" Traditionally a prominent argument for God's existence, the design proof has currency even among some biologists today, such as Edmund W. Sinnott, and some theologians, such as Robert E. D. Clark.

In 1802, theologian William Paley presented one of the best-known expositions of this argument. As was the custom of religious thinkers of his day, Paley called on a long list of examples from the sciences to demonstrate his argument. The migration of birds, the instincts of other animals, the adaptability of species to various environments, and the human's ability to forecast based on probable causation all suggested a plan and a planner.

More recent writers often think similarly. How, they wonder, can we otherwise explain our continued safety from the two zones of high-intensity particulate radiation trapped in the earth's magnetic field and surrounding the planet? As one writer says, "the ozone gas layer is mighty proof of the Creator's forethought. Could anyone attribute this device to a chance evolutionary process? A wall which prevents death to every living thing, just the right thickness, and exactly the correct defense, gives every evidence of plan."[9]

But critics have asked, "Does the appearance of order necessitate conscious design?" The order in the universe, they say, could have occurred by chance through an incredibly long period of evolution. Hume argues that in an infinite amount of time, a finite number of particles in random motion must eventually effect a stable order. After all, it is impossible to imagine a universe without some design. In fact, by definition, a universe must have design.

As Darwin later contended, the life around us has won in the "struggle for survival"—the fit have survived and the unfit have perished. Through a process of natural selection, in which those that can adapt survive and the rest die, a stability in things comes to pass. Concerning our safety under an ozone umbrella, both Hume and Darwin would point out that it is not explained by a God who made things and then shielded them but by an evolutionary fact: that only life that adjusted to the precise level of ultraviolet radiation penetrating this ozone has survived. In other words, life has adjusted to the ozone; ozone has not sustained life.

Objections to Theism: The Problem of Evil

The traditional proofs for God's existence, as we've seen, have obvious flaws. There are additional serious objections, of which the major is the problem of evil.

Clearly humans continue to be beset by all kinds of problems: sickness, poverty, suffering, and death. Yet theism insists that there is an all-good, all-powerful Creator. Is this not at least paradoxical? How is evil compatible with

9. *Arthur I. Brown.* Footprints of God. *Findlay, Ohio: Fundamental Truth Publishers, 1943, p. 102.*

an all-good Creator? If God is all-powerful, surely He could destroy all evil. If he doesn't, why not? Is he really not all-powerful? Or is it that he's unwilling? But if God is unwilling, then He seems to have evil intentions, which certainly aren't consistent with the nature of an all-good God.

In his *Dialogues concerning Natural Religion*, a three-person discussion of the chief arguments for God's existence, Hume considers this question of evil. His conclusion, in the words of one of his characters, Philo, is that one's experience in the world argues against the existence of an all-good, all-powerful being:

> My sentiments, replied Philo, are not worth being made a mystery of; and, therefore, without any ceremony, I shall deliver what occurs to me with regard to the present subject. It must, I think, be allowed that, if a very limited intelligence whom we shall suppose utterly unacquainted with the universe were assured that it were the production of a very good, wise, and powerful being, however finite, he would, from his conjectures, form *beforehand* a different notion of it from what we find it to be by experience; nor would he ever imagine, merely from these attributes of the cause of which he is informed, that the effect could be so full of vice and misery and disorder, as it appears in this life. Supposing now that this person were brought into the world, still assured that it was the workmanship of such a sublime and benevolent being, he might, perhaps, be surprised at the disappointment, but would never retract his former belief if founded on any very solid argument, since such a limited intelligence must be sensible of his own blindness and ignorance, and must allow that there may be many solutions of those phenomena which will forever escape his comprehension. But supposing, which is the real case with regard to man, that this creature is not antecedently convinced of a supreme intelligence, benevolent, and powerful, but is left to gather such a belief from the appearances of things—this entirely alters the case, nor will he ever find any reason for such a conclusion. He may be fully convinced of the narrow limits of his understanding, but this will not help him in forming an inference concerning the goodness of superior powers, since he must form that inference from what he knows, not from what he is ignorant of. The more you exaggerate his weakness and ignorance, the more diffident you render him, and give him the greater suspicion that such subjects are beyond the reach of his faculties. You are obliged, therefore, to reason with him merely from the known phenomena, and to drop every arbitrary supposition or conjecture.[10]

Hume is saying that if we presuppose an all-good, all-powerful God, then we, in effect, rationalize away the evil that we experience as being something beyond our ability to comprehend. But if we don't presuppose such a being, then our experience in the world lends no support to the claim that an all-good, all-powerful being exists. If we don't take God's existence for granted, then the experience of "vice and misery and disorder" in fact argues against a theistic God.

There have been a number of attempts to deal with the problem of evil. Augustine, for one, argues that evil is a negative thing—that is, the absence of good. To be real, said Augustine, is to be perfect. Since only God is perfect, only God is wholly real. God's creation, therefore, being finite and limited, must contain incomplete goodness—that is, evil. But this argument seems to

---

10. *David Hume.* Dialogues concerning Natural Religion, *pt. XI.*

dodge the issue. Call sickness lack of health, if you wish, and war lack of peace—the fact remains that people experience pain and suffering, which they commonly regard as evil. No amount of word play can ease their situation.

Others argue that evil is necessary for good, that only through evil can good be achieved. It is true that in many instances good seems to depend on evil, as in the case of having to suffer surgical pain to rid one's body of disease. But to say that God can bring about good in no other way than through inflicting pain is to deny God's omnipotence.

But the most common and serious attempt to escape the problem of evil is to claim human freedom as the cause of evil. Since we are free, we are free to do evil as well as good. Even an omnipotent God could not make us free in all other respects but not free to do evil, since this would be contradictory. Therefore, evil results from free human choice.

But there are several problems with this argument. First, it does not account for natural evils: earthquakes, droughts, and tornadoes. Humans apparently exercise no control over these. So the argument can pertain only to moral evils—that is, those perpetrated by humans on other creatures: war, murder, and torture. Undoubtedly we are free to do this evil, but why did an all-powerful God enable us to do such terrible things? After all, if He is all-powerful, He could have made us differently. Already we are vulnerable, limited creatures. Why not make us unable to do evil? Perhaps we do not really understand the nature of evil; what we perceive as evil may in God's eyes be good. But if this is so, even more complex questions arise concerning the nature and morality of the Supreme Being. We are also left puzzled about what goodness itself really is.

John Hick (1922–), lecturer in divinity at Cambridge University, has taken a novel approach to the problem of evil. In his *Philosophy of Religion*, Hick suggests that a world without suffering would be unsatisfactory. Consistent with the thinking of early Hellenistic fathers of the Christian church, such as Irenaeus, Hick seems to argue that while humans are made in the image of God, they have not yet been brought as free and responsible agents into the finite likeness of God as revealed in Christ. The world, then, "with all its rough edges," becomes the sphere in which this stage of the creative process takes place:

> Suppose, contrary to fact, that this world were a paradise from which all possibility of pain and suffering were excluded. The consequences would be very far-reaching. For example, no one could ever injure anyone else: the murderer's knife would turn to paper or his bullets to thin air; the bank safe, robbed of a million dollars, would miraculously become filled with another million dollars (without this device, on however large a scale, proving inflationary); fraud, deceit, conspiracy, and treason would somehow always leave the fabric of society undamaged. Again, no one would ever be injured by accident: the mountain-climber, steeplejack, or playing child falling from a height would float unharmed to the ground; the reckless driver would never meet with disaster. There would be no need to work, since no harm could result from avoiding work; there would be no call to be concerned for others in time of need or danger, for in such a world there could be no real needs or dangers.

To make possible this continual series of individual adjustments, nature would have to work by "special providences" instead of running according to general laws which men must learn to respect on penalty of pain or death. The laws of nature would have to be extremely flexible: sometimes gravity would operate, sometimes not; sometimes an object would be hard and solid, sometimes soft. There could be no sciences, for there would be no enduring world structure to investigate. In eliminating the problems and hardships of an objective environment, with its own laws, life would become like a dream in which, delightfully but aimlessly, we would float and drift at ease.

One can at least begin to imagine such a world. It is evident that our present ethical concepts would have no meaning in it. If, for example, the notion of harming someone is an essential element in the concept of a wrong action, in our hedonistic paradise there could be no wrong actions—nor any right actions in distinction from wrong. Courage and fortitude would have no point in an environment in which there is, by definition, no danger or difficulty. Generosity, kindness, the *agape* aspect of love, prudence, unselfishness, and all other ethical notions which presuppose life in a stable environment, could not even be formed. Consequently, such a world, however well it might promote pleasure, would be very ill adapted for the development of the moral qualities of human personality. In relation to this purpose it would be the worst of all possible worlds.

It would seem, then, that an environment intended to make possible the growth in free beings of the finest characteristics of personal life, must have a good deal in common with our present world. It must operate according to general and dependable laws; and it must involve real dangers, difficulties, problems, obstacles, and possibilities of pain, failure, sorrow, frustration, and defeat. If it did not contain the particular trials and perils which—subtracting man's own very considerable contribution—our world contains, it would have to contain others instead.[11]

Persons of faith may be largely indifferent to evil as an issue, since they "know" their God beyond rationality and can easily say that we can't begin to fathom God's mystery. In the last analysis, evil may be a problem only for those whose tolerance of mystery is minimal. The rationalist or empiricist must explain away mystery rather than confronting it and getting intimations of the divine and the holy. But for many people, evil just isn't a problem. The same can be said of the other criticisms made of theism.

One of those criticisms concerns God's all-knowing nature. If God is all-knowing, He is aware of what is going on. But can he be aware of our travail without suffering with us? Some say that is precisely why God became man. But how can the timeless and unchanging become incarnate in our world of change? In addition, God's knowledge of our changing world is said to be itself unchanging. How is this possible? Traditional theism, furthermore, speaks of a God that transcends creation; God is said to be different from and superior to what He made. But isn't perfect knowledge contingent on knowing something "inside out"? A parent never completely knows its offspring, for it can never fully know what that offspring feels, thinks, and desires. If God has perfect

11. *John Hick.* Philosophy of Religion. *Englewood Cliffs, N.J.: Prentice-Hall, 1963, pp. 45–46. Reprinted by permission.*

knowledge, isn't He then a composite of the many things that make up reality? But if this is so, how can God at the same time be separate and distinct from His creation?

These objections seem real and pressing. But again, people with a strong faith can write them off as irrelevant. The thoughtful person of faith may simply ask interrogators to stop flaunting their cognitivity and listen to other aspects of their being. Yes, reason may be one of our important tools. But it's hardly the totality of our being. Without direction from the passions, reason is impotent, to paraphrase David Hume.

Yet, some people cannot dismiss such concerns with a humble "Ours is not to reason why." Indeed, they answer this expression of simple faith with "Then why is it ours to reason at all?" As a result, some reflective theists today often find pantheism and panentheism more comfortable than traditional monotheism.

Pantheism and Panentheism

Pantheism means literally "all God." It is the belief that everything is God and God is everything. In brief, God and the universe are identical. Pantheists see God as an immense, interconnected system of nature, in much the same way as did philosopher Baruch Spinoza (1632–1677). Spinoza reasoned that if God is all-powerful, all-knowing, and all-present, as traditionalists claim, then God must be everything. If God is everything, He can't be separate from anything. If God is all-powerful, there can be no world outside God. Hence, all of nature, everything that is, must be God. But how can God be constituted of incomplete, changing parts, as we see manifest in nature? Spinoza's pantheism perceives things as necessary—that is, as incapable of being otherwise. If this is so, what happens to free choice? What happens to the human as an experience-confronting, choice-making entity?

Peculiar to the twentieth century is a brand of theism known as **panentheism**, which attempts to merge theism and pantheism. Rather than believing that all is God, panentheists hold that all is *in* God. God interpenetrates everything, as in pantheism; but God is also transcendent. Developed by G. T. Fechner, Friedrich von Schelling, and Charles Peirce, panentheism sees God as a Supreme Being whose original nature is fixed, unchanging, and inclusive of all possibilities. But at the same time God has a historical nature that exists in time as a growing, changing, expanding dimension. God, therefore, is a unity of diversity, being and becoming, the one and the many. He contains all contrast with Himself.

Still, problems of logic remain. How can such a fusion of opposites occur? Did God create His temporal nature? What precisely is the relationship between God's finite nature and His infinite nature? Was God "compelled" to exist in time? Panentheism may be more coherent than theism or pantheism, but it seems to raise further complexities that require an almost mystical grounding to be accepted.

The problems of establishing a panentheistic, pantheistic, or theistic God have led many to disbelieve God's existence. Such disbelief generally takes the form of atheism or agnosticism.

Atheism

Atheism denies the major claims of all varieties of theism. In the words of atheist Ernest Nagel (1937–), "Atheism denies the existence . . . of a self-consistent, omnipotent, omniscient, righteous and benevolent being who is distinct from and independent of what has been created."[12] Philosophical atheists today generally share a number of characteristics. First, although they often differ on how to establish claims to knowledge, they agree that sense observation and public verification are instrumental and that scientific method is the measure of knowledge and truth. As Nagel states, "It is indeed this commitment to the use of an empirical method which is the final basis of the atheistic critique of theism." Thus, by means of respectable methodology, the atheist claims to explain what theists can account for only through introducing an unverifiable hypothesis about a deity.

Atheists reject **animism**—the belief that supernatural creatures in the form of spirits exist and exercise control over the natural world. On the contrary, atheists deal exclusively with the natural, physical world. If we are to make any progress, they say, we must focus our attention on the properties and structures of identifiable objects located in space. The variety of things that we experience in the universe can be accounted for in terms of the changes that things undergo when relating with other things. At the same time, there is no discernible unifying pattern of change. "Nature," says Nagel, "is ineradicably plural, both in respect to the individuals occurring in it as well as in respect to the processes in which things become involved." In short, "An atheistic view of things is a form of materialism."

With their emphasis on empiricism and the physical world, atheists generally accept a utilitarian code of ethics. Such a code, as indicated in Chapter 3, holds that total social consequences determine the moral action. There is no code of morality apart from the results of human actions. The final standard of moral evaluation is no commandment, no divinely inspired code of conduct, but the satisfaction of the complex needs of the human creature.

As a result of these viewpoints, atheists focus directly on the world here and now, and they generally resist authoritarianism and stress individualism. Traditionally, they have opposed moral codes that try to repress human impulses in favor of some otherworldly ideal. At the same time, this stress on the individual has not made atheists forget the role that institutions can play in advancing human goals. Because atheists cannot fortify their moral positions with promises of immortality, threats of damnation, or guarantees of righteous recompense, they must rely on what Nagel calls "a vigorous call to intelligent activity—activity for the sake of realizing human potentialities and for eliminat-

---

12. *Quoted in Ramona Cormier, Ewing Chinn, and Richard Lineback, Eds.* Encounter: An Introduction to Philosophy. *Glenview, Ill.: Scott, Foresman, 1970, p. 224.*

ing whatever stands in the way of such realization." But there are objections to atheism.

Objections to Atheism

One objection to atheism is that its claim that God does not exist can no more be proved than can the theistic claim that God does exist. Atheists counter that there's insufficient evidence, in quantity and quality, to claim that God exists. However, perhaps a statement like "God exists" cannot be handled like a scientific statement. Furthermore, we are especially susceptible to a subjective interpretation of evidence for God's existence. This interpretation is based on various assumptions about knowledge and the world. These assumptions are open to question. Why are the epistemological bases of atheism sound and those of theism not?

But most people are not so analytical. Instead, they charge atheism with abandoning humankind to its own devices and with ignoring the persistent belief in a force superior to humankind, a force that often leaves us with hope, confidence, faith, and love in the face of apparently insurmountable troubles. To strip us of these qualities is to leave us both ill equipped to cope with life and, more importantly, morally bankrupt.

Immanuel Kant, although arguing against many of the proofs for God's existence, maintained that there was no basis for morality in the absence of a God from whom all good emanates. Without such a figure, what is the point of trying to do good? Why not just act according to your own impulses, according to your own idea of what is good or bad, or according to what is fashionable? If there is no God, notions of right and wrong are inconclusive. This fact dooms us, in turn, to ignorance, uncertainty, and anxiety. In brief, without God we have no basis for evaluating our actions. In this way Kant argued for the existence of God.

Finally, consider this observation about atheism, which is more of an insight related to the first objection than a criticism. Atheism, to use Nagel's own word, involves a "commitment," in much the way that theism or monotheism does. In other words, empirically minded atheists erect their position as much on a commitment of faith as those who hold religious positions. All the characteristics of atheism that Nagel cites are founded as much on a categorical commitment as are the characteristics of the religionists. The commitments obviously differ: The religionist's commitment is to nonrational, nonempirical ways of knowing; the atheist's is to empiricism. If this is so, we should ask the atheist for empirical-rational reasons for committing oneself to empirical-rational standards and subsequently to atheism. Lacking these reasons, by what criterion can we judge the empiricist-atheistic commitment of faith to be more sound than the theistic commitment?

Agnosticism

Having studied the arguments for and against the existence of God, many thinkers claim that neither side is convincing. As a result, they say they just don't know whether God exists—a position known as **agnosticism.**

" . . . the claim that God does not exist can no more be proved than can the theistic claim . . . "

The nineteenth-century English scientist Thomas Huxley was a well-known agnostic. For Huxley, agnosticism expressed absolute faith in the validity of the principle "that it is wrong for a man to say that he is certain of the objective truth of any proposition unless he can produce evidence which logically justifies that certainty."[13] Huxley would find sympathy among contemporary linguistic analysts, who go further and assert that the propositions "God exists" and "God does not exist" are meaningless because there is no possible way of verifying these claims. The linguistic analyst, however, is much harsher than Huxley ever intended to be. For Huxley the statements were at least meaningful, if insoluble. So he suspended judgment, as he did on the real nature of such ultimates as matter and mind. The agnostic position implies ignorance of the nature of such things. As Huxley puts it, "We have not the slightest objection to believe anything you like, if you will give us good grounds for belief; but, if you cannot, we must respectfully refuse, even if that refusal should wreck morality and insure our damnation several times over. We are quite content to leave the decision of the future. The course of the past has impressed us with the firm conviction that no good ever comes of falsehood, and we feel warranted in refusing even to experiment in that direction."[14]

Objections to Agnosticism

Agnosticism, unlike atheism, need not prove any claim, for it makes none that demands verification. But it is still open to all the other objections to atheism. In addition, one can validly wonder whether one can suspend judgment on the question of whether God exists.

13. *Quoted in Ramona Cormier, Ewing Chinn, and Richard Lineback, Eds.* Encounter, *p. 227.*

14. *Quoted in Ramona Cormier, Ewing Chinn, and Richard Lineback, Eds.* Encounter, *p. 230.*

To suspend judgment on whether unicorns exist is one thing, but to do so on whether God exists is quite another. Unicorns make no difference in our lives, but this cannot be said of God. Consider how much is tied up in our belief or disbelief in God's existence. For many, absolute proof for or against God's existence would mean a different life-style—a different way of thinking, seeing, and behaving. But whatever position we take, we are probably assuming it as if there were absolute evidence for it, even though we admit there is none. And in all likelihood we are trying to live according to this position. To suspend judgment on the question seems to be avoiding the issue, because the question evidently does not allow such a response. In short, critics of agnosticism argue that we are faced not with a false dilemma but with a genuine one: We must either believe that God exists or not believe it. We'll see this position developed fully later in James's "The Will to Believe."

In the last analysis, the existence or nonexistence of a theistic God cannot yet be proved. But lack of certain evidence does not make the question any less important, any more than our not knowing what to study in college makes the issue of an academic major unimportant The point is that, lacking sufficient evidence, most of us still believe or disbelieve. And the position we take affects how we see ourselves. Whether we see ourselves as surviving after death—as being immortal, being reborn, or experiencing resurrection—is a good example. It is also a question of fundamental concern in the philosophy of religion.

Life after Death

Any person who is conscious of death has wondered: Will I continue to live in some way after I die? This question has occupied humankind from earliest times and perhaps penetrates the issue of self more deeply than any other. For if we continue to live after death, we must wonder about the state, form, and condition of that existence; we must wonder whether our present life will affect those aspects of the next life, whether the departed currently live among us, and whether contact between this world and the next is possible. The belief in survival after death is closely connected with a belief in God: If we believe God exists, it is easier to accept this belief.

When speaking of personal survival after death, the term *immortality* inevitably comes up. We can speak of immortality in several ways. There is biological immortality, which is the continuance of germ plasm after death. In this sense, we are immortal. We are also immortal in the sense that we leave behind us a social legacy or contribution by which we are remembered. Some people also speak of an impersonal immortality in which, upon physical death, the self merges with the unity of all things, a world soul. Versions of this belief are popular in Eastern religions, in which the self assumes a different form after death—as a human, an animal, even an insect. Plato subscribed to the doctrine of transmigration of souls, or **metempsychosis**, the passing of the soul into another body after death. But these beliefs are not what people in the West generally mean by immortality. Rather, they view survival after death as the continuance of personal identity in some other world or realm. The issue, then, is whether the conscious self persists after death.

Although they generally agree on the existence of some kind of personal survival after death, religious leaders are divided over its nature. The source of the division stems from two traditions: the Greek and the Judeo-Christian.

The Greek influence originates primarily from Plato, who first attempted to prove the existence of the soul, or reason. Plato argued that the body belongs to the world known to us through our physical senses and shares the nature of this world: change, impermanence, and death. On the other hand, the soul, or reason, is related to the permanent, unchanging realities that we are aware of when contemplating not particular things but universal, eternal Ideas. Related to this higher and lasting realm, the soul, unlike the body, is immortal. After death, the souls of those who have contemplated the eternal realities will gravitate to the world of eternal Ideas, despite their bodies' turning to dust.

The Judeo-Christian tradition, in contrast, has generally substituted resurrection for immortality, although Judaism de-emphasizes, even declines in some sects, resurrection. Whereas Plato considered the soul immortal, the Jewish and Christian view, as found occasionally in the Old Testament and more often in the New Testament, is that the complete human—soul and body—may be resurrected by God. This belief posits the direct intervention of a theistic God and a special divine act of recreation. The human is utterly dependent on the love of God for survival after death. Christians argue that there is evidence for resurrection in the New Testament. But the belief arises as a necessary part of the purpose of God. It is argued that God would be contradicting Himself to have created humans for fellowship with Himself, only to have them extinguished and this purpose unfulfilled.

Apart from its religious aspects, the question of life after death has recently received new attention with the growing interest in **extrasensory perception**, the phenomenon of having experiences without relying on the normal senses. Although there are many facets of ESP, the one relevant to this discussion is **telepathy**, the name given to the phenomenon of a thought in one person's mind evidently causing a similar thought in another person's mind without normal means of communication. For example, one person will draw a geometric pattern and then transmit a mental impression of it to someone in another room, who then creates a similar pattern. Experiments have ruled out chance in instances of telepathy. S. G. Soal, for example, has reported experimental results demonstrating that the probability of chance operating in such cases ranges from 100,000 to 1 to billions to 1.[15]

Just how telepathic communication works is unknown. So far, only negative conclusions have been reached. Telepathy does not seem to consist of physical radiation, such as radio waves, for distance has no effect. Nor does the thought leave the sender's consciousness to enter the receiver's, for frequently the senders are not even aware of the thought until it is brought to their attention, and receivers often receive just a fragment of it. As a result, some believe that, although our minds are exclusive of one another on the conscious level, we are constantly influencing one another on the unconscious level. It is at this level that telepathy is believed to occur, particularly through

15. *S. G. Soal.* The Experimental Situation in Psychical Research. *London: The Society for Psychical Research, 1947.*

the link of emotion or common interest that may exist between two especially close people. Telepathy sometimes is used as evidence of survival after death, although it seems to be questionable evidence.

The Proceedings of the Society for Psychical Research in London contain many documented cases of people who had recently died appearing to people who were still unaware of their deaths. The Society for Psychical Research is a well-established institute with rigorous standards and an impressive membership list of scholars.

In the case of "ghosts"—apparitions of the dead—it has been established that there can be "meaningful hallucinations" through telepathic sources. The classic example is the woman who, while sitting by a lake, witnessed the figure of a man running toward the lake and throwing himself in. A few days later a man killed himself by doing precisely this. Presumably, as the man contemplated his suicide, his thought was telepathically projected onto the scene by the woman's mind.[16]

The Society for Psychical Research also reports that minds that operate in mediumistic trances, alleging to be the spirits of the departed, frequently provide information that the medium could not possibly know. How is this possible? Again, one currently popular theory is that the communication really results from telepathic contact between the medium and the client. This theory is dramatized in the case of two women who decided to test the spirits by assuming the personality of a completely imaginary character in an unpublished novel written by one of the women. Having filled their minds with all the characteristics of this fictitious person, they went to a medium, who proceeded to describe accurately the fictitious character as a spirit from the beyond and to report appropriate messages from him.[17] Thus, although ESP is opening fascinating vistas on the mind, it is doing little to support the contention that there is an afterlife or other world. This, of course, does not mean that one does not exist.

The belief in an afterlife, inspired by religious conviction, will undoubtedly persist, and many people will continue to live their lives with one eye on this world and one on the next. Although there is no conclusive evidence to resolve the question of God's existence, we live as if there is, incorporating corollary beliefs and ways of viewing ourselves and the world. Do we have any real basis for such beliefs? Lacking certain evidence, are those who believe in God irrational, or are they justified in perhaps allowing their hearts to rule their heads? Since this question of religious belief is so influential in our lives, it seems appropriate now to examine it fully.

Religious Belief

Whether or not the existence of God is an issue today, the question of whether or not to *believe* in a divine dimension is. Is the cosmos far-flung matter that originated in chance and is propelled by accident? Or is it, scientific

16. *John Hick.* Philosophy of Religion. *2nd ed. Englewood Cliffs, N.J.: Prentice-Hall, 1973, p. 106.*

17. *John Hick.* Philosophy of Religion, *p. 105.*

explanations notwithstanding, something sacred, something divine? How we answer these questions will greatly affect our self-concepts and consequently our lives. In this case, the belief is as important a question as the fact.

A simple example will illustrate the influence of belief in our lives. Suppose at some point in college you begin to question whether you should actually be there. You are finding it neither interesting nor manageable. Besides, you have a pretty good job that you like and, if you work full-time, you can make enough money to get married. On the other hand, limiting your education might restrict your personal and professional opportunities. What should you do: Stay in school or quit? You must choose; there is no escaping the issue. Obviously, there is no certain answer. The best you can do is open-mindedly collect and weigh the data and decide. But whatever your choice, you will undoubtedly *believe* you are doing the right thing. In fact, that belief will help make the decision, which will have important consequences for your life. The decision might be reversible, but it will steer your life in a certain direction. That direction will be full of experiences that another direction might have lacked, experiences that will help shape you. So, in believing you should choose that direction, you have really decided to a degree what you will become.

Like the dilemma of whether to stay in school, the answer to the question of God's existence is inconclusive. But the question of *belief* in a divine dimension—whether theism, pantheism, or panentheism—is not. Although you cannot resolve this question, you can decide whether to believe in some kind of divine dimension. And that belief, if you are true to it, will affect your life, because through it you relate yourself to the world and everything in it.

There are many responses to the question of God's existence. One is to become so overwhelmed by it that one gives up hope of ever believing anything. The unfortunate aspect of this reaction is that it is a decision—a decision to remain uncommitted. Another possibility is to avoid the anguish of decision making by choosing whatever belief is conventional, popular, acceptable, or fashionable—in effect, to choose to become one of the statistics that we allow to formulate our beliefs. On the other hand, we might face up to the anguish of decision making, consider its implications, choose to believe or not to believe, then live that decision. The decision is ours to make.

Aside from whether a theistic God exists, is there any basis for religious belief? Do we have any grounds for believing in a divine dimension of any sort? Perhaps religious belief ultimately is not based and cannot be based on any evidence. Perhaps it must be a personal decision made with the heart. In a classic address entitled "The Will to Believe," American philosopher William James confronted this issue. After delivering the speech, he wrote that he wished he had entitled it "The Right to Believe."

"The Will to Believe"

The thrust of James's address is captured in the following argument: "Our passional nature not only lawfully may, but must, decide an option between propositions, whenever it is a genuine option that cannot by its nature be decided on intellectual grounds; for to say, under such circumstances, 'Do not decide, but leave the question open,' is itself a decision,—just like deciding yes or no,—and is attended with the same risk of losing the truth."[18] Without understanding the terms as James understands them, we can easily misconstrue what he is saying.

First, consider the word *option*. By this James means a choice between two hypotheses, a *hypothesis* being anything that may be proposed for our belief. "There is a divine dimension to the universe" would be a hypothesis; so would "There is no divine dimension to the universe." Some hypotheses are *live*; a live hypothesis "appeals as a real possibility to him to whom it is proposed." For example, the proposal that you believe in the Mahdi (the Islamic messiah) would probably not be appealing to you because of your Western acculturation and perhaps ignorance of Islam. The hypothesis would be a *dead* one. On the other hand, to an Arab it would probably be very much live. The deadness or liveness of any hypothesis, then, is not a quality inherent in the proposal but a quality determined by the individual thinker. It is an indication of our willingness to act; a hypothesis is most live when we are willing to act irrevocably— that is, to believe.

James further points out that there are several kinds of options: (1) living or dead, (2) forced or avoidable, and (3) momentous or trivial. A genuine option is living, forced, and momentous.

By a *living* option, James means one in which both hypotheses are live ones. For example, the proposal "Be a theosophist or be a Muhammadan" would probably be a dead option, because neither proposal is likely to be a live one for you. On the other hand, "Be a Christian or be an atheist" would probably be a living option, because both choices are probably live for you.

Now, suppose someone proposed "Either love me or hate me." You could avoid a decision by remaining indifferent to the person. Likewise, if someone proposed "Either vote for me or vote for my opponent," again you could avoid the decision by not voting at all. Options like these are not forced; they are *avoidable*. On the other hand, if someone said "Either accept this proof or go without it," you would be forced to make a choice. When there is no way to avoid a decision, the option is *forced*.

Finally, an option is *momentous* when the opportunity is unique, when the stakes are significant, and when the decision is irreversible. For example, a friend comes by one night with some "surefire" stock. This once-in-a-lifetime opportunity, she promises, will yield incredible riches. To accept her offer or reject it would be a momentous option. On the other hand, whether to wear jeans or slacks to school would be a *trivial* option, because it is not unique, attended by high stakes, or irreversible.

Now, what does James mean by "our passional nature"? As an empiricist, James forsakes an objective certainty. He claims that we can never be absolutely sure of anything except that consciousness exists. But he does *not* abandon the quest for truth itself; he still believes that truth exists. This belief springs more from desire and feeling than from reason; it is more passional

18. *William James. "The Will to Believe," in* Encounter. *Ramona Cormier, Ewing Chinn, and Richard Lineback, Eds., p. 236.*

than rational. This belief provides the best chance of attaining truth, "by systematically continuing to roll up experiences and think." His point is that, since we can never know with certainty, there will inevitably be a nonintellectual, nonrational element to what we choose to believe—a passional element. James writes, "Instinct leads, intelligence only follows." The first two tasks of this passional element are knowing the truth and avoiding error.

Choosing between these two "commandments," we could end up affecting our lives in completely different ways. For example, suppose you regarded the avoidance of error as paramount and the search for truth as secondary. Since there is very little if anything for which there is incontrovertible evidence, you would probably draw no conclusions. The result would be lifelong intellectual suspension. Imagine a child who cannot choose one of thirty-one ice cream flavors for fear that his choice may not live up to his expectations or that he will regret his choice. James is suggesting that when we are more committed to avoiding error than to chasing the truth, we necessarily lose the truth, since there will never be absolute supporting evidence. But to make such a choice is to be "like a general informing his soldiers that it is better to keep out of battle forever than to risk a single wound. Not so are victories either over enemies or over nature found."[19] Or, we might add, over the self.

It is easy to misunderstand James. He is not saying that avoiding error should always be subordinate to attaining truth. In options that are not momentous, James claims that we can save ourselves from believing a falsehood by not deciding until all the evidence is in. This approach would apply to most of the scientific questions and human issues that we are likely to face. In other words, in most choices the need to act is seldom so urgent that it is better to act on a false belief than on no belief at all. But he also argues that there are forced and momentous choices that we cannot ("as men who may be interested at least as much in positively gaining truth as in merely escaping dupery") always wait to make. As he puts it, "In the great boardinghouse of nature, the cakes and the butter and the syrup seldom come out so even and leave the plates so clean."

Granted, for some people religious belief is not a hypothesis that could possibly be true. But for most it is a live option. To these people, James says that religious belief is a momentous option. They stand to gain much by their belief and to lose much by their nonbelief. It is also a forced option. If they choose to wait in order to avoid error, they risk losing the chance of attaining the good that religious belief promises. "It is as if a man should hesitate indefinitely to ask a certain woman to marry him because he was not perfectly sure that she would prove an angel after he brought her home. Would he not cut himself off from that particular angel-possibility as decisively as if he went and married someone else?" Or, more simply, should the ice cream shop close while the child is debating his choice, the result would be the same as if he had chosen to have no ice cream. On a question that cannot be answered on intellectual grounds, James argues that we not only can but *should* allow our "passional nature" to decide it. We must choose to chase truth, not to avoid

19. *William James*. The Varieties of Religious Experience. *New York: Longmans, Green, 1929, p. 74.*

possible error; for in fearing to be duped, we exclude the possibility of being right.

James's argument has relevance not only for those who believe in a personal God but also for those whose innermost feelings detect a divine dimension at work in the cosmos, but not necessarily a Supreme Being such as the one of traditional theism. Because he relies on the importance of personal experience in religious belief, James is providing a philosophical basis for a personal encounter with the sacred, whatever we may experience that to be. Just what constitutes a personal experience of the divine is a complex question, but today, perhaps more than ever, individuals are using it as their source of or justification for religious belief.

Personal Experience of the Divine

We said earlier that religious belief, in its most general terms, is the belief that there is an unseen order and that we can do no better than to be in harmony with this order. Our religious attitudes spring from this belief. But this belief need not be rooted in objects present to our senses. On the contrary, the *belief* in a thing's existence can evoke in us as powerful a reaction as the thing itself. As an example, consider this encounter between a young man and a young woman who meet in a park.

Young Man: Do you come here often?

Young Woman: Whenever I need to feel the presence.

Young Man: The presence?

Young Woman: Haven't you ever felt a void, an emptiness?

Young Man: A quiet desperation?

Young Woman: That, too.

Young Man: It's not something one can easily speak of.

Young Woman: True.

Young Man: And coming here helps?

Young Woman: It stills the loneliness.

Young Man: But there's no one here.

Young Woman: There's the sunshine and sometimes the rain. And almost always the breeze.

Young Man: I guess nature *can* be therapeutic.

Young Woman: No, it's the *presence* that brings me here.

Young Man: The presence of what?

Young Woman: Of something greater than myself.

Young Man: God?

Young Woman: If you want. I'd rather not name it, because words are so misleading. But I know there's something there. . . . Why are you looking around? You won't see it, you know. But it's there, all the same.

This young woman feels a sense of reality that is deeper and more real to her than her sense experiences. She cannot fully communicate what she experiences. It cannot be defined, it does not consist of sensation, it does not consist of specific hypotheses based on such facts. Yet what she feels is more convincing than those truths arrived at through rational methods.

Rationalism gives a small and sketchy account of the nonspecific, nonlearned parts of our mental lives. True, reason and logic can be used to argue, point out flaws, and refute. But in the presence of what James calls "dumb intuitions," rationalism invariably loses the fight. Thus, something in this woman absolutely *knows*, despite any rationalistic argument to the contrary.

The apparent weakness of rationalistic thinking shows up dramatically in discussions of religious belief, particularly in the issue of God's existence. Very few of us today believe in God because of rational proofs. Similarly, few do not believe or have stopped believing because the arguments are flawed. Many people, perhaps most, do not need any rational proof for their religious belief, any more than they need proof that they feel joyful or loving. Others might point out innumerable reasons for not feeling joyful or loving, but to those experiencing these feelings, such arguments bend like straws in the wind. It is this kind of personal, direct, nonrational experience that frequently characterizes the sense of a divine presence that is not the personal God of traditional theism. On the contrary, this experience often takes the form of mysticism.

Mysticism

Young Man: Can you describe what you feel when you experience the presence?

Young Woman: Not really. Words are really inadequate, and I think it all sounds very foolish to someone who thinks more than feels.

Young Man: But I'd like for you to try. You see, what you say may touch my life. And it would be terrible to lose that possibility because you thought I'd ridicule what you say.

Young Woman: All right. I'll try to describe what happened last week on this very spot. At first I was frightened. I was losing myself, I thought, perhaps losing my mind. Then suddenly I had a vivid impression of something indescribable—call it God if you wish. At that moment when I felt most abandoned, I became one with this infinite power, this spirit of infinite peace. Through my attachment to this prodigious power, I sensed myself as I never have before. I felt one with everything: trees, birds, insects. I gloried in my existence, of being part of it all—part of the blades of grass, the bark of trees, the drops of rain. It was as if my thoughts were piercing the great veil of confusion and ignorance that I had always looked through. Suddenly I saw why we suffer, why it's necessary to suffer, why there will always be suffering. I also saw the thread of love that weaves through nature and makes it all one. I saw all the terrible hatred as love and the love as potential hatred, the one serving as counterpoint to the other, the two together producing the song of the universe, a cosmic harmony that left me in a divine ecstasy. There was more, much more; but even now I feel the inadequacy of words, and I'd rather not reduce my experiences any further.

The young woman appears to have had a mystical experience. One problem in trying to speak of such experiences is that, by nature, they defy verbalization. Religious belief often finds its origins in such mystical states of consciousness.

In his *Varieties of Religious Experience*, James proposes two characteristics by which an experience may be termed mystical. First is *ineffability*; that is, the state defies expression. Like the young woman, the experiencer feels that the mystical experience cannot be adequately reported. Second, there is a *noetic quality* about these experiences: To the individual they appear to be knowledge. They provide insight into the depths of human experience that no amount of intellectualizing can plumb. They are revelations and illuminations that are full of meaning, truth, and importance.

Mysticism, then, is the experience of a reality more inclusive than that which we are generally conscious of. According to mysticism, we can truly know only when we surrender our individual selves and sense a union with the divine ground of all existence. Certainly, mystical experiences vary in content, but like the young woman's experience, they often involve an acute awareness of a divine presence and of a direct communion with divinity, although this divinity is more likely to be an incomprehensible entity than a theistic deity.

Like most people, mystics have sensed within themselves a desire or longing that goes beyond the imperfect world of which they are a part. They may feel an urge for something permanent and free that transcends sorrow and is of everlasting value. They may feel airborne, looking for a place to land. Most Westerners try to quell such feelings and desires by seeking outside themselves, but mystics believe that the outward search is a race on a treadmill.

Mystics turn to the self to still these uneasy inner feelings. What occurs is impossible to describe—it must be experienced. But the writings of mystics indicate that, above everything else, the inner way leads to an understanding that all is one and one is all; that the self is one continuous process with God, the cosmos, or whatever term a particular culture or individual chooses to call ultimate and eternal reality. Such an inner experience has been termed "religious experience," "mystical experience," and "cosmic consciousness." But none of these terms captures the nature of such experiences, any more than the phrase "in love" describes what we experience in that state. The philosophy of religion employs the term *numinous* to describe these mystical states.

The Numinous

Professor of philosophy Peter Koestenbaum lists several characteristics of the numinous experience.[20] One is a feeling of infinite dependence, of the experiencer and the mundane world being insignificant. Values change, and a new sense of reality supplants the old. Thus, Thomas Aquinas, a consummate rational theologian, underwent a mystical experience after completing his

20. *Peter Koestenbaum.* Philosophy: A General Introduction. *New York: Van Nostrand Reinhold, 1968, pp. 140–147.*

major work. As a result, he was led to describe his previous efforts as so much straw compared with what he'd experienced. He never wrote another line.

Another aspect of the numinous is mystery. Mystery is closely related to James's ineffability and to what the young woman in the park is experiencing. Since our language is designed to handle ordinary experience in the ordinary world, a numinous experience is often described simply as a mystery or miracle. You will recall from Chapter 2 that in his famous "Allegory of the Cave," Plato writes about a prisoner who escapes the cave prison where humankind is condemned to watch shadows on a screen, which it then takes for reality. Having escaped and contemplated the real world, the prisoner returns to the cave and attempts to enlighten his cavemates, but in vain. Their points of reference and his are different, and so he cannot convey his experience. A similar communication gap faces the mystic.

Terror is a third characteristic of the numinous. This results from the total annihilation of our world of experience as we know it, the removal of all stability and substance from our existence. Numerous Old Testament passages evidence the kind of dread that accompanies the numinous. Speaking through one of His prophets, the God of the Old Testament says, "Their slain shall also be cast out, and their stink shall come up out of their carcasses and the mountains shall be melted with their blood" (Isa. 34:3) and "For the indignation of the Lord is upon all nations, and his fury upon all their armies: he hath utterly destroyed them, he hath delivered them to the slaughter" (Isa. 34:2). Literally interpreted, these references suggest that God must be capable of evil. But viewed analogically, they represent the element of terror in the numinous.

A fourth characteristic of the numinous is bliss. References to heaven, paradise, salvation, and love all suggest a feeling of supreme fulfillment and satisfaction. The numinous satisfies the most profound yearnings of the human heart. Thus, Saint Catherine of Genoa writes, "If of that which my heart is feeling one drop were to fall into hell, hell itself would become life eternal."[21]

As Koestenbaum points out, there are many other characteristics of the numinous. The key point is that religion may be approached through a numinous interpretation. In fact, the mystical tradition in both Judaism and Christianity parallels the evolution of rational theology, and it is even generally supported by it. Today the numinous approach conforms to our emotionally and psychologically oriented times, which accommodate the nonrational. Especially among youth, there is intense and unprecedented interest in what we can call the transformation of consciousness. Much of this springs from a growing sense of personal estrangement from the world. Many feel out of touch and try to locate themselves in the scheme of things as a result. More and more, people are rejecting the traditional institutional prescriptions for inner peace and contentment and instead are following their own vague but pressing sense of what is good for them. This pursuit takes many forms: "self-healing," "consciousness expansion," "positive growth potential," and "survival experiments." But all forms have nonrational, mystical overtones. It is impossible to discuss all these movements, but we can introduce three phenomena that, although quite

21. *Quoted in Peter Koestenbaum.* Philosophy, *p. 146.*

different in content and methodology, are similar in their attempt to gain religious experience through a mystical transformation of consciousness. These are radical theology, the use of psychedelic drugs, and the study of Eastern religious thought.

Radical Theology

The nagging questions about the existence and nature of a Supreme Being have spawned a school of theology that deviates from traditional theism more radically than do pantheism and panentheism. Such "radical theologians," as these thinkers are often termed, perceive God not as a being among other beings but as an aspect of reality. As a result, they feel that our relationship with God is more experiential than rational. The modern roots of this view can be traced to thinkers like the Danish philosopher Sören Kierkegaard, whom we will showcase in this chapter.

The chief exponent of radical theology in our time has been Protestant theologian Paul Tillich (1886–1965). Tillich, an existentialist, contends that traditional theism has erred in viewing God as *a* being and not *being itself*, an error that he believes the proofs for God's existence, discussed earlier, have fostered. As a result, we have bound God to our subject-object structure of reality. *He*—notice the sexualization—is an object for us as subjects, becoming the target for our prayers, worship, and supplications. He becomes almost some *thing* to which we direct our lives. At other times we make ourselves object for Him as subject. Because theism posits an all-knowing, all-powerful God, and because we are neither, the relationship must therefore be one of superior (God) to inferior (us), controller to controlled, subject to object. An antagonistic tension results. As Tillich says, "He deprives me of my subjectivity because he is all-powerful and all-knowing. I revolt and try to make him into an object, but the revolt fails and becomes desperate. God appears as an invincible tyrant, the being in contrast with whom all other things are without freedom and subjectivity."[22] This image of God as "invincible tyrant," he feels, is a much more telling blow to theological theism than all the objections to the traditional proofs for God's existence. Tillich believes that his criticism is justified, for God as tyrant is "the deepest root of the Existentialist despair and the widespread anxiety of meaninglessness in our period." Notice that Tillich rejects traditional theism not on empirical but on theological grounds. For Tillich, theism is just bad theology.

If Tillich and other radical theologians reject the theistic concept of God, what do they offer as a substitute? What kind of God do they believe in? Tillich's God is a "God above God," "the ground of being." This God transcends the God of theism and so dissipates the anxiety of doubt and meaninglessness. This ground of being is not proved, because it cannot be. It is neither an object nor a subject. It is present, although hidden, in every divine-human encounter. Tillich grants that this notion is paradoxical. But he notes that Biblical religion and Protestant theology are already studded with paradoxes. Consider the

22.   *This and all other Tillich quotes are from: Paul Tillich.* The Courage to Be. *New Haven, Conn.: Yale University Press, 1952. Reprinted by permission.*

"God cannot be proved, as if He were an equation or a laboratory specimen."

"paradoxical character of every prayer of speaking to somebody to whom you cannot ask anything because he gives or gives not before you ask, of saying 'thou' to somebody who is nearer to the I than the I is to itself." Indeed, it is paradoxes like these, says Tillich, that "drive the religious consciousness toward a God above the God of theism, a God that is the Ground of our very being."

The "ground of being" is only one of Tillich's many slippery concepts. "Depth" is another. "Depth is what the word God means," he writes, but still we ask what depth is. The word seems to have no meaning. "If the word has not much meaning for you, translate it," advises Tillich, "and speak of the depths of your life, of the source of your being, of your ultimate concern, of what you take seriously without any reservation." Atheists might reply, "That there is no God—now *that* I take seriously, without any reservation." But Tillich would say that this is impossible, for to call themselves atheists they would have to forget everything traditional that they ever learned about God, maybe even the word itself. The only people who can rightly call themselves atheists are those who can say, "Life has no depth. Life is shallow. Being itself is surface only. If you could say this in complete seriousness, you would be an atheist; but otherwise you are not. He who knows the depth knows about God."

Like many existentialists, Tillich is not easy to understand. But clearly he believes that traditional theism has erred in making God an object. It does so in its definitions of Him and in its proofs of His existence. God cannot be proved, as if He were an equation or a laboratory specimen. Such "objectivation" not only limits the deity but also raises the very kinds of inconsistencies that are leading to a loss of faith. Tillich's God, therefore, defies traditional definitions and proofs. His God is closer to the concept attained by the mystic but still significantly different. Where the mystic would eschew sense experience and reason when taken as ultimate, and through intuition alone move to a knowledge of God, Tillich confronts the world of experience and its nagging questions. He is no escapist, no dodger of doubt. On the contrary, he faces the concrete world of finite values and meanings and uses all its imperfections, skepticism, and meaninglessness to confront what is ultimately real: being. And in this ground of all being he experiences God. Everyone does "who knows the depth."

Objections to Radical Theology

Besides having many elusive concepts, Tillich's theology provokes other objections. He seemingly says that those who do not recognize his God, the ground of all being, are not ultimately concerned. Suppose you tell an unaccomplished violinist that the reason she failed to become a virtuoso is that she never practiced long enough. "Long enough!" she protests. "Are you kidding? Why, I have practiced every day of my life!" "Obviously, it wasn't long enough," you reply, "because you never became a virtuoso." Clearly, by "long enough" you mean "until one becomes a virtuoso." Your directive to the would-be virtuoso, then, was nothing more than "Practice until you become a virtuoso, and you will become a virtuoso." In logic, a statement whose predicate repeats its subject, as this one does, is called a **tautology**. Is Tillich's argument tautological? Has he, as Anselm evidently did, defined something into existence? When Tillich says, "He who knows about the depth knows about God," he seems to be saying, "He who knows about God knows about God." When he argues "If one is ultimately concerned or has the courage to be, then one knows God," he appears to say, "If one knows God or knows God, then one knows God."

Tillich also claims to have an experience of divine presence, of a merging with some fundamental reality. No one may question his experience; it is as personal as a headache or a hunger pang. But his interpretation of his experience can be questioned. We can and should, it seems, ask for verification when he interprets that experience as resulting from contact with the ground of all being. Tillich must verify the reality of the ground of all being and establish it as the cause of his transcendent experiences.

Tillich would probably reply that the knowledge of his God is a completely different kind of knowledge from that which we customarily speak of. Taking his departure from psychology or from religious or mystical experience, areas open to all, he would argue that his knowledge transcends empirical data and defies scientific verification. It is knowledge whose source is much closer to mystical intuition than to senses or reason, although the latter are instrumental in generating the intuitive response. This knowledge is similar to the mystical knowledge of the young woman in the dialogue, who knows in her heart that what she feels plumbs the depths of reality. This knowledge is rooted in a personal experience, traditionally induced through prayer and meditation. Today, however, some seek a similar experience in less traditional ways.

Psychedelics and Religious Experience

The word *psychedelic* is defined as "of or pertaining to or generating hallucinations, distortions of perception, and, occasionally, psychotic-like states."

It is true that the five principal psychedelic drugs—LSD-25, mescaline, psilocybin, dimethyl-tryptamine (DMT), and marijuana—when used indiscriminately have produced these characteristics in certain people. But the same characteristics frequently accompany the so-called mystical or religious experience, the numinous.

Raynor Johnson, in his excellent collection of accounts of mystical experiences *Watcher on the Hills*,[23] lists some states of consciousness that mystical experiences invariably involve, all of which also characterize psychedelic experiences. First is a sense of timelessness. Mystics as well as psychedelic drug users frequently describe a loss of the sense of time. A minute may seem like an hour, an hour like a minute. Both groups fall into a state of such utter relaxation that they become oblivious to temporal affairs. Often accompanying these feelings is an acute realization that the purpose of life is to live and experience every moment as fully as possible.

Because of these similarities between drug use and mystical experience, the young man in our dialogue, who once used marijuana, can understand the woman's seemingly unintelligible mystical experience.

Young Man:　Funny, but as I've been listening to you describe your experience I've had a feeling of *déjà vu*.

Young Woman:　Then you know what I'm trying to describe.

Young Man:　I think I do. But let me ask you something. Did you have the feeling that time slowed down?

Young Woman:　Not only did it slow down, but it was as if I were anchored in the present. Every pore seemed to open to what was occurring *now*.

Young Man:　The past didn't exist.

Young Woman:　Nor the future.

Young Man:　You had none of the normal concerns about the future?

Young Woman:　I had neither anxiety about it nor anticipation of it. It simply didn't exist.

Young Man:　I once felt that way—that I had crossed the time barrier between the finite and the infinite, that time was just an illusion. And then I experienced something strangely wonderful, something very difficult to explain, and that was that everything was somehow integrated. Somehow, having broken through the bubble of time, I experienced the oneness of everything, things that before had somehow been separated by time.

Young Woman:　And spatial relationships.

Young Man:　Yes, time and space—they both struck me as illusions.

Young Woman:　And so long as we're committed to those illusions, we persist in perceiving reality in terms of opposing forces: good and bad, love and hate, right and wrong.

Young Man:　But there are no opposites. I felt this more strongly than I've ever felt anything. That all things are interconnected and intertwined with everything else.

23.　*Raynor Johnson.* Watcher on the Hills. *London: Hodder and Stoughton, 1959. See also Charles Tart,* Altered States of Consciousness. *New York: Doubleday, 1972.*

Here is another principal feature of the mystical and psychedelic experience: the loss of a sense of polarity. What we commonly view as opposites are seen as different sides of the same coin. There is an interdependence among all things, such as between heads and tails or between up and down. Self necessitates other; good, bad; solid, space; saints, sinners. In this state the mystic and often the drug user realize that each thing in existence can have meaning and definition only in terms of something else. There is, then, just oneness.

Such a loss of conventional classification labels can produce a heightened sense of the interdependence among all parts of creation.

Young Woman: I recall becoming engrossed in watching a tiny ant that was moving across my foot.

Young Man: Did you wonder at the ant's universe?

Young Woman: Really! I thought that the ant must think of itself as I think of myself, although it sounds silly to speak of an ant thinking. But then I recognized that I couldn't even begin to speak of myself thinking if it weren't for the ant, if it weren't for the apparent difference between us.

Young Man: Without the ant you would lack self-definition.

Young Woman: In a sense I would. And without everything else I stand in relation to, I would melt away, evaporate.

Young Man: The thought terrifies me.

Young Woman: And it did me, but then I was filled with marvel at this cosmic order that finds a place for everything and somehow ordains a role for each.

The young woman seems to be describing an experience of the relativity of all things, an experience similar to one that the young man experienced under the influence of marijuana. Such an experience frequently reveals a sense of the self as a link in an infinite chain that connects each life to all other lives. This hierarchy of processes and beings ranges from subatomic particles through bacteria and insects to human beings and supernatural beings.

There is a final feature that frequently accompanies both experiences. Some describe it as the awareness of eternal energy.

Young Man: I think the most marvelous part of my experience was the sense of incredible strength that I had.

Young Woman: A kind of energy.

Young Man: Yes, you could call it that.

Young Woman: I remember seeing an almost blinding light.

Young Man: Did you feel that this light was the source of all life, of all being?

Young Woman: More than that. I felt that the light was me.

Young Man: Yes, that the concentrated energy was your own being.

Young Woman: That I was the source of all life, that it all flowed from me, that I was——
Young Man: Divine?

Accompanying such experiences is the profound recognition that the totality of existence is a single energy. But even more often this energy is one's own being: It is a realization that the individual is the divinity and the divinity is all that is (see Philosophy and Life 10–2).

Obviously, not everyone under the influence of psychedelic drugs will experience these states of consciousness. Nor should everyone seeking a religious experience try psychedelic drugs. In too many cases, excessive and indiscriminate use ends tragically. Nevertheless, the similarity between the mystical and psychedelic experiences in altering states of consciousness raises philosophical curiosity about why society disapproves of drug use.

First, it is obvious that society disapproves of psychedelics because of their often deadly effects. But if their effect can be strikingly similar to that of a religious or mystical experience, are we, in effect, disapproving of that as well? Zen scholar Alan Watts, in his fascinating essay "Psychedelic and Religious Experience,"[24] says we are. He gives a number of reasons, two of which are noteworthy here.

Like the psychedelic experience, the mystical experience is not logical. Because it defies common sense, it runs counter to empirical and rational knowledge, the basis of Western epistemology. Such experiences are inconsistent with how we relate ourselves to the universe—that is, as separate, individual egos confronting an external and often alien world. Religious, mystical, and psychedelic experiences, then, are truly revolutionary. They suggest ways of seeing and knowing that contradict most of what we have grown up to accept.

Even more important, when we claim consciousness of oneness with God or with the universe, we fly in the face of our society's concept of religion. Our Jewish and Christian origins do not sanction the individual's claim to identity with the Godhead, even though this identity may have been peculiarly true of Jesus Christ. For anyone to claim that he or she is the all-powerful and all-knowing ruler of the world has traditionally been considered blasphemy.

Watts is suggesting, then, that the prohibition against such drugs, even in controlled scientific studies, is really a prohibition against questioning traditional secular and religious values. As evidence, he records how suspicious institutional religion has always been of mystical claims and how persecutive it has been, as in the case of Johannes "Meister" Eckhart, whose claims of equality with God resulted in his condemnation as a heretic. Western mystics who have received church acceptance, such as Saint Teresa of Avila and Saint John of the Cross, have always acknowledged a distinction between themselves and their God.

The Eastern philosophical and religious traditions, on the other hand, have always been sympathetic to mystical claims and experiences. For this reason

---

24. *Alan Watts. "Psychedelic and Religious Experience."* California Law Review, *1968, vol. 56, no. 100,* p. 74.

many today may be seeking the source of their religious experiences not in drugs or in radical theology but in these traditions.

Eastern Religious Traditions

As we mentioned in Chapter 2, Eastern philosophy refers to those systems of thought, belief, and action espoused by many peoples of the Near and Far East. It is neither our intention nor within our capabilities to mention all of these, let alone discuss them adequately. But we should mention at least two of the principal religions to which many Westerners are turning for meaningful religious experience: Hinduism and Buddhism.

Hinduism

One of the oldest of Eastern traditions is Hinduism, which has been practiced by hundreds of millions of people for about 5,000 years. Hinduism has

---

PHILOSOPHY AND LIFE 10-2
Distinguishing between the Drug- and Non-Drug-Induced Religious Experience

In his widely read essay "Do Drugs Have Religious Import?" professor of philosophy Huston Smith recounts an intriguing experiment he once conducted among a group of Princeton students.* He provided the students with accounts of two religious experiences. One occurred under the influence of drugs, the other without their influence. The students were asked to distinguish between them. Here are the two accounts:

> Suddenly I burst into a vast, new, indescribably wonderful universe. Although I am writing this over a year later, the thrill of the surprise and amazement, the awesomeness of the revelation, the engulfment in an overwhelming feeling-wave of gratitude and blessed wonderment, are as fresh, and the memory of the experience is as vivid, as if it had happened five minutes ago. And yet to concoct anything by way of description that would even hint at the magnitude, the sense of ultimate reality . . . this seems such an impossible task. The knowledge which has infused and affected every aspect of my life came instantaneously and with such complete force of certainty that it was impossible, then or since, to doubt its validity.† (Ignore footnotes until answering questions.)

* Huston Smith. "Do Drugs Have Religious Import?" The Journal of Philosophy, 1964, vol. 61, no. 18, pp. 517–530.
† Anonymous. In "The Issue of the Consciousness-Expanding Drugs." Main Currents in Modern Thought, 1963, vol. 20, no. 1, pp. 10–11. Experienced under the influence of drugs.

many divisions and subdivisions, and no leader or belief is accepted by every Hindu sect. In fact, so diversified is Hinduism that it is very difficult to describe it as a whole. Any attempt at description is bound to be an oversimplification. A further complication is the fact that our language has no precise equivalents for certain Indian terms and concepts.

Aware of these limitations, let us begin with the literary source of Hindu teaching. Although many texts form the body of Hindu scripture, one has influenced Hindu thought more than any other: the *Bhagavad-Gita*, the Song of the Lord, which is part of the great epic *Mahabharata*. Reading the Gita will introduce you to the principal concepts of Hinduism, as well as to beautiful poetry.

One concept common to all expressions of Hinduism is the oneness of reality. This oneness is the absolute, or Brahman, which the mind can never fully grasp or words express. Only Brahman is real; everything else is an illusory manifestation of it. A correlative belief is the concept of **atman,** or no self.

All at once, without warning of any kind, I found myself wrapped in a flame-colored cloud. For an instant I thought of fire . . . the next, I knew that the fire was within myself. Directly afterward there came upon me a sense of exultation, of immense joyousness accompanied or immediately followed by an intellectual illumination impossible to describe. Among other things, I did not merely come to believe, but I saw that the universe is not composed of dead matter, but is, on the contrary, a living Presence; I became conscious in myself of eternal life. . . . I saw that all men are immortal: that the cosmic order is such that without any peradventure all things work together for the good of each and all; that the foundation principle of the world . . . is what we call love, and that the happiness of each and all is in the long run absolutely certain. ‡

In Smith's experiment, twice as many students (forty-six) answered incorrectly as answered correctly (twenty-three).

‡ *Dr. R. M. Bucke. Quoted in William James.* The Varieties of Religious Experience. *New York: Modern Library, 1902, pp. 390–391. Not experienced under the influence of drugs.*

□ *Which account do you think reflects a drug-induced experience?*   □ *Does a difficulty in distinguishing between the drug-induced experience and the non-drug-induced experience argue for or against Watts's thesis about societal proscriptions against drug usage?*

What we commonly call I or the self is an illusion, for each true self is one with Brahman. When we realize this unity with the absolute, we realize our true destiny.

Also common to all Hindu thought are four primary values. In order of increasing importance, they may be roughly translated as wealth, pleasure, duty, and enlightenment. The first two are worldly, which when kept in perspective are good and desirable values. Duty, or righteousness, refers to patience, sincerity, fairness, love, honesty, and similar virtues. The highest spiritual value is enlightenment, by which one is illuminated and liberated and, most importantly, finds release from the wheel of existence. Repeated existence is the destiny of those who do not achieve enlightenment.

To understand enlightenment you must understand the law of **karma**, the law of sowing and reaping. All of us, through what we do or do not do, supposedly determine our destiny. If we are particularly evil, we may find ourselves reborn as subhumans. If we are noble, we may be reborn as especially favored humans. This wheel of existence turns until we achieve enlightenment, after which we are released from this series of rebirths.

Sri Sarvepalli Radhakrishnan, in *A Source Book in Indian Philosophy*,[25] lists characteristics common to all Indian thought. First is an emphasis on the spiritual. It is the spiritual that endures and is ultimately real. Second is the realization that our philosophy and our life are inextricably enmeshed. What we believe is how we live; if our beliefs are in error, our lives will be unhappy. Third is a preoccupation with the inner life. The road to enlightenment stretches not outward but inward. To understand nature and the universe we must turn within. Fourth is an emphasis on the nonmaterial oneness of creation. There are no polarities; a unity of spirit provides cosmic harmony. Fifth is the acceptance of direct awareness as the only way to understand what is real. Unlike the user of psychedelic drugs, the Indian believer finds this direct perception through spiritual exercises, perhaps through the practice of yoga. Reason is of some use, but in the last analysis we know only through an inner experience of oneness with all of creation. Sixth is a healthy respect for tradition, but never a slavish commitment to it. The past can teach but never rule. Finally, Indian thought recognizes the complementary nature of all systems of belief. Hinduism is not rooted in any single doctrine, nor does it claim a monopoly on truth or wisdom. It preaches tolerance of all sincere viewpoints and includes many of these within its own spiritual teachings.

Buddhism

Another major Eastern tradition is Buddhism, contained in the teachings of Siddhartha Gautama (563 B.C.–?), its founder. Since Gautama found no evidence for a belief in a personal God, his teachings are a diagnosis of and a prescription for the "disease" of living.

He preached the Four Noble Truths, which we mentioned in Chapter 2. It might be useful to show how they compare with some of Tillich's ideas. The

25. *Sarvepalli Radhakrishnan and Charles A. Moore, Eds. A Source Book in Indian Philosophy. Princeton, N.J.: Princeton University Press, 1957, pp. xx–xxvi.*

First Noble Truth, concerned with the suffering that we experience in living, Tillich might call "existential despair," although he would attribute it to theism. The Second Noble Truth identifies the cause of this suffering or, more accurately, this frustration: clinging or grasping based on **avidya**, ignorance and unawareness. This unawareness is characterized by commitment to the world of things and illusion, maya, and not to the concrete world of reality. This unawareness is also characterized by a doomed attempt to control oneself and the environment, which can lead only to a futile grasping that results in self-frustration and the viciously circular pattern of life called **samsara**, the round of birth and death. Tillich might see this as the false subject-object distinction that we customarily make. The Third Noble Truth concerns the ending of samsara, called **nirvana**, release or liberation. It is the way of life that results when we stop grasping and clinging. Tillich would call it experiencing the "depth," the "ground of all being"; in the nirvana state we are released from the round of incarnations and enter a state that defies definition. The Fourth Noble Truth describes the Eightfold Path of the Buddha's **dharma**—that is, the doctrine whereby self-frustration is ended. We outlined this in Chapter 2.

Zen Buddhism

Japanese scholar D. T. Suzuki, who has marvelously rendered the philosophy of Zen Buddhism to the Western mind, shows in "Zen Buddhism" how Zen has established itself firmly on a teaching that claims to be

> *A special transmission outside the Scripture;*
> *No dependence on words or letters;*
> *Direct pointing at the Mind of Man;*
> *Seeing into one's Nature and the attainment of Buddhahood.*[26]

These four lines, says Suzuki, describe the essentials of Zen Buddhism and provide insight into its religious impulses.

Suzuki points out that the first line does not imply the existence of an esoteric Buddhist teaching that came to be known as Zen. Quite the opposite is true. "A special transmission outside the Scripture" is understood by reference to the second line, which asserts Zen's lack of dependence on words and letters. "Words and letters" and "the Scripture" stand for conceptualism and all that the term implies. Zen abhors and eschews words and concepts, as well as the reasoning based on them. It views a preoccupation with ideas and words as an empty substitution for experience.

In contrast, Zen upholds the direct experience of reality. It does not brook secondhand accounts or authoritative renderings of reality. Zen followers aspire to drink from the fountain of life rather than to listen to accounts of it. The ultimate truth is a state of inner experience achieved by means of wisdom. This state is beyond the realm of words and discriminations. To discriminate is to be caught in the endless cycle of birth and death with no hope of emancipation, attainment of nirvana, or realization of Buddhahood.

26. *Daisetz T. Suzuki. "Zen Buddhism," in* The Essentials of Zen Buddhism. *Bernard Phillips, Ed. New York: Dutton, 1962, p. 73.*

How, then, are we emancipated? How does Zen help one to achieve nirvana or Buddhahood? In answering this, Zen reminds us that we live in a world of dualities, of contradictory opposites. To be emancipated from the world may mean to leave or to deny it. Some people have taken this to mean self-destruction, but Suzuki suggests that this is a misinterpretation of Zen teaching. It is the mere amassing of knowledge, the storing of shopworn concepts, that is self-destructive. Rather, emancipation consists of recognizing the inadequacy of explanations and discriminations, of rejecting the notion that an explanation of a thing or fact exhausts the subject. For Zen there is no better explanation than actual experience, and actual experience is all that is needed to attain Buddhahood.

Let's turn to the last two lines: "Direct pointing at the Mind of Man; / Seeing into one's Nature and the attainment of Buddhahood." To grasp the meaning here, we must understand what is meant by *Mind, Nature,* and *Buddhahood.*

Mind does not refer to our ordinary functioning mind, the mind that thinks according to the laws of logic and psychological explanations. It is the mind that lies beneath all these thoughts and feelings. For the Zen Buddhist, the Mind is also known as Nature, that is, reality. We may look on the Mind as the last point that we reach when we dig down psychologically into the depths of a thinking and feeling subject. Nature is the limit of objectivity. But the natural objective limit is the psychological subjective limit, and vice versa. When we reach the one, we find ourselves in the other. True, in each case we start differently: We go out to Nature, we go in to ourselves. But in the end there's a confluence of the two, a point of merging. When we have the Mind, we have Nature. When we understand Nature, we understand the Mind. They are one and the same.

Now we can speak of enlightenment, of Buddhahood. The person who has a thorough understanding of the Mind and whose movements are at one with Nature is the Buddha, the enlightened one. Nature personified is the Buddha. In effect, then, Mind, Nature, and Buddha are three different points of reference. The ideal of Zen, then, as expressed in the four lines, is to seize reality without the interference of any agency—intellectual, moral, or ritualistic.

The direct holding of reality is the awakening of **prajñā,** transcendental wisdom. Transcendental wisdom answers all questions that we can formulate about our spiritual life. Thus, wisdom is not the intellect in the ordinary sense. It transcends dialectics of all kinds. It is not analytical reasoning but a leap over the intellectual impasse, and in this it is an act of will. At the same time, it sees into nature. There is a noetic quality about it. It is both will and intuition. Zen is associated with willpower, because avoiding the tendency to analyze and intellectualize requires an act of will. This requires individual effort. Outsiders can only help by reminding us that all outside help is futile.

The literature of Zen glitters with anecdotal reminders of this. An especially graphic story involves a Zen Buddhist monk who is asked about the depths of the Zen River while he is walking over a bridge. At once he seizes the questioner and would have hurled him into the rapids had others not frantically interceded. The monk wanted the questioner to go down to the bottom of the river and to take its measure.

The basic principle of Zen is the growth or self-maturing of the inner experience. People used to intellectual exercises, moral persuasion, and devotional exercises will find Zen a disarming if not heretical teaching. But this is precisely what makes Zen unique in the history of religion. It proposes that we look within a thing in order to understand it. In contrast, we usually describe a thing from the outside in order to understand it; we speak of it in objective terms. While this objective method has its place and value, Zen proposes a method that for millions gives the key to an effective and all-satisfying understanding.

Obviously, there is much more to Hinduism, Buddhism, and Zen than we have outlined. Nevertheless, these sketches illustrate major differences between Eastern and Western thought. Let's consider these differences more closely.

Differences between East and West

First, the East rejects the West's "objectified" God. There is no claim of a personal, all-knowing, all-good, all-powerful, and all-loving God, as there is in the Western tradition. As a result, Eastern thinkers have never debated God's existence. As a corollary, Buddhism does not share the Western view that there is a moral law, enjoined by God or by nature, which it is our duty to obey. In contrast, Western religions frequently, if not always, include behavioral proscriptions that if violated may lead to eternal damnation. In short, our tradition presents a God who expects us to behave in a certain way. In contrast:

> The Buddha's precepts of conduct—abstinence from taking life, taking what is not given, exploitation of the passions, lying, and intoxication—are voluntarily assumed rules of expedience, the intent of which is to remove the hindrances to clarity of awareness. Failure to observe the precepts produces bad *"karma"* not because *karma* is a law or moral retribution, but because all motivated and purposeful actions, whether conventionally good or bad, are *karma* insofar as they are directed to the grasping of life. Generally speaking, the conventionally "bad" actions are rather more grasping than the "good."[27]

Finally, whereas the thrust of Western religion traditionally has been to align us with our divine creator, Eastern thought, like Tillich's emphasis on being, aims to ground us in what is real. To do so, Eastern thought generally prescribes discipline, self-control, moderation, and detachment. Although these values are frequently observed in Western religious practice, they are just as frequently seen as means to an end: salvation and reward. While they are ways of attaining wisdom and truth, they are also ways of avoiding damnation.

Perhaps these differences explain why, since the middle 1960s, there has been a growing interest in the United States in Eastern thinking and religions. Many people are turning away from traditional faiths in favor of Zen Buddhism, Yoga, transcendental meditation, the International Society for Krishna Consciousness, Vedanta, and so on. Obviously, converts to Eastern religions have not stopped asking about their places in the scheme of things. On the

27. *Alan Watts.* The Way of Zen. *New York: Pantheon, 1957, p. 61. Reprinted by permission.*

contrary, they are asking perhaps more intensely than ever. Apparently, the traditional Western answers no longer work for them. The traditional concepts of self, subject-object distinction, Judeo-Christian dogma, the egocentric emphasis on one's personal relationship with a theistic God, and the dismissal of nonhuman natural objects as essentially inferior and alien—perhaps all have conspired to send these seekers in other directions. Many features characterize these new directions: the emphasis on the workings of the mind and inner growth; the importance of discipline, practice, and method; a distrust of doctrines and dogmas; and hope for integrating body and intellect, feelings, and reason through a personal philosophy. But central to these features seem to be a reevaluation and a redefinition of one's traditional concept of the divine and one's relationship to it.

Showcase: Sören Kierkegaard (1813–1853)

The Danish philosopher Sören Kierkegaard is generally considered the father of both the "new" Christianity, which would include in its following thinkers such as Paul Tillich; and the nonreligious philosophy which we have spoken of elsewhere, existentialism. One author has noted that Kierkegaard's life was dominated by the most intense experiences of paradox.[28] For example, he broke off an engagement with a young woman he loved, then was anguished when she quickly took another man. His writings, too, writhe with images of paradox: the king who loves a servant girl but knows he cannot appear to her as the king without dashing all hopes of a loving relationship; the mother who blackens her breast to wean the baby she cherishes. "Always in the background of Kierkegaard's tortured and passionate thought looms the spectre of paradox: I must, but I cannot."[29] Indeed, it is this paradox which is at the core of Kierkegaard's relation to God, our central concern here.

In understanding Kirkegaard's thought, it helps to know a little about his society. The society into which Kierkegaard was born was thoroughly Christian. Everyone believed the same dogmas, although few gave much thought to their beliefs. By the same token, all attended the same Lutheran churches and church social functions, and mechanically mouthed the doctrines that they were raised to espouse. While this behavior passed for Christianity, Kierkegaard believed that it was anything but that. In his view, such behavior lacked passion, and so did the Christians who displayed the behavior. Where they should have felt fear, these people were complacent; where they should have shown intensity, they were secure. To put it bluntly, Kierkegaard was revolted by these self-professed pillars of the Christian community. Appropriately enough, then, in works such as *Philosophical Fragments* and *Concluding Unscientific Postscript*, Kierkegaard spent most of his short life expostulating a view of Christianity and of seeing oneself as a Christian which was at once new and yet very old.

28.   See *James Ogilvy*. Self and World: Readings in Philosophy. *2nd ed. New York: Harcourt Brace Jovanovich, 1980, p. 424.*

29.   *James Ogilvy*. Self and World, *p. 424.*

Unfortunately, Kierkegaard poses some problems for readers because many of his works were written under pseudonyms, thus making authorship problematic. Also, his writing can be rather turgid. At the same time, Kierkegaard's style is as paradoxical as the experiences of his life; for his prose can be brilliantly incisive, profoundly touching, and refreshingly amusing.

Today Kierkegaard is regarded by many as the most Christ-centered thinker in Christian history. Concerned with the question of God's existence, he focused on the linchpin of Christian faith: God made man in the person of Jesus of Nazareth. Kierkegaard's Christ-centered writings continue to provide Christians with fresh and challenging insights into and interpretation of their faith. And, for Christian and non-Christian alike, Kierkegaard stands as a penetrating psychologist who boldly engages the problems that beset those in quest of the authentic self.

Speaking about Kierkegaard can be as challenging as reading him, for his inner emotional life, his lifelong struggle with religious faith, and his rejection of the dominant Hegelian philosophy of his day are so intertwined that it is difficult to speak of one apart from the others. In what follows, we shall focus on his distinction between objective and subjective thinking and show the seminal role this distinction plays in his reconstitution of what it means to be a Christian.

Objective vs. Subjective Thinking

Central to Kierkegaard's religious thought is his distinction between the objective and subjective thinker, which is essentially a distinction between reason and faith. In Kierkegaard's view, the objective thinker is one who strikes an intellectual, dispassionate, scientific pose toward life. In effect, the objective thinker adopts the view of an observer. For Kierkegaard, the most ludicrous examples of objective thinkers are professors who produce systems of philosophy with no regard to their own existence as human beings who must confront the same problems as anyone else. Such persons feel no great commitment to the truth of what they are studying or advancing. Indeed, their approach to the whole question of truth is characterized by disinterest and impartiality; they are free of passion and directed principally toward the object under investigation.

In contrast, the subjective thinker is passionately and intensely involved with truth. Truth for the subjective thinker is not just a matter of accumulating evidence to establish a viewpoint, but something of profound personal concern. Because questions of life and death, of the meaning of one's human existence, of one's ultimate destiny, often preoccupy subjective thinkers, Kierkegaard sometimes calls them existential thinkers. Whether termed *subjective* or *existential*, thinkers of this cut are vitally involved with the truth of what is under consideration. The outcome, the upshot, the truth matters enormously to them.

While it is true that Kierkegaard is primarily concerned with subjective thinking, he never denies that objective thinking has its place. He simply asserts that not all of life's concerns are open to objective analysis. Indeed, from Kierkegaard's view, it would be fair to say life's most important questions defy objective analysis. A good example, which also happens to be Kierkegaard's preoccupation as a religious thinker, is religious faith. Religious faith, says Kierkegaard, is not open to objective thinking because it involves a relationship with God. Stated another and more exact way, religion and religious faith are a confrontation with the unknown, not something knowable. In the following passage from *Philosophical Fragments*, Kierkegaard demonstrates what he means:

But what is this unknown something with which the Reason collides when inspired by its paradoxical passion, with the result of unsettling even man's knowledge of himself? It is the Unknown. It is not a human being, in so far as we know what man is; nor is it any other known thing. So let us call this unknown something: *the God*. It is nothing more than a name we assign to it. The idea of demonstrating that this unknown something (the God) exists, could scarcely suggest itself to the Reason. For if the God does not exist it would of course be impossible to prove it; and if he does exist it would be folly to attempt it. For at the very outset, in beginning my proof, I would have presupposed it, not as doubtful but as certain (a presupposition is never doubtful, for the very reason that it is a presupposition), since otherwise I would not begin, readily understanding that the whole would be impossible if he did not exist. But if when I speak of proving the God's existence I mean that I propose to prove that the Unknown, which exists, is the God, then I express myself unfortunately. For in that case I do not prove anything, least of all an existence, but merely develop the content of a conception. Generally speaking, it is a difficult matter to prove that anything exists; and what is still worse for the intrepid souls who undertake the venture, the difficulty is such that fame scarcely awaits those who concern themselves with it. The entire demonstration always turns into something very different and becomes an additional development of the consequences that flow from my having assumed that the object in question exists. Thus I always reason from existence, not toward existence, whether I move in the sphere of palpable sensible fact or in the realm of thought. I do not for example prove that a stone exists, but that some existing thing is a stone. The procedure in a court of justice does not prove that a criminal exists, but that the accused, whose existence is given, is a criminal. Whether we call existence an *accessorium* [something predicated] or the eternal *prius* [first given or assumed], it is never subject to demonstration. Let us take ample time for consideration. We have no such reason for haste as have those who from concern for themselves or for the God or for some other thing, must make haste to get existence demonstrated. Under such circumstances there may indeed be need for haste, especially if the prover sincerely seeks to appreciate the danger that he himself, or the thing in question, may be nonexistent unless the proof is finished and does not surreptitiously entertain the thought that it exists whether he succeeds in proving it or not.

If it were proposed to prove Napoleon's existence from Napoleon's deeds, would it not be a most curious proceeding? His existence does indeed explain his deeds, but the deeds do not prove *his* existence, unless I have already understood the word "his" so as thereby to have assumed his existence. But Napoleon is only an individual, and in so far there exists no absolute relationship between him and his deeds; some other person might have performed the same deeds. Perhaps this is the reason why I cannot pass from the deeds to existence. If I call these deeds the deeds of Napoleon the proof becomes superfluous, since I have already named him; if I ignore this, I can never prove from the deeds that they are Napoleon's, but only in a purely ideal manner that such deeds are the deeds of a great general, and so forth. But between the God and his works there is an absolute relationship; God is not a name but a concept. Is this perhaps the reason that his *essentia involvit existentiam* [essence entails existence]? The works of God are such that only the God can perform them. Just so, but where then are the works of the God? The works from which I would deduce his existence are not directly and immediately given. The wisdom in nature, the goodness, the wisdom in the governance of the world—are all these manifest, perhaps, upon the very face of things? Are we not here confronted with the most terrible temptations to doubt, and is it not impossible finally to dispose of all these doubts? But from such an order of things I will surely not attempt to prove God's existence; and even if I began I would never finish, and would in addition have to live constantly in suspense, lest something so terrible should suddenly happen that my bit of proof would be demolished. From what works then do I propose to derive the proof? From the works as apprehended through an ideal interpretation, i.e., such as they do not immediately reveal themselves. But in that case it is not from the works that I make the proof; I merely develop the ideality I have presupposed, and because of my confidence in *this* I make so bold as to defy all objections, even those that have not yet been made. In beginning my proof I presuppose the ideal interpretation, and also that I will be successful in carrying it through; but what else is this but to presuppose that the God exists, so that I really begin by virtue of confidence in him?[30]

From this passage it is clear that Kierkegaard condemns the "proofs" for God's existence, as well as other attempts to "know" God. The reason is that, by Kierkegaard's account, God cannot be known; God is not subject to rational, objective analysis. But if the point of religion and religious faith is not to know God, then just what is their point? To *feel*, rather than to know. Paradoxically, it is the absurdity and irrationality of Christian doctrines that makes this rare intensity and feeling possible, as Kierkegaard points out in this snippet from *Concluding Unscientific Postscript:*

The absurd is precisely by its objective repulsion the measure of the intensity of faith in inwardness. Suppose a man who wishes to acquire faith; let the comedy begin. He wishes to have faith, but he wishes also to safeguard himself by means of an objective inquiry and its approximation-process. What happens? With the help of the approximation-process the absurd becomes something different; it becomes probable, it becomes increasingly probable, it becomes extremely and emphatically probable. Now he is ready to believe it, and he ventures to claim for himself that he does not believe as shoemakers and tailors and simple folk believe, but only after long deliberation. Now he is ready to believe it; and lo, now it has become precisely impossible to believe it. Anything that is almost probable, or probable, or extremely and emphatically probable, is something he can almost know, or as good as know, or extremely and emphatically almost *know*—but it is impossible to *believe*. For the absurd is the object of faith, and the only object that can be believed.[31]

In the end, rational thinking, which is the religious expression of objective thinkers, points to the existence of God but gives individuals little on which to

30. *Sören Kierkegaard.* Philosophical Fragments. *David Swenson, Trans. Copyright 1936, © 1962 by Princeton University Press. Excerpt reprinted by permission of Princeton University Press.*

31. *Sören Kierkegaard.* Concluding Unscientific Postscript. *David F. Swenson and Walter Lowrie, Trans. Copyright 1941, © 1969 by Princeton University Press. Excerpt reprinted by permission of Princeton University Press.*

erect a relationship with God. "I contemplate the order of nature," says Kierkegaard, "in the hope of finding God, and I see omnipotence and wisdom; but I also see much else that disturbs my mind and excites anxiety. The sum of all this is objective uncertainty." Faced with objective uncertainty, with the inconclusiveness of objective analysis and rational debate and the "proofs," we are anguished. This anguish, this suffering, is all compounded by the anticipation of our own death and our feeling of smallness and insignificance in the face of the eternal order of things. The debates go on, our lives ebb away. We must make a decision. This decision is what Kierkegaard calls the "leap of faith," which consists of a commitment to a relationship with God that defies objective analysis. Of course, we may choose not to make the leap of faith; we may, instead, try to minimize the suffering through professional understanding and knowledge, through objective analysis. But for this alternative, Kierkegaard has only sarcasm: *"The two ways,"* he says; "One is to suffer; the other is to become a professor of the fact that another suffered." In the language of the atheist Sartre, either make the leap of faith or be inauthentic; either establish a relationship with God or practice self-deception.

There are, then, several main currents in Kierkegaard's religious philosophy. First is the distinction between objective and subjective thinking. Second is the point that religion is a confrontation with the unknown, not something knowable. Third is the assertion that the decision to believe involves a leap of faith, which consists of a commitment to a relationship with God that defies objective analysis. In brief, Kierkegaard asserts that faith cannot be based on direct observation of God, nor on rational inferences from the nature of the world. Each individual is confronted by the central Christian claim of the God-man, as it is mediated by the Church. Since this claim cannot be resolved on the objective level, individuals, in responding to it on the subjective level, may experience the benefit of authentic existence. Finally, individuals should not be inhibited by doubts arising from the level of objective reason because objectivity is not applicable to this claim.

Even from as brief an overview as the preceding, the connection between the religious thought of Kierkegaard and that of "new" or "radical" theologians like Tillich should be evident in their (1) shared retreat to personal experience, (2) distinction between subjective and objective thinking (and truth), and (3) emphasis on establishing a relationship with God. What may not be apparent, though, is the comparison that can be made between the religious thought of Kierkegaard and the pragmatism of William James.[32]

Kierkegaard and James

Perhaps the first similarity between Kierkegaard and James that is worth noting is that both are concerned about established standards that will guard against superstition and nonsense. Like James, Kierkegaard believes that the higher level of subjectivity goes beyond or against the understanding that operates on the objective level. Also, Kierkegaard's concern about the status of Chris-

32. *See Malcolm L. Diamond.* Contemporary Philosophy and Religious Thought. *New York: McGraw-Hill, 1974, pp. 163–164.*

tian beliefs seems to run parallel to James's. As we have seen, Kierkegaard stresses the traditional view that Jesus Christ was both fully God and fully man. He doesn't believe that religious beliefs of this kind can be affirmed strictly on an intellectual level. Neither does James. Furthermore, both Kierkegaard and James reject the possibility of offering a theoretical account of truths about God. In fact, in order to understand the status of the central affirmation of the God-man in Kierkegaard's thought, it helps to consider James's pragmatic view of the truth.

Recall that, according to James, the function of thought is to form ideas in order to satisfy our needs and interests. This is why he is so concerned with the *difference* that a true idea makes. In science, the truth of an idea is determined by experiential verification. Inasmuch as verified ideas serve our needs to predict experience and cope with our environment, scientific truth satisfies practical interests. But, as James points out, science does not help in deciding cases of metaphysical and theological beliefs. Since the meaning of a world view, such as is involved in a faith like Christianity, is its effect on the attitudes of those espousing it, individuals are justified in regarding such world views as true insofar as the views provide them with vital benefits. Thus, on pragmatic principles, if belief in God works satisfactorily in the widest sense of the word, then it is true.

At this point, there is an important distinction to make between Kierkegaard and James. Kierkegaard does not urge individuals to become Christians because of its practical benefits. This would be self-defeating because, in effect, it would be basing religious faith on objective analysis. Thus: "Since there's a payoff in believing, I shall believe." But, like James, Kierkegaard does say that the lower or objective level of thinking and truth does not provide individuals with standards for judging religious belief. For James, we are entitled to affirm these beliefs at a higher level, because they provide benefits. Kierkegaard would acknowledge the possibility of these practical benefits, but would insist that these benefits are not available to those who think that they ought to believe *in order* to experience authentic existence. By Kierkegaard's account, individuals must first appropriate the truth, acknowledging that it is objectively absurd. This is the "leap of faith." The benefits of authentic existence may or may not follow. The very uncertainty of a payoff is, for Kierkegaard, as it should be; for faith involves risk. But precisely because of its risk element, Kierkegaard believes that faith can open up individuals to the possibility of peak experiences, of vital, practical benefits.

Summary and Conclusions

We opened this chapter by noting that all religions speak of personal commitment and experience and of our need to find our place in the cosmic scheme of things. Traditionally in the West, these phenomena have been sought through a relationship to a personal, theistic God, and many arguments have been assembled for God's existence. Seeing weaknesses in the theistic position, many have adopted pantheism or panentheism, others atheism or agnosticism.

Whether or not God exists, the question of religious belief persists and affects our lives. For many, this decision involves a relationship not to a personal God but to a divine dimension to the universe, which they sense through personal experience. There is a growing emphasis on this kind of personal experience as the basis of religious belief. In this connection we examined mysticism and contemporary movements with mystical overtones, such as radical theology, psychedelic drug use, and Eastern religious thought.

Clearly, the philosophy of religion has had a long and illustrious history that continues to unfold. The concept of religious experience is inextricably linked with a psychology of self, for religious experience is one way that we can integrate our personalities and lives and thereby achieve wholeness. Perhaps this wholeness is what psychologist Abraham Maslow means when he speaks of "peak experiences," vivid moments in our lives when everything seems to fall into place, when our vision is clear, our lives meaningful, and our place in the order of things certain.[33]

Up until very recently, it was thought that the experiences that Maslow describes happened only to saints, mystics, artists, and poets, but certainly not to average people. Maslow's "new psychology" suggests the contrary and offers a constructive insight into religious experience that might provide common ground for different viewpoints.

The moments that Maslow describes seem linked to feelings of self-fulfillment, achievement, and creativity. As such, they can happen to anyone. But we must allow them to happen; we must open ourselves to them. This element of personal receptivity has always been an integral part of religious teaching, of the numinous, but it is often buried under pomp and ceremony. Now, growing interest in humanistic psychology is suggesting ways of getting in touch with the self and thereby with religious impulses.

Humanistic psychology has spurred interest in expanding our awareness of self by increasing our creativity, improving our health, enhancing our learning and problem solving, and, most importantly, providing ecstatic experiences. As a result, there are a burgeoning number of mind and brain investigations that attempt to see the human from all sides. These are leading to new concepts of self that originate in a kind of religious experience, in which we experience self and reality in a new and different way.

Rather than viewing humans as a bundle of responses to stimuli, we now accept the richness and complexity of the human and the importance of each individual. Central to this emphasis on the individual is a recognition of wholeness. The centuries-old split between mind and body has been abandoned for the *holistic* approach, which recognizes the inseparability of mind and body and the influence of each upon the other. Appropriately, there is more recognition of the roles that emotions and spiritual feelings play in our lives and of the limitations of logic and rationality. As a result, subjective experience is gaining respect in scientific circles, a place heretofore reserved for objective experience. The realization that science and individual experience are not incompatible is growing. In addition, whereas we once had presumed our-

---

33. *See Abraham Maslow.* Toward a Psychology of Being. *New York: D. Van Nostrand, 1968.*

selves to be objects of Freud's subconscious forces, we have now found a new belief in our own capacity for growth, self-transcendence, or what Maslow calls "self-actualization." Related to this belief is the idea that we are not static or fixed systems; instead, we can more accurately be described in terms of energy flow and energy fields. Finally, purpose and meaning, which were once seen strictly as religious concepts, are now entering psychology, which is beginning to recognize a spiritual dimension.

The potential for what we have been calling religious experience is staggering. The next twenty-five years may open areas of conscious awareness that we hardly dream of today. This awareness will no doubt be accompanied by a deep and reverent sensitivity to the profound mystery of life and our wondrous part in it.

Section Exercises

The Ontological Argument

1. Anselm argues that a perfect being must exist because the lack of existence is an imperfection. Could you argue that, on the contrary, a perfect being must not exist because existence is an imperfection? Explain.

2. If you believe in God, do you believe on the basis of Anselm's ontological argument? If you do not believe in God, do you disbelieve because you consider the ontological argument inadequate?

3. Explain the difference between these two statements: "If there is a perfect being, then a perfect being exists" and "If there can be a perfect being, then a perfect being must exist." Which represents the ontological argument? Which the objection to it? With which do you agree, and why?

The Cosmological Argument

1. Evaluate these statements:
   a. God was the first event.
   b. God caused the first event.
   c. God is an uncaused cause.
   d. First there was a mind without a body, God, who then created matter, including bodies.

2. Do you agree that if there is no first cause, the universe makes no sense? Is an infinite regress nonsensical?

3. If you believe in God, do you believe because of the argument from cause? If you do not believe in God, do you disbelieve because of the inadequacy of the argument from cause?

4. Aquinas's proofs are based on analogical reasoning, in which he compares what we have experienced directly with what we have not. What is the source of his analogy in the cause argument? Is the analogy a good one?

The Design Argument

1. Explain what Hume means when he says, "A universe by definition must appear designed, for it shows design."

2. In what ways would you say organic evolution is compatible with the account of creation given in Genesis? In what ways is it incompatible?

3. If you believe in God, do you believe because of the argument from design? If you do not believe in God, do you disbelieve because of the inadequacies in the argument from design?

Radical Theology

1. In your own words, what is Tillich's objection to traditional or theological theism?

2. Are you sympathetic to Tillich's objections? If so, cite instances to illustrate that your sympathy is grounded in experience.

3. Anglican bishop John Robinson has said, "The traditional material is all true, no doubt, and one recognizes it as something one ought to be able to respond to, but somehow it seems to be going on around one rather than within. Yet to question it openly is to appear to let down the side, to be branded as hopelessly unspiritual, and to cause others to stumble." First interpret this statement, then explain it from the viewpoint of a church leader. Finally, ask yourself if it has any meaning for you.

4. Anselm's ontological argument claimed that existence was a necessary part of the meaning of a perfect being. Is Tillich similarly claiming that God is a necessary part of the meaning of "ultimately concerned"? Is he defining God into existence?

5. Some people claim that the mere fact that Tillich interprets his own knowledge of the "depth" as an experience of God does not make it so. Neither does it guarantee the existence of God. Are such critics distinguishing between belief and knowledge? How?

6. Some people compare Tillich's claim that experience of the "ground of all being" is an experience of God to the claim "I have a toothache because some mad genius has possessed my body and is causing the pain." Evaluate this analogy.

7. Do you think that Tillich's claims need public verification, as critics say they do? Is Tillich talking about a completely different kind of knowledge, a knowledge that transcends empirical data? In what ways is this a mystical knowledge?

Psychedelics and Religious Experience

1. Would you say that James's two characteristics of a mystical experience would also apply to a psychedelic-induced state of consciousness?

2. If through fasting, meditation, and prayer someone induced in himself a conscious state similar to a psychedelic-induced one, do you think

society would react as it does to the user of psychedelics? If not, why not?

3. A common objection to the use of psychedelics is that the user loses touch with reality. What does such an objection assume? Do you think that the validity of this objection depends on the circumstances under which the drug is used?

Eastern Religious Traditions

1. What would you say are the main sources of attraction for Westerners in Eastern thought?

2. What obstacles would you note that many Westerners might face in adjusting to Eastern thought?

The Death of Ivan Ilyitch

Leo Tolstoy

Most people would agree that there is no greater evil that can beset an individual than to be afflicted with a terminal illness. What possible value and purpose could it have? In "The Death of Ivan Ilyitch," master storyteller Leo Tolstoy (1828–1910) provides a glimpse of the inner torment of a man who faces up to the fact that he is dying. In sketching one man's struggle to deal with his own mortality, Tolstoy portrays dying as an opportunity for profound introspection. Keep in mind as you read the story that in all his work Tolstoy aims to show the presence and influence of God in our lives.

Chapter VIII

It was morning.

It was morning merely because Gerasim had gone, and Piotr, the lackey, had come. He put out the candles, opened one curtain, and began noiselessly to put things to rights. Whether it were morning, whether it were evening, Friday or Sunday, all was a matter of indifference to him, all was one and the same thing. The agonizing, shooting pain, never for an instant appeased; the consciousness of a life hopelessly wasting away, but not yet departed; the same terrible, cursed death coming nearer and nearer, the one reality, and always the same lie,—what matter, then, here, of days, weeks, and hours of the day?

"Will you not have me bring the tea?"

"He must follow form, and that requires masters to take tea in the morning," he thought; and he said merely:—

"No."

"Wouldn't you like to go over to the divan?"

"He has to put the room in order, and I hinder him; I am uncleanness, disorder!" he thought to himself, and said merely:—

"No; leave me!"

The lackey still bustled about a little. Ivan Ilyitch put out his hand. Piotr officiously hastened to him:—

"What do you wish?"

"My watch."

Piotr got the watch, which lay near by, and gave it to him.

"Half-past eight. They aren't up yet?"

"No one at all. Vasili Ivanovitch"—that was his son—"has gone to school, and Praskovia Feodorovna [Ivan's wife] gave orders to wake her up if you asked for her. Do you wish it?"

"No, it is not necessary.—Shall I not try the tea?" he asked himself. "Yes . . . . tea . . . . bring me some."

From "The Death of Ivan Ilyitch" by Leo Tolstoy. In The Death of Ivan Ilyitch and Other Stories. *Louise and Aylmer Maude, Trans. London: Oxford University Press, 1934. Reprinted by permission of Oxford University Press.*

Piotr started to go out. Ivan Ilyitch felt terror-stricken at being left alone. "How can I keep him? Yes, my medicine. Piotr, give me my medicine.—Why not? perhaps the medicine may help me yet."

He took the spoon, sipped it.

"No, there is no help. All this is nonsense and delusion," he said, as he immediately felt the familiar, mawkish, hopeless taste.

"No, I cannot have any faith in it. But this pain, ... why this pain? Would that it might cease for a minute!"

And he began to groan. Piotr came back.

"Nothing. . . . go! Bring the tea."

Piotr went out. Ivan Ilyitch, left alone, began to groan, not so much from the pain, although it was horrible, as from mental anguish.

"Always the same thing, and the same thing; all these endless days and nights. Would it might come very soon! What very soon? Death, blackness? No, no! Anything rather than death!"

When Piotr came back with the tea on a tray, Ivan Ilyitch stared long at him in bewilderment, not comprehending who he was, what he was. Piotr was abashed at this gaze; and when Piotr showed his confusion, Ivan Ilyitch came to himself.

"Oh, yes," said he, "the tea; very well, set it down. Only help me to wash, and to put on a clean shirt."

And Ivan Ilyitch began to perform his toilet. With resting spells he washed his hands and face, cleaned his teeth, began to comb his hair, and looked into the mirror. It seemed frightful, perfectly frightful, to him, to see how his hair lay flat upon his pale brow.

While he was changing his shirt, he knew that it would be still more frightful if he gazed at his body; and so he did not look at himself. But now it was done. He put on his khalat, wrapped himself in his plaid, and sat down in his easy-chair to take his tea. For a single moment he felt refreshed; but as soon as he began to drink the tea, again that same taste, that same pain. He compelled himself to drink it all, and lay down, stretching out his legs. He lay down, and let Piotr go.

Always the same thing. Now a drop of hope gleaming, then a sea of despair rising up, and always pain, always melancholy, and always the same monotony. It was terribly melancholy to the lonely man; he longed to call in some one, but he knew in advance that it is still worse when others are present.

"Even morphine again . . . . to get a little sleep! . . . . I will tell him, tell the doctor, to find something else. It is impossible, impossible so."

One hour, two hours, would pass in this way. But there! the bell in the corridor. Perhaps it is the doctor. Exactly: it is the doctor, fresh, hearty, portly, jovial, with an expression as if he said, "You may feel apprehension of something or other, but we will immediately straighten things out for you."

The doctor knows that this expression is not appropriate here; but he has already put it on once for all, and he cannot rid himself of it—like a man who has put on his dress-coat in the morning, and gone to make calls.

The doctor rubs his hands with an air of hearty assurance.

"I am cold. A healthy frost. Let me get warm a little," says he, with just the expression that signifies that all he needs is to wait until he gets warmed a little, and, when he is warmed, then he will straighten things out.

"Well, now, how goes it?"

Ivan Ilyitch feels that the doctor wants to say, "How go your little affairs?" but that he feels that it is impossible to say so; and he says, "What sort of a night did you have?"

Ivan Ilyitch would look at the doctor with an expression which seemed to ask the question, "Are you never ashamed of lying?"

But the doctor has no desire to understand his question.

And Ivan Ilyitch says:—

"It was just horrible! The pain does not cease, does not disappear. If you could only give me something for it!"

"That is always the way with you sick folks! Well, now, it seems to me I am warm enough; even the most particular Praskovia Feodorovna would not find anything to take exception to in my temperature. Well, now, how are you really?"

And the doctor shakes hands with him.

And, laying aside his former jocularity, the doctor begins with serious mien to examine the sick man, his pulse and temperature, and he renews the tappings and the auscultation.

Ivan Ilyitch knew for a certainty, and beyond peradventure, that all this was nonsense and foolish deception; but when the doctor, on his knees, leaned over toward him, applying his ear, now higher up, now lower down, and with most sapient mien performed various gymnastic evolutions on him, Ivan Ilyitch succumbed to him, as once he succumbed to the discourses of the lawyers, even when he knew perfectly well that they were deceiving him, and why they were deceiving him.

The doctor, still on his knees on the divan, was still performing the auscultation, when at the door were heard the rustle of Praskovia Feodorovna's silk dress, and her words of blame to Piotr because he had not informed her of the doctor's visit.

She came in, kissed her husband, and immediately began to explain that she had been up a long time; and only through a misunderstanding she had not been there when the doctor came.

Ivan Ilyitch looked at her, observed her from head to foot, and felt a secret indignation at her fairness and her plumpness, and the cleanliness of her hands, her neck, her glossy hair, and the brilliancy of her eyes, brimming with life. He hated her with all the strength of his soul, and her touch made him suffer an actual paroxysm of hatred of her.

Her attitude toward him and his malady was the same as before. Just as the doctor had formulated his treatment of his patient and could not change it, so she had formulated her treatment of him, making him feel that he was not doing what he ought to do, and was himself to blame; and she liked to reproach him for this, and she could not change her attitude toward him.

"Now, just see! he does not heed, he does not take his medicine regularly; and, above all, he lies in a position that is surely bad for him—his feet up."

She related how he made Gerasim hold his legs.

The doctor listened with a disdainfully good-natured smile, as much as to say:—

"What is to be done about it, pray? These sick folks are always conceiving some such foolishness. But you must let it go."

When the examination was over, the doctor looked at his watch; and then Praskovia Feodorovna declared to Ivan Ilyitch that, whether he was willing or not, she was going that very day to call in the celebrated doctor to come and

have an examination and consultation with Mikhaïl Danilovitch—that was the name of their ordinary doctor.

"Now, don't oppose it, please. I am doing this for my own self," she said ironically, giving him to understand that she did it all for him, and only on this account did not allow him the right to oppose her.

He said nothing, and frowned. He felt that this lie surrounding him was so complicated that it was now hard to escape from it.

She did all this for him, only in her own interest; and she said that she was doing it for him, while she was in reality doing it for herself, as some incredible thing, so that he was forced to take it in its opposite sense.

The celebrated doctor, in fact, came about half-past eleven. Once more they had auscultations; and learned discussions took place before him, or in the next room, about his kidney, about the blind intestine, and questions and answers in such a learned form that again the place of the real question of life and death, which now alone faced him, was driven away by the question of the kidney and the blind intestine, which were not acting as became them, and on which Mikhaïl Danilovitch and the celebrity were to fall instantly and compel to attend to their duties.

The famous doctor took leave with a serious but not hopeless expression. And in reply to the timid question which Ivan Ilyitch's eyes, shining with fear and hope, asked of him, whether there was a possibility of his getting well, it replied that it could not vouch for it, but there was a possibility.

The look of hope with which Ivan Ilyitch followed the doctor was so pathetic that Praskovia Feodorovna, seeing it, even wept, as she went out of the library door in order to give the celebrated doctor his honorarium.

The raising of his spirits, caused by the doctor's hopefulness, was but temporary. Again the same room, the same pictures, curtains, wallpaper, vials, and his aching, pain-broken body. And Ivan Ilyitch began to groan. They gave him a subcutaneous injection, and he fell asleep.

When he woke up it was beginning to grow dusky. They brought him his dinner. He forced himself to eat a little *bouillon*. And again the same monotony, and again the advancing night.

About seven o'clock, after dinner, Praskovia

Feodorovna came into his room, dressed as for a party, with her exuberant bosom swelling in her stays, and with traces of powder on her face. She had already that morning told him that they were going to the theater. Sarah Bernhardt had come to town, and they had a box which he had insisted on their taking.

Now he had forgotten about that, and her toilet offended him. But he concealed his vexation when he recollected that he himself had insisted on their taking a box, and going, on the ground that it would be an instructive, esthetic enjoyment for the children.

Praskovia Feodorovna came in self-satisfied, but, as it were, feeling a little to blame. She sat down, asked after his health, as he saw, only for the sake of asking, and not so as to learn, knowing that there was nothing to learn, and began to say what was incumbent on her to say,—that she would not have gone for anything, but that they had taken the box; and that Elen and her daughter and Petrishchef—the examining magistrate, her daughter's betrothed—were going, and it was impossible to let them go alone, but that it would have been more agreeable to her to stay at home with him. Only he should be sure to follow the doctor's prescriptions in her absence.

"Yes—and Feodor Petrovitch"—the betrothed—"wanted to come in. May he? And Liza!"

"Let them come."

The daughter came in, in evening dress, with her fair young body,—her body that made his anguish more keen. But she paraded it before him, strong, healthy, evidently in love, and irritated against the disease, the suffering, and death which stood in the way of her happiness.

Feodor Petrovitch also entered, in his dress-coat, with curly hair à la Capoul, with long sinewy neck tightly incased in a white standing collar, with a huge white bosom, and his long, muscular legs in tight black trousers, with a white glove on one hand, and with an opera hat.

Immediately behind him, almost unnoticed, came the gymnasium scholar, in his new uniform, poor little fellow, with gloves on, and with that terrible blue circle under the eyes, the meaning of which Ivan Ilyitch understood.

He always felt a pity for his son. And terrible was his timid and compassionate glance. With the exception of Gerasim, Vasya alone, it seemed to Ivan Ilyitch, understood and pitied him.

All sat down; again they asked after his health. Silence ensued. Liza asked her mother if she had the opera-glasses. A dispute arose between mother and daughter as to who had mislaid them. It was a disagreeable episode.

Feodor Petrovitch asked Ivan Ilyitch if he had seen Sarah Bernhardt. Ivan Ilyitch did not at first understand his question, but in a moment he said:—

"No . . . . why, have you seen her yet?"

"Yes, in 'Adrienne Lecouvreur.'"

Praskovia Feodorovna said that she was especially good in that. The daughter disagreed with her. A conversation arose about the grace and realism of her acting,—the same conversation, which is always and forever one and the same thing.

In the midst of the conversation, Feodor Petrovitch glanced at Ivan Ilyitch, and grew silent. The others glanced at him, and grew silent. Ivan Ilyitch was looking straight ahead with gleaming eyes, evidently indignant at them. Some one had to extricate them from their embarrassment, but there seemed to be no way out of it. No one spoke; and a panic seized them all, lest suddenly this ceremonial lie should somehow be shattered, and the absolute truth become manifest to all.

Liza was the first to speak. She broke the silence. She wished to hide what all felt, but she betrayed it.

"One thing is certain,—if we are going, it is time," she said, glancing at her watch, her father's gift; and giving the young man a sign, scarcely perceptible, and yet understood by him, she smiled, and arose in her rustling dress.

All arose, said good-by, and went.

When they had gone, Ivan Ilyitch thought that he felt easier: the lying was at an end; it had gone with them; but the pain remained. Always this same pain, always this same terror, made it hard as hard could be. There was no easing of it. It grew ever worse, always worse.

Again minute after minute dragged by, hour after hour, forever the same monotony, and forever endless, and forever more terrible—the inevitable end.

"Yes, send me Gerasim," was his reply to Piotr's question.

Chapter IX

Late at night his wife returned. She came in on her tiptoes, but he heard her; he opened his eyes, and quickly closed them again. She wanted to send Gerasim away, and sit with him herself. He opened his eyes, and said:—

"No, go away."

"You suffer very much."

"It makes no difference."

"Take some opium."

He consented, and drank it. She went.

Until three o'clock he was in a painful sleep. It seemed to him that they were forcing him cruelly into a narrow sack, black and deep; and they kept crowding him down, but could not force him in. And this performance, horrible for him, was accompanied with anguish. And he was afraid, and yet wished to get in, and struggled against it, and yet tried to help.

And here suddenly he broke through, and fell . . . . and awoke.

There was Gerasim still sitting at his feet on the bed, dozing peacefully, patiently.

But he was lying there with his emaciated legs in stockings resting on his shoulders, the same candle with its shade, and the same never ending pain.

"Go away, Gerasim," he whispered.

"It's nothing; I will sit here a little while."

"No, go away."

He took down his legs, lay on his side on his arm, and began to pity himself. He waited only until Gerasim had gone into the next room, and then he no longer tried to control himself, but wept like a child. He wept over his helplessness, over his terrible loneliness, over the cruelty of men, over the cruelty of God, over the absence of God.

"Why hast Thou done this? Why didst Thou place me here? Why, why dost Thou torture me so horribly?"

He expected no reply; and he wept because there was none, and could be none. The pain seized him again; but he did not stir, did not call. He said to himself:—

"There, now again, now strike! But why? What have I done to Thee? Why is it?"

Then he became silent; ceased not only to weep, ceased to breathe, and became all attention: as it were, he heard, not a voice speaking with sounds, but the voice of his soul, the tide of his thoughts, arising in him.

"What dost thou need?" was the first clear concept possible to be expressed in words which he heard.

"'What dost thou need? What dost thou need?'" he said to himself. "What? Freedom from suffering. To live," he replied.

And again he gave his attention, with such effort that already he did not even notice his pain.

"To live? how live?" asked the voice of his soul.

"Yes, to live as I used to live—well, pleasantly."

"How didst thou live before when thou didst live well and pleasantly?" asked the voice.

And he began to call up in his imagination the best moments of his pleasant life. But, strangely enough, all these best moments of his pleasant life seemed to him absolutely different from what they had seemed then,—all, except the earliest remembrances of his childhood. There, in childhood, was something really pleasant, which would give new zest to life if it were to return. But the person who had enjoyed that pleasant existence was no more; it was as if it were the remembrance of some one else.

As soon as the period began which had produced the present *he*, Ivan Ilyitch, all the pleasures which seemed such then, now in his eyes dwindled away, and changed into something of no account, and even disgusting.

And the farther he departed from infancy, and the nearer he came to the present, so much the more unimportant and dubious were the pleasures.

This began in the law-school. There was still something even then which was truly good; then there was gayety, there was friendship, there were hopes. But in the upper classes these good moments became rarer.

Then, in the time of his first service at the governor's, again appeared good moments; these were the recollections of love for a woman. Then all this became confused, and the happy time grew less. The nearer he came to the present, the worse it grew, and still worse and worse it grew.

"My marriage . . . . so unexpected, and disillusionment and my wife's breath, and sensuality, hypocrisy! And this dead service, and these labors for money; and thus one year, and two, and ten, and twenty,—and always the same thing. And the longer it went, the more dead it became.

"It is as if all the time I were going down the mountain, while thinking that I was climbing it. So it was. According to public opinion, I was climbing the mountain; and all the time my life was gliding away from under my feet. . . . And here it is already . . . . die!

"What is this? Why? It cannot be! It cannot be that life has been so irrational, so disgusting. But even if it is so disgusting and irrational, still, why die, and die in such agony? There is no reason.

"Can it be that I did not live as I ought?" suddenly came into his head. "But how can that be, when I have done all that it was my duty to do?" he asked himself. And immediately he put away this sole explanation of the enigma of life and death as something absolutely impossible.

"What dost thou wish now?—To live? To live how? To live as thou livest in court when the usher proclaims, 'The court is coming! the court is coming'?

"The court is coming—the court," he repeated to himself. "Here it is, the court. Yes; but I am not guilty," he cried with indignation. "What for?"

And he ceased to weep; and, turning his face to the wall, he began to think about that one thing, and that alone. "Why, wherefore, all this horror?"

But, in spite of all his thoughts, he received no answer. And when the thought occurred to him, as it had often occurred to him, that all this came from the fact that he had not lived as he should, he instantly remembered all the correctness of his life, and he drove away this strange thought.

Chapter X

Thus two weeks longer passed. Ivan Ilyitch no longer got up from the divan. He did not wish to lie in bed, and he lay on the divan. And, lying almost all the time with his face to the wall, he still suffered in solitude the same inexplicable sufferings, and still thought in solitude the same inexplicable thought.

"What is this? Is it true that this is death?"

And an inward voice responded:—

"Yes, it is true."

"Why these torments?"

And the voice responded:—

"But it is so. There is no why."

Farther and beyond this, there was nothing.

From the very beginning of his malady, from the time when Ivan Ilyitch for the first time went to the doctor, his life was divided into two conflicting tendencies, alternately succeeding each other. Now it was despair, and the expectation of an incomprehensible and frightful death; now it was hope, and the observation of the functional activity of his body, so full of interest for him. Now before his eyes was the kidney, or the intestine, which, for the time being, failed to fulfil its duty. Then it was that incomprehensible, horrible death, from which it was impossible for any one to escape.

These two mental states, from the very beginning of his illness, kept alternating with one another. But the farther the illness progressed, the more dubious and fantastical became his ideas about the kidney, and the more real his consciousness of approaching death.

He had but to call to mind what he had been three months before, and what he was now, to call to mind with what regularity he had been descending the mountain; and that was sufficient for all possibility of hope to be dispelled.

During the last period of this solitude through which he was passing, as he lay with his face turned to the back of the divan,—a solitude amid a populous city, and amid his numerous circle of friends and family,—a solitude deeper than which could not be found anywhere, either in the depths of the sea, or in the earth,—during the last period of this terrible solitude, Ivan Ilyitch lived only by imagination in the past.

One after another, the pictures of his past life arose before him. They always began with the time nearest to the present, and went back to the very remotest,—to his childhood, and there they rested.

If Ivan Ilyitch remembered the stewed prunes which they had given him to eat that very day, then he remembered the raw, puckery French prunes of his childhood, their peculiar taste, and the abundant flow of saliva caused by the stone. And in connection with these recollections of taste, started a whole series of recollections of that time,—his nurse, his brother, his toys.

"I must not think about these things; it is too painful," said Ivan Ilyitch to himself. And again he transported himself to the present,—the button on the back of the divan, and the wrinkles of the morocco. "Morocco is costly, not durable. There was a quarrel about it. But there was some other morocco, and some other quarrel, when we tore father's portfolio and got punished, and mamma brought us some tarts."

And again his thoughts reverted to childhood; and again it was painful to Ivan Ilyitch, and he tried to avoid it, and think of something else.

And again, together with this current of recollections, there passed through his mind another current of recollections about the progress and rise of his disease. Here, also, according as he went back, there was more and more of life. There was more, also, of excellence in life, and more of life itself. And the two were confounded.

"Just as this agony goes from worse to worse, so also all my life has gone from worse to worse," he thought. "One shining point, there back in the distance, at the beginning of life; and then all growing blacker and blacker, swifter and swifter, in inverse proportion to the square of the distance from death," thought Ivan Ilyitch.

And the comparison of a stone falling with accelerating rapidity occurred to his mind. Life, a series of increasing tortures, always speeding swifter and swifter to the end,—the most horrible torture.

"I am falling.". . .

He shuddered, he tossed, he wished to resist it. But he already knew that it was impossible to resist; and again, with eyes weary of looking, but still not able to resist looking at what was before him, he stared at the back of the divan, and waited, waited for this frightful fall, shock, and destruction.

"It is impossible to resist," he said to himself. "But can I not know the wherefore of it? Even that is impossible. It might be explained by saying that I had not lived as I ought. But it is impossible to acknowledge that," he said to himself, recollecting all the legality, the uprightness, the propriety of his life.

"It is impossible to admit that," he said to himself, with a smile on his lips, as if some one were to see that smile of his, and be deceived by it.

"No explanation! torture, death . . . . why?"

Chapter XI

Thus passed two weeks. In these weeks, there occurred an event desired by Ivan Ilyitch and his wife. Petrishchef made a formal proposal. This took place in the evening. On the next day, Praskovia Feodorovna went to her husband,

meditating in what way to explain to him Feodor Petrovitch's proposition; but that very same night, a change for the worse had taken place in Ivan Ilyitch's condition. Praskovia Feodorovna found him on the same divan, but in a new position. He was lying on his back; he was groaning, and looking straight up with a fixed stare.

She began to speak about medicines. He turned his eyes on her. She did not finish saying what she had begun, so great was the hatred against her expressed in that look.

"For Christ's sake, let me die in peace!" said he.

She was about to go out; but just at this instant the daughter came in, and came near to wish him good-morning. He looked at his daughter as he had looked at his wife, and, in reply to her questions about his health, told her dryly that he would quickly relieve them all of his presence. Neither mother nor daughter said anything more; but they sat for a few moments longer, and then went out.

"What are we to blame for?" said Liza to her mother. "As if we had made him so! I am sorry for papa, but why should he torment us?"

At the usual time the doctor came. Ivan Ilyitch answered "yes," "no," not taking his angry eyes from him; and at last he said:—

"Now see here, you know that you don't help any, so leave me!"

"We can appease your sufferings," said the doctor.

"You cannot even do that; leave me!"

The doctor went into the drawing-room, and advised Praskovia Feodorovna that it was very serious, and that there was only one means—opium—of appeasing his sufferings, which must be terrible.

The doctor said that his physical sufferings were terrible, and this was true; but more terrible than his physical sufferings were his moral sufferings, and in this was his chief torment.

His moral sufferings consisted in the fact that that very night, as he looked at Gerasim's sleepy, good-natured face, with its high cheek-bones, it had suddenly come into his head:—

"But how is it if in reality my whole life, my conscious life, has been wrong?"

It came into his head that what had shortly before presented itself to him as an absolute impossibility—that he had not lived his life as he ought—might be true. It came into his head that the scarcely recognizable desires to struggle against what men highest in position considered good,—desires scarcely recognizable, which he had immediately banished,—might be true, and all the rest might be wrong. And his service, and his course of life, and his family, and these interests of society and office—all this might be wrong.

He endeavored to defend all this before himself. And suddenly he realized all the weakness of what he was defending. And there was nothing to defend.

"But if this is so," he said to himself, "and I am departing from life with the consciousness that I have wasted all that was given me, and that it is impossible to rectify it, what then?"

He lay flat on his back, and began entirely anew to examine his whole life.

When in the morning he saw the lackey, then his wife, then his daughter, then the doctor, each one of their motions, each one of their words, confirmed for him the terrible truth which had been disclosed to him that night. He saw in them himself, all that for which he had lived; and he saw clearly that all this was wrong, all this was a terrible, monstrous lie, concealing both life and death.

This consciousness increased his physical sufferings, added tenfold to them. He groaned and tossed, and threw off the clothes. It seemed to him that they choked him, and loaded him down.

And that was why he detested them.

They gave him a great dose of opium; he became unconscious, but at dinner-time the same thing began again. He drove them from him, and threw himself from place to place.

His wife came to him, and said:—

"Jean, darling, do this for me (for me!). It cannot do any harm, and sometimes it helps. Why, it is a mere nothing. And often well people try it."

He opened his eyes wide.

"What? Take the sacrament? Why? It's not necessary. But, however . . . ."

She burst into tears.

"Will you, my dear? I will get our priest. He is so sweet!"

"Excellent! very good," he continued.

When the priest came, and confessed him, he became calmer, felt, as it were, an alleviation of his doubts, and consequently of his sufferings; and there came a moment of hope. He again began to think about the blind intestine and the possibility of curing it. He took the sacrament with tears in his eyes.

When they put him to bed after the sacrament, he felt comfortable for the moment, and once more hope of life appeared. He began to think of the operation which they had proposed.

"I want to live, to live," he said to himself.

His wife came to congratulate him. She said the customary words, and added:—

"You feel better, don't you?"

Without looking at her, he said:—

"Yes."

Her hope, her temperament, the expression of her face, the sound of her voice, all said to him one thing:—

"Wrong! all that for which thou hast lived, and thou livest, is falsehood, deception, hiding from thee life and death."

And as soon as he expressed this thought, his exasperation returned, and, together with his exasperation, the physical, tormenting agony; and, with the agony, the consciousness of inevitable death close at hand. Something new took place: a screw seemed to turn in him, twinging pain to show through him, and his breathing was constricted.

The expression of his face, when he said "yes," was terrible. After he had said that "yes," he looked straight into her face, and then, with extraordinary quickness for one so weak, he threw himself on his face and cried:—

"Go away! go away! leave me!"

Chapter XII

From that moment began that shriek that did not cease for three days, and was so terrible that, when it was heard two rooms away, it was impossible to hear it without terror. At the moment that he answered his wife, he felt that he was lost, and there was no return, that the end had come, absolutely the end, and the question was not settled, but remained a question.

"U! uu! u!" he cried in varying intonations. He began to shriek, "N'ye khotchu—I won't;" and thus he kept up the cry on the letter u.

Three whole days, during which for him there was no time, he struggled in that black sack into which an invisible, invincible power was thrusting him. He fought as one condemned to death fights in the hands of the hangman, knowing that he cannot save himself, and at every moment he felt that, notwithstanding all the violence of his struggle, he was nearer and nearer to that which terrified him. He felt that his suffering consisted, both in the fact that he was being thrust into that black hole, and still more that he could not make his way through into it. What hindered him from making his way through was the confession that his life had been good. This justification of his life caught him and did not let him advance, and more than all else tormented him.

Suddenly some force knocked him in the breast, in the side, still more forcibly compressed his breath; he was hurled through the hole, and there at the bottom of the hole some light seemed to shine on him. It happened to him as it sometimes does on a railway carriage when you think that you are going forward, but are really going backward, and suddenly recognize the true direction.

"Yes, all was wrong," he said to himself; "but that is nothing. I might, I might have done right. What is right?" he asked himself, and suddenly stopped.

This was at the end of the third day, two hours before his death. At this very same time the little student noiselessly stole into his father's room, and approached his bed. The moribund was continually shrieking desperately, and tossing his arms. His hand struck upon the little student's head. The little student seized it, pressed it to his lips, and burst into tears.

It was at this very same time that Ivan Ilyitch fell through, saw the light, and it was revealed to him that his life had not been as it ought, but that still it was possible to repair it. He was just asking himself, "What is right?" and stopped to listen.

Then he felt that some one was kissing his hand. He opened his eyes, and looked at his son. He felt sorry for him. His wife came to him. He looked at her. With open mouth, and with her nose and cheeks wet with tears, with an expression of despair, she was looking at him. He felt sorry for her.

"Yes, I am a torment to them," he thought. "I am sorry for them, but they will be better off when I am dead."

He wanted to express this, but he had not the strength to say it.

"However, why should I say it? I must do it."

He pointed out his son to his wife by a glance, and said:—

"Take him away . . . . I am sorry . . . . and for thee."

He wanted to say also, "*Prosti*—Forgive," but he said, "*Propusti*—Let it pass;" and, not having the strength to correct himself, he waved his hand, knowing that he would comprehend who had the right.

And suddenly it became clear to him that what oppressed him, and was hidden from him, suddenly was lighted up for him all at once, and on two sides, on ten sides, on all sides.

He felt sorry for them; he felt that he must do something to make it less painful for them. To free them, and free himself, from these torments, "How good and how simple!" he thought.

"But the pain," he asked himself, "where is it?—Here, now, where art thou, pain?"

He began to listen.

"Yes, here it is! Well, then, do your worst, pain!"

"And death? where is it?"

He tried to find his former customary fear of death, and could not.

"Where is death? What is it?"

There was no fear, because there was no death.

In place of death was light!

"Here is something like!" he suddenly said aloud. "What joy!"

For him all this passed in a single instant, and the significance of this instant did not change.

For those who stood by his side, his death-agony was prolonged two hours more. In his breast something bubbled up, his emaciated body shuddered. Then more and more rarely came the bubbling and the rattling.

"It is all over," said some one above him.

He heard these words, and repeated them in his soul.

"It is over! death!" he said to himself. "It does not exist more."

He drew in one more breath, stopped in the midst of it, stretched himself, and died.

Questions for Analysis

1. How would you describe the "same inexplicable sufferings," "the same inexplicable thought," that plague Ilyitch?

2. The more he suffers, the more Ilyitch approaches the unavoidable truth about his life. What is that truth?

3. What is the realization that allows Ilyitch to die peacefully?

4. What value does Tolstoy find in suffering, isolation, and death?

5. Do you find Tolstoy's response an adequate resolution to the problem of evil?

Paperbacks for Further Reading

Camus, Albert. *The Plague*. New York: Vintage, 1972. The theme of evil permeates this novel by a leading existentialist. Ultimately, Camus's is a humanistic posture, based on compassion for the meaningless plight that all people suffer.

Cheney, Sheldon. *Men Who Have Walked with God*. New York: Dell, 1945. A nice selection of excerpts from the biographies of seers and saints through the ages, with useful introductions and commentaries. Among those presented are Lao-tzu, Buddha, Pythagoras, Plato, Plotinus, Saint Bernard, Meister Eckhart, Fra Angelico, Jakob Böhme, Brother Lawrence, and William Blake.

Dostoyevsky, Fyodor. *The Brothers Karamazov*. New York: Signet, 1971. Especially relevant in this classic is book V, chap. 4, in which Ivan's philosophical crisis over the presence of evil in the world crystallizes.

Fynn. *Mister God, This Is Anna*. New York: Ballantine, 1974. A short, captivating, true story of a little girl whose presence, wit, and theology changed the author's life. Its theology seems to capsule and often to cut through Christian theology in a way that no other testament has.

Greeley, Andrew. *Unsecular Man*. New York: Dell, 1972. Sociologist Greeley argues that the human religious needs and the functions of religion have not changed significantly since the late Ice Age. The changes that have occurred make religious questions more critical rather than less critical in the contemporary world.

Huxley, Julian. *Religion without Revelation*. New York: New American Library (Mentor Books), 1957. Huxley argues for agnosticism and for religion as a way of life independent of revelation and theistic belief. Huxley supports his belief with scientific evidence.

Moody, Raymond. *Life After Life*. New York: Bantam, 1976. Physician Moody not only presents accounts from people of their experiences during intervals when they were pronounced clinically dead, but also compares these accounts with those found in ancient writings, including Plato's. This book is as provocative as it is intriguing.

Needleman, Jacob. *The New Religions*. New York: Doubleday, 1970. This is a clear and inclusive study of the burgeoning interest in new forms of religious expression. Especially well covered is Eastern thought.

Robinson, John. *Honest to God*. Philadelphia: Westminster Press, 1963. Anglican bishop Robinson is a leading spokesperson for radical theology. In this work, he argues that theism is untenable in modern times. He rejects absolute moral values and posits a new morality centered on the love principle.

Russell, Bertrand. *Religion and Science*. New York: Oxford University Press (Galaxy Books), 1961. Russell reviews the historical conflict between religion and science. He argues that the ascendancy of science has had positive intellectual and humanistic influences on religion.

Stace, Walter T. *Religion and the Modern Mind*. Philadelphia: Lippincott (Keystone Books), 1952. Stace argues for a divine principle, declaring that our lives are rooted in the mystical as well as in the natural. He contends that religious values are necessary to correct the distortions of science's own subjective relativism.

Tremmel, William. *Religion: What Is It?* New York: Holt, Rinehart and Winston, 1976. A highly readable attempt to define religion. Provides an analysis of religious phenomena that does justice to the practice of religion in many cultures.

Watts, Alan. *The Way of Zen*. New York: Random House, 1957. This is a very popular and readable presentation of Zen Buddhism, including its nature, history, and value. A more simplified version of the same material is found in Watts's *The Spirit of Zen* (New York: Grove Press [Evergreen Edition], 1960).

Glossary

Some of these terms are not used in the text but are included because they are part of the philosopher's working vocabulary. In many instances these terms carry nuances that are unmentioned here. Every attempt has been made to be concise without being misleading.

abstraction   the mental power of separating one part of an entity from its other parts or of inferring the class from the particular instance

accidental characteristic   a characteristic that is not necessary to make a thing what it is; an accompanying characteristic

act utilitarianism   in normative ethics, the position that an action is moral if it produces the greatest happiness for the most people

aesthetics   the branch of philosophy that studies beauty, especially in the arts

agnosticism   a claim of ignorance; the claim that God's existence can be neither proved nor disproved

analogy   a comparison; when you reason from analogy, you conclude that because two or more entities share one aspect, they share another as well

anarchism   the theory that all forms of government are incompatible with individual and social liberty and should be abolished

animism   the belief that many spirits inhabit nature

anthropomorphism   the attributing of human qualities to nonhuman entities, especially to God

antinomy   used by Immanuel Kant to refer to contradictory conclusions arrived at through valid deduction

a posteriori   pertaining to knowledge stated in empirically verifiable statements; inductive reasoning

a priori   pertaining to knowledge that is logically prior to experience; reasoning based on such knowledge

atheism   denial of theism

atman   the Hindu idea of the self after enlightenment; the concept of no self

authority   a common secondary source of knowledge; a source existing outside the person making the claim that the person uses as an expert source of information

avidya in Buddhism, the cause of all suffering and frustration; ignorance or unawareness that leads to clinging

axiology the study of the general theory of values, including their origin, nature, and classification

axiom a proposition regarded as self-evident or true

behaviorism a school of psychology that restricts the study of human nature to what can be observed rather than to states of consciousness

Brahman the Hindu concept of an impersonal Supreme Being; the source and goal of everything

categorical imperative Immanuel Kant's ethical formula: act as if the maxim (general rule) by which you act were to become a universal law; the belief that what is right for one person is also right for everyone in similar circumstances

catharsis a purging or cleansing of the emotions; used by Aristotle to describe the purifying of the audience through emotional involvement in a play

causality, causation the relationship of events or of cause and effect

cause whatever is responsible for or leads to a change, motion, or condition

classification the process of grouping like things

cognition the acquiring of knowledge of something; the mental process by which we become aware of the objects of perception and thought

coherence theory a theory contending that truth is a property of a related group of consistent statements

common sense the way of looking at things apart from technical or special training

common-sense realism the epistemological position that does not distinguish between an object and an experience of it

concept a general idea, distinguished from a *percept*, which we have upon experiencing particular entities; thus, we can have a percept when we see particular citizen John Smith, but we have a concept of man, a universal unexperienced entity

conditioned genesis the Buddhist formula consisting of twelve factors that summarize the principles of conditionality, relativity, and interdependence

consequentialist theory in ethics, the position that the morality of an action is determined by its consequences

contingent an entity that may be and also may not be

contract theory in social philosophy, the doctrine that individuals give up certain liberties and rights to the state, which in turn guarantees such rights as life, liberty, and the pursuit of happiness

correspondence theory a theory contending that truth is an agreement between a proposition and a fact

cosmology the study of the universal world process—the process by which the world unfolds and evolves

critical philosophy the analysis and definition of basic concepts and the precise expression and criticism of basic beliefs

deduction the process of reasoning to logically certain conclusions

defining characteristic a characteristic in whose absence a thing would not be what it is

deism a widespread belief in the seventeenth and eighteenth centuries in a God who, having created the universe, remains apart from it and administers it through natural laws

denotation a definition that is a verbal example of what a word signifies

designation a definition consisting of the defining characteristics of a word

determinism the theory that everything that occurs happens in accordance with some regular pattern or law

dharma in Buddhism, the doctrine whereby self-frustration is ended; the Eightfold Path

dialectic in general, the critical analysis of ideas to determine their meanings, implications, and assumptions; as used by Hegel, a method of reasoning used to synthesize contradictions

disanalogy a difference between compared things that lessens the likelihood of an analogical conclusion

divine command theory a single-rule, nonconsequential normative theory that says we should always do the will of God

dualism the theory that reality is composed of two different substances, so that neither one can be related to the other; thus: spirit/matter, mind/body, good/evil

duty theory in ethics, the position that the moral action is the one that conforms with obligations accrued in the past, such as the obligations of gratitude, fidelity, or justice

eclecticism the practice of choosing what is thought best from various philosophies

egoism a consequentialist ethical theory which contends that we act morally when we act in a way that promotes our own best long-term interests

emergence, emergent evolution the view that, in the development of the universe, new life forms appear that cannot be explained solely through analysis of previous forms

emotivism the metaethical position that ethical statements primarily express surprise, shock, or some other emotion

empathy a psychological and aesthetic designation of the motor attitudes, muscular reactions, and feelings that we experience when we identify with another person or object

empiricism the position that knowledge has its origins in and derives all of its content from experience

entelechy a nonmaterial power, vital force, or purpose that permits a form to come to realization

entitlement theory a theory of social justice contending that individuals are entitled to the holdings that they have acquired without harming anyone in the process

epiphenomenalism the view that matter is primary and that the mind is a secondary phenomenon accompanying some bodily processes

epistemology the branch of philosophy that investigates the nature, sources, limitations, and validity of knowledge

essence that which makes an entity what it is; that defining characteristic in whose absence a thing would not be itself

ethics the branch of philosophy that tries to determine the good and right thing to do

eudaemonism the view that the end of life is happiness—that is, a complete, long-lived kind of well-being; from the Greek *eudaimonia*, "happiness"

existence actuality

existentialism a twentieth-century philosophy that denies any essential human nature; each of us creates our own essence through free action

extrasensory perception   communication outside normal sensory activity, as in telepathy

fallacy   an incorrect way of reasoning; an argument that tries to persuade psychologically but not logically

false dilemma   an erroneous bipolarity resulting from the existence of positions between the two presented

fatalism   the view that events are fixed, that humans can do nothing to alter them

finite   limited

formalism   in ethics, the view that moral acts follow from fixed moral principles and do not change because of circumstances

free will   the denial that human acts are completely determined

Gestalt   a psychological view that the whole is not just the sum of its parts

Golden Rule   the ethical rule that holds: Do unto others as you would have them do unto you

hard determinism   the doctrine that every event has a cause that entails the denial of moral freedom

hedonism   the view that pleasure is intrinsically worthwhile and is the human's good

humanism   the view that stresses distinctly human values and ideals

human nature   what it essentially means to be of our species; what makes us different from anything else

hypothesis   in general, an assumption, statement, or theory of explanation, the truth of which is under investigation

idealism   in metaphysics, the position that reality is ultimately nonmatter; in epistemology, the position that all we know are our ideas

ideational theory   the theory of word meaning that stresses the emotional impact of words

identity theory   the theory that mental states are really brain states

immanent   indwelling, within the process, as God is frequently thought to be in relation to His creation

immortality   the belief that the self or soul survives physical death

indeterminism   the view that some individual choices are not determined by preceding events

individualism   the social theory that emphasizes the importance of the individual, his or her rights, and independence of action

induction   the process of reasoning to probable explanations or judgments

inference   a conclusion arrived at inductively or deductively

infinite   unlimited

infinite regress   the causal or logical relationship of terms in a series that logically has no first or initiating term

informal fallacies   common argumentative devices used to persuade emotionally or psychologically, but not logically

innate ideas   ideas that, according to some philosophers, such as Plato, can never be found in experience but are inborn

instrumentalism   synonymous with John Dewey's pragmatism; the view that emphasizes experience and interprets concepts, beliefs, and attitudes as ways in which an organism adjusts to its environment

interactionism   the theory that the mind and the body interact, originally associated with Descartes

intuition   a source of knowledge that does not rely immediately on the senses or reason but on direct awareness

judgment   asserting or denying something in the form of a proposition

karma   the Hindu law of sowing and reaping; determines what form and circumstances we assume in each reincarnated state

laissez-faire   in economics, politics, and social philosophy, the concept of government noninterference

language   an aspect of human behavior that involves the use of vocal sounds and corresponding written symbols in meaningful patterns to formulate and communicate thoughts and feelings

linguistic analysis   a contemporary form of analytic philosophy claiming that philosophical problems are partially language problems; the purpose of philosophy is to dissolve, not resolve, problems by a rigorous examination of language

logic   the branch of epistemology that studies the methods and principles of correct reasoning

logical empiricism (positivism)   a contemporary form of analytic philosophy that contends meaning is the most important feature of philosophical discourse; there are two kinds of epistemological meaning: (1) that expressed in analytic statements—that is, formal meaning that can be verified by logic and syntax; and (2) empirical—that is, factual meaning that can be verified by sense data

logical positivism   the philosophical school of thought that would restrict meaningful propositions to those that can be empirically verified or to those that state relationships among terms

logos   the term used by classical philosophers to describe the principle of rationality or law that they observed operating in the universe

materialism   the metaphysical position that reality is ultimately composed of matter

maximin principle   the social theory of justice which contends that inequality is allowable only insofar as it improves the lot of the worst off in a society

maya   in Buddhism, the world of illusion

mechanism   the view that everything can be explained in terms of laws that govern matter and motion

meliorism   from the Latin meaning "better"; the view that the world is neither all good nor all bad, but can be improved through human effort

mentalism   the view that mind or idea is all that exists

metaethics   the study of the meanings of ethical words and of the sentences in which they appear

metaphysics   the branch of philosophy that studies the nature of reality

metempsychosis   the belief that upon physical death the soul can migrate into another body

monism   the view that reality is reducible to one kind of thing or one explanatory principle

monotheism   the belief in a single God

morals   the conduct or rule of conduct by which people live

mysticism   the philosophy of religion contending that reality can be known only when we surrender our individuality and experience a union with the divine ground of all existence

naive realism   the view that the world is as we perceive it to be

naturalism   a version of materialism that rejects supernatural principles and maintains that reality can be explained only in terms of scientifically verifiable concepts; a denial of any fundamental difference between humans and other animals

natural law   a pattern of necessary and universal regularity holding in physical ratio; a moral imperative, a description of what ought to happen in human relationships

necessary condition   a way to refer to cause; for example, when *B* cannot occur in the absence of *A*, *A* is said to be a necessary condition of *B*

new realism   the view that the world is as we perceive it to be

nihilism   the view that nothing exists, that nothing has value; the social view that conditions are so bad that they should be destroyed and replaced by something better

nirvana   in Buddhism, enlightenment that comes when the limited, clinging self is extinguished

nominalism   the view that only particular entities are real and that universals represent detectable likenesses among particulars

nonconsequentialist theory   in ethics, the position that the morality of an action is determined by more than just its consequences

nonnaturalism   the metaethical position that ethical statements defy translation into nonethical language

nonnormative ethics   the scientific or descriptive study of ethics; or the study of ethical terms, including the notion of moral justification

normative ethics   the branch of ethics that makes judgments about obligation and value

objective   a term describing an entity that has a public nature independent of us and our judgments about it

objective idealism   the position that ideas exist in an objective state, associated originally with Plato

objective relativism   the value theory which contends that values are relative to human satisfaction but that human needs and what satisfies them are open to empirical examination

obligation   that which we must or are bound to do because of some duty, agreement, contract, promise, or law

omnipotent   all-powerful

omnipresent   being everywhere at once

omniscient   all-knowing

ontology   a subdivision of metaphysics; the theory of the nature of being and existence

ostensive definition   a definition that consists of an instance of a word's denotation

panentheism   the belief that God is both fixed and changing, inclusive of all possibilities

pantheism   the belief that everything is God

parallelism   the theory that physical and mental states do not interact but simply accompany each other

parapsychology   the school of psychology that studies extrasensory powers

paternalism   the care of someone in a manner suggestive of a father caring for his children

perception   the act or process by which we become aware of things

phenomenalism   the belief, associated with Kant, that we can know only appearances (phenomena) and never what is ultimately real (noumena); that the mind has the ability to sort out sense data and provide relationships that hold among them

phenomenology the philosophical school founded by Edmund Husserl which contends that being is the underlying reality, that what is ultimately real is our consciousness, which itself is being

philosophy the love and pursuit of wisdom

pluralism the view that reality consists of many substances

polytheism belief in many gods

positivism the view that only analytic and synthetic propositions are meaningful

postulate a presupposition used as a basis for establishing a proof

pragmatism the philosophical school of thought, associated with Dewey, James, and Peirce, that tries to mediate between idealism and materialism by rejecting all absolute first principles, tests truth through workability, and views the universe as pluralistic

prajñā in Zen Buddhism, transcendental wisdom

predestination the doctrine that every aspect of our lives has been divinely determined from the beginning of time

prima facie duties according to Ross, duties that generally obligate us but may not in a particular case because of circumstances

primary qualities according to Locke, qualities that inhere in an object: size, shape, weight, and so on

probability the likelihood of an event's happening or of a statement's being true

proposition a true or false statement

rationalism the position that reason alone, without the aid of sense information, is capable of arriving at some knowledge, at some undeniable truths

realism the doctrine that the objects of our senses exist independently of their being experienced

reason the capacity for thinking reflectively and making inferences; the process of following relationships from thought to thought and of ultimately drawing conclusions

referential theory a theory of word meaning which contends that words refer to things

relativism the view that human judgment is conditioned by factors such as acculturation and personal bias

religious belief in its broadest sense, the belief that there is an unseen order and that we can do no better than to be in harmony with that order

representative realism the position, associated with Locke, that distinguishes between an object and one's experience of it

right in ethics, act that conforms to moral standards

rights those things to which we have a just claim

rule utilitarianism the normative ethical position which contends that we should act so that the rule governing our actions produces the greatest happiness for the most people

samsara in Buddhism, the round of birth and life

scientific method a way of investigation based on collecting, analyzing, and interpreting sense data to determine the most probable explanation

secondary qualities according to Locke, qualities that we impose on an object: color, smell, texture, and so on

self the individual person; the ego; the knower; that which persists through changes in a person

self-determinism   advocates of self-determinism hold that our actions are determined but not solely by external forces or conditions

semantics   the study of the relationship between words and reality, including their linguistic forms, symbolic nature, and effects on human behavior

sense data   images or sense impressions

situation ethics   according to Joseph Fletcher, the doctrine that contends that the moral action produces the greatest amount of Christian love (agape)

skepticism   in epistemology, the view that varies between doubting all assumptions until proved and claiming that no knowledge is possible

social philosophy   the application of moral principles to the problems of freedom, equality, and justice

soft determinism   advocates of soft determinism attempt to reconcile freedom and responsibility with determinism

solipsism   an extreme form of subjective idealism, contending that only I exist and that everything else is a product of the subjective consciousness

soul   the immaterial entity that is identified with consciousness, mind, or personality

subjective   that which refers to the knower; that which exists in the consciousness but not apart from it

subjective idealism   in epistemology, the position that all we ever know are our own ideas

substance   that which is real; essence; the underlying ground in which properties inhere; that which exists in its own right and depends on nothing else

sufficient condition   a way to refer to cause; A is said to be a sufficient condition of B if, without exception, whenever A occurs B occurs

tautology   a statement whose predicate repeats its subject in whole or in part

teleology   the view that maintains the reality of purpose and affirms that the universe either was consciously designed or is operating under partly conscious, partly unconscious purposes

telepathy   in ESP, the name given to the phenomenon of thought transfer from one person's mind to another's without normal means of communication

theism   the belief in a personal God who intervenes in the lives of His creation

theology   the study of God, including religious doctrines

totalitarianism   the political view that the state is of paramount importance

universal   that which is predictive of many particular entities; thus, "woman" is a universal, since it is predictive of individual women

utilitarianism   in ethics, the theory which contends that we should act in such a way that our actions produce the greatest happiness for the most people

validity   correctness of the reasoning process; characteristic of an argument whose conclusion follows by logical necessity

value   an assessment of worth

verification   the proving or disproving of a proposition

vitalism   the view that there is in living organisms an entelechy, or life principle, that provides purpose or direction

Bibliography

Chapter 1

Boethius. *The Consolation of Philosophy*. New York: Modern Library, 1943.

Brinton, C. *The Shaping of Modern Thought*. Englewood Cliffs, N.J.: Prentice-Hall, 1963.

Bugbee, H. A., Jr. *The Inward Morning*. Bald Eagle, Pa.: State College of Pennsylvania, 1958.

Dakin, Arthur H. *Man the Measure*. Princeton, N.J.: Princeton University Press, 1939.

Fromm, Erich. *Escape from Freedom*. New York: Farrar & Rinehart, 1941.

Hocking, W. E. *Human Nature and Its Remaking*. New Haven, Conn.: Yale University Press, 1932.

Johnson, David W. *Reaching Out: Interpersonal Effectiveness and Self-Actualization*. Englewood Cliffs, N.J.: Prentice-Hall, 1972.

Lin Yutang, Ed. *The Wisdom of China and India*. New York: Random House, 1942.

Maslow, Abraham, Ed. *Motivation and Personality*. New York: Harper & Row, 1970.

Naranjo, Claudio. *The One Quest*. New York: Viking, 1972.

Ostrovsky, Everett. *Self Discovery and Social Awareness*. New York: Wiley, 1974.

Tournier, Paul. *Adventures of Living*. New York: Harper & Row, 1965.

Watts, Alan. *The Wisdom of Insecurity*. New York: Pantheon, 1962.

Wheelis, Allen. *How People Change*. New York: Harper & Row, 1973.

Chapter 2

Allport, Gordon. *Becoming: Basic Considerations for a Psychology of Personality*. New Haven, Conn.: Yale University Press, 1955.

Blanshard, Brand. *The Nature of Thought*. Vol. 1. New York: Macmillan, 1940.

Broad, C. D. *The Mind and Its Place in Nature*. Chap. 3. London: Kegan Paul, 1925.

Bronowski, Jacob. *The Identity of Man*. Garden City, N.Y.: Natural History Press, 1965.

Buber, Martin. *Between Man and Man*. R. G. Smith, Trans. London: Kegan Paul, 1947.

Descartes, René. *Selections*. Ralph M. Eaton, Ed. New York: Scribner's, 1927.

Erikson, Erik. *Identity, Youth and Crisis*. New York: Norton, 1968.

Frondizi, Risieri. *The Nature of the Self*. Carbondale: Southern Illinois University Press, 1971.

Hume, David. "Personal Identity," in *A Treatise of Nature*. Oxford: Oxford University Press, 1955.

Locke, John. *An Essay concerning Human Understanding*. Book II, chap. 27. A. C. Fraser, Ed. Oxford: Clarendon Press, 1894.

Matson, Floyd. *The Broken Image*. Garden City, N.Y.: Doubleday, 1964.

Niebuhr, Reinhold. *The Nature and Destiny of Man*. New York: Scribner's, 1943.

Rhine, Louisa. *Hidden Channel of the Mind*. New York: Sloane, 1961.

Strawson, P. F. *Individuals*. New York: Anchor Press, 1963.

Watts, Alan. *The Book*. New York: Vintage, 1972.

Chapter 3

Adler, Alfred. *The Time of Our Lives: The Ethics of Common Sense*. New York: Holt, Rinehart and Winston, 1970.

Aiken, H. D. *Reason and Conduct: New Bearings on Moral Philosophy*. New York: Knopf, 1962.

Aristotle. *The Nicomachean Ethics*, in *The Basic Works of Aristotle*. Richard McKeon, Ed. New York: Random House, 1941.

Barry, Vincent E. *Personal and Social Ethics*. Belmont, Ca.: Wadsworth, 1978.

Barry, Vincent E. *Moral Issues in Business*. Belmont, Ca.: Wadsworth, 1979.

Broad, C. D. *Five Types of Ethical Theory*. New York: Harcourt, Brace, 1930.

Bronowski, Jacob. *Science and Human Values*. London: Penguin, 1964.

DeWitt Hyde, W. *The Five Great Philosophies of Life*. New York: Macmillan, 1927.

Epicurus. "Letter to Menoeceus," in *Epicurus: The Extant Remains*. C. Bailey, Trans. Oxford: Clarendon Press, 1926.

Ewing, A. C. *The Definition of Good*. New York: Humanities Press, 1947.

Fletcher, Joseph. *Situation Ethics: The New Morality*. Philadelphia: Westminster Press, 1966.

Frankena, William. *Ethics*. 2nd ed. Englewood Cliffs, N.J.: Prentice-Hall, 1973.

Fried, Charles. *An Anatomy of Values: Problems of Personal and Social Choice*. Cambridge, Mass.: Harvard University Press, 1970.

Fromm, Erich. *The Art of Loving*. New York: Harper & Row, 1956.

Glass, Bentley. *Science and Ethical Values*. Chapel Hill: University of North Carolina Press, 1965.

Johnson, Ernest F., Ed. *Patterns of Ethics in America Today*. New York: Collier, 1962.

Kant, Immanuel. *Foundations of the Metaphysics of Morals*. Lewis White Beck, Trans. New York: Bobbs-Merrill, 1959.

Korner, S. *Kant*. Chap. 6. Baltimore: Penguin, 1955.

Ladd, J. *Ethical Relativism*. Belmont, Ca.: Wadsworth, 1973.

Lockland, George T. *Grow or Die: The Unifying Principle of Transformation*. New York: Random House, 1973.

Mill, John Stuart. *Utilitarianism*. New York: Bobbs-Merrill, 1957.

Moore, George E. *Principia Ethica*. London: Cambridge University Press, 1903.

Muller, Herbert J. *The Children of Frankenstein*. Bloomington: Indiana University Press, 1970.

Nietzsche, Friedrich. *Genealogy of Morals*. F. Golffing, Trans. Garden City, N.Y.: Doubleday, 1956.

Norton, D., and M. Kille. *Philosophies of Love*. San Francisco: Chandler, 1971.

Oraison, Marc. *Morality for Moderns*. J. F. Bernard, Trans. New York: Doubleday, 1972.

Parker, Dewitt. *The Philosophy of Value*. Ann Arbor: University of Michigan Press, 1957.

Plato. *The Republic*. Benjamin Jowett, Trans. New York: Random House, 1957.

Rachels, James, Ed. *Moral Problems*. New York: Harper & Row, 1971.

Ramsey, Paul. *Basic Christian Ethics*. New York: Scribner's, 1950.

Ross, W. D. *Foundations of Ethics*. New York: Oxford University Press, 1939.

Ross, W. D. *Kant's Ethical Theory*. Oxford: Clarendon Press, 1954.

Ross, W. D. *The Right and the Good*. Oxford: Clarendon Press, 1930.

Stace, W. T. *The Concept of Morals*. New York: Macmillan, 1965.

Warnock, Mary. *Existential Ethics*. New York: St. Martin's Press, 1968.

Chapter 4

Adler, Alfred. *The Idea of Freedom*. Garden City, N.Y.: Doubleday, 1961.

Arendt, Hannah. *Crises of the Republic*. New York: Harcourt Brace Jovanovich, 1972.

Barth, Alan. *The Price of Liberty*. New York: Viking, 1961.

Beauvoir, Simone de. *The Second Sex*. H. M. Parshley, Trans. New York: Bantam, 1961.

Benn, S. I., and R. S. Peters. *The Principles of Political Thought: Social Principles and the Democratic State*. London: Allen & Unwin, 1959.

Cahn, Edmond. *The Predicament of Democratic Men*. New York: Macmillan, 1961.

Cranston, Maurice. *Freedom: A New Analysis*. London: Longmans, Green, 1953.

Devlin, Patrick. *The Enforcement of Morals*. New York: Oxford University Press, 1965.

Hart, H. L. A. *Law, Liberty and Morality*. Stanford, Ca.: Stanford University Press, 1963.

Hobbes, Thomas. *Leviathan*, in *The English Works of Thomas Hobbes*. London: J. Bohn, 1839.

Hook, Sidney. *Political Power and Personal Freedom: Studies in Democracy, Communism and Civil Rights*. New York: Criterion, 1959.

Locke, John. *Of Civil Government*. London: Dent, 1924.

Machiavelli, Niccolo. *The Prince*. T. G. Bergin, Trans. New York: Appleton-Century-Crofts, 1947.

Marcuse, Herbert. *One-Dimensional Man*. Boston: Beacon Press, 1964.

Marx, Karl, and Friedrich Engels. *Manifesto of the Communist Party*. F. Engels, Ed. Chicago: Henry Regnery, 1954.

Mill, John Stuart. *The Essential Works of John Stuart Mill*. Max Lerner, Ed. New York: Bantam Books, 1961.

Muller, Herbert J. *Issues of Freedom: Paradoxes and Promises*. New York: Harper & Row, 1960.

Myrdal, Gunnar. *Beyond the Welfare State: Economic Planning and Its International Implications*. New Haven, Conn.: Yale University Press, 1960.

Nathan, N. M. L. *The Concept of Justice*. London: Macmillan, 1971.

Niebuhr, Reinhold. *Faith and History: The Irony of American History*. New York: Scribner's, 1949.

Nietzsche, Friedrich. *Beyond Good and Evil*. Walter Kaufmann, Trans. New York: Random House, 1966.

Oppenheim, Felix E. *Dimensions of Freedom: An Analysis*. New York: St. Martin's Press, 1961.

Rawls, John. *A Theory of Justice*. Cambridge, Mass.: Harvard University Press, 1971.

Rossiter, Clinton. *Conservatism in America: The Thankless Persuasion*. 2nd ed. New York: Knopf, 1966.

Sorokin, Pitirim A. *The Crisis of Our Age*. New York: Dutton, 1941.

Spengler, Oswald. *Today and Destiny: Vital Excerpts from The Decline of the West*. New York: Knopf, 1940.

Spitz, D. *Patterns of Antidemocratic Thought*. New York: Free Press, 1949.

Sweezy, Paul. *The Theory of Capitalist Development: Principles of Marxian Political Economy*. New York: Oxford University Press, 1942.

Whitehead, Alfred North. *Adventures of Ideas*. New York: New American Library, 1955.

Williams, Bernard. *Philosophy, Politics and Society*. 2nd series. New York: Barnes & Noble, 1962.

Wise, David. *The Politics of Lying: Government Deception, Secrecy and Power*. New York: Random House, 1963.

Chapter 5

Aristotle. *Poetics*, in *The Basic Works of Aristotle*. Richard McKeon, Ed. Ingram Bywater, Trans. New York: Random House, 1941.

Baxandall, Lee. *Radical Perspectives in the Arts*. New York: Penguin, 1962.

Beardsley, Monroe. *Aesthetics: From Classical Greece to the Present*. New York: Macmillan, 1966.

Berger, John. *Art and Revolution*. New York: Scribner's, 1970.

Berleant, Arnold. *The Aesthetic Field: A Phenomenology of Aesthetic Experience*. Springfield, Ill.: Charles C. Thomas, 1970.

Brown, Merle. *Neo-Idealistic Aesthetics: Croce-Gentile-Collingwood*. Detroit: Wayne University Press, 1966.

Croce, Benedetto. *Aesthetica*. Douglas Hinslie, Trans. London: Macmillan, 1909.

Dewey, John. *Art as Experience*. New York: Putnam, 1958.

Ducasse, Curt John. *The Philosophy of Art*. New York: Dover, 1966.

Edman, Irwin. *Arts and the Man: A Short Introduction to Aesthetics*. New York: Norton, 1939.

Else, Gerald F. *Aristotle's Poetics: The Argument*. Cambridge, Mass.: Harvard University Press, 1957.

Fallico, Arthur B. *Art and Existentialism*. Englewood Cliffs, N.J.: Prentice-Hall, 1962.

Feibleman, James K. *Aesthetics*. New York: Humanities Press, 1949.

Harries, Karsten. *The Meaning of Modern Art*. Evanston, Ill.: Northwestern University Press, 1968.

Hegel, G. W. F. *The Philosophy of Fine Art*. F. P. B. Osmaston, Trans. London: G. Bell, 1920. (Originally published 1832.)

Henn, Thomas. *The Harvest of Tragedy*. London: Farber and Farber, 1956.

Hofstadter, Albert. *Truth and Art*. New York: Columbia University Press, 1965.

Kant, Immanuel. *Critique of Judgment*. J. H. Bernard, Trans. New York: Hafner, 1951.

Langer, Susanne. *Feeling and Form*. New York: Scribner's, 1953.

Langer, Susanne. *Reflection on Art: A Source Book of Writings by Artists, Critics and Philosophers*. New York: Oxford University Press, 1958.

Munro, Thomas. *Oriental Aesthetics*. Cleveland: Case Western Reserve University Press, 1965.

Newton, Eric. *The Meaning of Beauty*. Baltimore: Penguin, 1962.

Parker, DeWitt H. *The Principles of Aesthetics*. New York: Appleton, 1946.

Plato. *The Republic*. Benjamin Jowett, Trans. New York: Random House, 1957.

Santayana, George. *The Sense of Beauty*. New York: Scribner's, 1896.

Sypher, Wylie, Ed. *Comedy*. Garden City, N.Y.: Doubleday, 1956.

Tolstoy, Leo. *What Is Art?* Louise and Aylmer Maude, Trans. London: Oxford University Press, 1896.

Tomas, Vincent, Ed. *Creativity in the Arts*. Englewood Cliffs, N.J.: Prentice-Hall, 1964.

Weiss, Paul. *Nine Basic Arts*. Carbondale: Southern Illinois University Press, 1961.

Wittgenstein, Ludwig. *Philosophical Investigations*. G. E. M. Anscombe, Trans. New York: Macmillan, 1953.

Chapters 6 and 7

Aristotle. *Posterior Analytics*, in *The Basic Works of Aristotle*. Richard McKeon, Ed. G. R. Mure, Trans. New York: Random House, 1941.

Ayer, Alfred J. *The Problems of Knowledge*. New York: St. Martin's Press, 1942.

Barry, Vincent E. *Practical Logic*. New York: Holt, Rinehart and Winston, 1976.

Berkeley, George. *Principles of Human Knowledge: Three Dialogues between Hylas and Philonus*. New York: Philosophy Series of the Modern Student's Library, 1901.

Blanshard, Brand. *The Nature of Thought*. Vol. 2, chaps. 25, 26. New York: Macmillan, 1939.

Copi, Irving. *Introduction to Logic*. 4th ed. New York: Macmillan, 1972.

Descartes, René. "Meditations on First Philosophy," in *Descartes Selections*, Ralph Eaton, Ed. New York: Scribner's, 1927.

Descartes, René. *The Philosophical Works of Descartes*. E. S. Haldane and G. R. T. Ross, Trans. Cambridge: Cambridge University Press, 1931.

Dewey, John. *The Quest for Certainty*. New York: Putnam's, 1929.

Hume, David. *Enquiry concerning Human Understanding*. Raymond Wilborn, Ed. New York: Liberal Arts Press, 1955.

Hume, David. *Treatise on Human Nature*. L. A. Selby-Bigge, Ed. Oxford: Clarendon Press, 1896.

James, William. *Pragmatism*. New York: Meridian, 1965.

Katz, Jerrold J. *The Problem of Induction and Its Solution*. Chicago: University of Chicago Press, 1962.

Khatchadourian, Haig. *The Coherence Theory of Truth*. Beirut: American University Press, 1961.

Locke, John. *An Essay concerning Human Understanding*. Books 2, 4. New York: Dutton, 1948.

Murphy, Arthur E. "The Pragmatic Theory of Truth," in *The Uses of Reason*. New York: Macmillan, 1943.

Plato. *The Apology*. H. N. Fowler, Trans. Cambridge, Mass.: Harvard University Press, 1914.

Plato. *Phaedo*. E. F. Church, Trans. New York: Liberal Arts Press, 1951.

Plato. *The Republic*. Benjamin Jowett, Trans. New York: Random House, 1957.

Price, H. H. *Thinking and Experience*. London: Hutchinson, 1953.

Ritchie, A. D. *George Berkeley*. New York: Barnes & Noble, 1967.

Russell, Bertrand. *Human Knowledge: Its Scope and Limits*. New York: Simon & Schuster, 1948.

Russell, Bertrand. *The Problems of Philosophy*. New York: Oxford University Press, 1912.

Woozley, A. D. *Theory of Knowledge*. London: Allen & Unwin, 1949.

Yolton, John. *John Locke and the War of Ideas*. London: Oxford University Press, 1956.

Chapter 8

Asimov, Isaac. *The Intelligent Man's Guide to Science*. New York: Basic Books, 1963.

Barkey, Stephen F. *Induction and Hypothesis*. Ithaca, N.Y.: Cornell University Press, 1957.

Barnett, Lincoln. *The Universe and Dr. Einstein*. New York: New American Library (Mentor Books), 1957.

Boas, George. *The Challenge of Science*. Seattle: University of Washington Press, 1965.

Braithwaite, R. B. *Scientific Explanation*. Cambridge: Cambridge University Press, 1953.

Bunge, Mario. *Causality*. Cambridge: Peter Smith, 1959.

Campbell, Norman R. *What Is Science?* New York: Dover, 1952.

Conant, James B. *Modern Science and Modern Man*. New York: Doubleday, 1953.

Dampier, Sir William Cecil. *A History of Science and Its Relations with Philosophy and Religion*. New York: Cambridge University Press, 1966.

Eddington, Sir Arthur S. *The Nature of the Physical World*. New York: Macmillan, 1937.

Frank, Philipp. *Philosophy of Science*. Englewood Cliffs, N.J.: Prentice-Hall, 1962.

Hart, H. L., and A. Hondre. *Causation and the Law*. Oxford: Oxford University Press, 1958.

Hempel, Norwood Russell. *Aspects of Scientific Explanation*. New York: Free Press, 1965.

Madden, Edward H., Ed. *The Structure of Scientific Thought*. Boston: Houghton Mifflin, 1960.

Mill, John Stuart. *A System of Logic*. London: Longmans, Green, 1959.

Nagel, Ernest. *The Structure of Science*. New York: Harcourt, Brace & World, 1961.

Reichenbach, Hans. *The Rise of Scientific Philosophy*. Berkeley: University of California Press, 1951.

Russell, Bertrand. *The ABC's of Relativity*. Rev. ed. Felix Pirani, Ed. Fairlawn, N.J.: Essential Books, 1958.

Russell, Bertrand. *Introduction to Mathematical Philosophy*. London: Allen & Unwin, 1919.

Russell, Bertrand. *Religion and Science*. New York: Oxford University Press, 1961.

Salmon, Wesley C. *The Foundations of Scientific Inference*. Pittsburgh: University of Pittsburgh Press, 1967.

Scheffler, Israel. *Science and Subjectivity*. New York: Bobbs-Merrill, 1967.

Werkmeister, W. H. *A Philosophy of Science*. Lincoln: University of Nebraska Press, 1965.

Whitehead, Alfred North. *Process and Reality*. New York: Harper & Row, 1960.

Whitehead, Alfred North. *Science and the Modern World*. New York: New American Library, 1948.

Chapter 9

Aristotle. *Metaphysics*, in *The Basic Works of Aristotle*. Richard McKeon, Ed. W. D. Ross, Trans. New York: Random House, 1941.

Aristotle. *Selections*. W. D. Ross, Ed. New York: Scribner's, 1927.

Ayer, Alfred J. *Language, Truth and Logic*. London: Victor Gollancz, 1936.

Ayer, Alfred J. *Logical Positivism*. Glencoe, Ill.: Free Press, 1959.

Berkeley, George. *A Treatise concerning the Principles of Human Knowledge*. Colin M. Turbayne, Ed. New York: Liberal Arts Press, 1957.

Bertocci, Peter A., and Richard M. Millard. *Personality and the Good*. New York: McKeon, 1963.

Blanshard, Brand. *Reason and Analysis*. London: Allen & Unwin, 1962.

Brazill, William J. *The Young Hegelians*. New Haven, Conn.: Yale University Press, 1970.

Cornman, J. *Materialism and Sensations*. New Haven, Conn.: Yale University Press, 1971.

Descartes, René. *Meditations on First Philosophy*, in *Descartes Selections*. Ralph Eaton, Ed. New York: Scribner's, 1927. (Originally published 1641.)

Descartes, René. *Principles of Philosophy*, in *Descartes Selections*. Ralph Eaton, Ed. New York: Scribner's, 1927. (Originally published 1644).

Harris, E. E. *Nature, Mind and Modern Science*. New York: Humanities Press, 1954.

Heidegger, Martin. *Being and Time*. Edward Robinson, Trans. New York: Harper & Row, 1964.

Hume, David. *An Inquiry concerning Human Understanding*. New York: Liberal Arts Press, 1955. (Originally published 1748.)

Husserl, Edmund. *Phenomenology and the Crisis of Philosophy*. Quentin Lauer, Trans. New York: Harper & Row, 1965.

James, William. *Pragmatism*. New York: Meridian, 1965.

Johnson, A. H. *Whitehead's Theory of Reality*. Boston: Beacon Press, 1952.

Kant, Immanuel. *Prolegomena to Any Future Metaphysics*. Paul Carus, Trans. New York: Liberal Arts Press, 1951. (Originally published 1783.)

Kierkegaard, Sören. *Fear and Trembling: The Sickness unto Death*. Walter Lourie, Trans. New York: Doubleday, 1954.

Krikorian, Yervant H. *Recent Perspectives in American Philosophy*. The Hague: Martinus N. Jhoff, 1973.

Lamprecht, Sterling P. *The Metaphysics of Naturalism*. New York: Appleton-Century-Crofts, 1967.

Lange, F. A. *The History of Materialism*. New York: Humanities Press, 1957.

Marcel, Gabriel. *The Mystery of Being*. G. S. Fraser, Trans. Chicago: Henry Regnery, 1950.

Marx, Karl, and Friedrich Engels. *Basic Writings on Politics and Philosophy*. Lewis Feuer, Ed. Garden City, N.Y.: Doubleday, 1959.

Mundle, C. W. K. *A Critique of Linguistic Philosophy*. Oxford: Clarendon Press, 1970.

Peirce, Charles. *Values in a Universe of Chance*. Philip Wiener, Ed. Stanford, Ca.: Stanford University Press, 1958.

Plato. *Phaedo*. E. F. Church, Trans. New York: Liberal Arts Press, 1951.

Plato. *The Republic*. Benjamin Jowett, Trans. New York: Random House, 1957.

Plato. *Timaeus*. Benjamin Jowett, Trans. New York: Liberal Arts Press, 1959.

Pratt, James B. *Personal Realism*. New York: Macmillan, 1937.

Radhakrishnan, S. *An Idealist View of Life*. London: Allen & Unwin, 1951.

Sartre, Jean-Paul. *Being and Nothingness: An Essay on Phenomenological Ontology*. Hazel E. Barnes, Trans. New York: Philosophical Library, 1956.

Sartre, Jean-Paul. *Existentialism and Human Emotions*. New York: Philosophical Library, 1957.

Schofield, Robert E. *Mechanism and Materialism: British Natural Philosophy in an Age of Reason*. Princeton, N.J.: Princeton University Press, 1970.

Sellars, Wilfred. *Philosophical Perspectives*. Springfield, Ill.: Charles C. Thomas, 1967.

Sellars, Wilfred. *Philosophy for the Future*. New York: Harper & Row, 1949.

Smart, J. J. C. *Philosophy and Scientific Realism*. New York: Humanities Press, 1963.

Taylor, Richard. *Metaphysics*. Englewood Cliffs, N.J.: Prentice-Hall, 1963.

Waismann, Friedrich. *The Principles of Linguistic Philosophy*. London: Macmillan, 1965.

Whitehead, Alfred North. *Process and Reality: An Essay in Cosmology*. New York: Harper & Row, 1960.

Wittgenstein, Ludwig. *Philosophical Investigations*. G. E. Anscombe, Trans. Oxford: Blackwell, 1953.

Chapter 10

Aquinas, Thomas. *Summa Theologica*, in *Basic Writings of Saint Thomas Aquinas*. A. C. Pegis, Ed. New York: Random House, 1945.

Augustine. *City of God*. M. Dods, Trans. Edinburgh: T. & T. Clark, 1872.

Augustine. *Confessions*. J. G. Pilkington, Trans. New York: Liveright, 1943.

Barth, Karl. *The Humanity of God*. Richmond, Va.: Knox, 1960.

Brightman, Edgar. *A Philosophy of Religion*. Englewood Cliffs, N.J.: Prentice-Hall, 1940.

Burrill, Donald, Ed. *The Cosmological Arguments*. New York: Doubleday, 1967.

Campbell, C. A. *On Selfhood and Godhood*. New York: Macmillan, 1957.

Christian, William A. *Meaning and Truth in Religion*. Princeton, N.J.: Princeton University Press, 1964.

Hick, John. *Arguments for the Existence of God: Philosophy and Religion*. London: Macmillan, 1970.

Hick, John. *Evil and the God of Love*. New York: Harper & Row, 1966.

Kierkegaard, Sören. *Philosophical Fragments*. Princeton, N.J.: Princeton University Press, 1967.

Knox, John. *Myth and Truth: An Essay on the Language of Faith*. Charlottesville: University Press of Virginia, 1965.

Koller, John M. *Oriental Philosophies*. New York: Scribner's, 1970.

Mao Tse-tung. *Four Essays on Philosophy*. Peking: Foreign Language Press, 1960.

Murray, J. C. *The Problem of God, Yesterday and Today*. New Haven, Conn.: Yale University Press, 1964.

Needleman, Jacob. *The New Religions*. Garden City, N.Y.: Doubleday, 1970.

The New English Bible with the Apocrypha. Oxford: Oxford University Press, 1970.

Northrop, F. S. C. *The Meeting of East and West*. New York: Macmillan, 1946.

Novak, Michael. *Belief and Unbelief: A Philosophy of Self-Knowledge*. New York: Macmillan, 1965.

Pegis, Anton C., Ed. *The Basic Writings of Thomas Aquinas*. New York: Random House, 1945.

Pike, Nelsen. *God and Evil*. Englewood Cliffs, N.J.: Prentice-Hall, 1964.

Plating, Alvin. *The Ontological Arguments*. New York: Doubleday, 1961.

Plato. *The Apology*. H. N. Fowler, Trans. Cambridge, Mass.: Harvard University Press, 1914.

Plato. *Phaedo*, in *The Dialogues of Plato*. B. Jowett, Trans. New York: Random House, 1937.

Plato. *Thaetetus*, in *Plato's Cosmology*. F. M. Cornford, Trans. New York: Harcourt, Brace and World, 1937.

Radhakrishnan, Sarvepalli. *East and West: The End of Their Separation*. New York: Harper & Row, 1956.

Russell, Bertrand. *Why I Am Not a Christian*. New York: Simon & Schuster, 1957.

Suzuki, D. T. *Zen Buddhism*. William Barrett, Ed. Garden City, N.Y.: Doubleday, 1956.

Teilhard de Chardin, Pierre. *The Divine Milieu*. New York: Harper & Row, 1964.

Tillich, Paul. *The Future of Religions*. Jerald C. Bower, Ed. New York: Harper & Row, 1966.

INDEX